Almost

Famous

Dwayne Jones

Published by:

Fortune Publishing Group

E-mail: info@fortunepublishinggroup.com

www.FortunePublishingGroup.com

For Large Book Orders Contact Fortune Publishing Group at: (410) 888-0508

Printed in the United States of America

Book cover designed by Skarr Akbar & Max Fortune

Contents

Introduction VII

Chapter 1 - The Beginning............................... 1

Chapter 2 - The Foundation.............................. 5

Chapter 3 - Dwayne Meets Hip-Hop 9

Chapter 4 - Bright Lights & Brighton Street 13

Chapter 5 - Holiness & Adolescence........................ 17

Chapter 6 - High School Obstacles........................ 25

Chapter 7 - Pushing Through............................... 31

Chapter 8 - You're A Leader 37

Chapter 9 - First Love 41

Chapter 10 - Senior Year 49

Chapter 11 - Voo Doo- Witchcraft 63

Chapter 12 - Freshman Year (UMES) 69

Chapter 13 - Sophomore Year (UMES) 81

Chapter 14 - Junior Year (UMES)......................... 87

Chapter 15 - Drug Dealer................................ 103

Chapter 16 - College Dropout............................ 113

Chapter 17- De'Martim Records 123

Chapter 18 - Musical Bonds 127

Chapter 19 - A New Beginning 145

Chapter 20 - Crazy Love.................................... 151

Chapter 21 - Mouse's Cousin 163

Chapter 22 - Music & Mayhem 183

Chapter 23 - Heartbreak Hotel........................... 193

Chapter 24 - The Aftermath 209

Chapter 25 - Whatever It Takes........................... 229

Chapter 26 - About To Blow............................... 243

Chapter 27 - Run It Back................................... 262

Chapter 28 - Green Light 275

Chapter 29 - Clarinda..................................... 293

Chapter 30 - Jackpot...................................... 323

Chapter 31 - Solo.. 359

Chapter 32 - Back To The Streets 389

Chapter 33 - A New Sheriff's In Town 400

Chapter 34 - Always 419

Chapter 35 - The Birth of Holla Back 433

Chapter 36 - Picking Up Steam 443

Chapter 37 - The Death of Holla Back.................... 495

Chapter 38 - Africa 517

Chapter 39 - Sisqo's Chain 553

Chapter 40 - Elliott's Ways 597

Chapter 41 - Local Moves.. 629

Chapter 42 - Falling Apart 653

Chapter 43 - Gut Blow.. 673

Chapter 44 - Rock Bottom 697

Chapter 45 - Welcome to Altanta............................. 717

Chapter 46 - Fix the Broken Pieces 733

Chapter 47- Gracefully Bowing Out 789

About the Author.. 799

Introduction

The living room is completely dark with the exception of the streetlights shining through the windows, bouncing against the flawless white paint on my mother's ceilings and walls. Ironically the shadows from the trees are starting to look like dragons as they dance from wall to wall when the wind blows. My legs are hanging over one end of the couch as I'm constantly adjusting a couch pillow (that my mother would kill me if she knew I was laying on) against the arm rest on the other end. As I'm gazing at my prom pictures on my mother's mantel piece, I vaguely hear my mentally challenged neighbor outside on his porch talking to himself along with trains and passing cars. I can't sleep. My mind is going a hundred miles and running, and I want it to stop. I look over towards the hallway leading to the kitchen and notice a beige trench coat hanging from a coat hanger on the wall. I grab the coat, ball up on the couch and toss the coat over my head searching for complete darkness and silence. I close my eyes for a few and adjust the coat over my head enough so I can breathe. Every time I open my eyes, I find myself looking at my mother's mantel piece with all of the pictures. I start to wonder, what's Tracy and Teresa up to these days (my junior and senior prom dates)? I hear my mother upstairs telling one of her foster kids to turn their TV off... The tree shadow- dragon moves faster each time I take notice. I shut my eyes tighter trying to avoid my thoughts when suddenly I hear a thump coming from next door. When my eyes open this time, still in the direction of the mantel piece, instead of focusing on the prom pictures I noticed Sisqo's- Return of Dragon CD cover (that my mother framed). My eyes start to water and I think to myself, how did I get here...

Chapter 1 - The Beginning

Two plus two equals four
Open up or I'm a break down the door
Because one plus four equals five
Work these problems and don't try to hide
This is DJ that your listening to
I work from nine to five and twelve to two
When I'm not working math I'm on the mic
I'll rock this school day and night
Because ten plus ten equals twenty
I work math problems even when its sunny
Cause I'm DJ the rapper of the school
I make all the other rappers look like fools
Because math is the word for me
And I know one plus two equals three
Okay I already kicked down the door
Cause my math room number is 104
Follow me and follow my path
Go and study so you can work this math
When you're dealing with fractions
you're dealing with parts
I got hundreds straight down my keeping score chart
I'm a mathematics man and I do exist
So, all you other rappers, bust this!

The school auditorium erupts and goes crazy as my rap about math ends as every other rapper on the stage that day.... With a UTFO Roxanne signature! The applause was more than any 10-year-old could ever imagine from his peers. Everyone was in awe even my teachers and principle as I walked off the stage. It was then when I realized the power of performance and I loved how it felt.

I was born in Baltimore Maryland in the winter of 1973. My mother Azalee moved to Baltimore from South Carolina when she was 19 and met my father George while working at a factory. My mother was country girl from a big family, 10 siblings while my father was a city boy the oldest of four boys. At time of my birth, my mother was 23 and my father was 43.

When my mom got pregnant, my father moved her in with him and his mother, my grandmother Blanch on the west side of Baltimore, a small block called Brighton Street. Two of three of my uncles Frank and Harry lived there as well. My other uncle Leroy (nicknamed Hercules) lived several miles away. My grandfather died a few years before I was conceived.

My father's side were Carter's but when I was born I was given my mother's last name Jones because they weren't married. When I was 3 my parents moved in an apartment building adjacent to my grandmother's house- Gwynn Crest Apartments.

I was my mother's only child but my father's 5th and youngest child. I never knew I had brothers and sisters on my father's side until I was a teenager. Growing up, it was just my mom, dad and me. My mother came from a family of gamblers; card players, dice shooters, drinkers and smokers while my Dad came from a more reserved background. Every weekend my Mom and I would go to one of my aunt's house where there would always be a card game. I would play with my cousins while my mom would gamble and smoke. My dad never engaged in these festivities. My father was a very private/ stay to himself type of guy but at the same time a peoples' person. He always knew what to say to make people smile and laugh, even when they didn't want to and his timing was always perfect! He came up in one of the roughest areas in Baltimore (Murphy Holmes Projects) yet he came across as a distinguished gentleman and charismatic. People often would ask if he was a doctor or a preacher judging from his demeanor. It seemed as if he and my mom were the total opposites but as the old saying goes, opposites attract! From the time I was born till now, I can never recall a time where my mom and dad had an argument or even raised their voices to one another.

Growing up as an only child, I always had to find ways to keep myself entertained. When I couldn't go outside to play, I would draw. I drew lots of pictures but the ones I would cling to would be the pictures that expressed what was on my heart. I would draw detailed pictures of super heroes and cartoon characters but the ones that I would tape to my wall were the No Smoking Signs simply because I wanted my mother to stop smoking. My father had asthma and every winter he would have to be admitted to the hospital from being around second-hand smoke. I was always afraid that he would die because he was so much older than me and my mom and he had gray hair (the thoughts of a young kid). Also, I didn't want my mom to get cancer from smoking so I would smother my walls with these drawings, hoping she would get the picture (pun intended) and stop smoking. When I wasn't drawing, I would be outside playing with my neighborhood friends. It was always the same group, Derrick, Jason, Peanut, Greg, Donny, Shawn Green & Terry. There were many others but this was the core. I was one of the youngest of the bunch so I often looked up to my older friends and followed in their footsteps. My father was very strict so I couldn't do a lot of the things and go a lot of places where my friends did. I always had to stay on the front of my buildings parking lot and I couldn't play any sports on Sunday because of the Sabbath. Like any other kid, of course I strayed off the front several times and needless to say when I got caught I received a whipping. In fact, I was known for getting whippings all the time. My friends would stand under my apartment window and laugh as they heard me begging for mercy and would tease me the next day.

Chapter 2 - The Foundation

The year was 1983 when my mom and dad sat on our couch anticipating the Temptation & Four Tops performance on Motown 25. I remember seeing the excitement on their faces as the two groups went back and forth competing and singing each other's songs. I was used to seeing my mom excited about music. She always played Teddy Pendergrass, Pattie Labelle, Donna Summers and Stephanie Mills on our record player (33 inch or the single 45 inch) and sung every lyric. At times when she thought I was asleep, she would even play Millie Jackson records! But on Sundays, she would only play gospel records. Her favorites were Willie Banks, Shirley Caesar, Mehaila Jackson & The Mighty Clouds of Joy. She would sing every song and praise God right in our apartment living room. So, I was accustomed to her excitement when it came to music. My father on the other hand never showed any enthusiasm at all musically. The most I remember is him playing the BG's when I was very small maybe four or five at my grandmother's house. But I never saw my dad excited until Motown 25 came on. They both were at the edge of their seats and laughed nonstop as the

Temptations and Four Tops went back and forth. That was the first time I witnessed the influence of music.

Then this happened.... Before a commercial I heard "Stay tuned for an upcoming performance by Michael Jackson & The Jacksons!" As each commercial aired, I grew more and more impatient as I anticipated the return of Motown 25 awaiting to see Michael Jackson. When the Jacksons took the stage, I was memorized. The songs, the dancing, the energy all seemed unreal. I thought I had saw it all until the Jacksons left the stage and it was time for Michaels solo performance. That magical performance changed my life forever! When Michael Jackson performed Billie Jean and did the moon walk for the first time, I was speechless. It was past my bedtime when his performance aired but my mom and dad were generous enough to allow me to watch Michael's performance but afterwards I had to go straight to bed. As I climbed into the top bunk of my bunk bed tears began to run down my face but I didn't know why. I silently cried all night tossing and turning as I played back every move, every note and every scream from the audience from Michael Jackson's performance. I didn't know why I was crying, all I knew was something magical happened. It was then when I knew music held a special place in my heart. Whatever I felt from Michaels performance, I wanted to possess and own it so I could make others feel the same way.

The next day, I decided I wanted to be a singer. I would write a song (to other artists melodies, subconsciously) and draw a nice cover page for it and present it to my mom and dad for approval. They would read the words, give me a pat on the back and send me on my way. I also started practicing my dance moves and of course, like every other human on the planet in 1983, I mimicked Michael Jackson. On the weekends when my mother would visit my aunts for their routine card games, music was always in the atmosphere. Otis Redding, Sam Cook, and Donny Hathaway were their favorites but when they wanted entertainment my aunts and uncles would always play Michael Jackson's Thriller album and watch me and my cousins dance. They even started collecting money from the adults at the card game and had contests for the best Michael Jackson impersonator. I would win 1st place every weekend. I had the socks, a leather jacket and of course the infamous glove. In my mind I was Michael Jackson whenever it was time to perform. The only problem was I couldn't sing.

Chapter 3 - Dwayne Meets Hip-Hop

Being as though my mother had 10 siblings in which all of them except one (Uncle Pook) had several kids, I had over 20 cousins ranging from older teenagers to babies. We all would come with our mothers to which ever house was the "spot" for the card game (Normally my aunt Gertie May or Aunt Izzy) that weekend so we all saw and spent time with each other on a regular basis. We all were close but of course depending on the ages, some of us were closer than others. During this time I was closest to one of my older cousin (by 2 years) Shawn and one of my younger cousin Kebo. Shawn was an only child at the time as well so we had a lot in common. I looked up to him like an older brother and I wanted to do everything I saw him doing.

In 1985 Shawn, Kebo and I went to see a movie that would forever change my life. We caught the bus to Reisterstown Plaza and watched the iconic movie Krush Groove. As I watched the movie, I remember getting the same feeling I felt when watching Michael Jackson on Motown 25, especially when Run told the audience that it was "HIS MOTHAF*CKIN HOUSE"!! When we left the movie theatre, all three of us were floating on clouds. We walked to the bus stop talking about our favorite parts and mimicking all of the featured artist. As we waited for our bus on North & Bentalou St. (West Baltimore) Shawn suggested an idea that would ultimately lead to this writing. He looked at Kebo and me and said "Let's start a rap group!" Of course, Kebo and I was down for it. Shawn was our big cousin. We looked up to him a followed his every footstep. Then he said, "I have the perfect name for us…. The Awesome 3!"

We rapped and performed the entire ride home that day, excited about our new endeavor. Shawn's rap name would be "Kool Jay Fresh". Kebo decided he would be the beat box and named himself "AJ". I wanted my rap name to be "DJ" (my initials) but the name was too common plus it doesn't define an MC. It's a title for someone on the turntables. So, I decided to add a "C" (for Carter- my father's last name) calling myself DJC.

The next weekend after watching Krush Groove, at the gathering at the family weekend card games, instead of the glitter gloves and socks and Michael Jackson impersonations, it was now Lee jeans, shell head Adidas and kangoo's. When impersonating Michael, I was always the star among the kids but I knew I wouldn't be the star in this group. Observing Run DMC, I was amazed at the confidence/ arrogance of Run. I loved how he was but I knew I didn't have what he had. My personality was closer to DMC, a solid artist but not so much up front and in the spot light. So Shawn would be Run, I would be DMC and Kebo would be Jam Master Jay. Every chance we got, we would write and practice our rhymes. Kebo would beat box and Shawn and I would recite our written raps. My raps were okay but Shawn's raps were phenomenal! No matter how hard I tried, my raps could never compare to Shawn's. I accepted that I wasn't as good as Shawn; I just didn't want it to be a drastic difference. I figured if I could just get closer to his rhyming level, people wouldn't tune me out when listening to the group. So "Shawn's level" was my bar and goal every time I wrote a rhyme.

As time went on and we got a little older, Shawn started to lose interest in rap. He was in his early teenage years and he decided to start working at McDonalds for income. That decision left Kebo and me in limbo, not only with our rap group but with all of our social activities. The three of us played football and baseball together against the neighborhood kids, we went to movies, fairs and wrestling matches together and one of our favorites, we played football on an electronic board with NFL action figures. We kept stats, had a schedule and took the league very serious. All of that diminished when Shawn started working. Kebo and I tried to do our normal routines without Shawn, but it just wasn't the same. Our group "The Awesome 3" was now just two and it was without our best rapper, leader and star of the group.

Chapter 4 - Bright Lights & Brighton Street

After the breakup of "The Awesome 3" I would still write raps and soon afterwards fell in love with pop locking and break dancing (Inspired by the movies Breakin' and Beat Street). I would often perform at my school's talent shows pop locking and break dancing till one day my Math teacher Mrs. Stokes asked the class to write a rap about math. The 10 best raps would be able to perform on stage in front of the entire school. I was a shy kid but whenever there was a chance to perform, I was always up for the challenge. I went home wrote and practiced my rap and performed it in front of my class the next day. Hands down I had the best rap in my class and was chosen to perform for the entire school.

On the day of the show, being as though Mrs. Stokes had already heard everyone's rap, she decided to place the performances in order from worst to best, saving the best for last. I had a feeling from the response I received in the classroom that my rap was the best but it was certified when I was chosen to go on last. After the show, I noticed a change in everyone's persona when I was in their presence. I noticed the stares from the younger students, the smiles from my peers and the acknowledgments from my teachers and principle, addressing me by name when before they never knew, each morning and afternoon. I remember saying to myself "Wow, this must be what stardom feels like" and I loved how it felt. The only problem would be how long will it last and how will I feel when it goes away; or does it have to ever go away?

A few days later while walking home from school my friend Derrick Stanfield was sitting on his porch and called me over to talk. "Yo, I heard that you rocked the house at the school the other day! How does it feel to be a superstar?" I dropped my bookbag and sat on his steps and told him about the show. As we're talking Derrick asked "Are you still rapping in the group with your cousins... The Awesome 3?" I explained to him that we weren't a group anymore because of Shawn's departure and then he says, "Jason, Greg, Donny, Orlando and I are forming a group and we want you to be down. The name of the group is Phaze One." I accepted without hesitation. Being in a group with my friends was the next best thing to being in a group with my cousins.

The next day me and the guys immediately started working on new songs as soon as we came home from school. I didn't want to use DJC as my rap name anymore so I decided to change it to Tornado D. Derrick was "Dub Devastating/ Devastating D" Jason was "Jay Bird" Greg was "Speedy G" and Orlando was "Jose D." Derrick had two older brothers that were heavily into music Mark and Tank. Mark had a connection with a guy that had his own recording studio (Woody) and Derrick made arrangements for us to go in and record our 1st song.

Once the date and time was set, I had to get permission from my father to go to a studio with someone no one knew except Derrick's older brother Mark. I knew this wouldn't go over well with my Dad. I was the youngest kid in the group. If I couldn't leave the block without getting a beating, how would I be able to get into a stranger's car and go to an unknown place to record rap music? Needless to say, I didn't tell my Dad where I was going. I lied and said I was going to be at Derricks house, snuck in Woody's car when he pulled up and went to the studio.

When we arrived, we all were super excited! I remember going over my verses in my head, thinking to myself this must be what Run DMC feels when they're on their way to the studio. I couldn't wait to record my verses and hear myself on a song for the first time. As we walked in, I thought to myself, this looks like somebody's house not a building with studio equipment. It looked like a house because that's exactly what it was. It was Woody's house and the "studio" was one of his rooms that he soundproofed and transformed into a recording booth. Woody and Mark sat at the keyboard, made a beat on the spot and we all rapped and recorded our verses. We all were so proud of the record. The name of the song was called "Phaze One". I was roughly 11 or 12 years old.

When back in the neighborhood, we did what everyone does after recording a song in the studio. We played it over and over again non-stop. We only had one cassette tape and Derrick had possession of it. Everyone in the group including other neighborhood kids would gather on Derricks porch and listen to our new jam for hours at a time.

Derrick was a huge Run DMC fan as well. In fact, he was the biggest fan of us all. All four of the walls in his room were covered with Run DMC posters. Whenever we or anyone came over to visit he would make us salute to one of the Run DMC posters with a hand over the heart saying a pledge of allegiance to Run DMC (all in fun)! Whoever showed resistance he would shoot with his BB gun! So, you either said the pledge or got shot with a BB! Derrick also had turn tables and mixers. He and Jay Bird were the only ones of our crew that had turntables. I wanted some but they were too expensive. It was Derricks house where I learned the true essence of hip hop. He had all of the latest records. From Run DMC, LL's and Fat Boys to later the Eric B & Rakims, EPMD's, Public Enemy's, Boogie Down Productions, MC Shan's and so on and so on's. Derrick's room was our club house. Its where we all came together and enjoyed hip hop in its purest form.

Chapter 5 - Holiness & Adolescence

The group Phaze One stayed together until everyone got a little older and real-life situation started to kick in. When I was in the 7th or 8th grade my mother started attending a Holiness Church and changed her lifestyle. She washed herself from her worldly ways and stopped gambling, cursing and eventually stopped smoking cigarettes. She also stopped wearing pants, make-up and jewelry. Gospel music was the only music allowed to be played in the house and church was mandatory every Tuesday, Friday and all day on Sundays (11am – 11pm). The sudden changes in her lifestyle were shocking but nothing shocked me more than when my Mom asked my Dad to move out. An unmarried couple living together was considered "shacking up" which was against God's will so my Mom insisted that my Dad had to leave. When asked to leave, my Dad didn't argue nor complain. All I remember him saying was "I'll have my things out by tomorrow morning." The next day, my Dad did what he said. He moved all of his belongings out of our apartment and into my grandmother's house adjacent to our apartment building. I was 12 years old.

Now that my Dad was out of the house and my mother was in church a lot, I had total freedom to do whatever I wanted. Whenever I could come up with a good excuse not to attend church (which wasn't often) I would just stay home alone or hang out with my neighborhood friends. Being as though my Mom didn't gamble anymore, we rarely visited my aunts and cousins.

Music wasn't on my radar at the time. I was more focused on surviving in a notoriously violent middle school called William H. Lemmel. My grades landed me in the Advanced Academic Program, so I was among some of the smartest kids in the school, as well as the city. Being in school was harmless, but getting to and from school was the issue. There was a gang called Chocolate City that hung out outside of the school on the top of a hill that terrorized the entire school as well as the community. I was fortunate enough to never have had any bad situations with Chocolate City (I was chased home a few times but never caught), finished my two years and moved on to high school which was Carver Vocational Technical High School (the same high school my Dad attended).

My 1st year in high school was typical I guess for every freshman. A new school, students and teachers would take some time to get used to. I remember before choosing a high school to attend, my neighborhood friends and I would all talk about who from around our way (neighborhood) was already attending the school (just in case we got into a fight and needed back up). That was a very BIG deciding point as to if we would attend the school. Carver was good for me because my older cousin Shawn was already there in his junior year and also a childhood friend named Diggs.

Midway thru the 1ˢᵗ quarter of my freshman year I remember sitting in music class when the teacher (Mrs. Stovall) introduced a new transfer student to the class. His name was Marlon Harper. "Oh shit. My homeboy is here" said Skeeter. Skeeter (Donnell Stokes) was a new friend I met and started to roll with along with Paul Grant. "He's from around my way so nobody ain't fucking with him" said Skeeter as he wrapped his arm around Marlon's neck and walked him to his desk. Before he sat down, Marlon blew a kiss at one of the prettiest girls in the class and started talking to her. All of the guys in the class looked amazed as Marlon openly poured on the charm and got her phone number in front of the entire class. I remember thinking to myself "Wow! This dude is BOLD! He hasn't been here 5 minutes and has already done what majority of all the guys were afraid to do (including myself), and we've been here for weeks! After class ended, Skeeter introduced me and Paul to Marlon and he instantly became the 4ᵗʰ member of our click.

As time went on and everyone was more comfortable with one another, me and the guys gradually started horse playing with each other. It started off with who gets the most girls. Then it moved on to "your mother" jokes. Afterwards came slap boxing. Everyday day after gym while in the locker room we would all square up and box. As time went on I started to notice that Paul, Skeeter and Marlon all focused their aggression towards me. They stopped going at each other and started jumping me 3 on 1. They wouldn't hit me in the face but everything else was fair game. Skeeter was always the first to start and the ring leader. The locker room antics soon moved from the locker room to the school hallways. I remember thinking to myself, "the locker room wasn't bad because it was just us (boys) in there but it's embarrassing to have this going on in the hallways. Girls are watching! These guys are supposed to be my homeboys. What's going on!?" Again, being as though we weren't fighting for real, it didn't warrant me reaching out to my neighborhood friends or cousins for back up. But it was embarrassing. What made it weird is if I had gotten into a fight with someone else these guys would have gone to war with me. One minute we're laughing and joking and the next we're slap boxing or wrestling. Every day it was name calling, teasing and then I was being jumped. It even spilled into the classrooms when we had substitute teachers. I remember one specific time when the had me pinned to the floor and Paul took one of my shoes off. They all stood in three corners on the classroom (Skeeter, Paul and Marlon) and tossed my shoe to each other as I tried to get it back. The entire class laughed as I ran from one person to the next.

I remember in that moment I thought back to when I was nine years old and my mother put me on a little league football team called Franklin Square. The age limit was 10 – 12 but the kids were at least 13 going on 14. It was based in Harlem Park; a tough neighborhood in Baltimore city. I remembered being scared to death every practice and I cried every time the older kids hit me. One day during practice right before we were about to do a drill call "Oklahoma" a guy name Wayne came up to me. He was one of the meanest and toughest boys on the team. As I was crying he wiped my face and helped me put my helmet on. As he snapped my chin strap he said "Don't cry shorty. We're only doing this to make you tougher." I remembered thinking to myself, when I get older I will never allow this to happen again.

Now here I am in the 9th grade (5 years later) running from person to person trying to get my shoe as well as dignity back. Meanwhile while dealing with what today's society calls "bullying" at school, at home I was either there alone or being forced to attend church with my mother. My mother sold life insurance for a living so her hours fluctuated. I never knew when she would or not be home. My Dad and grandmother were across the alley and available if needed. When I didn't want to be at home alone I would go to my Dad's house and HE would just talk. We didn't watch TV or sports together. He would just talk and I would listen. He told me all of his childhood stories as well as his experiences in the Korean War when he was drafted into the Army as a young man. He talked to me a lot but what I didn't know at the time was he was planting seeds of wisdom in me that I would later use in my adult life.

On Tuesdays, Fridays and Sundays my mother would take me to church with her. The name of the church was Holy Temple Holiness Church of Deliverance. The pastor, founder and overseers name was Julia Williams. Here is where I was first introduced to my Lord and Savior Jesus Christ. My Christian foundation was instilled in me here but I also witnessed things that I'd never experienced at previous churches.

Holy Temple was a small church (maybe 100-150 members) mostly all were family members to one another. They believed in praise so it was a lot of shouting (back then it was called catching the Holy Ghost) and hooping style preaching. As a young kid, the Bible was confusing enough and when the Preacher started hoop preaching, I never could interpret or understand what they were saying. I often fell asleep until I felt a pinch or nudge from my mother telling me to wake up. Pastor Williams was a prophetess so after every service, she would call people out of the congregation and tell them what the Lord said. When called, you would have to stand, raise your hands and receive God's word. I didn't like this part of the service at all. I was always afraid that she would call on me. Lots of times she would have the person run around the church and shout. Pastor Williams had prayer lines where she would pray for people and they would pass out. I was petrified of that. She also casted out demons. She would tell all of the kids to touch a Bible and while the men held down the person possessing the demon, she would pray, speak in tounges and splash holy water on them (or oil). Sometimes she would put the microphone to the person who's possessed mouth so the entire church can hear the growl and the foul mouth of the demon. Me being terrified is an understatement.

On prayer nights we would all come to the alter and pray for hours. Then we would tarry for the Holy Ghost. Tarrying is when you say Jesus over and over again, as fast as you can until you start foaming at the mouth. We were told as kids that the foaming was the sin coming out of us. My cousins, Shawn, Keacha, Tinika, Angie and Kevin all attended Holy Temple with me and our mothers. Holy Temple way of life was law to me and I never questioned anything until tragedy made its way to the forefront. My younger cousin Tinika (age 10) was diagnosed with leukemia and wasn't expected to live. Of course, being as though we had Pastor Williams I thought we had a direct connect with God and my cousin would be healed and cured. Pastor Williams prayed for Tinika and also prophesied that Tinika would live. Our entire family was ecstatic about the good news. A few months later Tinika died.

Chapter 6 - High School Obstacles

Going into my sophomore year in high school, I was determined to make sure that what happened last year wouldn't happen again. So, I decided that whatever my crew did to me I would do it 10 times back to them. I would go to the extremes on all levels! If you bump me with your shoulder, I would hit you with a chair. If they jumped me, I would chase only one of them and when I caught him (no matter how long it took) I would beat him nonstop. If you teased or called me names I would do the same about your mother or grandmother. EVERYTHING times 10. I also decided to focus my aggression on the lead troublemaker, Skeeter. If you chop off the head, the body will soon fall!

The first day of school was cool. Everyone was happy to see each other and show off their new clothes but after the excitement wore off, the crew gradually started back with the horse play. When going to one of my classes, I found a metal pole outside of the auto mechanic shop class (pocket size) and I connected it to my key chain. Later that day, while sitting in class, I felt someone pluck my ear from behind. Skeeter, Paul and Marlon were laughing along with a few girls. I got up, pulled the pole out of my pocket and cracked Skeeter on the knee cap. The sound was so loud the entire class said "DAMN!" As he held his knee screaming in pain, I punched him in his arm and said "what's up" smiling as I did so. Skeeter yelled "yo aight, aight. I quit!" laughing but holding his knee still in pain. While everyone was laughing, Paul asked me "Yo what was that you hit him with?" I said "It's the Skeeter beater!" The whole class burst out in laughter. "Every time he acts up I'm busting his ass with the Skeeter beater!" And that's exactly what I did. Even the least amount of horse play, I would pull the pole out and hit Skeeter even if he wasn't the one committing the act. Once I had Skeeter in check, Paul and Marlon fell in line and all of the horse playing stopped.

We all hung together as much as we could despite taking different classes and enrolled in different trades. Paul was in Carpentry, Marlon was in Printing, Skeeter was in Brick Laying and I was in Drafting. As our sophomore year went on, everyone started going their separate ways except for me and Marlon. We stayed close and hung out together every single day. Later that year, Skeeter dropped out and started hustling.

By the end of my sophomore year, Marlon and I were inseparable. Whenever you saw one, you saw the other. We did everything together from playing basketball, watching movies and reciting the lines (House Party, Harlem Nights, Jungle

Fever- Gator Scenes) to just hanging out doing nothing. Every morning before school I would walk to Marlon's house and his mom (Ms. Brenda) would fix us fried eggs and sausages. They were the best eggs ever! Marlon's house reminded me of the girl's house in the movie House Party with all of the family members everywhere. The house technically belonged to his grandmother. She was a very soft and kind elderly woman. Every time we came in and left out we would kiss her on the cheek and she would just smile. It was a three-story house and Marlon's aunts and uncles were everywhere. Marlon also had a baby sister name Jennifer.

Marlon was a lady's man. A true charmer. He always knew what to say and how to say it when it came to girls. Me on the other hand was shy and never knew what to say. Marlon would often "coach" me on how to talk to girls and what they liked. He taught me about keeping my room clean (damn near spotless) so when a girl comes over, she feels comfortable in the clean environment compared to the dirty rooms she may have been in before. Sprinkling baby powder under your sheets, lightly spraying your pillows with cologne all were plays from Marlon's playbook.

Marlon always had a girlfriend (sometimes two or three). When spending time with his girlfriend he always insisted that I came along with them. I was always the third wheel. Marlon made it clear to all of his girls, that if they wanted to spend time with him, they had to be cool with me around. He always tried to get whatever girl he was dealing with at the time to hook me up with their homegirls. I would drop the ball every time. Marlon felt bad for me and wanted me to experience what he was experiencing when it came to girls. I remember one time he and his girlfriend were making out on one end of the bed as I sat on the other end. He did this a lot but this time it looked as if they were about to go all the way. I felt uncomfortable because this wasn't some random girl that no one knew, this was Towanda, Marlon's main girl and a friend of mine. Before cloths started coming off, Towanda stopped Marlon and said "Why would you do this in front of Wayne?" She got up and walked into the bathroom to fix her hair. Marlon didn't mean any harm. He just got caught up in the moment and wanted me to experience making out (because he knew I wasn't doing it with anybody) the best way he could, even if it exposed his main girl.

I remember when I had a crush on a girl named Tracy Artis and I told Marlon to help me out. Marlon gave me the words but I didn't have the balls to approach her. Several days went by and I still hadn't approached Tracy. Marlon knew exactly what to say to get me going. School had just let out and Tracy was coming out of the main doors. He said "Look Slice (Slice is what we called each other), if you don't talk to her, I WILL!" Needless to say, I knew he would so I had no choice but to take action by approaching Tracy. Tracy and I soon afterwards began to date and later became boyfriend and girlfriend.

In my Junior year in high school I only had two things on my mind. Money and girls. I always worked odd jobs here and there throughout my childhood (pumped peoples gas at gas stations for spare change, shoveling snow, raking leaves, washing cars etc.). When I was 14 my childhood friend Donny got me a job where he worked (Burger King). This was my 1st "real" job and I made $3.35 per hour. Now at about 15 or 16 I figured if I had a good paying job, I could buy nice clothes and that would get me more attention to get more girls! My cousin Shawn was a crew leader at McDonalds and he convinced his manager to hire me at 15 (even though you had to be 16 to work there). I learned at an early age of how important connections/ relationships are in this competitive world we live in today.

I kept my passion for music hidden from those who didn't share the same passion. Me and Marlon were like brothers yet I didn't talk about my love for music until one day a school flyer surfaced asking for participants for a Talent Show. I thought back to when I was I elementary school and the response I received from that show. I wanted to feel that feeling again. I wanted to feel like I was important, I wanted to be noticed. I wanted to feel like a star and I knew I had what it took to be special when it came to music but I didn't want to do it alone. I told Marlon I wanted to enter the Talent Show and I wanted him to be my hype man. Of course, he was with it even though he never heard me rap. The first time I rapped for Marlon, he looked shocked, almost as if he saw a ghost. "Yooooooo, I didn't know you were nice like that!" We both laughed and started putting together our show. As we were putting the final touches on the show, I remember thinking to myself this is it! The whole school will know who I am after this! At the audition, a fight broke out and the Talent Show was canceled. I was crushed. Music was my superpower and that show was the only way to show it. After the show was canceled I gradually put rapping on the back burner and started focusing on making money and chasing girls.

Chapter 7 - Pushing Through

Maybe two or three days during the week and on the weekends, I would go to work at McDonalds. Like at school, I was quite and I stayed to myself. I didn't know anyone except my cousins Shawn and Chantell. Shawn introduced me to two of his close friends Rodney and Malcolm. They also went to my high school. Every day at work, all we would do is crack jokes on each other for the entire shift. We all eventually became very close friends. Shawn, Rodney and Malcolm created a name for their click called "JB" before I started working there. All of the girls at the job even some of the guys would ask them "what does JB stand for?" They would never tell. They had a saying "JB only 3... Malcolm, Shawn and Rodney!" The mystery of JB was always the talk of the job. Everyone wanted to know what JB stood for including the managers. Being as though I was rolling with them all of the time, I wanted to know what JB stood for. So, I asked them, and they all laughed but wouldn't tell. I even tried to pull my cousin Shawn to the side by himself and ask but he wouldn't tell me.

The summer of 1989 NWA's album "Straight Out of Compton" made its way to Baltimore and took the streets by storm. Everyone was in a frenzy about the subjects and language displayed on the album. I remember asking my cousin Shawn about what NWA stood for. When he told me "Niggas With Attitudes" I couldn't believe it! We talked like this all the time in the hood but I never heard this kind of language on a song. I immediately was drawn in and wanted to hear everything this group had to say. Not long afterwards, I knew every single lyric on the entire album by heart and so did Shawn, Malcolm and Rodney. Everyday after work, while waiting for the bus or even sometimes walking home, we all would recite the entire album (but more so Gangsta Gangsta and I Aint The One) all the way home. We gave a show to all who watched and an earful to all that could hear.

The more we performed these songs the more I began to get that musical itch again. The way Shawn, Rodney, Malcolm and I recited NWA lyrics, reminded me of when Shawn and I were younger (The Awesome Three) reciting Run DMC. One night after work while walking home, I suggested to the guys that we should start our own rap group. "You guys are already known as JB, so let's make it a group!" Everyone was excited about the idea and ready to go. The only problem was JB was "only three" Malcolm, Shawn and Rodney. I would be the fourth member and JB only four just didn't have the same feel. So, I suggested we keep the name as JB Only 3 but add "and the dope producer

Wayne." And there it was, we were officially called JB only 3 and the dope producer Wayne.

Being as though Shawn didn't rhyme since we were The Awesome Three and Rodney and Malcolm never rapped except for reciting NWA, I wrote all of the songs. As time went on, my passion for the group never wavered but I can't say the same for the rest of the guys. Music was my love but to them, it was just something to do. Eventually the rap group ended without us recording a single song. On a high note, the guys did finally tell me what JB stood for but I'll never tell!

The summer before going into my junior year of high school Marlon convinced me to try out for our high school's football team. At the first day of try outs I remember the smell of the grass reminding me of when I played with Franklin Square when I was younger. I thought to myself, this is my chance to redeem myself from being tossed around like a rag doll as a kid. While everyone else was simply trying out and going through the motions, I had a personal fire burning inside of me. I refused to let what happened to me as a young kid happen as a teenager. I also decided to use the "Skeeter Beater" approach. Whatever someone attempted to do to me, I would do it in return times ten! Every drill and every play, I ran into my opponent full speed and tried to take their head off. I played Strong Safety on defense and Marlon played wide receiver. One day at practice, the offense ran a reverse play headed my way with Marlon running the ball. As soon as I realized it was a reverse headed my way, I ran full speed at Marlon. When the running back tossed Marlon the ball I was a split second away laying a ferocious hit that knocked him completely off of his feet. The entire field went completely silent. I got up and ran back to the defensive huddle and never looked back. As Marlon slowly got up, everyone was looking as "if he would hit his best friend like that, imagine what he would do to someone else?" I immediately gained the respect of my entire team as well as all of the coaches. I felt redeemed. All of the turmoil I went through at Franklin Square was redeemed at the expense of a ferocious hit on my best friend.

After the football season was over, I decided to try out for basketball and I made team. Marlon didn't want to try out for basketball. He wanted to spend more time with his new girlfriend Angie. By this time, me and Tracy had went our separate ways. I can't remember why, but we just drifted apart. Basketball took up most of my afterschool time so I didn't hang out with Marlon as much out of school. While in school, we were two peas in a pod until it was time to go to trade class.

My trade instructor was Mr. Joseph Haus. He was a short Jewish man that resembled Mario from the Nintendo game (Super Mario Brothers). With the exception of my father, this man had the most significant impact on my teenage life. The trade was drafting but he taught me more things about life than he ever did about 90-degree triangles and T-squares. Growing up in Baltimore City, I never had interactions with other races except with the police or some sort of corporate setting (stores, courts, etc.). Mr. Haus was the 1st non-black that I ever had one on one interactions with. At the time I didn't even know what being Jewish was. To me he was just a white guy with a different accent. At Carver high school, when in your junior year, the school day was split in half. The first half, students would take academic classes and the second half of the day would be spent in your trade class. So, after lunch the remaining of the day would be spent in trade class.

The trade Drafting was not a popular trade so the class was very small, roughly about 10- 12 students. At the time I wanted to be an architect so this was the class to be in. Mr. Haus always found a way to sneak in a life lesson within his lesson plan. As he would be showing how to properly drag a pencil on an angle while spinning the point to keep the lines even, he would stop and ask me "What are you going to do with your life?" "What are your plans after high school?" I never thought about things like that before meeting Mr. Haus. Girls, money and clothes consumed the majority of my thoughts. Besides that, the goal for me and all of my friends was just to live to see 18. If we made it to 18, the next goal was 21. After that, 25. If we live to see 25 in our minds, we've made it!

Mr. Haus would often call me into his office after class and just talk. He was very concerned about my future. More so than I was. He talked about colleges, money, credit and anything you could think of that I would later face after leaving high school.

I retained some of the info but like most teenagers, some of the info was going in one ear and out the other. Preparing to be a grownup was the furthest thing from my mind. Its like he was giving me the keys but I wasn't wise enough to fully understand was he was doing.

The same goes for my Dad as well. My father would talk to me all of the time about everything. He would always say "Son if you ever ask me something that I don't know the answer to, I promise I know where to go to get the answer" (and this was years before the internet). My dad would always tell me that I was smarter than him and he kept his mouth loaded with encouraging words whenever I needed to hear them.

Chapter 8 - You're A Leader

Out of all my childhood friends (Derrick, Jay Bird, Peanut, Donny, Greg, Shawn & Terry) Derrick Stanfield was always the leader and Jay Bird was second in command. After Derrick and Jay Bird graduated from high school, they enlisted in the army and went away to boot camp, leaving a void of leadership on our block. The rest of us continued to hang out but the block just wasn't the same. When Derrick and Jay Bird returned, we all were like kids waiting for Santa Claus! Everyday we would all gather on Derricks porch and just hang out. One day after everyone had left to go in for the night, Derrick called me on the phone and asked me to come back to his porch. I went back outside and he told me that he was about to go away to college (University of Maryland Eastern Shore). Then he told me something that would change the way I thought forever. He said "Yo, do you notice that whenever we're hanging out and you decide to leave, everyone leaves right behind you? When you talk, everyone listens. You're a leader man and you don't even know it! The torch is passed. They're following you now, not me."

The end of my junior year was approaching and the junior prom was right around the corner. Prom night was always a big deal because it meant you were almost guaranteed to have sex that night. Marlon was dating a girl named Angie at the time and was practically living with her. On the weekends and even sometimes during the week Angie's Mom would allow him to spend the night. It wasn't the norm for a parent to allow this but Marlon had the kind of charm that could win over almost any female willing to listen to him. Needless to say, Marlon didn't need a "prom night" to have sex. There were many others before Angie was even in the picture. As for me, I had only had sex one time and it was with a girl I hardly knew. My childhood friend Greg had hooked me up with her after he had had sex with her. Her name was Michelle. I spoke to her for the first time on a Monday and had sex with her on a Tuesday. She was my first. Afterwards, I never spoke with her again.

I didn't want to attend the junior prom because at the time I didn't have a girlfriend but Marlon insisted that I'd go. He wanted me to find someone to experience what he experienced all of the time. He and his girlfriend Angie tried hooking me up with a few girls but they already had dates and the ones that didn't have dates needed me to pay for their dresses because their Moms couldn't afford one. That definitely wasn't happening. I could barely get money for my own outfit.

Just as I was about to give up, I decided to call my ex-girlfriend Tracy and ask her if she was willing to go. We didn't break up on bad terms, we just drifted apart. Also, we never had sex. We tried a few times but it never happened. Tracy gladly accepted and I was all set for the junior prom but more importantly to a 16-year-old boy, I had an appointment to have sex!

On the night of the junior prom I was on a triple date. Marlon and Angie, myself and Tracy and Angie's home girl named Nicole and her date (a fireman for Baltimore City). We didn't have money for a limo or a rental car so Nicole's date (never knew his name) drove his Van and took us all to the prom. After it was over, Marlon and I had a discussion on what would happen next. Normally couples went out to eat and then a hotel but we didn't have enough money for both so we decided to get some Chinese Food from a carry out that we were both familiar with (North & Longwood). I remember all of the goons on the corner giving me and Marlon high fives for "keeping it a hundred" and walking into the Chinese joint with our tuxedos on after leaving a prom. This move allowed us to have money for the hotel room. Nicole's date was the only one old enough to get the rooms so all three rooms were in his name. We all went into our rooms and Tracy and I slept together for the very first time. Even though I had technically had sex one time before, I consider this moment with Tracy as my first because it was with someone I knew and cared about. The next morning, I called my mother and she said Tracys father had been calling all night looking for us. I was afraid to bring her home thinking her Dad was going to kill me. Luckily when we dropped her off, he wasn't on the porch waiting. Once we saw Tracy get in the door we sped off and left. Me and Tracy never got back together but remained friends.

Chapter 9 - First Love

The summer before my senior year in high school (1990) was a summer that I would never forget. If I wasn't at work (McDonalds) I was either playing basketball at the neighborhood playground or hanging out with my friends. Around this time, me and my homies were starting to explore the club scenes and house parties. There were numerous clubs in Baltimore but our favorite spots were Odells and the Paradox. Sometimes instead of going to the clubs, we would go to the infamous house parties thrown by Vincent (DJ Vicious V). Vincent lived on the corner of Brighton and Ellamont St. Every time he threw a party the entire neighborhood would come. The house was always packed, so much you could barely move in there but we loved it. We were among all of our peers and we felt safe. Plus, we got to "freak" all of the neighborhood girls. Occasionally a fight would break out, but Vincent would always find a way to squash the beef and get back to the party. Everyone in the neighborhood had a high level of respect for Vincent. He was loud and kind of obnoxious. A lot of people were afraid of him but you would have to know him to love him. He was our DJ. The guy that kept our parties jumping.

One day while sitting on my father's steps, Jay Bird walked down the block calling my name. "Yo Wayne, what's up? What are you about to do?" I told Jay that I was just chilling... what's up? He went on to say "Yo, I got some girls on their way over here. My homegirl Teresa and her friend Adriene! I've been trying to get with Adriene for a while now and she agreed to come though if Teresa came with her!" I asked Jay, "What's up with Teresa!? How does she look?" He said "Teresa is fine but she's 18 years old and has two kids." At the time, I didn't care about how many kids she had. I just wanted to see what she looked like.

About an hour or so later, Teresa and Adriene arrived at Jay Birds house and he told her that I wanted to meet her. She agreed and I walked to Jays house and introduced myself. Teresa was fine, Just as Jay said. She was tall with a slim build and had a beautiful smile. I remember being nervous thinking to myself "she's 18 and I'm only 16! She has 2 kids so it's clear that she's experienced and I'm not!" But then I thought to myself, what would Marlon do? How would he approach this? I was around Marlon and other girls so much (being a 3rd wheel) I knew exactly what he would do and say. So that's what I did. I transformed into Marlon! We began to talk on one end of Jays porch while he and Adriene talked on the other. More time had passed and I suggested that Teresa and I walk to my house and leave Jay and Adriene some time for themselves. We went to my apartment and sat outside on the balcony. I couldn't have company in my bedroom so I figured the balcony was the best place for a little privacy. Teresa and I talked for hours. The more we talked, the more I felt comfortable and soon I didn't have to stay in "Marlon Mode". I was able to be myself. She told me she had a boy and a baby girl. Her kid's father was in and out of jail and she wasn't technically with him anymore but he's always around. She had her own apartment and he lived across the street.

A few weeks had gone by and Teresa and I talked every day during this time and became closer. On Friday's nights, when my mother went to church, Teresa would catch the bus to my apartment and later I would walk her to North Avenue to catch a hack (a Baltimore term meaning illegal cab) back home. The more she visited, the closer we became intimately and I knew it was just a matter of time before we slept together. One Friday night just moments before it was time for Teresa to leave, we began to kiss in my doorway. We've kissed before but this time was it was different. We kissed as if it was the last time we would ever see each other; passionate, meaningful and full of lust! As we were kissing Teresa slowly unbuckled my pants and gently started stroking my penis. The moment she grabbed it, she immediately stopped kissing me and looked at me with a look of surprise. Her eyes opened wide as well as her mouth. At the time I didn't know what shocked her so much so I continued to kiss her and then we went back to my room.

Teresa took off her clothes and so did I. As I sat on the side of my bed, putting on a condom, I remember thinking to myself "I really have to perform well or else this will be the first and last time she'll have sex with me". Up till this moment, I had only had sex twice and now I'm 16 in bed with an 18-year-old with two kids and lots of experience. The moment I entered inside of her I knew I wouldn't last long. Between the way she was moving her hips and the noises she was making, I didn't stand a chance. Within 3 to 4 minutes of having sex, it was over.

The next day I called Marlon and told him what had happened. He said "Man you gotta think of something boring while you're doing it. Its all in your mind! Think of baseball!" The next Friday Teresa came over and we had sex again. This time we started almost as soon as she got to my apartment which meant we had more time because my mother would usually be in church for about 3 to 4 hours. The mind trick worked. As soon as I felt myself getting too excited, I would think of sometime boring or switch positions to give myself time to calm down. We had sex all night giving each other multiple orgasms and then we both agreed it was official. We were now in a committed relationship (well at least on my part). Teresa still had her kids father lurking in the background. At this time, he was in jail but due to come home soon.

As the summer went on Teresa and I were inseparable. Friday nights weren't enough so I started going to her apartment to spend time with her. This was the same apartment that her kids father (as well as his family) lived directly across the street from. I remember being scared out of my mind as the hack was driving down her block approaching her apartment. There were so many dudes outside and I didn't know if one of them were related to her kids father or one of his homeboys. Her kids father name was Tyrone and he was well known for trouble in that neighborhood. I would never get out of the car directly in front of her house. I didn't want the attention of people asking "Who is that going into Teresa's house?" I would always get out a few houses down, linger around until I saw a moment and then sprint to the door. I would literally pray each time before I made that trip. The butterflies I had in my stomach were sometimes unbearable and my leg wouldn't stop shaking at times but I wouldn't let none of that stop me from seeing Teresa. By this time, we were doing so much more than just sex. We were now doing oral sex as she allowed and encouraged me to finish in her mouth. She taught me how to please her orally which in both cases were new to me. Taking showers together, full body massages, full course meals, waking up from naps to oral sex at the early age of 16; I was COMPLETELY sprung.

As the summer was coming to an end Tyrone was released from jail and things took a slight turn with Teresa and me. Tyrone was spending a lot of time at Teresa's apartment and the reason I was given was that he was visiting the children. Teresa stuck to the story of they were just co-parenting. Sometimes I would call her house and he would answer the phone. Each time, he would take the phone to her without any problems and Teresa and I would talk as normal. This kind of solidified Teresa's claim of the two of them just co- parenting. I didn't get the feeling of Teresa and Tyrone messing around but I didn't feel comfortable going to her house anymore. Yet still when she called, there I was, walking to North Avenue, waving down a hack, approaching her apartment praying with butterflies and a shaking leg. The stressful part was always making it in the house un-noticed. Once I was in, I felt better. One time, while spending the night at Teresa's, around 2 o'clock in the morning we heard a pounding at the door. I heard a man's voice yelling "Teresa! Open this muthafuckin' door! Do you got a nigga in there!?" Immediately my heart dropped. Teresa's phone wasn't on (disconnected) at the time and of course there wasn't any cell phones back then therefore I couldn't call anyone for assistance. I looked at the windows for an escape, only to notice the bars covering them in order to keep out intruders. I was trapped! No where to go and I couldn't call anyone. Teresa yelled through the door "No ones in here Tyrone! Take your drunk ass home! Leave before the police come!" Tyrone continued to bang on the door for another 15 minutes or so (which felt like hours) and then suddenly the banging stopped. Teresa looked at me and said "Don't worry about him. He always gets like that when he drinks. He doesn't know you're in here." She then attempted to kiss me leading towards sex. I kissed her but didn't sleep with her. I was so nervous, sex was the last thing on my mind (besides, we had already had sex three times before the encounter started). All I could think about was walking out of the front door tomorrow and being shot dead before I made it off the block. Tyrone was around 21 or 22 years old and Teresa told me a while ago that he carried a gun. The next morning around 6am, I walked outside with my head on a swivel, and saw no one! "Thank God" I thought to myself as I walked to West Side Shopping Center in search of a hack. When I got home I said to myself, I'm never going over there again. Four days later I found myself in a hack, praying with butterflies and a shaking leg on my way to Teresa's again. The power of a woman's touch! I was hooked and in love.

Chapter 10 - Senior Year

Twelfth grade year has arrived! I was officially a senior in high school. I had my best friend Marlon, my girlfriend Teresa and I felt like I was grown because I was doing grown man things. The only problem was I was broke! Marlon and I couldn't afford the clothes and sneakers the kids were wearing at the time so we decided to flip the script. We decided to dress up everyday in slacks, dress shirts and hard bottom shoes. We figured we would look nice/ professional, we would stand out from everyone else and the biggest point, it was cheaper!

One day while walking down the school halls, Marlon and I bumped into the Varsity Football Coach (Coach Shell). We tried to duck him out but it was too late. Marlon and I had tried out and made the varsity team that summer but quit right before school started. Coach Shell asked "Why did you two stop coming to practice? What happened?" I told Coach Shell that I couldn't play football because I had to work (at the time I was still working at McDonalds). That's when Coach Shell told me something that I would later tell all high school kids in the future... He said

"Son, you have the rest of your life to go to work. You only get a small window, chance and opportunity to play high school football. Once it's done, it's done. You can never go back. Enjoy your high school years to the fullest!" Then he walked away.

I missed out on playing Varsity football my senior year (I only played in a few pre- season games before I quit) but Coach Shells words stuck with me and when basketball season started I quit my job and made the team. Basketball took up a lot of my time during the week therefore Marlon and I couldn't hang out as much and I didn't see Teresa either. I played JV the year before but varsity was a whole different beast. Before junior varsity, I had never played organized basketball. I only played at my neighborhood playground and a few BNBL (Baltimore Neighborhood Basketball League) games. I could barely dribble with my left hand yet alone shoot with it. But I was tall and I knew how to position myself under the basket to get rebounds. That's how I made the team. My coach (Coach Durce Jackson) taught me from scratch how to play the game of basketball. At every practice he would always find a little time to work with me personally one on one to improve my game. I barely got in the game at times, my minutes were extremely low, but he always found time to get me in when it made since and when I could be successful. By mid-season, I was dunking (off the step and vertical) and finishing with both hands. My dad always inquired and asked to come to one of my games but I always pushed it off and told him not to come. Although I was getting better as a player, I was embarrassed about not getting playing time and I didn't want my dad to see me on the bench. My mom on the other hand, showed no interest. We won the Championship that year and I was named most improved player on the team. I sometimes wonder what could have happened if I had got an earlier start and been mentored by coaches like Coach Jackson well before my senior year in high school? Maybe this would be a different reading but that's neither here nor there.

After the basketball season ended, everything went back to normal. Marlon and I was hanging out during the week and Teresa and I spent time together on the weekends. One evening while sitting in my room watching TV, I heard Marlon outside of my apartment window. "Yo Slice!" he called. When I went to the window, I saw Marlon outside on a bike. He said "Yo come outside! Somebody was killed at the top of your block!" I went outside and saw a man lying in the street with a bullet hole in his head. His eyes were still open and it wasn't a lot of blood like you would imagine but still it was a horrific scene. That was the first dead body I saw but definitely not the last.

My mother was still going to church every Tuesday, Friday and Sunday and always pushed for me to join her. One Sunday I decided to go to church with my mother without putting up my usual fight. Little did I know that this Sunday would be a sermon that I would never forget. Morning service normally started at 10:30am and didn't end till 4pm or later. Roughly around 3pm this particular Sunday, Pastor Williams started prophesizing to random members of the church. This was always scary to me because I didn't like to be called on and put on the spot so I would slouch down in my seat and try not to make eye contact as she combed through the congregation. Suddenly Pastor Williams stopped and starred in my direction. I thought she was looking at me but actually she was looking at my mother. She began to prophesize to my mother and announced to the entire congregation "God has sent you a husband!" She then pointed to a complete stranger by the name of Douglass Zimmerman. "God said that's your husband!" The entire church started shouting and praising God while my mother and Mr. Douglass Zimmerman starred in shock.

A few days later I heard my mother on the phone with my aunts speaking about wedding arrangements. I couldn't believe it. I thought to myself, how can you marry someone you don't know? My mother's cousin was also prophesized to that day and was set to marry a complete stranger also. They were planning on having a double wedding. The reasoning behind the decision was because God said so through prophecy.

Not too long afterwards, my father found out about the wedding. At this point my mother and father barely spoke to each other. The only time they spoke is when it involved me. I remember sitting at the front living room window at my father's house hearing him plead with my mother not to marry Mr. Douglass. After about an hour of pleading his case, my father hung up the phone and started crying. That was the first time

I saw my Dad, my hero shed a tear. Of course, me seeing this broke me and I started crying. My Dad hugged me and said that he didn't want to lose me and that was the reason why he was crying. I didn't understand how he thought he would lose me just because my mother was getting married. At the time I was around 16 years old so my foundation was etched in stone in regards to who my father was. I believe that my father still loved my mother and her marrying a complete stranger was hurtful but he didn't want to tell me that. He stuck to the notion of he didn't want to lose me.

About a month later my mother married Mr. Douglass (a double wedding with her cousin) and Mr. Douglass moved into our apartment. Keep in mind that this is the same apartment that my Mom and Dad got together, the same apartment my Mom asked my Dad to leave, the same apartment that was adjacent to my father's house (only thing separating the two was an alley) and the same neighborhood where EVERYONE knew my father and some knew my mother as well. I remember feeling bad for my Dad because all of this was on display for all of the neighbors to watch. Watching Mr. Douglass move his things into the apartment while everyone starred and murmured "Who's this guy" and "Where did he come from?" was hard but my Dad being the class act that he was held his head high with his shoulders back and greeted Mr. Douglass with the sincerest smile and handshake. Once the neighborhood saw my father's warm attitude towards Mr. Douglass, everything fell into place and all of the possible drama seized before it even had a chance to start.

Mr. Douglass had three children. His oldest son was doing time in prison, his middle daughter was away at college and his youngest son (maybe 2 or 3 years younger than me) came over on the weekends. This was a major adjustment for my mother and me. I was an only child and used to my own space. Now on the weekends, I had to share my room with a kid I didn't know as well as share my mother with a complete stranger. Adjustments were made and we all did the best we could in order to get along. One day while dozing in and out of sleep in my room, all of a sudden heard Mr. Douglass drop the f bomb coming out of my mother's room (this was a HUGE deal because Holiness Christians never cursed- well at least that's what I thought). Half woke, I jumped up and ran into my mother's room to see what was going on. When I entered the room, my mother was on one side of the bed (standing) and Mr. Douglass was on the other. I couldn't tell if they had been physically fighting or not but it looked like they were about to. Mr. Douglass was screaming "Call your ex (speaking about my father) I want him anyway!" My mother then replied "I don't have to call him. I have enough brothers that can handle you!"

I don't remember much after that. Mr. Douglass left that night and never returned. Shortly afterwards my mother and Mr. Douglass were divorced. This experience similar to my cousins Tinika's death, made me feel a little weird about church and prophecy.

Once Mr. Douglass was gone and things were back to normal, I was back to kicking it with my neighborhood friends and my best friend Marlon. One day out of the blue Marlon says to me "Yo Slice, I think I'm going to break up with Angie. It's time for me to step my game up!" I brushed him off because I thought he was just having a moment but little did I know, he was serious. Marlon wanted a woman not a teen aged girl! Months before, he told me that he was sleeping with one of his mother's girlfriends (Ms. Patty). Ms. Patty was in her late thirties and Marlon was sleeping with her on and off since he was 15. Marlon's mother (Ms. Brenda) never knew. She would have killed Ms. Patty and to put the icing on top, Ms. Patty was married. "I'm tired of all of these immature little girls at the school" Marlon says. "I want one of the teachers!" "A teacher! Man, you're crazy!" I said. "What teacher is gonna holla at student??" Marlon said "Shid, you'll never know till you try!"

And that's exactly what Marlon did. Marlon wrote a love letter to our science teacher named Ms. Palmer. Ms. Palmer was cute, light skinned with a slim build. I remember Marlon letting me read the letter before he gave it to her and I thought to myself "Wow, he's really gonna try this!" The letter was very neat and respectful but also direct. He made his intentions perfectly clear. He also sprayed cologne on it so when she opened the envelope that would be the first impression. One day after Ms. Palmers class ended, Marlon and I waited till the students cleared out and Marlon went up to her and gave her the letter. My heart dropped as Ms. Palmer cracked open the envelope and reached in for the letter. Marlon bopped away as usual with the highest confidence possible. About an hour later, while in Mr. Davis English class, Ms. Palmer, another male teacher and the Vice Principle interrupted the class and asked to speak with Marlon privately. Marlon once again bopped out of the class with his head held high. I remember thinking to myself, this is it. He's going to get expelled from school and will not be able to graduate. Twenty minutes later, Marlon returned to the class room with a poker face and took his seat. The entire class was wondering why he got pulled out but only he and I knew. After the bell rang, Marlon and I huddled up in the hall way and he told me what happened. "Man Ms. Palmer was pissed! They were talking about putting me out of the school. I had to apologize and plead with them not to put me out! That was a close call."

A month or so had past and Marlon was back at it again. You would think that almost getting expelled from school would settle his urge but that wasn't the case. If anything, it probably added fuel to the fire. This time Marlon had his eyes set on the baddest female in the entire school, Ms. Lucas! Ms. Lucas was the school's secretary that worked in the main office. She was light skinned, had long black hair, green eyes and a body most men would kill for. She looked like a professional cover page model. The male teachers all would stare uncontrollably every time she walked by. We as students were mesmerized. It didn't matter what she wore, she couldn't hide her body features and when she walked, everything moved!

Once again, Marlon wrote another letter, neat, respectful and very direct. As soon as we arrived at school, he went into the main office and handed Ms. Lucas the letter. As before he walked out of the office bopping with confidence, head up high. While we were in first period, I kept starring at the door anticipating the Vice Principle (Ms. Diana) scooping him out of class once again. But it didn't happen. First, second and third period came and went, no Vice Principal. When we went to lunch, Marlon was constipating on whether he should go into the main office to follow up or do it after school. During lunch the office was always busy so we both agreed it would be best if he went in after school. When the dismissal bell rang I thought to myself, wow he made it though the entire day and didn't get pulled out of class. Marlon and I walked up to the main office and waited till some of the traffic settled down. "Yo Slice, this is it! I'm about to go in there and see what's up" I gave Marlon a pound and he walked into the office. Ten minutes later Marlon came out of the office bopping like George Jefferson. He came to me and said "Look Slice!" He turned his face to the right and showed me a lip stick kiss on his cheek! I couldn't believe it! He got a kiss from Ms. Lucas! He also had a note that she wrote back with her phone number! "See Slice! Anything is possible if you go hard! We jetted out of the school and went home both in awe and in somewhat disbelief. Marlon just booked Ms. Lucas!

As the weeks went by Marlon and Ms. Lucas continued to write each other every day. Even though he had her number, he decided to still give her romantic letters because he knew he was up against all odds. Marlon was only 17 and Ms. Lucas was in her mid-thirties. She wasn't seeing any one seriously but of course there were a few guys lurking coming in and out of her life and Marlon was determined to push them away. Ms. Lucas also had a son (older than us) but he was locked up for attempted murder. Ms. Lucas lived directly across the street from our high school so as more time went by eventually Marlon started walking her home from work/ school. Time went on and Marlon started sleeping with Ms. Lucas and eventually moved in with her. Now after school, instead of going home, Marlon and I were going to Ms. Lucas house! Unbelievable... and soon Ms. Lucas wasn't Ms. Lucas anymore. She was Denise. Marlon was in a full relationship with Ms. Lucas/ Denise. Some teachers and staff were starting to inquire about the relationship but Marlon, Denise and I remained silent. We didn't deny or confirm their assumptions. We simply said nothing. On the weekends Teresa and I would stay with Marlon and Denise at Denise's house. There was nothing you could tell us. We thought we were Gods for a lack of a better term.

At the end of our senior year, Marlon and I started planning for the senior prom. Of course, I would be taking Teresa but Marlon's situation was a little tricky. If Marlon took Denise, that would confirm all of the rumors going around about their relationship with the students as well as the school's staff. It would also solidify Marlon as a LEGEND for taking "Ms. Lucas" to his senior prom! And that's exactly what happened! We double dated and Marlon walked in with "Ms. Lucas" on his arm. All of our peers were in total shock! The guys couldn't believe what they were seeing and the girls were melting wondering what kind of super power did Marlon have to get Ms. Lucas. The teachers were the same! They couldn't believe what they were seeing. I remember thinking to myself "man I hope Denise doesn't get in trouble or fired for doing this." The room froze when we walked in, especially when Denise took off her jacket but Denise didn't pay them any mind. She danced and engaged with Marlon, Teresa and me as if we were the only ones in the room. We had a ball and all eyes were on us! Afterwards while the rest of the students were trying to get hotels rooms to have sex with their dates, we all went back to Denise's house and did what we normally would do. Marlon went down in the books as the greatest of all time with students, teachers and staff for dating "Ms. Lucas."

One week after the epic prom, Marlon and I graduated from high school and received our diplomas. I was accepted into several colleges but decided to follow in Stanfield's footsteps and attend the University of Maryland Eastern Shore. Marlon chose not to attend college. The entire summer leading up to my first semester in college (Fall 1991), I worked for a temp agency landing work where ever I could find it, warehouses, dock unloading, selling flowers on road sides, what ever it took to make some cash. Marlon on the other hand started selling drugs with one of Denise's cousins. As the summer progressed, I started noticing a change in Marlon's behavior. Not only was Marlon selling drugs, he started to use the very same drug he was selling. When I wasn't at work or at Teresa's, I would go and hang out with him at Denise's house. Denise's younger brother was living there at the time and introduced Marlon to "Coke Fugs"- cigarettes with cocaine sprinkled in the tobacco. As he would smoke, he'd always look at me and say "boy I better not catch you doing this" as if he's my big brother. We would laugh and I'd say "man you're only 9 months older than me!" Needless to say, I wouldn't entertain the thought of smoking cocaine or any other type of drug at that time. The death of superstar basketball player Len Bias shook me to my core when I was younger and I vowed to never use cocaine after his death.

As the summer was coming to an end, I began setting up my approach on a new life attending college. No one from my high school was attending UMES and Stanfield, my childhood friend, one of the main reasons I chose to go there, had transferred to Coppin State College. I literally didn't know anyone that was attending or would be attending the school. I decided to take advantage of the opportunity and reinvent myself. In high school I knew that I was quite and a little reserved causing a lack of socialization and I didn't want the same experience in college. I was smart enough to know that I wasn't going to change so I decided add a crutch to my issue and that would be a stand out name! If I had an unforgettable name, it wouldn't matter if I was quite/ reserved or not. As soon as others heard my "stand out name" they would always remember me as well as inquire about the name. I just had to figure out what to call myself. I got a sheet of paper and each day I would jot down a possible name. One day I was reminiscing about a time when I worked at a restaurant at the Inner Harbor and I met a guy who's name immediately stuck with me as soon as I heard it. I never heard anyone call themselves this before and I knew he wasn't attending UMES so I decided to use it for myself. The first day of college, when someone asked me what's my name, I'll say "Kool-Aid."

Chapter 11 - Voo Doo-Witchcraft

It was the Fall Semester of 1991 when I arrived on campus at the University of Maryland Eastern Shore. My mother and my oldest cousin "Bally" drove me there. After we arrived and as we were unpacking my mother's car with my things, I remember watching Bally as he moved with such speed and strength. His demeanor was so cheerful, and I could tell he was proud of me yet still I could still see flashes of a horrific Voo Doo experience I experienced with him as a young child.

In the summer of 1982, my family received a phone call from my grandmother (living in Summerton SC) saying to come home immediately, Bally is "sick". My entire family, aunts, uncles' cousins etc. packed up and drove to South Carolina. When we arrived, I remember walking into my grandmother's house and seeing my oldest cousin Bally, the slickest, the ladies' man, the coolest cousin one could imagine, run through the house thinking he was a horse! He ran from room to room galloping and making horse sounds. All of my aunts were in tears as my uncles attempted to calm him down. As a young child seeing this, I was both confused and afraid. I remember thinking to myself what happened to my "role model" cousin. After many attempts to calm down the situation, my uncles were finally able to calm Bally down.

Later that night, my grandmother along with my mother, aunts and uncles sat in the living room and discussed what happened to Bally. Apparently Bally and my Great- Uncle (my grandfather's brother) George were dating the same woman and had an argument over it. One night while home alone, someone shot my uncle George in the eye causing him to lose his eye. Being as though Bally and Uncle George just recently had a huge fall out, my Uncle George accused Bally of shooting him and swore revenge. Bally had no idea of Uncle George's feelings. A few months later Bally and Uncle George were sitting on Uncle Georges porch having a drink and conversating. It was then when Uncle George laced Bally's cigarette with some sort of 'Voo Doo" as well as his drink. Shortly after that Ballys mental health started to decline and before we knew it, he was galloping around the house like a horse.

"If Daddy was alive, he would get his shot gun and kill Uncle George!" one of my aunts yelled in anger. As everyone started to chime in and express their anger as well, my grandmother gently spoke suggesting that we go in prayer and everyone immediately calmed down. So that's what we did. My entire family prayed over Bally day in and day out. There were talks of my aunts taking Bally to see a witch doctor to have the "spell" reversed. Being as though I was a young child, I wasn't privy to all of the information. I got bits and pieces and so did my other cousins. From what I recall, the witch doctor told my aunt to take Bally to my grandfather's grave and perform some sort of ritual to help but it wouldn't completely resolve the problem. The only person that could remove the spell was the person who created it, which was Uncle George.

Uncle George lived in the next house down the road from my grandmother. The only thing that separated the two houses were about 100 yards of woods. While me and my cousins were outside playing in the yard, we would see Uncle George drive by in his green Chevy, He would always stare at us as he drove by and it scared me to death. I remember thinking, what kind of power does this man have that gives him the ability to make someone act like a horse or sit on the floor and drool like baby? Whatever it was, I just wanted it as far away from me as possible. One day while outside playing, Uncle George drove by but this particular time he decided to turn into my grandmothers' yard. I almost died! My cousins and I sprinted into the house and informed our mothers. None of my uncles were home at the time. My mother along with all of her sisters went outside to confront Uncle George. When Uncle George got out of his car and approached his nieces, I remember pulling my mother back towards the house. I didn't want her to get too close to Uncle George. I thought if she got close, he could put Voo Doo on my mother and make her act how Bally was acting. There were a lot of words being exchanged between

Uncle George and my mother and aunts but the only words I remember came from Uncle George when he said "Yeah I put it on him (the spell) and I'll put it on yall too! I'll have all of you crawling around this yard like a snake!"

A few days later my Uncle Zeek borrowed my mother's car to run a few errands. My cousins Shawn, Kebo and I went along for the ride. Bally went along as well. Shawn, Kebo and I (The Awesome Three) rode in the back seat and Bally sat in the front while my Uncle Zeek drove. After running errands while on the way back to my grandmother house, my Uncle Zeek spotted my Uncle George outside working in the field. Uncle Zeek pulled over on the side of the road and got out of the car (leaving the car running). He approached Uncle George with a warm greeting and they both began to laugh and talk. Till this day, I'm not sure why this happened. I can only speculate by saying Uncle George was Uncle Zeeks uncle as well and maybe they had a bond that I wasn't aware of.

Needless to say, I was scared out of my mind to be this close to Uncle George and so was Bally! Bally started rocking back and forth making strange noises as each minute passed. Finally, when Bally was fed up, he jumped in the driver's seat, put the car in drive and took off! My cousins and I were screaming at the top of our lungs begging Bally to stop the car. He drove around the narrow country roads at approximately 100 mph, recklessly, sometimes on two wheels when he couldn't handle the curves. If another car was coming in the opposite direction, there's no way we would be alive today. Not sure how he knew but Bally found my grandmothers house, turned into the yard and was headed full speed at the front of the house! At the last second, before crashing head on into the house, he spun out and we did about two and a half donuts until the car finally came to a stop! It rained the day before so very large mud puddles were all over the front yard. We spun out so hard, that we splashed mud all over the front of my grandmother's house. The roof, windows. doors all were covered in mud!

I don't remember much after that incident. All of the witch craft, voo doo and spells took a toll on my young mind. The reckless car ride was the icing on the cake. Subconsciously, I checked out. I'm not quite sure how it all came to an end. I do know that Bally continued to see other witch doctors to get rid of the curse/ spell and performed several graveyard rituals but only Uncle George could completely remove it. As years went by Bally got better and was starting to act like his normal self but sometimes, he gave off flashes of the curse. It might be a stare or a weird look in his eyes but he seemed to snap out of it before it went too far. It was a concern that Uncle George would pass away and never remove the spell and that's exactly what happened. Uncle George passed away of old age and the Voo Doo spell was never removed.

Chapter 12 - Freshman Year (UMES)

My mother and Bally helped me unload my things in my dorm room and returned back to Baltimore. I was on my own not knowing anyone on campus. I wasn't scared or nervous. I was actually excited! This was my chance to start from scratch and create my own narrative. My roommate's name was Mike. "What's up Mike. I'm Kool-aid!" Mike smiled and said "Why do they call you Kool-aid?" I replied "I don't know. Its just a name that stuck with me I guess." Mike knew a few guys in our dorm from his high school so everyone he knew he introduced me as "Kool aid" and the unique nick name received the same response. Before I knew it, everyone that I came across in my dorm was addressing me as Kool-aid. Some of which I didn't even know. When the girls caught wind of the name, they all were intrigued. The flirty girls would always ask "what flavor" which I would reply "Black Cherry!" My new name was always a door way for conversation. It did exactly what I intended for it to do.

Each floor in my dorm (Nuttle Hall) had a RA- Resident assistant and a RAT- Resident Assistant Trainee. The RA assigned to my floor name was Damon. The RAT was Joe.

Outside of my roommate, these two guys were the ones I quickly formed a bond with (along with a few others- Terrell, Croix and Chad). We were all from Baltimore except for Chad. He was from Prince Georges County. Typically, everyone would cling to others that were from where they were from. Baltimore students hung out with other Baltimore students, DC with DC, Philly with Philly and so on. Traditionally, it was always a big rival between Baltimore and DC/ Prince Georges County that would sometimes turn violent. It almost had a "gang like" feel to it. But I was cool with a lot of people from DC, Philly and New York. I was cool with everyone. I was Kool- Aid.

One day my roommate Mike had a visitor stop by our room by the name of Tip. Mike introduced us and Tip seemed to be a cool guy. After a few minutes, Mike and Tip left out for a class they had together. Two weeks later our dorm had a talent show in the lobby area. As I sat in the audience watching all of the talent being displayed, I thought back to when I rapped with my cousins as well as with my neighborhood friends. The music as well as the response the crowd was giving to the performers was giving me chills. The last act to go on just so happened to be the best act by far and the artist was Tip, my roommates' friend. He had the crowd going crazy and rightfully so. His performance was on fire.

The next day, I told Mike to tell Tip I wanted to talk to him about possibly doing the next talent show together. Mike relayed the message to Tip and he was all for it! Myself, Tip and a guy from New York (we called Bo) decided to put a song together for the homecoming Talent Show. We rehearsed every single day leading up to the talent show. I hadn't been on a stage since the 6th grade but I wasn't nervous at all. I was smart enough to team up with the hottest rapper on campus. All I had to do was maintain and get through the performance without any hick ups and my mission would be accomplished. I would be recognized and even more people would know my name as well as acknowledge my hidden talent. Besides, I heard Tips verse and I felt as though my verse was just as hot, maybe even hotter! We did the show and the performance was a major success. We received a standing ovation and our names began to spread all around campus.

A few weekends afterwards, I decided to go home for the weekend. I normally would call home and tell my mom or Teresa that I was coming home but this particular weekend I decided not to. When I arrived in Baltimore, I went straight to Teresa's house. When she opened the door, she looked surprised which I expected but her surprised reaction eventually turned into irritation after an hour or so. Before I knew it, we were in a full-blown argument over nothing at all. As usual, once the argument reached its climax, I grabbed my bag and stormed out of the house and walked to my aunt Izzy's house (Kebo's mother) who lived close by. I allowed some time to pass after I arrived at my Aunt's and decided to give Teresa a call. I figured enough time had went by and we should both be calm by now. When I called, Teresa answered the phone and was very quiet.

She allowed me to do all of the talking. When I finally stopped and asked for her opinion, I heard a noise sounding like the phone was being transferred from one hand to the other. All of a sudden, I heard a guy's voice.

His name was Marcus and he told me that he was Teresa's new boyfriend and Teresa didn't want anything to do with me anymore. I immediately hung up and headed back to Teresa's house. Before I left, I went in my aunt kitchen a took a butcher knife and hid it up my sleeve. As I walked back to Teresa's house, in a slight jog, I thought to myself, that's why she had that look on her face when I unexpectedly arrived and that's why she started a bogus argument. My blood began to boil. I was hurt, angry and scared all at the same time. I didn't know what to expect or what I was about to walk into. As I approached the front door, I allowed the knife to slide down my arm, just enough where as though the blade was in my hand. Teresa opened the door and stood against the wall in the living room. Marcus was sitting on the couch. Marcus looked like a typical street dude, rough around the edges, between the age of 25 – 30. At the time, I was 18 years old. As I stood in the living room questioning Teresa with a trembling voice because of the pain, I remember seeing the both of them trying not to laugh. I gathered all of my belongings that were there, placed them in a trash bag and walked home.

It took roughly about two hours for me to arrive home. Instead of going to my mother's apartment, I went straight to my fathers house. When my dad opened the door, I fell into his arms in an uncontrollable cry. My father brought me into his house and we sat in his living room and we talked. I told him what had just happened. His calm and reassuring demeanor along with wisdom coached me back to normalcy for the time being. He explained to me that the pain I was feeling would not go away immediately but in due time, everything would be okay. Pain comes in the package of life and unfortunately its something we all must go through in some sort of way. Teresa wasn't technically my first, but in all other ways she was. I couldn't imagine at the time not ever sleeping with her again and just imagining another guy making love to her or Teresa doing what she did to me orally, made me sick to my stomach. My dad understood that thought and addressed it without me having to say it verbally. I felt a thousand times better when I left my fathers house but by the time midnight came around, I was sick again. That night as I laid in my bed with tears rolling down my face, I remembered conversations from a few weeks ago with Damon and Joe in our dorm rooms. Damon was going through a similar issue with his girlfriend. She had left him for another guy and he was devastated. He talked about the situation all of the time. Often, he looked as if he wanted to cry when speaking about it. Joe and I laughed about it and made jokes. We teased Damon every chance we got. Fast forwarding to me now lying in the bed in the same situation. This was my first taste of the lesson "the same things that will make you laugh, will make you cry."

The next day I went to Marlon's house and told him what happened. As we sat at his mother's kitchen table, Marlon poured us two cups of Colt 45. I had never had a drink before this day. "Man fuck her. You are too good for her anyway! You're going to find a new shorty that's way better than her." We sat and talked for hours and drunk two 40 ounces of Colt 45. I remember thinking to myself, this beer his harmless. I don't feel anything. It wasn't until I tried to stand up is when I knew what state I was in. I stumbled into the wall and almost knocked Marlon's mother (Ms. Brenda) pictures off the wall. Marlon laughed and quoted our favorite expression when referring to one another "You're just a kid". We went to the living room and began watching our favorite movies, Harlem Nights and House Party and quoted every single line, verbatim (as always) but this time in a drunken slur.

After the weekend ended, I returned to campus still devastated from the hurtful event of losing Teresa. As much as I tried to hide the pain, it still showed all over my face as well as in my demeanor. Joe was the first to pick up on my vibe. He was becoming my best friend on campus and he could tell something was wrong with me. Joe was older than all of us. He didn't start college directly after high school like the rest of us. He started 6 years later which made him a freshman at the age of 23. When we found out how old he was, we labeled him as an old man and gave him the name "Ole Man Joe". When Ole Man Joe would ask "what's wrong" I didn't want to tell him because he was notorious for making fun of people and even though we were good friends, I was afraid that he would make fun of me the same way we made fun of Damon. I knew my heart wouldn't be able to take the ridicule and the jokes would have broken me, so I told him that Teresa and I were going through a rough patch and I wasn't sure if we would stay together. All of this happened after the Thanksgiving break therefore the end of the semester was soon approaching. I counted down each day, marking X on the calendar, till the end of the semester because I couldn't wait to get back to Baltimore to make an attempt to get Teresa back. It was a miracle that I passed my classes and more so exams because I couldn't focus on anything else. Two of my classes were intermedium due to the fact that I attended a trade high school a wasn't prepared for college courses when I graduated. Never the less, I made it through the fall semester and returned to Baltimore for the Christmas/ Winter break.

When I arrived home, I immediately started to pursue Teresa but to no avail. She changed her phone number and I didn't want to just show up at her house because I knew her new boyfriend would be there. I began to feel very depressed. To get my mind off of Teresa, I started hanging out with my childhood friends more. Jay Bird had a sky- blue Geo Prism, the first one on the block to have his own car, and we all piled in his car everyday and just rode around the city looking for things to get in to. One day while driving around, my childhood friend Peanut pulled out some weed and asked, "Wayne, are you smoking with us?" Me wanting to escape the pain I was hiding from losing Teresa, I immediately said "hell yeah".

When I took my first hit, I didn't know what I was doing. I thought back to when my mother used to smoke cigarettes and I mimicked what I saw her do, or at least what I thought I saw her do. I pulled the smoke in and blew it back out. I didn't feel anything at all afterwards. After several days of doing this I finally said to the guys "Yo I don't feel anything, are yall high?" They all replied "Hell yeah". Peanut then said "Yo, let me see you hit it to make sure you're hitting it right." Peanut watched as I pulled the smoke in and blew it out afterwards. He then laughed and said "Yo, you're not inhaling! You have to inhale, that's why you don't feel it" "How do you inhale" I asked. "When you pull it, slightly swallow the smoke so it enters your lungs!" I did what Peanut told me and immediately started to cough uncontrollably. Everyone in the car laughed. "NOW you're going to feel it!"

The remaining time during winter break was spent either hanging out with childhood friends or hanging with Marlon but not as much with Marlon. Marlon had just married Denise (Ms. Lucas) and I was the best man. He was also dealing drugs on a heavier scale than before. He was hustling on Pennsylvania Ave along with one of Denise's nephews from sun up till sun down. During that time, I would just ride around with Jay Brid, smoking weed and trying to meet girls.

The beginning of my second semester arrived and I was back in college. The pain had lighted up a little but still there. My entire college crew returned which was rare because between semesters you never know who's going to have a change of heart and not return to school. Ole Man Joe, Damon, Terrell, Croix, Chad as well as myself were all back for another semester. As more time passed, the sting of losing Teresa became even fainter and I was in full swing with college life. Partying with my homies and dating a few girls but the uncommon addition to my activities was I was now drinking and smoking weed. I remember thinking to myself, wow, I came from a very rough environment back home in Baltimore, where all kinds of trouble and bad habits reside and I wait till I escape and come to college to indulge in this type of behavior. The University of Maryland Eastern Shore was a BEAUTIFUL campus surrounded by farms in the middle of nowhere. But I witnessed more drug use, more wild life and more fights than I ever did growing up in the hood. After attending classes, there really wasn't a lot left to do with the time constructively. The SDC (Student Development Center) was available for socializing but other than that you were on your own. So, a lot of students smoked weed, drank alcohol and slept with each other. The acronym for the school is UMES (which was renamed by students as University of Much Easy Sex) simply because you were in the middle of nowhere and there wasn't anything else to do. Spring semester, I didn't come home much. The only time I recall coming home is when I received a call from Marlon telling me his little sister Jennifer had passed away from a brain aneurism. She was only 9 years old.

Summer 1992 arrived, and I was back home in Baltimore. Still a little hurt from the Teresa incident, I was determined to find a new girlfriend/ replacement. Marlon and I were back at it in full swing. Marlon wasn't selling drugs anymore. He and his wife's Denise nephew had a falling out, so he decided to get a job, by the time I arrived back in Baltimore, he had already quit. We ran the streets every day, looking for something or someone to get into. One day while looking for something to get in to, Marlon suggested that we should hook up with his mother's longtime friend Ms. Patty. Marlon wanted me to experience what he was experiencing with an older woman. He set it up where we all went to a hotel (Marlon, Ms. Patty and myself) just to kick it and have drinks. After a few drinks, Marlon and Ms. Patty laid on one bed while I laid on the other. Before I knew it, Marlon had removed Ms. Patty's blouse and was sucking on her breast. Ms. Patty began to moan, and Marlon removed all her clothes and performed oral sex on her. Ms. Patty's moaning was beginning to get me aroused. As I'm watching from the other bed, I see Marlon's hand in the air suggesting that I join. I walked over to the bed and Ms. Patty forcefully grabbed my waist, unbuckled my pants and started performing oral sex on me. Marlon then turned her over and had sex with her doggy style while she performed oral sex on me. Ms. Patty was so turned on by what was happening that she began to shake uncontrollably. Marlon previously said that her husband was older than she was and the two of them never had sex. Ms. Patty showed all signs of this aggressively by allowing us to have our way with her. We took turns having sex with Ms Patty in every way imaginable till the late hours of the night/ early morning. Afterwards, Ms. Patty drove both of us home. Marlon and I were 18 years old. Ms. Patty was 40.

This was just one of many escapades Marlon and I encountered that summer. We were together every single day. Marlon was still using drugs but he wouldn't use when we were together. By us hanging out all of the time, two birds were being killed by one stone. Marlon and I were having fun and Marlon was staying clean. I was practically living at Denise's and Marlon's house. I was there all of the time. I even started dating/ sleeping with one of Denise's cousins. Marlon didn't smoke weed and I didn't use other drugs so Marlon and I would drink Malt Liquor Beer. Often, we would go out looking for girls and even picking up prostitutes from time to time (girls that had sex for money- not the street walker kind).

Shortly after the fourth of July, I started to notice a change in Marlon's behavior. He was always agitated about something. He and Denise began to argue a lot and Marlon began to get physical with her. He was also falling into a slight depression. One morning I received a call from Denise saying that Marlon tried to kill himself by swallowing some pills. He was rushed to the emergency room and was revived. When he was well again, they placed him in a psych ward for evaluation. When he was finally able to come home, he told me sometimes he just doesn't want to live anymore. Marlon was having a hard time figuring this thing called life out. He didn't want to go to college and there weren't any good paying jobs out there for just a high school graduate. We talked and blamed a lot of his actions on the alcohol. We decided to slow down on the drinking so this wouldn't happen again. He told me about how he had to drink crushed charco and water to fight off the pills he swallowed. He said it was the most disgusting taste ever. He also told me that while he was in the psych ward, he met a girl there and was sleeping with her in the ward. Typical Marlon.

The summer had come to an end and it was time for me to return to college. My father's brother, Uncle Harry, was driving me back to Princess Anne, MD. Marlon was at my apartment as I packed up my things. Once the final suitcase was placed in the trunk, I looked over at Marlon and he had tears in his eyes. "Man, what am I going to do now?" My eyes began to tear up as well. I knew that without me being in Baltimore, as a positive distraction, Marlon would turn back to the streets, using and selling drugs. When my Uncle started the car and I got in and closed the door, Marlon took off up the block in a slight jog. As we drove up the block and caught up with him, our eyes locked for a second, both filled with tears right before we passed him. I fought back the tears as much as I could because I didn't want my Uncle to see me cry and rode back to UMES.

Chapter 13 - Sophomore Year (UMES)

Fall semester 1992 I was a sophomore at the University of Maryland Eastern Shore. At the end of my freshman year, I applied for the job of a Resident Assistant and was awarded with the position. Now as a sophomore, I had my own room and was in charge of an entire floor in the dormitory (Nuttle Hall- 3rd floor). Once I was settled in, I went searching for all of my college friends that I hung out with as a freshman. Ole Man Joe, Chad, Terrell and Croix were all present but unfortunately Damon didn't return. My childhood friend Donny enrolled and was now attending UMES. I was very excited to have someone that I've known all of my life down the "Shore" with me. Things picked up right where they left off. Attending classes but in between, partying, smoking, drinking, and pursuing girls. The girl pursuit was a bit challenging for me at the time because I didn't have money and couldn't afford the clothes that I wanted to wear causing my confidence to stagger. A lot of the sophomores, even freshman had cars. I barely had a decent pair of sneakers to wear. As a result, I started stealing. Croix, Donny and I began to go to the mall (it was only one mall in town) and steal Polo shirts from the department stores. Croix was the only one in our crew that had a car. Actually, Croix had clothes and money too. He didn't need or have to steal. Donny and I on the other hand were in a different ball club. We couldn't afford what was in style at the time so the only way for us to get it was to take it! We stole any and everything we could get our hands on, from polo and nautica shirts/ pants to groceries out of the food markets. We even rode around the Princess Anne neighborhoods late at night, kicking cable boxes over and cutting the cable extensions, bring the units back to our dorms so we could watch cable.

In between all of the festivities on and off campus, I still found time to write rhymes. Tip and I continued to perform together until one day Tip decided that he had had enough. The interest just wasn't there anymore. I immediately started looking for a replacement because I wasn't comfortable being on stage by myself. I also was looking for someone who would attract a lot of attention. That way ALL of the attention would not be on me. I was comfortable being the #2 guy. I liked being the "DMC" (of Run DMC) of performances. I figured you get the same accolades with less pressure. The problem was, I couldn't find any "Run's" to partner with. So I was forced to be the "Run" and I partnered with Donny to be my "DMC". Donny and I entered every talent show on campus and before I knew it my popularity was growing larger than ever on campus.

Meanwhile back home in Baltimore, I received word from Denise that Marlon tried to commit suicide again and was back in a psych ward. This news was devastating to me and there was nothing I could do. I was 3 hours away in Princess Anne and Marlon was home in Baltimore. By the time I was able to make it home, Marlon was out of the psych ward and back in the streets. He was using a lot more and also hanging with some weird new "friends". The first time I laid eyes on his new friends, I knew they were addicts but for Marlon's sake, I went along and hung out with them anyway. We would ride around looking for something to get into as usual but frequently stopped to buy drugs. We would go to Greenmount and 20th street and Marlon and his friends would buy heroin. Then they all would take turns snorting the heroin. Afterwards they would wet a napkin and sniff the wet napkin so the water can go down their nostrils directly after snorting the heroin. They called it the "drain" which was supposed to be the best part of the high. As I sat in the back seat watching all of their pupils turn glassy, I remember saying to myself, I want to hang out with my brother but not like this. I came up with an excuse because I didn't want Marlon to feel like I was abandoning him, to get the guys to take me home. Marlon always felt like I left him alone in Baltimore to attend UMES so every time I was home, he wanted to hang out. I found out later that night Marlon and his new friends robbed a Burger King at gun point.

The weekend came to an end and I was back down the Shore (a nickname for UMES). One day while attending a Residential

Assistant meeting, I met another RA by the name of Lamont. Lamont was in his Junior year and from Washington DC. We started talking at the RA meeting and before you knew it, we were hanging out all of the time. Lamont was an interesting character. He always wore a shirt and tie or khakis and a polo with hard bottom shoes. He spoke very articulate and was extremely intelligent. He always wore a smile especially when greeting someone and was very charismatic. He could win over almost anyone off of his initial introduction alone. He even walked around campus often with the Holy Bible at hand. But Lamont was also a ruthless, stone cold thug that would blow your brains out at the drop of a dime! I was used to thugs looking, dressing and talking a certain way. I never saw a person that looked and acted like a saint convincedly but at the same time conducted himself like a devil. We clicked immediately when I told him what neighborhood I was from back home in Baltimore. Lamont was from DC, but was very familiar with Baltimore. His child's mother didn't live far from where I was from so he knew what type of environment I came from. We took on a big brother/ little brother kind of relationship. He told me about how his child's mother had brothers that were in the streets. The brothers would get into altercations with others guys and reach out to Lamont (being as though he was from DC and no one knew him) to "handle" particular situations. Lamont told me about several shoot outs he would have in Baltimore and afterwards drive directly back to DC. When telling me these stories, I could see it in his eyes that they were true. Also, when talking to people back home about some of the incidents, everything lined up.

I learned a lot from Lamont. I watched and observed how he manipulated people with kindness and pleasantries. I used to say to myself, if they only knew. Lamont would say to me all of the time, "Man we got the street smarts already, once we get the book smarts, we'll be unstoppable!"

Chapter 14 - Junior Year (UMES)

Fall 1993 I was in my Junior year at UMES and a lot had changed. Ole Man Joe, Donny and Chad had all dropped out or transferred to other schools. The only one left from my original crew was Croix. I was fired from the job of being a Resident Assistant due to a practical joke. One day we (all of the RA's) were scheduled to have a meeting with our Dean in a designated dorm room. All of the RA's were in the room waiting for Dean Tilghman to join the meeting. Dean Tilghman was running late and decided to call and let us know. When Dean Tilghman called the room, one of the RA's answered the phone in a disguised voice and cursed Dean Tilghman out. We all snickered and laughed afterwards. When Dean Tilghman finally entered the meeting, he was FURIOUS! He demanded to know who answered the phone and said those horrible things. We all pretended that the phone never rung in our room and that he must've called another room by accident. Dean Tilghman was buying it. He told us if we didn't tell him who was on the phone, he would fire EVERYONE in the room! He walked out and said he would return in 10 minutes. We huddled up and said "He can't fire ALL of us! We're sticking to our story of him calling the wrong room." Dean Tilghman returned along with another Dean, Dean Chesterfield. "Well, do you guys have a name? Who was it that cursed me out?" We all said the phone never rang. The next day, Dean Tilghman fired all of us. I was forced to move out of my single room in the Dorm and live in an apartment on campus with a roommate. They purposely scattered us all over campus and made sure we all had roommates; something we weren't use to being RA's. Yet still we never told on the guy that answered that phone and cursed Dean Tilghman... and never will!

Meanwhile, back at home, Marlon was sick and tired of the street life and decided to join the Army. He left earlier in 1993 and we kept in contact by writing letters. When I would come home on the weekends, it was strange not having Marlon in town to kick it with. Majority of the time, I would just stay in the house. One weekend while home, I heard a knock on our apartment door. My mother opened the door and I heard a female's voice. Me being in hound mode, I immediately went to see who it was. When I entered my living room, I saw the most beautiful girl one could imagine. She was tall and slim with curves; her skin tone was caramel and she had long black hair. She stopped by to pay her life insurance (my mother was her insurance agent). When I spoke to her, she looked at me and smiled, then continued her conversation with my mother. The moment after she left, I immediately asked my mother who was she. My mother brushed me off and said "boy that girl is too old for you." From her looks, it appeared that she was in her mid-twenties. After harassing my mother for about an hour, she finally told me the young lady's name and who she was. She was actually the older sister of a childhood acquaintance I used to play basketball with when I was younger. His name was Mason and he was murdered in front of his house a few years prior. The young lady's name was Glow.

The next day, I started thinking of ways of how I could possibly be in Glows presence again. I knew I didn't have much time because on Sunday night, I'd be back at UMES. I had to move fast. I thought to myself, "what would Slice (Marlon) do?" That's when it hit me! My mother kept an information log book of all of her insurance clients. If I went through the book, I would find her name and contact info! So that's exactly what I did. I took my mothers book out of her brief case, and found her name and number. Now here comes the hard part. Calling Her! What would I say and how would I say it? I mean this girl was absolutely gorgeous! She probably had 100 guys pursuing her on a daily basis. What could I do to stand out? Is this even possible to achieve? But then I thought back to when Marlon pursued and gave Denise that letter back in high school. Who would have ever thought that a high school kid could date "Ms. Lucas"? Fast forwarding to now and they're MARRIED! I picked up the phone and dialed Glow's number. One of her sisters answered the phone and gave to phone to Glow. As soon as I heard her say "Hello" something came over me. I went into a cool calm mack mode and began to introduce myself. I apologized for the cold call but expressed how it was imperative that I spoke with her. The mode I was in was shocking even to myself. She asked me how did I get her number and I told her. In some way, my efforts impressed her and I had her attention moving forward. We talked for hours that night and I could tell by the end of the conversation that I had a serious shot of dating Glow.

A few weeks went by and Glow and I were doing very well. I would come home every weekend just to see her. My childhood friend Peanut would be on the block and see Glow walking to my house (we lived a few blocks away from each other). He would tell all of the dudes going crazy as she walked by to chill, "That's my man's girl" Glow would come over every Friday night when my mother went to church and we would have sex all night long. Actually, that's all we ever did but I didn't notice or maybe didn't even care back then. One weekend Marlon came home on leave. I told him about Glow and how I got her. I was so proud of the bold way I approached her as well as how beautiful she was. I couldn't wait to get Marlon's approval. Marlon and I arranged for us all to go on a double date to the movies. When I told Glow about the plans, she was hesitant at first but hen finally decided to go. That Saturday afternoon, the day of the double date, I called Glow several times but no one answered the phone. Marlon was at my house as I was making the calls. Finally, after the 10th or so call, Marlon asked "Yo, why don't we just go to her house?" When Marlon and I arrived at Glow's house I began to get nervous. It just hit me that during the past few months of dealing with Glow, I had never been to her house! She was supposed to be my "girl" yet I never met any of her family or girlfriends and we had never been out anywhere. We simply just had sex all of the time. I got out of the car and knocked on Glow's door several times. No one answered. Marlon and I returned back to my house. It was starting to look like I was being stood up. Just as we were about to cancel the date, Glow called and said she was out all day with her sisters. She apologized for missing the movie date and asked if she could come over. I accepted her apology and explained to her that although we missed the original time scheduled, there was a late-night movie we could catch. Once again Glow sounded very hesitant but agreed. Marlon, Denise and I picked up Glow and we all went to the movies. Glow looked beautiful as ever. While in line going into the movies, Marlon nudged me and whispered "Slice, I'm proud of you boy! You got a winner! She is BAD!" I felt so accomplished hearing that from Marlon. Through all of the years of being a third wheel not having anyone, to Marlon sharing his women with me, I finally had someone that made me feel elite! Even during the times with Teresa, I wasn't alone but I didn't have someone of Glow's caliber on my arm. Teresa was cool but Glow was drop dead gorgeous! She was in the same ball park with the infamous "Ms. Lucas". Not to mention, the bold approach of how I got her! I finally felt like Marlon and I were equals and I wasn't just the charity case he kept around. Once we were seated in the movies, I noticed that Glow was uneasy. She kept nervously looking around as if she was looking for someone or maybe not trying to see someone she knew. After the movie was over, Glow left out of the movie and almost ran back to the car ahead of the rest of us. We all went back to Marlon and Denises house. Glow and I went into one of the spare rooms and did what we always did, had sex.

A month or so later Glow and I were still on our same routine. One day she told me she had to move out of the house she was living in because her family decided to sell it. She and all of her siblings were going their separate ways. Glow and her son (whom I had never met) were moving into their own apartment. When I heard of the news, I thought to myself, this is great! When she moves, I'll be able to come to her house and spend the night. Her reasoning for me not coming to her house before was because so many people lived there. I thought everything was working in our favor, till the day came when she actually moved. Glow never gave me her new address. She just told me the apartment complex was in Walbrook Junction. A few days before Glow was scheduled to move her phone was disconnected. I had no way of calling her. The night before she told me she was actually moving, I went to the old house and it was vacant. Everyone was already packed up and gone. The next day, no calls. It was clear to me that Glow was gone and I had no way of reaching her. I didn't know any of her family or close friends so I couldn't reach out to anyone. I laid on the bathroom floor and began to cry. Not again, I said to myself. This is Teresa all over again! My pain and sorrow soon turned into anger and rage. I began punching holes through the dry walls in my mother's apartment. She wasn't home. As always, she was in church. I said to myself, I can't let this happen. The same way I got her will be the same way I'll keep her. I had to do something extraordinary. Something out of the box! Then I remembered, she told me she was moving to an apartment complex in Walbrook Junction. Now there were several apartment complexes in Walbrook Junction, all of which were tough neighborhoods but I didn't care. I decided that I would walk to Walbrook Junction and go to every single apartment complex and find Glow. I threw on some clothes and headed out of the door. As I came out of my apartment building and headed for the alley that took me to Walbrook Junction, I heard a voice call my name. I looked to my right and saw my father sitting on his porch. "Come here" he said. I still had tears as well as determination in my eyes but as I walked over to my Dad, I did my best to transform back to my origin. Till this day, I can't remember one single word my Dad said to me that day. What I do know is that he must have sinced and eventually saw the trouble in my spirit and felt the need to address it. The magic my Dad had addressed the situation without ever mentioning it. He never said one word about what he saw in my eyes. He just talked and conversed with me and nothing about the conversation had anything to do with Glow or any relationships. By the end of the conversation, I didn't feel the need to go on a wild goose chase for Glow. I went back to my apartment and watched TV. As I sat on the couch, I began to replay my entire relationship with Glow. Then it finally hit me. I was just someone Glow enjoyed having sex with. I was a young college kid with no income. All I had was youth and energy. That's why I never met any of her family and friends. That's why she really didn't want to go to the movies or be seen with me in public. She just wanted one thing and from past partners testimonies, I did that one thing very well, sex. That was the end of me and Glow.

Spring semester concluding my Junior year at UMES was going well. I was living in a 3-bedroom townhouse (we called it the efficiencies) on campus. It was 6 of us living there but Croix was my roommate. At the time, I was dating a girl named Tonya and things were smooth sailing for the most part. Croix was the only one out of my original freshman crew that still attended UMES. Everyone else had either transferred or dropped out. So now when I did shows Croix was my hype man. We performed at all most all of the school's talent shows but one particular show changed everything. It was a show I decided NOT to perform in. Croix and I went to the show to watch the others perform. As each act performed, I watched and listened to the crowd more so than the artist. I made mental notes when they cheered, laughed, drifted away, etc. It was like I was conducting an experiment on crowd engagement. Majority of the artist pretty much received the same reaction but there was one that completely stood out. His name was Shamari. I knew Shamari since freshman year and I knew that he rapped. We participated in numerous shows together in the past and I was familiar with his skills. Shamari always had good songs but this one was different. Shamari wrote and performed a song called "Cluster 3". You see, on campus each townhouse (which we called efficiencies) was grouped with 3-5 other townhouses which was considered as a Cluster. So when someone asked where do you stay, you would say "I stay in the Efficiencies, cluster 1" or 2 or whichever cluster you stayed. Now the Efficiencies were for upper classmen only but the freshman that were advanced (scholarship students) were allowed to live there as well but only a small portion. All of the freshmen stayed in one cluster and that cluster was "Cluster 3". Not to mention, the cluster was all girls!

Now being as though Cluster 3 was full of freshman girls, all of the guys preyed on the cluster. These girls were new to the school, just getting away from parents for the first time and naïve to the college lifestyle. So needless to say, it was a lot of interactions going on at Cluster 3 and Shamari was smart enough to make a song about it. At the end of his performance the crowd went absolutely crazy! It was then that I learned when you make music that connects with a human experience you can't lose!

The next show scheduled was the biggest show of the year. The Homecoming Talent Show. This was the show that everyone came to, alumni and all. All of the "Big Dogs" were scheduled to perform so I knew I had to step my game up. I decided to do a two- part show going off of the observation of the last show I attended. The first part would be uptempo- using a hot beat that everyone was familiar with and the last part I decided I would slow it down and connect with the audience. I knew the uptempo portion really didn't matter lyrically because at shows, if the crowd doesn't know your song, they're basically vibing to the beat and your energy and possibly a very simple catchy hook; generally speaking, and that's ALL performance. But with the slower portion, I knew I would really have to be witty with my word play and connect with the audience. I decided for the slower portion to use The Isley Brothers "Groove With You" instrumental, well actually it wasn't instrumentals back then. I had a DJ loop the part where there wasn't any singing, normally that's at the beginning or the end of the actual song. Inspired by Shamari's song "Cluster 3" I decided to write a song called "The DL (Down Low)". You see UMES was large but small at the same time. Everyone knew each other so when people were messing around with one another, they wanted to keep it a secret because it might ruin the chance of them messing with someone else in the future. EVERYONE was "creeping" meaning secretly sleeping with each other. This was going on throughout the entire campus so I decided to speak on it and give it light. Shamari's "Cluster 3" was just about a freshman complex but "The DL" would address the entire University!

So I wrote:

Now ladies and gentleman I'm about to touch an issue

That's funny to the brothers but other may need tissue

See I'm about to get real raw up on this stage

And pull somebodys card and let the cat up out the cage

Now it seems as if a lot of you dude out here hitting freaks

You hit it different ways and the next day you dont speak

You see them on the yard and disregard that they're around

And words are limited because you want to keep it on the down

Low so nobody else will Know

That behind closed doors on the sack or on the floor

You're going at it, sweating something like a drug addict

When he's running for that dope or when he's trying to kick his habit

Now ladies you're shady, you're just like my niggas

Except that your wants are just a slight bit bigger

You smile all the time yo like everything is funny

And tell them what you want so you can juice them for their money

You fuck them if you want with one Common thought in mind

They're out to get theirs so I'm out to get mine

Now people its cool if you do what you do

But just keep it to yourself, you know between you and you

Our creep game is loose and if we don't tighten up

Guys we'll never get the skins and girls you'll never get the bucks

Chorus

So yeah and ya don't stop
To all my fellas look around and spot a boot you knocked

And yeah as I get loose
To all my ladies look around a spot a fool you juiced

And yeah as I get ill
To all my fellas spot a girl yo that sucked your "Chill"

And yeah and you don't pout
To all my ladies spot a nigga yo that ate ya out

On the DL
The DL, The DL, The DL
Its cool if we keep it on the DL

On the DL
The DL, the DL, the DL
I's cool if we keep it on the DL

2nd Verse

Now the next time Kool is called upon to wreck shop
Yo I'm a bust some bubbles like 2Pac be busting cops
I might call you out or then again call the names
Of the fake want a be's that put the creeping name to shame
See creeping is our thang everybody know whats up
But creeping aint creeping if you wasn't taught to keep your Mouth shut
What the fuck Is that really hard to do
Keep your biz to your self you know between you and you
Creeping is an art and all the real creepers know
That if you want to keep creeping you gotta keep it down low.

Chorus (Repeat)

This song, this moment changed my life. It was Belmont Elementary 6th grade math talent show times 10 but instead of in front of a grade school grades K through 6, it was in front of a HBCU and Alumni! The crowd went absolutely insane after my performance! Even throughout the song, when I said key phrases and touched certain points, the crowd was going bananas; so much that it was hard to keep my flow and words on the beat because I was in awe of how much they were feeling what I was saying. As I walked off the stage, while the crowd still screaming, Croix followed me and jumped on my back filled with excitement. "Yo, you killed it Kool!" My demeanor was relaxed and calm in the mist of all of the excitement. Before this show as well as all of my other shows, I always felt sleepy right before I went on stage. It was my way of dealing with my nerves. I would shut all emotions down, so much that sometimes I could barely move. But right before it was time to perform and I mean literally seconds away from hitting the stage I would flip the switch back on and release everything I had in my performance. Afterwards, I'm completely drained; sort of like the scene in the movie "Ghost" with Patrick Swazye. When the ghost left a body/ host it could barely move. And that was me after every performance; emotionally drained.

Everyone back stage was so excited about my performance. I was surrounded giving high fives, hand shakes and hugs to everyone around. It got so overwhelming that I left the building while the show was still going on and walked back to my room. I just needed a minute to get myself together. My energy wasn't matching the energy I was receiving. Everyone was so excited but I was completely drained.

Once I got myself back together I walked back to the auditorium. When I walked in, everyone I came across congratulated me and asked questions about the song. "How did you come up with that?" "What made you say this and that?" I was even asked to rap it again without the music; standing right where we were! This was the moment that I knew without a doubt that I wanted to do this for the rest of my life!

A few weeks went by and the semester was coming to an end. I had probably rapped the "DL" a little over 100 times for friends, strangers and even faculty in small settings. Being as though no one recorded the show, the only way people could hear it again was for me to rap it. Girls came from all over asking me to rap it for them. One of my house-mates girlfriend consistently asked me to rap the DL for her. So much that eventually I ended up sleeping with her strictly off of her infatuation for the song. If the nick name "Kool Aid" didn't make me stand out, the song "The DL" gave me super powers for the remaining of my college days.

Chapter 15 - Drug Dealer

It was the summer of 1994 and I was home on break. Marlon was still in the military stationed in Germany. Being as though Marlon wasn't around, I started hanging out with my childhood friends Peanut and Jay Bird. At the time, Peanut was hustling on the corner of Baker St. and Rosedale St. It was a Korean store there and the bricks were all red so we called it the Red Front. That's where all of the hustlers in our neighborhood sold drugs. Jay Bird on the other hand just dibbled and dabbled. He sold drugs from time to time but hustling wasn't his thing. Peanut was 100 percent in. One day we were all riding around and Peanut asked "Yo Wayne, are you hustling with us this summer?" Without even giving it a second thought, I said yes. I was tired of being broke, not having things, having to steal just to maintain. Being as though I had so much notoriety at school because of the "DL" performance, I now wanted to look like a star.

I didn't live around the neighborhood anymore. While away at college, my mother moved to the east side of Baltimore on

Howard & 26th street. I didn't have a car so I had to wait until my mother came home from work, borrow her car and drive back to my old neighborhood. The first night out on the block with Peanut was a breeze. He gave me all of his nickels (5-dollar bags of crack cocaine). Peanut was selling dimes (10-dollar bags of cocaine). Whenever someone wanted nickels, I would serve them. Being green (naive) to the drug dealing game, I kept my stash in my mother's car parked up the block. As time went on, I started getting tired of going up and down the block for a couple of bags for a sale so eventually I started keeping a few on me. I figured if the police jumped out, I would take my chances and run. I also kept a few bags in a Mary J. Blige cassette case stashed in the gas tank of any parked car. One particular night while on the block, a fiend went to Peanut and ask for a nick. Peanut told her to come holler at me. When the fiend approached me, she said she didn't have any money but she would "suck my dick" instead. The fiend looked very familiar but I couldn't remember where I knew her from. Then it finally hit me. Her name was Emily and she was drop dead gorgeous back in the day. She was the girl all of the older hustlers around the way went after and all of the youngin's included myself dreamed about. Now she's offering me head for a five- dollar bag of crack. Just because she was who she was, "Emily" I went on with the offer. One of the neighborhood fiend's who lived on Brighton street allowed us to go in and out of his house as much as we pleased. I took her to one of the back rooms, placed a condom on and she began to perform oral sex on me. When she started, I thought to myself, damn that rubber has to taste nasty. I can't believe she would do this for a five-dollar high! Once I was done, I pulled up my pants and gave her the nickel. Emily wasn't and never will be Emily to me anymore, I thought to myself. She was now just another crack head from around the way.

That was my normal routine for several weeks. Being as though I could only come out at night, after my mother got home from work, my money wasn't stacking like everyone else's. Peanut along with everyone else on the block, were outside all day and night. I was only catching the night sales and I was selling for Peanut which means I had to give a lot of the money to him. As each night went by, I was starting to see the dangers of being on the block. I had to worry about the police when driving from my mother's house to Brighton street, then worry about the police we called knockers while hustling. Then you had to watch out for the stick-up boys. I always tried to sell everything I came out with because I didn't want to drive back to my mother's house dirty doubling my chances of getting locked up. I decided that I would look for a job during the day and hustle at night. I said to myself, when I find a job, I would stop selling drugs but, in the meantime, I didn't want to sell nickels for Peanut anymore. It was time for me to cop my own drugs and be on my own. I asked Peanut if I could buy weight from him instead of selling his nickels. Peanut didn't sell weight but he agreed to cop me an eight ball (1/8 of an ounce of crack cocaine) the next time he went to re-up (buy more drugs). An eight ball was going for $125- $150 at the time. I gave Peanut the money and he brought me back an eight ball. Peanut also taught me how to cut the eight ball and bag it up. Bagging up crack was tedious and I hated it but it was necessary and apart of the game. Peanut taught me everything about selling drugs. If I paid $150 for an eight ball and if cut up and bagged properly, I could make 30 dimes which is $300. Then I could take the $300 and buy a quarter (which was anywhere from $225 - $275) ¼ of an ounce and make close to $600. Afterwards, I could keep going up to a half of an ounce and then a whole ounce. Back then, on the block, an ounce was the goal.

After breaking down and selling a few eight balls and going to Peanut for more, Peanut pulled me up and said "Yo, I can't keep copping (buying) for you." "You're going to have to jump out there and start getting it yourself." I understood where Peanut was coming from but I didn't like it at the time. Getting my weight from Peanut was safe. No risk. I knew Peanut since I was 3 years old. Going to someone else brought all kinds of risk to the table but I knew it was necessary. I couldn't expect Peanut to carry me forever. Peanut taught me how to read the scale when coping weight. For an eight ball, the scale should say "3.5" for a quarter "7" and so on and so on. He also told me to make sure the crack is not still in the wrapping when being weighed and also make sure that it isn't wet or damp. Both situations will cause the crack being weighed to seem heavier that it actually is.

There was one guy that pretty much supplied the whole neighborhood with weight and his name was Mike. I didn't want to cop from Mike because whatever you bought from him, he would front you (advance) the same weight. Meaning, if you copped an eight ball, he would front you a second eight ball and now you owe him cuts (profits) off of the second eight ball. I didn't want to owe anyone. I wanted total control over what I was doing. No fronts. So, I decided to cop from another source; A guy named Willie. And actually, it was still Mikes coke because Willie copped from Mike. We all grew up and lived in the same neighborhood since babies and Mike along with a few others was the source for all of the drugs.

A few weeks later my cousin Chantell got me a job working at the BWI airport in the toll booths at the parking garage. Chantell had a hustle going on there that was bringing in a lot of cash and I wanted in. As I promised myself, once I was hired, I didn't go out on the block anymore. Instead, I gave my coke to my friend Terry and Terry went on the block to sell it. So at this point, I'm working a 9 to 5 and also I have drug money still coming in. But that wasn't enough. My cousin Chantell had serious cash coming in but she wouldn't initially tell me how. When I asked her to put me on, she said "Hold up Cuz. I want you to know the job's in's and out's first. Then I'll put you on!" You see Chantell was smart. She knew that in order for the hustle to work, the person had to be very knowledgeable about the job's functions. I had just started. If I would have tried the scam, I would have gotten caught and blew it for everyone because I didn't know enough yet.

Once Chantell felt as though I knew enough, she finally put me on. I must admit, it was the best hustle ever! You see, we worked the toll booths for the parking garages for people coming in and out of the airport. The garage charged $20 per day for parking. It also charged $1 per hour for drop offs and pick- ups. So, let's say today is April 10th. A car comes through your line and the driver gives you a ticket and the date say's April 5th. Immediately you as well as the driver knows that the car has been there for 5 days which is $100 (5 days x $20). What we would do is manually enter the information on the cash register saying the car had been there for an hour, causing the charge to be $1. The driver would give us the $100, we would then write a manual receipt claiming the register is broken (because we can't give them a receipt that says $1) that says $100. When the driver drives off, we would put the $1 in the cash register and $99 in our pocket! It was the easiest score ever! The only problem we came across was when the price showed up on the screen attached to the booth. We didn't want the driver to see the $1 charge on the screen. There were about 10 booths on the lot but one booth's screen wouldn't light up. So, every day, the workers that were on to the scam would literally run to that booth because of the broken screen. It was Booth E! I was able to get Booth E a lot but when I couldn't, it didn't matter to me. Even when my screen worked, I would still scam the tickets. I would pick and choose who to scam. If someone was preoccupied talking to family members in the car, scolding their kids, just not paying attention, I would jump on the opportunity. Once every so often someone would ask, why does it say $1? I would reply "The screen is broken. It always says $1. Its stuck!". The drivers bought it every time. On an average day, I could easily bring home anywhere between $500 - $1000 per day and no one wouldn't even notice. I even got Jay Bird a job there and put him on to the scam as well. We used to beep each other with the amounts we were getting each day. And on top of all of this, I was still making money with Terry on the block.

By the middle of July I had so much money, that I didn't know what to do with it. I was making so much money at the airport that I really didn't care about the drug money anymore. The airport money was easier and came with less stress but I continued with the drugs because I didn't want to leave Terry high and dry. Till one day Terry told me that he gave our drugs to one of the younger dudes in the neighborhood to sell for him and the dude came back and told him that someone hit his stash (stole the drugs from where he was hiding them). Terry was pissed. Terry had a gun and went looking for him, When Terry finally found the dude, he threatened to shoot him. Jay Bird was there that day and talked Terry out of shooting the young dude. I chalked it up as a loss and didn't buy anymore weight after that situation.

Everyone in the neighborhood was doing very well from drug dealing. The kids that were the poorest coming up were now swimming in money and almost everyone had a new car. The Acura Legend as well as the 300 Z was the popular car in the city at that time so that was all you saw flying up and down Rosedale. I decided that I wanted to buy a car as well. Being as though I was returning back to school in September, I knew it would be hard to get financing in my name because my work history wasn't stable. I had the cash but didn't know how to go about buying a car. I asked my mother for assistance. My mother told me if I was going to get a car, purchase a brand-new car because if I buy a used one, I'm just buying someone else's problems. Also, I would be driving back and forth from UMES so the car had to be reliable. I asked my mother if she could get the car in her name and I made the payments. She refused with the reasoning that she still had car payments left on her car and if she got another car, she would have two car payments if I couldn't pay. So, I asked her how much she had left on her current car loan. When she told me, I immediately went into my room and gave her all of the money to pay her car off. My mother didn't ask where I got the money from. She knew what I was doing at the airport but it was never discussed. After my mother paid off her car, we went to the dealership and I bought a brand new 1994 Hyundai Elantra, right off of the showroom floor.

After I bought my car, it seemed like I had it all. I already had the latest clothes and jewelry and once I put the tint on my windows, I felt like I was complete. But there was one thing missing, A bad girl to be on my side. I was dealing with a few girls here and there but nothing serious. The girl I was dating at UMES, Tanya, had a boyfriend so when we were back home in Baltimore, I didn't see her that much. We did our thing at school but when we were home, it was different. One day Jay Bird, Terry and I were at Reisterstown Plaza shopping for new clothes as always. I was wearing a Sergio Tacchini outfit with a gold link chain with a Jesus cross piece attached. I was standing outside at one of the mall's entrances when all of a sudden, this girl walks up to me. She didn't initially say anything, she just seductive grabbed the Jesus cross on my chain, observed it and laid it gently back on my chest. I asked her if she liked what she saw and she replied, "Maybe". Her name was Alexis and she was beautiful and just my type; slim build, long hair and a pretty face.

Soon after our initial meeting, Alexis and I started dating and began to go together (boyfriend and girlfriend). Alexis lived with her Mother and Uncle and had a baby girl named Ny. They were Trinidadian's. If I wasn't at work or hanging on the block, I was at Alexis house.

- Alexis story continues in another reading "Egregious Acts" Written By: Lakeacha Jett (my cousin).

Small world; But anyway, the summer was coming to an end and soon it would be time for me to return to UMES. My goal was to stack up as much money as possible because I knew I wouldn't be able to make any money while in school. I was hitting the parking tickets harder than ever and even went half with Terry on some crack to sell. One day while out on the block, a fiend took "somebody's" stash (drugs) and tried to run but some of the homies caught him in the alley behind some houses on Rosedale. The person's stash that was hit, started beating the fiend and when the fiend fell everyone started stomping him. In the beginning of the beat down I was watching out of entertainment but as the beating continued, I started watching out of concern. The homies were beginning to go too far. After stomping the fiend till he could hardly move, one of the homies went and got a center block brick. He used both of his feet to hold the fiend's head straight, raised the center block brick over his head and crushed the fiend's skull. Before the brick actually made contact, I turned away. Afterwards everyone gathered around to see how bad the fiend was injured but me and a few others kept our distance. Soon afterwards, an ambulance came but it was too late. That was the first time actually seeing someone get killed. I've seen bodies in the street prior, but not till then did I see it happen.

Chapter 16 - College Dropout

It was Fall 1994 and I was back at UMES for my Senior year of college. This was a very pivotal moment in my young adult life. Croix didn't return to UMES. He was in a program in Hotel Restaurant Management that sent him away on an intern assignment. My UMES "girlfriend" did not return. She transferred to Catonsville Community College back in Baltimore. I was all alone. I had associates because of my popularity but absolutely no one from my immediate circle was there. I ate lunch alone, studied alone and pretty much stayed to myself. I didn't sign up for any talent shows for two reasons. One, I didn't have a hype man anymore and two, I didn't want the pressure of topping the "DL" song. Every weekend I would drive home. I also went though a weird phase of feeling depressed. I tried to sleep with girls to make myself feel better but to no success. I remember one particular girl I was interested in named Shawnna. She was a very popular girl on campus. I approached her and gave her my number. A few days went by and I didn't here from her. I remember sitting on the floor in my room falling into a deep depression, hoping Shawnna would call. The girls I was seeing were okay at best but Shawnna felt like an accomplishment. Someone only the elite would date. And I wanted to be Elite. As I sat on the floor feeling lower and lower as each minute went by, I started to pray. I asked God to please touch Shawnna's heart to call. I needed to feel like I didn't have to settle, that I could actually have something or someone I actually wanted. As I continued to pray, I eventually started to cry. Not sure why but tears were falling uncontrollably. Then all of a sudden, my phone rang and it was Shawnna. That was the first time in my life that I felt like God immediately answered my exact prayer. Afterwards, Shawnna and I hung out a little but nothing more than that. The biggest reason for Shawnna being mentioned was the phone call. God literally used the "Shawnna Call" to pick me up when I was down.

About Mid semester, I had a conversation with my childhood friend Stanfield about music. He explained to me that he was starting his own record label and he wanted me to be a part of it. He was back home in Baltimore attending Coppin State College while I was still at UMES. Thoughts began to swim around in my head in regards to leaving UMES. I thought to myself, "why am I here?" I was alone and all of the money that I saved up was starting to run out. My girlfriend Alexis was in Baltimore, all of my family and friends were in Baltimore and most importantly at the time, my way of making money was in Baltimore! Coming off the success of "The DL" and going directly into the "prosperous" summer I had, changed me. I was becoming addicted to having things that I never imagined I could have. That's why when I returned to UMES even though I had the car and the clothes, I didn't have that "feeling" the feeling of appreciation, the feeling of "I see you", being recognized in a major way. And on top of it all, Stanfield was talking about starting a record company and making me his primary artist. There was absolutely nothing left to hold me to UMES. I decided at the end of the semester, that I would transfer to Coppin State College back home in Baltimore. When I spoke to the counselors at UMES in regards to the transfer, they all looked at me like I had two heads on my shoulders. "Why would you want to transfer in your Senior year? You might lose some of your credits!" I didn't care what they said. I was lonely, semi- depressed and going broke! I had a car payment that needed to be paid and money that needed to be made (or stolen). I figured I would finish school back home in Baltimore and pick up where I left off at the end of the summer. I transferred to Coppin State College in Spring 1995.

It's January 1995 and I'm back in Baltimore living with my Mom attending Coppin State College. The first thing I did when I returned was contact my job at the airport to get back on the schedule. I needed to get back to the money. While away at UMES, my mother started working there as well. My goal was to pick back up where my summer ended but as we all know, nothing in life stays the same. When I returned to work, the only shifts that were available was the graveyard shifts (11pm – 7am & 12am – 8am). This was a HUGE problem. You see, during the graveyard hours, it wasn't a lot of cars coming in and out of the garage. There was barely any traffic coming through at all. Therefore, I couldn't hit any tickets and make large amounts of money anymore. I knew if I wanted to get back to the money, I had to get off of that shift. The only problem was I went to school during the day and I couldn't be at two places at the same time.

I asked my supervisor if I could split my shifts in order to work some days when I didn't have class during prime hours and the rest overnight. He agreed but needed some time to work the scheduling out. Meanwhile, while waiting for scheduling I decided to team up with Terry again and sell drugs but I didn't go out on the block. Between going to school during the day and working at night, I didn't have time for anything else. I was barely spending time with my girlfriend Alexis. Terry was selling our drugs (crack- we called it "Ready"- short for ready rock) for the both of us. I was just putting up half of the money. We didn't have a lot, maybe juggling a few quarters of an ounce. My money situation was totally different being as though I couldn't hit the tickets at work so everything was extremely tight. I was buying coke with our profits as well as putting up money from my actual paychecks.

One day, I received a call from Terry and he told me the police took our stash. I was devastated. We had just re- up'd (bought drugs) and that was all of our money. We needed to flip the Ready in order to make our money back and profit. I didn't know what to do. It was the first of the month and the block was jumping! I knew we had to get back on and fast. I thought to myself, who can I call to get some money from in order to cop more Ready. I called Ole Man Joe and explained to him how the drug game worked. Ole man Joe agreed and gave me money to buy the drugs. The only problem was I never intended on giving him his money back. You see a quarter of an ounce wasn't enough to be splitting 3 ways (Myself, Terry and Ole Man Joe). It barely was enough to split two ways. I needed that money to get us on again and my plan was to give Ole Man Joe his money back after we flipped a few times over.

We were able to get back on and moved forward till something else happened later. That's the thing when selling drugs. Something always seems to eventually happen and if you're not financially prepared, you're done. I'm not sure if our stash was hit or if some young boy or fene ran off with it, or maybe Terry and I fell into a financial jam and spent the "Kitty" (the money reserved to buy the drugs), but soon after, everything just dissolved and we no longer had Ready on the block. Luckily for me by this time I was working prime hours at the airport and back to my old ways hitting tickets.

Things were going well. It was starting to look like the previous summer all over again. The only problem was school. I was beginning to slack up, not completing assignments and sometimes not going to class at all. My Dad tried talking to me about making sure I finished school. He had no clue of what I was doing at the airport and definitely not when I was selling drugs.

My mother knew about the airport but didn't know about the drug selling either. The two of them never talked so I could tell one of them one thing and the other something totally different. My Mom talked about finishing school as well but just not as influential as my Dad. Its not that she didn't care as much, I believe that she just didn't know. My father on the other hand, had older children, my sister who had graduated from Michigan State so he saw first hand the importance of a college degree/ education and he wanted that for me as well. I reassured them both not to worry and I would continue with school.

Thing were getting harder and harder. I would find myself dragging to class and when in class, falling asleep. My only concern was getting money at the airport. I made it through the Spring semester at Coppin State but I didn't enroll for the next semester. If I didn't transfer, I would have been graduating at that time with a Criminal Justice degree. But just like my counselors warned, I lost credits when I transferred. I needed 26 credits to graduate after I completed my Spring semester at Coppin State. I decided that I would go back to school at a later time. At that time, I was only focusing on getting money from the airport and pursuing my dream of becoming a Hip Hop Star!

Stanfield started a record label like he said he would and named it De' Martim Records. The name came from a combination of himself as well as his two older brothers' names. Stanfield's first name was Derrick. His two older brothers were Mark and Timothy (Tank). De- Mar- Tim records and I was the first and only artist at that time. Stanfield had big dreams of becoming a Hip Hop mogul, following in the steps of Puff Daddy and he looked at me as if I was his Biggie Smalls (Notorious BIG). We would meet up every single day and discuss plans on how to make everything work. I was all for the Demartim Records movement but at the same time, I was addicted to the money I was taking from the airport. At one point, I felt like I had it all, the car, the money, clothes and jewelry and the girl (Alexis) yet still I wanted more. My Hyundai Elantra, although brand new, wasn't giving me the notoriety that I wanted so I decided I wanted a new car. I barely had the Elantra for maybe a year and I was already going for something new. I went to the dealership and picked out a 2 door M30 Coop, gold with rims! I absolutely loved that car. I had the money to put down and the car payments were affordable but once again I needed my mothers approval because the Elantra was in her name. I wasn't able to trade the Elantra so I would have had two cars with two car payments. I tried to talk my mother into taking my Elantra and letting me buy the M30 but she said no. I begged my mother for two weeks to allow this to happen but she didn't budge. When I finally realized that she wouldn't give in, I gave up hope on getting the M30 and decided to blow all of the money I saved to put down on the car. I had maybe 5 – 6 thousand dollars. One day, I took Alexis to the mall and took her and her daughter Ny on a shopping spree. I bought her any and everything she wanted. I was 21 years old and Alexis was 19. I probably spend about three thousand dollars that day. Alexis wasn't into labels that much so 3 thousand dollars in 1995 stretched a long way. Once I was done at the mall with Alexis, I called Stanfield. I met up with him and gave him 3 thousand dollars cash in his hand. I told him to take the money and do whatever needs to be done to get Demartim Records off the ground. The only ask I had was for him to never tell anyone that I gave him the money. I didn't want any pats on the back or acknowledgements. I just wanted to help my friend get his company going. Stanfield looked at me with tears in his eyes and thanked me from the bottom of his heart. A few weeks later, Stanfield came to me with a surprise this time. He handed me some paper work that required my signature. Stanfield made me part owner of DeMartim Records and Senior Vice President! Now, I just wasn't an artist, I was part owner as well. I couldn't have been happier and I knew at that very moment I was wilingl to do whatever it took to make this work.

Stanfield used the money I gave him and registered Demartim Records as an LLC with the state of Maryland. He also rented out an office on Reisterstown Road so we could have a place to conduct our business. We got our logo designed, had business cards and all of the bells and whistles that would make any young entrepreneur feel like a true business man. Everything was running smoothly until one day, my cash flow came to a screeching halt.

I went to work and before I could clock in, I was immediately called into the office. One of the head managers informed me that an audit was done on my tickets and some were missing.

The missing tickets opened up a can of worms and the audit team went back and pulled several of my work days and found missing tickets on every shift I worked. You see, whenever I hit a ticket, I always kept the ticket. I couldn't turn the ticket in with the rest because if someone saw a $200 ticket being scanned as $1, it would be obvious of what I was doing. So, I would stuff the ticket in my shoe or sock and throw them away when I was completely away from the airport; usually somewhere in the city at a gas station or something. This was one of my biggest fears, an audit. They occurred all of the time and normally you could talk your way out of it. Out of 500 tickets, sometimes 1 or 2 may come up missing. But I was missing 10 – 15 tickets on a regular basis. Of course, I was questioned and asked where were the missing tickets and of course I said I didn't know. Being as though the tickets were not found, I couldn't be criminally charged but it was enough evidence to fire me on the spot. And just like that, my days of hitting tickets were over. At the time I wasn't too upset about being fired. I had a couple of stacks saved up and I figured I would just hook up with Terry again and sell drugs until other job came through and besides, this would give me more time to focus on my raps and Demartim Records. Little did I know there was more to come. The manager was so upset about not being able to bring charges against me, he did the next best thing to get to me and fired my mother as well. My mother was very upset about being fired for no reason. She never hit tickets. She didn't know how and even if she did, she would never steal due to her lifestyle and religion. I was cool with the firing of myself but firing my mother was a hit below the belt. The next day I drove back to the airport with the intention of fighting the manager. Stanfield rode with me. When I arrived, the manager and staff immediately locked the office doors. I stood outside of the office and tried to convince the manager to come outside and fight. He stood in the window with fear in his eyes and wouldn't come outside. I called him every name under the sun and made a big scene. I looked around for something to use to bust the windows but couldn't find anything. Stanfield urged me to chill because he knew the police were on the way. We left just as I heard the sirens from a far. As we drove home, Stanfield began to talk and as always, even since we were kids, everything he said made since. He knew that I had plans on going back to the block with Terry and he didn't want that. He stressed the fact that it was time to let the fast money appetite go and to focus on our promising future and that was music. Be thankful that I was able to get away with as much as I did without any serious consequences and move on. I never called Terry after that conversation. I decided to be completely locked in on making my dreams come true of being a hip-hop artist.

Chapter 17- De'Martim Records

The year was 1996 and all Stanfield and I did was live, sleep and breathe music. We added a few people to the Demartim Records family, Dave (a classmate of Stanfield's from Coppin State College) and Rodney (a long time friend). Dave was given the responsibilities of being the A&R of the label and Rodney was financial support. The four of us made up the board of Demartim Records and made all final decisions. Stanfield and I were together every single day but on Thursdays, we would all meet up at the office and discuss future plans. At one particular meeting, we decided that we needed more artist on the label other than myself. So the hunt was on. Stanfield was pursuing a girl he once had a class with at Coppin and this girl had a younger cousin that could sing. Her name was Lia. One day Stanfield and I drove to Lia's house (Columbia, MD) to meet and hear her sing. Lia was 20 years old, lived alone and had three small children. She had a nice shape, Asian type eyes and a beautiful smile. She gave off a hip-hop type vibe and that was exactly what we were looking for, our very own Mary J. Blidge. Strictly from her image alone and not to mention she could really sing; it was a done deal. We offered Lia a spot on the roster right there on the spot and Lia accepted. Actually, I believe Stanfield was going to sign her no matter what just to get in good with her cousin! Never the less, it all worked out. After we signed Lia, we then started looking for a hip-hop group. We decided to have auditions at our office and we invited the entire community to come out and perform.

On the day of the auditions, I was running late getting to the office. When I finally arrived, the room was jammed packed with artist, predominately from the Park Heights area. We were in a conference room with an oval shaped table and it was standing room only. When I walked in, the entire room got quite and all eyes were on me. Stanfield told the group that I was the only hip hop artist on the label and that I was also the Vice President. None of them had ever heard me rap before but because of Stanfield's way of persuasion, the whole room hung on to every word he said as always.

The auditions started as soon as I took my seat. Act after act performed but no one didn't really stand out until this one particular group performed. The name of the group was Shock Trauma. It consisted of two individuals, Mr. Butch and Mouse AKA Bad Dreams. The energy they brought to the room was unmatched by far. Lyrics, image, originality, these dudes had it all. Even the other groups in the room were looking at them in awe. It was a no brainer after they performed. Of all of the many groups we heard that day, we decided to offer only Shock Trauma a spot on the roster and they accepted. Soon afterwards, we decided that we wanted another R&B female artist to add to the roster. Lia was our hip hop/ R&B around the way girl but we wanted a traditional female R&B artist as well. I knew just the person we needed. I reached out to my old "girlfriend" Glow. Glow was an Amazing singer! She had voice and vibe similar to Whitney Houston. We signed Glow as well. There were others that came and went but this was the core. The executives were Stanfield, Dave, Rodney and myself. The artists were Lia, Shock Trauma, Glow and myself "The Architect of Styles- Kool- Aid".

Meanwhile on the personal side of things, I was still dating my girlfriend Alexis and every moment that I wasn't with Stanfield conducting Demartim Records business, I was with Alexis. Alexis lived her mom, uncle and of course her daughter Ny. I myself practically lived there as well. Being as though someone was always home at her house, Alexis and I hardly ever had intimate time alone. I mean we would watch TV and movies together on the couch but I never was allowed or even attempted to enter her bedroom. I had too much respect for her Mom and Uncle who thought the world of me; not to mention they were from Trinidad and I thought they would chop my head off!

Being as though we were never alone, we hardly ever had sex. I would be lucky if we slept together maybe one a month. Since I wasn't having sex with Alexis, I would cheat and sleep with Tanya (from UMES) on a regular basis. Tanya and her boyfriend were on and off all of the time but during the entire process, since our days at UMES, we slept together regularly and often. We loved each other. I even impregnated her once but she had an abortion. Every once in a while, she would suggest that I left Alexis and be with her but I could never bring myself to do it. You see right before I met Alexis, I asked Tanya to leave her boyfriend and be exclusive with me. She declined and we went our separate ways. Not long afterwards, we connected again but I was already in a relationship with Alexis. Alexis was loyal to me therefore I would never leave her for someone that had the chance to be with me but declined. So, I just kept it sexual but I still loved Tanya and considered her to be a close friend. Just not my girlfriend.

Marlon and I kept in touch by writing letters and once every so often a phone call. He was stationed in Germany. He and Denise had got a divorce and he had a new wife named Stacey. He told me in one of his letters that he had a son on the way. We always said that we would name our first son after each other. I later found out that he named his son Dominick. I didn't feel any type of way. I thought of it as a silly childhood promise. Marlon later had a set of girl twins as well, Jennifer (named after his late younger sister) and Jessica.

Chapter 18 - Musical Bonds

Demartim Records was in full swing. We had executives, artists and we even had a producer for hire by the name of DBA that made all of our tracks, but as time went on, we struggled in an important area, MONEY. Being as though I wasn't hitting tickets at the airport anymore, nor did I have any drugs on the block, my income was bare minimum. Stanfield and I worked every job you could imagine just to keep Demartim Records a float. From stacking boxes at warehouses (graveyard shifts) to sales, there wasn't a job we wouldn't do in order to make the money we needed. After all of the odd and ends temporary jobs we worked, I finally landed a permanent job as a living assistant. I worked from 12am- 8am (graveyard shift) which allowed me to conduct music business during the day. Every morning when I got off, I would drive straight to Stanfields house and we would start our day. Stanfield didn't have a car so the first thing I did every morning was pick him up and we would go to the main post office to check our PO Box. Then we would run any personal errands needed and head to the office. Stanfield was very intelligent and knew how to convince others to believe in his vision. I watched him, studied his tactics and sometimes mimicked his ways of doing business when I had to handle things when he wasn't around. He was my mentor. Everything I knew about the music business at that time, I learned from Derrick Stanfield. All of the do's and don'ts, the written and unwrittens but more importantly the art of dealing with people, I learned from Stanfield.

Our entire staff executives and artists would have meetings every Thursday to discuss plans and future goals. Being as though money was low, Stanfield decided to make everyone pay weekly and monthly dues to fund the label. The executive dues were a lot higher than the artist and being as though I was both executive and artist, I paid both. The logic behind it was when it was time to get paid, I would be paid as both so it goes both ways. Stanfield knew that being based in Baltimore, we didn't have the resources that other cities had so instead of booking studio sessions here in Baltimore, he decided that we would only record in the best studios in New York and Atlanta. He booked sessions at Unique and Quad Studios in New York regularly and Bobby Brown and Dallas Austin's studio in Atlanta.

Due to the weekly meetings and just hanging out all of the time, everyone started to bond with each other. When we weren't at our jobs, chances were we were with each other, going over music, sharing our dreams, and just having a good time. As time went on a particular bond between Lia and myself began to form. Going back to when I first met Lia at her apartment, I thought she was attractive but I never thought about pursuing her. It was just business at the time but the more I got to know her by being around her, my interest started to grow. One day Stanfield and I was driving to Lia's house to hang out. Stanfield said as we were driving "Yo do you see how Lia looks at you?" "I think she likes you!" When we arrived at Lia's house, my scanners were on ten! I didn't notice before but now that Stanfield said it, I was looking for "the look". Lia's kids were away at her aunt's house so it was just Lia, her friend Nell, Stanfield and me. We drank, listened to music and partied till about 2am. As the party was starting to wind down, I noticed Lia staring at me. Soon afterwards, Stanfield and Nell had started to doze off on the couch. Lia was starting to drift off as well. Once I was sure that Stanfield and Nell were asleep, I got up and gently grabbed Lia's hand lifting her from her seat. When she got up, I led her into her bedroom and closed the door. Once the door was closed, I ran my hand on the side of her face and grabbed the back of her neck and pulled her into a passionate kiss. As we kissed, Lia's hands were franticly trying to unbuckle by belt to get my pants off. Once she got my belt loose, she pulled my pants down and grabbed my penis with both hands. As I took a slight step back just to take my shirt off, Lia looked at my body with both hands massaging my penis and let out the most sexual moan I had ever heard. At that point both of our clothes fell off and we made passionate love for hours until the sun came up.

As time continued, so did Lia and I. Sex with Lia was amazing! She knew just what to do and when to do it every single time. There wasn't any area she was lacking in. Not to mention, we shared a musical bond and our passions were aligned. A connection through passion takes relationships to another level and when you add sex, it becomes emotionally dangerous. We were crazy about each other. The only problem was, one, I was still in a relationship with Alexis and two, I couldn't see myself being with a girl that had three kids by three different guys, especially at such a young age. Lia had her 1st child when she was 14 years old. I looked at her as someone to have a good time with but I could never commit and make her my girlfriend. Well at least that's what I tried to tell myself. It wasn't long till I left Alexis and committed to Lia. Our connection musically as well as sexually was too strong to deny but I still had thoughts swimming in the back of my mind about her character. Alexis didn't accept the breakup well at all. A few weeks afterwards, Alexis called me and asked if she could come to my house to get some help with a project she was working on for one of her college classes. When she got to my house, she zapped out and went crazy, saying she was pregnant and demanding and answer of how could I leave her. She started breaking my mothers lamps, knocking pictures off the wall, trying to destroy my mothers house. I grabbed her in order to stop her from wrecking the house, we both fell down the steps together and I dragged her out on the front porch and closed the door. She banged and kicked the door demanding to be let back in. When I didn't open the door, she went next door and called the police and told them I hit her. The police came and knocked on my door. I called my father because as always my mother was at church and I didn't know what to do. I told my Dad everything that happened. My father told me not to open the door because if I did, they would arrest me. I thought being as though I did nothing wrong, that the police would see the damage Alexis caused in my home and if anything, they would arrest Alexis! Boy was I wrong. Against my father's advice, I opened the door and the police arrested me. Alexis bit my leg in the process of me dragging her out to the porch and it was bleeding. The police offered to take me to the emergency room but I declined. I just wanted to get the booking process over with. This was my first time being arrested. I was booked and charged with assault. When the court date came, Alexis didn't show so the charges were dropped. That was the last time I saw Alexis.

Meanwhile Mr. Butch, Mouse (Shock Trauma) and I began to get very close. We would hang out together all time, smoking weed, drinking and partying. I introduced my college friend Ole Man Joe to Stanfield and he was now helping out and was apart of the Demartim Records family. Come to find out that had actually grew up with Mr. Butch and Mouse and knew them very well. All four of us would hang out on a regular basis.

Meeting and hanging out with Shock Trauma opened up a door of hip hop to me that I was never aware of. Mr. Butch and Mouse were hip hop in its purest form. Mr. Butch was a lyrical genius and Mouse had the energy of a thousand MC's. Together they were incredible. They introduced me to an element that I had never experienced before, FREESTYLING (reciting lyrics that haven't been written/ whatever comes to mind). You see before I met Shock Trauma, the only time I ever rapped was in a talent show or in a studio in front of a mic recording a song. Shock Trauma freestyled all of the time! We would be in the car driving and if a song came on the radio that had a tight beat, they would rap over top of whoever song it was. Of course, being as though Hip Hop is so competitive, they expected me to be on the same page. They wanted to see what I could do. So even though I never freestyled a day in my life, I had to step up to the challenge. Before I knew it, I was freestyling right along with them! Then we would have ciphers, something else that I never did before. We would smoke weed and afterwards, play Mobb Deep or Wu Tang, turn off all of the lights in the house, stand in a circle and spit (rap) right off the top of the dome (freestyle)! All you could see was the orange light coming from the blunt as we passed it back and forth. We would freestyle for hours nonstop. This shot my confidence to an all time high. Not only was I freestyling, I was loud and aggressive because I had to be in order to match their energy. My demeanor was always chill, since I was a kid but Shock Trauma was turning me into a Monster and I loved it!

Demartim Records was my family. I had my girl, Lia, my childhood friend as well as mentor Stanfield, my new found brothers Shock Trauma and my best friend in college Ole Man

Joe. Not to mention, my ex-girlfriend from back in the day Glow, along with Dave (A&R) and Rodney. We would take road trips to New York and Atlanta to record our music and we all featured on each other's projects. We stayed in hotels and rented homes whenever we were out of town. After studio sessions, we all would get food and drinks and have fun enjoying each other's company. We thought of ourselves as being a Bad Boy Records in the making.

After our Thursday meetings, I would always take Lia and her kids home. Lia didn't live in the city. She lived in Columbia, MD which was about an hour away. Sometimes Glow would ride with me when taking Lia home and afterwards I would take Glow home and then go to work. One night after dropping Lia off, while on the way to Glows house, Glow and I started going down memory lane and speaking about the times we had together back in the day. One thing led to another and before I knew it, I was in Glows apartment sleeping with her. Glow and I continued to sleep together after that night. I was sleeping with both of the female artist signed to the label. Glow knew about Lia, of course but Lia had no idea (well at least that's what I thought). Lia knew that Glow and I were together years ago but didn't know about what was currently going on. I thought I was the man at the time. We would be at meetings and I would sit between the two of them and one hand was feeling on Glow and the other hand was feeling on Lia. Glow knew what I was doing but Lia didn't.

Stanfield didn't like what was going on. He said it was bad for business. Everyone knew I was sleeping with the both of them except Lia. One day, right before our meeting Lia and I got into a heated argument. After the meeting Ole man Joe and I got into my car and drove off. I figured Lia would get a ride home from her Aunt like she always did when we argued. As I drove on my way to take Ole Man Joe home he began to say "Yo, I had no idea that my cousin knew Lia". "What cousin??" I asked. "My cousin TC. I saw him outside after the meeting. He said he was there to pick Lia up and take her home." I immediately saw RED! I made a u-turn in the middle of the street and headed straight for highway, flying to Lia house in Columbia. When I arrived, I jumped out of the car leaving my door open, popped my trunk and got a baseball bat and went storming to Lia's apartment. Ole Man Joe stayed in the car. I took the baseball bat and beat the door knob till it came off. I was yelling at the top of my lungs calling Lia every name in the book. All of her neighbors were outside watching. Once the door knob came off, I kicked the door in and Ole Man Joe's cousin TC was standing in the hallway with his hands up. I stormed by him looking for Lia. My beef wasn't with him. It was with Lia! I found Lia in her bedroom. I stood on the other side of the bed afraid that I would hit her. I called her every name I could think of but I didn't hit her. Something told me to leave because I knew I made a huge scene and the police was on the way and in Columbia in the mid 90's the police were a black man's nightmare! I left Lia in the bedroom and ran outside attempting to flee. As soon as I threw the bat back in the trunk a police car pulled up. I explained that me and my girlfriend was having an argument and I was just leaving. The policeman surprisingly allowed me to leave. I later found out that Ole man Joe's cousin TC was arrested because of an outstanding warrant.

The next day, I went back to my old neighborhood, Brighton street and borrowed a gun from one of my childhood friends named Rico. I kept the gun on me everywhere I went just in case I ran into TC again. Although he was Ole Man Joe's cousin and Ole Man Joe was one of my best friends, I still approached the situation like he was someone I didn't know and someone I didn't know or in a lot of cases did know, would kill you. So I was ready if it came to that. A few weeks went by and there were no signs of TC yet still I kept the gun on me. One day I went to meet up with the guys at Mr. Butch's house. I took the gun out from my waist before I sat on the couch and sat it on the table. The whole room got quiet. I didn't pay them any attention. I figured they may have been a little nervous because they didn't know if the gun was dirty (have been used) or not. I broke the awkward silence mode by starting a random conversation. As everyone started to lighted up a little, I looked around and noticed a pair of girl glasses on the kitchen counter. As I looked closer, I discovered that they were Lia's glasses. "Yo, are they Lia's glasses" I asked Mr. Butch. He said, "Yeah. Rick (Mr. Butch's roommate) was coming home from work the other day and saw Lia leaving her mothers house with the kids headed to her aunts. He picked them up and drop them off at her aunts but she left her glasses in his car. He brought them in and told me to give them to her at our next meeting." I thought nothing of it and said cool.

By the end of that week Lia and I were back together. I even had a man to man conversation with TC and he explained to me that he didn't know Lia was my girl. They used to mess around a long time ago and she called him that day and asked for a ride home. I had no quarrels with TC and honestly it didn't matter what he said in regards to Lia. I kept the gun on me because I didn't know how he felt about how I busted her door in causing confusion which led to him being arrested. I was in a relationship with Lia and that's where I expected honesty from. Lia sold me a story of she was just trying to make me jealous and nothing ever happened between them since we were together. I brushed it off, gave the gun back to Rico and moved on.

The next time we all went to New York and recorded, I made a song called "I'm In Love With A Freak". The entire room was in complete shock when they heard the song. I didn't say any names nor did I speak on any specific details, but everyone knew about what had happened at Lia's apartment and could connect the dots. Lia wasn't 100% sure that I was talking about her but I'm sure she had a pretty good idea. It was then that I realized that whatever I suppressed in my subconscious, would always come out in my music even if I didn't want it to.

A few days after we returned from New York, Lia and I were having one of our usual arguments. After the scene at her apartment with Ole Man Joe's cousin, Lia gave me a key to her apartment to help build my trust in her. Normally when we had arguments, I would stay away from her for a few days and then reconcile but on this particular night, I decided to drive to Lia's house to discuss our issues. I didn't call, I just jumped in my car and drove. I knew Lia wasn't expecting me because it was a little after 1am and I never liked driving in Columbia that late because I (like all other black males) was afraid of being harassed by the police. When I got there, I opened the door and there were several trash bags filled with clothes (laundry maybe) pressed against the door. I pushed the bags to the side and walked in. As I was headed to Lia's bedroom, I noticed someone sleeping on her living room couch. When I entered her room, Lia sat up and we began to talk. Lia had a younger brother that stayed with her from time to time so I assumed that's who was sleeping on the couch but when I asked her who it was, she said it was Mr. Butch. Mr. Butch job was close to Lia's house so he would stop and sleep there at times when he had to work a double (instead of driving back into the city). Lia and I talked for a few and then I left. I wasn't too sure about how long this relationship would last.

More time had passed and we still didn't have a distribution deal. A lot of money was being collected in dues and people were starting to get a little anxious. Not to mention, everyone had a job contributing to the cause except Stanfield. His reasoning was that he couldn't work a 9 – 5 because he had to run the daily operations of the company. People were starting to complain and question where a lot of the money was going. Was Stanfield using the dues money to live off? Was he using the money to pay his personal bills I.E. child support? A lot of questions were starting to surface. I always had his back because I was with him all of the time and I never saw anything that looked suspicious yet still I felt the questions were valid questions. Never the less we continued to press on. We even signed two new acts. A teen age girl group called the "Short Cutz" and a young female rapper named "Deceitful". Dave also brought in two girls on the executive side to help out with promotions by the names of Stacey and Shanna.

Stacey and Shanna were absolutely gorgeous! They both were light skinned, had beautiful hair, perfect smiles and model type bodies. All eyes were on them since the first day Dave brought them to a meeting. Their appearance as well as their bright spirits and energy gave Lia and Glow every reason not to like them. Not to mention that I completely over looked the two of them and had my target locked in on Shanna of the two. Dave had his eyes on Stacey. Shanna and I originally started off speaking a lot about plans and ideas to move the company forward but as time went by our conversations converted to personal. We spoke almost every day and I made it very clear that I was interested in pursuing her. Shanna brushed me off a lot because she knew that I was with Lia and she didn't want to start any confusion within the company. She was one of the "new girls" and she was already getting dirty looks from Lia and Glow, so she kept everything between us light. But I on the other hand was in hot pursuit.

A month or so passed since the new arrivals within Demartim Records and we were back in Atlanta for a studio session. Stacy, Shanna as well as the Short Cuts and Deceitful came along on the trip also. Around this time, things were beginning to heat up in regards to how money was being spent and who would get to record in the studio. You see, when Stanfield booked a studio session, he booked time for the entire label. Meaning if he booked 12 hours, he decided how many hours each artist or act would get to record. Being as though I was top priority, I always was first up to bat. After myself was Shock Trauma and then Lia. If anytime was left Glow would get a shot but normally that wasn't the case and of course Glow wasn't happy about that. Being as though there was a lot of static going around about money and priorities, Stanfield decided that he would show everyone who was the "HNIC" and flex his muscle. Instead of following the normal protocol with myself, Shock Trauma and Lia (in that order), he decided to put Deceitful, the rookie of the label, in first and afterwards the Short Cuts. Stanfield produced some tracks prior to coming to Atlanta and wanted me and Shock Trauma to record them. We didn't like the tracks and declined. With us declining his tracks along with the static about money, gave Stanfield the fire he needed to make that decision. Deceitful and the Short Cuts used Stanfields tracks and between the two of them used 90 percent of the studio time. When they were done, Stanfield told us we could record but we all declined. It was only maybe two hours left in the session.

Everyone was extremely pissed off at the egotistical power move Stanfield pulled in Atlanta. I defended him all the way until that moment. When that happened, I felt betrayed. I couldn't believe that he would put a rookie on the label before me of all people after all we've been through. I felt like our relationship was like Malcolm X and Elijah Muhammad. My mentor turned his back on me. The Atlanta trip put a lot of us in a financial bind and we came back home with nothing to show for it. The only plus out of the trip was the time we all spent together at the rental house. Once the anger simmered down, we all had a ball! I was even able to get a little closer to Shanna during the trip also. Other than that, the trip was a total bust.

When we arrived back home in Baltimore, Mr. Butch and Mouse said they were thinking about leaving Demartim Records. Glow and Lia felt the same way. I had thought of leaving as well but I wasn't sure of where I would go. Demartim Records was all I knew, again similar to Malcolm X and Elijah Muhammad. Mr. Butch and Mouse had made their mind up to leave. Even Dave was jumping ship as well. I told the guys to give me a few days to think about it.

A few days later I was home alone watching TV and suddenly I heard a knock on the door. When I opened the door, it was Stanfield. He came in and said "Yoooooo you wouldn't believe who I just ran into downtown this morning at a hotel!" "Who" I asked. "Yo, I ran into Jam Master Jay!!" "I told him about the label and everything we were doing and he told me to holla at him and gave me his pager number!" My jaw almost hit the floor. All I could think about was when we were kids, how much we loved Run DMC, how seeing the movie Krush Groove changed my life by planting that hip hop seed in me, how Stanfield used to shoot at us with a Bee Bee gun if we didn't salute his Run DMC posters! Fast forwarding to now and he's standing here saying he has Jam Master Jays beeper number! It was unbelievable. The only thing left to do was to page him and see if he calls back. Stanfield asked "Yo, do you think I should page him now?" I immediately thought back to Marlon and how he approached things. Marlon never played the waiting game when he met a girl or wanted something. He always stayed in attack mode and that philosophy was now instilled in me. I told Stanfield, "Why wait, page him now!" Stanfield picked up the phone and paged him and we waited. We both were quiet as a mouse for almost an hour sitting still waiting for the phone to ring. Then out of nowhere the phone rang. When I looked at the caller ID I saw a New York number so I knew it was him. I gave the phone to Stanfield and as he said hello, I remember jumping so high in my mother's upstairs hallway, that I bruised my knuckles on the ceiling. I left out of the room and allowed Stanfield to work his magical gift to gab. I didn't want to stand in his face as he spoke and make him nervous. They spoke for quite some time and when the conversation was over Stanfield said to me, "It's going to take some time and a lot of work but I feel good about the call".

A few days had past and it was time for our weekly meeting. Everyone was still upset about what happened in Atlanta. Before the meeting started Stanfield asked Dave to get a copy of the meeting agenda off his desk. When Dave went to search for the agenda, he found a receipt for a $300 phone bill Stanfield paid for a girl he met on a chat line that lived in Philly. This finding sent Dave through the roof because he knew Stanfield had to use the company's money to pay the phone bill because he had no other income. Dave kept everything to himself till after the meeting and afterwards Dave called his own meeting and told us all, myself, Lia, Glow and Shock Trauma what he saw. For me, that was the final straw. We all were going broke trying to keep the label a float and he's spending our money paying a stranger's phone bill!? Not to mention the slap in the face episode in Atlanta. It was then when I decided to leave Demartim Records and move on to new endeavors. Right after I made my decision final, Mr. Butch and Mouse made me an offer I couldn't refuse. Mr. butch said "Yo, since we're always together, freestyling together, writing songs and collaborating together, we might as well make it official! We would like for you to join us and become the third member of Shock Trauma!" I graciously accepted the offer and we all decided that Dave would be our new manager!

After Dave, Mr. Butch, Mouse and I left, Stanfield had a hard time sustaining things without our financial backing. He still had Rodney as a financial supporter. Lia and Glow were on the ropes and just waiting for the right time to leave and eventually they did. The Short Cuts left as well. The only act that stayed was Deceitful. Shanna and Stacey left immediately after the Atlanta trip. Stanfield owned the two-inch tapes with all of our music but we didn't care. We figured we would just make new and better songs.

The day after I officially left Demartim Records, I called Shanna and told her about my decision. After talking for a few minutes on the phone, we decided to hook up in person. I drove to Shanna's house and we took a long walk and talked. I had several conversations with Shanna before but none as deep and intimate as this conversation. We talked beyond music as well as beyond my advances. That day was the first time Shanna and I actually connected. I expressed my interest in her and told her Lia and I wouldn't be together very long. Before, Shanna would just brush me off when I said things like that but this time I could see in her eyes that she was hoping that would be the case. She told me "Lets revisit this conversation when you're completely over your relationship with Lia" and for the first time, Shanna expressed her interest in me as well. After several hours of conversation, I walked Shanna back to her apartment and went home. A few days later, I called Shanna and her number wasn't working. Back then, no one had cell phones, just home phones. Shanna and

Chapter 19 - A New Beginning

Shock Trauma was officially in full effect. Mr. Butch, Mouse aka Bad Dreams and The Architect of Styles Kool- Aid. I previously chose the name Architect of Styles because of my childhood career goal of being an architect. There was no way that I was giving up the name of Kool-Aid because of the notoriety it gave me in college so I combined the two but as the sound of hip hop went deeper into the dark basement sound, I decided to change my name to Baritone (a reflection of my voice). Almost every night we all hung out, drinking forties of Colt 45 and Old English, smoking weed and freestyling. We stayed in the streets going from club to club, battling other crews and jumping into ciphers whenever we came across one.

One day, we were all sitting outside on my mother's porch and suddenly an unfamiliar car slowly pulled up. We all stared at the car trying to figure out who it was. Finally, the window rolled down and I heard a familiar voice, a voice I haven't heard in years. "Slice!" It was none other than Marlon! I couldn't believe my eyes! He was supposed to be in Germany. He jumped out of the car and we dapped each other up (shook hands) and hugged. I introduced him to Mr. Butch, Mouse and Ole man Joe. Afterwards, I asked him "Yo, what are you doing back here in Baltimore?" Marlon said that he had some time off so he decided to come home and visit. We all sat on the porch laughing and talking when suddenly a girl I knew named Chrissy walked by. Chrissy was a girl I slept with occasionally and not long before that day, I discovered had a freaky side to her. A few weeks prior, after one of our many sex capades, I arranged for Mouse to sleep with her as well. I called Chrissy over and took her in the house. She thought I wanted to have sex and started taking her clothes off but I had something else in mind. I told her my brother just came home and needed some special attention. She looked at me and said "I got you". She went back out on the porch, grabbed Marlon by the hand and guided him back in the house and up the stairs. As Marlon walked by me, he had the biggest smile! It felt so good to be able to do this. For so many years the shoe was on the other foot and finally I was able to return the favor for my brother who was doing this for me since we were teenagers. Chrissy took Marlon upstairs and showed him the time of his life!

We later joked around about the situation by me saying I knew he needed that episode. You see since we were kids, we always used to say that we were so close that we had a mental/spiritual connection, meaning if he was mad about something, even if I wasn't in his presence, I would feel his energy and be upset too. And that went for all emotions, whatever one of us felt, the other would feel as well, no matter where we were. It was our little inside joke.

Night after night following that day, Marlon, Mouse, Ole Man Joe and I (Mr. Butch was at work) would go out partying. Besides the 40 ounces of malt liquor, we would also drink Bacardi 151 proof. We even named ourselves the 151 Click because we drunk it so much and also because of its potency. One night after getting drunk, we all decided to go out to a club. When we went outside to leave, we noticed that I had a flat tire. We didn't want to go to the club with a spare donut on the car so we decided that we would go out and steal a tire. We drove around the city looking for a car like mine with the intention of taking the tire right where we found it. We finally spotted a car that had tires that matched mine. Now when we initially started looking, we were on slightly lit apartment parking lots but as we continued to drink, our concern for discretion went completely out of the window. We spotted a car on the corner of Cedonia & Radeke Rd (highly lit and visible area) and decided to take action. We all got out of the car (everyone except Ole Man Joe), went to the other car, jacked it up, took the tire off and sat the car back on the ground, all while traffic was going up and down the block. As we were putting the tire in my trunk, I noticed a guy watching us from his front porch. Yet still we put the tire in the trunk and drove off. As we were headed back to my house, Marlon and Mouse saw some girls on the bus stop and decided to pull over in an attempt to get their phone numbers. I was all for the interaction at first but as more time went by, I started to worry. "Yo, come on, we gotta go!" I said to Marlon and Mouse. "Alright Yo, hold up, we're coming" they replied. Suddenly I looked on the opposite side of the street and saw a police car coming in the opposite direction. "Yo, we gotta bounce" I yelled. When Marlon and Mouse saw the police, there attention immediately shifted from the girls and we pulled off. It was too late though. Several police cars were behind us. One of the police cars pulled beside us and then swerved in front of us to cut us off. We were surrounded. When the police came to the car, he demanded to see our hands. He told us that someone called and said they saw us stealing a tire. Of course, we denied stealing the tire not realizing that our hands were jet black from handling the tire. They pulled us out of the car, checked the trunk and found the tire. The police arrested everyone except Ole Man Joe because the witness said that they did not see Ole Man Joe get out of the car. The arrest went pretty smooth with the exception of one cop (black I might add) that wanted us to give him a reason to hurt us. He kept flinching at us with his gun, mean mugging us and calling us names but we didn't care. We were so drunk, we barely paid him any mind.

When we arrived to Central Bookings, we were still intoxicated from all of the Bacardi 151 we were drinking earlier. After we were processed, somehow, we were split up. Marlon and I went to one holding cell together and Mouse went to another. This was the second time I was arrested so I had an idea of what to expect. I knew that we wouldn't get to see the commissioner till the next morning so it was going to be a long night. I attempted to sleep as many hours as possible but sleeping was difficult because just like before, it was extremely cold in there. Unlike the scenes in the movies, I didn't see a lot of "tough guys" in the holding cell this time nor the previous time I was arrested. The majority of the guys were drug addicts, picked up for petty crimes. The remaining were guys that got into domestic disputes with their spouses/ girlfriends and small-time drug dealers.

After several hours of dozing in and out of sleep along with freezing, my stomach started bubbling due to all of the liquor I drank earlier. The last thing I wanted to do in that holding cell was to have a bowel movement in front of 12 – 15 guys. The toilet was metal without a seat and of course there wasn't any toilet paper. Finally, when I couldn't hold it anymore, I ran over to the toilet and took a dump in front of everyone in the cell. I squatted over the toilet and made sure nothing touched the already urine and vomit drenched commode and released everything that I had. I didn't have any toilet paper so I gathered up the brown paper bags from the sandwiches that were given to us, rubbed them together as if I was trying to make a fire (to soften the paper) and used them as toilet paper. I stunk up the entire cell. Everyone had their shirts up covering their nose. I was anticipating someone saying something about how bad the odor was but no one said anything. Not long afterwards we were moved to another cell. The next day, after moving from one cell to another, we were finally able to see the commissioner. We were charged with theft under $300 and released on our own recognition.

Mouse was released before Marlon and myself. When Marlon and I finally was released, we didn't want to wait for anyone to pick us up. We just wanted to get as far away from jail as quickly as possible so we decided to walk home. With our belonging in that clear plastic bag, we headed home. On the way we walked past a popular night club called Volcano's and saw Dave along with a lot of our high school classmates in the line. They looked at us like "you guys are at it again". From the direction we were coming from along with the plastic bag on our shoulders, it was blatantly clear that we were just released from jail. Marlon and I didn't care. We just smiled and kept heading for home.

Our court date was scheduled for maybe a month after we were released. Marlon was scheduled to return to the Army before the court date and that's exactly what he did. Marlon returned to the Army causing a warrant to be issued for his arrest in Maryland for failing to appear in court. Mouse and I went to court and the charges were dropped due to the witness not showing up. The witness was actually a bouncer at a lot of night clubs in Baltimore. After Marlon returned to the Army, Mouse and I would see the bouncer all the time when we went out partying. Mouse and I would always mean mug him just to let him know that we knew he was the witness in our upcoming case. Not sure if that had anything to do with him not showing up to court or not but I'm glad he was a no show.

Chapter 20 - Crazy Love

Due to all of the partying and clubbing with Mouse and Ole Man Joe (Mr. Butch worked a lot so the majority of the time, he wasn't there), I lost my job as a living assistant so I took a job where my mother was working at the time; a long distance company called MCI. It was a telemarketing job and all I had to do was talk on the phone and try to convince people to switch their long-distance carrier. I thought it was the easiest job on earth! Not to mention, I sat at a desk (instead of throwing boxes in a warehouse) and it was beautiful girls EVERYWHERE! In my eyes, who could ask for more.

Day one I was on the prowl. Lia and I were on and off a lot and being as though we didn't see each other as much due to the dismantling of Demartim Records, the distance made things even worse. There were so many attractive, smart and goal driven girls at MCI that I didn't know who to choose. But going back to the lessons I had learned from Marlon, I decided to start at the top, the baddest one and go from there. Of all the girls at MCI, there were two girls that stood out and they were best friends, Anna and Jenine. I watched them both all of the time (like every other guy in the building) but I never had an opportunity to approach the one I was interested in, Anna till one day I came in early for some overtime. Being as though I was working overtime, my usual desk wasn't available so I had to sit in another area. The only available seat available was a seat directly behind Anna. I thought to myself, finally I'll get a chance to talk to her. I didn't make any sudden moves. I figured I would allow the moment to come to me and if it naturally didn't, then and only then would I force the issue. A few hours went by and the both of us were just working. Then my moment finally came. Anna tapped me on my shoulder and asked if I could pass her a folder that was on the desk in front of me. As I handed her the folder, the conversation began and before I knew it, we were exchanging numbers. Anna was gorgeous, had a perfect smile and a body that was out of this world! She was from the city but spoke very intelligent and her diction was border line perfect. All of the other girls that I had ever dated all had a Baltimore accent but Anna spoke like a professional or some kind of teacher and I loved it.

After a week or so after speaking with Anna constantly on the phone, Anna invited me to her apartment. She was only 19 years old, had a daughter, her own apartment and a car. The only thing was she didn't have a driver's license and could barely drive. When I arrived at her apartment, I taught her how to back up her car in a straight line and I took her to MVA to take her driver's test. She passed with flying colors! After she passed her driver's test, she was so happy that she jumped into my arms and gave me the most passionate kiss I had ever had, right outside on the parking lot in front of everyone. She told me to meet her at her apartment later that night and that's exactly what I did. Later that night, I went to Anna's apartment. We laughed, talked, had a few drinks and eventually we slept together.

The next morning, I knew for a fact that I wanted to see Anna again but there was one thing that could possibly be in the way that I didn't mention in the beginning. Anna had a boyfriend! Anna had a boyfriend by the name of Jeff and he worked at MCI as well. Anna and Jeff were a well-known couple at the job but for all of the wrong reasons. They were known to get into physical altercations constantly. Jeff would come to work all time with scratches all over his face and neck. Everyone used to gossip about how toxic their relationship was but I didn't care. Anna was so fine that I was willing to overlook all of the drama witnessed at the job.

Since the first night Anna and I slept together, we were together all of the time. It was almost as if she didn't have a boyfriend because we spent so much time together and Lia and I was gradually drifting apart. I even started leaving some of my clothes at her apartment. One particular item I left there (actually Anna would wear it around the house) was a hockey jersey that we (Shock Trauma) won in a major talent show at the Baltimore Convention Center. I loved that jersey and it held sentimental value because of how I got it. Anna worked from

8am – 5pm and I worked from 5pm – 10 pm. One night when I got off from work, as usual, I drove to Anna's apartment. I didn't call and I never called because Anna didn't have a house phone and of course, no one had cell phones back then. When I got there, I saw the living room lights shining from the bottom of her apartment door and I also heard the TV. When I knocked on the door, I noticed that the lights went off as well as the sound of the TV. No one answered the door. I immediately got pissed and started banging harder on the door. Finally, when I realized that she wasn't going to open the door, I yelled out "Anna, its cool if you want to be with your boyfriend. Just give me back my hockey jersey!" Still no answer and finally after several attempts, I left.

The next day, Anna called me from work and told me that Jeff was at her apartment getting some of his things when I got there. They were officially breaking up. She said that when I knocked on the door Jeff was afraid and told her she had better not open the door. She said he threatened her and told her to be quiet. When he left, he took all of his things and took my hockey jersey out of spite. I became livid! That jersey meant a lot to me. I was hesitant in the beginning to let Anna wear it and I also stayed on her about keeping it clean, meaning no spills and to think that her ex-boyfriend had it in his possession, made me furious! I told Anna to tell Jeff that he had better return my jersey ASAP and it better be in good condition.

A few weeks went by and there were no signs of Jeff or my jersey. Meanwhile Anna and I were getting closer. She gave up her apartment and moved back in with her parents. My mother stopped working at MCI and was now working an overnight job. Every night when I got off from work at 10pm, Anna would meet me at my house and spend the night. My mother normally got home around 7am so Anna would leave every morning at 6:30am. Sometime she would even bring her daughter Destiny with her. Every so often while at my house, a girl would call and Anna would grab the phone and tell them move on. Actually, that's how Lia and I officially broke up. We were already skating on thin ice and one night Lia called and Anna answered. That was the official end of Lia and I. Anna also pulled the same trick on Alexis but the conversation escalated to the point whereas a fight needed to happen. After calling each other every name in the book, Alexis hung up the phone and 30 minutes later she was pounding on my door. I didn't answer and eventually Alexis went away.

One night, Anna expressed to me that she didn't want to live with her parents anymore. Anna was the oldest of 5 siblings and there wasn't a lot of space there for her and Destiny. I told her I was ready to leave the nest as well so we both decided to move in together. A few days later we found a townhouse in Yale Heights, signed the lease and were scheduled to move in on the first of the month.

Anna and I were very excited about moving into our new townhouse. We were getting fed up with her having to leave every morning at 6:30am. Everything was going according to plans till one day while at work, things took a drastic change. I was sitting at my desk on a call with a customer and suddenly I looked up and saw Jeff walking towards me. He came up to my desk and tossed my hockey jersey on an empty chair next to me. Then he said "Yo, don't be telling nobody that I had better give you your jersey back! I will give you this jersey when I feel like it! Be glad that I decided to give it back! I should have thrown it in the trash!" I couldn't say anything back to him because I was on a call with a customer but my blood was boiling inside. After Jeff said what he said, he looked me up and down and walked back towards the break room. The customer I was talking to was still talking as Jeff walked away. I was hoping that the customer would finish talking so I could hang up and address what happened. Finally, the call ended and I immediately got up and followed where Jeff was heading to. I spotted him in front of the security desk, close to the elevators at the entrance. I grabbed him by his collar with both of my hands and said "Bitch don't you ever run up on me like that again! I will fuck you up!" Then I shoved him into the coat closet. Security rushed us both and separated the two of us. We both were called into the human resources office individually and was fired on the spot. I was devastated. I just signed the lease with Anna a few days prior and now I'm jobless.

A few days later, Anna and I moved into our townhouse. The rent was a little over $400 a month. Due to the debt I accrued when funding the movement of Demartim Records, I fell behind on my car payments and was never able to catch up causing the repossession of my car. I was jobless, without a car, had a new girlfriend and her 2 year old daughter (Destiny), new household responsibilities and the icing on the cake, had my first child on the way. I felt lost and afraid. I remember thinking to myself, "what in the world have I gotten myself into?" Instead of throwing a pity party, I went into grind mode. I applied for every single job in the news paper and finally landed a part time job at a place called Arbitron in Columbia Maryland. Being as though I didn't have a car anymore, I would ask friends and family for rides to work and Anna would pick me up when I got off. MCI scheduling wasn't working for Anna and her doctor appointments so Anna decided to quit MCI. While in the process of looking for another job, I told Anna not to. Instead of looking for another "job" I advised Anna to look for a "career"! Anna took my advice and enrolled into school studying to be a Dental Assistant.

A month or so had past and everything was running smoothly. I saved up some money and Mr. Butch took me to Virginia (for cheaper car prices) and I bought another car; a Ford Taurus. I had Anna, my house, a car and Mouse, Mr. Butch, Ole Man Joe and I were still doing our thing, performing at every talent/ showcase show in town, creating a buzz. Things were looking good till one day I was at work and received an alarming phone call from Anna. There were no cell phones back then (1997) so one of my supervisors informed me that I had an emergency phone call at his desk. When I got on the phone, all I heard was Anna screaming "You lying, cheating son of a bitch! Come get your shit! I'm throwing it all out of this house now!" At the time I had no idea why Anna was upset. I hung up the phone and told my supervisor that I had to leave due to an emergency. I jumped in my car and sped home. When I got there, I saw my stereo broken into little pieces along with my cassette tapes/CD's all over my front steps. My clothes were in trash bags thrown out also. I stormed in the house and asked Anna "What the hell is your problem!? What's going on!?" "You're a fucking liar! That's what's going on" Anna replied screaming at the top of her lungs. What actually happened was earlier that day while Anna was at work, she called me (at home) and I told her that I was on the other line with Mouse. Me and the guys would talk everyday and discuss the next song, talent show or whatever and usually we would call each other on a three-way call. On this particular incident, myself Butch and Ole Man Joe were on the call but for some reason Mouse wasn't. But when Anna called, I must have said Mouse instead of Butch and Ole Man Joe, probably rushing to get back to the call. Later that day while I was at work, Mouse called the house to speak to me and when Anna answered, somehow, she asked if he had spoken to me earlier and he said no causing Anna to believe that I was lying earlier. Now, I got that the sequence of events looked a little sketchy from the perspective of a 20-year-old (Anna) and a 23 year old (myself), but what I didn't get was how crazy she went once her mind was made up. That could have been addressed in a simple conversation but instead, she called my job causing me to leave work and miss money and destroyed my stereo and CD's. Not to mention, packed my clothes up in trash bags all without even having a conversation with me. After a lot of fussing and screaming, we finally were able to talk through the misunderstanding and things settled down. Afterwards, I immediately began to think back to when we were at MCI and all of the rumors of how Anna used to fight Jeff and scratch his face and neck up. This was the first interaction we had but it definitely wasn't the last.

Meanwhile musically, me and the guys were still at it. Talent show after talent show, showcase after showcase, cipher after cipher all over the city. We did any and everything we could think of just to stand out from the rest. I found an old Freddie Kruger looking hat at a flea market and started wearing it in all of our shows. I even changed my name from Baritone to the "Scarecrow". We all wore crazy clothes. Butch would sometimes wear the jumpsuit that Jason wore in the movie Friday the 13th and I would wear sweatpants on my arms with a Timberland boot on my hand looking as if I had three legs. We started our own label- Jiggy Blaugh Entertainment and started recording with a guy name Bill Pratt out of Woodlawn, MD. Bill was a guy that we met through mutual friends, well actually a group that we lost to in a talent show called Parafruit From the Bonedice. Parafruit was a hip-hop/ Caribbean group that would remind you of the Fugee's with their accents and melodic flow. Their sound was so clear in the showcases, we asked, "where do you guys record at" and that's when they told us about Bill. Bill was an older white guy, maybe in his fifties, that majority recorded rock music. Parafruit and ourselves were the only two Hip Hop groups he worked with. We learned so much from Bill. He taught us about matching the tones in our voices when stacking choruses and also punch in's. He also taught us a lot about the technical side of things; sounds, reverbs, when or when not to use certain effects. Bill was a perfectionist which made us perfectionist. If it wasn't perfect, it wasn't good enough. Bill's studio was like our second home. If we weren't in the clubs battling, chances were we were at Bill's. We kept an outstanding balance because a lot of times we didn't have all of the money to pay for the sessions but he always allowed us to make payments and continue to come. One day while in the studio, I received a call from my cousin Fat Boy. This call was disturbing because how did he get Bills number and why was he calling. Anna gave him the number. Fat Boy called to inform me that our uncle (Uncle Pook) had died due to an overdose (heroine). I hung up the phone in disbelief. A few days later, I found out that Uncle Pooks funeral (in Summerton, SC) was going to be on the same day that a talent show we signed up for was on. The winner of the talent show was supposed to be offered a record deal with a major label and we were locked in for months preparing for it. It was a tough decision but I decided to miss my Uncle's funeral in order to perform in the talent show. We didn't win the show nor get noticed by any of the celebrity judges but if I had to do it all over again, I would have made the same decision. I was determined to make my dreams as a hip hop artist come true. But one good thing did come out of that particular show. He wasn't a judge but some record label representative approached us and gave us some advice. "I love yall energy and lyrics but your sound is too muddy" "You guys need brighter tracks!" At the time, we were still riding the Wu Tang, Black Moon, Smith & Wesson waves but Bad Boy- Puff Daddy's sound was controlling the air waves at that time. It was time for us to brighten up our sound. We hooked up with a producer named K- New that lived in Washington DC but was from Baltimore and everything changed for us. The blend of K-New's bright/ up to date tracks, our lyrical talent and energy and Bill's perfection and sound, catapulted us to a whole different level. Now instead of just performing in talent shows, we were winning them! News paper articles, radio interviews etc. were now starting to come.

Once we had enough songs completed, we started shopping our demo. We mailed it to every single record label that existed. We got the addresses off the back of other artist CD's. We drove to New York on several occasions, all four of us, Old Man Joe, Mouse, Mr. Butch and I, all sandwiched up in Ole Man Joes GEO two door Prism and waited outside of studios hoping to see someone of importance and give them our demo. One time Bad Boy was doing a show in Baltimore so we decided that we wanted to meet up with Puff. We knew it would be extremely difficult to get in front of him because Biggie was recently murdered so we knew security was going to be tight. We bought a box of Honey Combs Cereal and placed our demo inside of the box, just trying to stand out and be different. The "Combs" was supposed to connect with Puffy's last name. We waited outside of the hotel Bad Boy was supposed to be staying in for hours. Finally, just when we were about to give up, we saw a tour bus pull up and Busta Rhymes got off. I jumped out of the car and tried to catch up with Busta, yelling his name but he just kept walking and eventually got on the elevator and was out of sight. Moments later we saw Kid Capri and we gave the cereal box to him and asked if he would pass it to Puffy. Kid Capri agreed but who knows what happened afterwards.

Chapter 21 - Mouse's Cousin

Meanwhile at the home front, Anna and I were still at it. The smallest disagreement would turn into an all out physical spectacle. Anna was pregnant at the time so her emotions were triggered very easily and when her trigger was ignited, all hell would break loose. The cursing, hitting, spitting and destruction of property was at an all time high. But on the other hand, when we were in a good place, Anna was the sweetest, kindest person anyone could imagine. She would do absolutely anything for you and her compassion always came from a genuine place in her heart. I remember when we would be in bed sleeping in the middle of the night, if she would hear my stomach growling, she would ask me if I was hungry and if I said yes, she would immediately jump out of bed and fix me something to eat. Sometimes she would stumble down the steps due to being half asleep, with her eyes barely open just to fix me something to eat. She loved hard and hated/ disliked the same. It was either hot or cold with Anna; no in between.

One night, September 23rd 1997, Anna and I were sitting on the edge of our bed thumb wrestling. All of a sudden, Anna stopped and said its time! We grabbed Destiny and jumped into my car. Anna's doctor (Dr. Previs) wasn't at his routine hospital. At the time he was at a different hospital, Saint Joseph on York Rd (Baltimore, MD). We dropped Destiny off at Anna's parents house and Anna and I went to Saint Joseph. Before I could blink, Anna was lying in a hospital bed going into labor. I remember standing by the door in the delivery room, watching the doctor and nurses coach Anna through the process. As I stared, I had a song on repeat playing in my head from beginning to end and that song was "A Song For Momma" by Boyz II Men. Not sure why, but this song was all I heard as my son was being born. On September 24th 1997 at 12:23am, my first child Dwayne Carter Jones was born. Peanut is what we affectionally called him. When Anna was about 2 or 3 months pregnant, she always would complain and grunt about how the baby was wearing her down. When we went and got our first sonogram, the nurse showed us the baby and Destiny (Anna's daughter) said "Look! There he is! He's the size of a little peanut!" Anna and I burst out in laughter almost to say "is this little peanut giving you this much trouble?" From that moment on, we have been calling our son "Peanut"! We both agreed that he would have my name but I decided to add a little twist. I always wanted my fathers last name which was Carter so I decided to give it to my son as a middle name. I was beyond happy when Peanut was born. I remember thinking back, before he was even conceived, I used to think to myself if I died today, I wouldn't have left anything on this earth to carry on. I thought that my existence was meaningless until I had a child and until I had one, my life was purposeless. So once Peanut was born, my entire perspective on life changed. If I died at that very moment, a part of me would still be here and that made my soul smile. A few hours after Peanut was born, I left the hospital and went home and took a nap. I had to be at work at 8am. I was working as a Telephone Man at Bell Atlantic at the time. When I got off from work, I went back to the hospital and brought Anna and Peanut home.

A few months after Peanut was born, Anna and I were back to our unusual normal. We fought all of the time. The pettiest argument would turn into a physical fight and a visit from the police. The police were called to our home at least once a week. It got so bad that when we would go to the malls, sometimes we would see the police officers (off duty) that frequented our home at the mall and we all would speak as if we personally knew each other. Sometimes they would give up this little sarcastic nod as if to say "we will see you guys next week" because they knew another call was bound to come.

In between all of the fighting with Anna, me and the guys were still recording and trying to land a record deal. Occasionally, Stanfield and I would conversate just to see how things were going with each other. Mouse, Mr. Butch and Ole Man Joe didn't want any parts of Stanfield after the Demartim Record departure but my outlook was a little different because of our history. On one of our sporadic calls, Stanfield told me that he kept in touch with Jam Master Jay and was now living in New York working for his label. He told me the next time I was in New York, stop by and that's exactly what I did. On one of our trips attempting to shop our demo, I stopped by JMJ Records and met with Stanfield. After a few moments of catching up, He told me that he was working with one of Jam Master Jays new artist and he was very excited about the guy. He guaranteed that this guy was going to be larger than life. I was hearing him but when he told me the guy's name, I sort of checked out. His name didn't make any sense to me at all. Then Stanfield said "Yo speaking of the devil, here he comes now!" The guy walked in the office and we both spoke and shook hands. "Yo, this is Cool, one of my childhood friends from Baltimore." "Cool this is 50 Cents!" Soon afterwards, I left the office and headed back to the car where the rest of the guys were waiting and we drove back to Baltimore.

It was always after a New York trip that we were charged up and ready to go. The next couple of shows, our energy was on one thousand! We would sometimes let our girlfriends come to our shows and Anna would get so excited, that sometimes she would run up on the stage, take Mouse's mic out of his hand and perform the song with us! It was crazy! Like I said, with Anna, it was either hot or cold, extreme love or extreme hate. There was no in between.

One night after a show, Mouse received a notification on his pager with a 911 code. We stopped at a phone booth and Mouse returned the call. When he returned to the car, he told us that earlier that day, some guys were picking with his younger cousin at a pool party and we might have to go and see what was up. He then went on to say "Yo, dudes be trying my little cousin because he sings. And he can REALLY sing! Only thing is, he's always trying to sound like Jodeci!"

It really didn't matter why the dudes were picking on his cousin to us. All that mattered was what Mouse wanted to do. It was his call. If he wanted to go fight for his cousin, that's what we were going to do. No questions asked. We all were like that. For example, one day I had to do laundry so Mouse, Ole Man Joe and I went to a laundry mat called Sudsville in the Westside Shopping Center (West Baltimore). I only had a twenty-dollar bill with one load of clothes to wash. I didn't want to put my money in the change machine and receive twenty dollars in quarters so I went around asking people in the laundry mat for change for a twenty. I approached this girl and asked if she had change and she mumbled something and walked away. All of a sudden, a dude (her boyfriend) approached me and accused me of trying to talk to his girl. We started arguing and just before we began to fight, Ole Man Joe pulled me away. "Yo, we don't know if this dude has a gun or not. Let's leave and come back!" We left the laundry mat and headed straight for my old neighborhood, Brighton Street. I pulled up on the corner of Brighton and Rosedale and spotted my friend Rico and told him what had happened. Rico handed me a loaded gun and told me to bring it back when I was done. We went back to the laundry mat and waited outside in the car for the guy but there were no signs of him. Just when we were about to leave, Mouse said "Yo, there he is right over there!" The guy was walking back into the laundry mat. I gave the gun to Mouse, got out of the car and headed into the laundry mat. Mouse and Ole Man Joe followed. I walked up to the guy and punched him in the face. He fell back into one of the dryers and as he was trying to get himself together, I two pieced him again in the face. His homeboys wanted to jump in but Mouse and Ole Man Joe's presence prevented them from doing that. His girlfriend was pleading for me to stop hitting him so once I saw that he wasn't going to fight back, we left.

Another incident was when Mouse, Ole Man Joe and I were driving home one late night around 1:30am. I had my son Peanut with me as well probably because Anna and I were having some sort of disagreement. At the time, Peanut was probably around 6 months old. Ole Man Joe was hungry and asked me if I would stop at a carry out spot on Park Heights Ave. Normally, I wouldn't mind but being as though I had my baby in the car, I didn't want to make any unnecessary stops; especially on Park Height Ave. Anything could happen in the hood, especially at that time of night and I didn't want to put my son at risk. As reluctant as I felt, I still stopped at the carry out. When Ole Man Joe went in to order his food, I scoped the area out and everything seemed to look quiet then out of no where a group of guys entered the carry out as well. I was hoping that Ole Man Joe would get his food and get out of there without any confusion because I couldn't do anything if something went down with a 6 month old baby in the back seat. Finally, Ole Man Joe came back to the car with his food and we pulled off. "Thank God" I said to myself. Then all of a sudden Ole Man Joe said "Yo turn back around. I left my wallet in the carry out!" I was pissed. Just as I thought we dodged a possibly sticky situation we now have to go back into the fire pit. When we got there, the dudes were still there. Ole Man Joe went in and saw his wallet sitting on the counter top. He grabbed the wallet and came back to the car. Once inside the car, he checked his wallet to make sure nothing was missing. All of his money was gone. "Yo, we gotta go back in there and get my money from these dudes" Ole Man Joe said. That's when I blew up. "Yo, that's why I didn't want to stop in the first place! How are we gonna go up in there, demanding money with my baby in the back seat!" I was pissed but I knew what had to be done. Mouse's mother lived one block away from the carry out so we decided that we would ask her to watch Peanut while we went back to the carry out to go to war with the guys that stole Ole Man Joes money. We banged on Mouses mothers door but she never answered. Being as though we didn't have anyone to watch Peanut, we decided to take a loss that night and went home. Just two of many situations that we were willing to go to bat for one another. We never went to see about the situation with Mouse's cousin. We assumed that the situation was resolved.

As time went on, we continued to make new music and performed in talent shows but it seemed like we were standing still. On the other hand, Mouse's younger cousin, the one we were gearing up to fight for, was beginning to get noticed. Mouse came to us one day and said "Yo, my cousin's R&B group got a situation with a Movie soundtrack. They're about to shoot a video! The name of their single is called Tell Me." Soon afterwards, the song was beginning to hit the airwaves on all of the radio stations. Word was going around town that an R&B group from Baltimore was buzzing and they named themselves after a well known park in Baltimore, Dru Hill. When I heard the song, I thought the song was hot but I was curious to know which voice was Mouses cousin. At the time, Mouse didn't know either. He just knew his cousin was in the group. One day I was at home watching music videos and the host made an announcement saying Dru Hill was up next. Finally I was about to be able to put a visual with the song, I thought to myself. I also wanted to see if I could guess which one was Mouses cousin. Before the video played, I prejudged the situation and assumed that Mouses cousin was one of the background singers in the group because I was going off of the vibe Mouse gave me when he spoke about the situation at the pool party but when the video played, I immediately knew which one was Mouses cousin. "It had to be this guy with the blonde hair!" I could tell by his energy. How hard he was going. He acted just like Mouse! They were exactly the same except one rapped and one sung! I later found out that Mouses cousin called himself Sisqo and he was the lead singer of Dru Hill.

As time went on, me and the guys didn't put too much stock into the "Tell Me" situation. It was a slot on a movie soundtrack. We were so used to seeing groups come out with one song and then never hearing from them again, that we didn't pay it any mind. But when we noticed that Dru Hill was signed and putting out an album we looked at the situation entirely different. And then the hits started to pour in. In My Bed, Never Make A Promise and 5 Steps all were ground breaking and the music video's were electrifying!

After 5 steps came out, Butch and I approached Mouse and suggested that he reached out to his younger cousin and ask him to help us out. "Yo, your cousin is the lead singer in the hottest group out! Lets give him our demo and see if he can put it in the right hands!" Mouse wasn't feeling the suggestion at all. "Naw yo, fuck that! We can get our own situation! We don't need nobody's help!" Mouse went on to explain that when they were younger, he and Sisqo would always perform for their family in group settings and the two of them were very competitive towards one another. Butch and I believed that Sisqo probably was getting more attention than Mouse at the family shows and that stuck with him to adulthood. Back then, singers always received more love than rappers and if Sisqo was anything like he was in these Dru Hill videos, Mouse didn't stand a chance. So Butch and I assumed that the two had love for each other but musically, there was a little animosity in the air. Since Mouse didn't want to ask Sisqo for help, Butch and I left it alone.

A few months had passed and Dru Hill was still on fire, selling over a million records of their debut album- Dru Hill and following up with another soundtrack single "We're Not Making Love No More" written and produced by none other than Babyface (my favorite songwriter). Yet still Mouse didn't want to ask for help. Finally, after feeling the pressure from Butch and I for some time now, Mouse agreed to give Sisqo our demo tape. Mouse told Butch and I that Sisqo was hardly ever home so he left the tape with his aunt (Sisqo's Mom). Butch and I wanted Mouse to call and push Sisqo to listen but Mouse wasn't up to it. Handing his aunt the demo was as far as Mouse was willing to go.

A few weeks later Mouse called me and Butch on a three way call and said he had something very important to discuss. He explained to us that Sisqo called him and said that he was creating a new hip hop group and wanted Mouse to join. He already had two others and was looking for a third and final piece to complete his hip hop group. Mouse genuinely didn't want to leave our group and join with two guys that he didn't know but Butch and I explained to Mouse that this was an opportunity of a life time and he couldn't pass it up. Our only ask was to look out for us, when he's at a level to do so. Mouse reluctantly agreed and left Shock Trauma to Join Sisqo's group.

Almost immediately after the decision, Mouse teamed up with Sisqo's other two rappers and they began working on new material. Sisqo's two rappers were named Kidd and Make It

Hot. Sisqo named the both of them. Kidd was a flashy/ pretty boy with little to no rap experience at all and Make It Hot was in the beginning stages of rap, had a little experience but more known for his distinct graspy voice (similar to DMX & Ja Rule). Sisqo had just purchased a luxurious five bedroom house in Randallstown, MD but being as though Dru Hill was on fire, performing all over the globe, he was hardly ever home. Kidd and Make it Hot (Hot) would stay at the house while Sisqo was out of town and Mouse would go there every night to vibe and write songs. After the first couple of nights, Butch and I asked Mouse about the other two rappers. We all were from Baltimore but Butch and I never heard of the two and couldn't figure out the connection between them and Sisqo. We were on the local scene for many years and anyone that had any type of skills, we came across but we never heard of these guys. Mouse explained to us that Make It Hot was some sort of distant cousin to Sisqo and Kidd was introduced to Sisqo through Make it Hot. We then asked "Yo are they nice?" "Fuck no" Mouse said laughingly. "Make It Hot is okay but his voice is tight but Kidd is trash. Kidd can barely stay on beat but he looks like a star." "I think my cousin is just trying to look out for them because he fucks with them but talent wise, it's not there".

Night after night Mouse would go to Sisqo's house to work with Kidd and Hot. The next day after, he would always tell me and Butch how it went. Once every so often Sisqo would be there as well and Mouse would let us know. One day while Mouse was telling us about what happened the night before, I asked

Mouse if we (Butch and I) could come out to the house and meet Sisqo as well as Kid and Hot. Here's how the dialog went. "Yo, do you think we can come out the house one day?" Mouse replied, "I don't see why not!" The only problem was, a day or time was never set. Days turned into weeks and every time I asked Mouse about going to the house, he would always say the exact same thing, "I don't see why not." One day Butch and I were talking and Butch said "Yo I'm not asking him (Mouse) anymore! Its obvious that he doesn't want us out there so I'm not sweating it" Me, on the other hand, refused to let up. I told Butch "Shid, I'm going to ask him EVERY SINGLE DAY until he agrees to take us out there!" And that's exactly what I did. I asked Mouse constantly until he finally gave in and agreed to take us to Sisqo's house.

When we finally arrived at Sisqo's house, I remember just taking in the calmness of the neighborhood. In the city I was so used to inner city noise but at Sisqos house, it was quite and peaceful. The smell of fresh cut grass was in the air and bird chirping was all I could hear. When we entered, the house still had that brand-new smell as if no one lived there. Everything was spotless and in place. I looked around and said to myself, this is what I would like to have someday and to think it can all come from doing something I love was mesmerizing! Kidd and Hot were in the kitchen standing around the bar as we entered. Mouse introduced Butch and I to Kidd and Hot and we all hook hands. Afterwards, Mouse asked Kid "Yo, where is Sisqo?" Kid replied "He's still out of town." I remember saying to myself "DAMN" The one time Mouse finally gave in and brought us to the house and Sisqo wasn't even here. And then I began to wonder if Mouse already knew this and that's the underlying reason why he brought us this particular night. Never the less I didn't have time to figure it out. I made up my mind that I was going to treat Kid and Hot as if they were Sisqo, meaning I was going to show every bit of my God given talent to THEM in order for the word to get back to Sisqo about how dope I was and Butch was thinking the exact same thing. You see Butch and I already pre-planned how this interaction would go. We figured once we got in front of anybody, whether it be Sisqo or Kid and Hot, that we would show off at a level so high that they would have no other choice but to rock with us. And that's exactly what we did. After the introductions, some small talk and a few drinks, the beats came on and Butch and I went bananas! We turned the entire writing session into a dark cipher. We started off spitting written verses and then transitioned into freestyle and to prove we were freestyling, we would name things in the room we were in or something someone was wearing and even picking up the last word Kid or Hot would say and continue from there, just to prove that we were for real! The cipher was a major success. Afterwards, Kid and Hot were like "Yo what are yall doing tomorrow? Yall should come back tomorrow night!" Those words were like magic to our souls because that's EXACTLY what we wanted to happen!

After that night, almost every single day afterwards, Butch and I would go to Sisqo's house to meet up with Kid, Hot and

Mouse and soon, we didn't need Mouse's invitation to come out. We were beginning to form our own bond with Kid and Hot. We didn't write their raps for them but we helped improve what they had already written and guided their delivery. Night after night we were right there helping when needed and freestyling in cipher mode afterwards. Kid and Hot were a little younger than me and Butch and were very immature. Everything was a joke to them. They constantly played and made fun of people. They didn't mean any harm. They just loved to have fun at any expense. They often would joke Mouse about his clothes or his appearance at times and Mouse wasn't feeling it at all. He barely knew them and when they went too far (like they would almost always do) he would let them know. Tension was beginning to brew between Mouse and Kid and Hot.

One day Kid and Hot asked us to come out to the house during the afternoon but Butch and I had jobs and had to work. Both of us called out sick just to make the trip. When we arrived at the house, Kid and Hot were outside in the driveway talking. We got out of the car, dapped them up (shook their hands) and all four of us began to talk. Mouse was on his way but hadn't arrived yet. As we all were talking and approaching the front door, suddenly the door opened and out walked Sisqo! He and a model type girl came out and headed for his Black Lexus that was parked by his garage. Kid said "Yo, this is Kool and Butch." Sisqo shook our hands, said whats up and he and his model type girlfriend got in his car and drove off. I remember thinking to myself, "We finally met him!" "The key to all of our musical dreams are now within arms reach!" We all went into the house afterwards and got to work. Mouse never showed up that day.

Several weeks later, Butch and I were still at it, going to Sisqo's house night after night coaching Kid and Hot. Sisqo was home a few times and sometimes he would peek in the room where we were working to see how things were going. Every time he would open the door to take a look and listen, I would always make an attempt to do or say something to let him know that Butch and I were molding his talent. It didn't work though. Sisqo would give Butch and I a short what's up and nod and then look right through us to focus and talk to Kid and Hot. It was almost like we weren't even there.

Mouse was beginning to miss a lot of the sessions. Mouse was engaged and his fiancé wasn't feeling him being out Sisqo's house every single night working on "music". I was going through the exact same thing on my end. Anna and I already had fighting issues and now I was at an emerging superstar house every night till the early mornings. A recipe for disaster. I refused to let the drama at home stop me from my pursuit but Mouse on the other hand was beginning to fold. The pressure Mouse was feeling from his fiancé in addition to dealing with Kid and Hot's childish ways, caused Mouse to slack up on coming to the house and eventually quitting the group.

When Mouse left Sisqo's group, Butch and I wondered if we would get the invite collectively or just one of us. It didn't matter to us. As long as one of us got in, we knew the other would always help the other. I knew in my heart if someone had to choose, it would be Butch. Butch was by far the best rapper out of Shock Trauma. Whether it was freestyles or written raps, Butch was always the ONE. Since the beginning days of Shock Trauma we all knew this and accepted our roles. Butch was the best rapper, Mouse was the energy and I was the voice. My goal on every song or cipher we did was to not get slaughtered by Butch. I knew I couldn't out rap him. I just wanted to get as close as I possibly could just to have balance in the group. Butch set the bar. Instead of Kid and Hot extending an invite to one of us, they reached out to a guy named Redz and put him in the group instead. Butch and I were very disappointed but we didn't let it show.

Redz was the pretty boy type- lighted skinned with green eyes and freckles. His lyrics were good and he didn't need any assistance like Kid and Hot. Butch and I were beginning to wonder how much longer our services would be needed. Being as though Mouse wasn't coming around anymore, our connection was totally in the hands of Kid and Hot, two immature guys that we've only known a few months.

More weeks went by and we were still at Sisqo's house every night faithfully but only during music sessions. We noticed that when Sisqo was home, they all would have house parties, Kid, Hot, Sisqo and now Redz along with a gang of pretty girls and we were never invited. The only way we ever knew the parties even happened would be because the next day they would be talking about the party or something that went down with the girls at the writing sessions. It was clear that they only wanted us around for one thing and that was to help them with their music. We began to feel like we were being used; almost as if we were the help. We were good to be around when we were helping them with their songs but when it was time to socialize, they didn't want us around. We then decided to use that energy to our advantage. If we were going to be treated like the "help" we decided that we would flex on Kid and Hot every chance we got just to remind everyone of who we were and what we brought to the table.

Kid, Hot and Sisqo were into the flashy hip hop. Popping bottles, fast cars, clothes, money and girls while Butch and I were on a more street lyrical vibe and since we felt like they were treating us dirty, we decided to rub their noses in the mess that they were creating. Every so often Sisqo would have a few people at the house during the writing sessions like his sister, his sister's boyfriend Charles and his female protégé Chinky along with others. Whenever Butch and I spotted company, we made it a point to spark up a cipher and once it started, we would own the entire process. We would purposely cut Kid and Hot off when they stumbled on words, pick up from where they fell off and absolutely dominate the cipher. We wouldn't even give them a chance to get back in. We were so loud and aggressive; it was intimidating to enter if you could match the energy. Redz would try to get in a little but his voice was too light so he couldn't keep up. We also denounced bottle popping and all the things Kid and Hot stood for and pushed street rap down everyone's throat. By the time we were done, it was clear who was the talented and who was there as a prop. We couldn't tell whether or not if we were gaining any points by dominating the cipher. Half of the people around didn't know much about hip hop or what it should sound like but we didn't care. If they didn't know, they were going to learn that day! Also, they wanted to like Kid and Hot so bad that it was hard for them to see two other guys out shine them. Kid and Hot were supposed to be the upcoming stars. Who are these two guys? But Sisqo's sister boyfriend Charles would give us this look of approval. He was from New York and knew what hip hop was all about. When Charles would give us his nod of approval, we thought to ourselves "One down. A million to go!"

After a few ciphers that always went the way I just described, Butch and I came to the realization that our style of music and Kid and Hot style would never work together so we were cool with not being in the group. Kid, Hot and Redz could be one group and me and Butch could be another group and that was our new focus. We will let them cover the shinny suit style rap and we would stick to what we knew best; lyrical hood rap. We just had to convince Sisqo to want to deal with us separately from Kid and Hot or blow Kid and Hot up and follow them through the industry door.

In the mist of all the areas of hip hop being addressed between the two groups, I took notice to what the girls and "non hip hop" people at Sisqo's house would respond to and came to the conclusion that changes were necessary on my end. I decided that I needed to change my name from Baritone to something brighter. The name Kool-aid was embedded in my identity and I did not want to move away from that. Even at Sisqo's house the name stuck with everyone, the same way it did since my days in college. One Saturday afternoon I was watching TV and one of my favorite movies of all time was on and it immediately hit me. I will call myself Cooley High! That way I get to keep the Kool portion of the name. So when people call me Kool or Cooley, its pretty much all the name. The only difference was I decided to spell it differently (C O O L I – H I). The first person I shared my new name with was Anna. One of Anna's younger sisters was around and Anna told her what my new name was. Anna's sister burst out in laughter! For a split second, I thought to myself, "Maybe Cooli Hi is a bad idea" but then I thought "My confidence will make the name work" I could call myself almost anything with confidence and people will fall in suit. I ignored the laugh and Cooli Hi was born.

Chapter 22 - Music & Mayhem

The every night writing sessions till early mornings were beginning to put a serious strain on my relationship with Anna. We had just moved into a new townhouse in Baltimore County (Rolling Rd.) and things were financially looking okay. I was working as a telephone man at Bell Atlantic and Anna had graduated from a Dental Assistant school and was currently working in a dental office, five minutes from our new home. Maybe a week before we moved into our new home, we had one of our worst fights ever. Anna was upset (as usual) about me spending so much time at Sisqo's house and began to accuse me of cheating. No matter how much I tried to explain that I was there creating music, she wasn't trying to hear it. She knew Sisqo attracted girls and assumed the worst. Once the argument escalated, Anna started destroying my things like she would always do. She smashed my stereo and began to throw my clothes out of the front door. When I tried to stop her by grabbing my clothes out of her hands, that's when the punches were thrown. Anna would punch and scratch my face in almost every altercation but I never punched her back. But I would take the palm of my hand and push her face with force to keep her away. I also would grab and hold her forcefully to keep her from hitting me. This was how ALL of our fights were. Anna swinging and scratching and me pushing and grabbing (and sometime throwing her to the floor) in order to stop the assault. After tussling over my clothes at the front door, Anna went upstairs to our room, grabbed my rhyme book and started tearing up the pages, cursing and calling me every name under the sun as she did so. That's when I lost it. I grabbed our stand-up lamp out of the living room, went outside to her car and smashed her two front headlights with the lamp, swinging it like a baseball bat. Anna followed behind me and jumped in her car as I was bashing the lights. She started the car and attempted to run me over. I jumped up and landed face down on the hood and held on to the car by the window shield wipers. When Anna began to pick up speed, I rolled off the hood and hit the ground. Anna sped off. I went back into our house and began to gather my things. Anna returned as I was packing. When Anna saw that I was packing and preparing to leave, she grabbed the phone and called the police. "Bitch you're going to jail!" she screamed. I knew how fast the police could get to my house due to all of the other times they came, so I dropped my bags and ran out of the door. I ran as far away as I could full speed before I ran out of breath and then began to speed walk. I left Yale Heights and walked to the place where I called home, Brighton Street. I didn't want to go to my father's house because I didn't know if Anna had told the police that I might be there so I went to my childhood friend Peanuts house. Peanut lived a few blocks down from my father with his girlfriend Denita and her Mom. When I entered the house, Peanut was in the bathroom bagging up crack with his police scanner on. He used the police scanner to hear the moves and calls the police were being dispatched to in the area. He bagged up the crack in the bathroom just in case if the police kicked the door in, he could just flush everything down the toilet. When I told Peanut about what had just happened with me and Anna he said "Yo, I heard the police dispatcher talking about you on the scanner! They described your clothes and everything. I didn't know that they were talking about you!" We both laughed and Peanut continued to bag up. I stayed they for a few hours and later caught a hack (illegal cab) back home. Anna was asleep when I arrived. I took off my clothes and got in the bed. Anna turned towards me and cuddled up in my arms. "I'm sorry" she said. I replied "Me too". She cried in my arms momentarily and then we made passionate love.

Fast forwarding to real time, we're now living in our new home but we have the same problems. We were arguing and fighting more than ever but it was more dangerous for me because we lived in the county now and the county police weren't as lenient as city cops. The city cops knew us and a lot of times, they would tell me to just take a walk and cool off but county cops didn't play. If they came to your house for domestic violence, someone if not everyone was going to jail. Every so often when returning home from Sisqo's house, I would see my clothes blowing down the middle of the street or hanging from a tree branch because Anna threw my stuff out of the window. One day I got so mad about all of the back and forth arguing and the destruction of my belongings, I picked up Anna's 40 inch TV and threw it down our steps attempting to break it. The television was extremely heavy. I left it in the middle of the living room floor on purpose. Later that day I went to Sisqo's house. When I returned home, the TV was back upstairs in the bedroom on the TV stand. I asked Anna how did she get the TV back upstairs on the stand? She said the she and her girlfriends collectively lifted the TV and placed it back on the stand. I thought nothing of it at the time.

Meanwhile in the music world, Dru Hill had just finished recording their second album Enter The Dru. They had a release party scheduled in New York and Sisqo decided to rent a bus so all of his family and friends could attend. This was going to be a star-studded event and Butch and I along with Mouse got an invite to attend. I remember thinking to myself "Finally, we're being treated like friends instead of help". Being as though I knew a lot of celebrities would be there, I decided to take full advantage of the situation. I put together a few demo packages that consisted of a tape/cd of our actual music (Butch and I) a promo pic and a biography. I had 3 packages ready to go in brown envelopes. I asked Butch if he wanted to take some packages as well but he said no. The packages were big and bulky and he didn't want to walk around with the envelopes in his hand at the party. Me on the other hand, didn't care. I figured this was a once in a lifetime opportunity and I didn't know if I would ever be around these kinds of people again so I wanted to take full advantage.

The day of the party, we all met at Morgan State University to board the bus. This was the first time that I saw and met the other members of Dru Hill. No one introduced me to them. Being as though I was there boarding the bus, it was safe on their part to assume that I was "family" and they all embraced me as such. When we arrived in New York at Dru Hill's release party, my scanners immediately went in search mode. I was scanning the entire club to see who was there and who I could approach. Being as though Butch didn't bring any packages, I only had three shots so I had to make them count. I also knew that I had to use my time wisely because after Dru Hill performed, the entire entourage would be headed out of the door back to Baltimore. Stars were all over the room. Everyone that was hot in 1998 was there; too many to name. Ole Man Joe was there with us also and he was holding some of the demo packages for me. My goal was to approach bosses so my first target was none other than Jay Z. Jay was leaning against a wall observing the spot by himself. I went up to him and said what up and shook his hand. Then I said, "Yo, I'm Cooli Hi and I rap. I'm in a group called Shock Trauma. I have my demo with me. Are yall looking for any new acts over there at Rocafella?" Jay looked at me and said "Naw. We're cool with who we have right now." Then I asked "Yo, do you know of anyone in here that might be looking for acts?" Jay Z replied "Naw, I'm pretty much just in here. Just like you are" I then said "Respect". We both shook hands again and I walked away. I then ran into Timberland and attempted to have a conversation but his security intervened. I was able to hand him our demo package; well actually I handed it to his security guard. Before Dru Hill performed, I was able to give a package to someone in the Lost Boyz camp as well as one other manager. Dru Hill then performed and blessed the party with a spectacular performance! After the show, we all got back on the bus and prepared for the ride home. Everyone that attended the party was given the Enter the Dru CD as a gift. I sat by the window and put my CD into my portable CD player but before I pushed play, I just starred at all of the excitement that was going on outside of the club. I remember seeing Nokio and Jay Z having a one on one conversation and I thought to myself two things. One was Nokio must be high up the food chain to be having such a detailed conversation with Jay Z and two was "I sure would like to be in that position one day". After the last person got on the bus, we pulled off and headed back to Baltimore. I played the CD over and over again, blown away from how dope it was. Historically, sophomore albums are scary in regards to success but after hearing what I heard; I knew that Dru Hill was on the path to be SUPERSTARS! All 17 tracks were smashes, especially the ballads and Sisqo was killing every note that he sung. I couldn't ask to be in a better position. I thought to myself, all I have to do is work hard and stay close.

The next day after returning from New York, we were right back at it; at Sisqo's house helping Kid and Hot with their material but at the same time working on our own. Redz had an emotional breakdown one night at Sisqo's and decided to leave the group for personal reasons so it was back to just Kidd and Hot. Sisqo was on the road a lot promoting Dru Hill's new album and lead single "How Deep Is Your Love".

Things were looking good musically. Sisqo was getting bigger and bigger and our relationship with Kid and Hot was getting stronger. Butch and I were starting to get more invites to the house that didn't necessarily have to do with making music. We were now getting invites just to chill and hang out. The only thing was, Kid and Hot didn't have jobs, rent, bills or a family like Butch and I. Me of course was living with my girlfriend/baby mother Anna (along with her daughter Destiny and our baby boy Peanut) and Butch lived alone but had a girlfriend and a young daughter. Kid and Hot were very spontaneous. At the blink of an eye they would call and say "Yo, come out the house! Sisqo just got home and we're about to have a party!" These calls would sometimes be at night when I was already settled in after a days work or sometime in the middle of the work day. The night calls were pure hell. You can only imagine what I would go through by getting up and leaving out of my house in the middle of spending quality time with my fire cracker for a girlfriend Anna. But even more risky, when I received these type of calls during work hours, I would leave work to hang out at the house. Being as though I worked as a telephone man (Bell

Atlantic), I drove a work van and traveled from assignment to assignment. Sometimes I would be high in the air, strapped to a telephone pole, get the call and pack up my tools and leave. I left assignments and drove my work van to Sisqo's so many times till finally my supervisor showed up at one of my assignments that I ignored and fired me the next day. I was devastated. Bell Atlantic was the kind of job that you could possibly retire from and I blew it by gambling with my time just to hang out with Kid, Hot and sometimes Sisqo. Not to mention, I had a family to provide for and a firecracker for a girlfriend. I didn't tell Anna the real reason why I got fired. I made up something about not performing well and Anna was very supportive. Not once did she flip out or throw it in my face. Soon afterwards I took a job as a cable guy (TCI Communications), installing and disconnecting cable. It didn't pay as much as Bell Atlantic but it kept food on the table. I didn't have the freedom that I had with Bell Atlantic so I would just make up a crazy excuse to leave work whenever I received a call. I was willing to risk almost anything just to be around because I knew that if I stayed close, an opportunity could possibly occur but if I'm not around, absolutely NOTHING could happen. Also, Sisqo's house was magical to me. Here we have these young guys, with legit money, cars, girls, a house and FAME. I had been around people with money before but never fame. Fame is an entirely different beast and once an aspiring artist gets a wift of fame, they immediately become addicted.

One day while at work, I received a routine call from Kidd asking me if I was coming to the house later that day. Of course, I said yes and then I called Anna to tell her about my plans. Anna complained for a little and then she asked me the question that I knew was bound to be asked for some time now; "If you're just hanging out and not working on music, why can't I ever come with you?" Just to prove that nothing was going on when we were at the house, I agreed to take Anna with me. You see, sure there were lots of girls at the house at times but Butch and I were the last guys on the "list". The girls that were there were for Sisqo! He was the star! After Sisqo, Kidd was next in line because of his physical appearance. Kidd looked like a model, light skinned, tall and muscular with a bald head. After Kidd, it was Hot. They had the house, cars, name brand clothes, jewelry and money, not us. These guys were the catch so when girls came to the house, all eyes were on them not us (Butch and I).

Later that night I took Anna with me to Sisqo's house. Anna had on a white pair a fitting pants and a tight t-shirt. Before we left our house, I knew that I would be placed in a compromising situation because of her outfit and how the guys respond to attractive women. Anna was very attractive and her body was amazing; particularly her butt. I would catch guys starring at her all of the time but that was just what came with being with a woman that had a voluptuous body. I was used to it but I didn't like it. When we walked in the door, I anticipated the stares as always and per usual the stares came. Kidd, Hot and Sisqo were the only ones there. Butch hadn't arrived yet. Anna and I sat at the bar in Sisqo's kitchen and smoked some weed as Kid, Hot and Sisqo sat in the living room on the couch. Everytime Anna got up to move around, all eyes were locked in on her. I immediately gave them the "look" as if to say "don't even think about it!" Kidd came to me laughing and whispered "Yo I think she wore that outfit for me!" I shoved him and said "whatever nigga!". He laughed and ran in the other room. Although it was said in a joking matter, I took note on how these guys moved. Where I was from, we all followed the bro code and the bro code stated that baby mothers and main girls are OFF LIMITS. Even though no one technically crossed the line, the vibe was there and that told me that these guys play by a different set of rules; rules that I didn't abide by. The stares and slick little comments made, in any other situation, I would have tried to crack someone's skull but being as though I looked at them as if they were my ticket to stardom, I had to fall back. I left a lot sooner that night because I didn't want something to happen and force my hand to act a fool. That was the first and the last time I took Anna to Sisqo's house.

Chapter 23 - Heartbreak Hotel

O ne day while Butch and I were at the house working with Kid and Hot on some music, out of the blue, we finally got the invite we were waiting for. We all were sitting at the bar in Sisqo's kitchen trying to come up with a hook for a song and suddenly Kid said "Yo, you know what we should do? We should all become a four-man group!" Hot chimed in afterwards and said "Hell yeah! That would be dope!" I couldn't believe what I was hearing! After all of the constant nights helping these guys, playing the background, losing jobs, fighting with Anna about being out, finally we were getting the ask that we wanted since day one! Butch and I never made eye contact but I knew that he was feeling the exact same way. Finally, we were being offered a seat at the table. Butch and I of course agreed and the four-man group process began. But there was only one other thing that had to happen in order to make it official. Sisqo had to approve it.

The next day, Kid ran the idea across to Sisqo. Sisqo didn't give a yes or no response. All he said was "Cool. Let me hear some records". Immediately we all got together and wrote and recorded about 3 – 4 songs together. We also added a few songs that Butch and I did separately as well as Kidd and Hot individual songs. The projected consisted of 8 songs. After everything was mixed and mastered, it was then time to present it to Sisqo for his final approval of the group. I remember thinking to myself, Sisqo has heard me rap live numerous times in his kitchen or outside on his front lawn freestyling but he has never heard me recorded on a song. I was beginning to doubt myself a little. I knew he would like Butch. After all, EVERYONE liked Butch! He was the hottest rapper of us all. It was actually discovered that when Sisqo initially called Mouse to join the group in the beginning, he had mistaken Butch for Mouse on the demo Mouse left at Sisqo's mothers house. So the whole time, Sisqo thought Mouse was Butch rapping on the demo and the invite came from Butch's lyrical talent. Never the less, I had faith that Sisqo would like my skills as well and I got on my knees and prayed to God that he would.

A few days later, I was working up on a utility pole, reconnecting cable and I received a beep from Kidd with a "911" code. That code told me that Kidd was with Sisqo and the verdict had been decided. As I was coming down the utility pole, the butterflies in my stomach almost sent me to the bathroom. I'm not even sure if I finished the job or not; I just packed up my tools, jumped in my work truck and drove to the closest phone I could find which was at my mothers' house. When I got there, my mother wasn't home so I was there all alone. I went into the kitchen where the phone was, picked it up and called Kidd. As the phone rung in my ear, I remember shaking almost uncontrollably. Kidd answered the phone and said "Yo, me and Hot are with Sisqo now. He just listened to the demo. Hold on, I'm calling Butch on the three way!" As I waited in silence for Kid to return to the line with Butch, I became even more nervous. Kidd returned to the line with Butch and now everyone was on the call. Then Kidd said "Yo, Sisqo liked everything on the demo except for one thing.... YOU Kool!" I replied "Yo stop playing. Now is not the time to be joking around!" Kidd then said "Yo, I'm dead serious. Sisqo said who is that dude with the deep voice? I don't like him. If yall want to keep him in the group, yall can go get a deal with someone else (possibly Mya's father) but if yall want to roll with me, cut him out of the group and I will fly yall to California later this week to start working on an album!"

*Side Note: Kidd and Mya were good friends. Kidd met Mya through Sisqo. Mya's father was a manager and Kidd wanted us to have him as a back up just in case Sisqo didn't want to move forward with the group.

I then replied "Yo are you serious!?" Kid then said "Yo I'm dead ass serious!" As Kidd was saying this, I could hear Hot slightly laughing in the background. Kid was also struggling with trying to hold in his laugh. Then Kidd said "Yo, I'll put him on the phone so he can tell you himself!" Kidd passed the phone to Sisqo. Sisqo then said "Yeah man, I don't think it's a good fit. You're voice and your delivery doesn't match with the rest of the group. But you put me in the mindset of an East Coast Snoop Dog and you should probably do your own thing by yourself but it's a no for the group" Sisqo then passed the phone back to Kidd. Kidd then said "Yo so what do yall wanna do? We still have Mya's father that willing to manage us. Which way do we go?" As the question is being asked, I can still hear the snickering in Kidds voice as well as Hot's in the background. With tears rolling down my face, I said "Yo, I cant hold yall up just because he doesn't like me. Yall go ahead without me and roll with Sisqo. Just look out for me on the back end." Kidd immediately said "Okay that's whats up! I'll call you back later" and hung up the phone. Two seconds later my phone rang and it was Butch. Butch said "Yo just say the word. If you don't want me to do it, I won't. This shit is crazy man." I told Butch "Yo, I can't ask you not to take the deal because of me. This is what we've been dreaming for. Go ahead and do your thing with them. Just look out for me on the back end." Butch asked me if I was sure and I told him I was and then we hung up. After hanging up, I burst out in tears and dropped to one knee on the floor. I couldn't believe that I came that close to fulfilling my dreams and missed the mark. I rolled from one knee to eventually sitting on my mother's kitchen floor with my back leaning against her dishwasher, with my head in my hands crying like a baby. Not only was I devastated about getting cut from the group, I thought to myself, what am I going to tell everyone? My mother, Anna, my cousins, aunts, uncles, friends etc. All of these people knew that I was directly tied into Sisqo's camp and I'm going to look like a failure when they see everyone blowing up except me! I couldn't go back to work after that news. I called my supervisor and told him that I was sick and couldn't finish the day. I didn't want to be around anyone because I knew the disappointment was all in my face and demeanor so I stayed at my mother's until maybe 30 minutes before she was expected home and then I went home.

The next day, Butch informed me that Sisqo booked flights for him, Kidd and Hot to fly out to California on the upcoming Friday as promised. He also said that Sisqo had come up with a name for the group which was Cuzzon and he hated it. Sisqo got the name Cuzzon from a Jodeci Remix song in which Raekwon from Wu Tang said "Wu and Jodeci is like Cuzzons" in his verse. Since the guys were scheduled to leave soon, Butch had to get all of his affairs in order (job arrangements, who would check in on his apartment, mail etc.) which meant the word was about to get out that I was not in the group. Butch was dating Anna's sister Ne Ne at the time so once Ne Ne found out of course Anna would know.

Before I could break the news to Anna, she approached me once she found out from her sister that Butch was headed to California soon. She initially had an attitude because she thought that I was going too but was trying to hide it from her. When I told her that I wasn't going, she felt relieved about me not hiding the trip from her but then her energy shifted to find out why. I told Anna that I was not going to be apart of the group. I didn't tell her that I was cut because my pride wouldn't let me. Besides, I knew Anna and I was due to get into a meaningless argument soon and I didn't want her to have that to throw in my face, so I decided to lie. I twisted Sisqo's words and told her that Sisqo wanted me to be a solo act; an east coast Snoop Dogg and after he completed the groups project, he would start working on mine. This was the same lie I told everyone that asked about the situation. By saying that Sisqo would start my project after the groups, that gave me time to work on my craft and get better. Although I was eternally crushed about getting cut, I was also determined to get better so that Sisqo would reconsider and possibly put me back in the group. But until that time came, I was going to tell that lie to anyone that asked. I told the lie so much that I honestly started believing it myself.

That Friday came and the group (now known as Cuzzon) flew out to California. I was left musically alone in Baltimore with absolutely nothing to do besides go to work and come home. Not only did I lose the ones I created music with, I also loss the "friendship" piece to the equation. These guys were the only ones that I hung out with and even the place where we hung out at (the house) wasn't available either. I began to find myself fighting hard not to fall into a state of depression. The only thing that kept me going was believing if I got better, Sisqo would possibly put me back in the group so I worked constantly on my delivery as well as on my lyrical content.

Every night or so, Butch would call me from California to check on me and give me updates. Butch was also advocating for me to get back in the group but being as though he was still looked upon as a "new member" he didn't have the weight that Kidd and Hot had so he had to tread lightly. One night around 2am the phone rang. Both Anna and I as well as the kids, were asleep. When I heard the phone ring, I knew it had to be Butch because he was on West Coast time which was 3 hours earlier, explaining the late call. As I was answering the phone, Anna was already complaining about the late call interrupting her sleep. As soon as I heard Butch's voice, I knew something was wrong. Butch didn't waist anytime. He immediately said "Yo I know its late over there but I had to call and tell you this. You're not going to believe what just happened! Sisqo just put another guy in the group. He goes by the name of Fame." He then went on to say "Yo and I aint even gonna lie, this guy is on fire! He damn near raps like Eminem plus he makes tracks that are just as fire as his raps!" Hearing Butch say those words sent a chill through my body. I almost couldn't breathe. I was lying in the bed next to Anna trying not to talk or make any noise because I didn't want to hear her mouth about me being on the phone so late but I had to say something. My last bit of hope was being taken away from me. I had all of my eggs in the basket of being readded to the group and now I'm hearing that a Rap-God just dropped out of the sky and killed any chance of me rejoining the group. As Butch and I continued to talk, Anna became more frustrated. "I wish you would get off the damn phone! Its 2am in the fucking morning. Shut the fuck up!" Out of frustration

I replied "You shut the fuck up!" Afterwards, I continued my conversation with Butch. Just as he was explaining to me how it went down in regards to Fame joining the group, Anna got out of the bed, and snatched the phone cord completely out of the wall, which of course disconnected the call. Then she yelled "Fuck you and Butch!" I got up and attempted to take to cord out of Anna's clinched fist and Anna threw the cord at me. When I saw that the cord was broken, I lost it. I pushed Anna and she fell into our closet. She got up screaming and cussing and stormed downstairs headed for the kitchen. I stayed in our room attempting to connect the cord back into the wall so I could finish hearing what Butch had to say about this new group member. Anna came storming up the steps with a butcher's knife. She came towards me with the knife and I raised my left arm as a shield and the point of the knife went into my fore arm. When I saw the blood, I tried to take the knife from her and grabbed the blade and my entire left hand was sliced open. Bleeding from two spots, my arm and my hand, I wrapped up my hand with a t shirt, threw on some clothes, grabbed my work uniform and left.

I spent the night at my mothers that night. When I arrived, of course she was in the bed (3am). She didn't say anything. She probably assumed that Anna and I got into it again but she had no idea about the stabbing till the next morning. I told my mother about what happened with me and Anna but didn't tell her about the new guy in the group. I mean, how could I? It would have contradicted my entire lie about being a solo artist.

My mother saw my wounds and was very upset. She went on to say that I should never allow a woman to mark up my body. I thought that was some sort of country/ South Carolina talk. My mother wanted me to go to the hospital and get stitches and shots but I refused. I just wrapped the cuts up and took Tylenol for the pain. I told my supervisor that someone tried to rob me and that I was stabbed in order to call out as well as keep my job. I had called out so many times before due to hanging out at the house or up all night fighting with Anna that I needed to have a solid reason for not coming in moving forward. My mother could see that I was in bad shape; not because of the stabbing but life as a whole so she did what she always did when she felt as if she couldn't help. She called my father. My mother and father never talked to each other. Only when it was necessary and when it involved me. After the call, my father called me and asked me to come see him. Whenever I got calls like that from my dad I felt like I was in the mob and was being "sent for".

When I arrived to my father's house, as soon as I hit the front door my eyes began to fill with water. It was just something about that house that made me feel vulnerable. That house was like my root in its purest form. Everything that mattered to me started and ended in that house. 3327 Brighton Street along with my father and grandmother was my safe haven. That was and is the only place on earth where I felt and feel safe from the dangers of this world. It was there where I could resort to being a baby and sometimes in life, that's needed.

I sat on the couch and began to tell my father about what had happened with me and Anna. I honestly didn't have to mention Butch or the group because my dad and I very rarely talked about music. I didn't have to tell my dad the lie. He only knew who Sisqo and Dru Hill was because I mentioned them to him. His main concern was always in regards to the lifestyle entertainers lived. Drugs, alcohol and fast life were all concerns of his and he didn't want me to get caught up in the madness. As I talked about what happened, and showed him my sliced open hand, I began to tear up again because not only was I going through the worst fight that I ever had with Anna, I was also dealing with her threats of keeping my son away from me as well as the door in Cuzzon being shut and sealed with no way of getting back in. It was just too much to deal with at one time. My father never judged or told me what I should do. Instead he just spoke positivity and assured me that everything would be okay. By the end of the conversation, I felt a thousand times better. When I left my fathers, I went back home to Anna. She apologized. I apologized. Then we went back into our normal routine.

A few weeks had past and finally Sisqo and the guys returned back to Baltimore. They brought their newest member Fame with them. Dru Hill was scheduled to go on tour the following month so immediately the group started working on new material. Sisqo arranged for Cuzzon to work with a producer from Baltimore that played in Dru Hills band named Dave Evans. The first session the guys had with Dave, everyone was there, Sisqo and Cuzzon as well as myself. Sisqo also was in the process of creating a female version of Dru Hill called Lovher so one of the lead singers Chinky was there as well.

Dave the producer lived in one of the grimiest neighborhoods (North Ave & Gay St.) in East Baltimore. Sisqo had a brand new 400GS Lexus, all black with rims that stood out like a sore thumb in that neighborhood. When I would pull up to Dave's house and see Sisqo's car I would think to myself, "he's asking to get kidnapped or robbed bringing that car around here". Sisqo on the other hand either blindly didn't know or didn't care. His main focus at the time was to complete two demo's; one for Cuzzon and one for Lovher. Sisqo had a production deal on the table with Def Jam for his new label Dragon Records so Cuzzon and Lovher were top priority.

Every night, the entire crew was at Dave's house and I was there also. I was the only one there that wasn't apart of the movement. I remember a few times catching Sisqo look at me as if to say "Why are you here?" I wasn't sure if that's what he was thinking but it felt that way. It could have been my insecurities playing tricks with my thoughts. Never the less, I stayed and continued to attend every session no matter what anyone thought. I believed strongly in the saying "out of sight, out of mind" so I was determined to always be around if allowed. Being as though I wasn't one of the "artist" the guys and everyone at Daves house was starting to treat me like a errand boy. If someone wanted something from the store, they would send me. If someone needed to be picked up from the airport or dropped off somewhere, they would ask me to do it. I wasn't doing anything else besides sitting there watching everyone create, vibe and record so I guess they figured they would make my presence useful.

I played this position for the entire recording of Cuzzons demo. I remember being in those sessions, hearing everyone bounce ideas off eachother and wanting to chime in but couldn't because I was looked at as the guy that wasn't good enough. Hearing Sisqo ad lib over the guys rap verses was amazing to me because he sung with so much feeling and soul. I remember thinking to myself "Man I'd give anything to be apart of this". One song that stood out to me was when Sisqo and the guys remade Phil Collins "In The Air Of The Night". Everyone's rap verses were cool but when Sisqo came in with the ad libs over the hook, it sent chills through everyone's body. It was absolutely electrifying! The energy in the studio was on ten and I genuinely was happy for everyone but at the same time, I was sad because I wasn't apart of it. Also, Sisqo, Kid and Hot made me feel like I wasn't apart as well. A lot of times while vibing and celebrating in the moment, they wouldn't even look at me. Sometimes even Butch would give me the same vibe but I honestly believe that he was in an awkward situation. The only one that was in a neutral position and showed me consistent love was ironically the new member in the group Fame.

Since day one, Fame was always solid. He wasn't like Kid and Hot. He was a real genuine guy. He didn't know about any of the back stories of the group and he really didn't care. His main focus was to make good music. When I told him about Sisqo cutting me out of the group, he was shocked. He listened to me rap and checked out a few older songs with me on them and liked what he heard. He would often say "Yo Cool, Fuck these dudes. I'm gonna make sure you are straight!" Fame was a pretty boy that rapped about the fast life; things Sisqo as well as mainstream listeners wanted to hear and he was incredible at doing it. But Fame was even hotter at producing music! His beats were off the charts. A one-man band. Fame would sometimes see the sadness in my demeanor at some of the sessions and would pull me to the side and say "Don't worry Cool. I got you." Of all the people in that room, I was receiving words of encouragement and affirmation from someone that I practically didn't even know; a stranger. Lesson learned.

Meanwhile on the home front, I was catching hell from Anna. By this time, she knew that I was cut from the group and Sisqo had no intentions on working with me as a solo act. Her knowing this made it even more stressful when I hung out at Dave's house while the group recorded. She would always say "Why in the hell are you still hanging with them!? Its obvious that they don't want you around! They cut you out of the group and you still keep coming around; like a little flunky!" Anna's words would cut and hurt me to the core of my soul, but I never let her know it. Every night before I left home to head to Dave's

I had to hear that and often it would almost break me, but I never stopped going. I just figured that I had to be there; just in case an opportunity presented itself.

One evening after a hard day at work, I came home with the intention of staying in. Sisqo was out of town so there wasn't a studio session that night. When I arrived home, Anna had just got in from work but accidently left her wallet at her job. Anna was working as a Dental Assistant at a dental office about 10 minutes away from our house. While rushing trying to get back to the dental office before the receptionist locked the doors, she accidentally left her pager on our couch. As I sat on the other end of the couch playing with my son Peanut, I kept hearing Anna's pager go off. I picked up the pager and saw that someone had left her 4 voicemails. Curious to know who it was, I grabbed our house phone, called Anna's pager, entered the last four of her social and just like that, I had access to the voicemails. As I listened to the voicemails. My entire body got hot and I began to sweat. I heard one of our neighbors on Anna's voicemail, saying how much he missed her and couldn't wait to see her again. This was a guy that I saw almost every day, with his wife and kids and sometimes had shorts conversations with. All I saw was red and I wanted to hurt someone badly at that moment. I called Anna at her job and told her what I heard. She couldn't say anything because she was caught red handed. All she could say was "I'm sorry". I hung up the phone, grabbed my son Peanut and drove to Butch's house. Butch lived maybe 15 minutes away. When I arrived at Butch's house, I asked him to take a ride with me. I really didn't want to tell him what was going on because I was embarrassed but I needed his assistance with what I was planning to do so I had no choice. I told Butch what I heard on Anna's voicemail and explained to him that I was going to beat my neighbor with a crowbar. I needed Butch to watch Peanut while I punished my neighbor and take Peanut to my mother's if I went to jail. I also had a heart to heart talk with Butch and asked him not to tell anyone about this because it was embarrassing. Butch understood and agreed.

When we arrived back to my house, Anna had already been there and was trying to pack her things and exit. When she saw me get out of the car, she dropped her bags and ran into the next-door neighbor's house (a girl we both knew). I banged on the door and was about to attempt to kick it in but decided not to. Butch stayed in my car with Peanut as he slept in his car seat. I then headed to the neighbor's house who I heard on Anna's voicemail. I banged on the door and the dude's wife answered. I told her what was going on and she was devastated. I had the crowbar in my hand, and I asked her where he is. Out of fear she pointed to the top of her steps. I walked past her and looked up the step and saw the dude standing there, holding his baby daughter in his arms. He was saying and pleading something (out of fear), but I couldn't make out exactly what he was saying due to his wife crying as well as his other two kids screaming out of fear. I saw the commotion I was causing, and I knew I wasn't going to hit him while holding a baby, so I turned around and left. I took Butch back home and my son

Peanut, and I went to my mothers and spent the night. That was the end of Anna and me. I could deal with the arguments, name calling, fights and even stabbing but one thing I couldn't deal with was cheating. I knew that I would never look at her the same afterwards so the next day I started looking for an apartment. Not long afterwards, I moved out and Ole Man Joe and I shared an apartment not far away. When everyone asked why we broke up, I told them it was because I was tired of all the fighting.

Chapter 24 - The Aftermath

About a month later, I was settled into my new apartment, now single with a baby momma instead of a live-in girlfriend. The only thing I took from Anna and I's townhouse was the brand new leather living room set (that I had recently just bought), the entertainment center along with the 40 inch TV and of course all of my clothes and personal items. Anna was pissed about me taking the leather couches and even more pissed when she found out that her father helped me move everything in his truck. I didn't have a bed so I just piled a bunch of quilts up and slept on my bedroom floor. Being as though my name was still on Anna and I's townhouse lease, Ole Man Joe agreed to put the apartment in his name therefore he had the master room in the apartment. I lost my job with the cable company for missing too much time at work, due to either fighting with Anna or staying up all night at Sisqo's house or Dave's studio but luckily Dave (from Demartim Records) hooked me up with a job where he worked; a customer service job, selling telephone accessories- a place called Tesco. Dave and I kept in contact even after Shock Trauma. We would party together all of the time and occasionally he would come to my house (when Anna and I was living together) and play video games. Everything was looking good for me personally except for one thing; Anna's bitterness.

Anna was very upset about me moving out and it seemed as if she was determined to make my life miserable. I didn't want her to know where I lived at so I would always pick up and drop off our son Peanut at our (well now her) townhouse. One day after a drop off one of Anna's girlfriends followed me home and my cover was officially blown. The next day as I was driving to work, cars were riding up beside me saying "hey man, your license plate is missing". When I arrived at work (Timonium MD), I looked at the back of my car and my license plate was gone. I was afraid to drive back home without a license plate, especially coming from Timonium, so I called the police and reported it stolen. I knew this was the work of Anna so on my lunch break I called her and convinced Anna to return my tags. When I got home from work that night my tags were leaning up against my apartment door. She also taped the phone bills to my apartment door for all my neighbors to see and circled the outstanding balances (over $1,000) from her calling Cleo the psychic- a 900 number for psychic advice about our relationship. I was so pissed about the high phone bill that she ran up which was in my name, that I attached my tags back on my car but forgot to call the police to inform them that the license plate was retrieved. The next day, I was driving home from work, taking a short cut through the back roads and a police car crept up behind me. Immediately butterflies began to swim around in my stomach because I knew he was running my tags and they're still reported as stolen. Soon afterwards, three more police cars were following me and out of nowhere a police car swerved in from a side street to my right causing me to have to slam on breaks. They all jumped out of their cars, pulled their guns and order me to get out of my car and lay face down on the ground. I did exactly what they said and spread my arms and legs out to make sure there was not any confusion. The ground was extremely hot so I couldn't lay my face completely on the ground, so my head was sort of dangling in the air as I laid on my stomach. I explained to the police officers that they were my tags; I just forgot to call back and say they were retrieved. The police made me wait, lying in the hot street face down, while they confirmed my story. Once everything was confirmed, they allowed me to get up and leave.

A few days later Dru Hill went on tour and Sisqo as promised, took Cuzzon with them, leaving me once again musically all alone. Mouse was getting married during this time and Butch was supposed to be the best man but being as though Butch was away on tour, I was next in line. I had the time of my life at Mouse's reception, partying with Mouse, Ole man Joe and Mouse's brother in law but it all was ruined at the end when a girl at the reception showed interest in me and Anna approached the girl and attempted to fight her. When we separated the two, I left with Anna and went back to "her" townhouse and had sex. The next morning, as I was leaving Anna suggested that

I move back in. When I declined, I saw it in her face that she finally realized that we were not getting back together.

A few weeks later, the guys came home for a few days because part of Dru Hill's tour dates were overseas and Sisqo decided not to take the group out of the country. They would reunite when Dru Hill returned to the states. One day Butch, Hot and I were headed to Sisqo's house, but I had to stop at a gas station for gas. As I pumped the gas, I saw a beautiful girl walking towards the door of the gas station. I spoke to her and she spoke back as she went inside. Butch, Hot and I all looked at each other as if to say "who's going to try and talk to her". When she came out of the store, I decided to take matters in my own hands, so I asked her if she had a moment. As soon as she stopped, I knew it was a go. I introduced myself and asked her what her name was. She smiled and said Chante. We talked for a few and then exchanged numbers. Afterwards I got in the car and we headed to Sisqo's house.

The next day, I called Chante and we spoke for hours as if we already knew one another. Chante was 18 years old, living in her own one-bedroom apartment, owned her car and was working as a legal assistant in a lawyers office; and had no kids. She was an only child like me and grew up in Joppatowne, MD. She didn't know a lot about the city life nor did she hang out in the local clubs or hang out spots. She always seemed happy and full of bubbly energy and to me that was like a breath of fresh air. She was the sweetest most innocent girl that I had ever met. I figured that I hit the jackpot by meeting her. She was not a sexual virgin but in almost every other category she was a virgin or the closest thing I would ever come across in Baltimore City. I knew that I wanted to make her my girlfriend.

Soon afterwards, the guys returned on tour with Dru Hill. Being as though there were no musical distractions, Chante and I were together almost every day. After work she would come to my apartment and we would just chill out and talk. Of course, I was always trying to sleep with her by the end of the night, but she always declined. We cuddled, hugged, and kissed but she would never allow things to go too far. I respected her for that and that made me want her even more! Of all of the girls I've ever dated, Chante made me wait the longest (by far) so I knew that she wasn't easy which was another A+ on the "girlfriends score card." After a little over a month of dating Chante and I made it official and became and item on May 21st 1999.

Meanwhile the guys were still on tour with Dru Hill and Butch would call almost every night to keep me updated. One day Butch called and said "Yo, we're going to be in New York in a couple of days. You should come up and hang with us!" I eagerly accepted the invitation. A few days later I caught the bus to New York and met up with the guys at the hotel. I was in awe of the entire tour life movement. Through Sisqo's Dragon Music Group, the guys had just signed a deal with Def Jam and received their advancement money. Phat Farm clothes and air force ones were everywhere! Avirex jackets and coogi sweaters as well. The guys looked like bonafide superstars. Butch had his girlfriend Ne Ne (Anna's sister) in town and decided to stay back at the hotel and not attend the show. He gave me his all access pass so I could attend in his place. Being escorted in the venue by security with all of the screaming fans felt like a dream come true even though I knew they weren't screaming for me. Just being apart of it made me feel good. The backstage, the dressing rooms with all of the fruit, snacks and drinks, lights and cameras, everything was just amazing to me. Kidd, Hot and Fame were used to it by now; this was every night for them but for me, it was my first time experiencing this fiasco and I was taking in every moment. The grand finale was when Dru Hill performed, this was only my second time watching Dru Hill live (the 1st was at the album release party). The show was absolutely amazing and the icing on the cake was when Dru Hill performed on of their hit songs "Beauty" and Sisqo flew around the arena in a harness singing his lungs out! I actually saw girls crying in the audience as Dru Hill was performing and I thought to myself, Wow! I'm right where I need to be. I am around the right people that can make my dreams come true!

After the show we all got back on the tour bus and Kidd said to me "Yo the next show is in Connecticut. Are you rolling with us?" I looked around the extravagant tour bus and everything in me wanted to say yes and ride to Connecticut but I knew I didn't have enough money for another bus ticket. Butch had paid for the original ticket. Besides, I had to go to work the next day. Even Sisqo gave me a nod as if to say "come roll with us to Connecticut." But I had to decline. Getting off of that tour bus and catching the greyhound back to Baltimore was heartbreaking. Another guy that was close to one of the band members rode back to Baltimore with me as well. His name was Jamari and he had hopes of breaking into to music industry as well.

When I returned home, I wasn't the same person anymore. The tour life experience was the straw that broke the camel's back. My blinders went completely up and all I could see was stardom! I was obsessed with becoming the greatest artist that Sisqo would ever come across. That morning I was supposed to go to work, but I didn't. I quit my job that day. I refused to leave the house until I felt like I got better. I wrote raps from sunup to sundown. While at Tesco, I met a producer named Ike and he gave me a track a while ago with the 112- Cupid sample. I remembered that I had the track and wrote one of the most influential songs (well the 1st and 2nd verse) "Always" that I have ever written. At the time, the song did not have a name. I was going through so much turmoil previously with Anna and seeing my son Peanut, that I decided to write about it, but the issue wasn't real time. It was a feeling that I had felt and had stored over a year prior to me writing the song. I also wrote a song called the Average Joe during that time as well as numerous freestyle/ battle raps. Not only was I writing, I was also working on my delivery and showmanship as well. I did this every single day until the guys returned home from Dru Hills tour.

The first day back from tour (well that night, after everyone got settled in) we all met up at Sisqo's house per usual. I couldn't wait for the opportunity to display to everyone what I'd been working on. We all sat in the kitchen and living room, drinking, smoking and talking and before you knew it, someone put on an instrumental. It was showtime! As soon as I heard the beat, I toned everyone out. I was determined to be by far the best artist in the house. I wanted to crush everyone in the room, including my good friend Butch. It was anything personal, but I knew that if I wanted to advance in this circle, I had to be far better than everyone. I couldn't leave it up to a toss up decision. The guys looked at the cipher as just recreational play, but I looked at it as an all-out competition! I knew that I would crush Kidd and Hot but with Butch and Fame, I had to be strategic about it. I decided to exploit what I thought was their weaknesses. Butch was an exceptional lyricist, but he lacked in showmanship so when I was rapping in the cipher, I made sure to turn up my "showmanship dial" in order to stand out and outshine him. In regards to Fame, he was damn near flawless. He had it all; lyrics, showmanship and delivery. But there was one thing that he didn't have that I did have and that was street experience. So that was his weakness to me, and I attacked it. Every time he kicked a rhyme about money, cars and ice, I followed up denouncing the flashy life and glorified the hood. Hood and street rap were an area that Fame couldn't and wouldn't touch so I stood on it and talked trash about rappers rapping about things that they didn't have in real life. I was the loudest and most aggressive one in the room. The touring and Def Jam deal had made the guys comfortable and my hunger was on a thousand and it showed. The guys couldn't even see what was happening. The only ones that could see it was Charles and Sisqo's girlfriend Nikki. After the cipher Nikki actually pulled Sisqo to the side and said "You should pay more attention to Cool." That was the day a savage was born! Not a lyrical savage or an artistry savage but savage in regards to going after something relentlessly and not taking no as an answer. From that moment moving forward I knew that if I kept applying the same pressure all the time, my opportunity would definitely come.

Meanwhile on the personal side, after I would spend the average workday hours working on my craft, Chante would come over and hang out. Often it was just me, Chante, Ole Man Joe and now Butch because the tour was over. Mouse was now married and didn't come around as much as before. Ole Man Joe and Butch became very cool with Chante. A lot of times, the two of them would be playing the game and Chante and I would be chilling on the couch. Butch would talk to Chante a lot to get a females perspective on relationship and life issues. Sometimes when I would go to Chante's apartment, I would see Butch's phone number on her caller ID. It was cool though. Sometimes Butch would call her looking for me and other times they would have friendly talks. Ole Man Joe used to joke about how much Butch liked talking to Chante but I didn't pay Joe any mind. Ole Man Joe joked about absolutely EVERYTHING!

One day Chante and I were having a very personal and intense conversation and she mentioned something out of innocence that blew my mind. She brought up the situation about Anna cheating on me with our neighbor and asked how did that affect me. I was in complete shock. For starters, I was totally embarrassed about that situation and also I wondered how in the hell did she know about it? It was only one person that could have told her and that was Butch. I thought to myself, "Why would he tell my current girlfriend something that was so personal about my previous girlfriend/ baby mother?" I also wondered if he told Chante, who else did he tell? He gave me his word that he wouldn't tell anyone! I felt anger and betrayal all at the same time. The next day I asked Butch why did he tell Chante something that was so sensitive and personal about me. He apologized and told me a long drawn out story of how it came up which didn't make any sense to me at all. Afterwards, I told Chante not to talk to Butch at all if I wasn't around. Ole Man Joe was very upset about the situation. He felt as though Butch was up to no good by telling Chante what happened between Anna and me. Chante was young and naïve to a lot of things so she wouldn't catch certain things. I couldn't confirmed or deny what Ole Man Joe's intuition was saying but to be safe the communication between Chante and Butch was cut off.

One night while home alone working on new material, I received a phone call from Lia. Every so often we would reach out to one another just to check in and make sure we both were okay. We hadn't been sexually involved since we were in a relationship. We talked for hours this particular night, reminiscing about the Demartim Records days as well as the bloopers in our relationship. I can't remember which one of us brought it up, but somehow, we started confessing things that went down when we were together. A lot of secrets were exposed but in laughter and fun. One of the secrets Lia revealed to me was one of her friends, Maria, who occasionally stayed with Lia was a bisexual and one night they planned to have a threesome with me. Lia vaguely mentioned it to me but at the time I thought it was a set up and declined. Lia confirmed that it was very real, and I missed the boat! Lia and Maria messed around the whole time and I never knew it till this conversation. I told her about some episodes I had with Glow and how bad I wanted Shanna but that was about it. Lia then asked me a question that would eventually release the ultimate skeleton out of the closet. Lia asked me "of all of my girlfriends, which one would you want to sleep with?" I though about it for a second and then answered. I named one of Lia's best friends; a girl named Shawnie. I then returned the ask to Lia, same question. Lia thought for a minute and then she said Butch. I then said to Lia "We should set it up! Hook me up with Shawnie and I'll hook you up with Butch!" Lia agreed. The next day I told Butch about the conversation that Lia and I had and asked if he was down for the swap. Of course he said yes. I even gave him details about how Lia has sex, what she liked, what she didn't like and also what she was good at. Butch was very excited about the swap and was eager to get it started. I also told Ole Man Joe about it too.

About a week or so later Ole man Joe came into my room early in the morning. "Yo, that's crazy! Why didn't you tell me it went down?" I didn't know what Ole man Joe was talking about, so I asked, "What do you mean?" He then said, "The swap!" I said "Yo the swap didn't happen yet. What are you talking about?" Ole Man Joe then said "Yo, last night Butch and I were playing the game and smoking. After we got high, Butch started talking and saying how good Lia's sex was. He was giving details blow by blow. This niggas eyes were closed and he was smiling ear to ear talking about how good it was!" I said "damn I didn't even know. No one told me."

I called Lia after Ole man Joe and I's conversation and asked her why she didn't tell me that it went down. Lia replied "Nothing happened yet. What are you talking about?" I told Lia about Ole Man Joe and Butch's conversation and Lia suddenly became quiet. She then said "Yo, there's something I need to tell you. Butch wasn't talking about something that happened recently. He's speaking about when he and I used to mess around back in the Demartim Records days!" She then went on to say "Butch and I were sleeping together almost the entire time of Demartim Records. I knew you were sleeping with Glow so I said to myself, two can play this game!" She went on to say, "do you remember the time when you came to my apartment and I had a lot of bags of clothes at the front door? Those bags were put there to slow you down just in case you came. When we heard you stepping over the bags, Butch ran out of my bedroom a laid on the couch pretending to be asleep. You asked me who was on the couch and I said Butch but you thought he was just there because his job was close by! We were just about to have sex. After you left, I wanted to continue but he was so shook about you coming there that he just left. Another time, you saw my glasses at his apartment and you asked him about it. He told you that his roommate Rick saw me on the bus stop, gave me a ride and I left them in his car. The truth was I was at his apartment all the time and I accidentally left my glasses. Rick and Mouse knew about it. Ole Man Joe did not." I didn't feel any animosity or anger after hearing what Lia had told me. I actually didn't feel any at all. Now if it was back in the Demartim records days, I'm sure I would have been livid but being as though so much time had passed and I didn't have any romantic feelings for Lia anymore, it didn't bother me. However, I was baffled as to why Butch didn't tell me. Why did I have to hear this from Lia? Especially after I arranged for him to sleep with her with this "swap" situation.

Later that evening I told Old Man Joe about Lia and I's conversation and Ole Man Joe became livid! Both scenario's made his blood boil- the first was the fact that Butch was sneaking around and sleeping with Lia back in the Demartim Records days (bro code violation) and two, not coming clean even after the swap was brought to the table. A few of Butch's actions in the past made Ole Man Joe question his character a little, but this was the straw that broke the camel's back! Ole Man Joe also had a hidden grudge against Butch that was suppressed because of the lack of evidence but this issue amplified the grudge and added fuel to the dim fire igniting fury in Ole Man Joe's soul. You see also back in the Demartim Record days, Ole Man Joe had suspicions of Butch flirting around and possibly messing around with his baby's mother. Ole Man Joe claimed that he caught a few looks being exchanged between the two but he didn't have enough proof to accuse anyone, so he let it go. But this situation with Butch and Lia proved that Butch would do something like this and now Ole Man Joe felt validity for the thoughts he had in the past.

Ole Man Joe looked at Butch as a snake and did not want anything to do with him anymore. He wanted me to pull Butch up and confront him for what he did but I had a better plan. You see, I agreed with Ole Man Joe's notion of Butch being a snake in regards to women, but I didn't agree with him on how I should handle it. I decided that I was going to expose Butch without him ever knowing.

I never told Butch that Ole Man Joe and I knew the truth and never mentioned my conversation with Lia. Instead, I told everyone else around us and made them give their word that they wouldn't mention it to him. I even told Sisqo. The entire squad knew except Butch. Butch and Lia went forward with the swap and Butch gave me all of the details pretending as if it was the first time. I played along with his antics and studied his ways as he continued to act as if this was something new. The more and more he slept with Lia during current times, I wondered to myself "damn is he ever going to confess?" As more time went by, the more I became disappointed with Butch. I was just waiting and waiting but he never said anything. Sometimes we would all be together, and conversations would come up about friends stabbing each other in the back. One particular time, Butch even had the nerve to go on a rant about how he thinks it's the dirtiest thing in the world for someone to sleep with his friend's girlfriend. As he was preaching so passionately about it on his imaginary soap box, we all were tapping each other under the table as if to say "I can't believe he's saying this!" That performance made Butch look like an imposter in everyone's eyes simply because he spoke so passionately about it, not knowing that EVERYONE knew what he did. His ways were exposed and that was satisfaction for me.

Unfortunately, this wasn't enough for Ole Man Joe. He was determined to make Butch pay in some sort of way. Ole Man Joe decided that the best punishment for Butch was to have the same thing did to him so Ole man Joe decided to pursue Butch's baby mother Ne Ne (Anna's sister). Prior to Butch dating his baby's mother, Ne Ne, Ole Man Joe and she would at times act "friendly" to one another but nothing more than that. So, Ole Man Joe thought that he would revisit the "friendly vibes" from years ago and attempt to sleep with Ne Ne as payback for what Butch did with Lia and possibly Ole Man Joes baby mother. When Ole Man Joe propositioned Ne Ne, she didn't know how to respond. She knew Butch and Ole Man Joe were close friends and couldn't figure out why Ole Man Joe would attempt to cross that line. Being confused and not knowing where that energy was coming from, Ne Ne told Butch about Ole Man Joes advances.

Hearing this news sent Butch through the roof! He immediately called me and told me what happened. I continued to act as if I didn't know anything and all of this was a surprise to me. I wasn't on board with Ole man Joes plan. I was okay with the exposing and knowing how he moves without him knowing I knew but Ole Man Joe had his own agenda. Butch didn't have a clue of what was going on. He just thought that Ole Man Joe was being a slime ball by trying to sleep with his baby mother which was actually his girlfriend as well. Butch called Ole Man Joe every name in the book and told everyone that he was going to punch Ole Man Joe in the face the very next time he saw him. Once again, everyone knew the whole truth except Butch. Even the other members of Dru Hill as well as Sisqo's female group Lovher knew as well.

A few days later we were all at Sisqo's house just hanging out having fun. Kidd being the instigator that he was sparked up the conversation and began to provoke Butch about fighting Ole Man Joe (in a joking way). At the time Ole Man Joe wasn't there. Kidd began to say things like "Butch I think I hear someone at the front door! It might be Ole Man Joe! You better run!" Of course, Butch responded with harsh words standing on his statement that they would fight the next time they crossed each other's path. After a moment of joking around, Kidd went into another room, called Ole man Joe and invited him out to the house. When Ole Man Joe accepted, Kidd returned to the kitchen where everyone was, with the jokes. "Ah shit, yall. Ole Man Joe is on his way out here!" Let's see what Butch is going to do when he gets here!"

Everyone at the house continued to joke around as we waited for Ole Man Joe's arrival but as more time went by, I could see it in Butch's eyes that he really didn't want to fight Ole Man Joe but being as though he said he would, he had to. About an hour later, the doorbell rung, and it was none other than Ole Man Joe. Everyone gathered around like kids in a school yard at the front door to watch to see what was about to happen. Butch answered the door, walked outside and asked Ole Man Joe to follow him so they could talk. I closed the door behind them leaving the two of them outside alone to talk. After every 15 minutes or so, one of us that were in the house would peak out of the door to see what they were doing. All everyone saw was the both of them just talking. After about 45 minutes, we all wondered what they were talking about for so long and finally we just went outside to join them.

Once Butch saw everyone come outside, his energy immediately went from talking to wanting to fight. Both Ole man Joe and Butch put their guards up and started to approach each other to fight. As they strategically walked around in slow circles, waiting for the opportunity to hit each other, no one threw a punch. The both of them were talking the entire time. Butch was telling Ole Man Joe that he was a snake for trying to sleep with Ne Ne. Ole Man Joe finally got fed up with Butch being in the dark and blurted out "Yo, everyone out here knows that you're the biggest snake of them all because we know that you slept with Lia back in the day!" Butch looked almost as if he saw a ghost when Ole Man Joe said that. Butch looked around at everyone almost as f he was trying to read our facial expressions, and then he just zapped out and charged Ole man Joe with a flurry of punches. They both slugged it out for a few seconds and then locked up and started wrestling. Once we felt that the two had gotten whatever they had off their chest, we pulled the two part.

Ole Man Joe jumped in his car and immediately left. Butch walked to the side of Sisqo's house and started to vomit. To me, it seemed as if the entire situation weighed heavily on Butch's spirit. He didn't really want to fight Ole Man Joe but he felt as if he had to. In his eyes Ole Man Joe had violated him in a major way as well as he had told everyone that he would fight Ole Man Joe the next time he saw him. But the biggest factor of them all was finding out that we all knew about what transpired between him and Lia back in the past. After Butch got himself together, he left as well.

A few days later, I was back at Sisqo's house again just hanging out when suddenly Butch walked through the door.

This was our first time seeing each other since the fight. I had to make a run to Columbia, MD to pick up a cd of tracks from a production team called One Up Entertainment and was headed for the door when suddenly Butch stopped me and said that we needed to talk. I said "Sure. Come ride with me to One Ups spot". Butch agreed. As I drove, headed to Columbia, Butch started off with small talk, claiming that he was really feeling the drink he was sipping before we got in the car, claiming to be borderline drunk. I saw the cup he poured before we left the house and noticed it wasn't much in there, so I knew that he wasn't tipsy or borderline drunk. I assumed he said that just to take the edge off what he wanted to say. He then went on to say "Yo, I just want to apologize for how everything went down with me and Lia in the past. When we first started messing around, I barely knew you. We had all just met and by the time me and you became friends, Lia and I were already in deep. I didn't know how to tell you; especially when I saw you beefing with Ole Man Joes cousin that time, and carrying guns. Then after yall broke up, I figured it was one of those things that I would just take to my grave." I told Butch how we all found out; about how he was high and told Ole Man Joe and then Lia telling me everything. Butch was once again in shock. He didn't even remember saying those things that night. I also told him thats why Ole Man Joe pursued his baby mother. It all started to make sense to Butch in regards to Ole Man Joe. I told Butch that I wasn't mad and I wasn't holding any type of grudge against him. I just wish he would have told me when the swap came up instead of having to hear the truth from Lia.

Whatever friction that was in the air between Butch and I was put to rest that night at that moment. Butch was my friend. He maybe wasn't my friend at the time he and Lia were sleeping together but at the current moment he was, so I let the past stay in the past. I forgave but the Scorpio in me would never allow me to forget!

Chapter 25 - Whatever It Takes

About a few months or so had passed since my New York experience with the guys and me quitting my job. All of my financial responsibilities were backed up and I didn't have my half of the rent money for me and Ole Man Joes apartment. We were facing eviction and it was all my fault; simply because I quit my job in order to work on my craft. As we approached the eviction date, I felt torn right down the middle. One half of me felt bad because I let Ole Man Joe down. He was depending on my half of the rent in order to sustain. Not to mention, the apartment was in his name so this was going to look bad on his credit report. The other half of me felt like this was needed in order to get to a place where renting an apartment wouldn't be necessary. Sharpening my skills will put me in a position where I will soon be able to buy a house!

By the time the actual eviction date arrived, Ole Man Joe had already moved his belongings out of the apartment. I couldn't tell if Ole Man Joe was mad at me or not. I believe he was torn too. Half mad and the other half believing in the process. I moved all of my clothes and small things to my mothers and Chante's prior to eviction day but I didn't have anywhere to put my living room set. I called everyone I knew and tried to sell my leather couches but couldn't get anyone to bite. Finally, the sheriff and the maintenance team arrived and placed all of my things outside in the grass. I sat in my car just to keep an eye on my things, praying it didn't rain. After a few hours Ole Man Joe came to the apartment complex and told me one of his co-workers wanted to buy my living room set but he wouldn't have the money till next week. I had no choice but to accept the offer or leave my set in the grass. Ole Man Joe's co worker came with a truck and took my living room set. Afterwards I went to my new home which was Chante's apartment.

Meanwhile on the musical side, Dru Hill had just returned from a show in London which caused turmoil within the group. It was rumored that a big fight broke out after a show which led to Dru Hill's van windows being shot out. Shortly after the group returned to the states, Woody left the group.

Dru Hill was now a three-member group and at the peak of the Enter The Dru album. They were scheduled to shoot a video for a song called "You Are Everything (Remix)" so Sisqo invited the guys out to the video shoot. I wasn't invited. Being as though it was only 3 members in Dru Hill now, the focus was split into three individual parts, Sisqo and his dance along with his crew (which was Cuzzon), Nokio and his rap along with his crew (The Entity) and Jazz. At the end, the three came together but for most of the video, it was individualized.

After the guys shot the video and returned home, we all met up, per usual at Sisqo's house. After a few drinks Kidd and Hot began crack jokes about Butch's performance in the video. They were saying that he was stiff with his movements and looked lost when the camera was on. When Butch wasn't around, they went into details claiming that Sisqo kept telling Butch to slide down to the end of the VIP couch in the scene, so much that Butch was completely out of the camera shot. When the video finally came out, we couldn't see Butch in the video at all. We barely saw Fame. We only saw Kidd and Hot.

A few weeks later, Def Jam blocked out a few weeks of studio time for Dru Hill's production company's. Sisqo had Dragon Records which involved Cuzzon and Lovher and Nokio had The Entity which involved three solo rap artist, Philly Frank, Freak Nity (both from Philly) and a female rap artist named Gray (from New Jersey). Fame was signed to them both- Sisqo as a rapper and Nokio as a producer. One day Sisqo and Nokio got into an argument over Fame and decided to make Fame choose which route he wanted to take. Fame figured that production was a lot more promising than being a rapper, so Fame chose to roll with Nokio as a producer. Sisqo was extremely pissed off about Fame's decision. So pissed off that he decided to cut all ties and revert back to the originals that he started with so he cut Butch out of the group and sent him home. He dropped the name Cuzzon and just rolled with "Da Kidd and Make It Hot".

Butch was devastated about being cut from the group. He quit his job at Bethlehem Steel (a job that was very hard to get in Baltimore) when he originally made the group and wasn't sure if he could return. He also gave up his apartment as well as his car when he went on tour with the group. Butch was so upset that he actually talked about physically attacking Sisqo for playing with his life like that. Of course, I felt his pain. Just because Fame chose production, in the blink of an eye, Sisqo snatched a deal with Def Jam away, sending him home to basically nothing without thinking twice. Not sure if Sisqo knew about the sacrifices Butch made or if he even cared.

I tried to approach the drastic situation on the positive side. I suggested to Butch that him and I could go back to recording again as a group and possibly sign with Nokio's production company. Butch was very neutral about my proposal. I honestly didn't think he wanted to do it. He was in the "circle" and signed to Def Jam. The last thing on his mind was rejoining with me and starting all over from scratch again.

A week later, Dru Hill hit the road again, this time leaving the guys behind. They left all of their acts in New York in order to work on new material while they were gone. They still had the block out of studio time. Fame was left sort of "in charge" of everything due to his production expertise. Being as though Butch was just released from the group, he wasn't feeling going back to New York in order to possibly record. Fame and I became good friends so as soon as I found out that he was in charge,

I asked if Butch and I could join the sessions. Fame insisted that we came. I had to do a little convincing and finally Butch decided to make the trip.

When we arrived at the studio in New York, everyone was working vigorously on their records. The vibe was very intense and it wasn't a lot of playing and joking around. Kidd and Hott as well as Nokio's acts were all locked in because they knew Sisqo and Nokio would have to turn in their records to Def Jam. Once we got there and settled in, once again I felt alienated. Being as though I wasn't technically apart of either team, I figured I would just hang around and possibly catch a feature on someone's project. I knew Nokio's acts, Philly Frank, Freak Nitty and Gray but I didn't have a close enough relationship with them for them to invite me on a song. So, I had to ask them. They didn't actually say no. They just stalled, by saying things like "lets see if we can figure it out" or "I'll let you know". Kidd and Hot were getting assistance from Butch and Fame, almost as if they all were still a group again. That left me on the sidelines once again.

Fame caught wind of my alienation and suggested that Butch and I do a song together. I was ecstatic about the offer but when I told Butch about what Fame suggested, he didn't seem excited at all. Fame gave me some tracks to pick through. I asked Butch if he wanted to listen so we could choose one, but he sort of brushed it off and continued to work with Kidd and Hot.

I sat in one of the smaller writing rooms and tried to come up with something to one of Fames tracks. Fame was walking by and saw me in the room alone. He came in the room and asked "Yo why are you in here by yourself? Where's Butch?" I told Fame Butch was in one of the other rooms. Fame and I began to talk and I told him that nobody wanted to do a song with me. Fame then said "Yo we are about to shock the entire studio. I will do a song with you! Just me and you and we're gonna kill it!" This was going to be huge! You see everyone wanted to do a song with Fame because they knew he was on fire, both with the beats as well as with the lyrics. And Def Jam loved him! But he refused because he didn't want to rap anymore, especially because of the Sisqo and Nokio altercation.

Fame went into the main room and played one of his tracks on the big speakers. The track was absolutely mind blowing! Everyone stopped whatever they were doing and came into the room going crazy, asking Fame who is the track for. Fame told everyone, "Yo this is me and Cool's new joint"! He then went on to say "This is just me and Cool's joint so don't nobody ask to get on it! Y'all didn't want to do a joint with him before so don't ask to do one with him now." Everyone looked stunned. Fame put everyone out of the room and we began to write our verses. Fame already had the hook. The name of the song was "Money Makes The World Go Round".

As I wrote my verse, I thought to myself, man I really have to bring it being on a track with Fame. If I don't, he's going to bury me on this song. It was almost like doing a song with Eminem. You have to be on your "A" game or you will definitely get slaughtered. The beat was on fire as well as the hook. All I had to do was survive.

I decided to take a realistic approach, the same way I did when the guys returned from tour and we were in Sisqo's kitchen. I would rap about things Fame couldn't because he didn't experience it. I also was very influenced by the Notorious BIG's "shock factor" methods, which means saying things that people might think, but wouldn't dare to say. Biggie did this routinely in a lot of his songs but the one that stood out the most with me was "Suicidal Thoughts." When we recorded the song, everyone at the session loved the record. They also were shocked that I was able to hold my own on a song with Fame. A portion of my verse went like this:

"Its' Cooli Hi (Cooli Hi) say my name twice

Fuck a chill life that comes with no spice like plain rice

I need that live shit, that do or die shit, the kind I had for years

Bulky white boys jumping out of beige Cavaliers

Frisking me, cause a nigga got a coke history

Momma found out and tried to put her size 6 in me

But fuck that, I buck back, don't hide shit, no loop holes

Pardon me but bitch you aint buying me no school clothes

I'm out here getting money making moves known on every block

Stash no, got a ass hole full of ready rock

Tripping with the neighborhood chickens and getting doe

I'm a corner nigga, run up on ya nigga bout to blow."

That song , that verse, gained the respect of everyone in both camps. Afterwards I felt bad a little about referring to my mother as a bitch. The entire line was fabricated but I knew I had to say something that my kind of people, hood guys, thought but wouldn't dare to say on a song; emulating the Notorious BIG. And it worked! The two main lines that stuck with everyone was "say my name twice" and "you aint buying me no school clothes". Till this day when Nokio's former assistant Coop see's me, he always says "Cooli Hi- say my name twice!" Mission accomplished. The song Fame and I did, never went anywhere nor opened any doors. It was just a major statement letting everyone know that I could bang with the best of them. I couldn't thank Fame enough for giving me that opportunity. It meant the world to me.

Soon afterwards Dru Hill was starting to cool off because their fan base wasn't gravitating to the 3 man group (Sisqo, Jazz and Nokio). Rumors began to float around about Sisqo possibly going solo stronger than ever before. It initially started when Dru Hill did a song with Will Smith (Wild Wild West) and Will Smith called Sisqo's name out on the song. The inevitable was soon to happen. Meanwhile Butch and I were back home in Baltimore trying to figure out the next move while Kidd and Hot were moving around on the road with Sisqo. Fame was still in New York producing records for Nokio's production company (The Entity). At the time I was zeroing in on Nokio's team and I was trying to get Butch to come aboard. I figured Sisqo had his favorites and made his choice. Let's go with Nokio. Nokio didn't have a hip-hop group, he knew hip hop better than Sisqo and he had Fame and Fame wanted to see us win! I talked to Fame about my plan and he was 100 percent on board. Fame gave Butch and me 3 tracks (all fire) and told us to record a demo for Nokio. Fame was beginning to rub shoulders with a lot of shakers and movers, and he told us if Nokio passed on our demo, he would shop us to others. He also gave us the song he and I did and removed his verse so Butch could replace him and it could be our song. Butch and I had 4 solid songs and were set musically.

One day Fame called and told me that Woody (formally of Dru Hill) was starting a solo project and he was asked to produce some tracks for the project. He suggested that I came back to New York to possibly help out and write to some of his tracks. I eagerly agreed. Fame called on a Sunday and told me the first session was on the following Friday. Anna at the time did not have a car and I did. I knew I was going to be in New York for at least a week or so, so instead of letting my car just sit parked somewhere I decided to let Anna borrow my car until I returned.

That way she and the kids (Destiny and Peanut) could have reliable transportation.

When Thursday arrived, a day before I was scheduled to leave for New York, Fame called and told me the session was postponed for a few weeks. I didn't think anything of it. The music business is sporadic, things get canceled all of the time however when I told Anna about the change of plans, all hell broke loose. We were riding on the highway Anna, myself and my baby boy Peanut when I told her about the cancellation. Anna immediately became irate. "If you don't want me to hold your car, just say so! You don't have to lie!" I assured Anna that I wasn't lying and I was telling the truth but she wasn't trying to hear it. "You know what, fuck you and your dumb ass car bitch!" Anna said. This immediately pissed me off. Here I am trying to be nice, offering to loan her my car and this is the thanks I get just because the plans changed. Anna and I began to scream at eachother as I drove down the highway headed to my mothers house. Things got so heated that Anna began to grab the stirring wheel, shifting my gears and attempting to take the key out of the ignition, all while we're doing about 70mph on the highway. Not to mention our baby boy Peanut was in the back seat in his car seat. I fought Anna off the best I could and finally made it to my mothers block and pulled over. By this time, she had both feet in the air attempting to smash my stereo with her heels and then attempting to kick out my front windshield. I jumped out of my car, walked around to the passengers side, opened the door and dragged Anna out of my car. My mother came outside when she saw all of the commotion. My mother had her cordless phone in her hand. I grabbed the phone and called my homegirl Paula and asked her to come to my mothers and beat Anna's ass.

Sidenote: Paula was a somewhat childhood friend from Brighton Street. I say somewhat because we actually didn't grow up together. We met when I was around 18 or 19. She lived across the hall from me with her Aunt Jackie. Marlon and I would always hang out at her apartment playing cards and of course trying to date her aunts. Paula was around 16 years old at the time. They all were sexy dark-skinned Jamaican's that barely wore clothes during the summer and used to dance very erotically. After we all moved from Brighton Street, Paula and I remained close and I considered her to be one of my best female friends. She even used to hang out with us (me, Mouse, Butch and Ole Man Joe) when we club hopped and ran the streets. All of this was of course after a few years and Paula was of age. Not only was she of age, she was bad and had the perfect body. Everyone wanted her and wonder why I never tried. I told everyone she was like a sister and that's what it was. But I wasn't blind. One night after hanging out, Paula and I crossed the friendship line and slept together. Afterwards our friendship was never the same. We were still cool but the hanging out slowed down and eventually we drifted apart. Paula said this would happen right before we crossed that line but of course I wasn't listening. I was in a relationship with Lia at the time and

Paula knew we couldn't be together so it only happened once. I lost a good friend but our intimate moment was unforgettable.

Paula knew Anna personally (through me) and kind of didn't want to get in the middle of it, so she told me to call the police before Anna did. So that's what I did. When the police arrived, they saw the scratches on my face and neck from Anna attacking me when I was driving and they also saw grass stains on Anna's knee's from when I dragged her out of the car. A high ranking white police officer was one of the officers there. He told the other officers to arrest the both of us and to put my son in foster care until one of us gets out. I told the officer "Sir, my mother is right over there. Please allow my son to go with my Mom". The officer refused. "Since yall want to be out her fighting like damn fools, your son is going to a foster home!" he said. I practically had to beg this white officer not to send my baby boy to a foster home. My mother pleaded with the officer as well. Finally, the officer gave in and allowed Peanut to go with my mother. Anna and I both were arrested.

When we were placed in the police wagon, Anna began to cry. This was her first time being arrested and she was afraid. I had to be very firm with her because I knew what she was in store for. I told her to suck those tears up and be strong and assured her that everything would be okay. Being as though this was my 3rd time being arrested, I felt like I knew the process like the back of my hand. I was happy that it was Thursday and not Friday because I figured I had a better chance to see the commissioner before the weekend hit.

Anna was released after a few hours, let out on her own recognizance but my situation didn't work out quite as smooth. For starters, central bookings (males) was crowded as usual so it took almost 24 hours for me to see the commissioner. When I finally did see the commissioner, I was expecting to be released on my own recognizance as well but I was sadly mistaken. The commissioner gave me a bail and for the first time, I had to go upstairs to jail. I was striped down to my underwear, given an orange jump suit and sent to general population. All of the cells were full so a couple of guys and I were given mats to lay anywhere and sleep on. After many hours finally a cell became available for me and I was placed in one with another inmate that had already been there for some time. He appeared to be a fene (drug addict) and he already had the bottom bunk. When I walked in, he was balled up in knot sleeping or pretending to be. I jumped up on the top bunk and just stared at the walls. I made a call previously to my Mom and told her what my bail was. I was hoping and praying that someone would bail me out. The next day, I went for another bail review and this time another commissioner reviewed my case and decided to drop my bail and allow me to leave on my own recognizance. When I got home, I later found out that Kidd had paid my bail before I saw the second commissioner. That was the last time Anna and I ever had a physical altercation, but it wasn't the last Anna would have in my presence.

Weeks after our arrest, Chante and I were sitting on my mothers porch with my son Peanut. Anna was scheduled to pick him up. Up until this point Anna and Chante had never met because I knew how Anna would act. When Anna arrived, she immediately started giving Chante dirty looks. Once she buckled Peanut into his car seat, she started calling Chante a bitch and said she didn't want her around Peanut. Chante just laughed at her and we both walked up the street hugging and kissing to antagonize Anna. More "bitches" and "fuck yall" came flying and finally she left.

A few days later Chante and I were at my mothers house again and Anna came to pick Peanut up as usual.

*Sidenote- I watched Peanut everyday at my mothers during that time while Anna worked. I couldn't afford daycare so I kept my son with me and took him everywhere I went.

When Anna came in, she immediately picked up right where she left off, by calling Chante all kinds of bitches for absolutely no reason at all. This particular day, Chante wasn't in a laughing mood like before. Chante began to throw shots back by calling Anna every name that you could think of and before I knew it, they were throwing punches in my mother's kitchen. I broke the fight up the best I could by pulling them apart and putting Anna out on the front porch. I picked Peanut up and placed him in Anna's arms to stop her from trying to get back in and continue to fight. After a few more name calls, finally Anna left.

Chapter 26 - About To Blow

After several months of rumors, it was official. Sisqo made the decision to go solo and was working in overdrive to complete his album. One day we were all at his house as usual, and Sisqo told us to gather around. He wanted to play the first song he recorded for his upcoming album "Unleash The Dragon". The name of the song was "Incredible" and the song was incredible! That was our first time hearing him without the other members of Dru Hill and it appeared as if Sisqo didn't miss a beat.

Sisqo kept Kidd and Hot with him the entire time as he recorded his new album. Butch and I were home in Baltimore working at a collection company/ call center call Credit Trust. A few weeks after hearing "Incredible", Kidd played "Got To Get It" for Butch and me which had Hot rapping on it. Kidd told us that the both of them wrote it together but Hot was the only one rapping on it. The song was hot, and it appeared to us that Sisqo was going to have a good album. Then suddenly Kidd said "Yo, if yall like that, wait to yall hear "The Thong Song"!" "The Thong Song" what's that? we asked. Kidd and Hot were smiling so hard that I thought their jaws would lock up. Sisqo just stood there with a slight modest grin nodding his head as if a beat was playing. Kidd said "Yo, check this out!" and played the song. When I heard the "Thong Song" I was completely blown away. Especially when the infamous Baltimore club music sample from "The Earth People" came in on the bridge. We all agreed, once the world hears this, its going to be over! Sisqo is going to soar out of this world. It was Sisqo, Kidd, Hot, Butch, Lovher and I in Sisqo's kitchen. We played the Thong Song on repeat all night that night nonstop.

Over the next couple of weeks, my adrenalin was on twenty. I knew when Sisqo dropped this album, he was going to be the biggest star in the game and we had access. What added to the adrenalin rush was finding out that "Got To Get It- (featuring Make It Hot) was going to be the first single. Kidd and Hot were on their way to stardom as well. They also rapped on another song on the album entitled "Unleash The Dragon" but Def Jam later replaced them with Beanie Segal.

Kidd knew that stardom was on its way as well, so he started preparing and making plans. He convinced Sisqo to rent out a three bedroom condominium in a gated community for him and Hot. Prior to Sisqo's solo project, Kidd would drive Sisqo's Lexus around town but when "Got To Get It" happened, Kidd went out and purchased a brand new 430 GS Lexus- burgundy with lamb- skinned seats and rims. Sisqo also rented a townhouse for Lovher as well. Being as though Kidd and Hot had a three bedroom condo and it was only two of them, they allowed Butch to move in and take the spare room. Things were about to take off in a major way.

Once the video for "Got To Get It" dropped with Kidd, Hot and Lovher in it, it was on and popping. Kid and Hot became instant stars all over the world but especially in Baltimore. The song was being played in rotation nonstop and everyone was talking about it. Kid stood out more than Hot in the video because Hot was moving around a lot and Kidd stood still so he was able to be recognized. In addition, Kidd looked like a model so the girls loved him. Even though his voice wasn't on the song, he received more notoriety than Hot. Not to mention, he was riding around town in a brand new Lexus looking the part. Hot was more conservative and actually cheap. Hot had money but never wanted to spend it. Kid knew how to play the game but Hot didn't. Hot didn't need Kid's help writing the "Got To Get It" verse but somehow Kidd convinced him to allow him to help which meant they had to split the publishing for the verse. Kidd also maneuvered his way into the web of the "Thong Song" as well.

Legend has it that the "Thong Song" came about this way. One day everyone was in Sisqo's kitchen hanging out when suddenly Kidd came in the house. Kidd was telling everyone about one of his escapades with a girl and said "Yo, when I took her pants off she had on a Thong the Thong Thong Thong" emulating a melody from a Tums commercial. Everyone in the kitchen burst out in laughter. Sisqo made a mental note of the joke and later wrote the Thong Song. As a thank you, Sisqo decided to give Kidd a percentage of the song but Kidd never wrote one word. He just said a funny joke. Kidd initially said he would split his percentage with Hot, the same way Hot split his "Got To Get It" with him, but after Kidd's percentage got cut down due to Rickey Martin claiming a piece of the song, Kidd went back on his word and kept his percentage all to himself.

Kid also brought in a three man production crew out of DC/ Columbia MD called One Up Entertainment (Rich, Loren and Kevin). Kid arranged for them to produce the title song of the album "Unleash The Dragon". Kidd had his hands in every pot available when it came to Sisqo and no one could figure out why or how it all came about. I was told that Kidd initially met Sisqo through Hot. Hot and Sisqo are allegedly cousins (I don't believe they're blood cousins- according to Mouse. Sisqo's family and Hot's family are very close so the two embraced the title of cousins). In the beginning of Dru Hill, Sisqo didn't have a car and would always call Hot when he needed a ride home from the airport and to get places he needed to go. One day, Hot brought Kidd along for the ride. Sisqo and Kidd became cool and when Hot couldn't pick Sisqo up from the airport, Kidd filled in and not long afterwards Kidd was driving Sisqo around all of the time. Once "Tell Me" took off, Sisqo felt a sense of loyalty towards Kidd because he was there when Sisqo had nothing or no one he could depend on, so he vowed to look out for Kidd when he was in a position to do so. When Sisqo bought his house, he allowed Kidd to move in. He also allowed Kidd to drive his cars as if they were his and the grand finally, he promised to make Kidd a star!

There were always speculations about Kidd and Sisqo being lovers or if the both or one of them was gay. I was asked this question 99 out of 100 times when people found out that I knew Sisqo and I always answered it the exact same way. Here's my answer: "There is only one person on earth that I can speak on in regards to their sexuality and that's ME! I'm not gay and I can't speak about anyone else because I don't know what anyone does when their bedroom door closes. However, if you asked if I "think" Sisqo is gay, my answer would be no. The demeanor Sisqo portrays on camera verses how he acts in real life are exact opposites. I'm around him a lot and I never caught a gay vibe from him. He walks and talks just like us and he's a girl hound just like us! The only difference is his choice of video games. He's more into the cartoon type games, Dragon Ball Z, Sonics, etc. and the only video games we play are Sport games like Madden. Other than that, everything is the same". As for Kidd, I never saw any signs however, several girls would spread rumors about weird sexual favors he would ask of them while having sex. Kidd was very popular so rumors came along with the territory and Kidd would deny every allegation.

Kid and Hot were on fire! They were on every radio station, all over television from the Apollo to Soul Train Music awards and on every video show out. You couldn't turn on the radio and not hear "Got To Get It". Butch and I on the other hand, were in shirts and ties in a call center Monday through Friday collecting money on phone calls. I remember sitting at work hearing girls go crazy over Sisqo and the guys. I would always try to interject and let them know that I knew them and they were like family. A lot of times, they would look at me like I was crazy as if to say "if they are like family, why are you working here?" But some would inquire and that's when I would invite them to the house (depending on how fine they were) to party. And all of this was happening BEFORE the Thong Song dropped. That was one of my infamous "go to" lines. I told girls at the job all of the time, "If yall like "Got To Get It" wait till yall hear the thong song!"

Sidenote: To attempt to keep up with the movement of Kidd and Hot monetarily, one time Butch and I hooked up with our supervisors husband and purchased some counterfeit twenty dollar bills. We gave our real money to our supervisor and she in return brought us a stack of fake money. We couldn't examine the money good while at work, but when we got home and looked at the money, we felt like we were scammed. The fake twenties almost looked like monopoly money.

Butch and I couldn't return the fake money but we were also not in a position to take a loss, so we decided we had to make the best of it. We bald each bill up and then ironed it with a hot iron to make the paper appear to be old. Then we hit the streets. We knew anyone with experience with cash could spot the fake money a mile away, so we decided to target the less experienced. We went to every fast-food drive thru in town, ordered a $3.00 meal and exchanged our fake $20 for $17 real dollars. What initially was a plan to make a profit turned out to be a hustle just to break even. Once we made our money back, we threw away the rest. Butch and I often referred to the fake $20's we had in our music as "grilled cheese!"

Once the Thong Song dropped the earth shook and the game was over! Everyone in pop culture went into a frenzy and Sisqo took off like a rocket into orbit. Before he was a star and now the impact of the Thong Song had certified him as a superstar! Sisqo was everywhere from TV commercials to movies as well as all over the radio and music video shows and Kidd and Hot were right by his side. He even had his own television show on MTV called "Sisqo's Shakedown".

When Kidd and Hot weren't on the road with Sisqo, they were here in Baltimore with Butch and me. The Vice President of Def Jam at the time, Kevin Lyles (a Baltimore Native) encouraged them to move to New York in order to work on the craft and be in the right hip hop circles, but they declined. Not only did they decline their bosses offer (because they were signed to Def Jam) they also started declining shows with Sisqo as well. A few times Sisqo needed them to travel over seas to perform

"Got To Get It" with him and they told him no because they didn't want to take the long flight or they had something else they would rather do. Sisqo had to fly Nokio in to perform Hots part on several occasions. Kidd and Hot had the city in the palm of their hands and were enjoying every moment of it. We would often all go to the clubs to party and the club owners would practically kiss their feet as they walked in, more so Kidd's feet. Butch and I didn't have the money that the guys had of course so we would borrow their clothes in order to look the part and fit in. Kidd would often joke us and say "Yo, yall not going anywhere with me, wearing that!" He would often go into his closet and give us a coogie sweater and some ice berg jeans along with some airforce one's (fresh out of the box). Kidd always looked out for us like that. He was very generous in regards to clothes, food and drinks when we were at the clubs. He would often pay for everything when we went out. Hot on the other hand never shared anything and paid for nothing.

Everywhere we went Kidd drew attention. When we would go to the mall, Kidd would go into the sneaker store and say "Give me a size 12 in white on white airforce ones". The sales guys would bring back the shoe (one pair) and Kidd would say "No, I want ALL OF THEM! Every pair that yall got!" We would leave the store with nearly 30 boxes of airforce ones, attracting all kinds of attention. Kidd would do things like this all the time. He did it so often tha when he returned to the stores a few days later, the store managers and even owners would greet him at the door again boosting his notoriety. He knew how to draw and keep attention. Butch and I and even Hot, the voice of "Got To Get It" often appeared as his entourage, just guys in the background.

Sisqo signed a crappy deal in the beginning of his career with Dru Hill causing his new money to be stalled to a degree but when he appeared in a Pepsi commercial as well as the movie Snow Dogs, an abundance of revenue came pouring in. Sisqo renovated his basement and built a state of the art studio along with a lounge room, an exercise room and full bathroom with shower. He also built an extension to his house, a pool house that resemble an island type vibe with palm trees and a bar. The pool was shaped like an "S" and had his dragon logo with lights around it shining from the bottom. The pool house had several lounge chairs and tables, a jacuzzi, glass walls with tints and a glass ceiling that opened a closed by the touch of a button. It looked like paradise in that pool house. It felt like you were on an island when in there. It even had bird chirping noises making you feel the entire experience. He also black fenced off his house but the home owners association in his neighborhood later forced him to remove it. So now, we had access to two spots. Sisqo's new and improved house with now a pool and studio as well as the guys condo. Kidd had his Lexus and Hot would either borrow Sisqo's 500 Benz or rent some sort of truck.

Sidenote: No one knew how Kidd was balling out of control by spending so much money as well as keeping up with the payments for his Lexus. Kidd and Hot were a group but it was evidently clear that Kidd had more access to money than Hot. It was speculated that Sisqo was paying the payments knowingly or unknowingly. More to come.

Soon after the Thong Song hit the airwaves, the video shoot was scheduled to be shot in Miami. This was going the be the biggest video ever and I knew that I had to be there. Kidd and Hot were telling Butch and I about all of the guest celebrities that were scheduled to be there. They were with Sisqo on the road at the time and asked Butch and I if we were coming to Miami for the shoot. Butch and I didn't have money for airfare as well as hotel. Kidd suggested that if we made it to Miami, we could sleep on the roll out beds the hotel has and share rooms with him and Hott. The flight tickets were very high because of course, everything is spur of the moment so Butch and I only had enough money for a one way ticket. Once again, Kid suggested that we still came and we would work out getting back home afterwards. I figured out of all of them, someone would help us out in regards to getting back to Baltimore. Myself, Butch and Kidd's cousin Rushie, flew to Miami and met up with the guys at their hotel as planned.

The next day, which was the day of the video shoot, we all headed to the beach and was waiting in Sisqo's trailer. Lovher was there as well. Soon after we arrived, all walks of life were arriving as well. There were half naked girls EVERYWHERE! All with bikini's or thongs on. I was determined to take full advantage of the situation. I wanted to meet and explore every situation possible. I had a disposable camera and Hot had one also, so we went from trailer to trailer, flirting with the girls and taking pictures with them. I took as many pictures as I could with everyone until the film ran out.

When Kid and Hot went to film their scene in the video, I went back to Sisqo's trailer to sit down an relax. I had been running around on the beach all day. As I was sitting there, just relaxing, suddenly the trailer door opened and two guys walked in and sat down. It was none other than Redman and Method Man. They spoke and I spoke back. The two of them were talking and Method Man was telling Redman a story about how some guy got beat up while in the barber chair in a barber shop. It was just us three in the trailer. I didn't say anything as they talked. Then out of nowhere, Redman asked me "Yo, do you drink?" I replied "hell yeah". Redman went and got 3 red cups and fill all three to the rim with Hennessey. He took one, and gave me and Method Man the others. "Whats your name?" he asked. To let them know that I rapped I said "My rap name is Cooli Hi". Redman smiled and nodded his head as he lit his blunt. He hit it a few times and then passed it to Method Man. After Method Man hit it, he looked at me as if to ask if I wanted it. I reached my hand out and he passed me the blunt. I couldn't believe it. I was sipping Hennessy and smoking weed with Red and Meth.

After the blunt was done and about a quarter of our cups, Meth said "Come on yall, lets see whats popping outside". We left the trailer and just walked around the beach flirting with the girls and drinking and smoking. They poured so much hennessy in the cups that It was overflowing, running down our arms. While talking to some girls, a radio DJ approached us and asked if they could rap on some sort of mix tape that he was in the process of making. He had a tent set up with a mic and recording equipment right on the beach. I had never seen anything like it before. We went to the tent and Method Man put on the earphones first and started rapping. He then passed it to Redman and he stared rapping. As Redman was spitting his verse, I was praying silently to myself hoping that they would allow me to spit something as well. When Redman finished, he looked at me like "you're up" and passed me the mic and headphones. I said to myself "Thank God". I put the headphones on and recited one of my favorite verses/ songs, a verse that I wrote when I quit my job, returning from the Dru Hill tour- a verse entitled "The Average Joe". After I was done, both Red and Meth dapted me up and we went back to the festivities. I hung out with Red and Meth for the entire video shoot.

At the end of the night, when I met back up with everyone, I told them who I was with and about the recording we made in the tent. Sisqo was amazed. He asked me "Where was Butch?" I said "I have no idea" Sisqo then said, "Yo you always find a way to be at the right place at the right time!" Everyone laughed. That was a moment that I will never forget. Red and Meth probably did forget. With all of the Hennessy and weed we drunk and smoked that day; you would think that I wouldn't remember a lot of what happened. But I remember every part of it. Not sure of whatever happened to that recording. I'm not even sure if the DJ kept my verse. But what I am sure of is both Red and Meth showed me love by allowing me to get on the recording with them. For that I am forever grateful.

The next day, it was time for Butch, Rushie and me to return to Baltimore. Rushie had his plane ticket already paid for but Butch and I did not. Sisqo left for London earlier that morning. Butch and I went to Kidd and Hot and asked if they could help us out with airfare like we talked about before we came to Miami. Kidd began to make jokes saying "I aint got it yall!. Yall might have to look for a job here in Miami" Kidd was being Kidd as usual joking about serious situations, but we knew that he would eventually come through. As the time got closer and closer to the flight we were scheduled to board, we noticed that Kidd wasn't letting up off the jokes and not loaning us the money. I said to him "Yo, you need to stop playing! We have to leave and head for the airport soon!" Kidd continued to laugh. Then he said seriously "Yo, yall are going to have to get Blondie to buy the flight tickets." Blondie is what we called Sisqo. "I'll call Ken (Sisqo's manager) and see if he can book it while yall are in route to the airport." Butch and I had no other choice but to believe that it would happen, so we headed out to the airport. When we got there, we waited and waited for as long as we could before the flight started to board. We called Kidd and he said he was trying to get in contact with Ken. More time passed and no word from Kidd. We called him back and didn't get an answer. Butch and I were officially about to be stranded in Miami. At the very last minute, Rushie transferred money out of his savings and paid for our tickets to fly home. We paid Rushie back when we received our paychecks the following week.

After all of the dust settled from the Miami trip, I began to think about the situation in regards to us getting home. What if Rushie didn't have the money to loan us? It was hard for me to believe that Kidd and Hot didn't have the money to loan us in order to get home. I started thinking about the moments when we were in malls and Kidd would buy out items from the stores inventory. Not once did he ever offer to or buy us anything. I mean its his money and he can do whatever he wants with it, but how can you buy 30 pairs of sneakers and not look out for the team that helped you get to where you are? In the hood, that's how guys get backstabbed, robbed and killed. One person having everything and everyone around him has nothing. Then it hit me. He only helps if it eventually helps HIM in the long run. When we go to clubs, he can't have us looking corny because that would affect his brand so he would give us clothes to essentially make HIM look good. The drinks at the clubs that he buys for everyone makes him look like a boss! It all comes back to him! If its not a full circle, he doesn't care as much. As for Hot, he was just tight and cheap. We never expected anything from Hot. I couldn't cut ties with the guys especially now with Sisqo being the hottest artist on the planet but once again I wanted to explore all options.

I reached out to Fame and asked if he knew any managers that were looking for new artist. Fame was living in Atlanta at the time. He introduced me to his friend from California that worked for Nokio named Aaron. Aaron was helping Nokio with his production company and had moved to Maryland. I gave Aaron me and Butch's demo (produced by Fame) and he loved it! He agreed to manage and help us find a record deal.

Shorty afterwards Aaron, Coop (Nokio's assistant) Butch and I took a trip to Atlanta to meet with Fame. Fame wanted to make new tracks for me and Butch in order to give us the best chance to get a record deal. At the time, Fame and Nokio's relationship was either severed or close to it due to production credits. Nokio had several hit records out at the time. He produced "How Can I Love You Tonight" on Sisqo's album as well as a few hip-hop hits. His biggest hip-hop hit was the record he produced for DMX entitled "What These Bitches Want" featuring Sisqo. This was another undeniable hit that was on the heels of the Thong Song enabling Sisqo to lock down the Pop market as well as the streets.

I spoke to Fame every single day leading up to us arriving in Atlanta. He told me that he had a catalog full of beats and a studio for us to record in however when we arrived in Atlanta, that wasn't the case at all. Butch and I thought we were coming there to work but when we got there all Aaron and Fame wanted to do was drink and party. The first night after we arrived, we went to a strip club. Butch and I didn't have any extra money for clubbing. We barely had food money so the strip club was the last place that we wanted to be but since we were there, I figured I'd might as well make the best of it. Of us all. Aaron was the only one with real money. I consistently asked Aaron to give me a stack of ones so I could enjoy the festivities the same way he was. The first few times he shewed me away but I kept asking and pressuring him in a joking but persistent way. After consistently asking and staying in his presence, he finally gave me 200 one's and told me to leave him alone. We both laughed and I went about my way in the club.

Butch came over to me as I was getting a lap dance and tipping and said "Yo! Where did you get that from?" I told him Aaron gave it to me. Later that night when we got back to Fames house, Butch asked Aaron why did he give me money and not him. Aaron replied, "Butch, you wanna know why I gave Cooli money and not you? Its because Cooli is ALWAYS around! Every time I look up, Cooli is right there! He never lets up! He just keeps pushing and pushing until he gets what he wants! You didn't get any money because you weren't around." Those words registered with me for life. That taught me that being consistent brings results. Pressure and being relentless brings results as well. I thought back to what Sisqo told me when he found out that I recorded with Redman and Method

Man at his video shoot. From that moment moving forward I knew that I would give it my all to be in the right places at the right time and always apply pressure!

Fame was a heavy drinker and at the time I wasn't sure what Aaron was in to. Aaron would take one drink and absolutely lose his mind. He would become very irate in the blink of an eye. Butch and I would say to each other, how can one drink do that? One day we all were at Fames place drinking beer and Aaron went in another room and minutes later came back with all of his clothes off (except his boxers) drenched in sweat. He only drunk one beer. He was completely done. Fame got up from his couch, forced Aaron back into the room and made him put his clothes back on. We later found out that Aaron was addicted to cocaine. He even bragged and laughed about being the one who turned the actor from Different Strokes, Todd Bridges on to cocaine. Fame and Aaron together were a total disaster. One was a drunk and the other was an addict. Every morning while in Atlanta, we asked Fame when we would be able to record and he gave us an excuse every single time. By mid-afternoon he was drunk and putting it off till the next day.

When sober, Fame would talk about a publishing deal that he had in the works for the songs he produced with Nokio. He claimed that it was going to be huge and often talked about a Lamborghini that he was planning on purchasing. Fame claimed that he was the one that actually produced DMX's "What These Bitches Want" along with the other Hip-Hop hits

Nokio had scored. He told me that being as though he was signed to Nokio's production company, Nokio took credit for the work. Fame said that Nokio had the connections, but he had the music. Collectively they made it work. I can not confirm if that's true or not. I wasn't there when they made the song however, I will say that DMX's track has Fame's sound all over it.

After about 5 days of this routine, we finally decided to go back home to Baltimore. We never heard one single track and needless to say, we didn't record anything. Butch and I were very disappointed. We didn't get any new songs however we still had the previous songs that Fame did for us prior. We stopped dealing with Aaron after that Atlanta trip. A few months later, Fame did close on his publishing deal, bringing in close to a half of a million dollars. Aaron allegedly worked with and helped Fame get the deal. Fame and Aaron had a fall in regards to who did what to make the deal happen and when the check came, Aaron drove to Atlanta to meet with or confront Fame. A day after Aaron arrived in Atlanta, Aaron was found dead in his car due to a shotgun wound. His death was ruled a suicide.

Fame caught a lot of heat after Aaron died. I spoke to him a lot and he assured me that he had nothing to do with Aaron's death. He stated Aaron helped a little in regards to the publishing deal but he did over 90% of the work to close. Fame said he was willing to give Aaron a small portion for what he contributed but Aaron was asking for a lot more and that's where the conflict came in. Fame said that he never saw Aaron when he came to Atlanta. In my eyes Fame was a good guy. He had his demons with the drinking, but we all struggle with something. When absolutely no one wanted to work with me, Fame did, and he always was the same since the first time I met him. I believe that he had nothing to do with Aaron's death. Rest In peace Aaron.

Chapter 27 - Run It Back

Butch and I had loss our jobs at Credit Trust due to all of the traveling and calling out from work. We took another job at a warehouse that stored social security files called Riojas. Meanwhile Kidd and Hot were still traveling with Sisqo, touring, and doing shows. But being as though the guys were only doing shows and making appearances with Sisqo and not making music, Def Jam was starting to lose interest. Def Jam signed the guys when they were a four-man group, with Fame and Butch and kept them because of Sisqo's wishes but Def Jams primary concern was Lovher; the female version of Dru Hill. Kidd and Hot still had to prove to Def Jam that they weren't just Sisqo's little science project that he was trying to force on the label. More time passed and Def Jam had enough. Sisqo was at the peak of his career and Def Jam dropped Kidd and Hot and focused solely on Lovher.

Kidd as always, was one step ahead of the game. Right before Def Jam dropped the guys, Kidd had arranged with a female artist that he met through Sisqo, named Mya to co-star in her music video "Best of Me- featuring Jada Kiss." Once the video came out Kidd's popularity skyrocketed to an all-time high! Before the Mya video, some recognized him from the Sisqo appearances, but it was more so his demeanor. You could just tell that he was somebody "important" by the car he drove, the clothes, the model type girls he dated and the impact he had when he entered a room. But when the Mya video dropped, he was now known as "the guy that's in the Mya video- Kidd." Kidd also took full advantage of Sisqo giving him a percentage of the Thong Song and started embracing the title of being a writer of the Thong Song.

Being as though Sisqo was traveling all over the world due to the success of the Thong Song, Kidd was the celebrity of our team and the head guy in charge. Girls would literally scream when they saw him. He had all of the baddest girls on rotation and the dope boys in town envied him. There were lots of guys in Baltimore that had just as much and even more money than Kidd but they didn't have that showmanship like Kidd had. When Kidd walked into a room, all eyes stayed on him. There were speculations that he was dating Mya but that wasn't the case. The two of them spent a lot of time together and Kidd would play on that by driving around town with Mya riding shotgun in the front seat. He would even take her to clubs with him again boosting his notoriety but that's as far as it went. He tried his hand several times but according to him, that's as far as it went. However, he did date other celebrities that I will not speak on. Kid was the man and me, Butch and even Hot were just his boys in the background.

After a few months of crushing all of the music charts, Def Jam decided to do a remix to the Thong Song. Sisqo wasn't happy about it at all. He felt as though the record didn't need a remix. He especially didn't like the fact that Def Jam was putting Foxy Brown on the song. Sisqo had a slight grudge with Def Jam. He felt as though he did his album all on his own and Def Jam jumped aboard at the end. Normally when signed to a label, the label will arrange for the artist to work with producers and writers and have songs submitted for the album, but Def Jam didn't do any of that. Sisqo went to producers on his own, recorded the album and sold it back to Def Jam. The only record Def Jam brought to the table was a song called "Incomplete." And now they want to jump in and call shots by forcing the Thong Song Remix. Sisqo had no other choice but to comply.

Sisqo shot part of the Thong Song Remix video in Baltimore and of course all of us were there. The video was shot outside at Dru Hill Park. Being as though we all were outside at the park, I was able to invite my cousins to the video shoot (Fat Boy, Shawn, Tim Brown and Kebo). Chop, a very close friend to the family was there also. As always, when my family got together, gambling would occur. My cousins began to shoot dice off to the side of where the video was being shot and before you knew it, a mob of guys were surrounding and joining in. Nokio was one of them. One guy came up, dropped a one hundred dollar bill and asked "Who gonna fade me?" We all looked around like naw we can't cover that. The guy picked up his money and walked away. The guys name was Cliff Jones- a manager from Washington, DC that was currently managing Jazz. Rumor has it that he was like an East Coast Suge Knight, known for running up in executives' offices with baseball bats, imposing his will.

After the Thong Song remix video dropped, Sisqo's relationship with Def Jam started to go south. Def Jam was putting a lot of restrictions on him that he didn't like. Sisqo recorded a song with Lil Kim called "How Many Licks" and the record was an undeniable smash hit! When it was time to shoot the video, allegedly, Def Jam refused to sign off on his appearance because of the feud Foxy Brown and Lil Kim had going on, causing Sisqo to miss the video. Lil Kim was extremely pissed off about the situation and had to result to a toy type robotic video instead. If Sisqo would have been in that video, that song would have blown through the roof! Sisqo was very upset about missing the video. He felt like he let Lil Kim down but there was nothing that he could do. He also felt that Def Jam was attaching themselves as much as possible to the Thong Song's success by putting Foxy Brown on the remix because Jay Z wrote Foxy's verse which tied him and Def Jam into the publishing of the song.

The biggest conflict and probably the straw that broke

the camel's back was when Sisqo wanted a live band when performing instead of using DAT's (Digital Audio Tapes). Def Jam said no to the live band and Sisqo was furious. He had sold over 5 million records and he felt like Def jam was being cheap by not providing him with a live band. He started to compare himself with other male solo artist that had live bands but didn't sell as many records as he did at the time. One of the names he mentioned was Usher. Sisqo didn't have any personal beef with Usher. In fact, Sisqo, Usher and Ginuwine were once in talks of creating a super group until Usher's Mom pulled out at the last minute. Sisqo and Usher were cool. He was just using him as an example of how one label treated their artist compared to Def Jams treatment. Sisqo is very competitive. Competition is what drives him. He felt like he was better than Usher and at the time he was, but Def Jam wouldn't budge.

Meanwhile back in Baltimore, Butch and I were at a standstill. We still had our 4 songs produced by Fame but outside of that we had nothing. I decided that it was time for us to record again. I reached out to a local producer in Baltimore by the name of Dukeyman. Butch and I met up with Dukeyman and he made us an original beat right on the spot. Butch and I took the beat home and wrote our verses as well as the hook. We then took it back to our origins and booked a session with Bill Pratt- the guy we recorded all of our Shock Trauma music with (The four songs we recorded produced by Fame were

recorded in Fort Washington, MD at a famous studio in the

DMV area- Stacey Latisaw's husbands Kevin's spot). The name of our new song was "Keep It Right There" and the song was a smash! This was the record that I really showed growth on in regard to my delivery. Butch used to tell me since the days of Demartim Records, "Yo, your voice is amazing! Once you master how and when to use certain tones, you're going to be undeniable!" This was the song where I figured it all out. We took the song to Sisqo's house the next day and played it for Kidd and Hot. They loved the song. Kidd had this expression on his face while listening. I could tell that he was up to something, but I didn't know what.

Everyone that we played the song for absolutely loved it! I suggested to Butch that we should press the song up as a single and put it out in the streets. Butch didn't like the idea at all, but I was determined not to just sit on a hot record. Since Butch wasn't feeling the idea of putting the song out, I decided to do it on my own. I used a picture that Butch and I took at a picture shop in Security Square Mall (Baltimore, MD) and paid a graphic designer to create a CD cover. At that time, our name was MBC- Mr. Butch & Cooli Hi. I had a cd duplicator at my house and it copied one cd in roughly 2 to 3 minutes. Night after night, I would burn one CD at a time until I had enough for the next day. I bought cases of blank cds, some cd stickers (that I designed myself on my mother's computer) and some cd cases and began to give the single out as promotion to everyone I came across. I had everyone at our job banging the cd and giving us props. Co workers were approaching us all the time asking for additional copies. When they asked Butch, he had to direct them to me because he didn't have any. I purposely didn't give him any because he shot down the idea and didn't put any effort into the distribution process. I even left a stack of CD's at Sisqo's house for everyone to just grab and go as they pleased. Sisqo caught wind of the process and was very impressed and when he listened to the song, he was blown away. That was the first song that I was a part of that Sisqo said he liked and actually listened to on a regular basis. I finally had his attention.

Kidd and Hot also had new music as well. While spending time in LA with Sisqo, they connected with a producer from Atlanta named Mattie P and recorded 6 new songs. This was the first time the two made music together as a two man group and the songs were good. The producer Mattie P did all of the hooks for them so all they had to do was lay their verses down but still the songs were good. A lot better than anyone expected. Kidd and Hot's money was running low and they needed another situation to generate more money. Especially Kidd. His profile was at an all time high and he was willing to do whatever it took to maintain and keep a float.

Sisqo's manager Kenneth Crear attempted to shop Kidd and Hots new songs to a few record labels but everyone passed. One day after listening to our single "Keep It Right There" Kidd suggested that the four of us take a swing a being a group once again. When he made the suggestion, I thought to myself,

"That's what he was thinking when I saw that look on his face when he first heard the song!" Kidd had already ran the idea by Sisqo and being as though Sisqo loved our song, he was willing to give it a chance. Kidd convinced Sisqo to block out a few days of studio time at Horizon, a popular studio in Washington DC.

Sidenote: Once again I learned another valuable lesson. The song "Keep It Right There" being a good song wasn't enough. It took the pressing of the CD's, the entire display, the look of it all, and the hype to penetrate. If I didn't take these extra steps, the song would have never gotten Sisqo's attention which led to other opportunities. Being good isn't enough. You have to be good and smothered in glitter in order to be noticed!

The first day in the studio we all decided to create a story line of two individual groups coming together as one but first we had to come up with a name. After several suggestions that were all shot down, Hot came up with the perfect name for the group- The Associates. Butch and I was from West Baltimore and Kidd and Hot were from East Baltimore. Two groups combined into one. We used the songs Fame produced for us and of course "Keep It Right There" and Kid and Hot used the songs they recorded with Mattie P. In addition, we recorded four new songs collectively as a four man group. We even got Lovher to feature on a few of the songs as well.

The recording process was very tough for Butch and I. Kidd,

Hot and Lovher as well, didn't work jobs. They were receiving living expenses from Sisqo. Butch and I were not. The very first day at the studio, Butch and I left work and drove directly to DC. We were there for so long, by the time we drove back home to Baltimore, we only had three hours to sleep and then it was time to wake up and go back to work. Kidd and Hot would go to the condo and sleep until Butch and I got off from work, then we would all head back to the studio. This process repeated itself for about four to five days straight; until the demo/ album was done. Butch and I were so tired after studio sessions, that when we were at work, we would sneak off to one of the stairways in the warehouse and take turns sleeping/ napping on the steps. Butch would take a nap while I looked out and then vice versa. That was the only way we could get rest. After work, we headed right back to the studio in DC. When the project was finally over, we both crashed for two days straight.

The day after we completed the project, Kidd sent a copy of the CD to Sisqo and his manager Ken via Fed Ex. They both were in California. After waking up from a two-day rest, my nerves were spiraling out of control. I was thinking to myself "what if Sisqo still doesn't like me? Could I accept being cut twice??" I almost gave myself a stroke worrying about how Sisqo would respond to the project. The CD consisted of 16 songs so we called it "Sweet 16". From a positive standpoint, Sisqo had already loved Butch and I's song "Keep It Right There" and he approved and paid for the studio lockout, knowing I would be on the project, so I at least had a shot. I figured all I had to do was not blow it!

The day Sisqo and his manager, Ken received the CD, Ken called Kidd later that evening and told him what they thought. When Butch and I got off from work we went to the condo, walked in and Kidd was in the kitchen making himself something to eat. When he saw us, he immediately said "Yo, I just hung up the phone from talking to Ken. Yo he said he and Sisqo absolutely LOVE THE CD!! Ken said they have been playing it on repeat nonstop since they received it!!" I couldn't believe what I was hearing. Just to make sure, I asked Kidd "Yo, was he cool with me being apart of it?" Kidd looked at me and said "Nigga, didn't I just say that they LOVED the CD!? And aint you on it!? Well then." He then went on to say "Yo Blondie (Blondie is what we called Sisqo) was quoting your lines and everything! You good yo! We are officially a four man group!" Out side of my son Peanut being born, that was the happiest day of my life! Finally, I was on.

The very next day, I decided to go in late to work. As I was driving to work, my mind began to play tricks on me. I was so used to the back and forth wishy washy games that people play in the music industry and I had been burned and left out so many times that I began to second guess Sisqo's decision. "What if he changed his mind after listening all day yesterday?" "What if Ken liked it but Sisqo didn't?" "What if Kidd was lying at the time because he didn't want to crush my spirits and he's planning to call me today with a different answer?" All of these thoughts were running through my mind as I drove to work. I figured the best way to handle this would be to hear the words straight from the horse's mouth, well maybe not the words, even better the actions!

Since Sisqo's album "Unleash The Dragon" was released Kidd and Hot would always get "loans" from Sisqo by contacting Ken. Ken would then contact Sisqo's accountant and a check would be sent overnight via Fed Ex. Kidd and Hot received these "loans" all of the time. Whenever their money ran low, they would say "Man, I'm about to call Ken so they can send me another loan." Well since I was officially in the group now, I figured I should have the same access as Kidd and Hot so I'm going to ask for a loan. I ran the idea by Butch as I sat outside of our job in the car and Butch said "Naw yo. Its too soon. Remember, we are not Kidd and Hot. They don't fuck with us like they fuck with them. I wouldn't do it." Butch got out of the car and walked into the job afterwards. I sat in my car and thought about what Butch said. He was right. It was soon and we were not Kid and Hot but then I also thought back to what Aaron said when we were in Atlanta, about me pushing and being persistent. There was only one way to be 100 percent certain that I was apart of this group and that was to see if Sisqo and Ken would cut a check. I called Kidd and asked for Kens number. I then called Ken and when he answered I said "Yo Ken, being as though I'm in the group now, do you think that I can get a "loan"? Ken immediately said, "How much do you need?" I replied "3". Ken then said "Send me your address. The check will be there tomorrow." I sat in my car and thanked Jesus like never before. When I was done, I started my car and drove away. I quit my job on the spot. The next day, I received the check in the mail for three thousand dollars.

Later that night, I met up with Butch and the guys at the condo after Butch got off from work. I told them that I got a "loan" for three thousand! I felt like I was walking on clouds that day, not only because of the money but because the money certified that I was finally in the "musical circle" that I'd been striving for, for some time now. When Kidd heard me say the amount of the check, he said "Nigga, you should have asked for 10!" and started laughing. Butch couldn't believe it. He now wanted to ask for a "loan" as well but he didn't want to come right behind me asking. He decided to wait for a few days and then ask. Butch also kept going to work for another 2-3 weeks and then he finally quit as well.

Chapter 28 - Green Light

One Saturday evening around 7pm, I was at my mother's house getting dressed and preparing to head over to the guys condo when suddenly the phone rang. It was my childhood friend Donny from Brighton Street on the line. Donny worked as a manager at a movie theatre. When I answered the phone he said, "Yo, I'm at work and you wouldn't believe who I just saw walk in here." "Who" I asked. "Yo, ya girl Shanna from back in the Demartim Record days!" "Yo, she's still fine too!" I couldn't believe it. I hadn't spoken to Shanna since the day we took that walk at her apartment complex. All I had was one picture in my drawer that she gave me and memories. Shanna was my all time crush and on the top of my bucket list. I asked Donny was she there with someone. Donny stated she was with some kids. I then told Donny that if he saw her after the movie, try to keep her there. My plan was to meet her at the theatre before the movie let out. As Donny and I were talking, Shanna just so happened to walk out of the theatre and approach the counter where Donny was standing attempting to buy popcorn. Donny said "Yo, you aint gonna believe this. She's standing right here in front of me now!" I said "Yo give her the phone!" As

Donny attempted to give Shanna the phone, I could hear her sounding confused like "why is this movie guy handing me the phone and who could it possibly be on the other end?" Shanna didn't remember Donny, so she was baffled as to what was going on. Reluctantly she took the phone and when I told her it was me, she screamed! We talked for a quick minute because she has left her younger cousins in the theatre by themselves (to get popcorn) and had to return. We exchanged numbers and Shanna returned to the movie.

The next day, I called Shanna, and we talked for hours. Shanna had informed me that she was now married and had adopted her nephew as her son. Her husband was away in the military so she, her new adopted son and her mom shared and apartment together. I was heartbroken to hear she was married but although it should have, it didn't stop my pursuit. After all, I was still in a happy relationship with Chante and Shanna was now married but Shanna was my ultimate crush and I had to have her.

A few weeks went by and Shanna and I talked on the phone every single night. One night while on a routine call with her, I decided to turn up the heat with sexual topics and conversation. Shanna's husband had been away in the Army for 2 years so I knew she was in desperate need of physical attention. I was at my mothers house having this conversation while my mother was away at church. Shanna and I got so involved on the call that she wanted to have phone sex but couldn't because she didn't have the kind of privacy she needed. I suggested that she came to my mother's house. Shanna lived close to an hour away from my mothers and claimed by the she got there; the feeling would be gone. I kept talking seductively, saying everything I could think of to convince her to come and finally she gave in and said "I'm on my way!" I was so excited I didn't know what to do. I looked at the clock at it was around 10pm. My mother normally got home from church between 11 and 11:30pm. I knew we would be cutting it close. I took a shower, splashed on some cologne and before I knew it Shanna was at the door. When she came in, we embraced each other with a hug and I slightly kissed her cheek. We left the living room and as soon as we walked in the kitchen, my mother was putting her keys in the lock unlocking the door. I felt deflated. My mother walked in the kitchen and I introduced Shanna to my Mom as one of the assistants, from back in the days at Demartim Records. My mother didn't think anything was going on due to us being in the kitchen with the TV on. Shanna was a people's person with a vibrant personality so after being introduced, she warmed my mother up with lots of friendly conversation and smiles. After a few minutes of talking, my mother was tired and said she was heading up stairs to go to bed. Shanna and I looked at each other and Shanna said "If we would have gotten started, your mother would have walked in on us!". She laughed and then said "I guess it just wasn't meant to be." I couldn't believe it. I couldn't believe that I came that close to sleeping with Shanna- my crush, and just like that the moment was over. I knew if I allowed this moment to pass that I would not get another, so I grabbed Shanna, pulled her close and started kissing her. As we kissed, I gently allowed my hands to move down her back until her ass was in the palm of both hands. I put one hand down the back of her thin pajama type pants and made my way to her vagina gently rubbing it through her panties. Shanna was trying her best to keep her moaning down but couldn't control it at times. I slightly bit her lip and pulled her hair to expose her neck fully and then proceeded to passionately kiss her neck. As I did so, I gently moved her panties to the side and put my finger inside of her. She was soaking wet. After a few strokes of my finger, Shanna couldn't take it anymore. She pushed me away, unbuckled my pants and started stroking my penis. She then looked at me and slowly took her thin pants and panties off, bent over and looked back at me. I entered her from behind. Shanna had to bite her jacket in order not to wake my mother upstairs. We went at so hard that I thought my mother would hear the dishes in her china closet moving around. We aggressively yet passionately made love and both orgasmed at the same act time. Afterwards, my confidence was at an all time high. First getting the green light from Sisqo to be in the group and now sleeping with the girl of my dreams. Things were looking great!

A week later Sisqo was in New York scheduled to appear on the MTV award show. He was up for several awards and we all were eager to see if he would win. The night of the show we all (The Associates) were at the condo watching it play out live on TV. When the moment came and Sisqo was nominated, we all got quiet and stiff watching in suspense. When the host announced that Sisqo won, we all cheered but to our surprise, when Sisqo accepted his award, he thanked all 4 of us individually by calling our names out live, on TV! I couldn't believe my ears! For everyone that ever doubted that I knew him or was an important piece to his musical family (especially the girls at one of my former jobs- Credit Trust), this was 100% validation. He didn't thank a lot of people which made the shout out even more prevalent. Just his manager Ken, Lovher and us, individually I might add! The guys and I were so excited about the international shout out that we decided spontaneously to go to New York, right at that moment. We all jumped in Kidds car, drove to the train station and boarded a train headed for New York.

The train ride headed from Baltimore to New York was one to remember. We played around running from one car to another, laughing and joking as if we were 10-year-olds. The train was practically empty, so we didn't have to worry too much about complaints. When we were recording "Sweet 16", we had a rule. No one was allowed to fall asleep in the studio. If someone did fall asleep, the other group members would pour whatever we could find all over them and take pictures. Nothing was off limits. Your clothes could be brand new; it didn't matter! You would wake up covered in whatever we could find. On the train ride, Kidd fell asleep and Hot, Buch and I took action. We drew smiley faces on his brand-new Phat Farm sweat with ketchup and mustard, and filled his white on white Airforce One's with relish. We opened about 30 packs of ketchup and drenched his sweatpants as well. When Kidd woke up, all he could do was laugh!

When we arrived in New York, we jumped in a cab and went to the hotel Sisqo was staying in. Sisqo had no idea we were coming. We wanted to surprise him. Sisqo never used his real name when staying at hotels of course because of fans and paparazzi but we knew all of his aliases. We went to his suite and knocked on the door. The door opened and the person standing there looked like a goddess! It was none other than Lisa Raye. Lisa Raye appeared and starred in Sisqo's music video "Incomplete" and was his date to the MTV awards. She was very nice and invited us in. She looked at Kidd covered in Ketchup, mustard and relish and said "Damn, what happened to you!?" We all burst out in laughter. Sisqo came out from the bedroom portion and laughed as well. We all hung out for a few hours, just enjoying the MTV win and the moment and then me and the guys returned home.

A few days later Sisqo was back in California. Def Jam rented a mansion on Moholland Dr in Beverly Hills for Dru Hill in order for them to bond and work on a new album. After a few weeks of staying and recording in the mansion, the members of Dru Hill weren't seeing eye to eye and the guys decided to part ways again. When the other members of Dru Hill left the mansion, Sisqo decided that he would work on his sophomore album "Return of Dragon" but he didn't want to be there alone so Sisqo made arrangements to fly us- The Associates as well as Lovher out to California to record as well.

When we arrived in LA and was on our way to the mansion, I couldn't believe what I was seeing. I had never seen palm trees before and the cars the people were driving were straight out of car magazines. I was thanking God silently the entire ride, extremely grateful. Being as though this was my first trip whereas my expenses were arranged and paid for, everything was brand new to me and I was taking in and appreciating every bit of it. I mean, I was simply blown away initially by the driver standing at baggage claim holding a sign reading, "The Associates", taking our bags and treating us like royalty. That alone made my day, but I noticed Kidd and Hot didn't pay it any mind. They were used to it.

As we drove closer to the mansion, I noticed that it was very foggy in certain spots (I later learned it was because we were up in the mountains and driving through clouds) and when we arrived, I was speechless. There were four cars out front, a Benz, Navigator, an Expedition and another foreign car, all there at our disposal (but we only drove the Navigator). Once we stepped inside, we all were blown away. We ran around the entire house, claiming rooms and trying to figure out where everything was. A few times I actually got lost and had to figure my way back to the front door. The house had everything you could imagine. It was a four-story mansion with about 8 bedrooms, several living rooms, a game/ entertainment room with a pool table and projector style TV, a work out gym (which was turned into a recording studio) several dining and lounge rooms and too many bathrooms to count.

After we scoped the entire house, I went to the room I picked and started to unpack. When I was done, I sat on the edge of the bed, grabbed the diamond flooded dragon piece on my chain and began to silently give thanks to God again.

Sidenote: Receiving an iced-out dragon chain from Sisqo meant you were officially apart of his family. When Sisqo approved the idea of the four of us being a group again- The Associates, Kidd made arrangements for Butch and I to receive our dragon chains but of course like always, Kidd had ulterior motives. Kidd gave Butch his dragon chain and convinced Charles AKA Murda to give me his. Kidd then called Sisqo and asked for money to buy new chains. When the money came, which was for the entire group, Kidd got Charles his chain and spent the rest of the money on his new jewelry only. He bought a GIGANTIC iced out Associates chain that covered his entire chest. Hot was extremely pissed because he felt as though Kidd manipulated the money, but I could care less. I had my iced out dragon chain and I could care less about what Kidd had. Hot went back and told Sisqo what Kidd had did. Hot demanded that if Kidd had an Associates chain (literally 4 times bigger than our dragon chains) than the entire group should have one. Sisqo agreed and made Kidd return the Associates chain.

After my private praise break, I met up with everyone in the game room and the LA life began.

The house consisted of Sisqo, me and the guys (The Associates), a producer named Al West, Sisqo's body guard Big Rich, Charles (Sisqo's personal assistant) and an engineer named JP. Lovher didn't want to stay in a house full of guys so Def Jam rented them an apartment not too far away. We had a personal chef that cooked us breakfast and dinner every day. For lunch, we were on our own. We received per diem, which was $245 per week. The refrigerator stayed full of food, the bar stayed stocked with alcohol and we had the best weed in California. We couldn't ask for anything more.

Sisqo was working in overdrive as usual on his new album "Return of Dragon". When Sisqo wasn't recording, we would. Sisqo's manager Ken wanted us to create new songs with Al West so he could shop us to record labels. Al West gave us a few tracks and we got to work. Lovher would come over every day and hang out with us as we recorded. At the time Kidd was in a relationship with Butta. After recording, we all would just hang out in the game room drinking and smoking weed. Kidd didn't smoke but the rest of us did. The majority of the time it was just us and Lovher. Sisqo would be in his room with the door closed usually either with a bad model type girl or playing his video games. Being as though we all spent so much time together and shared the same passion it was natural to be attracted to each other and when you throw alcohol and weed into the equation, there's no telling where things could lead to. I was still in a relationship with Chante, but Chante was home in Baltimore, and I was in Beverly Hills being exposed to an entirely different lifestyle. I had my eyes set on the lead singer of Lovher, Chinky for quite some time and now I was finally in a position where I felt like my status was high enough to pursue her. One night after partying and drinking, I made my move, and we spent the night together. We started seeing each other from that point on.

Everyday me and the guys followed pretty much the same routine. We would usually be up all night so we routinely missed the breakfast our personal chef would cook. The chef would leave the food he prepared for us to warm up and eat when we woke up but we rarely did. We would eat something light and head to the gym. Prior before coming to California, we all would work out 5 days a week with Kidd's cousin Rushie. Rushie was our personal trainer. So now that we were in LA, we continued the process. After the gym we would get something to eat and sometimes play basketball at a local playground we came across. Afterwards, we would go back to the mansion, shower, turn on a track and start writing. Occasionally we would go to the Beverly Center (a mall in Cali) and hunt for girls. Everytime we met some girls and invited them back to the mansion to hang out, we would have to sneak them in certain parts of the house so that Lovher wouldn't see them. Lots of times Lovher came to the mansion, saw that we had company and would scare the girls until they felt uncomfortable and left. Lovher would laugh afterwards, all except Butta because she and Kidd were in an "exclusive" relationship. They argued all the time. Chinky and I were seeing each other but not exclusively so we didn't have any type of drama going on at all.

One night me and the guys went to a strip club to hook up with some girls that Kidd knew. When we got there, we all sat in our section drinking and socializing watching the dancers. The type of girls Kidd pursued and dated were nothing less than center fold magazine models. It was quite intimidating when we were with him and he brought these girls around because I knew they were totally out of my league yet still I shot my shot. That particular night one of the models beamed me her 2 way info before we left the club. About a week later, me and the guys were looking for something to get into and like always, we would ask each other to "call some stews" (Stews was what we called girls- and I have no idea where that name came from). The conversations would always be like "Yo, who got some stews?" Then we would all pull out our two-way pagers and start searching for someone to call to come over. Of course, we all would go back and forth about who had the most stews or who never brought any stews to the table. This was an ongoing debate that almost all guys have and never ended. I thought about the girl I met at the strip club and decided to call her. After speaking for a few, I invited her over and told her to bring some friends. When she and her girlfriend arrived at the mansion, we brought them in one of the side doors where the gym/ studio was. As soon as we walked the girls in the house,

JP our studio engineer was having a threesome with two girls in a bed set up adjacent to the studio equipment. When JP saw us walk in he said "Oh don't mind us yall! We're just having a little studio fun!" The two girls giggled and continued what they were doing. Me and the guys along with the two girls I invited over walked passed them and went into another section of the house. Once we were settled, I asked the girls if they wanted something to drink. The girl I knew, named Jade replied "Yes, we would like some drinks but we'd like to go back to that room we initially came in even more!" I replied "Oh yall wanna go back in there!? Shid lets go!" We all got up, grabbed a few bottles and went back into the room where JP was with the two girls. By this time, JP and the girls were done. There were just laying in the bed and smoking. We all sat on the other side of the room on a large love seat. "Surprise! We're back!" Jade said to JP and the girls when we walked in. JP replied "Welcome! The more the merrier!" Everyone laughed. We poured a few drinks and turned on our music and out of nowhere Jade and her girlfriend started kissing. The song we played was a song called "All the Way" produced by Al West. The track consisted of a lot of gothic type sounds and could easily put a mind under the influence in a different state. During these times almost everyone was doing ecstasy and I assumed Jade and her friend probably did a half of a pill before they came. Before we knew it, Jade and her girlfriend were completely naked having sex with each other on the floor. Then Jade got up, came over to me, unbuckled my pants and pulled my penis out. She performed oral sex on me like I never had before. Before I knew it, I was having an orgasm as Jade continued in a slow passionate way. I looked over and Jades girlfriend was performing oral sex on Kidd as well. Afterwards, the guys praised me for coming through with Jade and her friend. Normally it was always Sisqo and Kidd bringing in the girls, but that episode put my name in the basket as well.

The next day, we all were talking about the wild night we just had. We thought back and gave credit to our song "All the Way". "That's what got them open" we all said. We told Al West about what happened, and Al said something very alarming. Al said "Yo I think that track is possessed with evil spirits." He then went on and talked about how he was seeing and hearing things in the house and how the track had demonic undertones. I heard everything Al was saying but I also knew that he and almost everyone in LA at that time were popping ecstasy like candy and ecstasy made people act very emotional, horny and weird. I remember one time Al had left some of his invoice stubs in the studio and we saw how he was receiving 30K for a Nas song, 50K for Mary J. Blige, 40K from the Trackmasters and so on and so on. He had damn near a half of a million dollars' worth of invoices just laying there. He once told us "Yo if yall ever see money laying around in my room and need it, just take it. I don't care how much it is. If you need it, take it. Its yours! I always have more coming in!" When he said this, I thought that he was high and didn't know what he was saying and now he's talking about demonic spirits are talking in the background of the music, so again, I thought he was high, or was he? The next day, we went to look for Al in his room and he was gone. He packed up his things and his cars and left. We never saw him again.

A few days prior to Al West leaving the mansion, he produced our biggest song as the Associates called "Head Won't Stop-featuring Sisqo" The song was a party track with a very catchy hook that Sisqo and I wrote. Sisqo wrote the singing portion and I followed up behind him with the rap portion. This song was a HUGE deal to me because it was the first song that I had ever did with Sisqo. When we recorded the song, after I layed down my portion of the hook as well as my portions of the verses, I remember being so excited to hear Sisqo ad lib over my voice. All I could think about was the sessions we had at Dave's studio back in Baltimore when Cuzzon was re-making Phil Collins "In The Air of the Night" and hearing Sisqo go crazy with ad libs on everyone's verse's. I wanted that so bad back then and now it was happening in a mansion in Beverly Hills.

The song was a certified banger! After it was mixed, we played that song every night non-stop on repeat, just like we did with the Thong Song when we first heard it. Whenever we partied, we always played our own music. We never listened to anything if we didn't create it. That's just how we were. Sisqo, Associates and Lovher. That's it. We didn't even listen to Dru Hill. Just us. Once we had "Head Won't Stop" Ken felt like he had what we needed to land us a record deal. Sisqo was so hot at the time that almost any label would take us just because we were affiliated with him. Ken had a major deal on the table with Priority Records for us. One night we met up with the A&R's and VP at a nightclub and performed our entire CD live in the limo. The Priority reps loved it!

One day while in our favorite place, the game room, we were all sitting around playing in a John Madden tournament between us, Big Rich and Charles (We all would put $50 into a pot and the winner of the tournament would get the money). Ken came in and announced that we were having a house party that night to celebrate the completion of Sisqo's new album. Ken said it would be a star studded event so don't worry about recording today; lets just relax and have a good time.

I went into my room and picked out one of the iceberg jean suits that Sisqo bought us weeks ago (Kidd would always arrange these shopping extravaganza's for us by going to these expensive boutiques, picking out clothes and then calling Sisqo's accountant demanding that she okays the purchases). I, Butch, Hot and Charles put up some money and called our weed guy to bring us the best that he had. Ken was having the party catered so that was all that we needed.

Later that night, the party began, and it was everything that I expected. Gorgeous model type women were all over the house. Celebrities filled the house as well, Ja Rule, Dave Chapelle and Pauly Shore were among many just to name a few. As the party continued, I was on the prowl trying to get to know as many girls as I could but something just wasn't right. From a far, the girls at the party looked absolutely amazing but when I got close, face to face and talked with them, they looked like demonds. Their eyes were glassy from doing coke, their skin was pale and they were the size of tooth picks. The best way I can describe it is to compare what I saw to a scene out of the movie "The Devil's Advocate" when the gorgeous women turned into demonic monsters in the blink of an eye. As I was seeing this, I began to think about what Al West was saying prior. I also learned that the mansion we were staying in was often used to shoot porno movies, so all kinds of energies were in the mist. The girls at that party actually scared me so I wanted nothing to do with any of it. I eventually went to my room with Chinky and called it a night. Oh, I forgot to mention, Sisqo stayed in his room the entire night. He had a girl and his video game as usual. Not once did he come out.

After that night, Chinky and I began to spend almost every night together. Besides being physically intimate, Chinky and I began to bond mentally as well. We talked about everything from our musical dreams of becoming stars to the drama inside of our Dragon family circle. Chinky didn't know about Chante and if she was dating any other guy, I didn't know about him either. We never brought up others or even bothered to ask. We just enjoyed each other's company to the fullest with no strings attached.

About a week or so later, our time was up, and it was time to return to Baltimore. We spent Christmas as well as brought in a New Year (2001) in California. We were living in the mansion for about 2 or 3 months. Again, this mansion was for Dru Hill's project but when they had the fall out, we the Associates and Lovher stepped in and took full advantage of the opportunity. There were so many memorable moments that happened in that house. I could actually write a book about Muholland Drive all by itself. From the drinking games we played, certain individual's passing out and the rest of us taking pictures, Kidd and Hot almost getting into fist fights from arguing, Kidd and Butta beefing all of the time and then making up, the practical jokes we played on each other, the porn star girls JP the engineer had living there with us, the laughs as well as several escapades that I won't mention, we had the time of our lives and in addition, we made some great music!

Chapter 29 - Clarinda

Once I returned from LA back to Baltimore, I knew I had to make the best of my time. We were scheduled to go back to LA in a couple of weeks. Def Jam had arranged for Sisqo to move in another house just for him. He still had a few more records to complete for his new album. I saw my mother and father when I came home but I spent the majority of my free time with my son Peanut and Chante. I also visited my cousins and aunts as well.

One night, I was on my way to Sisqo's house and decided to stop at my aunt Gertie's house while in route. My grandmother (my mothers mom) was in town and she was there. My grandmother was in town for about a week or so and was scheduled to return to South Carolina that night. My grandmother had liver issues and was on dialysis. When I came in my aunts house, everyone was very excited to see me especially my grandmother. I went to her, hugged her, and kissed her on the cheek, the same routine since I was a kid. I remember when I went in for the kiss, holding back a little at first because when I was a child, it was so many grandchildren that we would line up to greet grandma and depending on where you were in the line, when you kissed her cheek, you caught all the light saliva from the cousins that went before you. When I kissed grandma, her skin was soft as feathers. We all sat and talked and I answered all of the questions everyone had about being in LA. Finally, when it was time for my grandmother to head for the car and leave, I saw several of my aunts crying. At the time, I didn't know why. My uncles were preparing to drive her back to South Carolina. Me and my cousin Shawn each grabbed my grandmothers' arm and walked her down the steps and to the car. When she got into the car, I kissed her again and told her that I loved her. She replied "I love you too. Write me a letter when you have time while on the road! You hear me?" "I will grandma" I replied. After the car pulled off, I went back in the house and asked my mother why everyone was crying. My mother said "Because this might be the last time we ever see her alive."

I left my aunt's house and drove to the guys condo before heading to Sisqo's. Kidd, Hot and Butch were all there. Butch and Hot were playing a track that One Up gave us a while ago, trying to come up with a hook. The track was on fire! Butch came up with a melody and was trying to fill in the words. We were all so excited, that we decided to work on the song instead of going to Sisqo's but Kidd had other plans. He didn't want to work on any music that night because he had arranged to hook up with some girls. We told Kidd that he should stay and work on the song with us, but he refused and out the door he went. Butch, Hot and I continued to work on the song. When Butch finally filled in the words to his melody he said "Yo, you know what would be dope? If we got Blondie to sing this hook!" Butch sung the hook to me and Hot and we both agreed. Before you knew it, we were in the car headed to Sisqo's. When we got there, we played the track for him and Butch sung the hook. Sisqo loved it but of course he changed the melody a little to his liking. We all agreed that it would be 3 verses and being as though Kidd ditched us to hang out with some girls, he wouldn't be on the record. The name of the song was "Off the Corner".

A few weeks passed and we were back in California. This time Sisqo wasn't in a mansion but in a very extravagant house on Clarinda Dr. Being as though this house was for Sisqo and not Dru Hill, there weren't a lot of rooms like the mansion had so Sisqo and Ken decided to put us in a hotel about 10 minutes away from the house. Kid and Hot were pissed initially but of course Butch and I didn't care. We were grateful to be there.

The house on Clarinda wasn't big like the mansion on Moholland Dr. but it had more bells and whistles. It had a tennis and basketball court, a pool and beautiful palm trees everywhere. After we got settled in our hotel rooms and made our way to the house, as soon as I walked in, I heard music blasting from Charles room. We all followed the sounds and greeted Charles with pounds and hugs as he was mixing with two turn tables and a mixer. He had the entire house jumping.

Sidenote: Charles was from New York and he took hip hop very seriously. Whatever you said in a verse, he would hold you to it. I remember in one of the Moholland Dr. songs I said in a verse "a fifth of Hennessy is in me but I'm still sober" and till this day Charles still teases me about drinking that much Hennessy without getting drunk.

Charles being who he was, immediately started mixing instrumentals because we entered the room. He was testing to see who would want to spit. When a real MC hears an instrumental beat, how can he not rap? As the record played, I watched Charles as he watched the demeanor of the guys. If Charles eyes could talk, they would say "I know yall hear this beat! Who's gonna jump on it!?" but Kidd and Hot paid him no mind. To my surprise even Butch didn't show any interest but me on the other hand was locked in and loaded. I told Charles to pass me the mic that he had hooked up and I went for broke. Once I started freestyling, Kidd, Hot and even Butch left the room and went to another section of the house. I continued to freestyle saying raps off the top of my head as well as verses I previously written. Charles kept switching the beat and I kept going nonstop. After about an hour, Charles faded the music out and shook my hand. From the look in his eye, I could tell that I earned his respect as an MC and the rest of the guys probably lost it. We then sparked up some weed and went to join the rest of the guys.

Later that night the girls (Lovher) came over to the house. When we left the mansion and returned to Baltimore, the girls stayed in LA at their apartment because Def Jam had them working on their debut album. This was my first time seeing Chinky since the mansion. I wasn't sure if she was still feeling the same as before because in Hollywood things change in the blink of an eye. Never the less, I pursued and Chinky and I picked right back up where we left off. That night, instead of Chinky going back to her apartment with the girls, she stayed with me in my hotel room.

The next day as well as days moving forward, our days were pretty much the same as it was before. We would start the day off by going to the gym (we all were in tip top shape due to the extensive workout plan Rushie had us on back in Baltimore), get something to eat, play basketball against each other (me and Hot verses Kidd and Butch), shower and hit the mall (the Beverly Center- hunting for girls) and then return to the house to party and make music. Being as though this house was more accessible there was a lot more traffic coming through. Every so often you might look around and see a celebrity just chilling on the couch or getting something out of the kitchen. La La Anthony stopped by often (at the time she was a radio personality in LA), Christina Milian came through occasionally and sometimes Mya. One day Raven Simone stopped by to see Kidd and we joked him for days because she was a teenage girl at the time.

One night while in the studio (that was built again in the exercise room) with One Up (Rich and Loren) we decided to record the song we started back home called "Off the Corner". At the time, all we had was the hook that Sisqo agreed to sing. Butch, Hot and I all locked in and began to write our verses. Right before I started to write my verse, I received an anonymous tip that Rich from One Up said that he was tired of hearing me rap about drugs and street life. That comment awoken a monster in me. The street life was my edge, especially in this camp. With the exception of Butch, no one else could even touch on the subject. I used that comment as fuel to ignite an already lit fire. I didn't even know if he actually said it or not. I didn't care. The kill switch was turned on and there was no turning back. I was totally focused on drilling it even harder than ever before and crushing baller raps so here's what I wrote:

"A yo we bash in brains

Then hit a nigga pockets for the last of his change then put a slash through his veins

Bullies of the block, we harassing the game

With a sound that's so hot we're turning gas into flames

Yall keep jumping around like my raps entertain

Fuck around and get beat down with some bats and some chains

When yall was on them lots dropping cash on a range

I was tounge kissing blocks bump and stashing them thangs

And now that I'm on only half of it changed

See the corners in my past but my ass is still deranged

I rumble in ya ear like that flash when I rains

When I hit ya get the picture knock the glass out the frames

I rap for the name of dope, crack and cocaine

And I'm a drill it in ya ears till you collapse from the pain

And after the fame I'm going back to Dwayne,

But for now nigga (Blaugh) feel the wrath of the pain"

Up till this point, this was by far the best verse I ever had written. The flow, lyrics and delivery were all peaks of my career. I took shots at everybody and everything that in my mind were against me, just for the hell of it.

Sidenote: When Ken told us about the deal we had on the table with Priority Records, Kidd convinced us all to go to the Range Rover dealership and test drive some Range Rovers. He told us that it would be awesome if all of us had brand new Range Rovers. We all went but after running our jacked up credit and finding out how much we had to put down (not to mention the car payments) we all declined. Well, not all of us. Kidd went through with it and purchased a dark green 2001 fully equipped Range Rover.

Everyone absolutely loved my verse on the song. Especially Rich from One Up. Again, till this day I'm not sure if he said what was mentioned to me or not. Maybe I needed to hear that to ignite the beast in me. Never the less, I couldn't ask for a better end result. Butch and Hot blessed the song with amazing verses as well and when Sisqo laid the hook and ad libs, the song went into orbit!

Once all the vocals were done and we were listening to the song on repeat as usual, I looked at Kidd and saw a disturbing look on his face. It was clear that he was upset about not being on the song. We explained to him that this was the song that we came up with back at home when he ditched us to hang out with some girls.

A few days later, Sisqo was hanging out with Tom Hanks son and played off the Corner for him. Tom Hanks son told Sisqo that he absolutely crushed all three of us on the record. Sisqo came home and stated that he didn't like the record anymore and that we should scratch it. Butch, Hot and I couldn't believe what we were hearing. Two days ago, he was crazy about the song and now "Tom Hanks son" is making him second guess. Or was it Tom Hanks son? I was beginning to think that maybe Kidd went behind our backs and hated on the song because he wasn't on it. With these guys you never knew.

I knew I had to get Kidd involved with this song in order for it to stay alive. I suggested that Kidd do a skit, calling Sisqo and asking him to come to the studio and sing on the record. Kidd loved the idea. He just wanted to be a part of the record by any means. Sisqo liked the idea too and decided to go along with the skit but he also decided to alter his voice almost as if he was singing through a telephone just so his pure vocals wouldn't "crush" us like Tom Hanks son said. So that's what we did. Kidd and Sisqo did the skit at the beginning of the song and Sisqo's ad lib vocals had effects on them sounding like he was singing through a phone. Everyone was happy and the song was alive and scheduled to appear on Sisqo's new album! This situation taught me a very valuable lesson. If we wanted to make any power moves, Kidd absolutely had to be involved. There was no way around it.

About a week or so later I was at my hotel room and received a call from my cousin Big Flood (aka Fat Boy) but wasn't able to answer. I was rushing trying to get dressed because me and the guys were heading to Sisqo's and I was running late. We all shared an Expedition truck so when one of us went somewhere, we all went somewhere. The only exception was early in the mornings, I would leave out with the truck with Chinky to take her to media training classes. I would drop her off and then return to our hotel and go back to sleep. On this particular day, I had overslept and now rushing to get downstairs to the guys in the truck.

As soon as I got in the truck, Kidd looked at me and said, "Yo, I'm sorry to hear about your grandmother" I was confused. "My grandmother" "what do you mean?" I asked. He then replied, "Yo did you talk to Fat Boy?" That's when it hit me. Fat Boy was calling to tell me that our grandmother had passed away. When i didn't answer, he called Kidd. I got out of the truck and returned Fat Boys call and he confirmed that our grandmother was gone. I went back to my room and cried. After I got myself together, I came back downstairs, and the guys were still there. I thought they may had left because I was in my room for quite some time. I got in the truck, pulled out a pint of Hennessy that I had in my jacket and began to sip it as we headed to Sisqo's. By the time arrived at the house the pint was done and so was I. All I wanted to do at that point was bury myself into a song and that's exactly what I did. I turned on some beats and began to write in order to take away the pain.

About a day or so later, my mother told me that my grandmothers funeral date was set for the following week and it was going to be in South Carolina. I went to Ken and told him about the situation. Ken gave me his condolences and advised me that he could arrange for a flight to South Carolina, but he could not arrange for a flight back to California. His reasoning was at this point, we the Associates were just hanging out in LA. Sisqo's album was done and he had all the music from us that he needed to close a deal. It didn't make business sense to fly me back and forth. So I had to decide. Fly to South Carolina and then return to Baltimore with my family afterwards or stay in California and miss my grandmother's funeral.

I was completely torn. I didn't know what to do. I thought to myself, if I leave California I wont be able to return and I knew first hand about the rule of out of sight, out of mind. Things change in the business in the blink of an eye and I didn't want to miss out on any unexpectant blessings but on the other hand, what kind of person would skip his grandmothers funeral for a vague possibility that something "might" happen. If I missed my grandmothers funeral, how would that make my mother feel? How will my family look at me and to top it all how would my grandmother feel if she was still here? The decision was driving me crazy so I went to who I always went to when I needed words of wisdom. I called my Dad.

I explained to my father the situation and the dilemma I was facing. My dad said to me, "Son, keep in mind, funerals are for the living, not the dead. It's a way for family and friends to pay their respects, and come together to cope and deal with the loss of a loved one. The persons whose funeral it is, is gone. Don't feel like you're doing your grandmother a disservice by not attending the funeral. You have to do what's best for you. I'm sure that's what your grandmother would want." After speaking to my Dad, I made the tough decision to stay in California and miss my grandmothers funeral. I called my mother and told her about my decision, and she was okay with it. I never picked up an ill vibe. I'm sure she caught slack from my aunts about me not attending the funeral but like any good mother, she shielded me from those comments in order to keep my mind intact, therefore the comments never landed on my emotional doorsteps. Years ago, I missed my uncles funeral to perform in a talent show and now this. Missing my grandmother's funeral (with no guarantee's) was one of the toughest decisions that I ever had to make. On the day of my grandmothers funeral, I stayed in my room at the hotel for the entire day. I didn't come out till around 9 or 10 that night. I just needed to be around people and music in order to cope.

A few days after the funeral, the guys and I went to Sisqo's house after our routine workout and getting something to eat. Sisqo had called us and told us to come.

Sidenote: The day before, Ken informed us that we were no longer negotiating with Priority Records. We were now very close to closing a deal with RCA Records. RCA was offering more money than Priority.

When we arrived, Sisqo looked at me and said "Yo I got some good news for you!" At first I thought the meeting was about the Priority to RCA switch but when he said the news was directly for me, I was lost. We all gathered in the room where Charles had his DJ equipment set up and then Sisqo looked at me and said these words "Yo they want you to rap on CAN I LIVE!!"

Can I Live was a song produced by Teddy Riley and was scheduled to be Sisqo's first single off of his new album. We all had heard the song and absolutely loved it. The version we were hearing up till that day was the version with only Sisqo on it but we were told Teddy Riley was rapping on it as well. When Sisqo told me that "they" wanted me to rap on "Can I

Live", I was in a complete shock. Who were "they", how did this happen and what about Teddy Riley's verse were all questions that swam around in my head but I didn't question the offer at all. "Alright bet" I said to Sisqo. Sisqo then gave me a CD with the instrumental and told me to get to work. I took the CD and went straight to my hotel room and wrote my verse. Here is what I wrote:

"Lets nip this in the bud I feel fatally attracted

And I aint tryna go home to the smell of boiled rabbits

That's why we gotta chill till I instill it in your cabbage

The meaning of space and to clarify your status

You aint my Gina and I aint your Martin

So chill with that crazy bullshit that you're sparking

Paging off the hook like you bent off of hen rock

Replies and your signature smothering my inbox

You call all the time but never saying nothing

So now when you call boo you get the end button

I never understood you aint in the woods hunting

So why you keep binoculars at hand like cufflink

You're gray hairing me no better yet fuck that boo you're scaring me

Talks that you wanna marry me

Naw go stalk another nigga

I aint breathing is the reason that I'm pulling out the scissors
Now bounce, bounce."

A few days later, Teddy Riley flew in town and booked a session for me to record my verse on Can I Live. The guys went with me to the studio session. Sisqo did not attend. As we were in route, I began to feel nervous about recording with the legendary producer Teddy Riley. I started thinking about all of the hits he produced from Doug E. Fresh (The Show) to Michael Jacksons Dangerous Album. I spit the verse over and over in the truck in order to shake off nervousness. The guys liked my verse. All I needed now was Teddy Rileys approval.

When we arrived Teddy Riley was already there, track loaded and in full motion. We all greeted each other with smiles and handshakes and immediately got to work. I was extremely nervous right before we went in the studio but once I saw Teddy a calmness came across me and I was no longer nervous. I believe it was because of our height differential. On TV these stars look and appear to be larger than life, both physically as well as their presence but in person I towered over him due to my height (6'4") and when face to face he barely was at my shoulders and had to look up at me.

After a little small talk, Teddy asked me if I had my verse ready and I told him yes. He suggested that we get started immediately. It almost felt as if he was in a rush. I went in the booth and Teddy cued up the beat and asked if I was ready. Normally, I would warm up a little, spit the verse a few times to the beat and work out the kinks in my voice and get comfortable before recording but I could tell that I wasn't going to be given that luxury in this session. Teddy was ready NOW. Teddy started the beat and I began my verse. As soon as I started rapping, Teddy stopped the track and said "Yo, you're off beat." Can I Live had an abnormal drum pattern that was hard to catch but that's what made the track so hot. I wrote my entire verse to the pattern I heard in my head which was the exact opposite of how Teddy heard and created it. Once Teddy counted me in and showed me where I should start, it threw my entire flow off and my verse didn't sound as good to me anymore. Now the pressure was really on. Here I am, with the legendary Teddy Riley on the other side of the glass at the board, with high expectations of me nailing this verse on the 1st or 2nd take and my flow is completely thrown off because I'm basically rapping to a beat that I didn't write to melodically. I had no time to figure it out. Everything I had in my head, I had to erase on the spot and start from scratch (melodically) at that moment. Teddy played the track and I went for broke. As I was rapping it felt so awkward to me. Imagine speed writing with your off hand or running up and down some steps backwards. That's how it felt. I got halfway through the verse, stumbled and Teddy stopped the track. "Fuck" I screamed out loud as I always did whenever I messed up when recording. "Bring it back" I said to Teddy. From the first half of the verse, before I stumbled, I could tell Teddy liked it because he was nodding and smiling as he listened back. Once I saw that I had him in a good space, it boosted my confidence. The 2nd take I went through the entire verse without any mess up's. Teddy was feeling the verse. "Yo, that was it! Lets stack it!" he said. I said cool. I was very happy that he liked it but in my mind I felt like I could have done it better. Butch felt the same way. Butch actually said to Teddy, "Yo I think he can do it better" but Teddy told Butch he liked what I just did so there's no need to do it again. After I stacked the verse, Teddy asked me to do an intro for the song. I did the intro in one take and the song was a wrap. We all shook Teddy's hand again. Hot took a picture with him and we left.

That night, Chinky came over to my hotel room and asked about the session. I told her that I didn't feel comfortable about my delivery of the verse. For one, I had to recite my verse to the same beat but different drop, causing me to alter my flow significantly on the fly and I also felt like I was being rushed. I didn't have time to warm up and I felt like I could have done it better. This was an opportunity of a lifetime and I just didn't feel like I did my best. After venting to Chinky for about an hour she chimed in and said "We all hold ourselves to higher standards. Higher than anyone could imagine. I believe you when you say you could have done it better, but I also believe that the legendary Teddy Riley wouldn't allow you to leave if he wasn't happy with what you spit on his track! Relax babe. You got this!" Chinky's soothing words were able to resonate my worried soul and soon afterwards I felt a lot better about the session.

The next day, Ken's assistant Marcus Grant came to my room with the splits (paperwork) for the song as well as a check for 15 thousand dollars. I was so excited and grateful, not only for the money but for the opportunity to keep my publishing percentage of the song. Teddy Riley could have easily demanded to keep all of the publishing for himself as well as his nephew (who wrote the song) because he was who he was, but he allowed me to keep my percentage instead of writing me off as a work for hire.

Sidenote: A "work for hire" is when you're paid one time for whatever you did and that's it.

By allowing me to keep my publishing percentage meant that I would be paid for the song for the rest of my life (as long as the song was being played somewhere in the world). Now all I had to do was pray that nothing changed, and the song was released.

After Marcus left, the guys came to my room to celebrate. When I told them how much the check was for, Kidd jokingly said "Yo, I know I'm getting at least half right?" I replied "Shid, I'm keeping this all to myself!" We all laughed about it and then headed out the door to Sisqo's. While driving to Sisqo's, I sent Kidd and Butch a two-way message and told them that I was going to give them some of the money. I had no intentions on giving Hot any money. You see, I thought back to the days when I didn't have and how Kidd would allow me to borrow his clothes, give me sneakers, attempt to bail me out of jail and so on and so on. Butch was a no brainer. Of course, I would look out for him. But Hot on the other hand, never helped anyone, especially me. I remembered on several occasions I asked and damn near begged Hot to borrow one of his many coogie sweaters in order to fit in when we went to parties with them and Sisqo back years ago and he told me no. If it wasn't for Kidd, I would have looked totally out of place when hanging with them. I gave Kidd $2,500 and I gave Butch $2,500. I kept the remaining $10,000. They both promised that they wouldn't tell Hot. Hot thought I didn't share the money with anyone, and he didn't think nothing of it because that's something he would've done but I didn't get down like that. To me, it was all free money. I did something that I had be doing all my life for free and was given a check for it. Also, we were scheduled to sign our recording contracts with RCA soon and was expecting a very large signing bonus, so the lack of money wasn't a concern.

A few days later, I was beginning to hear rumors about Sisqo keeping Teddy Rileys verse on the song instead of mine. All kinds of crazy thoughts were running through my head after hearing this. Maybe Teddy Riley didn't like my verse; maybe that's why it felt like he was in a rush. He just wanted to get it over with because he knew he was keeping himself on the record. But that didn't make sense because why would they have me sign paperwork and pay me? Or maybe Kidd went behind my back to Sisqo and talked him out of using my verse because he knew that I would blow up being on Sisqo's first single following the Thong Song album? Again with these guys, you never knew. I was so confused and what was frustrating was I couldn't say anything to Sisqo because I wasn't supposed to know that these conversations were even happening. One day Sisqo would say he's using Teddy Rileys verse. The very next day, he would change his mind and say he was using my verse. Back and forth, back and forth he went. Sisqo's girlfriend at the time Tera (Nikki) had my back as she did years ago and would tell Sisqo he needs to keep me on the song. I also had Charles vouching for me as well. Charles stayed in Sisqo's ear saying that I was a true MC and my verse was hotter than Teddy Rileys. To put a cherry on top, Charles would play a CD that he recorded of me in the car wherever he and Sisqo went. What I didn't know was the very first day that we arrived in LA and I freestyled over the instrumentals Charles was mixing, he secretly recorded the entire thing. Being as though he was Sisqo's personal assistant, he was with Sisqo all the time and when they went places, Charles would pop the CD in and blast it the entire ride. So Charles was forcing me and my skills down Sisqo's throat yet still he kept going back and forth. Charles would keep me posted daily on which way Sisqo was leaning. I didn't know what to expect. I was beginning to think to myself "I knew it was too good to be true". I started leaning to maybe Kidd was pulling strings behind my back but then it was revealed to me about how I was invited to get on the song in the first place.

I was told that although Kidd did the introduction skit on "Off The Corner" he still wasn't satisfied. He wanted to be heard rapping on Sisqo's album so he went to Sisqo and suggested that since Butch, Hot and I was on Off The Corner, he should be allowed to rap on the album as well. Kidd knew that Can I Live was Sisqo's first single, so he "suggested" that Sisqo replaced Teddy Riley with him on Can I Live and Sisqo agreed. When Sisqo went to Def jam with the idea, allegedly Def Jam laughed at the idea because they knew Kidd couldn't rap. Sisqo got upset about the laughter/ disrespect and Def Jam said "I tell you what. Let us hear this rap group that you have". Sisqo played Off The Corner and after the song went off Def Jam said "Who's the guy on the 2nd verse? He's on fire! He can be on "Can I Live"! Not Kidd." So Kidd's plan to backdoor the group and get on Can I Live backfired and the song fell directly in my lap!

Our time in LA was coming to an end. We were scheduled to leave LA and fly to Miami to shoot the video for Can I Live as well as sign our recording contracts with RCA records. At that point I still didn't know if I was on Can I Live or not. Two days before we left, I needed my hair braided for the video. The whole time I was in LA, Serenade (from Lovher) would braid my hair but for the video I wanted it professionally done.

Sidenote: During the entire time in LA, although I was seeing Chinky, Serenade and I would flirt with each other all the time, majority by two way texting. Our conversations would get very heated at times and if giving the opportunity, we probably would have cross those lines but the opportunity never presented itself so it never happened.

I decided to call the only person I knew that lived in Cali for assistance and that was Jade (the girl that came to the Mansion with her friend). I told Jade about my dilemma and she suggested that we meet up at her apartment so that she could take me to a hair stylist. I agreed. Being as though our first escapade was at the mansion, I wasn't sure if she thought I had a lot of money or access to it therefore I didn't trust her. I decided to bring Butch along for the ride just in case Jade was trying to set me up to get robbed.

When we arrived at Jade's apartment, everything appeared to be okay. She was there alone and the apartment was in a high scaled neighborhood. When Jade answered the door she only had on a T-shirt and panties. She didn't mind at all that Butch was with me. "Just give me a minute guys. I'll get dressed" she said. Jade began to walk around the house with a speed walk causing all of her "assets" to shake. Jade was absolutely gorgeous with a perfect body! As she looked at a few pair of jeans to wear she asked Butch and I if we needed anything. We told her no, we were good. She then went into the kitchen and I thought that she was returning offering us a soda or water but instead she came out of the kitchen with a tray full of cocaine lines and asked if we wanted any. Butch and I declined. Jade snorted a line of coke and continued to get dressed. Then she asked us the question that explained the episode we had at the mansion as well as the high scale apartment we were in. "Have you guys seen any of my movies?" she asked. "Naw, I didn't know you were an actor" I replied. Jade laughed and said "Well, I'm not exactly an actor. I'm a pornstar!" "Get the fuck out of here!" I replied. Jade laughed and said "Naw seriously!" Jade then opened one of her closets and showed us her collection of movies. She was on the cover of every VCR tape in the closet. As Butch and I looked through the tapes, Jade asked "Cooli, I did give you some head the last time we were together. Didn't I?" "Yeah, you did" I responded. We all laughed and soon afterwards we headed out of the door in route to the hair stylist jade had arranged for me.

When we arrived at the hair salon, Jade introduced me to a stylist named Kandi and then she left. She had to run some errands so we agreed to hook up later that night (but we never did). Butch stayed in the car as I waited to get my hair braided. While sitting in the shop, waiting for my turn to get in the chair, another one of Kandi's clients came in and sat next to me. It was none other than Tracee Ellis Ross. We talked for almost an hour until it was my turn to get in the chair. She was so cool and down to earth. You would think that someone that was born and raised under the star umbrella would be a little standoffish but she was the exact opposite. Tracee was dope and it was a pleasure conversing with her that day.

Two days later, we're all in Miami preparing to shoot the video for Can I Live. At this point I still didn't know if my verse was on the song or not. We all picked our outfits out while we were still in Beverly Hills, Averix leather jackets, iceberg jeans and t shirts so we were all set for the video. For fun, Kidd asked Ken to rent us all scooter's so during the day, we were weaving through traffic, having a ball but at night, we used a car service.

The first night in Miami, we decided to go to a night club. Sisqo did not attend. It was just us, the Associates. The DJ at the club must've gotten the word that we were in the club and decided to give us a shout out. A few moments after he shouted us out, I heard the instrumental of Can I Live blending with another song. Before I knew it Sisqo's verse was playing and the song was in full motion. As the song continued to play, my body stiffened as it came closer and closer to the rap breakdown. "Who will I hear?" I thought to myself. Teddy Riley or myself. Kidd, Hot and Butch were thinking the same. We all stood like statues, waiting for the rap to come in. As the bridge rolled in, I closed my eyes and took a deep breath. I thought about everything that I had been through in a flash up until that moment and then the rap came in. It was my verse! That was how I found out that I was officially on "Can I Live". In a nightclub, a day before the video shoot!

The guys jumped on my back joking around in celebration as my verse played through the speakers in the nightclub. I was happy and relieved at the same time but I also thought to myself "Oh shit, I have to get ready to perform this verse in the video!" Before I knew that I was officially on the song, I figured we, the Associates, worst case scenario would be guest cameos in the video but now that I knew that I was on the song, a performance scene was necessary. That night instead of going to sleep when we got back to the hotel, I stayed up half the night, going over my verse, trying to come up with animated things to do as I performed the verse. You see I knew that Sisqo would be dancing as I rapped, and his dance moves would absorb almost all of the camera time so I knew that if I wanted the director (Dave Myers) to show little old me instead of Sisqo (even for a split second) I had to do something worth showing. So, I acted out everything that I said in the verse with hand motions and animation in order to give the director something to work with.

After I had every move down to a science, I sat on the edge of my bed, thanked God and replayed everything in my mind. Just two years ago I was on my mother's kitchen floor crying like a baby because Sisqo had cut me out of the group and now I'm scheduled to sign a major record deal with RCA records and featured on Sisqo's 1st single from his new album "Return of Dragon".

Sidenote: Initially when me and the guys found out about Ken taking us to RCA instead of Priority Records, we were upset. RCA wasn't known for breaking any hip-hop artist. The only RCA artist that we knew of were SWV and Tyrese. Priority had a ton of hip hop so we thought it was a better fit but Ken explained to us that RCA was offering a lot more money, so we let it go. RCA offered us a 2 million dollar recording contract (1 million was set aside because Def Jam made RCA agree to spend 1 million dollars on our first single/ video because Sisqo was their major artist and Def Jam wanted a guarantee that the video would be up to their standards). After a lot of back and forth and negotiating, (which took months) RCA finally agreed. The other 1 million was for the budget of our album, Sisqo, management (which was Ken and his younger brother Cedric Crear) our lawyers Scott and Evan Friedfield and us, the Associates.

I thought about everything from the talent shows in college, to Demartim Records, then to all of the ups and downs dealing the Sisqo movement; losing jobs, damaging relationships, but the most influential thought of them all was how I came from the very bottom of them all to now being the 1st up at bat. The whole thing was surreal to me. It was like something you would see in a heroic movie. But never the less I was here and ready for what was in store and then a final reality thought hit me. If I had attended my grandmother's funeral, I would have missed this opportunity and none of this would have ever happened. I shot the dice and won.

The next morning the guys and I all met up in Hots hotel room and waited for our A&R rep from RCA, Tye-V, to arrive with our recording contracts. Tye- V along with Darrale Jones (A&R) and Angela Thomas (Marketing) all came to Miami to meet us and close the deal. Before Miami, we only talked on the phones and on two-way pagers. When Tye-V entered the room, she was full of energy and had our contracts in her arms like a baby that were as thick as a bible. Our moment had finally come. Our lawyers went over all of the details with us extensively before we arrived in Miami so we had an idea of what was in the contract. Every 5 or 10 pages or so, a yellow tab was sticking out of the contract saying, "sign here". We all joked around with Tye- V pretending that we would read the entire contract page by page before signing. It took some time but each of us signed on the dotted line and were officially signed to RCA Records. Afterwards, we all asked the same question, "When will we get our advance!"

After signing our contract, we all got dressed and headed to the club where Can I Live was being shot at. We weren't scheduled to shoot our scenes till later that evening, so we were there just hanging out and enjoying the scenery, especially the ladies. We all mingled through the club flirting with every girl we came across, took pictures, and watched Sisqo perform his solo scene's. Lovher was in the video also and had a dance routine. We all watched as they killed their performance scene, especially Chinky as she finessed the camera with perfect seductive facial expressions.

After Lovher finished, the guys and I went back to our rooms to get dressed for our scene's. Once we were dressed, we all met up at Kidd's room because he was taking the longest to get ready, being a pre-Madonna as usual. The reps from RCA, Tye-V, Darrale and Angela were there as well. They wanted to make sure that we were good from top to bottom because we now represented RCA. Finally when Kidd was ready and we were about to leave out, I went to the patio to get my jacket. Tye-V was grabbing her purse that was on the table next to my jacket. She told me that she really liked my verses on the CD we made at the mansion. She went on to say how she really enjoyed the song "All The Way" and I told her that my verse originally was set to be last. Tye-V then said, "Well I'm glad that you went first!" Then she whispered, "As a matter of fact, you need to go first on all of the songs." I didn't know what to say when she said that, so I just smiled, grabbed my jacket and we both headed out the door.

As soon as we arrived back at the club, it was time to shoot our first scene. We took a few pictures outside and then went straight inside to prepare for the scene. Our first scene was pretty basic. We were posted up at the entrance of the club, talking to females as Sisqo walked and danced through the doors. Our next scene was the four us, standing against a bar, checking out the girls as they walked past us. I remember asking the director Dave Myers, if we could touch them as they walked by. Dave told me to do what I would normally do if I was in the club and this was a real situation. On the very next take, when the girls walked by, I reached out and grabbed on of their hands attempting to pursue her. Dave Myers as well as his producers loved the gesture but little did they know that just like in the first scene when we were at the entrance, I was really trying to talk to those girls. It wasn't fake at all for me. I was shooting my shot in real life in every scene.

After the bar scene, the guys and I along with Sisqo, sat down and did an interview with MTV's Making the Video crew. Sisqo spoke very highly of us as well as Lovher saying that we were destined to take the music world by storm. After the interview, it was time for me to shoot my solo scene. I had no idea of what it would look like in regards to the scene. One of the producers came to me and said "Cooli, we're going to have you saying your rap to a girl, sort of standing off to the side in the club, as if you two are having a conversation." I replied, "Cool, lets make it happen!" At that time, I was so amped up that I could have shot through the roof! My confidence was on one thousand. I felt like my time had arrived. There wasn't a nervous bone in my body. This was what I had dreamed about practically all of my life! Kidd loaned me his iced out watch and I had a pair of scissors in my back pocket as a prop. Again, I knew Sisqo would be dancing during my rap so I wanted to do any and everything I could to keep the camera and edits on me!

When it was time to shoot, ironically the girl that the producer chose for me to do my scene with was the same girl I met at the Thong Song video shoot. We talked for a while at the

Thong Song shoot and took a few pictures but that was it. I was a nobody at the Thong Song shoot and now a little over a year later, I'm signed to a major record label and the main rapper in my group, featured on Sisqo's first single. The girls name was Tascha. When she saw it was me, she ran over and greeted me with a huge hug. My life and status literally did a 360 from the Thong Song shoot to Can I Live.

As soon as Dave Myers producer said "action" I went for broke. I gave it everything that I had. I acted out almost every single line that I said with hand gestures and facial expressions. I showed off Kidd's watch when I referred to time as well as pulled out some scissors when I mentioned it in the song. I remember hearing the producers yell "Good Cooli, Good!" as I was performing my verse. This reassured that I was doing well and my confidence grew higher and higher as I performed for each angle of the scene. When I was done, I felt like a certified star. All the Def Jam representatives were coming to me saying that I did an awesome job and of course my new RCA family was right there congratulating me as well. After I was done with my part, I went and sat with Sisqo and watched the guys shoot their scene without me, conversing with girls. I was on such a high from the adrenalin rush from nailing my scene that I was telling the producers where each of the guys should stand to make the scene look hotter. And the producers actually listened to me and followed my lead! The producers as well as Sisqo agreed with all of my suggestions.

Sidenote: This taught me that when you are good at something and add confidence and an authoritative demeanor/voice, people will listen and fall in line.

After the guys shot their scene, we watched Teddy Riley and Cuba Gooding Jr. shoot their cameo scenes and called it a night. The next morning the guys and I flew back to Baltimore with the Can I live video completed and newly signed RCA artist.

Chapter 30 - Jackpot

Once back in Baltimore, I did what I always did after returning. I spent time with my son Peanut, visited my Mother and Father and made up for lost time with my girlfriend Chante. Being as though we had just signed with RCA, me and the guys weren't in record mode so we didn't hang out at Sisqo's house 24/7 per usual so the majority of my time was spent with Chante.

Everyday me and the guys would call our lawyers to find out when we would be receiving our advances from RCA. Between the four of us we were expecting the first portion of our advance in the amount of $125,000 (a little over $31,000 per member) and once the completed album was turned in, another $75,000. Sisqo was expecting $100,000, our lawyers $80,000, Ken and his brother Cedric $90,000 and the remaining was our budget and 1 million set aside for the first video.

The checks seemed to take forever to get to us. Finally, after about 4 or 5 weeks we received a call from our lawyers saying the checks had arrived at their office and asked where they should send them. The guys and I all agreed to send them to my mother's house via Fed X- overnight. The next morning Hot and Butch arrived at my mother's house bright and early around 8am. Kidd was in LA shaking and moving as usual. We all sat in my mothers living room and waited for the Fed X man like kids waiting for Santa Claus. When he arrived, we almost pulled my mothers door off the hinges opening the door. Once I signed for the package, I opened it and gave Hot and Butch their checks. We all jumped around and celebrated in my mothers living room, taking pictures of us with the checks and acting crazy. Afterwards we went straight to the bank and deposited our checks. Hot was making jokes saying he was going to ask the teller to give him $1,000 in quarters just for the hell of it. We all were floating on clouds that day. Since Kidd was in LA, I took his check to his mothers and gave it to her. I also had Sisqo's check for $100,000 in my possession as well. I kept telling myself that I actually had almost a quarter of a million legal dollars in my hands, all from making rap songs- wow unbelievable!

The first thing I did with my advance money was I gave my mother and father an undisclosed amount of money as well as my church, by writing them a check because the advance check needed time to clear. Then I paid off all of my college student loans. I still had the $10,000 I received from recording "Can I Live" as well as all of the per diem I was receiving while in LA and Miami. I also bought Chante a diamond ring. It wasn't an engagement ring, but it was a ring to show her that I appreciated how she stuck with me and was loyal when she didn't have to.

Later that evening we all met up at Sisqo's house to celebrate as well as watch the first edit of "Can I Live". When I walked in and entered the kitchen, where we all congregated, I had Sisqo's check in my hand. Sisqo was in the middle of a conversation with his friend Chuck. I gave him a handshake and handed him his $100,000 check. Sisqo glanced at the check and then tossed it in his junk drawer, where he kept his mail and take-out menu's. When I saw him do that, that's when I knew Sisqo was beyond rich! He just put a $100,000 dollar check in a junk drawer with unwanted mail takeout menus.

Afterwards we all poured ourselves a drink and gathered around in the living room in order to watch the first edit of Can I Live. Lovher was there also (all except Kenji aka Ms Thang). Our normal crew was present- Sisqo, me and the guys (minus Kidd- was in LA), Charles, Big Rich (Sisqo's bodyguard), John (Sisqo's studio engineer) Lovher, Sisqo's sister (which was Charles girlfriend- Donisha) and Chuck (Sisqo's friend). Sisqo played the video and as I watched leading up to my performance, I thought it looked absolutely amazing! I remember thinking to myself, I hope they kept a lot of my parts and didn't pan out to Sisqo's dance performance as I rapped but when my part played I was completely satisfied. I did just enough not to get drowned out by Sisqo's dance scene. The guys scene was awesome as well. Lovher's dance scene was on fire and Chinky's solo shots were absolutely amazing. Her facial expressions were mesmerizing but there was only one "problem". Sisqo didn't like the fact that Chinky's braces were showing when she smiled. We asked if the editor could digitally remove the braces but Sisqo just brushed the thought off. Chinky was pissed but I encouraged her to don't overreact because we haven't seen the final version yet. When the final version did come through almost all of Chinky's solo scene's were deleted. I wish they would have kept some. She absolutely crushed that video!

A few days later, the checks had cleared at the bank and I was in rare form. Butch and I rented 2001 Ford Expeditions, I got a black one and Butch rented a gray one. After I rented the truck, I went straight to my cousin's Fat Boy (aka Big Flood) and Shawn's (aka Little Flood) house, picked them both up, took them to the mall and bough them sneakers and an outfit. The reason why I only did this for those two was because of all of my cousins, they were the two that were struggling financially the most. After we left the mall, I dropped them off back home and went to my mothers. When I arrived, my aunt Cynthia was there with my mother. She said she needed to speak with me. My aunt went on to say that she was behind on her gas and electric bill and needed money or else BGE was going to turn off her service. I asked her how much she needed. I thought she would need maybe $1,000.00 or so but she only needed $200. She then went on to say that she promised that she would pay me back. Two hundred dollars was nothing to me. I told my aunt that she didn't have to pay me back and that she could have it. My aunt broke down in tears and began to cry and praise God right on the spot. It felt good to be able to be a blessing to my aunt and I was happy that I was in a position to help her.

That scenario with my aunt sparked something in me and I wanted to give as many as I could that same feeling. I remember going to visit my cousins and someone would say "Yo Cool, I like that shirt" and I would take it off and give it to them and leave without a shirt on. I also picked up pointers from hanging with Kidd in regards to shopping. I took Anna to the mall with me and spent thousands of dollars on her, myself and Peanut in a store just to get the managers attention and watched as she watched the manager treat me like royalty, all skills I learned from being around Kidd. One time I was on the phone with Kidd while in a shoe store and told the manager to give me all of the items that you have in the entire store. Kidd got so excited! He loved for any of us to ball out. He shouted in the phone "Yo Cool! You're balling out like that!?"" What are you cleaning them out of, air force ones?" I replied "Naw, headbands!" We both burst out in laughter and joked about that incident for years!

Meanwhile Chinky and I were as close as ever. We were at the point of telling each other that we loved the other when we hung up on calls. The only problem was, we were back in

Baltimore and when in Baltimore, I was with Chante. At times Chinky was expecting me to spend nights with her at her hotel but I couldn't because I had to go home to Chante.

One day Chante called me and told me that she missed her period. Jokingly I said "Shorty I might have knocked you up!" Chante later took a pregnancy test and the results came back positive. Chante and I were expecting a baby. Once I found out that Chante was pregnant I knew I had to slow down with Chinky so I decided to tell Chinky about the pregnancy. I didn't tell Chinky that Chante was my girlfriend of 3 years and was pregnant. I sold the illusion of I got someone pregnant that I was casually dealing with and I needed to get my priorities in order. Chinky didn't sound to be upset (this was a phone conversation). She seemed very understanding and supportive, but it was clear that we weren't going to see each other anymore. There were no hard feelings on either side. We agreed to remain friends.

On May 8th, 2001, Can I Live was released for the world to hear and see. Every radio station across the country was playing the song. I was still in Baltimore when the song was released and Can I Live was in heavy rotation on all of the Baltimore stations. I was very grateful and happy to hear myself on the radio but I didn't get that "feeling" that I heard a lot of artist talk about when they heard themselves on the radio for the first time. Maybe it was because it wasn't my first time. Back when Butch, Mouse and I were Shock Trauma, we heard one of our songs entitled "Mystery" play on Morgan State College radio 88.9 (strictly hip hop) and lost our minds. But this of course was on an entirely different level. Again I was happy but I wasn't "go crazy happy". I think one of the reasons was because it wasn't my song (it was Sisqo's) and the main reason probably was because my name was rarely mentioned. The DJ's that knew me would shout me out after the song played but the song was entitled "Sisqo featuring The Dragon Family" instead of "Sisqo featuring Cooli Hi".

Sidenote: Lovher sung the background vocals on Can I Live. Sisqo and Lovher were signed to Def Jam. I was signed to RCA. Def Jam wasn't going to promote me as a feature on Sisqo's single because I wasn't signed to them so instead of using "Sisqo featuring Cooli Hi", they went with "Sisqo featuring the Dragon Family" because the song had Lovher as well as myself.

Even on the video the title read "Sisqo- Can I Live" or "Sisqo featuring the Dragon Family". My name was in the credits on the album of course but I wanted my name desperately to rang out along side of Sisqo's name because I knew what that would do for my career. In Baltimore, everyone knew it was me but outside of Baltimore how would they know.

A week after Can I Live was released, I met up with Anna and told her that I wanted to enroll our son Peanut into this private high end day care school. The day care was in Reiserstown Maryland and the kids that attended were the sons and daughters of Baltimore ravens players, lawyers and doctors. Anna was blown away when she saw the school. She asked "Are you sure you can afford this? Because I know I can't". I replied "Don't worry. I got it!" As I said this, I started the truck and my voice came blasting out of the speakers because as usual "Can I Live" was on the radio. We both looked at each other and started laughing.

The next day, I received a phone call from Sisqo's road manager, Huggy Carter. He informed me that Sisqo needed me to fly out and perform Can I live with him on a TV show. Absolutely, I told Huggy. Just tell me where and when. Huggy said "Good, we need you in London!" London! I don't have a passport I replied. Huggy then said "Don't worry, we're going to pay to have your passport expedited. You have to go to Washington DC today. Get the passport and you plane leaves tomorrow!" Oh shit, I thought to myself. Things are getting real.

I got myself together, gathered all of the paperwork needed and Butch and I went to DC to get my passport. The next day, I didn't have time to return my rental truck so I left it with my mother and flew to London by myself.

When I arrived, I got my luggage and afterwards I saw my car service guy waiting for me with a sign that had my name on it. I felt like a superstar! Before, back in LA, when we arrived the same situation was in place except the sign said "The Associates" but this time I was alone and the sign said

"Cooli Hi". I felt like I had made it! I got into the car and rode to the hotel. When I arrived, everything was laid out for me, no hassel, no confusion. I was given my room key and off to my room I went. I took pictures of everything with a disposable camera, the room, my view outside of my window, the room service food, everything that I could take a picture of, I did.

After about an hour or so after I arrived, Huggy called my room and told me to be downstairs in the lobby in 15 minutes. We had to go to the venue for rehearsals. I met up with Huggy, Sisqo, Charles, Big Rich and Tammy (Sisqo's hair stylist) in the lobby and we all jumped into a limo and went to rehearsals. Sisqo thanked me for coming to London on such a short notice and I looked at him like he was crazy. "Yo you're thanking me. I should be thanking YOU!" "I never experienced no shit like this before!" Everyone in the limo started laughing. I guess Sisqo was so used to Kidd and Hot's ungratefulness that he actually thought I was doing him a favor. I asked Sisqo, what was the name of the show we were about to perform at and he said "The Top of The Pops". At the time I had never heard of the show, but I later found out that it was one of the biggest TV shows in London!

When we arrived at the venue and started rehearsing, I didn't have much to do. The majority of the rehearsal was for Sisqo and his dancers. All I had to do was make sure my mic was at the level I wanted.

The next day when we arrived back at the venue for the actual performance, I saw something that almost brought a tear to my eye. I saw a dressing room with my name on the outside of it! I was completely blown away. I couldn't believe that I had my very own dressing room. After I took a picture of the door of course, I went inside and just sat there by myself taking the moment in. It was small, had a few waters and soda's and a small fruit basket, and it was all mine. I was very appreciative. After I took it all in, I left and went to Sisqo's dressing room where all the action was. Sisqo's dressing room looked like a suite and had all the bells and whistles. Sodas, waters, alcohol, hot tea, fruit, candy anything you could think of. As I watched everyone prepare for the show I began to get a little nervous. I wasn't sure if I could hold my own on a stage with Sisqo. I've watched him perform over the years and hes absolutely amazing and full of energy. Me one the other hand, I'm cool, calm and reserved and all by myself- no Butch or Mouse not even a hype man by my side. How is this going to work? What if Sisqo doesn't like my stage presence? But then I thought to myself, I'm here because I deserve to be here. This is my chance to perform with Sisqo and I plan to take full advantage of it. I 've been waiting for this day since I was a little kid dancing like Michael Jackson in my family talent shows. It's go time! I gave my disposable camera to Tammy and asked her to take as many pictures as she could. We went out and did the show and when my part came, I delivered! Sisqo was very pleased with my performance and so was I. My first show ever with Sisqo- Top of the Pops in London, the year 2001.

The next day we all left London and returned to the States. Sisqo went to LA and I returned to Baltimore. I was scheduled to be in Baltimore for 2 days and then I was headed to LA as well. BET (Black Entertainment Television) was planning their award show and we were not only scheduled to perform but scheduled to be the opening act to start off the show! This was HUGE! To open for any award show was an honor but to open for the 1st Annual BET Award show was not only an honor, it would go down in history.

Sisqo wanted to show love to our hometown, Baltimore for this great honor so he invited a legendary DJ from our hometown, 92Q Jams own DJ Reggie Reg to perform on the show as well. I had been knowing Reg for years, prior to meeting Sisqo, from being on the music scene and partying in Baltimore. Reggie Reg and I flew from Baltimore to LA together to meet up with Sisqo and prepare for the show. We both were excited about being on the award show and we laughed and talked the entire flight.

The day before we arrived in LA, Sisqo was in New York promoting the album on BET's popular TV show 106 & Park. Prior to this day, Sisqo did a few interviews and claimed to be the best R&B singer in the game. A lot of people frowned upon his claim to be the best because they thought he was being arrogant but actually that wasn't the case. Sisqo was still furious with his label Def Jam and was trying to make a statement. He felt like he was top notch, which he was, but

Def Jam wasn't treating him as such so he figured "who do I have to crush to get the respect I deserve around here!". So Sisqo claimed to be better than every R&B artist out at the time and when reporters started dropping names, he didn't back down. One reporter asked him "What about Usher?" and Sisqo doubled down and stuck to his claim. This started a frenzy in the gossip columns and magazines. Now, to fast forward to Sisqo being on 106 & Park, the hosts AJ & Free brought up the highly talked about subject and asked Sisqo if he actually said he was the best in the game. Sisqo, paused and looked directly into to camera and said "Yeah, I said it and now I'm saying it again!" When I saw this, I thought to myself "Damn Blondie is going hard! He's moving like a rapper! Rappers normally make claims like that. I never saw or heard of an R&B/ Pop singer moving like that". I also thought to myself "This will either go really good or really bad. No in between".

Now we are in LA preparing for the award show. The first day there, we all went to this tower, where Sisqo had to film his entrance to the stage. It was set up as an intro where Sisqo appeared to jump off of a roof and drop down from the sky, landing on the BET performance stage. I remember literally climbing up the side of the building where he was filming on several ladders until I reached the top. I kept my eyes up to the sky because I knew if I looked down, I would get dizzy and in one false move my life could be over. That's how high we were in the sky.

The next day we had rehearsals. Being as though Sisqo had just said what he said on 106 & Park, the media was instigating the feud between him and Usher. Everywhere we went, he was asked about his comments. As soon as we walked into rehearsal, who do you think we saw? It was none other than usher himself leaning against a stairway rail directly in our path as we walked in. Sisqo walked right passed him and didn't even make eye contact. He acted as if he wasn't even there. I on the other hand attempted to make eye contact because I wanted to see what Usher was made of.

Sidenote: The media had hyped up the feud so bad that although it wasn't an actual beef, with all the talk, rumors and hype it felt like a beef which turns it into a beef! Usher was clapping back in interviews as well.

I stared at Usher all the way until I passed him and he never looked me in the eye. Once he felt my stare, when I was directly in from of him for a brief second, he looked down at the floor and that told me everything I needed to know. I wouldn't say he was scared. Uncomfortable would be a better word. In Ushers defense, he was alone and we had close to maybe 15 people with us, but the energy wasn't street or violent at all. We had dancers, Lovher and road managers with us. Charles and I were as street as it was in our entourage (with the exception of Big Rich- Security).

Once we walked by Usher and made our way to the stage, we waited until the act that was rehearsing before us finished. It was none other than Jay Z and his RocaFella crew, Beanie Segal, Memphis Bleek and Damon Dash. As they walked off the stage pass us I stared at them as well, trying to make eye contact because I wanted to see who they really were. I couldn't catch all of them but I did catch Beanie Segal's eye as well as Jay Z. Both of them looked me back in the eye and we sort of gave each other a head nod as to say "what up".

Afterwards we ran through our performance full throttle. Contrary to belief, rehearsals are nothing but live shows without an audience. We go just as hard in rehearsal as we do when the actual show takes place. Each time we went through the performance, I would give it my all times ten just in case Jay Z or his crew was still there watching. After going over the performance, the producers walked me through where the pyro would explode so I wouldn't be in the wrong place at the wrong time and get set on fire. After we had it all worked out, we left and returned to our rooms.

It was two days before the BET Award show and I didn't have a clue on what I would wear. Ken told me not to worry. Def Jam's stylist would make sure I had everything I needed. When I finally saw what the stylist had for me to wear, I almost lost my mind! They picked out some red velvet looking shorts and a white tee shirt with Cooli Hi spray painted on it, in graffiti mode. I couldn't believe Def Jam thought that I would wear this. I was pissed because I did not have a lot of time to make adjustments. Hot just so happened to call me while I was still in rage about the outfit. I told him what had happened. Hot said to me "Yo, don't worry I got you!" "I can't have my man looking crazy on the BET awards!" "Send me the hotel address yall staying at". Hot sent me a Cal Ripken Orioles over night and saved the day!

Finally, June 19th 2001 had arrived, the day of the BET Music Awards. Never in my wildest dreams could I have ever imagined that I would be here. A little less than two years ago, I was on my mothers kitchen floor crying with a cable uniform and tool belt around my waist, being an errand boy while in studio sessions, alone in writing rooms in NY because no one wanted to do a song with me and now I'm in Vegas getting ready to perform on TV in front of millions of people.

When we arrived at the Paris Hotel, I remember seeing all of the empty chairs with the celebrity's names on them as people were coming in taking their seats. Growing up as a kid, when watching award shows, everything seemed so big and extravagant but now that I'm actually here, the environment was no different than the homecoming shows I performed at in college. That is what the setting felt like.

Sisqo didn't want to sit in the audience with the rest of his peers. He only wanted to come out and be seen when it was time to perform. That meant his seat was going to be vacant.

Sisqo and Ken were arranged to sit next to one another. Being as though Sisqo didnt want his seat, I suggested that I take it and Ken agreed. Before I knew it, I was sitting on the 3rd row in the audience catching all kinds of camera time surrounded by stars! I sat on the end of the row, so the camera stayed on me as I watched the show. A few seats to my right was Luther Vandross and Snoop Dogg. Behind me was Jermaine Dupree and Bow Wow. In front of me was Destiny's Child. This moment was so surreal to me. When Destiny's child was performing, I was so close to them that I could almost see up their skirts (they wore shorts under their skirts). Everyone you could imagine was within arm's reach from Jay Z to Babyface to Whitney Houston.

After watching a few performances as well as artist receiving their awards, finally it was time for us to go on. Whenever there was a commercial break the entire audience seemed to go into a frenzy, people moving everywhere and when it was time for the show to start back up, everyone had to hurry and get back in their seats. When the commercial break came before we went on, I got up and went backstage. When I got there, I saw Lovher talking to Steve Harvey and Cedric the Entertainer. I walked over to join them and introduced myself. They both were cool. Once the commercial break was over Lovher went to their assigned spot backstage and I stayed where we were all talking because that was the part of the stage that I was entering.

Cedrick the Entertainer went out on stage and introduced Sisqo and before I knew it, he was dropping down from the ceiling as if he was falling from the sky headed for the center of the stage. Reggie Reg was on a tower, high in the air behind Sisqo in the background. The dancers, Lovher as well as myself were still backstage waiting for our cue. As I watched Sisqo perform from the side of the stage, I tried to take a look at all of the stars sitting in the audience without exposing myself. The audience seemed dormant as Sisqo was performing and at the time I didn't know why. I later realized that when you're performing in front of other celebrities, you're not going to get the same response as when you're performing in front of fans. Fans scream, celebrities just watch.

As my cue approached, I was amped up and ready to go. Not a nervous bone in my body. When my part came up, Sisqo sung my name as an introduction to let people know who I was. When I entered the stage, I made sure I avoided the pyro explosion that the producer warned me about at the rehearsal. Normally when I perform, I can never see or recognize anyone in the crowd. Its all a blur to me but on this particular performance one person of all the celebrities stood out to me and I could see him as clear as day. That celebrity was none other than Shaquille O'neal aka Shaq! He was so huge sitting in those small seats, that I couldn't help but to notice him. He stood out like a sore thumb. As I performed my verse, I looked at him the entire time.

After I did my thing and walked off the stage, Lovher and Sisqo made their way to the front to close out the song. Sisqo and Chinky began to riff, going back and forth feeding off one another but Chinkys microphone was very low, barely on at all. Once they were done and we all were backstage, Sisqo was extremely frustrated. He was very upset about Chinky's mic level as well as DJ Reggie Reg scratching a record during the entire performance. I believe that Sisqo was upset about those things but I also believe that he was even more upset about how the audience responded to the performance. Sisqo is very prideful, especially when it comes to his performances and as I mentioned before, the crowd was full of celebrities which meant no one hardly cheered or clapped after we were done. The response was very dull and minimum. If the audience was full of fans, the results would have been completely different however it wasn't. I believe this was the real reason why Sisqo was so pissed afterwards. As soon as we all gathered together backstage, Sisqo said "Yo we're out" and headed for the door. We all reluctantly followed him, especially me because I wanted to return to my high-profile seat and watch the rest of the award show. None the less, we all walked out with him and left the award show.

After the BET Award Show, we went in full promotion mode city to city, radio station to radio station, promoting the new album and single. We performed on Fox Teen of Palooza show (where the crowd went absolutely bananas because it was full of actual fans), The CBS Morning Show (where I lost my cool and threw my microphone in the sky, upset because it wasn't on while I was rapping my verse. Sisqo actually had to break out of his dance routine, give me his mic and when I was done, I had to rush and give it back to him. Thank God that the mic didn't hit any fans when it finally came down. We possibly could have gotten sued.) and MTV infamous show TRL (Total Request Live) just to name a few.

About a month or so prior to the release of Can I Live, Sisqo took me and the guys to Key West to celebrate the season finale of his MTV show "Sisqo's Shakedown". This was another star-studded event where he brought us out with him live on stage at the end of the show. While in Key West we hung out with Carson Dailey and partied with him that night. He was a very cool down to earth guy.

Now fast forwarding to the performance on TRL. In my opinion this was my best performance with Sisqo. The TRL stage is very small and the audience is right in your face so the experience is more personable. I absolutely loved small stages because that meant I didn't have to work so hard moving from east to west. I could basically just stand in one spot and do my thing and that's exactly what I did on MTV's TRL. I stood in one spot, finessed the camera with my expressions and nailed my delivery of the verse because I didn't have to manage my breathing as much. When I finished my verse, as always I exited the stage. After Sisqo and Chinky completed the riffing at the end and the song was over, the crowd went crazy! Carson

Daily came on the stage, congratulated Sisqo and then he didn't something that no one could have ever expected. Carson Dailey looked around and said "Wait, hold up. Where is my man Cooli?" I couldn't believe it. He actually remembered me from Key West and called me back on stage in front of millions of viewers. I returned to the stage and the fans went crazy! Carson came to me and gave me a pound (handshake) and said "What's up man! I didn't even see you creeping back there!" Another surreal moment that I will never forget.

After the TRL experience, we all flew out to London with the exception of Lovher. Def Jam didn't like how Lovher was being portrayed while on the promo tour with Sisqo. You see, being as though Lovher was a female R&B group, they required things that at the time Sisqo was not providing. Things like a hair and makeup stylist on deck, to make sure they were always on point and also a wardrobe stylist that could put them in the correct outfits. Traveling with us, the girls were doing their own hair and make up and wearing jean suits with their names on the back. Def jam made an executive decision to remove them in order to start working on their image and completing their project and although I knew I would miss them, I agreed with the decision.

In London, we did several shows and even had a private jet fly us from London to Scotland to perform as well. All of our shows seemed to have the same acts on the card. It was usually us, Destiny's Child, Lil Bow Wow, Shaggy and sometimes Nelly and the Saint Lunitics. In London is where I first met the members of Destiny's Child individually. Sisqo introduced me to each of them and they all were very polite and cool. Back then, I thought to myself "Oh my God, that's that bad girl from Case's video "Happily Ever After!" She was Beyonce then, but I didn't have no idea that she would be the Beyonce that we all know and love now!

In Europe, everything seemed amplified times ten. The venues were bigger, the crowds were bigger and the fans seemed to be more loyal and obligated to support. The girls seemed to be more opened to do whatever we asked as well. We were there for only a short period of time but I slept with several girls in the short time span. Back in the states, the hot girls were only focused on Sisqo and we were always looked at as the alternate options but overseas , everyone was fair game. One of the girls I slept with was a virgin and actually she was 1st and only virgin that I've ever slept with. I didn't know she was a virgin until right before the act of having sex. I mean literally as I was about to enter her she whispered "Oh my God, please be gentle. This is my first time." I felt so bad after hearing that because I didn't even know this girls name and she's about to allow me to be her 1st But she was gorgeous and she had that London accent. The combination of the two was an undeterrable turn on. Since I knew it was her 1st time I was very gentle with her and I tried to make it as pleasurable for her as possible. I remembered hearing so many horror stories from girls telling me how it was when they lost their virginity, and I didn't want that to be the case with us. I asked her often if she was okay as I gently moved in and out of her and softly kissed the side of her face as tears were rolling down. When we were done, she left her phone number on desk in my room and left.

London was awesome. One of Def Jams A&R reps from back in the day named JaHa was there and was now the President of Def Jam- Europe. Jaha being from the states, showed us extra love so anything we asked for, he made it happen. Jaha had an assistant named Safiya and I as well as every other human that came across her, had the biggest crush on her. I shot my shot constantly but she politely always declined. I was told that EVERYONE from Redman and Method Man to every other artist that came from the States pursued Safiya and she respectfully declined everyone. She had been in the music industry for a long time and she knew how entertainers moved. Dating one was not an option.

Outside of Sisqo, Huggy and the bodyguards, it was just Charles, Tammy (our hairstylist- Sisqo, Charles and I all had braids) and me. Charles and I would often go out and just see what we could get into. One time Charles arranged for me to go to an underground radio station in one of London's grimiest hoods. I didn't even know London had hoods but they did and it was real. We went in and I did an interview, kicked a few freestyles and then we left.

Tammy (our hair stylist) and I became very cool on this trip as well. We laughed and talked all of the time. She actually would try to help me win over Safiya because she knew how much I liked her. We also hung out with some Def Jam reps from London that showed us a good time, taking us to the best restaurants and hottest night clubs. London was great. Once we were done with the promo tour and it was time to return to the States, I called the virgin that I had slept with a few days prior. I really didn't have much to say but I just didn't want to be responsible for another horror story. She was very happy to hear from me and also surprised. She told me that she didn't think that she would ever hear from me again. I told her that I enjoyed her company and hopefully one day I would see her again- wishful thinking. We both hung up with smiles in our voices. A few hours later, I was on a plane headed back to the States.

When we returned to the states, our next stop was New York to do an interview on Hot 97. There was a very popular DJ/Radio personality there at the time that was known to stir up controversy. As the interview progressed, I noticed that he was trying to antagonize Sisqo and get him to talk about the beef with Usher. Sisqo was being as diplomatic with his answers as he could but the DJ kept pushing and I knew exactly what he was doing.

Prior to this interview, when we were on other radio stations, Sisqo was starting to brag about my freestyle capabilities to everyone. "Put any beat on and my man Cooli Hi will crush it" he told the DJ's. "He will drop 100 bars in a heartbeat! Cooli Hi is the hottest MC out! Can't nobody touch him." The DJ's would never call his bluff because they all were trying to get him to talk about his album or the Usher beef so they just took his word that I was a beast but I always was prepared just in case someone wanted to pull my card.

Now we're in New York with this asshole DJ trying to provoke a beef. I saw right through him and I started to get upset because I felt like he was trying to manipulate Sisqo. When Sisqo did what he always did and started telling everyone how dope I was, the DJ attempted to manipulate me the same way he did Sisqo. He asked "What about you Cooli Hi? Since Sisqo says he's better than Usher, are you better than DMX? Do you want to...." I immediately cut him off and said "Yo I aint with that Bull you're tryna stir up! I see right through you and I know what you're tryna do. Try that bull crap with somebody else cause I aint the one!" As I was saying this, I was looking him directly in his eyes letting him know that this can go however he wants it to go. The DJ laughed it off and moved on to the next topic. Charles looked at me as if to say, "My Man. I'm glad you put him in check"

Sidenote: A few months later when Aaliyah passed away when her plane crashed, I was told that the same DJ was playing plane crash sound affects while speaking of her on the radio. I was told allegedly Dame Dash came to the radio station and pistol whipped him. The DJ was later fired for his actions.

After the New York interview, we all went to Philadelphia to continue the promo tour. When we arrived in Philly, we stopped at a KFC to get something to eat. Everyone had gotten their food and was back in the car except Ken and me. While we were waiting for our food, Ken turned to me and said "Yo Cooli, I have some news for you. As you probable already know, "they" want you to leave your group and go solo but if you do, you might have to deal with bad karma!" I didn't respond to Ken verbally when he said this. I just looked at him and shook my head. I actually didn't know what to say.

Once we got our food and returned to the car, I thought to myself, that's why Tye V from RCA whispered to me while in Miami that I should go first on every song and that's why the RCA reps seemed to cater to me on the Can I Live video set. They were planning for me to go solo the entire time. Later that day I spoke with Sisqo about the situation to get his advice. He pretty much told me the exact same thing that Ken told me. He said ultimately its up to me but if I did, I would be leaving my group behind which in return could lead to bad karma in the future. Sisqo then went on to tell me about how much he missed being with Dru Hill. "Singing with Dru Hill always pushed me" he said. "I always had to be on my "A" game because as we know, they aint no joke! It was always like an unmentioned competition to see who the best was!" I knew exactly what Sisqo was talking about. I had mad love for my group members but when it was time to lay a verse on a song, or perform, I always wanted to be the best and I'm sure they all felt the same way. "Just take some time, think about it and let us know what you want to do" Sisqo said.

Later that night we were all in the hotel lobby in Philly and Beanie Seagal and his crew popped up. Beanie had rapped on Sisqo's "Unleash the Dragon" record and they both were affiliated with Def Jam. Beanie and Sisqo shook hands and began to chat a little. I stood off to the side because I didn't want it to seem like I was trying to be in their mix. Charles kind of stayed in their vicinity. After Beanie spoke with Sisqo for a few, he then started talking to Charles. As they were talking Charles looked over at me and waved his hand asking me to come join the conversation. When I walked over to them, Charles said "Yo Beans, this my man Cooli Hi" Beanie shook my hand and said "Yo, you killed that verse on "Can I Live" my nigga. That was some good shit!" "If you need anything while yall here, just let me know!" I thanked him for the love shown, we shook hands again and then we went to Charles room to smoke the weed that Beanie Seagal gave him. As we walked to Charles room, Charles said to me with excitement "Yo, that's big that Beanie Seagal knows who you are and he fucks with your verse!" I agreed. I felt validated that another MC that I respected, recognized and respected my work. Another surreal moment.

The next show we had was schedule in Chicago. I remember when we arrived I saw guys wearing green and red suits and I thought to myself "These must be real pimps!" After we did our sound check for the upcoming show, as we were sitting in our limo just about to pull off, suddenly the car door opened and it was none other than the actor/ singer Tyrese. Tyrese got in the limo, spoke to everyone and then he and Sisqo began to talk. I remember Tyrese being so excited about being in Sisqo's presence. It was very obvious that he was a big fan. He kept quoting Sisqo's ad lib from a song entitled "What Are We Gonna Do" when Sisqo was calling out Nokio's name at the beginning of the song. Sisqo just laughed as Tyrese kept mimicking his parts.

After we all talked and laughed Tyrese asked us if we had saw his new movie yet. We told him no. "Well there no time like the present time" Tyrese replied. "Lets all go and check it out now!" We told the driver to take us to the closest movie theatre that was showing Tyrese's movie. The name of the movie was Baby Boy.

When we arrived at the theatre, security had already blocked off a portion of the theatre for us only. It was me, Sisqo. Tyrese, Murda and one of Tyrese's friends.

Sidenote: Tyrese's homeboy that was with us actually played a small role in the movie. He was the one that was having sex with a girl while she was on the phone and told Taraji P. Henson that she would call her back.

We all sat in our blocked off section and watched the movie. At the time I didn't know who Taraji P. Henson was so after seeing the sex scene, I asked Tyrese "Yo did you hit that forreal?" Tyrese laughed and replied, "Naw I didn't smash but I show you the one I did smash!" Tyrese showed me who he was talking about but I won't say.

After we watched Baby Boy, we did our show and then headed out to a night club. The club was very high scale and appeared to be one of the best in Chicago. As we were parting, the club promoter came over and told us that Michael Jordan was there. We all got excited and asked the promoter to take us to him. We left our VIP section and headed over to Michael's. He was sitting on the arm of a couch smoking a cigar. When we walked over to greet him, I remember Michael extending his left hand to all of us as he continued to smoke on his cigar. Where I'm from, extending the left hand is a form of disrespect. I wasn't sure if Michael was being disrespectful or not because I realized that some people were raised different, so I shook his hand anyway and so did everyone else. After all, it was Mike! When the night was over and we got back to the hotel, Sisqo was upset about the Mike situation. He felt the same way I was thinking when we were at the club but it was over now, so we let it go.

After the Chicago show we all headed to our hometown Baltimore to perform. We were schedule to perform at the Baltimore Arena. I think I was more excited about performing here than I was at the BET awards. Performing home, in front of my hometown and in the building formally known as the Civic Center, the same place where I used to watch Ric Flair, The Four Horseman and The Road Warriors, also where I watched Biggie and Puff perform when I was older, was epic to me. I couldn't wait to hit that particular stage.

We arrived in Baltimore a few days before the show, so I had time to visit my family. As always, the first stops were Mom, Dad, Peanut and Chante. Sisqo decided to throw a huge pool party at his house since we were in town for a few days. On the day of the pool party, I made sure to spend as much time as possible with Chante because I knew I would be out late that night. When I arrived at Sisqo's house that night, the party was already in full effect. Being as though I left directly from Chante's apartment, I came to the party alone. Butch and Hot were already there. Kidd was still in LA working on who knows what. He always kept a trick up his sleeve. I was happy to see Butch and Hot because I hadn't seen them in a while. Lovher surprisingly was there also. The party was one for the record books. Everyone who was someone was there. My confidence was on an entirely different level, higher than ever before due to all of the exposure I was receiving from being seen on the BET Award show. Everyone in the party knew who I was and they looked at me as if they were looking at a star. I even heard girls whispering to one another "That's Cooli Hi- the rapper that's on Can I Live with Sisqo".

I walked around the entire pool house introducing and conversating with every single group of females in the house. I knew that they knew me yet I still introduced myself to show the humility in me. Being around Sisqo and Kidd taught me how to work a room and that night I was working in overdrive. I was having the time of my life until a group of dudes decided they wanted to try me.

As I was conversating with a group of girls, some guys that grew up with Sisqo came over and introduced themselves to me. They told me the name of their crew and said that they rapped and wanted to know if I wanted to battle. "Battle" I said to them. "Yo we are in a pool party with all of these pretty girls around and yall want to battle?" One of their leaders then said "Yo, Sisqo claims you're so much better than everybody else so we're trying to see what's up!" And then it hit me, just like Sisqo did at the radio stations, hyping me up to the world, he probably did the same to these guys. If they grew up with Sisqo, they're probably feeling slighted, as if to say "Sisqo, why did you put this dude on, when you've been knowing us all of your life and didn't put us on?" It was about 10 to 15 of them and they all looked like they wanted to rip my head off.

Once I saw the energy they were bringing I said to myself "Fuck it, lets do it!" I was determined to show these dudes exactly why Sisqo said what he said and chose me over them. The battled started off with me going head to head with one of the guys. Then he stopped and I went back and forth with another guy, then another guy and another one. They were coming out of the woodwork non stop. I thought to myself "Damn, do all 15 of them rap?" And then I thought to myself "Where the hell is Butch and Hot?" They were no where to be found. Here I am battling damn near 15 guys all by myself. It was just me and Charles surrounded by a team that called themselves Swansen Bay (I believe).

As more time went by, the battle started to get more intense. I began to feel a little uneasy. I didn't like the fact that I was alone surrounded by click of dudes that clearly felt animosity towards me. I was holding my own lyrically with each of them, but I just didn't like the vibe. I felt like at any moment something could pop off. As one of the guys rapping began to spit another verse, I saw his body language and to me it seemed like he was positioning himself to swing. I could have been tripping. Maybe it was the drinks or the weed but whatever it was, it prompted me to act. I stormed out of the circle and went upstairs headed to a bedroom closet where I knew Sisqo kept his gun. Chinky must have saw me go upstairs and knew exactly what I was going up there for. I grabbed the gun out of the closet, cocked it and headed back towards the steps. As soon as I turned to go down the steps, Chinky came out of nowhere and dived on my back attempting to tackle me. I didn't go down so I literally walked down the steps with Chinky on my back and a gun in my hand. I'm not sure who, but I think it was my cousin Tim Brown and Butch who saw this and they all grabbed me and wrestled the gun out of my hand.

The next day was the anticipated day I'd been waiting for. It was the day to perform in front of my hometown at the Baltimore Arena. Before the show, Sisqo and I did radio interviews with all of the radio personalities on Baltimore's 92Q. The show, like all of them, was a part of a Summer Jam sponsored by radio stations so not only us, but a lot of acts were on the card. Jay Z, Ja Rule, Destiny's Child and Lil Bow Wow (still) and a host of other acts that I vaguely remember.

The show was a major success! The crowd per usual went crazy over our performance and I enjoyed every minute of it, especially because it was coming from Baltimore. Before we performed, I remember being in our dressing room and everyone who was anyone was there to greet us and wish us well. The heavy weight boxing champion of the world, Hassim Rakman was there, and he and I laughed and talked before the show. Everyone from radio was there as well. It was like a Baltimore All Star event behind stage.

Normally after we perform, we head straight for the door but being as though we were home in Baltimore, I didn't have to follow Sisqo out the door as usual so I decided to stick around for a few. As I walked down the hall leaving our dressing room, I remember seeing Ja Rule walking in my direction. He was alone and so was I. As we crossed each others paths, I looked at him and he looked to the side and sort of downward at the ground. I spoke and said "what up" and then he looked up and spoke back. I never could read what that look meant. I saw that in a lot of celebrities. Usher did it at the BET Award rehearsal and when we were in LA running through the Beverly Center looking for girls, we would often run into Marlon Wayans and he had that same look in his eyes. In an ordinary street setting that look would come across as timid, or fear but I can't say that it was the same when celebrities are involved. The look could mean that they don't want to be bothered or noticed. I was never exactly sure but what I do know is that I didn't get that look when saw Jay Z, Beanie Seagal or Nelly and the St. Lunitic's.

After I passed Ja Rule, Vita from Murda Ink followed shortly afterwards. When we saw each other, we smiled and embraced in a friendly hug. I met Vita though Kidd when she and Kidd used to date and had been cool with her for quite some time. I even wrote a few verses for her that she recorded at Sisqo's house, but the songs were never released.

After the Baltimore show, we continued to go city to city promoting the single and album but I was starting to hear murmurs that Sisqo's movement was coming to an end. I was told that Sisqo and the President of Def Jam, Lyor Cohen had a big argument that turned into a shouting match. I was also told that Sisqo even attempted to remove his platinum plaques off Def Jam's office wall. I can not confirm that any of this happened because I wasn't there. These are things that were told to me and I began to worry. Lyor Cohen ran Def jam which was the machine that made Sisqo's brand work so I didn't see any advantages coming from pissing him off. The final rumor that I heard that really made me panic was when I was told that Lyor Cohen told Sisqo that he was the "chainsaw scene in the movie Scarface!" When I heard this, I thought to myself "Oh my God! This Def Jam relationship is a wrap!"

Shortly afterwards, the radio promotions shows started to slow up. After that the record spins started to slow down as well. At one point I would hear "Can I Live" at least twice in any car ride going from point A to point B and now I wasn't hearing the song at all. The video that played in a regular rotation on MTV and BET now wasn't being played at all. In a blink of an eye, it was like everything just stopped.

Feeling the momentum of the album coming to a screeching halt, the "powers that be", decided to move to the next single which was "Dance For Me". Dance for me was written by Sisqo and Kidd (Kidd actually did write on this record) and produced by One Up Entertainment. We all flew out to LA to shoot the video and RCA sent a camera crew to follow us around and get behind the scene footage of us working with Sisqo. This was our first project with our new label that actually had nothing to do with Sisqo. It was about us, the Associates.

This was the first time in a while (since the "Can I Live" video shoot) that me and the guys were all together in the same place. I had been touring with Sisqo, Hot and Butch were home in Baltimore and Kidd was in LA. "Dance For Me" was being filmed at Universal City and me and the guys were in rare form, doing what we always did, flirting with the female talent and acting the fool and our camera crew filmed it all. We had a ball showing out for the cameras and the camera crew enjoyed our shenanigans. We all had very small cameos in the Dance for Me video but we didn't care because we were having so much fun on the set.

Between scenes, while in Sisqo's trailer just hanging out, out of nowhere, Kidd decided to call Ken out in regard to management. You see, Ken Crear was a very high profiled manager. Not only did he manage Sisqo, he also had 112, Teddy Riley, and even Janet Jackson, just to name a few (He also later managed Cierra and discovered Mindless Behavior). Being as though Ken had all of these high profiled artists, he didn't want to take on the day to day management process with our group the Associates so he brought in his younger brother Cedric to run the daily activities while he hovered in the background and made final decisions. The only problem was, Cedric didn't know a thing about the music business. I believe he knew business but he had no experience in music and Kidd wasn't feeling it at all. Butch, Hot and myself could care less about what Cedric knew or didn't knew. We figured as long as we had Ken overseeing things, we would be okay. Kidd wanted a more experienced manager, with more connections. Kidd felt like Ken was just trying to get his brother paid off our situation. He felt like Cedric was just a waste of time and he voiced his opinion very loud and clear in front of both Ken and Cedric. The situation got so ugly, Ken suggested that we find all new management and stated that he and his brother would step down. After the temperatures cooled down, Butch, Hot and I went to Ken and told him that Kidd cannot speak for the entire group and we still wanted him and his brother to represent us. Ken said okay but I could tell from his body language that he didn't want anything to do with anything that Kidd was attached to.

When the Dance for Me video shoot was over, we all returned to Baltimore with the exception of Kidd. He stayed in LA. Dance For Me soon afterwards was release but to little if none success. The song never hit the radio and the video hardly ever played. Around this time even more rumors and murmurs were surfacing. I was told that Def Jam was in the process of blackballing Sisqo and had been for quite sometime. I was told that they never intended for the second album "Return of Dragon" to see the light of day and that they actually paid radio stations NOT to play Sisqo's music, particularly Can I Live. I also was told that even Ken knew about it and a few side deals were discussed to keep it under wraps. Again, all of this was speculation. I wasn't there and I heard or saw none of these actions. They were just told to me in rumors but I did see the promotion of Sisqo's brand spiraling downhill with my own two eyes.

Chapter 31 - Solo

Now that I was back in Baltimore and Can I Live was at a standstill, I decided to give a lot of thought to the solo offer that Ken and Sisqo mentioned to me. As I was in the process of deciding what I wanted to do, I was hit with another life altering situation, this time on the personal side of things. Anna called me and said that the high end day care that I had my son Peanut enrolled in wanted to have a conversation with us both, in regards to his behavior. "His behavior?" I thought to myself. Peanut is a great kid and doesn't give anyone any problems. What could they possibly have to say about "his behavior"?

The next day, Anna and I went to the day care and spoke with Peanuts teacher. The teacher informed us as soon as we sat down that this conversation had nothing to do with a behavior problem in a bad way. She told us that she noticed that Peanut didn't interact with the other kids at all and that he stayed to himself. She also told us that he wasn't speaking as fluent as the other 4 year old kids and that he played with his hands and toy cars the entire time while there, lining them up in single file lines very neatly. The computers and all of the advanced technology that the day care provided, Peanut showed no interest in and she believed that he wouldn't be able to grasp the process because it was too advanced for him. The Teacher (Ms. Jody) took a liking to Peanut and he liked her as well. She was the only staff at the day care that he would interact with. Ms. Jody suggested that we removed Peanut from the day care, not because she didn't want him there but because she believed that he wasn't getting the benefits (the advanced technology) that the day care offered, and the cost outweighed the gain. Finally, Ms. Jody mentioned a term that would forever change all of our lives. She asked us if we were familiar with the term "AUTISM". She then went on to explain that Peanut showed signed of being on a light spectrum of Autism called "Asperger's". She suggested that we have him evaluated and gave us some literature to read as well. At the time Anna and I only knew about the basics of Autism, not the levels or spectrums. We followed Ms. Jody's advice and had Peanut evaluated and it was confirmed that he had Asperger's Autism.

The confirmation of Peanut's autism in addition of me and Chante expecting a new baby, caused me to entertain the solo move even more. The only reservation I had was Butch. As I stated before, I knew what it felt like to be cut from a good situation and I also remembered when I was cut, it was Butch and Butch only who called me and said if I didn't want him to move forward, he wouldn't. Butch had loss the first deal with

Def Jam when Sisqo cut him from Cuzzon and I didn't want to him to experience it all over again. But still I had myself as well as my family to think about also.

One day my cousin, Big Flood and I were riding round town and I told him about the solo offer and asked for his opinion. He immediately said I should go solo with no hesitation. "Yall can be like Nelly and the St. Lunatics" he said. "The St. Lunatics are still eating, just not as good as Nelly!" he went on to say. I agreed. I decided at that moment that I would accept the offer of going solo and just made sure that the rest of the group would be okay.

I called Butch and Hot and told them to meet me at Sisqo's house so we could talk. Soon afterwards, Kidd called me from LA and asked me what I was going to do. As I was explaining to Kid about the Nelly and St. Lunatic scenario, Kidd laughed, cut me off and said "Nigga just say you're going solo!" Kidd and I both burst out in laughter. You see, Kidd had so many things going on in LA, that he wasn't solely depending on the success of the Associates. The Associates was just one of many hustles he had going on. With that being said, Kidd was the least of my worries. It was Butch and Hot that would be impacted the most.

When Big Flood and I arrived at Sisqo's house, Hot and Butch were already inside downstairs in the studio. Sisqo was out of town as always. There was a garden on the side of the house with a fake rock in it. The back of the rock slid off and contained a key to the house and we as well as Sisqo's family were the only ones that knew about it.

Once inside, downstairs in the studio, before I could open my mouth Butch said "Yo, before you say anything, I already know what you're going to say." "We know that you are about to tell Ken and Sisqo that you are going to take the solo deal but don't do it!" "We have a plan. Instead of going solo, we can just cut Kidd out of the equation because of the beef he has with Ken and Cedric!" With Kidd out of the group, everything will run smoothly with Ken, we will be a better group lyrically, and after our first album you can then go solo if you choose. Kidd is going to be good regardless. This way everyone wins!"

I thought about it for a moment and decided to decline the solo deal. What Butch said made sense. Kidd was going to be okay, if not better regardless, we would be a better lyrical group and Ken would be back in full swing because of the absence of Kidd. Also, I wasn't sure what a solo album on RCA would look like. I didn't know any hip hop artist that they ever broke, group or solo. Either way I couldn't lose but by staying in the group, everyone was guaranteed an opportunity for success.

After I made my decision, we called our A&R team Tye- V and Darrale and told them about us moving forward without Kidd. I didn't mention anything about the solo deal. Tye- V and Darrale didn't care at all about us moving forward without Kidd.

As long as Sisqo was still on board was all they cared about. Me and they guys were so excited about the three of us making records, we decided to rent out the same studio we recorded our first demo's for Sisqo, invite all of our neighborhood friends and family and make a mix tape. We decided that the mix tape would be called- Purple Haze!

We all drove down to DC, roughly about 30 to 40 of us to the studio I believe called Horizon. We took about 3 or 4 gallons of Hennessy and several ounces of weed. Charles introduced us to his old friend from New York, Wayne aka DJ Ricochet and Wayne brought his turntables along with a crate of instrumentals. We decided that we would record everything live without any punch in's or do over's. We wanted the mix tape to feel like a live experience. Once Wayne connected his turntables and started playing the beats, we all began to drink, smoke and just vibe. The booth was open and the mic was live. Once the Hennessy and weed kicked in, Hot Butch and I took turns walking into the booth and spitting verses and the crowded control room cheered us on as we did so. As stated before, we didn't do any of the verses over if we messed up or stumbled. Everything was one takes. We even kept the parts where we stumbled or fell off the beat. We also allowed our neighborhood friends who may have had a rap they wanted to spit, come in and rap their verses. Anyone that wanted to be a part had the green light to spit. That was a day that we all would never forget. The mix tape came out blazing and everyone had a good time.

Once the mix tape was mixed down, mastered and done, we sent the tape to our A&R's at RCA. We also sent it to our marketing rep Angela Thomas. Angela admired the fact that we took the initiative to pay for and create a mix tape on our own instead of waiting for our label and decided that she would help. Angela pressed up a few thousand copies of our mix tape and sent them to us to use as promo. Hot, Butch and I passed out the CD's for free all over Baltimore City and before we knew it, almost every hood was blasting our CD "Purple Haze".

Shortly after the Purple Haze frenzy, Butch, Hot and I began to put a little pressure on our A&R reps, Tye-V and Darrale to open our budget so we could get started on our album. At first Tye-V and Darrale were saying we needed Ken's approval to open the budget and start the album but after constant pressure from me and the guys, RCA finally gave in. Tve-V and Darrale opened the budget and Butch, Hot and I moved to New York in order to start working on our album.

RCA moved us into The Time, a hotel located in Manhattan. Our very first night in town Darrale took us all over New York, introducing us to the shakers and movers and people that he thought we should know. One of the last stops we made before heading back to our hotel was a stop at the legendary DJ Clark Kent's studio. As soon as we got there, shortly after the introductions and handshakes, Clark Kent immediately asked us to spit something. Butch, Hot and I were ready so without any hesitation we kicked it off and started spitting. After a few verses, Clark Kent called in some of his rappers from another room and they started spitting also. We all began to go back and forth, verse after verse, freestyle after freestyle. Afterwards the cipher was over, Clark Kent looked at Darrale and gave him a nod, sort of like a nod of approval of us. After we left, Darrale said to us "Yo Clark Kent fuck wit yall. That's big coming from him. He's a hard one to please!" It felt good to get a stamp from a legend in the game but I couldn't help but to think to myself "I'm glad Kidd wasn't there. He would have melted in that hostile situation and made us all look bad!" When we got back to the hotel, Butch and Hot said they were thinking the same way.

A few days later, One Up Entertainment (Rich and Loren) came to New York to produce some records on us. We were in the studio night after night and basically slept during the day. One night after a short session at the studio, I was on the phone talking to a girl that I met at a party at Sisqo's house named Kelly. It was around 1:30am and she was just leaving a club back home in Baltimore. She was upset with the guy she was seeing at the time and didn't want to go home because she knew he would try to come over. She asked me where I was and I told her New York. In a playful way she said "I'm so pissed that I could drive straight to New York from here!" I replied "Shid, come on. I'll wait up for you!" Before I knew it, Kelly was on 95 North heading to New York.

Kelly arrived at my room a little after 6am. When she came in, we embraced and then she went and took a shower. While she was in the shower, I thought to myself, should I try to sleep with her now or should I wait till later because of the long drive and night. I had slept with Kelly only once before but it wasn't a full session. Meaning, one night I was over her house watching TV on the couch and just as I was about to leave, we hugged at the door, and before I knew it I had her bent over on the arm of her couch. When it was over and I left, I felt like a king because earlier that day I had slept with this bad Korean girl that I met at Sisqo's house also. Two girls, (one Korean) that I had never slept with before, I slept with on the same day.

When Kelly got out of the shower, she climbed into bed with me, and we had sex. This time it was real sex. I take pride in everything that I do and although we had been together before, I felt like I had to show her how I really got down because before was just a passionate quicky.

Later that night, I took Kelly to the studio with me and introduced her to Hot and Butch. Kelly spent the night again and the next morning she returned back home to Baltimore. That following night while in the studio, instead of calling Chante on my cell, I called her on the studio phone because my battery was dying. Chante was scheduled to catch a train to New York and stay with me for a couple of days. When we were done talking, I told Chante that I loved her and hung up the phone. Well at least I thought I did. The studio phone had this weird way of hanging up. After you put down the handheld part, you had to press a button as well, otherwise the call is still live. Once I put the handheld part of the phone down, I began to tell Butch and Hot that I had to make sure my room didn't have any signed of Kelly being there, condom rappers, earrings, hair on the pillows etc. Chante was on the other end listening the entire time.

As we were leaving the studio, I received a call on my cell from Chante. As soon as I said hello, I heard her crying on the other end. My heart immediately sunk. Everything came to me in the blink of an eye about that studio phone not hanging up. I wasn't sure what she heard so I asked her what was wrong when I already knew. Chante told me that she heard everything that I said but I didn't know what "everything" meant. When she went into details, I tried to clean it up saying that me and the guys were smoking and drinking in my room and I had to clean it up before she got there. I wasn't sure if she actually believed me or not. I just begged her to get on the train and come to me and she did. I loved Chante. At the time she was the only thing in my life that was pure and true to me so the last thing that I ever wanted to do was hurt her. Chante came New York while pregnant and stayed with me for a few days and then returned to Baltimore.

A few weeks later while in the studio, Darrale came in and asked us if we had spoken with Ken lately. We hadn't. He then told us that Ken was upset about the budget being opened without notifying him. I told Darrale that I would call Ken after our studio session. After the session I called Ken and he explained to me that RCA should have told him about the budget being opened. That way someone on our side can watch the money to make sure things are being done properly. Then Ken said that Sisqo was about to go on tour with the Backstreet Boys and Kidd was going with him. I asked Ken "what about us?" Ken replied, "You're going to have to talk to Sisqo about that" That's when it finally hit me. The main purpose of Cuzzon, The Associates, all of the deals Def Jam and RCA was all for Kidd! Kidd was the priority! All of these groups were just assembled around him in order to make sure that HE was successful. I thought back to a conversation I had with Kidd shortly after we put out the Purple Haze Mix Tape. When I told him that we decided to move on without him, he gave me this laugh, as if to say "oh really". Little did I know, there is no Associates without Kidd, Kidd IS THE ASSOCIATES!

After the conversation with Ken, I immediately went to Butch and Hot and told them we have to leave New York and get on that tour. I knew that we couldn't allow Kidd to be alone with Sisqo for a three month tour without being there to monitor what he's saying. Allowing Kidd that much time with Sisqo without us being around would be the death of us.

The next day we packed up all of our belongings, checked out of the Time Hotel and headed to Penn Station to catch a train back to Baltimore. I remember us having so many bags from buying things while in New York, clothes, electronics, radios etc. that we could barely maneuver through the crowded train station. Once back in Baltimore, I immediately called Sisqo and suggested that we be on the tour as well. Sisqo initially gave me the impression that he didn't want us to come. He said "Yo, there isn't any opening acts. Its just me and the Backstreet Boys. Yall won't be able to perform so why even come?" I replied "Maybe we can do Off The Corner in your set and Hot can do Got To Get It!" I could hear in Sisqo's voice that he was considering the offer so in order to seal the deal I said "Yo, you don't even have to pay us. We just want to be apart of the tour!" With that being said, Sisqo agreed and allowed us to join the tour. When I told Butch and Hot, they both were happy about going on tour but wasn't happy about not getting paid. I told the guys "Don't worry. Once we get there we can renegotiate. We just need to get there first."

At this time, the tour had already started and Sisqo had performed in Milwaukee and was now in Cleveland, Ohio. Hot, Butch and I decided we would meet them at the next stop which was in Cincinnati. We paid for our own plane tickets and flew out to Cincinnati. The date was August 25th 2001. I remember that day because that was the same day Aaliyah passed away in a tragic plane crash. When we arrived at the hotel, a few hours before the show, we didn't feel like we were welcomed by everyone that was already there. Kidd had a nonchalant demeanor about us being there and it was hard to read what Sisqo was feeling but I didn't care. Past experiences taught me that in this business more than often you must force your hand and that was exactly what I did by practically forcing us on the tour.

Once we checked in our rooms, Huggy (Sisqo's road manager) came and gave us the lay out of the tour. We had two rooms per city, so we shared rooms between the four of us. Sisqo inserted "Off the Corner" into his set, but only the first and second verse, so Hot didn't have a part (but it was okay because Hot performed "Got To Get It" with Sisqo) and there was no pay, only per diem which was $235 per week.

That night right before the show, which was our first show together as a group, me and the guys were determined to make an impact by having a stellar performance because we wanted to have leverage in order to renegotiate the "not getting paid" agreement. And we did just that. Kid and Hot nailed their "Got to Get It" performance and Butch and I killed our Off The Corner performance along with Hot and Kidd on stage hyping the moment! It was clear and evident that we brought a hip-hop energy to Sisqo's set.

After the show we all went back to the hotel and was greeted by a gathering of fans and club acquaintances in the lobby. Everyone was still in shock about Aaliyah's sudden passing. After socializing for a few everyone individually headed back to their rooms. I met a gorgeous girl and she agreed to go up to my room with me but I was sharing a room with Butch. I told Butch about the situation and he agreed to hang out in Kidd and Hots room for a few. Me and the young lady went to my room and had sex but before we did so, I remember looking at her as she was undressing thinking to myself, my God this girl is absolutely gorgeous! She looked like a model. If it wasn't for music, I wouldn't even be in the same room with her yet here I am about to sleep with her. Right before I entered her she stopped me and asked what was my sign. I told her I was a Scorpio. She shook her head and said "Oh my God, I hope I don't become too attached" and then she closed her eyes as I entered her. When it was over, she just kept starring at me saying "I knew this was going to happen". The look in her eyes were telling me that I could have told her to leave Cincinnati and come on tour with me and she would have done it. I could tell I had my hooks in her and if I didn't have Chante back home, I probably would have entertained the thought of keeping in touch with her but I knew I would never return to Cincinnati and I classified her as a groupie so that's where it ended. This was day one of the tour and I thought to myself if the rest of the tour goes like this, I am going to have one hell of a time. I took her number before she left but never called.

The next morning before we headed out to the next city, me and the guys met with Sisqo to renegotiate our pay. Sisqo said that for the entire tour he would pay us $1,500 individually. Take it or leave it. I thought we had leverage because of the successful show but actually we didn't. Sisqo's show would move forward with or without us. Butch, Hot and I accepted the offer. Kidd declined. He said $1,500 for a 4-month tour is ridiculous! "$1,500 a show is what the offer should have been" Kidd said. Instead of boarding the tour bus to head to the next city, Kidd and his girlfriend Butta caught a taxi to the airport and flew back to LA.

With Kidd being removed from the tour, leaving the 3 of us, meant one of us had a room to ourselves and the other two shared. We decided to alternate the single room in each city. That way everyone had a chance to have their own room periodically.

Tour life was everything! We had two tour buses and each bus had a kitchen, two lounge areas, 6 bunk beds and two large TV's. On the back of the bus was where all of the action was. That was the lounge area where we played John Madden, smoked, drank, and just partied. We rarely slept in the bunk beds. The majority of the time we stayed up the entire ride and slept when we arrived at the next city.

Being as though we were touring with the Backstreet Boys, everything was HUGE! All of the shows were in the biggest venues and before every show we had catered food awaiting for us behind stage. The adrinalyn rush from hearing and entire arena go crazy at the sight of you is mind blowing (and addictive). We would always pray as we stood under the stage waiting for our que to go on and when our que came, we would come up the steps from beneath the stage with an abundance of energy! The crowd did whatever we told them to do. It was absolutely amazing! After we performed, as always we left the building headed either back to our hotel or off to the next city. The Backstreet Boys came on after us, but we never watched their set until the very last show.

After several shows ranging from Kansas City, Houston, San Antonio and Dallas, Sisqo agreed to give us more time on stage by extending our set. So after we performed Off the Corner, Sisqo would run off stage to take a breather and change his clothes. Thats when Butch Hot and I would take over. We did the normal crowd engagement by make the left side of the arena compete against the right side and then the middle as to who was the loudest. After we had the crowd at its peak, we all performed a freestlye rap that we wrote to Eve's "Blow Your Mind" instrumental (produced by Dr. Dre).

September 1st 2001, we were on our tour bus headed to New York. Our next show was scheduled for the 4th at the Nassau Coliseum. While in route for some reason Shanna crossed my mind so I decided to give her a call. Shanna and I talked for hours about everything from the tour to how things were going in her life. Just before the call ended, I suggested that she come to New York and hang out with me while the tour was as close to Baltimore as it would get. Shanna was a little hesitant at first but after a little persuading, she finally agreed to come.

I was so excited when Shanna agreed to come out for so many reasons. For one, she was still my all-time crush and although we had the sexual episode in my mother's kitchen that one time, I still felt like I didn't have a real sexual/ intimate experience with her. Her coming New York would give me the privacy and time that I had always wanted. Also, Sisqo and Kidd were the only two that brought beautiful girls in from out of town (we used to call it "importing stews"). Me bringing Shanna in made me feel like I was on their level in regards to beautiful women. I almost couldn't wait for Sisqo to see her because I knew my level of respect would go up even higher than it already was because that's just how the game went. A bad girl on your arm always raised a guy's status, point blank.

Shanna caught a train to New York and arrived at our hotel around 5 or 6pm the next day. When she got out of the taxi and walked in our hotel lobby, a few of the dancers were in the lobby along with me. "Yo, Oh my God! Who is that!?" one of the dancers said as Shanna walked in. As they all were checking her out, and making comments, I said nothing. When Shanna finally saw me, she smiled, ran over to me and we greeted each other with a long intimate hug. All of the dancers jaws damn near dropped to the ground. Mission accomplished! I grabbed Shanna's bags and we both headed upstairs to my room.

Once Shanna was settled in, I gave her an all-access pass to the show and we both headed out to the tour bus in order to go to the arena. When I walked on the bus with Shanna on my arm,

I felt like a certified superstar! All eyes were on us. Shanna had on some ripped jeans, exploiting her amazing body/ ass, some heels and a small cut off t-shirt showing off her six pack. Her hair and makeup were all on point and she actually looked like the girl of a rap star. When Sisqo saw Shanna, he looked and gave me a nod, sort of like a nod of approval. I could tell that he was very impressed. He later asked me "Yo where did you get her from??" I told him she caught he train up from Baltimore. Sisqo shook my hand and said "My man! She's dope! I see that you're now importing them in huh!?" We both laughed. Mission accomplished!

Sidenote: The crowd we were entertaining on this tour was a pop crowd. The Backstreet Boys were the main attraction, so the majority of the fans were white or non-urban. That's why Shanna's vibe shined so bright when she walked on that bus with me.

We did the show and as usual we killed our performance. I made sure I especially performed well because Shanna was there watching. She was on the front row and I remember as I was performing, our eyes connected and she gave me such a passionate look, winked her eye, pointed at me and then smiled (I can still see that look till this day).

After the show we all went back to the hotel to get dressed for a night out on the town. Sisqo was scheduled to appear at a few nightclubs and of course me and the guys were going with him. I didn't want to take Shanna with us, so I introduced her to one of the girls that was on tour with us and told Shanna to hang out with her and we'll link up afterwards.

Sisqo, along with me and the guys went out that night and had a ball. Afterwards, I returned my room and Shanna was already there. She was just getting out of the shower as I walked in. I had been drinking, I wasn't drunk but definitely tipsy. I asked Shanna how was it hanging out with the girl on tour and she said she had a good time but for some reason her vibe was a little off. I thought that she had maybe been a little upset about me ditching her to hang out with Sisqo and the guys. Shanna got under the covers and attempted to go to sleep. I, of course wasn't having it. I got undressed, and into the bed also. I said Shanna "I'm sorry if you feel like I ditched you tonight, but those club appearances were on our schedule prior to you arriving. I just didn't know about it till after the show. Let me make it up to you." Shanna and I started kissing and then we slept together.

The next day we were scheduled to leave New York and head for Boston. I asked Shanna if she would go with me to Boston and she agreed. Still tired from the night before, when we got on the tour bus, Shanna and I immediately got into one of the bunk beds and closed the compartment for privacy. Shanna cuddled up in my arms and we both fell asleep as we headed for Boston.

Midway through the trip, the bus pulled over and Big Rich (Sisqo's bodyguard) came to my bunk and said "Yo Cool, Sisqo wants to holla at you". I got up and told Shanna that I'd be right back.

Sidenote: We had two tour buses when traveling but only used one when going to and from the arenas. Sisqo had his own bus and me and they guys rode on the other bus.

I got off our bus and went to Sisqo's bus. Sisqo and a few of his dancers were in the back in the lounge area. When I went back in the lounge area to join them, I felt like I was on one of those intervention tv shows. Sisqo said to me "Yo sit down bro". As I sat down, he went on to say "Yo, I didn't know your girl got down like that!" I replied "What are you talking about?" Sisqo then said "Yo you didn't know? Ronnie and the "girl on tour" smashed your import last night!" "What?" I replied. Sisqo said "Yo, Ronnie, tell Cool what happened." Ronnie, one of Sisqo's dancers then said "Yo Cool, last night when yall went out, I went with Shanna and the "girl on tour" and we partied for a bit and had some drinks. Afterwards, we invited her to my room and one thing led to another and before I knew it, we were having a threesome!" I couldn't believe what I was hearing. I couldn't believe that the same girl that I had been chasing and crushing on for years, came to New York and in a matter of hours allowed two strangers to sleep with her! I was so shocked, but I had to keep it together because I didn't want Sisqo and the dancers to know how this news was impacting me. Sisqo then said "Yo that's why I told Big Rich to come and get you. I'm thinking since she let that happen, she's down for whatever and I want to smash too! Can you go get her and bring her over here?" Me trying not to show that I care, agreed to bring Shanna over to Sisqo's bus.

I went back to our bus, went to our bunk and told Shanna that we were going to ride on Sisqo's bus. Shanna looked confused and asked why. I made up some bogus story and took Shanna over to Sisqo's bus. We went to the back in the lounge area, and everyone was sitting on the couch watching TV. Beside Sisqo was an empty spot. As soon as we walked in Sisqo said "Shanna you can sit right here" Shanna sat down beside Sisqo with a confused look on her face. I sat on the edge of couch, maybe three people away from Shanna. As we all sat there, watching TV and talked, I noticed that Sisqo would occasionally place his hand on Shanna's knee. Shanna looked so uncomfortable, and I felt like I was stuck between a rock and a hard place. A part of me wanted to help her but the other part of me was saying how can I help her when she put herself out there like that. My hands were tied. I couldn't stand up for her after she had a one-night stand/ threesome with a dancer and the "girl on tour".

When we arrived in Boston, I grabbed our bags from our bus and headed to my room. Shanna followed. I never gave her the impression that I was upset nor if I had known about what happened. Once we were settled in, I sat Shanna down

and asked her very calmly, "Shanna is there something that
you want to tell me?" She replied "No, why would you ask me
that?" I asked her was she sure and she said yes. We went on
and on for quite some time and Shanna wouldn't budge. She
was sticking to the "I don't know what you're talking about"
theory and I refused to let her off the hook by telling her that
I knew. I wanted to see how far she would take it and Shanna
took it to the ultimate high. She cried and looked me dead in
the eyes, almost as if she was looking at my soul and blatantly
lied. Finally I told her that I knew about the threesome because
I had seen enough. Shanna burst out in tears and ran out of
the room.

After about 45 minutes or so Shanna returned to our room.
She came in, gave me a hug, apologized and said "Can we
talk?" She began to tell me what happened that night. She said
"When I went out with Ronnie and the "girl on tour" everything
was cool and on the up and up. We partied and had some
drinks. We all were having a good time. When it was over, you
were still out with Sisqo and the guys and I didn't want to go
back to the room by myself, so I accepted their offer when they
asked if I wanted to go to Ronnie's room and smoke. We went
to his room and started smoking in the bathroom so the smoke
wouldn't be in the actual room and go out into the hallway.
Ronnie had the hot water running for some reason and the
bathroom was very hot and steamy. The drinks along with the
weed had my heading spinning. Then all of a sudden Ronnie
and the "girl on tour" started kissing on each other and before

I knew it, they both were kissing on me! I don't think I have to tell you the rest. Afterwards I felt so bad that I ran to our room and jumped in the shower. That's when you came in. I felt so ashamed. I tried to get in the bed and go to sleep but you weren't having it. You thought I was upset about you being out with Sisqo but the real reason was because of what I had done. The next day when we were on the bus and Sisqo's bodyguard came and got you, I KNEW that they were going to tell you. I was so scared. I didn't know what you would do. Then we go to Sisqo's bus and this nigga starts feeling on my legs and shit. All I was thinking was Shanna what have you gotten yourself into now! Now we're here in Boston and you're asking if there's something that I want to tell you, but you're not upset so I was thrown off. I didn't know if you knew or didn't knew. I was so confused because you were so calm about the situation but once you actually said that you knew, I fell apart. This was something that I was gonna take to my grave and now the whole tour knows!" Shanna began to cry again. I comforted her with a hug and explained to her that I was upset. I just didn't show it. What Shanna didn't know was I was more upset about her not coming clean when I asked her and how she looked me in the eye and lied like that. At that very moment I knew that I could NEVER trust her, but I wouldn't let her know it. Shanna and I talked some more, cuddled and then we slept together several times all through the night into the next day. In some sort of weird way, that situation, well the aftermath, brought us closer to each other.

We were scheduled to head for Canada immediately after the Boston show, so Shanna left Boston before the show and headed back to Baltimore.

The drive to Canada was a historic day; one that no one will ever forget. We were all spread out on the bus, blasting Jay Z's new album "The Blueprint" that just came out. While listening to the album, we had the TV's on with the sound muted. Not long after we crossed the Canadian border, I remember being in the front part of the bus, sort of like the dining and kitchen area still listening to Jay Z but watching the television at the same time. As I was watching, I saw an airplane fly into a tall building. At first, I didn't think anything of it. I wasn't sure if I was watching a movie or a sci fi channel meaning I didn't think that what I was watching was real but as I continued to watch, I saw reporters speaking but I couldn't hear them because the sound was muted. I stopped the CD and turned up the sound and realized what I saw was real! Initially I thought the crash was an accident but as I continued to watch and could now hear what the reporters were saying, I learned it was an attack. The day was September 11th 2001.

I went through the bus and began to wake everyone up so they could see what was happening. I then tried to call home to my mother, but my phone didn't have any service. All of our phones were down. We all sat around the TV in silence watching as not one, but two planes collided into the World Trade Center buildings and watched as the buildings collapsed. We couldn't believe our eyes.

Finally, we arrived at our Canadian hotel and everyone immediately went to their rooms and called home to check in with their families. The first call I made was to my mother to let her know that I was okay. Afterwards I called my Dad, Chante and Anna to check in as well. Minute after minute, more information was coming in and we learned that a third plane had crashed at the Pentagon. It was obvious that America was about to go to war and here I am stuck in Canada. Later that day we found out that one of the stage crew guys on our tour was on one of the planes that crashed into the towers. The flight was leaving Boston and headed to Los Angeles. We also found out that the terrorist that hijacked that plane stayed in the hotel around the corner from where we stayed while in Boston. The next day, before the 1st of 4 shows at Air Canada Centre, a picture was shown of the guy on our tour that lost his life on the projector along with a moment of silence.

After our 2nd show (September 13th 2001) in Canada, the guys and I were hit with some news that we will never forget. Still coping and dealing with the shock of 9/11, we were told that RCA decided to discontinue their black/ urban division of the label. All of the acts that BMG (the parent company) wanted to keep were moved to Jive Records, artist such as Tyrese, SWV and few others. Everyone else would be released from the label and we The Associates were among the "everyone else".

We were told the news immediately after we got off stage and all I remember is Sisqo saying "Great! That's the best news ever! Now yall are free!" You see, Sisqo was still at odds with his record label Def Jam and although that may have been something he wanted for himself, we on the other hand did not want to be released. Our situations and Sisqo's were night and day. He was rich with a creditable name and catalog. We were not rich and no one knew of us outside of Sisqo's fans which involved being associated with him.

Getting the news that we were dropped from RCA was devastating. It felt like someone took a machete and sliced my legs off and left me squirming on the floor. We just signed our contracts in April and five months later its over. My brain began to race and I immediately started thinking of ways to fix it. The next day me and the guys had a meeting in my room to discuss the next move. Someone had informed us that the 9/11 incident caused RCA to drop their black/ urban division because of the uncertainties of the economy. We were also told that the reason why Jive Records didn't pick us up was because it was rumored that Kidd was in and out of the group which caused Sisqo to straddle the fence with us as well. It was even said that right before the tour started, while we were in New York recording, Sisqo called RCA and said he wasn't backing the group anymore (possibly a call influenced by Kidd). I'm not 100% sure that this call ever happened. This is just what we were told but at the end of the day the narrative was the

Associates had too much drama and that's why we weren't chosen.

Once I heard the why behind us not getting picked up by Jive, I immediately grabbed the phone and called RCA. I wanted to plead my case to whoever I needed to in order to assure them that we were not a problematic group and Sisqo was still behind us 100% (even if he wasn't). I called the office thinking I would get a secretary but to my surprise the President of RCA himself, Jack Rovner, answered the phone. When he told me who he was, I must admit I was shocked. Never in a million years would I expect Jack Rovner to answer the phone. That's like calling Def Jam and Russell Simmons picks up on the 2nd ring. I told Jack my name and he knew exactly who I was, which was also a shock. I told him that we were in Canada on tour with the Backstreet Boys, trying to boost our stock, I then went on to plead my case for him to push the envelope in order for us to go to Jive. Jack heard me out and was very pleasant in conversation. He told me that once everyone gets situated, we can revisit the conversation but for now he had to exit the building. He told me that he was the only one in the building, that's why he answered the phone. I told Jack to be safe and he said the same and then we hung up. Although the call went exceptionally smooth, I knew that I would never hear from Jack again. Our time at RCA had come to an end.

We finished our run in Canada and then headed back to the States, Buffalo to perform at the HSBC area. Afterwards we went on to Cleveland, Detroit, Chicago, and Minneapolis. After Minneapolis, we headed back to Canada to perform at the Saddledom in Calgary, AB but this trip did not go as smooth as the first. Due to the 9/11 incident the officers at the border were extremely cautious of who they were allowing to cross the border. After running extensive background checks on us all, the officers rejected my entry into Canada, Charles as well, because of our criminal backgrounds. Being as though we couldn't enter Canada, Huggy the tour manager decided to split the two tour buses up. One bus, with everyone except me and Charles, continued across the border to go on with the tour and the other bus, which had me, Charles and the bus driver, drove to Portland, which was the next stop after Canada, and waited for the rest of the tour to join us.

Charles and I stayed in Portland for roughly about 7 days before the remaining of the tour joined us. We were scheduled to perform at the Rose Garden, so our hotel was close to that area. Each day, Charles and I would just roam around in the area looking for people that looked like us but the majority of the people we were around were non-blacks. Eventually we did run into two black girls with an urban edge and began to hang out with them. They told us about a hip-hop club (I can't remember the name) and Charles and I went to check it out. The club was cool. It had been a while since we were in an urban hip-hop environment. We even saw Rasheed Wallace in the club and that let us know the club was on a high level, but the night was cut short because a fight broke out and police cleared out the building.

October 2nd 2001, the tour arrived in Portland and Charles and I were reunited with the crew. We performed at the Rose Garden that night but before the show, me and the guys played basketball with the lead singer Nick from the Backstreet Boys. He was very cool and down to earth and could actually play.

After Portland, we went on to Idaho, Utah, New Mexico, Denver, Arizona, 3 shows in California (one in San Bernardino and 2 in San Jose) and then we headed out to Reno, Nevada. The tour was coming to an end and as each day went by the guys and I began to worry because we didn't know what we were going to do after the tour. The tour was our distraction from the reality of us losing our record deal and although we weren't getting paid a lot of money, we were living the life of rock stars, being musically productive and most important of all, we were not back home in Baltimore doing nothing. Kidd was working his magic in LA trying to get us another deal and suggested that we went with a different manager once again. This time he had a guy in mind that went by the name of Demetrius Spencer.

We had 3 shows remaining on the tour after Reno- Bakersfield, Las Vegas and San Diego so Demetrius decided to meet us in Las Vegas to discuss coming on as our manager with Ken and Sisqo. In the very beginning of the tour, me and the guys would always wear a sports jersey of whatever city we were in (that also helped us to remember where we were because being on a stage night after night, sometimes we would forget what city we were in). Shortly after, we started wearing Ravens jerseys to rep where we were from and that became our stage uniforms for the remaining of the tour. While in Las Vegas we were told that the San Diego show was canceled so Vegas was the last stop. Since this was going to be the last show, we decided to wear whatever we wanted instead of the Raven jerseys. I had braids at the time but for the last show, I called a female friend that I met while on the Can I live run along with Sisqo and she came, picked me up from the hotel and took me to a barbershop in the hood and the barber transformed my blown-out hair from braids into a full afro.

We met up with Demetrius Spencer before the show and he seemed very cool, and we were comfortable with moving forward with him however Sisqo and Ken kind of gave him a cold shoulder. They didn't know him or of him so that's where it started and ended for them. After the show, we finally stayed at the arena and watched the Backstreet Boys perform and it was amazing.

Once the show was over, Huggy was preparing to book our flights back to Baltimore when we over heard one of the bus drivers mention that he had to bring his bus back to the east coast. We then asked him if he would mind if we rode with him and could he drop us off in Baltimore. The bus driver agreed so instead of catching a flight, we rode the tour bus from Las Vegas to Baltimore. We just did not want the moment to end. Anything that would prolong us going home to nothing, we were down for.

A few days later we were back in Baltimore. The tour bus driver dropped us off at M&T stadium. We each had $1500 to our names. The day was October 25th, 2001. The tour as well as our record deal with RCA was officially over.

Chapter 32 - Back To The Streets

T he very next day after arriving back home in Baltimore, I only had one thing on my mind and that was MONEY! I had gotten used to having more than enough money and the thought of going back to being broke was petrifying! While on the Can I live run with Sisqo, I made some money for performing on TV shows such as the BET Awards, CBS Morning Show, MTV's TRL and so on but the radio promo shows were unpaid. I only received per diem. By this time, I had run through practically all of my money. We were still expecting the backend of our advancement from RCA which before we were dropped was a little over $20,000 per member but now that we were dropped, we were only looking at about $3,000 per member. The record business is unpredictable so we didn't know when to expect that last check to come in or if they would actually send it. That year (2001) I made well over $100K, but I can't recall where or what I spent that money on. It was coming in so fast, I thought it would never stop and now I'm in my mothers living room, fresh off a major tour with only $1,500 to my name with a 4 year old son and another son on the way. I knew I had to make that $1,500 dollars work for me, so I decided to take it to the streets. I called one of my homies and bought an ounce of crack cocaine. Normally an ounce would go for around $900 but at that particular time, the prices were higher than normal so I paid $1,200. After I bought the ounce, I hooked up with my cousins Big Flood and Little Flood so they could sell it on the block.

I sat down with both of my cousins and we worked out the amounts of how each of us would get paid. We bagged up the ounce in $10 bags (dimes) in order to stretch the ounce as much as possible. We were able to stretch the ounce to $2,000- an $800 profit. My cousins didn't know how much I paid for the ounce. They didn't need to. All they knew were how much they would get off every ounce we sold. Being as though my cousins were known for messing things up and sometimes a little shady, I didn't trust them with the packs (bundles of crack cocaine). That ounce was all that I had and I couldn't afford to lose it. I decided to give them a little at a time so if something crazy happened, it would be a huge loss. So that's how we moved. It was a lot of back and forth on my end because if they sold what I gave them in an hour, I would have to stop whatever I was doing and drop off more product. They kept suggesting that I just left all of the packs with them because they would miss sales waiting for me to bring them more when they ran out but. I wasn't trying to hear it. It was a huge inconvenience, but it kept my money safe.

Meanwhile on the home front, Chante and I were expecting our baby boy. A few weeks before the baby shower, Chante and I laid in the bed and went over some names for our son who was due to arrive in 4 months. We decided to name him Darrian. I explained to Chante the reasoning behind Peanuts middle name being "Carter" (named after my father) and Chante was okay with Darrian's middle name being Carter as well. On the day of the baby shower, I remember sitting in a chair, Chante and I, in the middle of everyone playing baby shower games, thinking to myself "how am I going to support my girlfriend and children financially without a record deal?"

After the baby shower, I immediately went back into musical grind mode. Kidd was back and forth from LA to Baltimore and was trying to transition into being a songwriter. The majority of the time, he had his girlfriend Buttah with him. She would demo the songs the both of them wrote together. Since Sisqo literally gave Kidd songwriter credit on the Thong Song, Kidd was taking full advantage of the title. Instead of saying he was apart of the Thong Song, Kidd was telling people that he wrote the Thong Song!

With Kidd being focused on his songwriting agenda, I knew that me and the rest of the guys didn't have a chance at getting another deal as a group because Sisqo's support wouldn't be the same without Kidd being apart of it so I decided to venture out as a solo artist. I figured since RCA was interested in me as a solo act, maybe there are other labels interested as well. I still had some steam lingering from Can I Live so if there was a time to make a move, the time would be now.

I called Demetrius and told him about the situation. Demetrius was very supportive and was down for whatever move I was trying to make. Unfortunately, by Kidd writing songs and me being featured on Can I Live, Hot and Butch weren't major focuses and didn't have a leg to stand on which made them expendable. Demetrius sent a CD full of tracks from one of his producers named No ID. Once I received the tracks, I went to One Up Entertainment (Rich & Lauren) and asked if they would supply me with tracks also as well as record what I would write to Demetrius tracks. One Up agreed.

The first solo song that I wrote was to one of One Up's tracks. The song was called "Time After Time". One day while in a record/ CD store shopping for music, I heard a song playing in the store with an acoustic guitar. The acoustic guitar arrangement caught my attention and I knew from after 10seconds of listening that I wanted to use it. I asked the clerk at the register who made the song and he told me. I cant remember the bands name but I bought the CD and took it straight to One Up and told them I wanted something that sounded like this, and played the song. The next day One Up had the track completed.

When I heard the track, it made me feel that exact way I felt when I heard the rock band song in the record store. I decided that I wanted a singing melodic hook and as I continued to listen, Cindy Lauper's record "Time After Time" began to play in my head. "That's the hook!" I said to myself. The only difference is I wanted to tie the emotions of the song to three separate scenario's that were not romantic attractions. I decide for the 1st verse, I would talk about a step father and step son relationship that was inspired by a story Marlon told me he had with one of his mother's ex-boyfriends. On the second verse, I wanted to appeal to females so I told a story about a brothers love for his sister that was in an abusive relationship. On the third and final verse, I decided to make it personal and thank Sisqo for the opportunity he gave me and let him know that I would always have his back. I initially wanted Chinky to sing the hook but on the day scheduled for us to record it, she was a no show. Kidd was with me that day and as always, he had Buttah with him so I asked Buttah if she could sing the hook for me and she agreed. Time after Time- my first solo record.

The second song I recorded was actually a song that me and the guys were working on in New York, right before the Backstreet Boys tour. One Up produced the track and I came up with the hook but we left New York before we were able to lay down our verses. The track and hook was a banger so I asked one up if I could use it as a solo record. They agreed. The day I recorded the song, I called Lia, my ex- girlfriend from Demartim Records to come in and say some things that I arranged for her to say. You see I was very aware of my strengths and weaknesses. I knew that my voice was deep and had a monotone feel to it. When in a group, it was cool to hear my tone for a fraction of the song but to hear my tone for an entire song could be challenging. By me knowing this, I always was thinking of a way to lighten up the song or add spice to it by adding a females voice/ ad libs to highlight certain parts and break the monotony. The name of my second record was "Dat Shit".

The next two records I recorded were tracks from the CD Demetrius sent me "The Set Up" and "The Block". "The Set Up" till this date is the fastest full record (three 16 bar verses and hook) that I've ever written. I wrote the entire song in less than an hour when usually I would write one part of a song per day because I wanted to critique and polish every syllable and word. Again with "The Set Up" I infused Lia's voice with mine by writing and arranging her parts on the record. The Block was me showing love to the hood and embracing the fact that I might not ever get played on the radio because of my lyrical content.

Sidenote: All four of these songs are on my first album-Crown Victoria. When submitting the credits, I listed Demetrius as the producer because when I received the CD he sent, it had "No ID" written on it. I had no idea that "No ID" was actually the producer's name. I thought it meant that the CD didn't have an ID. No ID is now a world-famous producer that has worked with the likes of Jay- Z and Kanye West.

After I completed the last of the four records (The Block), I sent them to Demetrius for his approval. Demetrius liked the records and told me that he would use the CD to shop me around to his executive connects. I just had to be patient. Meanwhile, I was getting tracks from every producer I knew, gearing up to record as many new records as possible.

A few months had passed, and I was still in grind mode. I was still getting ounces of crack cocaine, traveling back and forth dropping packs off to my cousins and recording new songs every chance that I got. Sisqo had a brand-new state of the art studio in his basement but without a studio engineer it was useless because none of us knew how to use it till one day Kidd came in from LA and taught me what he learned being in the studios in Cali. Kidd didn't know a lot of the technical and difficult stuff, but he did know the basics. He knew how to record, stack and fly hooks, punch in when needed and load tracks for two tracking in pro tools. Kidd taught me everything he knew as we recorded each other. What ever we didn't know or when we ran into a problem, we would call John Gordon (Sisqo's studio engineer) and John would walk us through. It wasn't long before we were able to record a full song without any assistance. All we needed an engineer for was mixing and mastering.

My days were very routine around this time. I would spend the night a Chante's apartment. She was on bed rest and due to have our son any day now. In the morning, I would meet Anna at my mother's house and take Peanut to school. While Peanut was at school, I would drop off some packs to my cousins. In the afternoon, I would pick Peanut up from school and take him to a bridge that overlooked some train tracks because he loved to watch live trains travel on the tracks. I would then take Peanut back to my mother's house and write to whatever song I was working on at the time while Peanut danced to the instrumental. When Anna got home from work, I would drop Peanut off with her, check on my cousins to make sure everything was good with the packs and then drive out to Sisqo's to record.

One Friday afternoon (January 25th, 2002) after a doctor's visit, Chante and I were told that if the baby didn't come on his own over the weekend, they would induce the labor. The weekend came and went so bright and early Monday morning Chante and I headed to Mercy Hospital to have the labor induced. I had Butch's camcorder at the time, and I recorded everything; from Chante and I leaving for the hospital to the delivery of our baby boy Darrian and even leaving the hospital a few days later. My second child, Darrian Carter Jones was born on January 28th, 2002!

A few days later, after Chante and Darrian were settled in at home, I was back on my daily routine. The only difference was I didn't stay at the studio too late because I knew that Chante needed me to help out with Darrian. With my daily schedule being so tight, I knew that I had to adjust some of my moves.

The only obligation that I saw that had a little wiggle room was the back and forth with my cousins, dropping off the packs. There would be times when I was on my way to the studio (Randallstown, MD) and they would call saying they ran out and I would have to go back to East Baltimore, get the packs, take them to my cousins (Park Heights- West Baltimore) and then drive back to Randallstown. This scenario happened quite often and I was beginning to lean towards leaving all of the drugs with my cousins so I wouldn't have to run back and forth. My cousins kept suggesting that I did this and finally I gave in.

A week or so after the new arrangement kicked off, I noticed that my cousins wouldn't call me as much. Now its me calling them. The normal time it took for them to sell an ounce was now being extended. When I would ask why it was taking so long, they would say it was slow today or it was hot (meaning the police was out). It seemed to be a lot of excuses since they had all of the drugs at one time. I stopped calling them and just started popping up on them just to see what was really going on. A few times when I got there they were on the block but the majority of the time, they were in the house with a mouth full of reason why.

One day, right after we re-upped (bought new drugs) and bagged everything up, while on my way to the studio, I received a call from Big Flood saying Lil Flood had just been arrested for attempting to sell drugs to an undercover police officer.

"Damn!" I said to myself. "How in the hell are we going to be able to get him out of this?" I told Big Flood to call me when he gets a bail so we can get him out. All that night, I kept touching bases with Big Flood to see if Lil Flood had called to tell us what his bail was. Finally the next morning Lil Flood called and told us the amount of his bail. I can't remember what the amount was but what I do remember was we didn't have it. Well at least not in cash. I went to my cousins house in order to retrieve the drugs that were not sold yet. My plan was to take the drugs around my old neighborhood (Brighton Street), sell it and use the money to bail Lil Flood out. But to my surprise, when I got there, all of the drugs were gone! "Yo, we just bagged everything up earlier that day! What happened??" That's when Big Flood confessed and told me what they were really doing.

The moment I stopped dropping the packs off a little at a time and left all of the drugs with them, my cousins started finagling. They would quickly sell the ounce I gave them, use the money to buy another ounce (without telling me), sell that and then buy another and so on and so on. That's why they were stalling me because they were profiting off the ounce 2,3,4 times before they would come back to me. In regards to what happened with the most recent package, who knows. All I knew was all of the drugs were gone and Big Flood only had about $500 of my money and to add salt to an open wound, I had my Aunt Bert (Big Flood and Lil Flood's mother) one of my mother's younger sisters coming down hard on me saying "Whoever put Lil Flood out on them corners should be the one who gets him out of jail!" Everyone knew the "whoever" was me. Big Flood and I gathered up some resources and bailed Lil Flood out of jail after a few days or so. The bail along with the money I had tied into the drugs was all the money I had. We had no money for a lawyer, so Lil Flood had to use a Public Defender. Lil Flood had to serve 9 months in jail.

Chapter 33 - A New Sheriff's In Town

Without the steady flow coming in from the drugs, I literally had no stream of income. RCA did come through with the back-end advancement checks so I had that along with a few publishing checks from Can I Live. The pressure to get another record deal was heavier than ever before. Sisqo's studio was like my second home.

One night when I arrived at Sisqo's, headed for the studio, I noticed an unfamiliar voice coming from the kitchen. Instead of going down the basement I detoured and went into the kitchen to see who it was. When I walked in the kitchen, I heard the same voice yell out "Cooli MOE!" The guy with the voice came over and greeted me with a smile and a handshake as if we'd known each other all of our lives. Sisqo then said "Yo Cool, this is my homeboy Mupp! We grew up together."

Mupp (AKA Sway Lo Gee) had just recently been released from jail. There was a group that went by the name of 80 Dimes that had a very big record all over Baltimore entitled "Whoa Now" and Mupp claimed to be a very important part of that group. Sisqo wanted to be attached to the movement in someway because in the music industry, when you're a super star that comes from a small market, you should know who's hot coming out of your hometown and actually, it should somehow be coming through your channel! Since Mupp claimed to be apart of the 80 Dimes group and he and Sisqo grew up together, Sisqo saw a huge benefit of having Mupp around and of course Mupp wanted to be around.

Mupp was an inspiring music producer that had an enormous personality. It wasn't big or loud, it was just unique. The best way to describe it is sort of like a 70's pimpish personality. Mupp used words that he made up on the fly that were always very catchy or said words that we use every day and put his own twist on them. For example, the first time we met, he knew my name was Cooli Hi, but he decided to call me Cooli Moe (and he held and dragged out the Moe as if he was singing it!). He could walk into a room full of strangers and minutes afterwards, he would have everyone smiling and trying to mimic his style and grammar. The way he moved, talked, and danced were all authentic and if you were around him long enough, you wouldn't be able to help yourself from quoting something that he said.

Mupp had a plan. You see Mupp was in jail the entire time that Sisqo was blowing up as a solo artist with the success of the Thong Song so when he was finally released, he was determined to link up with his childhood friend, Mark aka Sisqo and the success of 80 Dimes new single "Whoa Now" was the perfect avenue into Sisqo's life. Mupp used the success of "Whoa Now" as a bargaining chip with Sisqo as if to say, "Sisqo, you'd better get with me on this because this is about to blow and you're going to look crazy if you're not apart of it!" None of us knew 80 Dimes personally so we couldn't verify if Mupp was actually an intracule part of the group. All we knew was he did know them because they all grew up in the same neighborhood.

Shortly after meeting Mupp, I noticed that he was coming around more and more. Every time I was there, he was there. Kidd was permanently back in Baltimore from his back-and-forth Cali trips, and he couldn't stand Mupp. Rightfully so. Mupp was beginning to gradually take Kidds place as being Sisqo's right hand man. Before we knew it, Mupp had moved in Sisqo's house and had started working on his own project. Mupp had a plan to produce his own rap group and the name of the group was "King of the Hill". Sisqo agreed to allow Mupp to produce and record in his studio. Mupp's idea of the perfect group to produce consisted of taking the best three rappers from different groups and combining them into one; his very own "King of the Hill". Mupp's three choices were Kevin, a rapper from Mupp and Sisqo's neighborhood from a clique called Swansen Bay, his cousin Daron aka Big Status and the final piece to Mupps puzzle was me.

One day while in the studio, Mupp pulled me to the side and asked me if I would be apart of his "super group". He went on to explain that it would only be for one album, with no commitments afterwards. Initially, I was on the fence about being apart of the group but after I saw all of the support Mupp had from Sisqo as well as Nokio, I decided it was at least worth a conversation. I met with my group, Kidd, Hot and Butch and told them about the offer. No one objected so after the meeting I agreed to record an album with Mupp and be a part of his group "King of the Hill". At this point, I had nothing to lose. Besides, this was a perfect opportunity for me to test my skills on songs with other MC's. In my group, I felt like I was the best and I wanted to see if I would be the best in this group also. I remembered a conversation Sisqo and I had during our "Can I Live" run when we were discussing the solo option I was presented. While riding in a limo on our way to a venue, Sisqo told me that he never really wanted to go solo. He loved singing with Dru Hill. He went on to tell me that singing with Dru Hill brought out the best in him. It was always a friendly competition on every song! I told Sisqo that I felt the same way. I always wanted my verse to be the best verse on the song and I'm sure the others felt the same way. Another incentive I had for being the best in "King of the Hill" was Kevin was apart of the squad that I had a confrontation with at Sisqo's party, the time when I was battling all of Sisqo's neighborhood and went to get the gun. It wasn't any beef, but I would use anything to add a spark to my lyrical killer instincts.

A few days after I agreed to the group, we started working on the project. Nokio was assisting Mupp with the production so I knew the beats would be tight. Prior to starting this project with Mupp, I was in talks with Jazz's former manager Cliff Jones to see if he would consider managing us as a group or myself as a solo artist. After I completed the four songs that I sent to Demetrius Spencer, our conversations started to dwindle and soon afterwards faded away. It was no hard feelings. Demetrius was in Cali shaking and moving and I was in Baltimore. I believe if he could've made something happen, he would have but like us all, if one avenue isn't working, we move on. It's just a part of the game.

Right around the time Mupp started coming around, me and the guys met with Cliff and told him about the RCA situation. After hearing what happened, Cliff suggested that Sisqo and Ken had possibly bam boozled us by getting RCA to pay THEM and afterwards, Sisqo and Ken paid the A&R's for setting it all up and once that was done, drop us. Cliff was very respected in the music industry so his opinion of what could have happened held weight and after time I started to believe it.

Side Note: It was later determined that this was not true. Sisqo and Ken allowed us to sign directly to RCA to avoid situations like this. We didn't sign to Sisqo's production company (Dragon Records). We were sign directly to RCA.

The first day of recording Mupp and I had a conversation and I told him about what Cliff had told us. I was very upset at the time and considering doing something crazy but Mupp sort of talked me off the ledge. After my conversation with Mupp I was cool but as always, I couldn't help but to express it in song. On the first song we recorded as "The King Of The Hill" I spoke on the issue on the last four bars of the verse.

"Cooli Hi, Crown Vicing aint got no problems sticking"

"So shorty rock that owe me that doe, your time's ticking"

"If it wasn't for my loyalty and words with Big Mupp"

"Boy I put it on my kids you would have been got touched"

Sidenote: I later used this verse on a freestlye (2nd verse) entitled "4,3,2,1" on Purple Haze Volume II.

The mentioned went right over everyone's head. The only one that caught what I was saying was Butch and of course Mupp. Sisqo didn't catch the line either. After all, he did not owe me any money because there was no foul play in regard to the RCA deal. If anything, I owed him!

Another point I was determined to drive home was the identity of my newfound click. Right before me and the guys left for New York to start working on our album with RCA, my childhood friend Jay Bird helped me to find a particular car I was looking for. That car was a 1989 Crown Victoria. The car was owned by an elderly white couple in Virginia. Ole Man Joe drove me to Virginia and I bought it on the spot and drove the car back to Baltimore with no tags. I absolutely loved that car. That car symbolized my entire childhood. It had the old feeling that I loved and reminded me of the card and dice games at my aunts house. The laughing, drinking and partying with my family and the most important part, the music. The Otis Redding, Sam Cookes and Gene Chandler's of the world; this Crown Victoria was all of that to me and that's who I was as an individual so when I rapped with the Associates I represented one way but when I rapped as a solo artist, I represented me and my blood family by referring to us as the Crown Vic Click!

After recording about 3 or 4 records for the King of the Hill project, the new group was presented with an ultimate challenge. This was around the time when Jay Z and Nas were going back and forth with diss records towards one another. On one of Nas disses to Jay, he used Sisqo's name as a prop, dissing Jay Z. When Mupp heard the mention, he immediately got upset. Sisqo on the other hand really didn't care one way or the other. He was used to people saying things about him because of the level of stardom he was on. In his eyes, it came with the "superstar package" but Mupp wasn't cool with this at all. Mupp being fresh out of jail and still with a street mentality couldn't understand why anyone would allow people to blatantly show disrespect and not address it so Mupp started a campaign throughout the house to make a diss record and address Nas for what he said about Sisqo. Mupp also campaigned to go after R. Kelly for saying a line in an older song calling Sisqo a bum when R. Kelly was taking shots at Sisqo for saying he was the best R&B singer alive. Mupp used his influence to convince everyone in the house that enough is enough. "We're not gonna just sit around and allow niggas to keep dissing or using Sisqo's name as a punch line in songs! I don't care who it is! Fuck Nas, R. Kelly and whoever else! We're from Baltimore! We don't play that shit around here!" Mupp said. Before you knew it, Mupp had everyone on board and ready to fire off on Nas, R. Kelly and anyone else who dared to mention Sisqo's name in a song.

Sidenote: Mupp also made us, The Associates look bad because we were Sisqo's rap group and should have stood up for him when anyone mentioned his name in a negative way. Mupp's fire back campaign raised his stock even higher in Sisqo's hierarchy and Kidd and the rest of us were gradually fading to the background.

Mupp and Nokio were like two peas in a pod. They were in separatable. They both were HUGE Prince fans, smoked like chimneys and had the same style of production. Mupp also was a huge fan of David Ruffin. Mupp brought a sample of one of David Ruffins songs to Nokio and together they produced a track entitled "This Is A Heart" for the King of The Hill.

The chorus still had David Ruffin singing in the background while Sisqo sung over top and the three verses consisted of Kevin going at Nas, Daron going at R. Kelly and I addressed all before and after beefs but no one specifically. I was very strategic in what I would address in the song because of the three rappers, I was the one with the most exposure and still in hot pursuit of a new deal. Nas and R. Kelly were very powerful artist so I had to make sure that I didn't ruffle any behind the scene/ machine feathers that would possibly kill my shot at getting a new deal. After the three verses Mupp said a few words in his signature tone and lingo followed up by Sisqo calling out Nas and R. Kelly.

Once the song was mixed and released, it immediately took off on all of the beef mix tapes on the east coast. Baltimore's station 92Q played it on their mix shows along with DC's 93.9 WKYS. It was also placed on New York's own K-Slay beef mix tape which gave national exposure to the gritty underground sounding song. I remember Kidd joking saying to me "Yo when Nas and R. Kelly hear that song, they're gonna end your career before it even gets started!" I'm not sure if Nas or R. Kelly ever heard the record. I was told that Nas heard it and afterwards he didn't say anything. He just slightly laughed. The hype lasted for a minute but like all waves, it eventually settled down and nothing came of it so we moved on.

After "This Is A Heart" settled down, Mupp found himself at a crossroad. Around this time the King of the Hill project had only about 4 or 5 records recorded but a lot of the songs still needed work on the production side. Mupp was depending on help from Nokio but Nokio was gearing up for another Dru

Hill album (Dru World Order) which of course was top priority. Without Nokio's help, Mupp was stuck and I could tell that he really was relying on the "This Is a Heart" record to launch his entire movement and when that didn't happen, he was lost. There were also rumors and speculations about Mupp's affiliation with the group 80 Dimes; the root of how he got into the mix. Several months had past, we were always having big parties at Sisqo's house and not once did anyone from 80 Dimes show up and no one was able to vouch for Mupp's participation in the group. The main person pointing this out was Kidd.

Soon the King of the Hill project slowed down and came to a screeching halt. Nokio was in full Dru Hill mode and had no time for anything else. Once the King of the Hill project paused, I immediately went back into recording solo songs for myself as well as group songs with the guys.

Kidd gave me a track one day that he got from an unknown producer that I absolutely fell in love with. After writing "Time After Time" when I used other people's situation (except for the last verse), I decided that I would make my writings more personal and speak from my own perspective as much as possible in order to be able to stand on my words more. When I got this track from Kidd, a melody and soon afterwards, words began to play in my head and I decided to write a make believe story about something that was very real to me. I decided to use the experience that I witnessed when I was a kid and my cousin Bally had witchcraft/ voo doo put on him. I wrote a song about a girl putting voo doo on me and the name of the song is "Lorraine". The song Lorraine features Butch and none other than Mupp singing the chorus and talking his signature lingo at the end of the song. Mupp brought so much character to every vocal track I ever heard him on, so it was only right that I had to get some of what he had on one of my very own songs.

Another stand out song I wrote during that time was a song called "The Realist". The Realist was a group song with Hot and Butch that was produced by Nokio. Although Nokio was in full Dru Hill mode at the time, he had a CD full of Hip Hop beats that he produced, so we went through the CD, picked the track, loaded it in pro tools, and recorded ourselves.

The track had a very slow and soulful feel to it and as always, I allowed the track to dictate the mood of what I wanted to say on it. I wrote the hook and in it, I decided to denounce all of the glam and glitter the hip hop world was conforming to and speak on the realist truths that I was feeling at the time. Once I recorded the hook and then laid my verse, Butch and Hot knew exactly how to follow. Kidd wasn't on this song because Kidd wasn't lyrical enough to survive on the slow soulful track. Kidd had to rap to party upbeat tracks because party tracks didn't require a lot of lyrical content.

After Hot and Butch recorded their verses on "The Realist" I remember playing the song for Kidd in the studio. After the song finished, he had no expression on his face. Although Kidd was the least talented rapper in our group, I respected his opinion on songs tremendously. He had an ear for hit records and no one could deny that. When the song ended Kidd said, "Yo its cool but its too slow!"

A few days later, I was in the studio working on another song and Kidd came through with a few girls. Kidd had just recorded a new solo record that had a party/ club vibe to it. When the girls were chatting amongst themselves, Kidd whispered to me, "Yo, play both of the songs- my solo record that I just recorded and then play "The Realist" and let's see how they react to the records".

I played Kidd's solo record first and the girls went crazy! They were up and dancing throughout the entire song. Afterwards, I played "The Realist" and within the first 30 seconds of the song, the girls had stopped dancing, sat down and began talking amongst themselves again, completely ignoring the song. "See what I mean now" Kidd said to me afterwards.

Once I saw the night and day reaction to the songs, I started to 2nd guess the style of music I was making. I knew that myself, Butch and Hot were 10 times more talented than Kidd however Kidd's way of doing things seemed to work out better than ours. Butch came to the studio later that day and I told him that I wasn't feeling "The Realist" anymore. He looked at me like I was crazy. I told him about what happened earlier with the girls and Butch said to me "Yo, of course girls are going to lean more towards a party track but I guarantee you songs like the song Kidd make will be forgotten after a month or so. Songs like "The Realist" will be remembered forever! It will stand the test of time!"

Hearing those words from Butch snapped me back into my reality. Butch was right however its such a thin line between being true to yourself and creating content from your heart and creating content that will sell, appeal to mass audiences and possibly convince another record label to sign you. The response from the girls Kidd brought to the studio almost persuaded me to lose my identity but thanks to Butch for bringing me back down to ground level.

Hot came through later that day after I left and he and Butch played "The Realist" for Nokio. Nokio loved what we did and played it for Sisqo. The next day when I came back to the studio, Hot and Butch were already there. When I walked in they both had the biggest smiles on their faces. "What are yall cheesing about?" I asked. They both said "Yo check this out!" and then played "The Realist" but this time something was different. Sisqo was ad libbing through the entire song which took the record to an unbelievable high and Nokio spoke at the end. The song was already hot but adding Sisqo and Nokio blew the doors off the hinges! Apparently the both of them liked the record so much that they felt as if they had to jump on it. Getting Nokio on the record was big but getting Sisqo on it was astronomical! Sisqo hardly ever came downstairs to the studio so just getting him downstairs and even singing on a track was big!!

Seeing Sisqo in the studio was almost like see a ghost. The majority of the time he would be upstairs in the living room playing video games. He could always hear the music coming through the floor (when we turned it up purposely for him to hear it and possibly get his attention) and every so often when he heard something that intrigued him, he would come downstairs and ask "Yo, what that?" So, when I heard his voice on "The Realist" I knew he had to love the song.

Side note: A few days after Sisqo and Nokio recorded their parts on "The Realist" the hard drive crashed, and we lost the files to the song. Luckily, I had burned a rough copy onto a CD. The rough copy I had was the only version left of the song. I later released the song on my debut solo album "Crown Victoria" and yes, the version on my album is the same rough unmixed version from the CD I burned just before the hard drive crashed.

The entire vibe of "The Realist" sort of breathed life into the Associates. It had been a while since we were "headlining" in the house due to Mupp's hostile takeover and I had to admit, it felt good. I was involved on both sides being as though I was a part of the King of the Hill, but it was nothing like the feeling I had when I recorded with my group, the Associates.

Mupp took notice of how the tides were beginning to sway back towards the Associates and so did Kidd. As Mupp began to worry, Kidd became more aggressive. Kidd knew that this was the perfect time to push the envelope and take back what he felt was ours, or his. Kidd proceeded to push the narrative that Mupp was never a part of the 80 Dimes group and he just used that to sneak his way into our circle. Kidd also began to allege that Mupp had plans on getting rid of all of us and bringing in new rappers for Sisqo, rappers that grew up in Sisqo's old neighborhood; the ones that I battled a while ago.

"We should do a brand-new album and crush any and every thought of us being replaced by anyone" Kidd said to me, Hot and Butch. I always was looking for something or someone to doubt me, something that I could use as ammunition, and turn it into motivation so I fed right into to Kidd's plan and as always, what I felt came out in song. The first song we recorded for our new album was a song called "How You Wanna Carry It" and although it was never said, the energy of that song was directed to Mupp and his movement. When Mupp heard the song he came to me and said "Cooli Moe, man I thought we were better than this. Why yall come at me like that?" I explained to Mupp that it wasn't personal at all. It was just competition. When its time to swing axes we don't care who's head gets chopped off. As long as its not ours. I had no beef or felt any ill way towards Mupp. I had no reason to. But if I felt threatened by someone, musically in the hip hop realm, it was natural for me to attack. I would do that to anyone, even the members of my own group!

After "How You Wanna Carry It" me and the guys went on to record the rest of the album finishing with about 12 songs. It was this album where I felt my lyrical skills as well as my delivery and tone all coming together better than ever before. Before this album, I could always look back on several songs and say to myself "I could have said that line better" or "I should have said this or that instead of that and this" but on this album, I practically nailed everything and moving forward there was no looking back.

Once the album was done, we recorded a freestyle to Scarface's "Guess Who's Back" Instrumental for the mixtapes just to get a buzz going while we shopped the album. In my verse I talked about the rise and fall of Can I Live as well as Def Jams part in it, going back to selling drugs with my cousins and back to the music all within 16 bars. Everyone held their own on the song including Kidd. We played it for Reggie Reg and he loved it. That same night he started playing on the radio 92Q Jams. All was looking good. Now we just had to get it in the right hands to land us another deal.

Sisqo wasn't in the same space as before so he couldn't or wouldn't help us. The Return of Dragon didn't work out as planned and he was now focused on recording Dru Hill's new album- Dru World Order so Kidd was our next best and only option. Kidd reached out to all of his connections but unfortunately no one offered us a deal. Not long afterwards, our hopes of getting another record deal as a group began to fade and I began to lock completely in as a solo artist. That was the last album we the Associates recorded as a group. We never named the album so several years later I released the album on Soundcloud and named it "The Last Supper".

Not long after the unsuccessful campaign of "The Last Supper" Sisqo and Dru Hill flew out to Jamaica to finish recording Dru World Order. After about a month or so they returned to Baltimore with the album about 90% done. The day they arrived in town, we all planned to have a huge party at Sisqo's to welcome Dru Hill back home and to celebrate completing the new album. On this particular day, I was one of the last ones to arrive at Sisqo's because I was getting my hair braided by a girl I was dating named Evette.

Sidenote: Evette was a girl that I knew of since I was a child but she didn't know me. She was older than I was and the baddest girl in our neighborhood. She dated the biggest hustler in the area and was adored by EVERYONE. Fast forward time, now I'm all grown up with a celebrity status and run into her at the hair salon where Charles cut hair when we weren't touring with Sisqo. We exchanged numbers, well actually she made me work; at first I only had the salon shops number, then I moved up to her cell and finally I got her home number. Evette was one of the most challenging women I ever dealt with before being intimate. The only one that made me work harder was Chante. After some time, we dated regularly but the majority of our time spent was at her apartment.

When I left Evette's apartment and headed to Sisqo's being as though I was running late, I was weaving through traffic trying to make up for time when suddenly I ran into standstill traffic. As I inched my way up Liberty Road approaching Washington Ave, I saw the police blocking the entire road off and putting up yellow tape. I was on the phone with Evette telling her that someone may have gotten killed as I followed the detour along with the other cars. When I finally arrived at Sisqo's and walked in, the entire house was silent. I walked over to Kidd and asked what was going on and that's when Kidd told me that Mupp had just been killed on Liberty Road.

Sisqo had a few motor scooters at the house and apparently Mupp had borrowed one of the scooters to visit a friend before the party. While on the way back to Sisqo's house, Mupp turned from Washington Ave. onto Liberty Road and was struck by a stolen car driving full speed. The accident that I saw when on my way to Sisqo's was Mupp's accident. He died on the scene.

Chapter 34 - Always

Shortly after Mupp's death, the status quo of the house went back to "normal". Sisqo of course was the head guy in charge (as always) and now Kidd was back in the 2nd command chair, without any threats now that Mupp was gone.

I had started connecting more with Cliff Jones in search of a solo deal. Again, originally I took the group to Cliff but similar to other situations, Cliff leaned more towards managing me as a solo artist instead of the group. I think it always went that way because for one, its a lot easier to manage one person instead of four (personalities, work ethics, etc.), two, because of the buzz from being on "Can I Live" and three my music was better than the groups music.

When I told Kidd about me dealing with Cliff Jones, Kidd just shook his head and told me to be careful. Kidd was intimated and afraid of Cliff. You see Cliff Jones was from Washington, DC but was notoriously known for being loud and aggressive. He had some size to him and it was rumored that he was bullying and threatening record executives in order to get deals done. It was also rumored that he would go into executive offices with a few of his goons carrying baseball bats! They used to call him the east coast Suge Knight.

I never felt threatened or intimated when I was around Cliff. Sure I could see that aggression and the street in him but coming from where I was from, that was normal behavior. But I could also understand that if you're not cut from a certain cloth, Cliff could scare you.

After a few meetings with Cliff in regard to me being a solo artist, Cliff called up some of his New York connections and set up some showcases for me to perform in. Leading up to the time before the showcases, I was spending a lot of time in DC hanging out with Cliff and his protégé producer Davey Boy and started to bond with them. They were starting to be my 2nd musical family.

When the time came, Cliff, Davey Boy and I jumped on the train and went to New York. All I took with me was a CD full of my solo instrumentals. The day before I left for New York, Butch played a track for me that one of his homeboys made that had a very slow soulful feel to it. I asked Butch if he was going to use the track and he said no and that I could have it. I added the track to my instrumental CD without any chorus or ad libs (unlike the rest that were on the CD). It was the raw beat only.

When we arrived in New York, Cliff took me to three record labels. I don't remember the first two but I do remember that last of the three which was Jive Records. The A&R's at Jive that I met that day were Jimmy Maynes and Toi Green. The showcase was nothing like I expected. I thought that I would be on some sort of stage performing in front of a small audience. Instead, I was in conference rooms performing in front of maybe 3 people at the most. I do remember being on a small stage on one of the first two showcases and after my performance was over, I remember the executives nodding their head in a gesture saying yes, looking in Cliff's direction. I assumed that it meant they liked what they saw and heard. After the first two showcases, Cliff told me that both labels liked me but he still wanted to go to Jive as well so we could weigh out our options and possibly get the best deal.

When we arrived at Jive Records, I performed in a conference room and used a TV remote control as a "make believe" microphone. Being as though I had just done two showcases right before this one, I was warmed up and in rare form. Every song I did, I nailed the performance, and I could tell that Jimmy and Toi was feeling me. The last song I did was to the track Butch gave me right before I left for New York. I decided to rap the song I wrote a while ago (1999) dedicated to my son, Peanut when I returned from Dru Hill's tour and quit my job. I originally wrote the song to 112's Cupid instrumental but Butch's track gave me the same feeling and actually fit the song better.

The song at that time did not have a chorus or a 3rd verse. It wasn't formatted at all. So when the track started to play, I decided to narrate the song and walk Jimmy and Toi through as if I was telling them a story. Both Jimmy and Toi were absolutely amazed by the song! They liked my other songs, but they loved this song! After the showcase, all they talked about was "the song about your son!". They asked what the name of the song was and could they get a copy and I had to explain to them that the song didn't have a name and I didn't record it yet. Jimmy told me "Cooli when you record it, lay it down EXACTLY how you did today in the showcase!" I told him I would. Jimmy, Toi and Cliff congregated for a few privately while I waited in the conference room. When Cliff came out of Jimmy's office, we left.

When we walked out of the door, Cliff looked at me, smiled and said "Joe (a DC term for all men) they want you! We are about to GET THAT BAG!!" Cliff and Davey Boy were very excited about the news but me on the other hand wasn't as excited. I was happy but I couldn't feel what they were feeling because the news wasn't delivered directly to me. It was delivered to Cliff. I think I would have felt more excited if I were included in that private conversation. Also, when we were leaving out, I didn't get the vibe of a label wanting to move forward with a deal. I knew what that felt like due to my previous experience with Priority Records and of course RCA. With Jimmy and Toi, I got the vibe that they liked me but it felt like they needed approval from someone higher up the food chain or some other component was needed to seal the deal. I could've been wrong, but it just didn't feel complete.

Once back in Baltimore, I was zeroed in on recording "the song about my son" and making it a real record. I called Toi Green at Jive Records and asked her what she thought about me getting Sisqo to lay down a chorus for the song. I did this for two reasons. For one, I wanted to see if me being affiliated with Sisqo would hurt me because Jive was the home of R. Kelly and Sisqo and R. Kelly had issues (not to mention, I was just apart of a diss record directed towards R. Kelly with Mupp's King of the Hill). Two, if the affiliation didn't hurt me, I wanted to let them know that I still had Sisqo's support and possibly that could get me closer to closing the deal. Toi Green loved the idea of getting Sisqo on the song. She also suggested that I added a 3rd verse.

The next day, I recorded the song and followed Jimmy's suggestion by doing it EXACTLY how I did in the showcase. I talked the audience through the same way I did at Jive Records. The only thing I added was an introduction; as if I was performing live at a club, and I also added a short 3rd verse like Toi suggested. I followed Jive's suggestions exactly. The only thing left to do was to get Sisqo to sing the chorus.

As I stated before, getting Sisqo in the studio was always a challenge. I hated the fact that I had to ask him because I knew he probably wouldn't want to but I knew I needed him to complete what I was selling to Jive Records. I went to Sisqo as he was playing video games in his living room (as always) and explained to him the situation that I had on the table with Jive. I told him about Toi Green and Jimmy Maynes but I did not mention Cliff. The reason being is that by mentioning Cliff, Sisqo would or could think that by helping me, he would also be helping Cliff and maybe that's not something he would want to do. The music industry is funny like that. You have a lot of moving parts/ people behind the actual artist and sometimes those moving parts or people are just as influential or even more influential than the artist when it comes to handling business. After a short talk, Sisqo agreed to lay down the chorus!

The stage was set. All my vocals as well as the intro had already been recorded. The only thing the song needed was the chorus. A few hours after Sisqo and I had the conversation, he finally came downstairs and into the studio. Normally when Sisqo came downstairs to record, everyone in the entire house stopped whatever they were doing and came in the studio to watch. We all were always so amazed by his talent, especially because we only caught glimpses of it. Sisqo never just walked around the house singing and dancing so the only time we saw and heard him was when the world saw and heard him! We almost never saw his blonde hair when in the house because he ALWAYS had on a hat or a doo rag! Sightings of the blonde hair were for shows only! If he wasn't performing, 10 times out of 10, his head was covered. So when Sisqo entered the studio, it was always a BIG deal. But on this particular day, it was only me, Charles and Sisqo at the house.

Sisqo came in, walked into the recording room, and put the headphones on. Charles was at the board preparing to record Sisqo's vocals. I was sitting at the board next to Charles. I didn't write a chorus because I didn't want to limit or clash with what Sisqo may have heard when he listened to the track. I purposely left it wide open in order for him to have complete control over what he sang. Sisqo listened to the song and track over and over again attempting to come up with the chorus. As the song played on repeat, I thought to myself, this is going to be EPIC! I couldn't wait to hear what Sisqo had came up with. After about 30 minutes or so of listening to the song on repeat, Sisqo took off the headphones, came out of the recording room and said that he'd be right back. He said he was going upstairs to get something to drink.

Charles and I sat at the board waiting for Sisqo to return. Fifteen minutes passed and then thirty. As the clock started to approach 45 minutes, Charles and I began to wonder what was going on. After about an hour, I went upstairs to see what was taking Sisqo so long to return. When I went upstairs, Sisqo was nowhere to be found and his car was gone. I went back downstairs and told Charles what I saw. Charles couldn't believe it. He grabbed his phone and called Sisqo but the calls were going straight to voicemail. Charles and I stayed in the studio for hours that day. Sisqo never returned downstairs to the studio. Later that night, as I was about to leave and go home, I went upstairs, and I heard Sisqo in his living room playing video games. I didn't see him, but I heard his voice from around the corner. I didn't go in the living room where he was. I just walked out of the door and went home.

The next day, I returned to the studio and called Ru-Scola (Scola for short), told him about the entire situation, including what just happened with Sisqo, and he agreed to do the chorus. Scola was a solo R&B singer (out of Baltimore of course) that I had been knowing for quite some time. Scola had a lot of local success which led him to being added as a member of Dru Hill when the guys weren't sure if Jazz was coming back to the group or not for the Dru World Order album. Jazz did return but Scola was such an influential part of the project, they decided to keep him as the 5th member of Dru Hill.

Scola was a cool down to earth guy. He didn't have that weird "industry" energy. Scola moved and acted like guys from around the way. We actually went to the same high school (He came out earlier than me). I could relate with Scola far better than the others simply because of our street mentality.

Scola came in, listened to the song maybe 2 or 3 times and laid down the chorus. Within 15 or 20 minutes the song was complete. I named the song Always because of how Scola concluded the chorus. I sent the completed song to Jimmy and Toi and told them I didn't get Sisqo on it but I got Scola from

Dru Hill. They absolutely LOVED the song! They also said that it was probably a good thing that Sisqo didn't sing the chorus. I didn't ask what they meant by the comment. I just left it alone.

Till this day Sisqo and I never talked about what happened that day in the studio. I have no idea why he left and never came back. If I had to guess, I would say that he might've gotten stuck lyrically. The song was so deep and had so much meaning that you couldn't get away with saying just anything on the chorus. Who knows but one thing I do know and you should know by now is I had to move on to the next. Time waits for no man and neither did I.

Now that "the song about my son" which was now titled "Always" was completed and Jive loved it, I was now in the process of playing the waiting game. Just waiting for Cliff to work out the deal with Jive. In the meantime, I was still recording solo records, a lot of which were coming from Davey Boy, Cliffs producer. Although Cliff had his own set up in DC, I still would take Davey Boys tracks to Sisqo's house and record them there. Sisqo's studio was my home base so if I had a choice, I would always be there.

More time passed and as the deal became closer to be finalized, Cliff needed to get our business in order first. Cliff suggested that I signed to his production company first. Once that was done, he would take his production company to Jive to close the deal. At the time, Cliff had 3 acts, me an R&B soul singer out of DC and a kid rapper. Cliff wanted to take us all to Jive under his production company and he had my contract ready. He just needed my signature. The only problem was, he needed my signature fast! We didn't have a lot of time to play with. I wanted to sign the contract but I wasn't going to sign before a lawyer took a look at it on my behalf. The only problem was, I didn't have a lawyer at that time. I thought that the lawyers I had when I was signed to RCA would still represent me but without a retainer in place, I couldn't even get them on the phone. I told Cliff that I wanted to sign but after a lawyer took a look at the contract. Cliff said it was cool, but I could tell he wasn't feeling it. Time was of the essence and Cliff wanted to close the deal asap.

After that conversation with Cliff, our business relationship came to a standstill. I wouldn't sign without a lawyer's assistance and at the same time looking for a lawyer but couldn't find nor afford one. Cliff on the other hand respected my stance but at the same time had to move forward. It was nothing personal but we parted ways at that point and went in separate directions.

Sidenote: Not sure if Cliff ever did the production deal with Jive. What happen between us happened, I'm not sure what happened with the kid rapper, but Cliff did land a situation with the R&B singer at Jive. His name is Raheem Devaughn!

After the situation with Cliff fell through, I was lost and didn't know where to go. Sisqo's steam was settling down which made the little steam I had left, continue to go out and Cliff's situation needed a lawyer. I was running out of options. Around this time, Kidd and I were hanging together every day and the majority of the time without Butch and Hot. Kidd and I were always trying to come up with a way to get a new deal, any deal that would cut a check. Although they were having problems here and there, Kidd was still seeing Buttah and Buttah's group Lovher was blowing up! They had a new single in heavy rotation on the radio stations all over the country called "How It's Gonna Be".

One day Kidd suggested that he and I go to New York and hang out with Lovher. Def Jam had rented an apartment for them there because they needed them in New York for recording and promoting their new hit song. Kidd and I figured we'd go and hang out with them in order to rub elbows with the shakers and movers in order to increase our chances of falling into a good situation. So off to New York we went.

When we arrived at Lovher's apartment, the girls showed us love but it wasn't the same. I felt like it was "Hollywood" love instead of the love we shared when we used to drink and smoke together, sleep on each other's laps when doing overnight sessions in the studio and laugh and talk for hours not even a year ago. Not to mention the personal relationship that I had with Chinky. Now, we were getting the "Hollywood" Hi's and the side hugs along with the calculated smiles.

Kidd picked up on the "Hollywood" vibe as well and began to call them out on it. "Don't be acting brand new because yall got a song on the radio now!" Kidd said in a joking way. When Kidd said that, it sort of broke the ice and the girls relaxed a little and began to act normal to a certain extend. We all chopped it up for a few and then headed to a photoshoot the girls had scheduled at some warehouse. When we arrived, Kidd and I were completed blown away. Def Jam's machine was in full effect. There were hairstylist, wardrobe personel, A&R's, assistants, lights and camera crews everywhere! It looked like one of Sisqo's photo shoots. The girls went straight into celebrity status as soon as we hit the door. Some Def Jam person grabbed them and rushed them in the back to prepare for the shoot. Kidd and I looked around and said to each other "Yo, they made it!"

After watching the high profiled photo shoot, we all went back to Lovhers apartment. It was late and the girls had an interview scheduled early the next morning. When it was time for everyone to go to bed, Kidd came to me and said "Yo, are you gonna go in the room with Chinky?" "I don't know" I replied. "We haven't been in that space in a while." I added. Kidd then said, "Well I'll holla at you in the morning" and then he went in the room with Buttah and closed the door. Chinky was in her room and then she came out with some blankets and a pillow. "Here you go Cool" she said as she handed me the linen. Once I saw those blankets in her hand, I knew I didn't have a shot at getting in her bed so I laid on the couch and went to sleep.

Early the next morning, as I laid on the couch, I heard several voices and people walking around the apartment that were not the girls or Kidd. "Chop Chop! Come on yall! Let's make it! We can't be late!" said one of the voices. I opened my eyes and looked through the blanket and saw Def Jam reps everywhere! They all were walking around the apartment helping each of the girls get ready for their morning interview. I though to myself "Oh my God! Here I am lying on their couch, looking like I'm homeless!" I kept the blanket pulled over my head so no one could see me. I was hoping that the girls would move quick enough so the Def Jam reps would leave without actually seeing me but then, all of a sudden, I heard one of them say "Who is this on the couch?" Chinky replied, "That's Cooli Hi" The rep then said, "Cooli Hi?? The guy that rapped on Sisqo's Can I Live song??" "Why is he sleeping on yall couch??" I felt soooo embarrassed and ashamed. I pretended as if I was still asleep and didn't budge. I couldn't wait till the girls were completely ready and all of them walked out of the door. It seemed like it took forever but finally they all left. As soon as the door closed shut, Kidd came running out of Buttah's room crying laughing and rolling all over the floor! He heard the entire conversation. He said laughing uncontrollably "Yo, when they came in, I said to Buttah, Oh My God! Cool is gonna look crazy out there laying on that couch!! I'm so glad they didn't see me!" Kidd continued to laugh. The Def Jam reps didn't even know Kidd was there. I felt like the Def Jam reps looked at me like I fell off and was a failure. That was one of the most embarrassing days of my entire life.

Chapter 35 - The Birth of Holla Back

After the New York fiasco at Lovher's apartment in New York, I began to feel down in the slumps but as always, the sadder I felt, the more I indulged myself into the process. Recording new songs, thinking of ways to get another record deal and the entire musical grind itself, was my way of coping with what some may call being depressed.

As for my personal life things were pretty much the same. Chante and I were still together but I hardly ever spent any real time with her. I would come to her apartment at night after studio sessions and then I would have to leave early in the morning in order to get my son Peanut because Anna had to go to work. Anna would drop Peanut off at my mothers and I would take Peanut to school and pick him up afterwards. When Chante had errands to run, I would have our baby boy Darrian as well. The guys used to joke me and call my situation "Daddy's Daycare".

Due to Peanut's Asperger Autism diagnosis, Anna and I always had appointments scheduled, whether it be speech therapy or some sort of evaluation so we both were always at appointments. Sometimes we alternated and took turns taking him but a lot of times we went together. At the time Peanut was enrolled at an elementary school just two blocks up from my mother's house so that was a major convenience for me being as though my car (the Crown Victoria) was down due to me not having car insurance and also a boat load of unpaid parking tickets.

Sidenote: During this time in my life, I had absolutely no sense of real responsibility. Outside of music, the only thing I cared about were my children. I mean I cared about others like Chante, my mom and dad and even Anna but my kids were the standouts. Bill's, childhood friends, other girls I dated, nothing mattered. I was completed focused on music. If it didn't involve music, I wasn't interested at all. I was borderline obsessed with getting another record deal.

I had no real source of money. I had no drugs to sell and the Can I Live checks came in quarterly (once every 3 months). My only sources were my mother at times would give me a little here and there and once a month I would pick my dad up from his house and take him to run his important errands like going to the bank, grocery store and the pharmacy to fulfill his prescriptions. Afterwards, he would always give me a lump some of cash that would hold me over for a few weeks or so. I still had an abundance of clothes from when I did have money so by the looks of things, I didn't look broke but in reality, I was as broke as they came but it didn't bother me. I just knew and believed that if the right song was played for the right person, I would be back on my feet again in no time.

This was a very dark time for me as well as with the rest of the guys including Sisqo. One night we were all sitting around in Sisqo's kitchen having drinks when Sisqo said something that I will never forget. "Yo Cool is one of the realist dudes I ever met. Did yall know that Def Jam offered him a solo deal and he turned it down because he didn't want to leave his group behind?" When Sisqo said this, I couldn't believe what I was hearing. There were others there with us outside of our immediate crew so I didn't want to address anything that should be addressed when it was just us so I just let him talk. Sisqo continued to go on and on about how he admired my decision and the others joined him with praises. Me on the other hand felt devastated. All of this time I thought the solo proposal was coming from RCA, not Def Jam! Every time Sisqo or Ken would mention the solo deal, they would say "they" want you to go solo and since I was already signed to RCA, I thought "they" were RCA. No one ever mentioned or said it was Def Jam! If I would have known that it was Def Jam that was offering me the solo deal, there's no way that I would have turned it down. It was every rappers dream to be signed to Def jam, the mecca of Hip Hop!

It all started to make since to me now. If Def Jam offered me a solo deal and they thought I turned it down, that explained why they didn't give me my feature credit on Can I Live. Instead of Sisqo featuring Cooli Hi, they went with Sisqo featuring the Dragon Family because I wasn't and wouldn't sign with them. Why would they assist in blowing up an artist that wasn't signed to them? Hearing that from Sisqo rocked my world but I couldn't dwell on it. I decided that I would make it apart of my comeback story and moved on.

My kids during the day, the studio at night and sleeping at Chante's was my life. Kidd and I were still hanging thick as thieves trying to come up with ways to get another big check. Kidd was kind of going back and forth between being a hip hop artist and writing R&B and Pop songs. A few times, he would have sessions with One Up Entertainment and he would be writing songs to their tracks. I would be there with him so I started inquiring about the writing process. Kidd taught me about publishing and how much money could be made by writing songs for other people. I knew about publishing prior but I only thought of publishing for my own work, such as my lyrics for my songs. Kidd opened my eyes in regard to writing for other people.

I sat in a few sessions with Kidd and One Up and once in a while they would allow me to write portions of a verse or a bridge but after a few songs or so, I was done with that and wanted to get back to the Hip Hop. Kidd kept telling me that he was working on something very big but he didn't want to tell me what it was until it was completed.

Maybe about a month or so later, one day I was in the studio working on some new material when I got a phone call from Kidd, telling me to come outside. As I walked outside, Kidd was pulling in Sisqo's driveway, but he wasn't driving his Lexus nor his Range Rover. Kidd was in a brand-new Blue 745 BMW with 20-inch rims! The car damn near looked like a spaceship. "Yo hop in. Let's roll" he said. I got in the car and asked "Yo, who's whip is this?" 'Its' mine!" Kidd replied. "Remember I told you I was working on something big? It came though!" At the time I had no idea what the "something big" was but I later found out that Kidd landed a huge publishing deal for his involvement with the Thong Song.

A publishing deal is what we all wanted as artist at the time. In addition to the record deal, a publishing deal is when you sell your rights to a committed number of songs that you have written or will write, in exchange for a large amount of money. In Kidd's case being as though the Thong Song was so huge, his deal was a large six figure deal.

The publishing deal Kidd landed raised his stock in the city once again to an all time high and I was right there beside him as his side kick. We would club hop night after night and Kidd would buy drinks for almost the entire club. There was no limit to how much money he would spend. Shot after shot, bottle after bottle, Kidd would always keep the drinks coming. He was known all over town for this behavior as well as having a good time. Everyday, Kidd would pick me up from my mothers, we would go to a restaurant and eat and afterwards just ride around looking for girls and popping in and out of clubs and bars.

This was fun in the beginning but as time moved on, I began to question the situation. Things were not balancing out. Kidd was sitting on close to a half of a million dollars and I barely had fifty dollars to my name. When we drove around town, hunting for girls or doing whatever, I couldn't eat until he was ready to eat because he was buying the food. When we were somewhere and if I was ready to leave, I couldn't because he was driving, and it was his space ship outside, not mine. I was totally at his mercy when we hung out together. Now granted, he was very free hearted and would give you almost anything you asked for (after a slight joke or two) but what kind of man is cool with constant handouts?

I began to think of ways that I could get a publishing deal also and I asked him if he would help me get a publishing deal from my percentages of Can I Live and Off the Corner. Kidd said he would look into it but never did. You see Kidd was just like so many other guys in the music industry and life in general. He was okay with having me by his side as a side kick but wouldn't dare help to get in a position to be his equal because if we were ever on the same level, I might surpass him.

I even offered to split whatever deal he could assist me with, but he never acted on it. I wasn't even sure if Can I Live and Off the Corner was enough to land a publishing deal and maybe it wasn't but if that was the case, I just wanted some guidance on what I needed to do to win also. Kidd never mentioned or talked about anything when it came to me or anyone else in our group getting a publishing deal. He kept the information all to himself. You see keeping me at the bottom was safe for him, so Kidd had no intentions of helping me get a publishing deal. He would rather spoon feed me here and there because by doing so, I would always need him, and he would always have the upper hand.

Once I was convinced that Kidd wasn't going to help me get a publishing deal nor point me to right direction to get one on my own, I decided to shift the energy. I realized a long time ago that Kidd, again like many others, was all about himself so if I wanted to bring an offer to his table, it had to be something that appealed to his ego.

One night Kidd and I, along with a few others were in Sisqo's basement, right outside of the studio, lifting weights. I said to Kidd "Yo, every day we do the same shit. Go eat, ride around looking for stews (girls) and pop bottles in these clubs. All of this money is going out and nothings coming back in and its YOUR money only! We should put out a single, an album or maybe even start our own record label! You could be like P Diddy or Dame Dash. Shit, you're already killing the club scenes like them!" Kidd was bench pressing at the time and stopped for a second to think about what I just said. I could tell by the look in his eyes that I had his interest. I then said to Kidd "Yo, we should start our own label and put out a single!"

A few days prior to this conversation, Kidd and I along with a local female artist named Ms. Kitty, recorded a new song with a very catchy hook called "Hang Low" that everyone who heard it absolutely loved. I wanted Kidd to invest his money on me because I had enough songs completed to release as an album, but I knew that Kidd would not spend his money on something that he wasn't directly involved in. Although I had lots of records that I would have loved to release as a single and were better songs, I suggested to Kidd that we should put out "Hang Low". The reason for my suggestion was because he was featured on it and that played into his selfish ego.

Sidenote: Hang Low wasn't one of my favorites but it was politically correct for the situation because I knew Kidd would move quicker at putting out a song the he was rapping on. To balance it out, I put a song called "My Life" on the B-side, a song that I actually loved.

When Kidd heard me say "Hang Low" should be the single we release, his eyes lit up like a Christmas tree. "Yo, that's a good ass idea!" "Let's get it cracking" Kidd said. "Cool" I replied. "I'll call Teddy (One of Sisqo's studio engineers) and get him to mix and master the record tomorrow" "After that we should press up the single on some vinyl records" I suggested. Kidd agreed. I then said "Yo, what should we call the record label?" Kidd was still bench pressing and as he went up and down with the weights, he yelled in a playful way "We should call the label Holla!" I replied, "How about Holla Back!" That was the moment Holla back Entertainment was born.

Chapter 36 - Picking Up Steam

The next day, Teddy came to the studio and mixed and mastered "Hang Low". The next and final step was to send it off to get pressed up. This was the ultimate test. You see people talk and make promises all the time in this business, but nothing is real until someone cuts a check. This same theory applied to Kidd and our new record label. It sounded good the night before, but it wouldn't mean anything if Kidd didn't cut the check in order to get the record pressed up. I knew that if he cut that check, he was serious and that's exactly what he did. Kidd cut the check and the vinyl records were in the process of being pressed up.

I now knew that Kidd was serious, so the next step was to go downtown and start a LLC with the state of Maryland. Kidd and I agreed to spit the company into three. Forty five percent between the two of us and ten percent to John Gordon (one of Sisqo's studio engineers). Our roles were cut and dry, very simple. Kidd was the financial backing and the business face of the company, I was the talent, managed all daily operations, and the man with the masterplan to make things work and John mixed and mastered all of the music to make sure the sound was right.

Once we had the infrastructure in place, Kidd began to add the bells and whistles. Kidd formed a partnership with a Korean bar/restaurant/ club owner on Calvert Street in downtown Baltimore. The name of the club was Alpha and Omega. When you walked in, it was a bar/ restaurant on the leveled floor but to the left were stairs that lead to an open club dance floor with an office in the back. Kidd struck a deal with the owner to allow us to have full access to the upstairs which was the club version of the establishment.

Once we had the club we started having parties on Tuesday Nights only to avoid competing with other larger clubs in the city that had the weekends locked down. We also hired the hottest up and coming DJ (DJ Quick Silver) as our main DJ.

Although we had what we considered as "our club" on Tuesday nights Kidd and I would also go to every other club in the city with our "Hang Low" vinyl records in hand, passing them out to every DJ, asking them to play our song. With my "Can I Live" status and Kidd's Thong Song/ Mya's video/ baller status, we hardly ever got any pushback about playing the record. Everyone wanted to be on our side. I would tell Kidd all of time that we had the perfect mixture for success! I told him

"Yo, between the both of us, we have all bases covered. You have all the music industry connections along with the appeal to the females, high popularity, flash and money and on the flip side, I have the music, the street music that Baltimore hoods respected along with the goons (Crown Vic Click) to back it up and I also had the know-how, discipline and plan on how to make a record company run successfully (due to my experience with Stanfield and DeMartim records back in the day)! We will put my album and movement out first, one because my albums about 95% done and two, it appeals to the market that we are in (Baltimore streets). Then we will bring your album out after the foundation has been laid so your sound (which was more like pop rap- targeting girls, fast life and clubs) will be easier accepted but in the meantime, feature you on my songs so it will be a smooth transition!" Kidd was totally on board with the plan.

As our Tuesday night parties began to grow, Kidd and I decide to put together a team of people that could help our vision blossom. In the beginning it was just me, Kidd, John Gordon and Butch. Hot didn't want any parts of what we were doing. You see Hot never really got over Kidd cutting him out of his "promised" percentage of the Thong Song. When Hot wrote his verse to "Got To Get It" on Sisqo's "Unleash The Dragon" album, Hot allowed Kidd to help him write the verse although he didn't need Kidd's assistance. Hot was a better writer and rapper than Kidd but he allowed Kidd to help with the writing so they could share the publishing in which they did. The tradeoff was Kidd was supposed to share his portion of the Thong Song with Hot. Kidd initially planned to do so but when Ricky Martins people came in and took a lot of the publishing of the Thong Song, that made Sisqo give Kidd a smaller percentage, so small that Kidd decided he couldn't share. Hot felt betrayed and his feelings multiplied as the Thong Song reached all time highs in record sales and revenue. The two of them remained cordial but that situation was always very sensitive when brought up. Sometimes we (Butch, Kidd and I) would joke about it and Hot would cuss us out and leave the room. He'd then return a few minutes later like nothing ever happened. That's just how we were. Almost nothing was off limits when it was joke time. But now Kidd has this new publishing deal and is sitting on almost a half of a million dollars from the Thong Song and Hot is pissed all over again. There was no way that Hot was going to participate in this movement.

As Kidd and I were looking for people to bring in for assistance, I was taking a business approach but Kidd as usual was taking more of a recreational approach. "Yo we need to have some bad ass stews (girls) around us at all times and take them everywhere we go! That's always a good look!" Kidd said. Me never objecting to having pretty girls around said "Alright cool" set it up. The next day Kidd called up a few girls, some he previously dated, some he wanted to date and was using this situation as a steppingstone and told them to meet us at Sisqo's house for a meeting. Originally, we all, me, Butch, Kidd and John were supposed to gather up the baddest girls we knew and invite them to the meeting but of us all, Kidd numbers outweighed us all 10 to 1. Hell, I didn't even bother to make a single call because I knew Kidd had that department covered.

I arrived at the meeting a little late that night but when I got there, I couldn't have been more pleased from the looks of things. There were about 10 girls in the lounge area outside of Sisqo's studio. To name a few, there was Ashley (a college student that Kidd was dating) and her best friend Sheena (whom I casually dated). Also there was Jene, someone that Hot dated but we all were very cool with. A girl named Christina (who looked like a super model) whom Kidd was pursuing at the time and last but not least there was Tanja (a girl that Kidd dated) and her former sister-in-law (her ex-husbands sister) Jackie. There were others there, but these were the stand outs and all of them looked absolutely amazing.

Kidd was the external business face of our company, but I was the internal face, so I conducted the meeting and every meeting afterwards. I explained to the girls what our goal was and what we needed them to do. I also made it very clear that it was no pay involved and that it was strictly volunteer work. Once our label got picked up by larger label or distribution company, we would be open to pay. I discussed a lot of my ideas and visions I had for the company but more importantly, I allowed the girls to chime in and share their thoughts and views as well. Although I knew some of the girls were a little star struck from being at Sisqo's house discussing record labels and deals, I didn't want them to feel like they didn't have a voice or this would be some kind of dictatorship. I made it clear that Kidd and I were in charge, but I also made it clear that everyone's opinion mattered, if not, they wouldn't be here. The whole ambience of being at Sisqo's house, the affiliation with him as well as with Kidd and myself made everyone want to be a part of the movement. By the end of the meeting, all the girls were on board and Holla Back Entertainment was fully staffed.

After the girls went home, Kidd and I went into the studio to work on new songs. I pretty much had the run down on every single girl at the meeting regarding who brought them in and basically who slept with them or was trying to sleep with them, but there was one girl that I was very curious about. I asked Kidd "Yo whats up with the girl Tanja?" Kidd replied "Yo you know she one of my old stews. I smashed her a few times." "How was it" I asked. "It was good! Real good!" Kidd said. Then he added "Yo she got three kids!" "Damn 3 kids!? Are they all by the same dude?" I asked. "Yeah I think so. She has a daughter and a set of twins by her ex-husband" Kidd said.

Of all the girls that were in the meeting, Tanja stood out to me the most. She was just so pretty to me. Her hair looked like she was mixed with another race, naturally curly and wavey with length, her eyes were golden brown and her smile looked like it was stolen off the face of an angel. She had a slim build and a slight tom boy vibe that gave her a hip hop edge. She even had her hair platted in two plats going to the back and down her back with a New York Yankee's fitted hat looking like a Hip Hop Cherokee Indian. Being as though Kidd had already slept with her, I didn't think too much about pursuing her (at the time) but I thought to myself, if an opportunity surfaced, I would definitely take it.

The following Tuesday I decided to have another meeting but this time at the club. I called all the girls and told them to meet us at the club in the back office before we opened at 8pm. I also added a few more members to the team, Mouse, his wife Melinda, Ole Man Joe, Jamal (one of Dru Hill and Sisqo's security guards who also just so happened to grow up in the same neighborhood as I) and last but not least Shanna, my all-time crush. I hadn't talked to Shanna that much after the situation we had on tour, but I knew that she would be a great asset to our movement because of her business skillset as well as many connections across the city. I also wanted her around for personal reasons also. Shanna and Jene just so happened to be close like sisters so although Shanna still felt a little embarrassed about what happened on tour, she was still willing to join the team.

Before the meeting I wrote down an agenda and had every minute planned out. I wanted to make sure that everyone present felt like their time was being valued, appreciated, and wasn't taken for granted. I gave each individual their role and title in the company and told them I would later have a one on one with each of them to discuss our expectations. Afterwards, I opened the floor and listened to their ideas and views and collectively figured out a way to implement the good ones into our game plan. Once all subjects on my agenda were discussed and the open floor came to an end, Kidd told everyone to go to the bar and get whatever they wanted. The club was about to open soon, and it was time to party! The vibe from everyone was like an instant connection. That was only the second time that everyone was together, and it seemed like we all had been knowing each other for years. I could tell that this was going to be a magical movement! That night we all partied and had a ball.

The next day I decided that Tuesday night meetings would be the norm and we would always end the meeting with a party. Being as though we weren't paying anyone, I wanted to make everyone's experience as fun and pleasurable as possible. Kidd decided that he was going to get sweatsuits and t-shirts made with our label, Holla Back Entertainment and logo on them. Everyday after that meeting, Kidd would call me as soon as he woke up, which was usually early in the morning, regardless of what he did the night before and ask me "Yo, what are our plans for today?" Kidd financially provided the mothership and depended on me to fly it.

My single "Hang Low" was still being played in the clubs but the song was so raunchy that it could never be played on the radio. My album was pretty much done but I still wanted to add another song or two. One day while riding around town with Kidd, an old school classic came on the radio called "I Got Five On It" by the Luniz. The melodic track put me in a trance and as the song played, my mind began to block out the Luniz and melodies of my own lyrics began to spend around in my head. It was always something about a R&Bish track that drew me in. I think back to when I was in college and performed my "DL" classic song to the Isley Brothers "Groove with You" and to go back even further, when I was a kid writing R&B before I saw Krush Groove and started rapping. Hip Hop drums with an R&B sample or even a straight R&B track always brought out the storyteller in me and usually I would expose my own ugly truths. I guess that was my way of releasing.

A few days later, I wrote sort of like a sequel to my popular song "Always" to the "I Got Five on It" instrumental entitled Crazy Love. Crazy Love is a song that I wrote about my relationship with Anna detailing all of the ups and downs but more shockingly, the dark side- visually describing the arguments and physical fights. I put it all in the song. I even brought our son Peanut to the studio and told him to say "Hi Mommy" at the beginning of the song and to really bring the song to life, I wrote a very graphic detailed hook and got Woody from Dru Hill to sing it. Scola was at the studio one day and while the song was playing, he kept telling me how much he liked the record so I asked him if he could jump on it and lay down some ad libs and riffs behind me and Woody's main vocals. Scola as always, (no pun intended) was down for the cause and just like that, I had two members of Dru Hill on the song which gave me the green light to entitle the song: Cooli Hi featuring Dru Hill- Crazy Love.

Sidenote: A few years later, I re- recorded Crazy Love but this time Jazz (from Dru Hill) laid down the ad libs behind me and Woody's main vocals. The version with Scola is on my Crown Victoria album. The version with Jazz is only on You Tube.

After Crazy Love was completed, I felt like my album was done. Everything else was just extra at that point. All of the subjects, emotions and topics I wanted to touch were in place. I was satisfied.

One day Kidd called me per usual in the morning to get the days agenda and told me that a local DJ was putting together a mix tape and wanted us to record a song for it. That night Kidd and I went to the studio and picked a track from and instrumental CD that had a party type vibe and began to write to it. Till this day, I don't know who the track actually belonged to. Since the track was an instrumental and going to be on a street mixtape, I didn't put a lot of creative thought into it. I just went with the vibe. I decided to use an old Onyx hook that I liked called "All We Got Is Us" (with a slight twist) as the chorus of the song. I went first on the song and Kidd followed with the second verse. The record came out amazing! So amazing that Sisqo heard us banging the song on repeat through the floor and vents and came down to the studio and jumped on the hook! A few days later, Lil Mo was at the studio (she and Kidd were close friends at the time) heard the song and jumped on it also! And just like that, almost in the blink of an eye, we had a song featuring Sisqo and Lil Mo! Being as though I used Onyx hook, the song really didn't have an identity to me because I looked at it like it was just a freestyle, us having fun on someone else's track but the more we played the song for people at Sisqo's house, the more people started to respond to it in a major way. The only problem was it didn't have a name. I decided to name the song "Trust'.

When the song was released on the mixtape, it immediately took off. Every DJ in the city was blowing up Kidd's phone asking for the song. Before we knew it, "Trust" was being played in every club and was gradually making its way to the 9pm radio mix shows. Kidd and I couldn't believe it! This was a freestlye that we made to someone else's track and its being treated like it's a single! No one knew that the track didn't belong to us, not even Sisqo or Lil Mo. It wasn't that Kidd and I manipulated them; it just never came up. Sisqo and Lil Mo both liked the song and jumped on it and Kidd and I didn't think to mention it because it was originally for a street mixtape. The record just organically took off!

Once Trust started picking up steam, Kidd and I decided that we would make the streets of Baltimore feel our presence by appearing EVERYWHERE! But unlike the other local record labels in town that moved around almost like a gang, with 50 plus guys in t-shirts causing mayhem, Kidd and I decided that we would have our Holla Back Team move on a higher level. We gave the girls Holla Back t- shirts, hoodies, hats, sweatsuits etc. and allowed them to always be in the forefront. The girls would cut up their t- shirts in a sexy way, exposing their six pack stomachs, throw on some tight jeans and absolutely kill the scene with their presence! So when we walked in the clubs, we had between 7 – 10 of the hottest girls in the city with us, all dressed in Holla Back apparel and my team (street dudes) - the Crown Vic Click dressed in all Black appearing to be down for whatever. Kidd's cousin, Derrick was a security guard/ club bouncer (6'6"- 280lbs) and he was with us all of the time, so it appeared as if we had security which made us look like stars, but actually he was just Kidds cousin rolling with us. The entire movement looked BIG! Not to mention, we had a hot song with Sisqo and Lil Mo playing everywhere!

Understanding the momentum, I knew we had to move fast in order to capitalize off of what was happening. I sat down with each member of our Holla Back Team and had a conversation with them in regard to what was needed from them individually. When it was time for me to sit down with Tanja, I felt a little intimidated. Again, she was so pretty to me. I knew I wanted her but although I had my accolades, I felt like she was still out of my league. She seemed like the types of Kidd and Sisqo's which explained why Kidd had already had relations with her.

Sidenote: Kidd ONLY dealt with the hottest of the hot! He wouldn't even speak to girls who weren't in model conversations.

The night Tanja and I had our conversation, we were downstairs at our club sitting at a table sort of tucked off in a corner. I did most of the talking. Tanja just nodded her head and listened. I kept it very professional and delivered the message that I wanted to get across. When it was over, we both went upstairs to the office, had our collective team meeting, and partied afterwards.

The next day Tanja called me to further go over what we had individually talked about. Tanja and I began to talk about last night's discussion and before we knew it, we had drifted off and started talking about everyday life. Soon afterwards we were laughing and talking about everything under the sun. She actually confessed and told me the reason why she was just nodded her head and didn't say much at our initial one on one conversation was because he had just finished smoking some weed and was high out of her mind. "I had forgot that we were supposed to have our one on one conversation and smoked right before the meeting!" she said. "I figured I would just be quite because I didn't want to say anything crazy and have you thinking I was a little off" she added. We both burst out in laughter.

Tanja and I talked on the phone every day after that conversation. She told me about her relationship with her ex-husband and how it ended, and I told her about my relationship with Chante. Everything was platonic and neither of us crossed any lines till one day we were talking on the phone and Tanja said in casual conversation that she needed to wash her hair. "You should let me wash it for you" I suggested. "Really!? You actually wanna wash my hair?" she sarcastically replied. "Hell yeah" I said. "Okay, so when and where would you like to do this?" Tanja asked. "Lets link up tonight after our routine Tuesday meeting when the club closes" I responded. Tanja agreed and we both hung up.

Later that night after our Holla Back staff meeting, I was so ready to skip the party and hook up with Tanja. I wanted her since the first time I laid eyes on her and tonight it was finally going to happen. We talked about me washing her hair but we both really knew what that meant.

Roughly around 1am, shortly before our club closed, I asked Tanja was she ready to leave and she said yes. We didn't want anyone to know what we were up to, so Tanja left out first and I followed a few minutes later and met her at her car. When I got in her car, Tanja looked at me and said "Where to?" "Lets go to Sisqo's house" I replied. We drove to Sisqo's house and the whole time while we were in route, I was hoping and praying that no one was there. Sisqo was out of town like always but I was hoping none of his sisters were there because they would stay at the house from time to time. Kidd was still at the club so I knew he wouldn't be there. When we arrived, the drive way was empty and all the lights were off in the house. I thought to myself thank God.

I went around the back of the house to the pool room and opened one of the sliding doors that we always left unlocked. Once inside I came to the front door and let Tanja in. Tanja and I went upstairs to one of the guest rooms and closed the door. Tanja took off her shoes, laid across the bed on her stomach, turned her head to the side while resting her head on her crossed arms and closed her eyes. I turned off the lights and being as though the shades were closed the room went immediately black.

I kneeled over top of Tanja, gently slid my hands up the bottom of her shirt and gently began to massage her lower back. As I slowly worked my way up her back, I could hear Tanja began to breathe heavily. As I made my way to her shoulders, I straddled her back in a way whereas my penis was pressed and pulsating between her back legs at the bottom of her ass. I then kneeled and whispered in her ear "You still want me to wash your hair?" We both slightly laughed and began to kiss. I then undressed Tanja before undressing myself, placed a condom on and we had sex. While in the mist of things, I made sure that I did everything I could think of to please her, and Tanja returned the same (we both are Scorpio's). So there we were, two pleasers trying to out please each other. Sexual bliss! When we were done, Tanja immediately got up out of the bed and turned the lights on. "What are you doing??" I jokingly asked. "I just wanted to visually see what was making me feel like that!" Tanja replied as she was staring at my penis. I grabbed Tanja, pulled her close to me, kissed her, turned off the lights and we had sex again.

The next day we both were floating around on cloud nine. Tanja sent emails to my two-way pager all day saying how much she enjoyed our time together and I felt the same way. Sex with Tanja was absolutely amazing! She didn't lack in any category, from how she moved her body, to how she felt, what she did, everything was amazing and let's not forget she was drop dead gorgeous to me!

Sidenote: Tanja was a Tomboy and had Tomboyish ways so a lot of people would overlook her beauty under the New York Yankee Baseball fitted, t- shirt and jeans but I could see through all of that and I would constantly remind and tell her how beautiful she was. She even one time expressed to me in a love letter that at one point she was confused and didn't know which lane she wanted to explore but after we connected, she was very clear of the direction she wanted to go in.

A few days passed and Tanja and I were secretly in separatable. We talked on the phone every chance we got and at night we would go wherever we could just to be together. The only problems were, for one, she slept with Kidd prior to me (I told Kidd the very next day that I slept with Tanja to make sure I didn't violate the Bro Code) so my pride wouldn't allow me to fall too deep for her and number two, I had my perfect girlfriend Chante at home with our baby boy Darrian. Also Tanja had 3 small kids that included a set of twins and collectively that all was a lot.

Meanwhile, outside of the romantic fling I was having with Tanja, Kidd and I, along with our entire Holla Back Team were preparing for the release of my debut album, following our single "Trust" entitled Crown Victoria. The release date was scheduled for March 25th, 2003. Shanna was my personal assistant as well as my creative partner so whenever I had an idea, all I had to do was mentioned it to her and she would bring it to life. Shanna arranged my photo shoot with a music producer that Butch and I worked with a while ago when we were Shock Trauma that switched professions and turned photographer by the name of Michael Clark. Shanna also used one of her many connections and linked us with a graphic designer by the name of Jer Olsen and sat with me for countless hours as we detailed every inch of the CD booklet as well as the CD itself. Shanna was also involved with setting up the company's website, our PO Box, business cards and 800 numbers. She had her hands in every pot that you could think of business wise.

Meanwhile, as we were continuing to appear everywhere in the city with our high-profile image, the cost of things was beginning to take a toll on Kidds pockets. He was funding the entire movement by himself. All of the posters, flyers, promotional CDs, t-shirts, sweatsuits, etc. were all being paid by Kidd alone. Not to mention he was still balling out of control in the clubs to maintain his image. The only thing Kidd didn't have to pay for was my album because everything involving cost, I took care of prior to us deciding to create a record label. In order to balance things out, Kidd decided to bring in another investor/ partner. The guy Kidd chose to bring in was a guy from DC by the name of Morris "Balldy" Henry. Balldy was a real estate investor that owned several properties between Baltimore and DC and even some apartment buildings. Balldy was business smart but didn't know much about the music industry. However, he was open to learning, a cool guy, and fit right in with our Holla Back family.

With the addition of Balldy, we were now able to do even more than before. Instead of one financial source we now had two! Everything enhanced! My posters were all over the entire city of Baltimore. The girls went out every weekend and ran my posters up every pole on every major corner and hotspot in town. Tanja was in charge of promotions and she made sure that my face was plastered EVERYWHERE!

Musically, the song Trust was still being played in the clubs as well as on the radio mix shows. Normally there was only one urban radio station in Baltimore and that was 92Q but out of nowhere came a new urban radio station called X105.7. X105.7 had the streets buzzing because people wanted something new. It was rapidly making its way to being the number one station in town. Our DJ who DJ'ed at our club and also when we did shows, DJ Quick Silver landed the job as the primary DJ on X105.7 and Kidd immediately saw an opportunity to excel.

One day Kidd came to me and Balldy and said we needed to talk. Kidd told us that he had a conversation with Quick about Trust being placed in rotation on X105.7. For those that don't know, the difference between being played on mix shows and being in rotation is when your song is being played on the mix show, its usually when a DJ has anywhere between 30 minutes to an hour and the DJ is mixing song after song sort of like a party atmosphere. Normally it's a 12 o'clock midday mix, a 5pm traffic jam mix and a 9pm night mix. When your song is in rotation, your song just naturally comes on the radio without a DJ mixing it in with other songs. It just comes on over and over again. That's why it's called rotation.

Balldy and I were very excited about the news till Kidd said "There's a catch. Quick hinted around about an iced out watch that he was very interested in and its safe to say, if we get him that watch, our song will be in rotation." "Fuck that! We ain't getting that nigga no watch! The song is hot! He should put it in rotation on the strength of the song!" Balldy said. "Yo Balldy, that's not how this music game is played. Sometimes you gotta give a little to get a little. I guarantee you, once X105.7 puts it in rotation, 92Q will follow! Trust me" Kidd replied. Balldy still wasn't trying to hear it. "Well its up to Cool" Kidd said. "You're the tie breaker. What's it gonna be?" I voted to buy Quick the watch. Business wise I figured, if it wasn't going to break us, it was definitely worth it and as an artist, there's nothing more fulfilling than hearing your song on the radio every hour. Balldy was still against it. Not sure of how things worked out, meaning I cannot confirm whether or not if Kidd bought Quick the watch or not because I personally didn't see it happen nor did I contribute to or buy the watch, but what I do know is a few days later, Trust was being played on the radio in rotation. I saw Quick later the night Trust debuted, at our club and he was wearing a brand new iced out watch.

Sidenote: When Quick Silver introduced the song or spoke of the song after it went off, he didn't know who the song belonged to. He would say "That was Sisqo, Lil Mo, Kidd and Cooli Hi's new song Trust!" Me knowing how Kidd operated, I knew that he wouldn't correct it because deep down Kidd didn't want me to get too much notoriety. I believed Kidd didn't mind that people didn't know Trust was MY song and everyone else was just featured on it. Kidd, in the long run, was looking out for himself. There's absolutely no way on planet earth that Kidd would have pushed for the rotation of Trust if he wasn't rapping on it. Kidds main objective was to have me kick in the door in order to make it easier for him when he came out with his solo project. I knew this. I would often refer to Kidd as Blade (from the movie), the vampire character played by Wesley Snipes. Kidd was naturally a vampire but I had to keep giving him serum in order to function as a human. But I knew it was just a matter of time before the vampire in Kidd came out and stayed out! I sent Quick a two way text and told him moving forward, the song is Cooli Hi ft. Kidd, Sisqo and Lil Mo- TRUST!

Now that Trust was in rotation, Kidd and I, as well as our Holla Back Team officially had Baltimore City in the palm of our hands. We were performing all over the city and even heading lining at some shows. Like Kidd said, shortly after x105.7 added Trust into rotation, 92Q followed behind and added it as well. Even our DC neighboring station 93.9 was starting to pick up and play the song. Trust was being played everywhere in our region and no one knew that it was just a mixtape record. When it was time to send the final version of my album off to be packaged and pressed up, Kidd asked me if I wanted to put Trust on my album. Again, Trust was SOMEBODY ELSE's track, someone else's song! We were just playing around with it and it took off. Although Trust had the city on fire, I decided not to put it on my album. I felt like I didn't need it. My album was hot enough without it.

In handling the business details of my album, Kidd and I didn't follow any of the rules. My album had 19 songs on it and we didn't pay any of the producers at all. We didn't pay any of the few features as well. We didn't pay anyone. The only thing we paid for was mixing and mastering (and I paid for the majority of that because again, the album was close to done prior to us creating the label). Our thought process was once we get picked up by a major label or distributor, we will circle back and compensate everyone. Everyone received their publishing splits, but we didn't pay anyone at all. All of the producers on my album were okay with the process because they saw the impact we were making around town. The only producer that kicked up some dust was Nokio. He called me and Kidd and was kind of upset about us putting "The Realest" on my album without his permission. He explained that he created the track with some of his partners and their permission was needed as well. Kidd and I didn't care. The song was hot and had Sisqo and Nokio on it. There was no way that I wasn't using that record. We basically told Nokio the same thing we told the other producers; when we blow, you blow!

As my March 25th 2003 release date approached, Trust went from normal rotation to heavy rotation and was now the number one requested song in the city on x105.7. This accomplishment got Sisqo's attention. You see in the beginning, Sisqo knew that we started the label but like all things, it had to be BIG or make some kind of noise to intrigue him. Hearing our song in rotation, not to mention him being on the record, got Sisqo's full attention and he started to be more open and receptive in our movement. He even started doing shows with us which of course took our performances to an all time high! I would complete my entire set and close the show out with Trust and bring Sisqo out and sometimes even Lil Mo!

Sidenote: Lil Mo and Kidd were close friends and she would hang out in the studio at Sisqo's house with us a lot. As I mentioned previously, that's how she got on the song. Lil Mo was very cool and down to earth. She cracked a lot of jokes and was very fun to be around. She was an incredible songwriter (she wrote a song for Lovher that I loved entitled "A Girls Gotta Do What a Girls Gotta Do") and she and I along with Butch recorded a freestyle type record to one on Nas's tracks in addition to Trust. Lil Mo's involvement with our Holla Back Team and the record Trust is how she met Quick Silver (our DJ at the time) and the two of them later went on to do big things! Of course, us being guys, I asked Kidd the golden question, if he was sleeping with Lil Mo. Kidd said he wasn't.

Kidd began to book us shows everywhere and Sisqo was starting to come around more often. One of our more memorable shows was when we performed at UMBC for their homecoming along with Ludacris. As usual we had our entire crew, the Holla Back girls in their sweatsuits, the Crown Vic Click and Sisqo and Lil Mo to close the show out. Shanna would always bring her camcorder and record everything from the audience. According to the response of the crowd, we blazed that performance and the crowd lost their minds when Sisqo came out at the end. Ludacris and his DTP crew went on after us. The reason why this show stands out to me is because while Ludacris was performing, one of the bouncers back stage came to me and said "Hey man do you mind if I give you a little advice?" "Sure" I said. "What's up". The bouncer then went on to say "Yo I listened to your songs as you were performing and all of them are hot, but your performance energy was low. Do you see how Ludacris is moving out there? That's how you have to move! I can tell that you're a laid back kind of guy but if you ever boosted up your performance, it would take your show from a 5 to a 10!" I shook the bouncers hand and thanked him for his feedback.

The next day, I asked Shanna to bring me the footage of the show and I began to watch and analyze my performance. The bouncer was right. I didn't move like I thought I was moving in my head. This taught me valuable lesson. Sometimes you can't see yourself until you actually "see" yourself. In my mind as I was performing, I was killing it but when I watched the video tape, it was the total opposite. The lyrics in my bars were very wordy and it didn't give me a lot of spaces to breathe when performing live so moving forward I started relying on Butch and Kidd (who were my hype men) to catch my ending words more in order to breathe better. I strategically picked my spots to do so and that allowed me to breathe better which in return gave me more energy to be active on stage.

After the UMBC show and seeing the response and impact we had on the city, Sisqo wanted in. He came to me and Kidd and told us he wanted to partner up with us as owners of Holla Back Entertainment. He then began to go through my entire album to find a song that he could jump on as a feature. The only problem was, my album was already packaged and pressed up, and scheduled to be released. Sisqo decided that he wanted to do a remix to one of my songs entitled "Grown Ass". He was already featured on "The Realest" but Sisqo knew

"The Realest" was a slow grimy track and he wanted to be on a more up-tempo party track. Sisqo jumped on "Grown Ass" and added an additional spice to the already catchy chorus.

In addition to Sisqo jumping on one of my songs, Kidd suggested that Sisqo should invest money into the company. Kidd's thought process was since he funded Holla Back all by himself until Balldy came aboard, if Sisqo now wanted to be apart of the movement, he needed to give him some of the money he already invested back or fund the movement alone moving forward until Sisqo's dollar amount matched his. Kidd had his eyes on this Play Back machine (a device that could store hundreds of songs as well as many sound effects- for performing purposes) for a long time and he decided to use this opportunity to grab it. He asked Sisqo to purchase the machine and Sisqo agreed. At the time, the machine was maybe $2,500.

Once we had the playback machine, our already top notch performance rose to even a higher level because at the push of a button we could start and play any track we had loaded. At shows, Kidd and I would often play around with that advantage by stopping a song dead in the middle, speak to the crowd to get them hyped up and drop the song all over again with bombs going off and exciting sound effects. It was a dream tool to have as a performer. Before this tool and like the other artist in the city, we had to perform off a CD, so if the CD skipped, we were in bad shape or if we wanted to stop or start over, someone would literally have to stop the CD and play the track from the very beginning. With this playback machine, we could do whatever we wanted, and it didn't take long for Quick Silver to master every feature. I remember going to shows and hearing other rap crews whisper to each other as we set up "Yo watch this! These dudes got some kind of machine that plays all of their music at the drop of a dime!" Kidd and I both would hear the murmurs so when it was sound check time, we would show off and give our peers a show before the show by highlighting all of the bells and whistles of the Playback machine.

Meanwhile on the personal side, I was still spending nights at Chante's, waking up early to take my son Peanut to school (picking him up also), taking my father on his monthly routine runs (grocery store, pharmacy, the bank etc.) and having Darrian until Chante finished whatever she was doing, then linking up with Kidd to get back to work (Chante breast fed Darrian so my time with Darrian without Chante was at a minimum. She would pump out a few bottles and return just before the bottles ran out). I wasn't driving my Crown Victoria anymore because I kept getting violations and tickets for having such a dark tent on the windows (that I refused to remove). I also had insurance violations, so my tags were suspended. My mother would allow me to drive her car and that's how I got around.

This was my normal routine except for my nights with Chante were beginning to slow down because I was getting closer and closer to Tanja. Tanja had a house that she used to live in that had some pipe issues which caused the house not to have any heat. Tanja couldn't afford to have it fixed so she let the house go. Tanja and her three kids were living with her uncle but she still had access to the house. Every night after clubbing, promoting, or doing a show, Tanja and I would go into that ice cold house and have sex all night long. It was like we could never get enough of each other.

When Tanja officially lost the house, Tanja and I didn't have anywhere to go so we began to get creative. We did the normal things like when her uncle wasn't home, or when my mother wasn't home, and even going to a friends house but when those options weren't available, Tanja and I would make love any and everywhere! You name a place, and we probably were intimate there. From the back seat of cars to public parks, laundry mats, playgrounds, on trails in the woods, outside openly on the hood of cars, there was no place or nothing off limits. Our physical attraction to one another was almost like something you would see in a fantasy sex movie. Our bond was so strong that we couldn't detach from one another.

One day while at my mother's house, Tanja stopped by and to me to come outside, she wanted to show me something. When I went outside to her car, she smiled and showed me her wrist. Tanja had gotten a new tattoo. The tattoo was in the form of a bracelet with a heart shaped charm at the end. Inside the charm it had the initials "DJ". When I saw the tattoo and the initials, it didn't hit me that they were MY initials, so I asked her "What does DJ stand for?" "They're your initials fool!" Tanja replied as she punched me on my arm. The reasons why the initials didn't register with me were because for one, everyone called me Cool, Kool aid, or Cooli (short for Cooli Hi). I hadn't referred to my initials "DJ" since I was a kid and secondly Tanja and I had just started seeing each other. It couldn't have been more than a little over a month since we first slept together so I didn't think that she would get my name tattooed on her. But that's just who Tanja was. She loved extremely hard and when she liked or loved someone, there was absolutely nothing on earth that she wouldn't do for them.

There were a lot of assumptions going around within our Holla Back family about Tanja and I but no one knew for sure until they saw the tattoo. The tattoo confirmed what everyone thought and Tanja and I didn't hide our relationship moving forward. We were official yet unofficial because I was still with Chante and I didn't have any intention of leaving her. At this time, Chante had moved out of the city (Hartford County, MD) and she never had any ties in the streets of Baltimore so I didn't have to worry about someone seeing Tanja and I out somewhere and going back to tell her. Besides, worst case scenario, I could always say that Tanja works on our Holla Back team and that was the truth.

Once Shanna found out about Tanja and I, she became a little jealous and started taking shots whenever the opportunity presented itself. "Wow, she got your name tattooed on her!? What did you do to that girl Cool? Oh I know, the same things you used to do to me huh?" Shanna would say. Shanna and I would go back and forth with the sassy convo and before I knew it, we would be at her apartment or at Sisqo's house having sex. So at the time I was sleeping with Tanja constantly and Shanna sporadically. Not to mention, I had Chante at home and occasionally I was with Evette, my childhood crush which was now the girl who braided my hair. Shanna of course knew about Tanja but Tanja did not know about Shanna. I told Tanja that Shanna and I dated in the past, but she had no idea that I was still sleeping with her.

Tanja and I had so much in common that it was scary. I discovered new things and grew more attracted to her every single time we were together. She was the smartest girl (book smart) that I had ever met yet she was hood at the same time. Normally you get one of the two traits in a person; both are very rare. She was a tomboy at heart but at the same time the most vulnerable in intimate situations and a sex goddess in the bedroom. We both liked and loved the same way and we showered each other with what we both craved for effortlessly. Some nights when we didn't have anywhere to go, we would spend the night in each other's arms in the backseat of a car. We would make love sporadically anywhere without thought broad day or night. You couldn't leave us together anywhere because we would always find a way to be intimate, whether it be oral, touching until someone climaxed or actual intercourse and to put the icing on the cake, she genuinely wanted to see my career take off and would do anything to see that happen.

Tanja and I were dangerously perfect for one another but there were just a few things that always kept a slight wall up on my side. I couldn't get over the fact that Kidd had slept with her prior. Tanja also revealed to me that she slept with Balldy also (it was years before Holla Back. They met at a club, dated for a few and slept together. Didn't speak in years and then Balldy walks though the Holla back doors…. Go figure). Now, not only do I have Kidd in the back of my mind, but I also now have Balldy too! On top of that Tanja had three small kids and I had Chante and Darrian at home. There was no way that I was going to leave my "perfect" girlfriend and child to be with someone with three kids and had previously slept with two of my friends/ business partners but being with Tanja felt perfect so I wasn't going to stop.

Meanwhile Kidd knew that I was sleeping with both Tanja and Shanna and his energy began to slightly shift a little. Kidd wasn't trying to sleep with Tanja again, but he did want to know (like the average man in regards to someone he slept with) that if he wanted to, he could but when he saw the tattoo and how much Tanja was into me, he began to feel a certain way. Tanja wasn't mean to him but when she was in Tomboy mode and friend-boxed him and then came over to me and turned into an angel, Kidd didn't like it. Kidd also tried to test the waters with Shanna occasionally, but Shanna shut him down.

I began to see the "Blade" in Kidd oozing out because it appeared as if I had the girls "plural" as well as the album about to drop with Trust being proclaimed as MY song all over the radio. When I saw the envy in Kidds eyes, I immediately gave him a shot of human serum to bring him back to normal. "Yo as soon as my album drops, we should start working on yours so there's no down time between the albums." I said to him. "Yeah you're right" Kidd replied. I then suggested that we should get John to mix two records that Kidd did a while ago so that they can kick off the start of HIS project. Kidd was all for it. Then Kidd said to me "Yo I have the perfect idea for the release of your album! We are going to perform live in the middle of Mondawmin Mall!

Mondawmin Mall is a popular urban mall on the west side of Baltimore that had a hood/ ghetto type reputation. Other artist had in store appearances at the FYE Record store there, but no one, local or national had ever performed in the middle of the mall. Kidd used his influence, along with our affiliation with Dru Hill and Sisqo and got the green for us to perform. In addition to the performance, Dru Hill and Sisqo were scheduled to make a guest appearance and afterwards we all would sign everyone's CD after purchase. Afterwards we were topping the night off by having an exclusive pool party at Sisqo's house and the entire event was sponsored by 92Q.

A few weeks before the release of my album and the big show at Mondawmin Mall, Tanja and our promotional team had my posters and flyers EVERYWHERE! Tanja was doing such a great job with our promotions, other record company promo directors were offering her positions on their team but Tanja respectfully declined. Tanja was as loyal as they came.

Once every so often, we all would go to X105.7 as guest on Quick Silvers night show. After a brief interview Quick would always put on some instrumentals and allow us to burn down the air waves. Kidd never rapped live on the radio or anywhere so times like this Butch would step up. I also would bring Big Status (Mupp's cousin) from the King of The Hill project and the three of us would freestyle live on the air representing Holla Back Entertainment and the Crown Vic Click. Per usual, Shanna was always there videotaping. One day Quick invited us to come join him on his radio show for and interview only. On this particular night, it was just myself and a local upcoming solo female artist by the name of Paula Campbell. Kidd and Shanna were there as always but I conducted the interview alone. The interview went well and Trust was still the number one requested song in the city.

The very next morning, Kidd called me and said "Yo, turn your radio on to X105." I got up and turned the radio on. When the station connected, all I heard was rock music. I checked the dial to make sure I had the correct station. When it was confirmed, I asked Kidd, "Yo what the hell is this?" "Yo, they fired the entire radio station and changed their format!" Kidd replied. "Damn! We were just there last night!" I said. Kidd went on to say "That's the nature of the beast." And just like that, my number one song was gone.

Now that X105.7 was gone Kidd and I knew we had to get 92Q fully on board. The only problem was, we lost our leverage. 92Q now was the only urban radio station in town so they held all of the cards. Trust was being played there but no way near as much as it was being played on X105.7. This was going to be an uphill battle. We put all of our energy into X105. We were always there doing interviews, drops and freestyles, rightfully so because Trust was in heavy rotation over there. Not to mention we had Quick Silver over there as well. At 92Q we knew everyone over there but we weren't in "business" with anyone over there. Kidd and I decided that we would address the situation after the Mondawmin Show.

The big day March 25th 2003 had finally arrived and my debut solo album "Crown Victoria" was released. This was also the day that my biggest solo show to date, in the middle of Mondawmin Mall was going down also. All day leading up to showtime, 92Q was promoting the show as well as the release of my new album. The turnout was expected to be record breaking.

Being as though my name was ringing all over the city and radio and it was the release day of my album, Chante decided she wanted to attend the show. I always told her before that I didn't want her at my shows because sometimes hip-hop shows got out of hand and it would be a distraction for me because I would be worrying about her safety. I couldn't look out for her, being in a protective mode and be who I needed to be to perform at the same time. My mind needed to be free from all distractions. This was the truth but not the whole truth because I also didn't want Chante around all of the shenanigans I had going on. I wasn't worried about Tanja or Shanna saying something to Chante about our relationships. They both knew that Chante was top priority however I didn't want to put Chante in a bad position where everyone knew what was going on except her. I convinced Chante to stay at home with our son, well at least I thought I did because I later found out that she came to Mondawmin Mall anyway, with our baby boy Darrian and watched the performance from a far so I wouldn't see them.

Before the show, when we arrived at the mall, the security officers escorted us into a business room that I never knew existed in Mondawmin. Kidd and I, along with our entire Holla Back team, including Dru Hill and Sisqo were in the room preparing for the show. The vibe reminded me of when we were on tour with the Backstreet Boys backstage eating fruit and drinking Red Bulls gearing up for the performance.

As always, independent clothing lines would give me and Kidd clothes to wear to promote their brand and for this show we agreed to wear the clothes but when we got the sweatsuit, Kidds fitted perfect but mine was too small. I didn't bring any back up outfit because I was solely depending on the promo sweatsuit. I was pissed. I didn't know what I was going to do. I started stretching the sweatpants, sagging them around my waist, trying to see if I could make it work. It was a lot of commotion going on but I remember looking for Tanja to get her opinion on how the too small sweatsuit looked, but I couldn't find her. Then all of a sudden, out of nowhere, Tanja pulled me to the side and said "babe, put this on!" When Tanja saw that the sweatsuit was too small, she ran out into the mall, went to several stores, bought me a pair of jeans, a white t shirt and a hat and got back just in time for me to throw it all on and head to the stage. Tanja saved the day once again!

Sidenote: The only thing I didn't have was a belt so I had to hold my pants up the entire time while I performed.

When we exited the dressing room and headed to the stage, you would have thought the President of the United States was entering the room. The Holla Back girls lead the way followed by 5 or 6 security/ bodyguards. Following the security you had my Crown Vic Click and then Butch, Kidd and me. The turnout was amazing. There were people as far as the eye could see. My posters were plastered everywhere! Quick Silver was DJing and Reggie Reg was the host. We blazed the show and closed it out with Sisqo performing Trust. After the performance, Sisqo and I autographed every purchased CD and then we all headed to Sisqo's house to kick off the Album Release pool party!

This pool party was one for the books. We had so many people attend that we had everyone park their cars at a nearby shopping mall parking lot and had a shuttle transport them to and from Sisqo's house. The pool house was packed as well as the pool and we set up a stage on the balcony and I performed my entire set again at the party. Some would say that it was my best performance to date! You name it, from radio personalities to magazine and newspaper writers, everyone who was anyone was there. We had the time of our lives, got drunk and celebrated all night long.

The very next day Kidd and I were back on our grind, on the phone trying to figure out a way to get 92Q fully on board, similar to what we had with X105. Even if we could, I knew another "watch" situation wasn't going to happen so I had to come up with something that would get us over the top. Kidd and I both decided that we would attempt to force 92Q to put Trust into heavy rotation by using heavy promotion.

A week after the release of my album, 92Q was still playing Trust on the mix shows but just here and there in rotation. Kidd and I decided it was time. On a Sunday night, we all went to the radio station (92Q) and plastered my posters everywhere! All on the front doors, up and down every single pole in the area, even in the tree's outside of the office and we sprinkled my flyers all over the ground surrounding the front door like confetti. We went completely overboard. It was border line vandalism. When the program director (Nikki) came to work Monday morning, she was beyond pissed off. She immediately called Kidd and told him if we didn't send someone there to remove what we did, 92Q would never play another Cooli Hi record again. Mouse and his wife Melinda went to the radio station and cleaned up the mess. That was strike one.

A few weeks later, everything was still going according to plan. We were still performing and showing up everywhere with our dominant presence and the CD was selling out of the stores. Every so often someone would ask me why Trust wasn't on the album and I would tell them that it was a promotional song only but as you can see the album is doing fine without it. Crown Victoria was doing very well and people were beginning to see me like I thought they would once they heard my collective work. This was my initial plan all along. I knew I always had the gift and the music, but I had no way of getting out to the masses. I believed that once people heard what I could do on a song, I could not be denied.

People were beginning to see me outside of Sisqo as well as outside of Kidd's right-hand man and my popularity began to soar. Now a power struggle was beginning to brew. I was no longer just the guy that rapped on Sisqo's song nor the guy that's seen with Kidd all of the time. I was now Cooli Hi, the guy we see and hear all over the city that put out the album called Crown Victoria! Kidd began to notice how much my popularity was growing and I could tell that he wasn't too fond of it. Not to mention, he was still feeling a way about my access to Tanja that he no longer had.

Kidd was the type that always wanted to keep the ones around him, needing him. I believe that he thought "as long as they need me, I'll always have the leverage but the moment they don't need me, they will leave." That's why instead of putting people in position to get things on their own, he would rather buy it for them, or give it to them. A weak-minded person would think that he's looking out or helping them when actually he's manipulating them. I saw right through this from day one and I must admit, I used his ambition to shine to my advantage and pushed for the start of the record label. I wanted my talents to be showcased so I could be seen and heard and I used Kidd to make this happen. But on the flip side, he was using me also. He needed me to validate him in these grimy Baltimore streets with my style of music, in order to open the door for his pop/party style that would follow.

While Kidd and I were secretly playing chess against one another, Sisqo was starting to feel a way about Kidd's upcoming. You see Sisqo knew about the publishing deal Kidd signed and was patiently waiting for Kidd to at least offer some type of compensation or just acknowledge that he played a major part in Kidd getting the deal. But more time was going by and Kidd never said anything and on top of it all, Sisqo see's 745 BMW's (Two of them. Kidd originally had a blue one and then switched it for a silver one. He also bought Butta a BMW but soon took it back after an argument) a secret condominium that no one knew the location of (except me) and a record company that had the entire city in the palm of its hands. Sisqo's patience was running thin and I could tell a confrontation was on the rise.

One-night Sisqo, Kidd and I, along with our entire Holla Back family went out to a club. I cant remember if I performed that night or not but something big had to be going on because Sisqo wouldn't have been there if it wasn't. During the party portion of the night, Kidd got extremely drunk, so waisted that we had to carry him out of the club. Once outside, Butch and I put Kidd in the backseat of his Range Rover and Kidd passed out. As everyone was getting into their cars preparing to leave the club, I thought to myself "How can I get Kidd to his house without revealing where he lived?" Kidd didn't want ANYONE to know where he lived and I promised that I wouldn't tell anyone but now we have to drive him home because he's passed out. Sisqo came to me and said "Yo throw me Kidd's keys. I will follow you to his house since you're the only one that knows where it is." At that point, I was all out of options, half-drunk myself, so I decided that was the best route to go.

When we arrived at Kidd's condominium, Sisqo and I along with a few other cars that were following, all parked in front of the cluster of condo's that included Kidds. Charles was driving Sisqo's truck. Me and a few of the guys that were there got out of our cars and helped Kidd get out of his truck. Everyone stood around as I searched Kidds jacket pockets for his house keys. While this was going on, someone leaned Kidd up against the hood of Sisqo's truck to hold him up. Kidd had already thrown up all over himself and now he was leaning on Sisqo's hood drooling at the mouth. When I found Kidds house keys, I said to everyone "I got em. His house is over here" and I pointed to the cluster (four condo's combined). Sisqo saw the cluster and must have thought that the entire cluster belonged to Kidd. "Yo is this is house!?" Sisqo asked in amazement. "I can't believe it!" he went on to say. As Sisqo continued to question the house, I interjected and said "Naw Yo, this is a cluster of four condo's! Kidds condo is around on the other side." I saw a big relief on Sisqo's face when he realized that Kidd house wasn't bigger than his. We all then went over to Sisqo's truck to get Kidd and noticed that Kidd had accidently drooled all over Sisqo's hood while waiting. When Sisqo saw what Kidd had done, he went into a rage. "Since he wants to spit on my car, I'm a spit on his!" Sisqo walked over to Kidd's truck and spat on the hood. It was that very moment that I knew the two of them were approaching their demise. Sisqo was a little drunk as well, but as the old saying goes, drunks and kids will always tell or show their true feelings! We helped Kidd get in his house, got him situated and then we all went home.

The next day, I told Kidd about everything that happened. Kidd didn't pay it any mind. He knew exactly where Sisqo's energy was coming from and I honestly think that he didn't want to address it but a few days later the taboo topic finally hit the fan.

Butch, Kidd, Ole Man Joe and I were all standing outside in the drive way at Sisqo's talking when Sisqo and his girlfriend Tera pulled up. Tera was driving and Sisqo was in the passengers seat. Sisqo got out of his truck and walked over to us. Somehow almost immediately the conversation flipped and Sisqo and Kidd began to discuss Kidd's publishing deal.

Kidd's demeanor was very cocky when speaking of the deal. "Yo I got that publishing on my own! Sisqo you didn't have anything to do with it. I negotiated this deal, not you!" Kidd said. "Yo you wouldn't have anything to negotiate if it wasn't for me! Yeah you got the deal but you got it on the strength of what I gave you! And when you closed the deal, you didn't offer me any type of compensation or nothing! You're acting like you don't owe me anything!" Sisqo replied. Kidd then went on to say "I don't owe you nothing! This was MY deal! I don't owe you nothing and I'm not giving you nothing! Not even a thank you!" Kidd went on and on about how he didn't feel like he owed Sisqo and how he did it all by himself, so much that it broke Sisqo's heart right on the spot. Sisqo's eyes actually began to water up as he said "Well since you feel like I didn't help you get to this point, just go ahead and do you. All of yall, leave my house and don't ever come back!" Before an actual tear could fall, Sisqo went back to his truck and he and his girlfriend drove away.

It was an awkward silence for a moment after Sisqo drove away and then we all began to discuss what had just happened.

Butch and I told Kidd that he was dead wrong for what he said to Sisqo but Kidd kept defending his actions. You see Kidd thought just because he went through whatever channels he went through, sat in the many meetings and offices and negotiated his deal, he had only himself to thank for that. He also thought that Sisqo didn't need any money because he was a millionaire but Kidd didn't take into consideration the principle aspect. Kidd was also missing the fact that if it wasn't for Sisqo putting him on and practically giving him a percentage of the Thong Song, he wouldn't have a leg to stand on and wouldn't be in a position to negotiate ANYTHING! Sisqo birthed his entire musical existence. He even named him "Kidd" for Christ sakes and for Kidd to dismiss Sisqo like that was very hard to watch.

A few weeks went by and our movement was beginning to run a little dormant. Being as though Sisqo and Kidd had the big fall out, Sisqo cut us all off because he felt like if Kidd (his right hand) would betray him, who's to say if the others (including me) wont do the same so the access to Sisqo's house (but more importantly the studio) was cut completely off. I was pissed about the entire situation but Kidd just kept saying "Give him some time. Eventually it will all blow over".

Trust was still being played on the radio but it had hit its peak and was beginning to simmer down. This was a huge problem for me because I knew that Kidd would not financially put out or push a "real" single of my Crown Victoria album, one without him on it. The only two he backed were Hang Low (a song I labeled as a bonus track on my album because it wasn't a "Cooli Hi" record. It was strictly political) and Trust, both of which he rapped on. For the first time since we started the label, I couldn't see where our direction was going.

Kidd also began to pass over some of the business negotiation responsibilities to me. Kidd had set up a meeting with a Regional music mogul named Shawn Ceasar to work out an additional distribution deal with his company DTLR. Usually Kidd would handle these types of meetings but for some reason he asked me to handle. Before I went to the meeting, I called and asked Tanja if she would go with me.

When Tanja and I arrived at Shawn Ceasar's office, I was nervous. I felt like a fish out of water. My area of expertise was on the music side and organizing what needed to be done for the company to be successful, not negotiating deals. I didn't know the going percentages nor what I should ask for. Luckily, I had already knew Shawn Ceasar from performing at his events back in the days of Shock Trauma so we had a relationship however when it was time to talk business, I wasn't sure of myself so I didn't speak with authority and confidence. Several times Shawn had to ask me to repeat myself because I was talking so low that he couldn't hear what I was saying.

After the meeting was over and we came to an agreement, Tanja and I left. When we got in the car, Tanja looked over to me and said "Babe, no one should ever have to ask a grown man to speak up. Even if you're not sure, say it like you're sure and if you have to, make them believe a lie with an authoritative voice!" This was just one of many things Tanja taught me. In addition to many life lessons, Tanja also taught me the basic fundamentals of how to use a computer. Kidd taught me how to use Pro Tools in a recording studio- using Apple products, but Tanja taught me the basic fundamentals of a PC, Ctrl Z & C, how to send attachments in emails, etc. Tanja as well as Shanna filled in all of the gaps on my administrative side (but more so Tanja).

Since we didn't have access to Sisqo's house anymore, we began to use the club even more as a melting pot. Our Tuesday night crowd was beginning to slow down a little because of fights that broke out (majority of the fights were my cousins and their Park Heights crew beating up on other crews). In order to bring in more revenue we began bringing in female strippers and charged higher entry fees for the guys to come in and watch the show. We even had a "special" room for the guys to go in if they wanted a private one on one with a stripper and whatever happened in the room, stayed in the room! I knew a girl name Justice and she would bring her girls along with some girls Kidd and Balldy knew and the club turned strip club would be on fire! Even my ex girlfriend from DeMartim Records, Lia was there stripping also. This went on for several weeks until the crowd began to get too large and the Korean owners of the club started to worry that the club would get shut down because of restrictions.

After the stripper phase ended, we went back to our normal Tuesday nights. One night after our Holla Back weekly meeting, Shanna came to me and said we had to talk. Shanna told me that Jene (one of our Holla Back girls) was stealing money from the front door when we were having the stripper parties.

Kidd and I had been knowing Jene long before Holla Back was even thought of. When we decided to put together our Holla Back team, Jene was the very first girl we called. She and Hot used to date. Jene worked at Footlocker and used to give us all discounts whenever we bought sneakers from her store. She had been down with us since day one. Ironically, she and Shanna just so happened to be as close as sisters also.

I could tell from the look in Shanna's eyes that she felt uncomfortable telling me about what Jene did. Apparently when Jene was collecting money at the front door, she pocketed some of the cash. She told Shanna the reasoning was because of all of the hard work she put in promoting Holla Back that she felt like she deserved some sort of compensation. Shanna said that she told Jene that she was wrong for taking the money but Jene showed no remorse. I told Kidd and Balldy what happened and we all decided to cut ties with Jene and I was left with the responsibility of letting her know.

The next week, after our meeting, I pulled Jene to the side and said "Lets talk". Jene and I sat at a table in the corner of the club. This was very hard for me. How do you quote unquote "fire" someone that you have never paid one cent? Everything she and the rest of our team did and was doing was strictly volunteering up to this point. I was extremely grateful because I knew, without Jene and the others, my album would just be stored on a hard drive. They were just as important as the music to me and to top it all off, Jene was a long-time friend. Nevertheless, I told Jene that we knew about what she had done, and her services were no longer needed. Before Jene left, she turned to me and said, "Wow, I can't believe my sister ratted me out over some dick!" We both casually laughed and Jene left.

Sidenote: The money stolen didn't mean anything to us. It was the principle. Jene and I still remained friends after this incident. I flirted with Jene before this incident and even after. Hell, I flirted with every pretty girl I came across back then. We even messed around one time, came close but did not have sex. Jene was a good person that just made a mistake.

Not long after the Jene incident, Kidd's intuition came to past. I'm not sure if the two of them talked it out or not but somehow Kidd and Sisqo squashed their beef and we all were back at the house. Sisqo and Kidd were still working out the details of Sisqo's partnership with our label. Up until this point, Sisqo had only purchased the Play Back Machine. Kidd suggested to Sisqo, that since he funded the majority of the expenses up till now, Sisqo should fund the remaining until they both are equal. I'm not sure if Sisqo even knew that Balldy even existed financially. Just like before with the Playback Machine, Sisqo agreed but this time he gave Kidd access to one of his credit cards. Not sure of what kind of limitations were discussed. All I knew was Kidd had Sisqo's credit card and was off to the races.

One night, I had a show in DC and everyone was at Sisqo's house preparing as we always did. Tanja along with her right hand in promotions, a guy that Kidd brought to the team by the name of Pig, had already been to the DC club and plastered my posters and flyers all over the area. Everything was set and waiting for our arrival. Moments before we left out to head for DC, I was sitting on the couch next to Tanja and I noticed Kidd starring at us through my peripheral vision. The look wasn't good, and I could tell that the vampire in Blade was about to surface, and I was all out of serum.

When we arrived at the club in DC, everyone that was anyone in our region was there from radio personalities, DJ's, program directors, new paper reporters, they all were there. As we were walking in, I saw Kidd starring over to his far-left mean mugging someone. Kidd was never the type that liked confrontation, so I was shocked to see him act that way. I followed his eyes in the direction where he was looking and I only saw girls in the area, one of which was the Program Director at 92Q (Nikki). I looked back at Kidd to make sure I didn't read his facial expression wrong and then I saw him lip talking saying "Fuck you" without actually saying it (just moving his mouth). Then he put up his two middle fingers! I tapped him and said "Yo, who are you talking too?" Kidd never responded as he kept starring in Nikki's direction. Soon afterwards I got distracted and before I knew it, it was time to perform.

A few days after the show, I noticed that I wasn't hearing Trust on the radio at all. I called a few people I knew that worked at the station and was told that there were signs up everywhere in 92Q saying "Do not play any music by Cooli Hi"! I had officially been black balled. Now I'm not sure if what Kidd did at the show caused this to happen or not but what I was sure of is Kidd was the reason I got blackballed because I had no dealing with the "powers that be" at the radio station. Kidd handled all of that. Maybe Kidd and someone had a big argument and that was the reason he acted the way he did at the show. Who knows? The only thing I did know was that signs were up and I needed them to come down.

Shortly after this, I spoke with Jamaal and he told me some alarming news. First, he confirmed that Kidd was beefing with the program director (not sure of the reason) and that was the cause of my music being blackballed at the station. Secondly, he told me that Kidd was in the process of pressing up promotional posters to promote his album. Jamaal then went on to inform me that Kidd was done with the Crown Victoria push and ready to move forward with his own project.

I was extremely pissed. Kidd was attempting to kill my project before it even had a chance. Not one single was released from my actual album. Only promo songs that he was featured on. The vampire in Blade was out and there was no turning back.

Being as though Jamaal told me Kidd's plan in confidentially, I didn't let Kidd know that I knew what he had planned. At our weekly Holla Back meetings conversations were short and you could tell that tension was in the air. The entire staff was beginning to split in half and choose sides. Kidd was secretly attempting to recruit as many as he could to support his movement because he knew that I would not nor anyone that was down with me. Like I mentioned before, not one song from my album was released as an actual single so how could I be okay with pulling the plug. Our Holla Back team slowly divided into two separate teams and I knew it was just a matter of time before it all ended. Then I got a call from Sisqo that sealed the deal on everything.

Sisqo called and asked me to come out to his house. When I got there, he dropped a bomb in my lap in regard to Kidd and I knew there was no coming back after this. Sisqo told me that Kidd was stealing money from him. "Check this out" Sisqo said as he handed me his credit card statement. The statement showed Kidd spending money at grocery stores, clubs (popping bottles), gas stations, etc. All personal purchases when he knew the credit card was given to him for Holla Back business purposes. It was also revealed that even before Holla Back, Kidd was stealing money by inflating prices of purchases for Sisqo and keeping the remaining for himself. For example, when Sisqo wanted new rims for his Benz or truck, he would send Kidd to take care of it. Kidd would tell him the cost was $10,000 but actually it may have been $7,500. Sisqo never questioned the cost. He just cut the check and Kidd would pocket the difference. Running up Sisqo's credit card for personal reasons, inflating prices and pocketing the difference in addition to the big fall out they just had about the publishing deal was the death of their relationship. That was the final straw and the reason why Sisqo called and told me all of this was because he had an alternatim. Sisqo told me if I continued to roll with Kidd, that he couldn't support my movement and rightfully so. This wasn't a problem for me because me and Kidd's business relationship was on the brink of destruction anyway. I told Sisqo that I was rolling with him, and I would cut ties with Kidd.

The next day Kidd called and told me that Sisqo accused him of stealing. His explanation for how he used Sisqo's credit card was he figured Sisqo "owed" him that money and he was using the card to break even. "Yo I footed the majority of the expenses up until now! How can Sisqo just come in now and expect to not pay what I had already paid? He gotta catch up!"

Kidd said. I replied, "Yo, we really haven't even cracked the surface! We didn't even release a single off the album yet!" This was me using this situation to drive home one of my own points. I then went on to say "Sisqo could have funded the entire movement moving forward until yall numbers evened out! That would have really helped the album take off but now its dead because he aint dealing with you no more." Kidd had no response because of ulterior motive. He wasn't thinking that way because he had no intentions on moving forward with my album.

The following Tuesday, the night of our weekly meeting, no one showed up including Kidd and myself. Somehow Kidd got the word that I knew of his plan to stop my album and start working on his. The situation was so touchy that neither one of us wanted to discuss it with each other, so we just gradually drifted apart. Kidd had his portion of the Holla Back staff and I had mine. I felt bad about putting our Holla Back Team in a situation where they literally had to choose a side, but it was what it was.

Kidd and I went from talking to each other all day everyday to not speaking to each other in weeks. Balldy tried to save the situation by getting both Kidd and I on the phone to discuss the matter and possibly resolve things. While Balldy was mediating, Kidd and I both didn't have too much to say to one another. I had my mind made up. I had ridden this train to its final stop and my mission was accomplished. The entire region knew who I was and recognized my talent. I felt like I didn't need Kidd anymore especially when I still had Sisqo. And the icing on the cake was I didn't have to be reminded of him and Tanja previously being together if he wasn't around because I had fell in love with her. The only thing that needed to be worked out was the revenue from the album sales.

Me not fully understanding the business side of things thought that since I wrote, arranged and put together my entire album, the revenue should come to me. Not some of it, all of it. I didn't consider the fact that Kidd and Balldy put out money to press the album up, promote it with posters, flyers, etc. and funded the entire Holla Back movement (regardless of motive) which made my brand soar. My logic was "Since you want to kill my album with your selfishness, I'll pocket all of the money!"

I called our distributer and told him that Holla Back was no more and the payment should come directly to me. Our distributer told me "Wow, that's funny, I just hung up with Kidd and he said the exact same thing! The payments should go to him!" I immediately became irate and started yelling and screaming at the distributer but then he stopped me and said "Cooli, relax man! I run into these situations all the time and whenever I do, I always side with the artist!" The distributer sent me all of the proceeds of my album and I didn't give Kidd or Balldy one penny of it. The nature of the music industry was turning me into a monster just like the rest of them and I didn't

Chapter 37 - The Death of Holla Back

Holla back Entertainment was officially over. I used Kidd and Kidd used me. I used Kidd to get my voice and talents out to the world and Kidd "attempted" to used me as a foundation to catapult his pop/ hip hop style of music in the hood environments of Baltimore Hip Hop.

The first thing I did when Holla Back was over was record a semi mix tape entitled "Free" to let everyone know that I was no longer affiliated with Kidd. On the title song "Free", I used Philly Freeways instrumental track FREE, and did a freestyle addressing the breakup. Like all of my songs, I always put it all in the music, whatever was on my mind, not holding back any punches by being very blunt, exposing what I felt. I would often tell on myself in songs all the time but a lot of people never caught what I was saying. For example, I would say it all the time in several freestyles that Holla Back was just a hustle to me. Crown Vic was what I cared about. I even said it at the end of my verse on our biggest radio song TRUST, "Holla Back be the hustle, Crown Vic the Click/ Cooli Hi need a doctor cause what I'm dropping is sick"

Sidenote: The women in my life would always say, "Dwayne won't say a word but Cooli Hi will tell it all! Whenever you want to know what's going on in his head, listen to his songs!"

I threw a few jabs at Kidd lyrically as well as verbally on the song "Free" and the remaining of the mix tape was just snippets of what was on my album and a few other freestyles. It wasn't nothing major. The main objective was to let everyone know that I was not affiliated with Kidd anymore, especially 92Q so the band could be lifted from my name.

Now that I didn't have Holla Back and all of the bells and whistles that came with it, I was now forced to move around town in a different way. Of the entire Holla Back staff, the only ones that came with me were Tanja and Shanna (for personal reasons of course) Ole Man Joe and Butch. Kidd took Sheena and Ashly. Jamaal and Pig initially went with Kidd also, but later left and joined forces with me. The rest of the team went back to their normal lives. With the absence of Kidd, Hot started coming back around as well.

Since I didn't have the Holla Back girls and Kidd's flash, My movement began to look very different. Instead of beautiful girls, I now had a bunch of dudes with me, primarily my Crown Vic Click (which were my cousins and my cousins homeboys) that knew absolutely nothing about the music industry. They were there just for a good time and trouble if trouble presented itself. I knew the importance of appearance (I learned that from Kidd) so I would always have Tanja or Shanna on my arm, looking like a million bucks to offset all of the thugs I had around me. Sometimes I would even go places with just Tanja or Shanna or even by myself.

One particular time, I remember going to a pool party where all of the local rappers and their teams were attending. It was being given by a group called JI 900. JI 900 was a two man group- Omar Little & Mr. Wilson both of which I knew personally. Omar and I grew up together since kids and Mr. Wilson (Mike Wilson) and I went to college together (UMES).

When I arrived, it felt like everyone at the party was starring at me. It was a hood event to the fullest, meaning a million guys, very few girls and of the few girls that were there, had a rough vibe. They were used to seeing me with the big entourage, pretty girls and flashy cars, but now here I am solo, all by myself and that's exactly what I wanted them to see. Kidd wouldn't have ever agreed to come to a function like this because of the rough vibe but I wanted to let everyone know that didn't already know that there was a big difference between me and Kidd. That's why I didn't bring anyone, not even my cousins. I wanted them to see me by myself, with an iced-out dragon chain on, moving around confident with no worries.

I received a lot of stares, but no one said anything offensive. I kicked it with JI 900 for a few and then I left but that party made me realize that being around the locals would always be an awkward situation. They will always look at me like an outsider because of my affiliation with Sisqo and Kidd. Only a few of them knew my back story and that my journey was entirely different from Kidd and Hots. Some even remembered my Shock Trauma days but not many. The only thing they couldn't deny was my music, my Crown Vic Click and our affiliation with the streets and where I was from (Brighton Street). That, along with my Sisqo affiliation, made me a force to be reckoned with.

Not long after the pool party, I went to the Maryland state office and created an LLC for my own record company and named it "Crown Vic Establishment." Jamaal and I would talk on the phone every day, brainstorming and trying to devise a successful plan for my new label. I later gave Jamaal the title of President of Crown Vic Establishment. I also assigned Pig as the A&R of the company. Tanja was now my personal assistant and Shanna was my advisor. These titles really didn't mean a lot to me, but I learned a long time ago that people feel better and are more eager to work when "titles" are involved. There wasn't any money involved so I had to somehow keep everyone motivated.

Since my superpower was music, the very next thing I did was put together a layout for a new mixtape. I decided to pick up where we all left off back in 2001 and create a sequel to our Purple Haze project and called it, Purple Haze- Volume II. Hot and I along with Sisqo had previously recorded a freestyle to Camron's "Welcome to New York" track and called it "Welcome to Bmore" that was absolutely amazing, so I knew I already had the main song (the body) to push the mixtape. I just needed to add the arms, legs and other components to complete the frame but just to make sure we kicked the door off the hinges, Hot, Butch and I recorded another freestyle with Sisqo called "Revolution." This really put the CD over the top! On the Revolution freestyle I spoke on the Holla Back situation again for those that didn't hear my "Free" freestyle. I also used the energy I felt from the local pool party that I attended and swung at the local crews in town also. I didn't have any beef with anyone. That was just the competitor in me. I would use anything to get me going even if I had to make it up. I heard Michael Jordan was like that also.

I asked Mouse to do the intro, to pay homage to him for initially bringing me into Sisqo's world. I also asked Charles (that I later nicked named Murda- short for C-Murda because we always would call Charles "C". I just added Murda at the end, inspired by the No Limit artist and eventually we all dropped the "C" and began to call Charles, Murda) to MC the mixtape paying homage to him for having my back during the Can I Live process. I invited a few guest appearances like Ms. Kitty (who rapped on me & Kidd's "Hang Low" record). Ms. Kitty and I became very cool over the years and she was always my "Go

To" whenever I needed a female voice or lyricist. She was the dopest female rapper that I had ever came across. I also invited JI 900 as well (Mr. Wilson couldn't make it but Omar Little came through). Everyone else on the mixtape were in house.

The vibe of the house was very exciting and energetic while we were in the mist of creating Purple Haze- Volume II. As always, there were a lot of small projects being worked on in the studio but when we started Purple Haze II, we drowned out everything and all the attention went into our project. Sisqo noticed the wave that was taking place and how everyone was following my lead and in the blink of an eye, I became Sisqo's right hand (musically). With Mupp's passing and Kidd being exiled, the position was open for the taking. I didn't have the personal relationship that Kidd had with Sisqo, but I was loyal, I respected him and most importantly I was grateful for the opportunities and I didn't take him or his house for granted. I had his back, but you know the old saying "with great power comes great responsibility".

One day Butch called and told me that one of his old Navy buddies was in town by the stage name of Body Bags (we called him Bags for short). I originally met Bags back in the day during our DeMartim Record days when Butch brought him and his then rap group to me and Stanfields attention. Bags was a part of a three-man group at the time. The other two members were from Virginia but Bags was from New York. Stanfield and I were thinking about signing them back then but for some reason we never did. Now fast forward 8 or 9 years later, Bags is back but this time he's solo.

Bags was a very dangerous human being. He was a killer that secretly suffered with mental issues. Bags and Butch met in the Navy years before I met Butch. According to Bags, one day back in New York, he got into a shoot out with two individuals, shot both (one of which he thought he killed) and ran directly to a navy enlisting place and signed up for the Navy. He hid out until it was time to head off to the Navy. Bags left New York and never looked back. Bags and Butch instantly clicked when they met each other and became close friends. They both got into some trouble together but only Butch was caught. Butch was sent to the Brigg and never ratted on Bags. From that point moving forward, Bags was forever loyal to Butch.

The first night Bags was in town, Butch brought him out to the house to hang out. Back in the DeMartim Records days I heard that Bags had a secret vendetta against me, simply because I was the "Number One Guy" and he felt like he was a better MC but when we saw each other, it was all love. Butch introduced him to everyone at the house including Sisqo. After we smoked and had a few drinks, I asked Bags if he wanted to record a solo freestyle for Purple Haze II. Bags was more than excited about the opportunity and went in and laid down a powerful verse. Bags energy was so animated and violent when recording I believe he scared some of the people that were there.

Bags was a killer that looked like a killer. There wasn't anything pleasant or pretty about his appearance at all. On top of that he was very loud and aggressive so for some folks who weren't used to that kind of energy, they looked shook because they were intimidated and there were a lot of people at Sisqo's house that weren't used to that energy. I brought every ounce of street to that house when I came with my crew so if you ever saw anyone that was official at Sisqo's house, chances are they were affiliated with me.

These affiliations would soon lead to one of my most challenging altercations to date. You see I had my immediate circle. Fat Boy (Big Flood), Tim Brown, Shawn (Lil Flood), Kebo, Chop, Ole Man Joe, Butch, Mouse and Murda but all of these dudes had homeboys of their own which I knew but were not a part of my immediate circle. They were extensions of my circle. In certain circumstances, if an extension was around long enough, I would embrace them and bring them in and consider them an immediate. I did this with Pig, one of Kidd's homeboys and this also happened with one of Fat Boys extensions, a guy named Shaggy.

When the final version of Purple Haze- Volume II was burned to a CD, Butch, Hot and I immediately went to work. We didn't have a way to press up large quantities of CD's so we went to Staples, Rite Aid, Walgreen etc. wherever sold blank CD's and bought CD's by the bulk as well as cases. We didn't have a sleeve so we brought the press on stickers, created a design and stuck the stickers directly on the actual CD. Each of us had CD burners, but they only burned two CD's at a time. We individually burned close to 1000 CD's two at a time! A very tedious and drawn-out process but we had no other option.

Once the CD hit the streets it took off! Purple Haze (part one) was labeled "by the Associates" but Purple Haze II was labeled "by Cooli Hi and the Crown Vic Click". This was something I learned from Sisqo and Dru Hill. The dynamics of Butch, Hot and I had changed drastically and I was the face of our Hip Hop movement so moving forward it would always be "Cooli Hi and the Crown Vic Click."

Things were looking good. I still had my Crown Victoria album in stores selling and now I had Purple Haze II buzzing in the streets. People were coming to me from all walks of life, wanting to collab, manage me, wear there clothing line etc. but I always pushed them away until I could get a good read on their true intentions. The only offers I would seriously consider were the ones suggested by someone in my eternal crew.

Around this time Shanna was heavily involved on the acting scene here in Baltimore. She often performed in live stage shows and plays across the region. Shanna knew a lot of the shakers and movers in town and one day she introduced me to a guy named Rodney from a company called "New Breed Films." Rodney and his partner Corey Grant created, produced, and directed independent movies. Shanna gave them my CD and they loved it and wanted to work with me in some compacity. Corey, the head of New Breed Films loved my story telling capability and was blown away on how I painted pictures with words. "It's like I can see your songs Cooli" Corey would always tell me.

My song "Always" was Corey's favorite, like a lot of peoples. Corey loved the song so much that he offered to shoot the music video for free! All I had to do was feed the people involved and Corey said that he would handle the rest. Corey and New Breed Films had never shot a music video before; they only did movies and short films. I was very excited about shooting the video and couldn't wait to get started.

Corey, Shanna and I sat down and came up with the treatment for Always (A treatment is a layout of what will happen in a music video). Since Shanna connected me with Corey and was an aspiring actress, it was only right that I casted her as the leading lady (which was my baby's mother) in the video. I wasn't sure if Tanja would be upset about or not but my decision was made. Tanja knew I would put her in the video. Just not as the lead role and she was cool with that. Still till this point, Tanja did not know that Shanna and I would occasionally sleep together. She just thought we were together in the past however Shanna knew about everything that was going on with me and Tanja. Like everyone did. Tanja was practically my girlfriend.

Sidenote: I still was with Chante and had no intentions on leaving her but both Tanja and Chante had major advantages over each other. Chante was the perfect girlfriend, I was with since she was 18, her body count was low (practically a virgin), she wasn't running the streets so no one had any dirt on her, she stayed home mostly to herself and read books and I was the father of her only child. It couldn't get any better than that. Tanja's advantage was she knew how to love me the way I wanted and needed to be loved without me having to give her instructions! She always knew exactly what to do whether it was sexually, mentally, educationally, or motherly but most important of all, Tanja was connected to my passion! Tanja was one with Cooli Hi. Chante was one with Dwayne but at this time Cooli Hi ran the show.

Simply put, man law says that you marry Chante, not Tanja. Tanja had three small children and previously slept with two of your partners. That kills all talks of prioritizing. But it was almost as if Tanja knew the cards were stacked against her, so she went overboard in all other categories to make up for her "short comings". I was in a tight situation and couldn't see how it would end.

Since the song was about my son Peanut of course he was going to be in the video but I also decided to put my baby boy Darrian in the video as well as a younger form of Peanut. That way both of my kids would be in my first video. The only challenge would be there's no Darrian without Chante which meant Chante, Tanja and Shanna would all be in the same room for the very first time!

The Always music video was scheduled for a 3-day shoot. Darrian was only needed for a day and a half so Chante would only be around for the same times also. The first day of the shoot, all of my guys were there and they knew about the entire situation and had their popcorn ready, waiting to see if something popped off. I was so focused on making sure the video came out right that I barely paid any of the nonsense any attention. I only cared about protecting one person and that person was Chante. She was innocent and in the blind so I was going to make sure that no one played with her or tried to make a fool of her by saying little slick comments or giving her dirty looks. I previously had a conversation with both Tanja and Shanna and they both were cool about the situation.

Day one completed without any hick ups. Everything went according to plan. Chante, Tanja and Shanna all were in the same rooms for long periods of time and nothing out of the ordinary happened. Chante did mention something to me when we got home. "That girl Tanja was watching me like a hawk the entire day! Everywhere I went, I could feel her eyes beaming on me!" I told Chante Tanja was probably starring so hard because they all knew she existed but never actually saw her. "She probably was just looking at you like that to be nosey! I mean you are Cooli Hi's girlfriend!" I told Chante. Chante smiled and moved on.

Day two was a lot more challenging than Day one. Corey, being in the dark to all of the soap opera drama, decided to put in a scene where Shanna and I kiss while sitting on a bench in a park. Both Shanna and I objected but Corey pushed until we finally gave in. "I need this scene guys. It can be just a 3 second peck!" Corey said. Both Shanna and I pretended like it was going to be difficult to pull off but in reality kissing was nothing compared to what we really were doing behind closed doors.

Before the kissing scene, I went to both Chante and Tanja individually and explained what was about to happen. Chante was upset but no way near as upset as Tanja. I eased the blow by telling them both that it was going to be a slight peck and it was just a part of the job that I signed up for when I decided to be an artist. Chante decided that she did not want to witness the kiss so she would stand on the other side of the park when the time came but Tanja decided that she wanted to be there front and center. I believe Tanja wanted to see if she could detect any chemistry between Shanna and I by dissecting the kiss.

When it was time to shoot the infamous scene. The entire cast came over to watch. Even random people at the park came over as well. We were surrounded by a mop of people, everyone there except Chante who purposely walked on the other side of the park so she couldn't see it. Tanja was up front directly behind the camera.

The moment came and Shanna and I kissed. We secretly talked before the kiss and said that we would make it look as innocent as possible but before we kissed, Corey gave us this prep talk about making it look real. "If it doesn't look real, yall are going to have to keep doing it over so yall might as well knock it out on the first go around!" Corey said. So, Shanna and I decided to kiss like we always kissed, slow and passionately. After the kiss, the entire mob got quiet. Then out of nowhere Corey yelled "Damnnnnn! That's what I'm talking about! Two professionals! Clap it up for them yall!" Everyone started clapping and congratulating us both. After the crowd scattered, Corey came to Shanna and me a second time and asked us to kiss again for a different angle. This time to avoid all the madness, we snuck off and shot another kissing scene without anyone watching. The scenes at the park were the last scenes I needed Darrian for so afterwards Chante and Darrian went home. When Chante left, all of my guys individually came to me to give me praise for how everything went down or didn't go down I should say. "Yo you had your wife and both of your mistresses all in the same room and you never flinched" they were saying. A bunch of handshakes and "You're the man" statements were thrown around but honestly, I didn't feed into any of it. My main concern was the success of the video and making sure Chante was not disrespected. That's all that mattered to me at that moment.

The next scene was set to be shot at an indoor swimming area. Corey rented out a pool room at a hotel for a scene where I would get caught flirting with a girl at the pool and Shanna would push the girl in the water. The pool room was full of beautiful girls, all in bikinis and bathing suits and of course all my guys were there as well.

When it was time for us to shoot our scene, Shanna and I went into the bathroom where everyone changed their clothes. The bathroom was huge but the lights in the ceiling were broken, and it didn't have any windows, so we had to leave the door cracked open a little to see. The door was extremely heavy and without it being opened, the bathroom was completely black. We had a door stopper at the edge of the door to keep it slightly opened. When Shanna and I walked in the bathroom, Tanja was already there about to put on her bathing suit. When a random person walked out, they accidently kicked the door stopper and the door shut closed. Tanja, Shanna and I were completely in the dark. Tanja and Shanna began to comment on how dark it was in the bathroom. As I was changing my clothes I jokingly said "Yeah its so dark, anything can go down and no one would ever know!" Out of nowhere something went "Pop!" I had been slapped right upside of my head! As soon as I realized I was slapped, someone came in the bathroom causing the door to open which brought in light. As the bathroom lit up, I immediately looked at both Tanja and Shanna to see who hit me because I had no idea due to the darkness. Both Tanja and Shanna were casually getting dressed without any alarming facial expression. I couldn't tell which one of the hit me. Whoever did it, played it off so well. I couldn't say anything because if I accused the wrong one it would have caused a conflict between the two of them. Both girls had reasons for hitting me. Shanna knew about how spontaneous Tanja and I was so that comment could have hit a sensitive button and Tanja was just giving me the blues on the ride to the scene because of the kiss she just witnessed at the park. Anyhow, I couldn't figure out which one hit me, so I never mentioned it to either of them. To this day, I STILL don't know!

We wrapped up the pool scene and the next day completed the video by shooting a few club scenes and some performance scenes on my mother block in the street. I was even able to get Sisqo to stop by (which was like pulling teeth) and bless the video with a cameo. When Sisqo arrived, he didn't want to get out of his truck, so Corey had to improvise, and we shot a quick scene at his truck.

Once we were done shooting the video, it was now time for the most important part of all visual content, the editing. The editing is the most detailed and tedious part of it all. It's the part where you choose what content will be used in the video. You can have hours of footage but somehow you must narrow it down to 3 to 4 minutes (or however long the song is) and piece the best clips together like a puzzle. The visual story line of Always had to connect to the musical line so I wanted to be present during the edit but Corey insisted that he had everything under control.

When Corey and his team completed the 1st edit, Shanna and I went to his house to review it. The edit was okay but it didn't line up with what I envisioned. Shanna felt the same way. Shanna and I took a copy of the 1st edit back to Shanna's house and dissected the entire video. We both took notes and wrote down the times of the frames that we wanted taken out and chose new frames to add in their place. We even decided to remove the kiss completely from the video. Reason being was it looked too natural and real. Anyone who saw this kiss would be able to tell we had something going on. Seeing the kiss for a few seconds live was one thing but being able to watch it over and over would have definitely let the cat out of the bag. Shanna was still married, and I had my whole situation going, so the last thing we both needed was this kiss analyzed.

This process took long hours over several days to complete. During this time Shanna and I bond became stronger toward one another, even stronger than after the situation we had when I was on tour. During Holla Back, Shanna and I sporadically slept together. We never planned it. We would just so happen to be together taking care of business and afterwards, thing would just happen. The majority of the time I was with Tanja so

Shanna and I were hit and miss but the Always video bonded us like never before.

Sidenote: Here is something regular people should know. Artist are weird. Not in a bad way but a creative way. We are driven by passion and we attract and are attracted to passion. Our thoughts and lifestyles only make sense to each other. That's why typically you will always see artist dating other artist or someone that has some sort of weird passion because we make sense to one another. The average person will not understand why we do what we do or make the sacrifices we make because they're not wired like us. This is why you will see a gorgeous female artist dating a band member or a producer or engineer. Not to mention we're all in the same circles literally for long periods of time. We connect to one another. To add more weird-ism we can sleep together, be in relationships, fall in love, all of the normal processes and then disconnect from all of those things and still function as true friends, almost like a family member! Its because of the passion we have dwelling in us. We are weird in that way.

Shanna's passion for acting and my passion for music had aligned through the creation of "Always- The Music Video" and for about a week or so Shanna and I were inseparable. Between the editing sessions, Shanna and I would take walks around Columbia Lake to clear our heads. She would tell me about her dreams of becoming and actress and I would talk about getting another record deal. I always would tell Shanna that she should leave Baltimore and pursue her dreams but Shanna always told me she couldn't. She didn't want to leave her Mom and her adopted son (which was her nephew by blood). She was so selfless. Always put others before her. That was one of the many attributes that I loved about Shanna.

After the walks we would dive back into the editing and when the late hours arrived, the editing ceased and we were all over each other. Before the Always music video, we would have our moments and then go our separate ways but now we were spending the night with each other and falling asleep in each other's arms.

After the 3rd edit, Always- the Music Video was finally complete and ready for viewing. Back then (2004) there wasn't any internet outlets such as YouTube or social media so I had to depend on local music video shows possibly picking it up and playing the video. The Video landed on a few local stations but that was it. This process was way harder than getting a song on the radio. After a few spots on the local shows the video eventually went dormant and was at a standstill until many years later when I was able to upload Always on YouTube and other internet outlets.

Shortly after completing Always the music video, Corey asked me to appear in a movie he was directing called "Under Pressure". Needless to say I agreed. The movie was about an undercover cop attempting to take down a king pin. I initially only had two parts in the movie. One was a studio scene with me in the booth rapping and the other was with me performing in a club on stage while the actors did their parts. I also agreed to allow Corey to use a few of my songs in the movie, one of which is called My Life. Corey offered me a 3rd part in the movie after a fatal car accident that took the life of one of the actors. The accident happened while in the process of shooting the movie so Corey wanted me to fill in and complete the scene the actor unfortunately couldn't complete.

This 3rd scene had nothing to do with music. It was a fighting scene. I had to wear the same clothes as the actor that passed way wore so the audience couldn't tell it was two different people. I also had to wear a hoodie to cover portions of my face.

Shooting this scene was eye opening to me. The dialog portion was easy because I really didn't have many lines. Corey allowed me to impromptu my parts, meaning I could say whatever came to mind, so I was good with that. It was the fighting portion that was challenging. Up till then, I didn't know that fight scenes were rehearsed. Almost like a dance. Me and the star of the movie had to go over punch by punch, kick by kick, to make sure everything went according to plan but more importantly, to make sure no one got hurt. One false move, or if you forgot where a punch or kick was coming from, you could get hit for real! After a few takes of the fight scene, my job was done but I made such a good impression on my first swing at acting (that didn't have anything to do with music), Corey promised me that he would use me in his upcoming projects!

Sidenote: Corey Grant was also the first one to recommend that I write a book. He loved my storytelling in songs so much that he kept suggesting that I write a book so hopefully one day it would turn into a screenplay directed by him! I started writing the book back then but was sidetracked because I was still in full throttle chasing my musical dreams.

Chapter 38 - Africa

A little time had passed since Always- the video shoot and my acting debut in Corey's independent film "Under Pressure". I was still doing what I did best, creating new songs night after night in Sisqo's studio. One day before a routine studio session, Sisqo asked me if I wanted to do a show with him out of the country. "Hell yeah! Where?" I replied. Sisqo then said "Yo, we're going to South Africa to perform for the Mandela Family!" I didn't say anything but I'm sure my eyes lit up like a kid at a toy store. "You're getting a 15 to 20-minute set. We leave next week!" Sisqo went on to say.

That night instead of creating new material, I went downstairs to the studio and mapped out my 20 minute set by choosing the songs as well as the transitions between songs, sound effects, explosions, things of that sort. Charles aka Murda was there with me every step of the way as always. To pay homage to Murda for helping me put my show together, I added to the show one of the freestyle songs that Murda rapped on, on our Purple Haze II CD so that Murda would have a chance to spit his verse.

Murda could dance very well and was always full of energy. He had already agreed to be my hype man in Africa so it only made sense to give him a moment to shine on his own. This would also give me a moment to catch my breath while performing as well.

The following week Sisqo, his girlfriend Tera, his Dad, Murda and I all flew out to South Africa. At that time there wasn't a straight flight from the states (Baltimore) to South Africa so we had to fly to the United Kingdom first and then fly out to South Africa.

When we arrived it was almost like I had died and went to heaven. Everything was absolutely GORGEOUS! The scenery, the people, their smiles and hospitality, the weather, the water, the air, everything was breath taking.

The Johannesburg South Africa trip was by far the best experience I had as a performing artist. Before we performed for the Mandela family we had lunch with them, very nice people, and took lots of pictures. At that lunch is where I first met the international recording artist named "Speedy". Speedy was a very close friend to the Mandela's and a great performer. So good, that Sisqo allowed him to come out and perform in his set.

After the 5 star lunch and show we all had planned to attend a night club that was across the street from our hotel but right before the party Sisqo and I made and appearance on a Johanesburg Live Video show (South Africa's version of MTV). Sisqo and I stood live on air and answered questions coming from the host of the show. After the interview the host asked me to kick a freestyle and lead them to a commercial break. An awesome moment that I will never forget. Afterwards, I had plans to party!

The woman in South Africa were incredibly gorgeous and their accents sent their vibe over the top. Sisqo was with Tera at the hotel so he didn't go to the club however Murda and I went and danced and conversated with women all night long. Murda was always in a sticky situation during times like this because Murda was in a relationship with Sisqo's sister. Murda would have fun but there was always a limit to how far he would go. Me on the other hand, was down for the moment and everything it involved. I met so many beautiful woman that night it was ridiculous. There was no need for getting their phone numbers because I wasn't going to be there much longer so the only option was a one night stand. After talking to several, I finally chose one to shoot my one night stand shot at, and she accepted. We went back to my hotel room and had amazing sex! The only detail I specifically remember is her legs trembled the entire time I was inside of her. She was gorgeous! Dark smooth skinned with a body out of this world. When we were done she said to me "Now you can tell all of your friend's that you had some REAL African booty!" We both burst out in laughter.

The next day, I went to the gift shop and purchased my Mom and Peanuts grandmother, Ms. Marlene some African sculptures as souvenirs. I also picked up a few rocks off the ground for Ms. Marlene as well. She would always ask me to bring her rocks from wherever I went so she could have a part of that town in her possession. Murda and I smoked some African weed and had a few drinks before it was time to head back to the states (Murda actually brought some back home with him). I wish we would or could have taken more pictures, but back then pictures were not a priority like they are now. There was no such thing as a camera phone so the only pictures that were taken was with a disposable or actual camera.

This trip was one for the books! The only hick up that I didn't mention earlier was a stupid decision made on my part the first day we arrived in Johannesburg. That night we all went out to a night club. Sisqo wore this BIG gold chain with colorful diamonds flooding the spinning dragon plate attached to it. When the flashing lights from the club hit his diamonds, it looked like his entire chest was glowing. Murda and I had on our iced out dragon chains as well. Our entire entourage was sitting in a private VIP section.

So I'm standing at the edge of the ropes, sipping my drink and looking over the crowd when suddenly I see this guy with this beautiful girl trying to get my attention. They both looked like they were Indian, light brown skinned with smooth long dark hair. I went over to the two and the guy said to me "My sister likes you! She recognized you from Sisqo's video "Can I Live". She wants to hang out with yall. Is that okay?" His sister was beautiful; could have easily been mistaken for a model (with the exception of her height) so I of course said "Sure". I grabbed her by the hand and escorted her into the VIP section.

After a few minutes of dancing with her, I noticed that she kept starring at my chain. Then she started rubbing on my chest and touching the iced-out dragon emblem as well. I asked her if she liked the chain, and she smiled and said yes. Then she said to me "Can I have it? I will do anything you want if I can have the chain!" "Anything" I asked. "Yes, anything" she replied and slightly touched my penis.

I remembered seeing a closet/ facility room not too far from our section when we first entered the club and I thought to myself "this would be a perfect creep off spot". I took her by the hand and lead her to the closet. When we got inside, she immediately unbuckled my pants and began to perform oral sex on me. Every so often while in the act, she would reach up attempting to grab my chain and I would gently move her hand from the chain and encourage her to finish. While this was going on, a few of the club employees opened the door but when they saw what was taking place, the immediately closed the door and left.

I thought since I was being treated like royalty ever since I stepped off the plane that I couldn't be touched. I was tipsy from the drinks, high from the weed and getting head in a closet from a beautiful girl, while the club was in motion and the staff at the club was allowing me to do so. I felt like I was untouchable. Then in the blink of an eye things changed.

Out of nowhere the door busted open, and it was three police officers! The girl immediately stopped, and I began to pull my pants up. "What the hell are you doing" one of the policemen said. This is grounds for an arrest!" One of the other policemen grabbed the girl and escorted her out of the room. The other two officers were still in the room with me. The main officer just kept going on and on chastising me about what he just saw. I thought I was about to go to jail. The last thing I wanted to do was get arrest in another country!

I could tell the main officer was trying to figure out if he was going to arrest me or not. Being as though I wasn't from there, I had no idea what their laws were and that's what I kept saying. I pretended like I didn't know what we were doing was wrong and in the states these things happen all the time, especially with celebrities. Finally, after a moment of the policemen contemplating and me playing the naïve role, they decided not to arrest me and allowed me to return to our VIP section.

About an hour or so later when we were leaving the club, I saw the girls brother outside. Security had a path made for us to enter our car so the brother couldn't get to close but I heard him yell "Cooli, where's my sister?" I ignored him and got into the car. I had no idea what the police decided to do with the girl.

Not long after we returned home from South Africa, maybe a month or two later, another opportunity presented itself again! Sisqo asked if I wanted to go back to Africa for a second time, but this time it was for three shows and a longer stay. Me being blown away from the first trip, anxiously accepted and couldn't wait to return. Sisqo also mentioned that we were going to a different part of Africa, which was Angola. At the time, I didn't care what part we were going to. All I knew was I just had the best time of my life in South Africa, was well compensated and I'm about to get a chance to do it all over again. When I told Tanja about the second trip to Africa she said "Babe you should research what part of Africa you're going to. Every part of Africa is not like Johannesburg!" I couldn't hear anything Tanja was advising. All I could think about was having a good time and getting paid.

On the day we were leaving to go to Angola, Tanja drove me to Sisqo's house where a car service was scheduled to take us to the airport. When Tanja and I arrived at the house, Sisqo told me that the car service got the times screwed up and wasn't going to be able to get us to the airport on time. Tanja said "I can take yall to the airport!" Sisqo said "Thanks" and Sisqo, his girlfriend Tera, Murda and I packed our bags in Tanja's sisters truck that she was driving and headed out to the airport.

Sisqo, Tera and Murda were in the backseat. Tanja was driving and I was in the passengers seat. When we arrived at the airport, I decided to check my voicemails one last time before powering my phone off. I had a flip phone and I knew once I boarded the airplane, I wouldn't have access to my cell phone until I returned back to the states (which would be in about 10 to 12 days). As I entered my four digit passcode, the moment I hit the last digit, I looked over at Tanja and I thought I saw her head sort of snap back to looking straight ahead; almost as if she was looking at me enter my code but when I looked at her, she tried to pretend she wasn't looking. I wasn't sure if she saw me enter the code. I tried to read her facial expression afterwards but it was nothing there. Something told me to change my passcode as soon as I got out of her truck but I didn't. I gave Tanja a kiss and we all got out of the truck and headed into the airport.

The process to Angola was the same as Johannesburg. We flew to London first and then to Angola. The flight was brutal, just like the first, totaling around 18 hours. When we finally landed and got off the plane, I remember smelling the most horrible smell. It smelled like the arm pits of someone who did not wear any deodorant. Normally you would smell this on a person but in Angola, well at the airport, it was in the air!

As we walked through the airport to get our bags and head for our car service, I quickly noticed that Angola was nothing like Johannesburg. It was the exact opposite. Everything looked ran down and second hand. The smell was overbearing and the people were rude and very aggressive. The police or army men had rifles on their shoulders and even some pedestrians had visible hand guns. Also, one of the biggest surprises to me of them all was they did not speak English! They spoke Portuguese.

The language barrier was a huge challenge because everything was moving so fast and we couldn't understand what people were saying. We were being rushed from one point to another, security/ police officers had their guns out being overly aggressive with the locals, people were swarming us wanting autographs, it was hot and smelly, and we couldn't understand a word anyone was saying.

Once we got to our car and headed to our hotel, I remember thinking back to what Tanja advised when she said I should research what part of Africa I was going to. Her words were playing through my head as I saw buildings half way torn down yet people were going in and out of them, I saw small children no more than 8 or 9 years old walking on dirt roads with no shoes on carrying hand guns and rifles. I also saw military tanks that were blown up still sitting in the middle of the streets. The town looked like total chaos. There were no signal lights or stop signs; no traffic laws what so ever so everyone just drove like maniacs and fended for themselves. I couldn't believe what my eyes were seeing.

When we arrived at our hotel, things did began to look a little better. Our rooms were very nice. The only downside was the air conditioning there wasn't like it was at home. It was almost as if the system didn't blow cool enough air so it always felt like a fan was on instead central air. The food was amazing. We had everything downstairs at the hotel to our disposal from lobster tails, steaks, shrimp, you name it. We also had security 24/7 around the clock and an interpreter to be with us at all times so we could find out what was being said to us and vice versa.

We had two interpreters. A young white woman and an elderly old white man with long white hair down his back. Our first night in Angola we were scheduled to go to a club but before we went, our female interpreter gave us the run down on how to move while in Angola. The first thing she told us was to stay together. Do not wander off. She feared for our safety and advised that it was best that we all stayed together when not at the hotel. Next, she told us, not to leave the hotel when the sun goes down (when it got dark). Chances were, we would not make it back. She told us a few other things but the one other jewel she gave that stuck with me was to tell our drivers to slow down when driving through small villages. "If you're driver hits and kills someone, the village will murder everyone in the car! The only ones they might possibly allow to live are white people!" she said.

That night when we headed out for the club we all stayed together like instructed. We originally were just going out to have fun but when we arrived we saw Sisqo's posters and flyers everywhere. Sisqo was very upset to see this because the posters and flyers meant they knew he was coming which also meant this was arranged, which finally meant someone got paid to bring him there and he didn't know about it or was paid.

Sidenote: Our regular road manager Huggy Carter didn't attend this trip. Sisqo fired the stand in road manager because of this club fiasco.

Once we got settled in and the drinks started flowing, it was party time. Since we couldn't understand what anyone was saying our interpreter would ask us which girl we liked. We would point the girl out to the interpreter, and she would go and talk to the girl for us. If the girl wanted to move forward, our interpreter would bring her to us and we would just dance.

The interpreter brought over several girls to me and I would always ask them if they spoke English. They all would always answer by saying "More or less". I think that was the general statement they all knew because almost everyone that we all asked, said the exact same thing and that was all the English they knew.

At the end of the night, we all picked a few girls and headed back to our hotel. Once we arrived at the hotel, everyone posted up in the lobby and started to socialize, transforming the lobby into a lounge. The hotel manager wasn't okay with this so he advised security to tell everyone that they had to go to a room or else leave the hotel. I grabbed one of the girls that came with me by the hand and started walking towards the elevator, heading to my room.

Once we arrived at my room and all the noise calmed down, the girl and I came to a standstill. Of course, I didn't have our interpreter in my room so I couldn't understand what she was saying and vice versa. We began to attempt to communicate by saying things to each other as slowly as possible, but it was no use. Portuguese is nothing like English. None of the words remotely sounded the same.

Once we figured out talking was useless, we began to attempt to use sign and body language to communicate. We both laughed at each other as we tried to guess what each other was trying to say. Finally, I decided to get a pen and a piece of paper and decided to draw. I drew a girl taking off her clothes to let her know I wanted her to get undressed. Once she saw the picture, she smiled and began to take her clothes off. We both figured out the next steps from there.

The next morning when we awoke, we went downstairs to the lobby and I attempted to walk her out of the hotel. She immediately stopped me at the door, almost as if to say "Stay here, I got this!" and then she left.

Sidenote: The girl came back to my room every single night for the remaining of the stay in Angola and we slept together. When we were out at a club or performing at the show and I returned to the hotel, she was always there waiting for me. We didn't talk. We couldn't talk. I didn't even know her name.

The next few days were full of eventful excursions. On our days off (when we didn't have a show) we would often ride around to sightsee and experience Angola culture. When in town, we didn't get out of the car much (for security reasons), but we did experience one of the towns most famous meals by getting a "chicken in a bag". The "Chicken In a Bag" was a meal prepared on the streets of Angola (literally on the streets). The cook would light a small fire, cook a chicken, smother it in some sort of African seasoning (that was to die for) and place it in a clear plastic bag. That's why we called it the "Chicken In a Bag". I'm not sure how they cooked the chicken nor if any of it was clean but one thing for certain was the chicken tasted delicious!

One day I was in my room chilling when Murda called and told me to meet him downstairs in the lobby. When I got downstairs everyone was there, Sisqo, Tera, Murda and Sisqo's dancers. "Yo we are about to go on a Safari! You trying to go?" Murda asked. I was a little hesitant with my answer because

I needed details so I asked the interpretuer how close do the animals actually get to the car. The interpretuer insured me that the animals don't get too close and that the safari was safe. Me judging from what I had already saw in Angola made me doubt the interpretuers words a little but Murda chimed in and said "Yo we're in AFRICA! How many people we know will get an opportunity to go on a Safari in our Motherland?" Murda had a valid point. I decided to put my fears and doubts in my back pocket and took an adventure leap.

We all piled up in a mini van and headed out to the safari. The driver told us it would be about a two-and-a-half-hour ride. While in route to the Safari, the driver was driving extremely reckless. Again there were no traffic rules, no traffic lights, signals, etc. It was every car for himself. Our driver drove extremely fast, on both sides of the road, swerving around oncoming cars and almost turning the van over on numerous occasions going around curves. As we were traveling through the town I often saw cars packed to the capacity, people hanging outside of the windows, holding on the side of vans and trucks, riding in the trunk, just holding on to vehicles for dear life trying to catch a ride and all of this was going on in chaotic traffic!

Once we cleared the town area and started making our way into the country/ village areas, the driving wasn't as bad because of the open roads. The only issue was the speed. The driver was driving so fast that the van was shaking almost out of control. He had to literally have his foot pressed all the way to the floor. At times I just buried my head in my lap because I just couldn't bear to look.

During the time I was able to look, I saw the most amazing things. I saw huts and small homes made out of tree branches and leaves. I saw a tree that fell over, and someone gutted out the root of the tree and was living in it. I saw small kids maybe 5 years old walking with machetes and fishing rods on the hunt for dinner. In this part of Angola, it was clear that the villages did not have any electricity, plumbing or running water. They were out in the woods for real, just like what I used to see on TV when I was a kid regarding Africa.

While still in route to the Safari, our interpretuer (this time the older white man) saw a shoppers mart (sort of like a flea market) between the villages and suggested that we stop. When we got out of the van, the entire market swarmed us. They were so happy to see Sisqo. They didn't speak a word of English but they knew how to say Sisqo!

Sidenote: I was told that there was a civil war in Angola less than 20 years ago when we were there. That explained why I saw blown up tanks still in the middle of roads as well as buildings crumbling. I was also told that Angola was under a colonial rule for a long time causing the influence of the Portuguese language.

As we walked through the outdoor market, the crowd walked with us step by step. The natives were amazed by our clothes, especially our accessories like our head and wrist bands, sun visors and hats. At times when I needed a break from the natives getting to close, I would take my wrist or head band off and throw it in the opposite direction and the entire mob would run and almost fight eachother to retrieve it. It sort of looked like being at a baseball game watching the crowd fight and wrestle over a homerun ball.

Hearing the natives yell Sisqo's name and for them to know who he was, was amazing to me! Murda and I said to Sisqo "Yo how do they know you if they don't even have running water yet alone a TV or a radio!" Sisqo just smiled and shook his head as if to say, "Who knows?"

After buying a few souvenirs from the market, we fought our way through the mob back to the van and continued to head for the Safari. As we were driving, again at full shaking speed, I could tell that the driver was going to blow the engine. He was driving entirely too fast. I kept telling the interpreter to tell the driver to slow down but the driver would only slow down for a few and eventually he would pick the speed back up. I felt like I was sounding like a broken record so eventually I stopped saying anything and before I knew it, just like I predicted, the van over heated and we broke down in the middle of nowhere and when I say nowhere, I mean literally nowhere!

I was so pissed off, I began to cuss and fuss. Not only was I pissed, I was scared also. We were stranded in the middle of a jungle with no one to turn to for help. No one had a cell phone and even if they did, I'm positive that it wouldn't have worked where we were. As we sat on the side of the road stranded for a few hours, suddenly a man walked out of the woods, maybe returning from a trail he was walking and tried to help. The man gave us a few pales of water to pour into the radiator and allowed us to keep the pales for refills. Once the van cooled down, we started to head back to the hotel, which was maybe two hours away. The driver would run the van going up hills and turn it off when going down hills to allow the van to cruise without the engine. Whenever we saw people we would pull over and ask them for water to refill the radiator in order to keep going. We did this for two hours until we made it back to the hotel. After that trip (with the exception of the shows) I vowed to never leave the hotel again.

Over the next few days, we performed at our sold out shows and each show was a major success. Murda was my hype man and he did an amazing job getting the crowd pumped as well as he nailed his verse on one of my songs. Sisqo even came out and danced as Murda and I rocked the amped up crowd. After the shows, I would return to my room and wait for my African lady friend to arrive.

Although I vowed not to leave the hotel after the breakdown of the van incident, I did manage to get the nerve up to go on a boat ride with everyone and it was amazing. The water was the clearest blue water that I had ever seen and we all had an amazing time.

After the boat ride, we all went back to Sisqo's room to hang out. One of Sisqo's dancers, Ronnie was seeing one of the native girls on the regular since he met her the first night we arrived. Everywhere we went, he brought her with us. While we were all hanging out, Ronnie left Sisqo's room to take a shower and left his female friend with us. I saw this as an opportunity to get sort of "even" for what took place when Shanna came out on tour with me a few years ago (the threesome). Ronnie's friend loved to dance so I went over to her, grabbed her hand and started freestyling a melodic melody just to get her moving (half of what I was saying was gibberish but it didn't matter because she could understand me anyway). Once I got her moving, I started to dance with her in a sexual way. I could tell that she was down for whatever simply by how close she was dancing on me. After a few minutes, I grabbed her hand, lead her out of Sisqo's room and took her to my room. Once inside, in order to keep the vibe going, I pulled out my Walkman CD player, placed the headphones on her ear and played one of my songs "Feeling It" off my Crown Victoria album to keep her dancing. As she continued to dance, very provocative I might add, I came up behind her and started removing her clothes. Needless to say, moments later we were having sex. Once we were done, I couldn't understand a word she was saying but I did understand the hand gestures she was making describing the size of my manhood. I must admit, I had been hearing that practically all of my sexual life but I was hearing that from girls in Baltimore but to literally be on the other side of the earth on another continent hearing the same thing was pretty cool!

After we cleaned up, we both went back to Sisqo's room. Ronnie was back by then. When we walked in, she went over and sat beside Ronnie. I went about my business and continued to socialize. Ronnie was cool though. We all knew not to trip over any girl that was on the scene. The rules were anyone that wasn't someone's main girl or baby mother was for the taking.

The following day was a day that I will never forget for as long as I live. Like the last time, I received a call from Murda asking me to come downstairs to the lobby and like last time Murda was delivering his pitch to go on another Safari. "Yo this time we have two cars that are practically brand new! I guarantee these wont break down." Murda said. Me ignoring every part of me saying not to go, decided to jump in and give it another shot.

Since we had two cars this time, our group was split into two. Sisqo, Murda, their security and the driver were in a small Mercedes Benz leading the way while me. two of Sisqo's dancers, Ronnie and Frank, our interpreter (white older guy) and driver followed behind in a small SUV. Just as before, the drivers were driving recklessly and out of control heading out to the Safari. So many times we came inches away from hitting people walking in the roads, not to mention oncoming traffic. All I kept hearing in my head was what the female interpreter told us the very first day when we arrived, "If you hit someone and kill them, they're going to kill everyone in the car!" So again, I'm telling the interpreter to tell the driver to slow down but our driver is so focused on keeping up with Sisqo's car that's in front of us, that he wasn't hearing me.

Once we got out of the town area and into the country, I felt a little better because the roads were open, except for when we went through small villages. The first couple of villages were okay. We sped through them without any scares but then something happened that changed my life forever.

As we were going through one of the last villages before we arrived at the Safari, out of nowhere a man walks across the road. Sisqo's car just missed him but our car hit him dead on and we were doing well over 100 mph! When we initially hit him, it seemed like he went up on our hood but his foot must have been caught on something because he immediately snapped back to the ground and we ran over him. All I could feel was his body being dragged under our car, as if we were riding over speed bumps at full speed. We were going so fast it took quite some time before we could stop. When we did stop, the man had come out through the back of the car and was disfigured in the middle of the road. When I looked out of the back window and saw him, it looked like his head was in his stomach!

Now we are stopped in the middle of the road and everyone in the car is completely quiet and in shock. All I could hear was what the white female interpreter told us on day one. "Tell your driver to slow down because if you hit and kill someone, the village will kill everyone in the car!" Sisqo's car kept going and was out of sight. Our driver decided to get out of the car to go take a look at the body he just dismantled. Once our driver got out of the car, one of the natives in the village reached his hand through the window, turned the car off and took the keys! I thought to myself, "Oh shit! I am about to die!"

Our interpreter was in the passenger seat and me and the two dancers, Ronnie and Frank were in the back. Our interpreter got out as well to go look at the body, leaving us three in the back. As seconds ticked away, the natives in the village began to gather in large crowds, around the body as well as around our SUV. The dancers and I immediately began to roll up the windows and lock the doors. Just as I went to lock my door, one of the natives grabbed the door handle trying to open it. The native and a few others began to pull the door open but the fear in me must have given me super powers that day because I managed to close and lock that door!

The mob began to get bigger and bigger around our car and things didn't look good at all. Then the natives began to throw rocks at the windows and hit the car with sticks. I began to think, its just a matter of time before they get in or turn the car over with us in it. One of the dancers Frank, began to cry and honestly I couldn't blame him. I remember saying to myself, "I can't believe I survived all the madness in Baltimore just to come to Africa and die in a jungle!? Naw, I can't go out like this" I told the dancers that we have to get out of the car. "Hell no" Frank said. "They are going to kill us" I replied "If we stay in this car, they're going to kill us! Its just a matter of time before they bust this glass out! We have to get out now!" The dancers agreed so we all got out of the car but before I got out, I took off all of my wrist and headbands. I even took off my shirt and was bare chested. I don't know what I was thinking. I thought somehow, I would look like them when we got out and maybe blend in with the natives I guess.

When we got out of the car, the natives grabbed me very forcefully and kind of pushed me around. I allowed them to toss me around like a rag doll and didn't give any push back at all. It was at least one hundred of them all irate and speaking a language that I didn't understand. It wasn't nothing but God that got me out of that situation because as each aggressor grabbed me forcefully, there was one small man with the calmest voice that kept saying "NO". Each time this man said "NO" someone would let me go! After several "NO's" eventually no one was holding me at all.

Once I realized that no one was holding me, I started to ease my way out of the mob, to the outskirts and eventually on the road. Now keep in mind, I was in the middle of the jungle so even if I got out of the mob, I didn't have a clue on where I would go but when I got to the road and looked, I saw Sisqo's car about a few hundred yards away. Murda was in the middle of the road waving both hands trying to get my attention.

Sidenote: I thought that Sisqo's car didn't see what happened and kept going but actually they did. They weren't going to drive back into all of that madness, but they did stop and thank God that they did!

Once I saw Murda and the car up the road I began to walk heading that way. I didn't want to run because Sisqo's car was so far away that if the mob saw me running towards the car, they might have caught me before I made it there. So I walked and walked just so I didn't get any attention and once I felt like I could make it, I turned on the jets and sprinted to Sisqo's car. Ronnie and Frank were right behind me.

Once we all made it to the car, we all piled in and took off. The Benz was so small we literally were laying and sitting on each other's laps but I didn't care. I just needed to get the hell out of there.

When we got back to the hotel, we all immediately started to pack up our things. Our intentions were to hop on the very next flight out of Angola. My mind all was all over the place as I threw by belongings into my suitcase. I didn't know the laws in Angola so I wasn't sure if we would get arrested or anything. Everything just seemed so unorderly and chaotic. Once I was done packing, I bought a calling card and called home to tell people what had happened just in case I came up missing. I wanted to make sure all bases were covered.

When the promoter got word of what had happened and that we were packed up and ready to go home, he did something that made me worry even more. The promoter advised our female interpreter to inform us that there weren't any flights leaving Angola for the next three days! We still had one more show left to do and Sisqo wanted to cancel the show so we could go home but going home wasn't an option (well at least not for another three days).

Sidenote: I didn't believe the Promoter when he passed the word of no flights leaving for another three days. I believe he just said that because he didn't want us to leave. He wanted that last show to happen. From the moment we stepped off the plane, the promoter was very charismatic towards us but brutally rude to the natives and all of his staff. He came across as a dictator, an Angolan gangster! I once saw a documentary with Angie Martinez interviewing Ja Rule and Ja Rule talked about how a promoter in Africa attempted to kidnap DMX. This was the same promoter we were dealing with.

Once we all came to grips about the fact that we couldn't leave for another three days, we all just hung out downstairs in the hotel lobby discussing what just happened. We later found out that the mob allowed our interpreter, the old white man with long hair to live (he returned to the hotel later that night) but they killed our African driver. At this point, I was completely done with Angola. I didn't want to perform in any shows, see any girls or none of that. I just wanted to go home.

A few hours later, I went back to my room to relax. I was watching TV when suddenly my phone began to ring. Not only was it ringing, it was ringing in double rings which meant someone was calling me from outside of the hotel.

Sidenote: Normally whenever we are on a tour, the only calls we receive are from each other, meaning room to room and those calls have the standard sounding rings of a phone but if someone called from outside of the hotel, for example if I gave Chante or my Mother my room number and they called, the ring would have a very distinctive sound.

As I listened to the distinctive ring, I thought to myself, I don't know anyone in Africa! The girl I was sleeping with every night never called. She just came over. Who could possibly be calling me from outside of this hotel!? When I answered the phone, I heard a very faint and distant females voice saying "Hello". As we both went back and forth saying "Hello" for a few, I realized that the voice belonged to none other than Tanja!

"Tanja?" I said. "Yes. Can you hear me?" she replied. I couldn't believe it! I hadn't spoken to her since she dropped us off at the airport. Back then, no one talked on the phones internationally because the rates were too high. Only in extreme emergencies were calls made.

After we greeted one another, I asked "How did you find me?"

Sidenote: Keep in mind, the only thing Tanja knew when she dropped us off at the airport was that we were going to Angola. She didn't know what part of Angola, what town, what hotel we were staying in or any of those pertinent things. All she knew was what COUNTRY we were going to! Also, Sisqo never used his real name when staying at hotels (because of fans) and the only people that knew his fake names were us. Tanja didn't know.

Tanja replied "That's not important but I need to ask you something." As soon as she said this, I immediately got nervous. Tanja somehow found me in Angola and called to ask me a question! There is no chance of this being good for me. Tanja then asked "Are you still seeing Shanna?" In a split second, just like in the movies, my mind started moving in reverse, all the way back to when I was entering my voicemail code while back home at the airport when I thought Tanja saw the numbers I entered. Tanja's question verified that she had my voicemail code and was listening to my voicemails the entire time while I was in Angola.

Sidenote: Long after this happened Tanja confessed and told me she vaguely saw me enter my voicemail code at the airport but didn't catch all of the numbers. Since I was in Angola, my phone was going straight to voicemail for almost two weeks so she had time to use what she saw and play around with options until she finally broke the code.

When I first arrived in Angola, I bought a calling card and checked my voicemails from time to time. One day Shanna left me a voicemail saying how much she missed me and that she was going through withdrawals by not having me in her bed (we had gotten a lot closer since the Always Video situation). Something told me to delete it after I listened but instead, I saved it. Not sure why, but I think I saved it because it was very rare to hear Shanna in a vulnerable state. Of course, when we were intimate, she was very vulnerable but just casually speaking, especially when leaving a voicemail, it was rare. So by me saving the message and then Tanja following behind hearing Shanna's message, led to me getting a phone call in Angola, Africa!

Of course, I denied my relations with Shanna, claiming that the voicemails were old messages. I then tried to deflect by telling Tanja about the car accident and that they were not allowing us to leave the country for another three days. Tanja was no fool by far but being as though the whole car accident fiasco was more important than who I was sleeping with, she let it go and focused on the fact that I needed to get out of

Angola. The call ended on a good note (I believed) because Tanja seemed to be concerned with getting me home, but I knew that wasn't the end of it.

The next day, the promoter got word that although we couldn't leave Angola, we still were not doing the final show. That's when he instructed the female interpreter to tell us that the native that we ran over, didn't die. She told us that at the guys funeral, he woke up from an alcoholic coma! That's when I really got scared. "These people will say ANYTHING to get us to do that show!" I said to everyone. I saw the natives head in his stomach, his intestines and blood splattered all over the road and they're telling us 24 hours later, he woke up from and alcoholic coma! From that point moving forward, I didn't trust anything anyone said that was from Angola.

The third and final day finally arrived and we were scheduled to go home but before we left, we had to do the last show (somehow the promoter convinced Sisqo to complete the tour). The plan was to do the show and head straight to the airport.

When we arrived at the show, the venue was packed. When we were pulling up to the venue, the police and security were outside of our tour bus beating the natives and fans off the side of our bus with Billy clubs. The natives were holding on to the side of the bus and the police were literally beating them so they would let go. Sisqo went on and did the show but I refused to go on. I was done with Angola. I just wanted to go home.

After Sisqo completed his set, we all ran back to the tour bus and headed for the airport. We were on a tight schedule and had no time to waist if we wanted to catch our flight. When attempting to leave the venue, the fans were surrounding our bus and yelling Sisqo's name. The bus driver came close on several occasions of running people over. As I watched this, I said to myself "Not again". The police were steady beating the crap out of the people that surrounded the bus till finally we had a clear path.

When we arrived at the airport, we received the same treatment as the venue. Natives holding on to the side of the bus, screaming Sisqo's name while now the airport security officers are beating them off with sticks. Due to all of the madness, we were running late and in danger of missing our flight. We got off the bus and ran into the airport only to find out we were too late. We had missed out flight. The next flight was in another 24 hours! The only problem was we had checked out of our hotel, it was almost midnight, and we had no place to stay.

Luckily the tour bus was still at the airport so we all went back and boarded the bus. Not knowing what to do next, we reached out to the promoter for help. The promoter said he had a place for us to spend the night but it was on an island and we had to get on a boat to get there.

Our tour bus driver drove us to the dock where a boat was awaiting to take us to the island. When we got off the bus and headed for the boat, we were expecting to see a nice sized boat because it was so many of us and we all had our luggage. Instead, we saw a small paddle boat with a motor on the back with two African sailors. "How are we all supposed to fit on this little ass boat!" I asked rhetorically. One of the sailors replied "Don't worry, we will be okay!" (surprisingly he spoke English). As each of us boarded the boat, it felt like we were sinking more and more into the water. Finally after we all were on board, luggage and all, one of the sailors started the motor and the small boat struggled, but eventually began to move.

It was a little after 1am in the morning so the sky and absolutely everything around us was pitch black. The boat did not have a top but it did have a big light in the front and a few small lights on the side. As we began to make our way, I looked back at the dock until I couldn't see it anymore. Soon afterwards, all I saw was darkness and fish (or what I thought were fish) jumping out and back into the water all around us. In fear of seeing something that I didn't want to see out there, I buried my head in my lap and prayed while the small boat slowly cruised across the African sea. The boat rocked recklessly a few times and often I thought we were going to sink or turn over because it was too much weight on the little boat but after an hour or so, miraculously we made it to the island. Exhausted from the long eventful day, once we got off the boat, we all went to our rooms and went to bed.

The next morning, we were awakened to a pleasant surprise. Being as though we arrived in the we hours of the morning, we couldn't see the beauty of where we were but now the sun had rose and we could see everything. The island we were on looked like paradise! The scenery was very tropical and colorful, surrounded by the prettiest blue waters that I had ever seen. I believe the island belonged to some rich person that the promoter knew and he agreed to allow us to spend the night due to us missing our flight. We were the only ones on the island (except for the staff). The owner even rolled out the hospitality by having servants wait on us hand and foot. When we all sat down and placed orders for breakfast (or brunch rather) we noticed that it took several hours for us to receive our food. We began to murmur and complain a little when finally we were told why it took hours for our food to arrive and it blew our minds! Whatever we ordered, the staff would actually go out and CATCH, KILL and COOK it! I was completely blown away. Everything we ate that day was as fresh as fresh could get!

Once we were done with brunch, we explored the beautiful island for a little and then we all boarded the boat to head back. This time the ride wasn't as bad. I guess my mind was at ease because I knew if we made it there we could make it back. Also, it was broad day light so I didn't have to worry about a strange night creature jumping out of the water and eating us.

When we arrived back at the dock, we still had about 8 hours before our flight so the promoter arranged for us to be taken to another one of his friends house until it was time to head to the airport. This friend of the promoters lived in a huge mansion but the weird thing about this mansion was it was located directly in the middle of an African hood!

I saw building barely standing, cars that were set on fire, children walking around with guns in their hands and strapped to their shoulders on one "block" and on the very next "block" here is this beautiful mansion sitting dead in the middle of all of this madness.

The promoters friend was very nice and hospitable. He gave us full access to his home. He had a beach and what looked like the ocean directly out back and he offered us Jet skiing while we waited. Food, drinks, relaxation, you name it were all at our disposal. A bonus was the friend and his sons spoke English. Murda kept joking with the friend asking him to adopt him and receive him as a son. The friend as well as everyone else laughed and soon afterwards Murda and the friend jokingly started calling each other "Dad" and "Son".

After a few hours at the mansion, our time was up and we all headed back to the airport, this time without any distractions. We arrived in good time, and everything seemed to be going according to plan. Then all of a sudden, we were advised that there weren't enough seats for our entire party. Three people had to stay in Angola and catch the next flight which wasn't leaving until the next day. That was the straw that broke the camels back. Ronnie (one of Sisqo's dancers) went crazy! He began to scream and threaten to call the US embassy. For a moment he was completely out of control. You see all of us knew that the only one anyone cared about in our entourage was Sisqo. If Sisqo got on that plane and left three of us behind, theres no telling what would happen to those three. I was going to make SURE that I was not going to be one of the three. Wherever Sisqo went, I was going! That wasn't up for debate but I'm sure everyone else felt the same. Things were getting very intense. No one wanted to be one of the three.

Everyone was looking at Sisqo to decide who was boarding the plane and who was staying behind. Before Sisqo could make a decision, an airport representative came over and told us there was another flight we could all board but it wouldn't take us to Baltimore. It would take us to New York. Thank God, we all said. We didn't care where the flight took us. As long as it got us out of Angola and ANYWHERE in the United States. We all boarded the plane and headed out to the United Kingdom (The UK was always the connecting flight between Africa and the United States). I remember when the plane started moving down the runway right before liftoff saying to myself, Thankyou Jesus! I'm never doing this again.

Once we arrive in New York, everyone in our entourage went their separate ways. The dancers got on another flight headed for California, Murda actually stayed in New York for a few days visiting his family and Sisqo and I rode to Baltimore in a lemo that he had waiting for us at the airport.

This was the first time in a while that Sisqo and I was alone and was able to talk. Normally it was always a crew of people around. Before this car ride, the last time I had a one on one with him was during the "Can I Live" run. We talked about a lot during the ride. Outside of music, we talked about our girls, he told me things about him and Tera and I told him about Tanja calling and questioning me about Shanna. And of course, we talked about all the events of the Africa trip, especially the killing of the native.

When we arrived in Baltimore, the limo dropped me off at my mothers and Sisqo went home but here's what was going on in the background of life that I didn't know. Shortly after Tanja and I hung up when she called my hotel room in Africa, she hooked up with Shanna and the two of them discussed our relationships. They both told each other when, where and how and compared notes as to what I was telling each of them and how often I was sleeping with the both. I was completely busted.

Tanja somehow knew about the flight back to Baltimore (the one where three of us had to stay in Angola) but she didn't know that we took the other flight to New York. So they both decided to meet me at BWI for a confrontation! If I would have gotten on the original flight, I would have came home to total chaos but they didn't know about the New York flight so while they were at BWI airport waiting for me, I was in a limo riding to Baltimore. I totally dodged a bullet and didn't even know it.

Sidenote: Tanja later told me that Shanna suggested that the both of them tell Chante about everything. Although Tanja was upset with me for sleeping with Shanna she didn't want to go that far and decided not to take part in telling Chante. She told Shanna that she wasn't down with it so Shanna didn't move forward with it either.

Chapter 39 - Sisqo's Chain

O nce I was home, back in Baltimore, I went through my usual routine by seeing my Mom, Dad, my son Peanut and of course Chante and Darrian. I told them all about what happened in Angola especially about the killing of the native. Everyone was shocked and amazed but grateful that we all were able to make it home safely.

Once the home front was addressed, I went back into Cooli Hi mode by hooking up with Tanja and getting back into the studio. Tanja was still upset about the Shanna situation but I apologized and promised that it would never happen again and I actually meant it. When I found out that Shanna wanted to tell Chante about everything and Tanja stopped it from happening, somehow in a weird way, that drew me even closer to Tanja and further away from Shanna. Again my top priority was to protect Chante by any means because she was the innocent one. Everyone else, especially me, were the dirt bags because we all were willing participants in this situation. By Tanja ignoring her own hurt to protect me by sparing Chante took our relationship to an even higher level.

I still was amazed of how Tanja found me in Angola. As I stated before, she didn't know any details because I didn't even have the details before we left. Also, keep in mind, the internet wasn't like it is today (back in 2004). The most anyone had if any was AOL dial up.

Tanja was always good at finding out things. Even after the Always video shoot, somehow Tanja had every detail about Chante's life. She knew her full name, birthdate, where she worked, home address and phone number. I found out because one day Tanja wanted me to attend a block party in her old neighborhood but I couldn't because I promised Chante I would spend time with her that day. Tanja got so upset, feeling like I chose Chante over her, that she called Chante's apartment. When she called, Chante was in the bathroom and I was close to the phone. I picked it up and hung up twice because Tanja called back to back. I did this because I didn't want Tanja to leave a voice message on Chante's phone. Afterwards, I deleted the number from the caller ID. The next day, I told Tanja I didn't want to see her anymore because of the phone calls. She apologized and promised that it would never happen again. That's how I found out that she had Chante's information. Till this day I still have no idea of how she got Chante's information or how she found me in Angola. Chante's info could have probably come from her license plate on her car, but Angola is a head scratcher.

As time continued to pass, I was still practically living in Sisqo's studio, recording new material day in and day out. Tanja was there with me every step of the way. Shanna was technically still around but because of the personal situation, I only dealt with her when it related to business and when necessary. I also had my entire team at Sisqo's house practically every night which caused the vibe of the house to change drastically. What used to be pretty Holla Back girls blended with a few average dudes had now turned into a gang of street thugs and one pretty girl, which was Tanja. Smoking, drinking and recording was all we did.

One day while in the studio, I decided to write a song to one of One Up Entertainments tracks that had a very melodic guitar playing in the background. Normally the more melodic the track was, the more I was inclined to say whatever was on my heart. I wrote a song entitled "Sleep For Days" and practically spilled all of the beans of my inner thoughts.

Sleep For Days is a song that I wrote that talks about me being tired of how I was living. It's a conversation that I'm having with God about everything that was going on in my life. Again, Dwayne was very reserved but Cooli Hi would tell it all! Some of the main points I hit in the song was that I didn't trust some of the guys in my inner circle. In one line I said "I got snakes all around me, some waiting in cuts. Laugh and smiling in my face but really hating my guts!" In the very next line I addressed my Chante, Tanja, Anna and Peanut's situation by saying "My personal's a reck so I just focus on business. And I can't leave my wife but I'm in love with my mistress. And my baby mother's crazy and my son's autistic. If I show you where its broke, can you fix it (speaking to God)?" When I said these lines in the song, I said them with so much passion and conviction that the entire room froze when they heard it. Sisqo even came downstairs from hearing the song through the vents and insisted that he jumped on it. He even got his female friend that was there visiting at the time to say the Lord's Prayer in French at the beginning of the song. Once Sisqo laid his vocals along with the French Prayer, the song went from hot to revolutionary! The only thing was you had to truly know me to feel the record the way it was intended to be felt.

Sidenote: Sisqo told me a long time before I wrote "Sleep For Days" that I wrote songs like I already had a record deal. Meaning the songs I wrote needed big budgets behind them. They needed visuals because the songs were so visual! He always suggested that I made songs a little lighter, something that didn't require too much thought. Dance or party records. Those are the records that normally break an artist! I heard and understood where Sisqo was coming from, but I didn't want to compromise my craft. Emotional songs were my strength. They were the core of who I was as an artist. I wanted my songs to be able to live forever and stand the tests of time and in order to do so I believed I had to attach to human emotions not party records.

When Tanja heard Sleep For Days (the part when I said I'm in love with my mistress) she came to me with water in her eyes and said "If this song doesn't get you signed, nothing will" and then she smiled and kissed me. I believe Tanja was so emotional because she knew that what I said in emotional songs were true and came directly from my heart and to hear me say in a song that I was in love with her, validated what we had was very real.

As for the part when I addressed my circle, so much was going on internally that the energy could have been coming from anyone. My Crown Vic Click had many groups of guys that all combined as one team, Again, originally the Crown Vic Click was Big Flood, Shawn (Lil Flood), Tim Brown, Kebo and Chop. They all were my blood cousins (with the exception of Chop). Then I had the musical side of Crown Vic which was Butch, Hot, Mouse and Murda. I also had my business side of Crown Vic which was Ole Man Joe, Pig and Jamaal. And the final pieces were all of these dudes had homeboys and crews that I took in and treated like family for example Butch's extension was Bags and Big Flood's extension was Shaggy. These are just two of many who came in as extensions but made it into my inner circle. Ole Man Joe was my right hand man and he would always try to warn me about the jealous vibes he would pick up when he saw something. Ole Man Joe thought that he was telling me things I didn't know but actually I saw it all. I just didn't have time to address each and every issue. I chose to ignore things for the greater cause until one day things turned for the worse.

One night we were having a party at Sisqo's house and per usual my entire Crown Vic Click was there. As always there were girls everywhere, Sisqo had his friends over as well as a few extensions of others that I vaguely knew. The entire night while the party was going on, Tanja and I were in the studio as I was editing some new music I had just recorded.

Not long before the party ended, my cousin Big Flood came to me and said he was leaving with some chick. We both dapped each other up and he left. About an hour or so later as the party was coming to an end, Big Flood's extension Shaggy (someone that I considered as one of the immediate now) came to me and said he was about to leave but as we dapped each other (shook hands) he looked at me with this strange look in his eyes and said "Yo word on the streets is Crown Vic ain't shit! Nigga's are out here saying that we're soft!" I didn't pay Shaggy any mind because I could tell he was high and drunk. "Alright cool. We will handle it." I replied. Shaggy walked out of the basement door and left.

A few hours later roughly around three or four in the morning, Tanja and I were sleeping on a futon in the studio when all of a sudden Murda comes over and says "Yo Cool wake up! Sisqo is upstairs going crazy because he can't find his chain! We gotta help him find it!" Tanja and I immediately got up and my brain began to race.

You see I knew that all fingers would point to me and my click. Whenever anything came up missing or broken around the house, my click always got blamed which actually meant I was being blamed. About a month or so prior to this night, one of Sisqo's Play Stations came up missing and everyone INADVERTENLY swore that someone on my team had something to do with it. I understood where the energy came from because my guys looked and acted like the type that would rob and steal and to be honest, not any of my immediate but the extensions would steal but I knew that if they did take the Play Station someone would have told me. I stood up for my crew and told Sisqo and everyone in the house that no one in my crew touched that Play Station. It later came out that Hot took the Play Station home with him one day to play it and a few days later he brought it back.

Now fast forwarding back to waking up out of a dead sleep and now Sisqo's colorful iced out chain (the one that I said lit up the entire club in South Africa) was missing. As we all looked frantically all over the house, I thought to myself "I hope nobody in my crew wasn't stupid enough to steal Sisqo's chain" And this wasn't any ordinary chain. This gold chain had a dragon plate that spined around with the prettiest colorful diamonds money could buy. I can't even imagine how much it was worth. The more and more we looked and couldn't find it, the more I began to worry. Sisqo always kept the chain in a box on one of the counters in his kitchen. It was always there visible for everyone to see. Sisqo never put the chain up because he trusted everyone that was there and felt no need to.

Finally, after an hour or so of everyone practically ripping the house apart looking for the chain, I called Big Flood and asked him if anyone on our team had taken the chain. Big Flood told me no. He left earlier than everyone else, but he assured me that no one on our team was stupid enough to take Sisqo's chain.

As more time passed Sisqo began to get very frustrated and upset. So upset that he began to cry. He was just so hurt from the fact that someone he considered close to him had stole from him. He even went on to say how much he opened his house up to everyone, showed a lot of people love, didn't treat them any different no matter where they came from and for them to steal something that was so valuable and dear to his heart was heartbreaking. I felt so bad for him because everything he said was right. No other celebrity would have opened their doors to people they barely knew. The majority of the people there were extensions of ME!

The sun was beginning to rise and we had been looking for the chain for hours and couldn't find it. Sisqo was scheduled to leave for New York at 7am to attend a recording session with

Timberland. He was so upset that he said he wasn't going. After a long talk with his sister, Murda and myself Sisqo changed his mind and decided to go to New York with a broken heart. I felt his pain. This was the ultimate betrayal. We couldn't find the chain anywhere, so it was obvious that someone took it. Hell, I subconsciously knew that after the first 30 minutes of searching.

I went home that morning and tried to go back to sleep but I couldn't. I needed to make sure that no one in my crew had anything to do with that chain being missing. Although Big Flood said what he said (and he was the "leader" of that portion of Crown Vic) I still had to keep in mind that he left earlier than everyone else so maybe he didn't know when I initially asked. That's what made me call Shawn (Lil Flood) and question him. When I called Shawn and asked him about the chain, he told me that Shaggy took Sisqo's chain! "Yo I didn't know he had it until we had left and were at the pancake house getting something to eat! Shaggy was sitting at the table and said Yo look what I got. Then he pulled the chain out! I asked him, why would he take Blondie's chain and he said that Blondie wasn't doing anything to help us! Its time for us to help ourselves! I told him he was stupid as fuck and he should give it back but he said that he's keeping it!" Shawn said.

No one could ever imagine how angry I was hearing this. I hung up with Shawn and immediately called Big Flood. When he answered I cursed my cousin out in the worst way. I thought that he knew Shaggy took the chain and had lied to me, but I later found out that Big Flood actually didn't know. He found out after Shawn and I had talked. Big Flood left the party earlier with a girl so he didn't talk to anyone in the crew till the next morning. Shawn on the other hand was with Shaggy. That's how he knew.

After cursing Big Flood out about not telling me what Shaggy did, I then called Shaggy. Of course, he wouldn't answer his phone. That's when I decided that I would get that chain back by any means necessary.

Sidenote: The entire time while everyone was looking all over the house for the chain, I could feel people cutting their eyes at me. I knew they quietly were blaming my crew and by blaming my crew they were in essence, blaming me. Now that it was confirmed that someone on my team took the chain, I had to get it back or else Sisqo might look at me as if I was in on it! Whether he thought that way or not, I am the one who brought these people to his home, so I felt responsible.

Since Big Flood was the leader of that part of my team and Shaggy was the thief, I didn't know who I could trust on that side so I cut everyone off in order to figure things out. Tim Brown, Chop and Kebo had nothing to do with it and Shawn was the one that told me but I was so pissed at Big Flood for not telling me, I severed ties with them all. Everything I did with my cousins was filtered down through Big Flood. He was like my lieutenant and to feel like I was crossed by him, made everyone suspect.

Later that day, I called Butch and Bags and we all decided to have a meeting at Sisqo's house. Sisqo was still in New York working with Timberland. Bags brought along his friend Tony (a white boy from Florida) to attend the meeting also.

Sidenote: Tony wasn't you're average white boy. He was down for whatever similar to Bags and always kept a gun on him.

When I told Butch, Bags and Tony about what Shaggy had did, they all were furious especially Bags. Bags was big on loyalty and to find out that someone was disloyal for no reason other than greed, made his blood boil. "Yo lets go find this nigga and break both of his hands!" Bags said. We all agreed and the hunt was officially on.

That upcoming weekend, Butch, Bags, Tony and I went to the club I knew my cousins and Shaggy liked to attend, hoping to find Shaggy. We didn't go in the club. We sat outside in the parking lot (next to Big Floods car) and waited for them to come outside. As always Bags and Tony had guns on them.

As the club was closing, everyone started leaving the club heading for their cars and we were waiting to see if Shaggy would come out. Finally Big Flood and the rest of my cousins came walking out but there was no sign of Shaggy. Bags knew that I was upset with Big Flood as well so since we didn't see Shaggy, Bags figured Big Flood was the next best thing. I made it specifically clear before we came looking for them that Shaggy was the target and Shaggy only. I wasn't dealing with Big Flood at the time but I didn't want anything to happen to him. Bags agreed but you could never really tell how things would turn out with Bags. He was a loose canon and very unpredictable.

We all were standing outside of the cars when Big Flood and my cousins walked up. When they saw us, Big Flood looked like he just saw a ghost. He knew how Bags got down so he figured if we were outside of the club at 2am waiting, we came there for violent reasons and he wasn't sure if we were there for him, Shaggy or the both of them. "Yo let me holler at you real quick" Bags said to Big Flood as they walked up. Bags put his arm around Big Flood and walked him over to our car. Just as Big Flood was about to get in the car, Tim Brown said "Come on Big Flood, We gotta go!" Big Flood and the rest of my cousins got in their car and pulled off. As we were leaving Bags asked me if I knew Shaggy's address. I knew where he lived but I didn't know the actual address so I told him I would find out.

The next day (which was a Saturday) before I met up with everyone at Sisqo's house, I drove by Shaggys house and wrote down the number address to his house on a piece of paper. When I arrived at the house, Bags, Butch and Tony were already there. Sisqo was there also. He had just got back from

New York. I told Sisqo that Shaggy had stolen the chain and we were in the process of getting it back. After talking to Sisqo for a few, we all went down to the basement to finish talking in the studio. Bags asked me "Yo Cool, did you get Shaggy's address?" "Yeah" I replied as I handed Bags the piece of paper. "Yo but we really don't have to go to his house. I know all of his whereabouts. Let's find him in the streets. Eventually he will pop up." I said. Bags replied "Alright cool" as he slipped the paper in his pocket.

Sidenote: Bags was determined to get that chain back by any means. You see Bags looked at this situation as an opportunity to do what he did best to put him in a better position in the crew. He knew that of us all, he and Tony were the only ones that would shoot without hesitation and this situation was perfect for showcasing that. Bags thought that if he got the chain back, it would raise his stock significantly with Sisqo and could possibly crown him as the king.

The next day was Superbowl Sunday. The previous night I went to Chante's spent the night and watched the Superbowl at her house. After the Superbowl was over, I jumped in my car and headed back in the city towards my mothers house. As I was driving, I received a call from Butch, a call that would change things forever. Butch called me and said "Yo you wouldn't believe where Bags and Tony are right now." "Where?" I responded. "Yo Bags and Tony are in Shaggy's house right now and they have his mother tied up! They have someone else gagged and nailed shut in a closet!" "What!?" I replied. "I thought we said we were gonna catch Shaggy in the streets!?" "Yeah but you know how Bags is" Butch replied.

Bags decided that he didn't want to wait so he and Tony went to Shaggys house. Tony knocked on the door and when Shaggys mother answered, he told her that he accidentally hit her car and wanted to give out his insurance information. Being as though Tony was a white boy, Shaggys mother probably thought everything was legit but when she opened the door, Tony forced his way in with Bags following close behind. Once inside they both pulled their guns out and scanned the entire house to see if any one else was there as well as if any guns were in the house. I think an older uncle or someone also was there. Bags and Tony did construction work so they brought a nail gun also. Bags plan was to torture Shaggy by shooting nails in him until he gave up the chain. After he got the chain, there's no telling what Bags would have done but the only problem was Shaggy wasn't there. So Bags and Tony tied up Shaggy's Mom, nailed the old guy in a closet and just sat there and waited for Shaggy.

An hour or so had passed and still there was no sign of Shaggy. The entire time while in the house, Bags was loud and irate, being the loose canon that he was, yelling out things that would lead back to me by saying "This is what happens when you fuck with Crown Vic!" Shaggy's mother knew exactly who I was and she knew that Crown Vic was essentially Cooli Hi. But

Bags was being Bags not giving any of this any thought and was practically yelling out my name the entire time.

Sidenote: Bags and Tony also did not wear a mask so that usually mean that it will not end well for the victims. Maybe that's why he was yelling out "Crown Vic"

A few more hours had passed and still no signs of Shaggy. Bags would call me every so often and tell me what was going on. One time he called me and said that Shaggy's mother had to use the bathroom and when he took her, a thought crossed his mind. I told Bags not to do that. Don't even think about it. You see I only wanted to get the chain back and whip Shaggy's ass for taking it. Bags took this situation to another level and now he was thinking about doing the unthinkable. After I talked him out of it, Bags finally decided that it was time to leave. He then asked me the life changing question by saying "Yo Cool, how do you want this to end?" Without actually saying, Bags was asking me if he should kill Shaggy's mother or not. I replied, "Yo we just want the chain. Let that lady be. She had nothing to do with it" Bags agreed and then he and Tony placed Shaggys mother in another closet, nailed it shut and left.

Later that night Shaggy called me sounding hysterical. It was as if he couldn't believe what had just happened and of course he blamed me. I told him "Don't blame me, blame yourself! You stole that mans chain and there are some folks willing to do WHATEVER to get it back!" We both went back and forth with some unpleasant words and then we hung up. After that call, I knew I had to prepare for a comeback. You see Shaggy knew where my mother lived also and in my mind it was just a matter of time before someone would be knocking or kicking at my mothers door.

The next day, Butch, Bags, Tony, and I, all met up at Sisqo's house. I thought about asking Bags why he went to Shaggy's house, but I didn't. It was pointless. What was done was done. When things like this happen, there's no point in questioning anything. The only thing to talk about is what's the next move. I initially gave Bags Shaggys address so if I wasn't with them while they were on the hunt, they would know where to wait for Shaggy to return (after clubbing) so we could get Sisqo's chain back because it would be a strong possibility that he would have the chain on him. Instead, Bags had his own agenda and acted on it as soon as he got the address. Bags reckless act put me and only me in the fire because Shaggy thought the move came from me and he knew where MY mother lived. I didn't have a gun at the time so Butch gave me his gun. It was on and popping from there.

There were so many moving parts going on regarding what took place that it was ridiculous. I kept Butch's gun on me at all times. At night, after studio sessions instead of being with Tanja, I went to my mothers to practically guard the house. Tanja and I would circle the block a few times before I got out of her car and the gun was always cocked and ready to go. Big

Flood, in fear of Bags coming to his house, stayed home with a gun waiting for a knock at the door.

Sidenote: I never gave Bags Big Floods address. There was no need to. The goal was to get the chain back, not to go running up in people's houses. Big Flood didn't have the chain, so his address was pointless.

As I said, there were a lot of moving parts, but here are the most disturbing of them all. After the home invasion, my cousins had a meeting of their own to take a vote as to if Shaggy should give the chain back. All my cousins were there, Big Flood, Shawn (Lil Flood), Tim Brown, Kebo, Chop and Shaggy but there was also one other person there that I would have never expected, Kidd!

Sidenote: I didn't find out about this meeting till quite some time after this all went down. Knowing that Kidd was in the mix brought all kinds of spectulations. Like what if Kidd put Shaggy up to stealing the chain in the first place? Shaggy had been around Sisqo and that chain many times before and nothing ever happened. Then Shaggy made that stupid comment about Crown Vic just as he walked out of the house with Sisqo's chain. When dealing with Kidd, you just never knew.

Kidd had already had his fangs deep into my cousins by then. He would wow them by taking them to clubs, buying them drinks and showing them a good time. He would bring them around female celebrities like Mya and show them things that they never experienced. He once flew Big Flood to California just to hang out and experience LA life. He even bailed a few of them out of jail a few times so they felt like they owed him. You couldn't tell them anything bad about Kidd because they thought the world of him but they couldn't see that he was manipulating them, trading petty gifts for their loyalty.

After they took a vote (and till this day I don't know who said yea or nay) they decided to keep the chain and sell it. Shaggy took the chain to New Jersey or New York (not sure which of my cousins went with him) to meet with some guys that wanted to buy the chain. Somehow, the buyers took the chain from Shaggy by telling him they would bring him the money AFTER they had the chain in their possession and ran off with it. Shaggy then returned to Baltimore with no money and no chain.

The stealing of Sisqo's chain put a serious strain on my cousins and I relationship. I felt like I shouldn't have had to go hunting for Shaggy. They should have kicked his ass and took the chain back themselves. If they didn't want to kick his ass, cool but they definitely should have gotten the chain back. And for them to sit around and vote on it was absolutely crazy to me! They had to know that the chain being stolen from someone that I brought to the house would kill my relationship with Sisqo, which in turn could kill my chances of progressing in the music industry. Sisqo was my musical PLUG! To me they chose money over family and that was a very hard pill to swallow.

In addition to the chain situation, I was now dealing with a more serious matter because of the home invasion. I didn't understand how could my cousins still be cool with a dude that tore our click apart, ruined any chance of them ever coming to Sisqo's house again and someone that might be thinking of harming their aunt (my mother)? Needless to say, I couldn't deal with any of them at all.

Moving forward without my cousins by my side felt a little weird but the show had to go on. Sisqo never blamed me for what Shaggy did, but I believe his family members may have a little. The entire situation was embarrassing to me especially being as though I couldn't get it back. What kind of "boss" cant manage his own crew? That's not a boss at all. Stealing that chain from Sisqo was like stealing the chain from me and I will always feel responsible.

At night I watched over my mothers house when I was there but I couldn't help but to worry about the times when I wasn't there. I didn't want my mother to be in the blind so I told her an altered version of the story and warned her that it could be a possible retaliation. My mother had already gotten wind of the situation through family gossip and already knew. One day I was trying to get my mother to keep the main door closed (she liked to leave it open and only have the screen door shut for the sun light) and she stopped me and said "Look don't worry about it. This house is protected by God and in the Blood of Jesus! I will not live here in fear!" What my Mom said registered in my soul. I kept a gun on me for about a month or so afterwards but eventually gave it back to Butch. But I kept my antenna's up at all times.

As time went on, I continued to make new music and started new projects. Although the music video "Always" received tremendous positive feedback, I decided to take Sisqo's advise a push a party track out into the atmosphere. I decided to do a remix to a song on my Crown Victoria album called "Grown Ass" and reached out to a Baltimore producer named KP for the track. KP gave me an up-tempo party track for the remix and I renamed the song and called it "Off The Chain."

Around this time, I was working with Corey Grant on a new project. Corey like what I did in his movie "Under Pressure" so much that he gave me a leading role on a Red Bull project that he was directing for his partner and girlfriend at the time name Nakia Warren. I played the role of a basketball star that was cocky and arrogant and ended up losing the final game to a nerdy guy who drunk Red Bull to get an edge. Shanna also had a small role in the film as well which reunited us because we hadn't talked much since the Angola incident. During the shooting of the small film, I played "Off the Chain" for Corey and he loved it and offered to shoot another music video, free no charge (just feed the talent). Video number two was in the making.

For the "Off The Chain" video, Corey and I wanted to shoot two versions. Back then BET had a late night show called BET Uncut where they show very sexually explicit videos and we wanted one of the versions on that show. The second version would be more mainstream. Corey had a casting call at Howard University and had thee most beautiful girls in the DMV area show up for casting. Again since Corey was Shanna's plug, I had Shanna with me along with Pig to pick the best girls for the video.

Meanwhile while the ground work of the new video was being set, I was still in the studio creating new songs. One day as I was writing in a separate room, I heard Murda playing a track that he had just made. Murda was Sisqo's personal assistant, but he also recently had just started making tracks a few years prior. Murda would always play tracks for me but I hardly ever chose any. I did chose one of his tracks for my Crown Victoria album (Interlude) but that was just me talking over the track. It was very rare that I heard one of Murda's tracks and wanted to rap on it but this track was different.

The track was everything I was looking for in a dance/party record. I was actually surprised that Murda made it! All producers have a distinct sound and this track sounded nothing like Murda's pattern. I stopped writing whatever I was writing at the time and ran into the studio. "Yo play that again!" I said. Murda smiled and replayed the track. I literally lost my mind. As I continued to listen, the melody of the hook began to form in my head. I didn't have the words just the melody. I asked Murda to bounce the track to a CD and I drove home with the track on repeat.

The next day, I returned to the studio with the entire song written and ready to record. I called Scola and asked him if he could come to the studio and sing what I had written. Scola agreed and a few hours later he arrived. By the time Scola had arrived, I had already recorded the 1st and 2nd verse. I walked Scola through the chorus and he blazed it, just as I heard it in my head. After Scola recorded the chorus, Murda and I kept playing the song non stop blasting it as loud as we could. The track and song made anyone that listened want to dance. By chance the other members of Dru Hill just so happened to be at the house that day, having a group meeting. Murda and I had the whole basement rocking to our new song. Dru Hill couldn't help but to hear the thumping that was coming from downstairs.

As we kept playing the song, Woody from Dru Hill came downstairs and asked "Yo what's that?" I told Woody its my new joint that Murda produced. As we all danced and vibed as we listened Woody began to sing. As soon as I heard Woody singing, I told Murda to add a few tracks and asked Woody to lay down what he was singing. Before we knew it, Woody had recorded an intro to the song.

Now we had Woody and Scola on the record. We continued to blast the record on repeat, while everyone in the house danced. Before I knew it, Nokio, Jazz and Sisqo were in the studio along with the entire house dancing and singing the record. Since it was so loud I couldn't hear what was being said but I saw Nokio and Sisqo talking as the nodded their head uncontrollably to the record. Before I knew it Jazz asked for some tracks and went in and blazed the song. After Jazz, Nokio went in and put harmonies on the hook. The only one left was Sisqo.

I didn't have a third verse, so it was the perfect set up for Sisqo to close out the song. I got Chinky to talk sexy on the intro and throughout the song and I added a few talk ad libs to set things up for Sisqo. When Sisqo went in the booth to record, I had no idea what he was going to say. Instead of coming up with something new, he just re-sung the chorus and added his own twist to it! Sisqo was feeling the record so much when he recorded his part that if you listen closely to the record, you can hear him stomping his foot in the background. Per usual it was one hell of a performance just watching him record his parts! This was the 1st and only hip-hop record to date that has ALL 5 MEMBERS of Dru Hill on it! The name of the record is "Out of Control"

Sidenote: We were so excited when recording this record that we didn't pay attention to our vocals! A lot of Jazz's and Sisqo's vocals came out distorted because they may have been too close to the mic but at the time, we didn't care! We were just caught up in the moment. I had Dru Hill singing MY WORDS! When Teddy Davis (an engineer from Fort Washington, MD- my favorite, RIP Teddy) mixed the record, he did the best he could with the distorted vocals. I had to live with it because there wasn't a chance in hell that I was going to be able to get all 5 members to record their parts all over again!

Once "Out of Control" was completed (mixed and mastered) we continued to play it non stop in the studio. At the time, Dru Hill was working on the "Dru World Order" album. On several occasions, Def Jam representatives would be at the studio listening to what Dru Hill had recorded for their album and we would play "Out of Control". The Def Jam reps loved the record! One time, one of Kevin Liles right hand men, Tony Austin suggested that Out of Control should be on Dru Hill's "Dru World Order" album and a lot of people agreed but me being naive to the business side of things, declined. I was so caught up on the artistry side of things that I couldn't see that allowing Dru Hill to use the song on their album could have catapulted me as a songwriter and possibly could have changed my current circumstances. Instead, I was thinking that "Out of Control" was my way of blowing up as an artist but what I didn't realize is that Dru Hill had a machine behind them (Def Jam). I had absolutely nothing behind me. All I had was a hot song.

Sidenote: Instead of allowing Dru Hill to use "Out of Control" on their album, I kept the record for myself. I thought this would be the record that would finally kick the industry door in for me. I borrowed money from associates and had vinyl records pressed up and gave it to all of the DJ's but nothing came out of it. If I knew what I know now, I would have definitely allowed Dru Hill to use it. Hindsight is always 20/20 vision.

While in the mist of all the "Out of Control" hype, I still was in the process of shooting the "Off the Chain" video. I had three locations I was using. One of the most popular clubs in Baltimore at the time, Club One, the most popular strip club in Baltimore, Norma Jeans and last but not least, Sisqo's studio.

Since this was a party record, there wasn't a lot of planning involved in this video. Outside of the choreography, everything else was just club scenes, partying and performing. The first scenes were shot at Club One and it was pretty basic, girls dancing and me performing the song. Being as though I still wasn't dealing with my cousins at the time, instead of them being on my side as I performed, I had Murda and Hot with me and sometimes I alternated by adding in a few local rappers that I was cool with. I invited everyone I knew to the club scene shooting because I rented out the entire club. Everyone in the video was there for the shoot, meaning we didn't just bring the cameras while the club was in process. What was seen in the video was specifically for me.

The club scene shots were so live, you would have thought the club was open to the public but it wasn't! We were shooting these scenes in the afternoon long before club hours. Even Sisqo came to the club just to watch and of course check out the "talent" (girls)! While shooting at the club, Corey made an announcement and told the girls that we were shooting and uncut version also that may involve some nudity. For those that wanted to participate he made them sign a waiver and shot separate scenes with them. Surprisingly the finest of the girls were all down for the uncut scenes.

After we finished shooting at Club One, we then went to the strip club, Norma Jeans and shot a few scenes there as well. Tanja was with me every single step of the way making sure I was straight by being my eyes for things I couldn't see. She watched over me and made sure that I looked the way I wanted to look because she knew. You see when you're performing in a video, you can't see if your shirt is crooked or if you're looking greasy or sweaty because of the hot lights or if somethings out of place in regards to your appearance. There are no mirrors around so its best to have someone to be your "eyes" and watch over you to make sure everything's in place and Tanja did that to perfection. Not to mention, she was looking absolutely gorgeous as she did this, making me look like a true star by having this bad ass "assistant" taking care of me. Often while shooting, people would ask Tanja why she wasn't in the video and she would reply by smiling and saying "Cool doesn't want me to be in a video like this." Which basically meant she was too good to be half naked and shaking her ass in a camera.

After the Norma Jean shots, we went to Sisqo's house to finish the video shoot. The only girls that were invited to Sisqo's were the ones that signed up for the uncut scenes. We got some shots of girls in bikini's and stripper outfits in the clubs but there was a limit to how far we could go. Now that we were at Sisqo's, there weren't any limits, and we were willing to go as far as the girls would allow.

We all gathered up in the studio portion of the basement as I shot a scene with me pretending to write the song as I envisioned sexy girls dancing as I wrote it. When we shot the scene, I decided to instead of playing "Off The Chain" play "Out Of Control" just to see how the girls would respond to it. All of the scenes we were about to shoot were non performing scenes (cut a ways) meaning they were action scenes so it didn't matter what song was playing.

When "Out of Control" started playing, Murda dimmed the lights in the studio and the girls went nuts! But not in a wild way but a sexual way. It was almost as if the song was hypnotizing them! Before we knew it the girls began to take off their clothes and dance totally nude! The vibe in that room was so sexual that I believe everyone wanted to just grab the person beside them and start having sex!

As several girls in the studio danced provocatively in the nude while Corey and his cameras recorded, Tanja and I were secretly touching on each other feeling the heat of the moment. Then out of nowhere, one of the girls started dancing and kissing on another girl! The two of them didn't know each other but like I said the vibe and the walls of the studio were screaming sex! As the two girls continued to make out, things got so heated that the two of them decided to go all the way. One of the girls grabbed the others hand and walked her into the recording room. They both were totally nude. Once inside, they laid on the floor, passionately kissed for a moment and then one of the girls went down on the other and began to perform oral sex on her. We all stood around in a circle, very quiet respecting the intimate moment while Corey and his camera continued to record. As this was going on Tanja and I were so close to the girl that was receiving the oral sex that her foot would occasionally rub up against my leg. I was sitting on the floor watching and Tanja was standing beside me. While everyone was focused on the two girls, I gently eased my hand up Tanja's leg as she watched also. Tanja had on a short mini shirt without any panties on. I knew watching the girls was turning Tanja on just like it was doing to everyone else who was watching so I continued to ease my hand up her leg until I touched her vagina and of course it was already dripping wet.

I played with Tanja's vagina the entire time as we all watched the two girls pleasure themselves.

When the girls were done, everyone began to slowly clear out of the recording room. A few other girls were topless and kissing in certain areas of the room but no one went as far as the two on the floor. Once the room cleared out a little, Tanja and I went and leaned against the back wall where it was the darkest. Before everyone left out Tanja lifted her skirt as I began to take down my pants. Tanja backed up on me and before I knew it, I was inside of her. People were still walking around the dark recording room and we were watching them but at the same time having sex. They didn't have a clue of what we were doing. Two other girls saw and walked over to us as I was slowly moving in and out of Tanja. As the girls got closer Tanja began to moan. Neither of us cared that they were close. It was actually turning us on even more. One of the girls realized what we were doing and said "Oh my! I know that's right! You better work it girl! Lucky you." And then they walked away. It wasn't long afterwards before both Tanja and I climaxed. That entire experience made Tanja and I realize that we were the true definitions of Scorpio's and ready to explore!

Sidenote: When the Off the Chain Uncut video was released, none of the Studio footage was used. It was entirely too much! If we would have used that footage, it would have been a porno tape instead of a music video! I'm not sure what Corey did with the footage. I'm guessing he still has it somewhere. Who knows?

Before the studio episode, Tanja and I were already adventurous but now it was clear that we both wanted to explore even more. We couldn't be anywhere alone and not ending up having sex but now we were finding ways to have sex even when we were not alone. Every single time that I had a show and we had to travel, Tanja and I would always sit next to each other in the back seat of the van or car. Tanja would pretend as if she was going to sleep and lay her head on my lap with her coat covering her entire head. Then she would perform oral sex on me until I climaxed and all of this would be going on in the mist of laughter and conversation throughout the car! I would then return the favor by using a coat to cover Tanja's lap and then I would touch her until she climaxed! We did this ALL the time, and no one never knew.

One day Tanja told me that the studio lights turned her on and although we had the quicky in the recording room during the "Off the Chain" video shoot, she wanted to do it again but this time have a full session! The next night Tanja and I waited until everyone left the studio dimmed the lights just perfectly and made love in the recording room but this time we took our time and we also vocally recorded everything. After we were done, I burned our sex recording to a CD so we could always playback that beautiful night.

Often when Tanja and I were together, I couldn't help but to think about how turned on Tanja was when watching the two girls so at times when we were intimate, I would whisper things in her ear while I was inside of her that pertained to another female. When I said these things, Tanja would go crazy so I knew she was open to the thought of being with another woman.

Soon afterwards, Tanja and I began to have the conversation of bringing someone to bed with us. Tanja was with it, but she had restrictions. The first restriction was we both had to agree on the girl and the second and final one was I could not enter the girl! Tanja said she couldn't watch me being inside of another woman. "I know how you make me feel when you're inside of me and I don't want to witness anyone else having that same feeling" Tanja said. I agreed to the terms. It really didn't matter to me really. Turning Tanja on turned me on so if she was good, so was I. "Besides, things could always change while in the heat of the moment," I thought to myself. Tanja and I decided to refer to whoever we brought in as our "toy". Someone we could play with and then put back in the box when we were done.

So now Tanja and I were on the hunt. I suggested calling one of the girls we watched at the video shoot (She was very attractive. The spitting image of Cierra Wilson) but Tanja declined. Although Tanja was down for the threesome, she didn't want to choose just anybody. "That girl slept with a total stranger in front of a room full of strangers! There's no telling what she might have." Tanja said. I thought about it and agreed. My brain then began to race. I didn't want to wait for Tanja to find someone because I thought that she would overthink things and take too long recruiting. I also knew that whoever I brought to the table had to be just as fine as Tanja or else she wouldn't be attracted to her. Then I thought about an old acquaintance of mine, someone I used to deal with, and she was bisexual and pretty. Tanja knew her as well because she would often be at the studio with us from time to time. "The old acquaintance would be perfect!" I thought to myself. She checked all the boxes for both Tanja and I's requirements. Instead of revealing the "acquaintance" name, I 'll just call her "Toy" (Me and Tanja's toy).

When I suggested to Tanja that we should invite Toy into our bedroom, Tanja was okay with it. Tanja knew that I had slept with Toy in the past and was okay with it. Now that I had Tanja on board, the next step would be to get Toy to agree.

Toy and I were friends before we dealt with each other and even after we separated, we still remained close friends so it was always easy to talk to her. One night while at the studio, I asked Toy what she thought about Tanja. "Tanja's beautiful!" Toy replied as she blushed a little. Right then, I knew she would be down for the proposal. "Tanja and I are interested in having a threesome. She's never been with a girl and we want to experience this with you!" I said to Toy. Toy smiled and said "Okay, I'm down with it. Just set it up and let me know when!"

Over the next couple of days, I tried to arrange the threesome but our schedules kept conflicting. When Toy was free, Tanja didn't have a babysitter. When Tanja was free, Toy was in a studio session and so on and so on.

Finally, one night both Tanja and Toy was at Sisqo's house in the studio with me along with many others. Almost every night, 9 out of 10 studio sessions, Tanja and I would always creep off to have sex while everyone was socializing in the studio. On this particular night, Tanja and I snuck off to do our usual. We went into the bathroom and locked the door. Toy must have seen us so after maybe 10 minutes or so we heard a light knock on the bathroom door. I knew it was Toy from the light knock. When I went to open the door, Tanja stopped me and said "No, I don't want it to happen in a bathroom! I want us to be able to fully enjoy the experience. She will have to wait until another time." Tanja and I ignored the knock and continued.

Later that night when it was time to go home, Toy needed a ride so I offered to take her home. As I drove, Tanja sat in the passenger seat while Toy sat in the back directly in the middle. We all laughed and talked as I drove but as we got closer to Toy's house, I began to get silent and allowed the two of them to talk. While Toy was conversing with Tanja, I reached my right hand over to Tanja and started touching her vagina through her pants. The more I touched Tanja, the more aroused she got and eventually she became very quiet and was just breathing heavy. When Toy caught on to what I was doing, she became quiet too and began to watch. Soon it was silence throughout the car and Tanja had taken one of her pants legs completely off and my fingers were inside of her. When we arrived at Toy's house, I parked the car and began to perform oral sex on Tanja, while Toy watched from the back seat. Every so often, I would look up and I would see Toy touching Tanja's legs as I was orally pleasing her. Just before Tanja began to go into convulsions from climaxing, I looked up and Toy was leaning over the seat kissing Tanja in the most passionate way. The kiss made me go into overdrive orally and within a matter of seconds, Tanja had a huge orgasm all while still kissing Toy. Afterwards, Toy softly ran her fingers through Tanja's hair and caressed her face as Tanja fought effusively to catch her breath.

When Tanja came back down to earth, I pretended to gently touch her vagina and she smacked my hand away. Toy then joking said "Stop it Cool! You know we are extremely sensitive down there after we cum!" All three of us busted out in laughter and then Toy got out of the car and went home.

About two weeks later, as usual Toy and I were at the studio working on some records but on this night Tanja wasn't there. As the night came close to an end, I called Tanja to let her know I would be there soon. It was late and I didn't want her to fall asleep. Tanja was living with her uncle at the time but on this particular night, her uncle was out of town and her kids were with her sister. When Tanja and I talked, I told her that Toy was in the studio with me. "Should I ask Toy to come also" I asked Tanja. "Yes" Tanja replied.

I then went and asked Toy if she had any plans after we left the studio. "No. Why what's up?" Toy replied. "You should come hang out with me and Tanja" I said. Toy agreed and then we both left the studio and headed to Tanja's house.

When we arrived, Tanja and Toy went upstairs to the bedroom and I stayed behind in the kitchen. For some dumb reason (maybe because I had been drinking) my mind reverted back to when Shanna told me how Sisqo's dancer, Ronnie and the other girl manipulated her by getting her in the bathroom and turning on the hot water causing the bathroom to get hot and steamy so I went to the thermostat and turned the heat up as high as I could. I then went upstairs and joined the two.

We all sat on the bed and talked for a few but we all knew what we were there for so it was just a matter of time before someone kicked things off. As we were talking, I said something that was kind of funny and Toy began to laugh. When Toy laughed she raised her hand in the air and when she brought it down she placed it on Tanja's thigh. Toy began to slowly move her hand up Tanja's thigh until she was close to her vagina. As Toy continued to touch on Tanja, Tanja and I began to kiss and then Toy and Tanja began to kiss. Soon afterwards, we all began to take each other's clothes off and the threesome began.

We started out with Tanja and Toy taking turns performing oral sex on each other. When Toy performed oral sex on Tanja, I kissed Tanja and caressed her breast but when Tanja performed oral sex on Toy, I entered Tanja from behind. As the threesome continued, Tanja got up and went to get some water (because I had the heat up so high). When she left the room. Toy and I touched each other but I didn't insert myself inside of Toy because that was one of Tanja and I restrictions. Instead, I allowed Toy to perform oral sex on me. When Tanja returned from getting some water, she ran back into the room with a startled look on her face, almost as if to say "He'd better not be in here fucking her!" When she saw that Toy was only performing oral sex on me, she looked relieved. Then she joined and they both performed oral sex on me.

When we were done, I drove Toy home and immediately returned to Tanja. Tanja and I made love that night (after the threesome) like we never had before. It was something about the threesome, that drew us into each other even more, kind of hard to explain. We had gotten to the point where we were not just in love anymore. We were now madly in love or infatuated with one another. Probably both.

The next day Tanja and I talked about the threesome in detail and discussed what we liked and didn't like. There weren't too many dislikes. The only thing Tanja and I were mainly concerned about was our performance. We both were competitive like that. Tanja always took pride in how good her sex was and so did I. Tanja felt like she could have made the experience more pleasurable for everyone but she didn't want to do a do over. Instead she wanted to find a new "Toy" and I was cool with that. We both decided that we were not going to aggressively hunt, but if someone became an option, we would jump on it (if she checked the required boxes).

The threesome along with everything that came before it, made Tanja and I two peas in a pod. We walked around in total bliss and didn't even know it. One day while at Sisqo's, Tanja was sitting on the kitchen counter and I was leaning against a wall, maybe a few feet away from her. For some reason Tanja and I locked eyes and just continued to stare at each other. Butch saw how we were looking at each other and came to me and said "Yo, it's just a matter of time before yall make it official! You two look like a scene out of a love story!" Everyone could visually see how Tanja and I felt about each other but still I wouldn't fully commit. Chante was technically still my number one but all of my time and effort was going to Tanja.

A few weeks later Tanja brought a very interesting proposal to our table. "Would you be interested in going to a sex club with me?" she asked. "I found one on line and I think it will be fun" she added. "Hell yeah! Let's do it!" I responded.

Tanja set up our memberships and paid whatever cost was involved and the following week, we were at the doors of the sex club. Initially we were worried that someone would be there that knew us but when we got in that wasn't the case at all. The club was hidden in plain sight, right off of Route 40 West in Baltimore County. When we walked in, there were hardly any black people there at all. Before going, I had envisioned the party looking like a scene from the movie "Eyes Wide Shut" where everyone is wearing a mask and having sex freely all over the club but it wasn't exactly like that. Some women had on lingerie and some were topless. As for the guys, a lot of them were fully dressed and some may have had their shirt off but no one was having sex out in the open. It was porn playing on all of the TV's and for the most part, everyone just walked around and socialized. This was the scenery on the main floor.

The lower level was a little more intense. Downstairs were bedrooms but you had to sign up for a time slot in order to have access. Once inside the bedroom, you had the option of leaving the door open, which meant it was okay for others to come in, watch, or join or you could close the door and have the room all to yourself.

Tanja and I stayed to ourselves while we were there. Being as though it was our first time and we were maybe the only black couple there (there may have been others sprinkled around but hard to tell) we didn't feel too comfortable letting our hair all the way down while there. We danced, had a few drinks and just observed on the main floor but we did make our way downstairs to watch a few couples that had their door open. When it was time for us to have our room, Tanja suggested that we closed our door. "Those people look creepy babe. Lets just do us and move on!" she said. Tanja and I both took turns and pleased each other orally and then we went back upstairs to the party area. After a few more drinks and conversation, we left.

Meanwhile on the musical side of things, I was still working on new material while at the same time trying to push my vinyl single "Out of Control" as well as get my music video "Off The Chain" seen on some sort of video platform. One night while at the studio, Scola and I were talking and he told me that he knew a guy that worked for Rocafella Records named Chubbs. Scola thought that I would be a good fit for Rocafella and told me that I should meet with him. The next day Scola got us both on the phone and scheduled a meeting the following week in New York.

I caught the train to New York the following week alone and met with Scola's guy, Chubbs at the Rocafella/ Def Jam office. When I arrived, I saw a girl from Baltimore that I knew by the name of Tracey who was working at Def Jam at the time. Tracey was always cool and it was good to see a familiar face in the building. After talking for a few with Tracey, I went into Chubbs office and we began to talk. After greeting each other and me telling him my story finally it was time to play my records. The first record I played for Chubbs was a song off my Crown Victoria album called "Dat Shit". As the song played, I remember thinking to myself, should I get up and perform the song as it plays (to sell the performance also) or should I just sit back with a hard head nod and vibe as the song plays. I decided to do the latter because of the size of the office (wasn't a lot of room for performing). Chubbs absolutely loved "Dat Shit" as well as all of the other records I played for him and as always, I only played the first verse and chorus of every song (which was the normal protocol when judging music). The last record I played for Chubbs was "Always" which completely blew him away. As Chubbs went crazy listening to my music, my heart beat began to race. I was thinking to myself, "Damn I'm here in Rocafella Records, Jay and Dame's label and this guy Chubbs is going nuts listening to my music! Is this real? Am I about to get signed to Rocafella Records?" I used to hear stories all the time (and you have probably heard stories too) about an artist getting hooked up with a meeting, playing their music, someone liked it and the rest was history! So I began to think that the clichés story was about to happen to me!

Just as I began to think that my dreams were about to come true, Chubbs walked out of the office and said he'd be right back. When Chubbs returned, he brought another dude with him and asked me to play the records again. That's when I realized that Chubbs was not the guy that needed to say yes and although I was very grateful and appreciative for the opportunity and happy that Chubbs liked my music, I knew that I had more hurdles to clear.

The guy Chubbs brought into the room loved my music also but after a few minutes of hearing him and Chubbs talk, I could tell the he wasn't the guy either. "Well at least I have two of them in my corner" I thought to myself. The only thing left was to find out who the actual "guy" was that I needed to say yes! As Chubbs and the other guy continued to talk, I heard the other guy say "We gotta get him in front of Kenny!"

The "guy" I needed to say yes was a guy by the name of Kenny Burns. Kenny Burns was the Vice President of Rocafella at the time but unfortunately for me, he wasn't in New York that day. "Yo Cooli, I want you to come back for another meeting when Kenny gets back in town" Chubbs said. "Okay cool. When will he be back?" I replied. Chubbs told me that Kenny would be back in a few days.

The following week I returned to New York very excited about playing my music for Kenny Burns. I knew that if he only liked my music or was on the fence about it, Chubbs and the other guys enthusiasm could possibly push me over the top. There was no way that he would think my music was trash so I thought my chances were pretty high. The night before the meeting I could barely sleep. Rocafella Records was the hottest label in hip hop at the time.

When I arrived in New York, I sped walked and damn near jogged to the Def Jam office on 8th or 9th Ave. When I arrived at the front desk, the security guard asked me for my ID which was needed to get a pass to go upstairs. When I reached in my pocket to get my wallet, I noticed that it wasn't there. I began to check all of my pockets frantically, but I couldn't find my wallet. Then it hit me. I was so excited about the meeting that I accidently left my wallet on my bedroom dresser. I asked the security officer if I could use the phone and called home to my mother and she confirmed that my wallet was there.

I then pleaded with the security officer to allow me to go upstairs and stressed how important the meeting was with Kenny Burns. The security officer would budge. "I need some form of identification in order to allow you in the building. Without ID, you cant come in" he said. My brain began to race. "What can I do to fix this?" I thought to myself. I called Chubbs several times but his phone was going straight to voicemail. Then I remembered that Tracey worked there and was probably upstairs also. I called Tracey and explained to her my situation. As always, Tracey tried to help. She didn't have the pull to get the security officers to bend so she did the next best thing and began to search for someone who did. "Hold tight Cooli. Let me find someone that can help!" Tracey said.

I stood at the security desk patiently waiting for the potential help. I was already about an hour late for my meeting. As I continued to wait, suddenly I heard some loud voices coming down the stairs. When I looked to see who it was, I saw that it was none other than Kenny Burns, Chubbs and a few other's from the Rocafella staff. "Yo Cooli where you been? We were waiting on you!" Kenny said. I was shocked that he knew who I was because we never met. I assumed Chubbs must have told him who I was. "I didn't have my ID so they wouldn't let me upstairs" I told Kenny. "Damn yo. Call Chubbs tomorrow and lets reschedule." Kenny said as they all walked out of the door appearing to be in a rush. I was devastated. I felt like this was a big opportunity for me and I blew it by forgetting my wallet and on top of it all I had spent my last dollar on my train tickets so if the reschedule was any time soon, I didn't have money to return to New York. Feeling totaling deflated, I walked back to the train station and went home.

A couple days later I called Chubbs to reschedule but Kenny's schedule was always booked up. Often he was out of town and when he was in town, it was sporadic. After many attempts to reschedule to no avail, Chubbs suggested that we all meet in Washington, DC. Kenny was from DC and was having a birthday party at a club so Chubbs thought it would be a good idea if I came through. I agreed and told Chubbs I would meet them there. Since they were coming from New York headed for DC, I tried to make a good impression by offering to bring them girls that would show them a good time. DC wasn't my town but it was close enough for me to have some sort of influence.

The night of the party, I called up some of the girls I met at my "Off The Chain" music video and I took them to DC with me. I also had a few others with me, none of my normal crew but one guy that I had with me was a guy I met though my cousin Big Flood that I became cool with named Kevin.

Sidenote: Kevin (we called him Cuzzo) was a street dude known for putting in work in Baltimore City. Although a lot of people feared him around town, he was a real cool guy. I remember he would always tell me that he had a sister that worked with Diddy and Bad Boy Records but to be honest, I didn't totally believe him. He didn't seem like the type that would lie so I just thought that maybe his sister worked in promotions or on some sort of street team. I later found out that he knew exactly what he was talking about. Kevin's sister was Makeba Riddick (Grammy Nominated Songwriter).

We attended the birthday party and partied with Kenny, Chubbs and their crew but that wasn't the place or the time to discuss business. Kenny was in party mode, socializing and drinking and although the party was lit, I didn't have a good time. I wasn't able to push the needle in my Rocafella process so to me the night was a dud. After that night I never heard from or saw Chubbs or Kenny again so needless to say I never got a chance to play any of my records for Kenny Burns.

Chapter 40 - Elliott's Ways

T he year was 2005 and I was still recording new music and at the same time attempting to land a new business plug that could walk me through the music industry doors. After the Rocafella situation, I decided to reach back out to Cliff Jones for assistance. As always Cliff was willing to help. Cliff and his producer Davey Boy provided me with tracks so I would record some songs in DC with them and some I would bring back to Sisqo's house and record there. My goal was to create a new demo for Cliff Jones to shop around but before I knew it, I had enough material for a new album (if I decided to release independently).

I decided to prepare for both scenarios. The demo for Cliff was easy. That only required putting about 4 to 6 songs on a CD and hand it off to Cliff but another independent album would require strategic planning and execution. To prepare for a possible new album, I decided to record a new mix tape. I didn't want it to be just an ordinary mixtape, I wanted it to be special and have meaning. This was going to be my first mixtape as a solo artist

(Purple Haze One & Two were me and the Crown Vic Click and Free was just a few songs mixed in with snippets from my album). Inspired by Dr. Dre and Snoop Dog projects, I decided to make my mixtape in a story mode, with lots of skits, comedy, and features. The title I chose for my mix tape was Elliott's Ways.

The title Elliott's Ways came from a line I said in a song called "Gangsta Strut (feat. JI 900)". I was speaking about my grandfather (my mother's father) when I said "followed Elliott's ways and now they're stuck with him" meaning I was following in my grandfathers footsteps and now I'm stuck with how he did things.

My grandfather's name was Elliott Jones. He passed away when I was 5 years old. Although I barely knew and remembered him, I decided to make a mixtape showing the similarities of how he did things in the past compared to how my family and I did things currently but in order to do this I needed my family as well.

Big Flood and I had began talking again after months of silence due to the stealing of Sisqo's chain and the events that happened afterwards. Big Flood told me that he wasn't dealing with Shaggy anymore and explained his side of the story. As I stated before, Big Flood wasn't there when Shaggy took the chain. "If I was there I would have made him put it back before he left Sisqo's house!" Big Flood said. "Once he had the chain, getting him to give it back was hard. All Shaggy saw were dollar signs! Shaggy's a bitch. Fuck him" he went on to say.

Sidenote: Big Flood and Shaggy also got into a fist fight and Big Flood beat Shaggy up, but I don't know what caused the fight.

Once Big Flood and I started talking again, me and all my cousins began talking again and things began to go back to normal, but I still felt a little salty about how things played out. Nevertheless, I pushed the salt to the side and let bygones be bygones.

The temperature at Sisqo's house wasn't how it used to be in regard to my cousin's but Sisqo knew that they didn't steal his chain so I was able to get the green light to allow Big Flood and Shawn (Lil Flood) back into the house. The entire entourage was obviously a no go but when Big Flood and Shawn slowly began to come around again, friction began to surface around the house.

There were a lot of hidden feelings swimming around among lots of people that were regulars at Sisqo's house but the two main culprits that I witnessed were with Murda and Bags. Murda was big on loyalty and I believe it was hard for Murda to separate Big Flood from Shaggy. He looked at them all as the same. Bags on the other hand was very hard to read. He was always on the edge because of the lifestyle he lived. You just never knew when it came to Bags.

Sidenote: Another twist to Big Flood and my cousins coming back around was leverage. With my cousins gone, some people thought it was an opportunity for them to "move up" and get closer to me but when they returned, they knew I would always choose my cousins over them and that caused friction as well.

When I started recording "Elliotts Ways" I brought Big Flood to the studio and said that I wanted him to host the mix tape. Big Flood was always down for whatever I asked and agreed. Big Flood has a very unique personality. He can make anybody love him without even trying. He always said things that the average person would think but wouldn't dare to say and people gravitated and loved him for that. I knew that Big Flood personality would take Elliott's Ways where I wanted it to go.

Sidenote: My decision to allow Big Flood to host "Elliotts Ways" brewed the friction in the house even more. I was told that Murda wanted to host the mix tape (the same as he did on Purple Haze- Volume II) and when I chose Big Flood instead of him, he wasn't feeling it. Right after Elliott's Ways was released, Murda parted ways with my Crown Vic Click and started his own team and called them the Greedy Boys. I can't confirm if this was the reason for creating the Greedy Boys or not. Murda and I never discussed it. At the time I thought Murda just wanted to do his own thing and I was cool with it.

With Big Flood hosting and my lyrical talent and production, Elliotts Ways was on its way to success! I also invited everyone that I had a musical connection with to be featured on the mixtape as well. I even had Minister Louis Farrakhan's granddaughter, a good friend Yonasda (we called her Yo Yo) do an introduction skit (playing the role of my mother) to start the mixtape. I wanted the mixtape to feel like a movie and from the feedback I received, I did just that.

Every night Sisqo's studio was packed with people coming in and out laying down the parts that I had specifically designed for them. As I was focusing on putting together my masterpiece, Ole Man Joe would often pull me to the side and give me a run down on the things he was observing. Ole Man Joe noticed a lot of jealously and underhanded gestures coming from the vibes of many people that were so called "Crown Vic Click". A lot of the things he mentioned, I saw too but didn't feel the need to address. I just made personal mental notes but there was one situation that I couldn't ignore that both Ole Man Joe and I observed and that was the jealously coming from Bags.

Being as though Bags was a loose cannon, his feelings were always all over the place. One minute he loved you and the next minute he hated you. Bags didn't like the fact that I was the "main guy" of the house (with the exception of Sisqo of course). He felt like since he was the one that would bust his gun, he should be the number one guy especially after what he did at Shaggys house (which I believe was the main reason why he did it). Bags didn't like the fact that I was the number one guy but he couldn't deny the music I made as well as the Crown Vic movement I had going. So like a light switch his love for me went on and off often in a blink of an eye. Another attribute to Bags jealousy towards me was he also had the biggest crush on Tanja!

Many nights at the studio after drinking and smoking, I would pretend to be zoned out bopping my head to the music or snugged up on a chair with Tanja but what I was really doing was watching the facial expressions and body language of everyone in the room. Often I would catch Bags starring at me with an evil eye especially when I was all over Tanja. Tanja's beauty along with her tomboyish ways (being able to fit in with the guys without even trying) was appealing to Bags and when she wasn't around, he would always bring it up. You see, everyone including Bags knew that Tanja wasn't my main girl and that Chante was so Chante got the respect and Tanja was looked at as the side piece. That's why Bags felt comfortable speaking about Tanja because he knew that we as guys don't claim the side pieces.

Sometimes Bags would vent to Ole Man Joe and tell him things like I stole some of his lyrics or I only invite him to Sisqo's house when its an all-male studio session but when girls are invited and it's a extravagant pool party, he doesn't get the invite. Ole Man Joe would tell him that the lyrics he claimed that I stole from him were written and recorded long before he arrived in Baltimore and as far as the parties, a lot of them are not planned. We will be at the house and someone might decide to make a few calls and before you know it, it's a party. Ole Man Joe had to talk Bags off the paranoia ledge in regard to me several times but to be honest Bags was right in regard to the parties (sometimes).

You see Bags was very rough looking, hardly ever had a haircut, very intimidating and obnoxious when drinking. Bags and Sisqo's crowd did not mix at all. Sometimes when the pool parties kicked off and Bags was there, the type of girls Sisqo had at the house would look at him and actually be afraid. And of course he would take offense and start calling them stuck up bitches which made the situation even worse. So to avoid the inevitable, I would sometimes not invite him to the house if I knew what kind of people Sisqo had coming over. But to be honest, I did this with a lot of people, not just Bags. Everyone wasn't meant for every crowd. Hell, in the beginning Kidd and Hott used to do that to me!

One-time Sisqo had an exclusive party for Ray Lewis at his house and I didn't invite anyone. I was grateful that I got the invite myself. That party was star studded, filled with Baltimore Ravens and women that I had never seen in Baltimore before. Very classy and high scaled. Everyone there was somebody so Bags and anyone else that hadn't accomplished something on the entertainment scale wasn't happening.

Another thing about Bags was trouble seemed to follow him everywhere he went which meant it followed me also because he was with me. You see whenever we were out in the streets and something broke out, just like when we had Holla Back Entertainment and the night club, AND when Bags was in Shaggy's house tying up his mother, everything always came back to me, Cooli Hi. The Crown Vic Click is essentially Cooli Hi. Sometimes I didn't want to take him to certain events because I was afraid of what might happen.

One time I had a meeting with JI 900 (Omar Little & Mike Wilson-RIP) at their studio and decided to bring Bags along with Butch and a few others. I was a little hesitant to bring Bags because I knew what kind of crowd JI 900 kept around and sometimes, well almost all of the time, Bags feels like he has to prove that he's the toughest dude in the room (which always leads to trouble). As me and JI 900 were discussing a song that we were about to do for their project, out of nowhere Bags and one of their homeboys stood up and began to square up, preparing to fight. When I was talking to JI 900, I noticed through my peripheral vision that Bags and the guy kept staring at each other but I didn't pay it any mind. When the two got up and was about to fight, I immediately got in between them to break it up. I knew I had to act fast because I didn't want Bags to pull out his gun and start shooting. I grabbed Bags and JI 900 grabbed their guy but after several attempts to break it up, JI 900 let their guy go. "Yo Cool, they're grown men. If they want it that bad, let them go outside and handle it like men!"

Mike Wilson said. I still refused to let Bags go because I knew if the two of them went outside, Bags was going to kill him and then come back and kill the rest of them in the studio. To avoid what I knew would happen, we left.

Sidenote: I later found out that the reason Bags and the guy got into it was because the guy was sizing Bags up and offered him crack. Bag took offense as if to say "Do I look like a crackhead!?" and that's why they both stood up and prepared to fight.

Another incident was one time we all went to a club where all the local hip hop artists were displaying their music and if you've ever been to a local hip hop show, you know its usually one million guys and two girls. This crowd was filled with hard heads and local gangsters. The vibe in the club was very intense. It seemed like every artist there brought their entire neighborhood with them so of course we were in there deep as well. One of the promoters saw me and wanted to take a picture of me and everyone with me (The Crown Vic Click) but where we were standing, it wasn't enough room because the club was so packed. When Bags saw that it wasn't enough room, he opened his arms as wide as he could and just backed up and pushed everyone back and out of the way. Dudes we spilling their drinks and getting pushed almost falling while Bags kept clearing the way. After the area was clear, the promoter took the picture and got out of there as fast as he could. The dudes that got pushed were mean mugging looking confused like "I know this dude didn't just push us!" I just knew we were about to fight because there was no way that these type of dudes were going to let that slide. I stayed maybe 30 minutes or so after the "push" and then I told the team that we were out. I had Tanja with me as always and I didn't want to put her in a bad situation. I knew that the guys Bags pushed were plotting on us.

When we got outside I had some flyers so as we walked to our cars, I began to put some on the windshield of cars. Bags was drunk that night and I noticed that he was a little too friendly with Tanja so I had to keep telling him to chill out. When I got to my car, I gave Bags and Butch a pound and the Tanja and I headed out. Bags and Butch stayed because they had some of my promo CD's and they wanted to hand them out before heading home. Butch told me the next day that after Tanja and I left, Bags attempted to hand a CD to some guy and the guy replied "I don't want that bullshit!" Bags took offense and went to grab his gun out of the car but by the time Bags got his gun, the guy sped off!

This is just two of many of Bags incidents/ encounters. So in addition to Bags running wild I had Murda branching off doing his own thing, my cousins back around but still a little salt on my end, Pig appearing as a loyal comrade but he was originally Kidd's friend so I had to keep an eye on him, Barrs and Holla which were extensions of Murda so I knew they would roll with him when he moved, Butch, Hot and Ole Man Joe which were solid and Tanja who had been recently hounding me about leaving Chante and being with her exclusively. There were many others but all extensions of the ones I just mentioned.

As I was still working on Elliott's Ways, I reached out to Shanna to do an acting skit playing the role of an elderly southern woman speaking about my grandfather. Shanna did such a good job on the skit, I decided to use her on another skit also, playing the role of my girlfriend but this skit was in comparison of me and my grandfather. The first skit, played by Tanja and I, described my grandfather attempting to be intimate with my grandmother but before it could start, he vomited because of being out drinking all night. Me and Shanna's skit was me in the present doing the exact same thing my grandfather did, following his ways.

When recording the skit Shanna and I were in the studio alone. In order to make it sound as real as possible while Shanna stood in front of the mic, I stood beside her and touched her in her favorite places to be touched so that her sexual moans sounded real. I also kissed her passionately in order for the microphone to catch the vibe I was trying to send. The skit came out perfect!

Sidenote: I also allowed Shanna to rap on a freestyle on Elliott's Ways called "Shine" feat. Big Status. I wrote her part on the hook and produced her vocally.

608 | Dwayne Jones - Almost Famous

When Tanja heard the skit, she questioned whether or not the scene was real. "That shit sounds like yall were in there together really kissing and touching on each other!" Tanja said. I denied it and told Tanja the kissing noises were me kissing my arm on a separate track to give off a real kissing effect. Tanja had no way of proving her assumption so eventually she let it go.

Shanna's reemergence somehow struck a chord with Tanja and she began to put the full court press on me about leaving Chante. You see Tanja hated losing. She almost had the drive and competitive spirit of a man. Losing or coming in second made her skin crawl. She was good at everything and I mean everything! Tanja would doll up at night and look like a super model and the next morning throw on some overalls and paint on a construction site. One time she even fixed my mothers water heater! I also remember another time when I played her in a one-on-one basketball game, and she could really play; had a left hand and all! I won the game of course but it wasn't as easy as I expected. I say all of this to say losing was not apart of Tanja's vocabulary and Shanna coming back around sort of reminded her that she needed to be number one.

According to Tanja, she had been asking me for a long time for an answer regarding when I was leaving Chante. Me on the other hand don't remember these asks. I can admit sometimes it vaguely came up in conversation, but I always skipped right by it because although what Tanja and I had was special, there was no way I was leaving Chante. Still up until that point I couldn't see myself leaving a perfect situation (girlfriend and son) to commit to someone that slept with two homie's (former homies) and had three kids. I never wanted to be the guy that was around someone else's kid more than I was around my own. In addition, I mentioned on several occasions all of Tanja's attributes but didn't mention her Achilles heel, and that was her personal life. Tanja's personal affairs were a mess. She didn't have a job nor a place to stay (she and her three kids lived with her uncle). Often she would drop her kids off with her sister or a friend to be with me and although we were having the time of our lives, in the back of my head I always thought about where her kids were. Anonymously people would call child protective services on her but the cases never had legs to stand on. But just the fact of someone having the nerve to go down that road caused concern.

One day Tanja and I got into an argument about me leaving Chante. Tanja claimed she had been asking for quite some time and I would tell her I was going to leave but never did. Till this day, I don't recall ever telling Tanja I would leave Chante. I didn't have to. Tanja was giving me EVERYTHING already knowing about Chante so I didn't have to lie. I could tell Tanja was close to being fed up. In the heat of the argument, I walked away from Tanja and ignored her calls when she called. She hated to be ignored.

Later that day I went to Chante's house to spend time with her and Darrian. As I was running around the house playing with Darrian suddenly the phone rang. Chante answered the phone with "Hello" and after that it was silence. When I noticed that Chante wasn't talking, I looked at her and she was staring at me shaking her leg as she listened to what was being said on the phone. I walked over to the caller id and saw Tanja's phone number. I immediately grabbed my keys and walked out of the door.

As I drove to my mothers house, I thought to myself "Damn, the cat is officially out of the bag!" There was no way of lying my way out of this. Knowing Tanja, she's telling Chante EVERYTHING under sun about our relationship that had been going on for almost two years.

When I arrived at my mothers house, Tanja was already there parked and waiting for me. I got out of my car, walked up on my mothers porch and unlocked the door. Tanja was still sitting in her car. Before I walked in the house, I asked Tanja to come also. Tanja got out of her car and came inside with me. As we both sat in my mothers living room I began to ask Tanja why would she call Chante. As Tanja began to speak, out of nowhere I heard a loud sound as if a window was being busted. I ran to the front door and saw Chante outside busting all of the windows on my Crown Victoria with a golf club. After she busted all my windows, including the windshield, she took a knife and stabbed all four tires. I called the police as she was flattening my tires. Once she was done with the tires, she ran up on the porch with the golf club and started swing at me. To avoid being hit in the head with the golf club, I put my left hand up to block the contact and a sharp piece of the club split my hand completely open. Chante charged her way in the house and begin to hit me with her fist because I had managed to take the golf club from her. I covered my head as Chante swung and scratched away while Tanja sat there watching. As Chante continued to swing, I kept telling her to leave because I knew the police were on the way and they would arrest her after seeing my hand. After pleading with Chante about the police finally she stopped and ran back to her car and left. At the time I didn't know but in the mix of all the confusion my dragon chain came off and was on the floor. Chante picked it up and left with my chain.

By the time the police arrived, Chante was gone. I didn't want her to get arrested but I did want her to stop demolishing my car. About an hour after the incident a tow truck came and towed my car to the junkyard per Chante's request.

Sidenote: I had outstanding violations with insurance and parking tickets so I put my Crown Victoria in Chante's name in order to drive it again. The car was paid for but Chante paid my insurance for me and technically it was her car!

Tanja stayed the entire time and helped me bandage my wounded hand. Although she was the whistle blower, she felt sorry for me after everything played out because she knew what my car and chain represented to me but more importantly, she knew that I didn't want to be separated from Darrian.

The next day, I decided that I had to do my best to fix things and do it fast. I called Chante nonstop until she finally took my call. I explained to Chante that yes, I was messing around with Tanja, but I downplayed how serious we were. Chante asked question after question about Tanja and me and I answered every question as best as I could without adding salt to the already open wound.

Every day I pleaded with Chante to take me back till finally she agreed. One of the terms Chante had for taking me back was for me to fully move in with her and spend more time with her and Darrian. Without hesitation I agreed. Chante came to my mother's house, we packed up my clothes and I fully moved in her apartment in Harford County, MD. I hadn't spoken with Tanja since the day of the incident.

So now Chante and I are back together but in a healing phase. Tanja was completely out of the picture. As days and weeks continued to go by Chante and Dwayne were getting better but the Cooli Hi in me was starving for attention. I hadn't been in the studio for weeks because I didn't have a car to get there and even if I could, I wouldn't be able to go because Chante knew that's where Tanja and I spent most of our time. I loved Chante and of course my son Darrian but the Cooli Hi in me was putting pressure on the newfound family man named Dwayne. Tanja was feeling it as well.

One night while I was asleep, Tanja texted me a very seductive message of how she missed the things we did together intimately. Chante saw the text and erased it out of my phone before I could read it. Tanja also started hanging out at the clubs to get her mind off me. One night she was with a couple of her male friends and they must have asked about me. When she told them that we were not seeing each other anymore and why, they told her that she knew the rules before we even started dealing with each other so she can't be mad. Tanja got so upset that she cried and left the club.

To make ends meet, Tanja would sometimes take odd jobs here and there. Bags and Tony did construction work. When Bags found out that Tanja could paint, he would always offer her jobs (he did this just so he could be around her). Since Tanja needed to stay busy to keep her mind off us, she took a job with Bags and Tony. While on the job, Bags made advancements on Tanja suggesting that she should join him and his current girlfriend in a threesome. Tanja declined and never worked with him again.

Sidenote: I received all these details weeks after they actually happened.

After almost a month of being away from the studio and my norm, I finally couldn't take it anymore. I pleaded with Chante and told her that I needed to get back in the studio to finish Elliott's Ways and be who I am. After some convincing, Chante gave in and took me to my mothers so I could borrow her car and go to the studio.

Sidenote: I never could drive Chante's car because she drove a stick and I didn't know how to drive a stick.

Once I got back into my normal. I gradually started slacking up on spending my nights with Chante. I was now practically sharing my mothers car so when I was done at the studio, instead on driving from Randallstown, MD to Harford County, MD (a little over a two hour drive), I would go to my mothers so I wouldn't have to wake up early in the morning to give my mom her car back.

As I slowly began to go back to my old ways of being out all the time, Chante's suspicion began to grow, assuming that I would start seeing Tanja again. Quite often while at the studio working, I would hear the sound of someone walking from the back entrance, headed to the studio with keys and I knew that sound very well. It was always Chante. Before the Tanja incident, Chante never came to Sisqo's house. Now she would pop up just to make sure I wasn't doing anything.

One night she popped up and when she saw that no one was there but me and Murda, she ran outside with tears in her eyes. I followed her and we began to talk outside. Chante told me that her suspicion was beginning to drive her crazy. I assured Chante that I was only working on music and that my cheating days were over but she found that very hard to believe. In a rage Chante jumped in her car and pulled off.

In order to bring some calm to Chante's emotional storm, she began to reach out to the worst person for peace. She started calling Tanja. Chante had so many unanswered questions that she decided to go to Tanja for answers because she knew I wouldn't tell her the entire truth. The two of them began to talk quite often and God only knows what they discussed. I kept trying to get Chante to stop calling Tanja because I knew Tanja had information that would deeply hurt Chante but she wouldn't listen.

Tanja then used her and Chante's conversations as a gateway for us to start talking again. Tanja would call me and I now would answer because I needed to know or at least have an idea of what was being said to Chante. I now needed to keep Tanja as calm and emotionless as possible so she wouldn't hurt Chante anymore that I had already done. As I stated before, my main concern was protecting Chante because she was the innocent one. I didn't care about anyone's feelings including my own. That's why I allowed Chante to beat my car with the golf club and beat on me also. I deserved it.

As Tanja and I began to talk more, feeling started to brew again and before we knew it, I was seeing her again. Tanja didn't start coming back to the studio because Chante was doing random pop ups so I started going to Tanja's new apartment. Tanja had rented out a basement of a house about 20 minutes away from the studio. I would leave the studio a little earlier than normal and stop at Tanja's before making my way back to my mothers or Chante's apartment. Chante somehow knew where Tanja lived so I would park my mothers car several blocks away and walk to Tanja's house.

One night while on the phone with Tanja headed to her house, Chante called. Before I clicked over to answer Chante's call, I said to Tanja "Hold up, this is Chante. Hold on." When I clicked over and began to talk to Chante, I could tell from her tone that this wasn't a good night for me to creep off so I decided to skip going to Tanja's and head "home" to Chantes. While in route, Tanja kept calling back, but I refused to answer. It was after 1am in the morning and if I clicked over from Chante, I would have had to answer a million questions about who was calling me that time of the night. Tanja kept calling back-to-back and I continued to ignore her calls as I drove to Chantes then all of a sudden, the calls stopped.

As I continued to drive and talk to Chante, I approached a red light ironically across the street from Druid Hill Park. I was the only car there. As I waited for the light to change, out of nowhere a car came from behind me and swerved in front of my car blocking my way. Then the driver's door opened, and the driver ran to my window (which I had rolled all the way down) and reached in the car and turned it off. The person was none other than Tanja!

I hung up the phone with Chante, put the car in park and attempted to get out to retrieve my keys from Tanja. "What the hell are you doing!?" I asked her as I got out of the car in rage. "I'm tired of you putting me and my feeling on the back burner for her!" Tanja said. Tanja then took a swing at me but missed. After she missed Tanja attempted to grab my penis with the intentions of bringing me to my knees. Back then (2005), I wore baggy sweatpants with basketball shorts under them so all she had was a handful of sweatpants.

Tanja had the grip of a thousand Pitbull's and would not let go. No matter what I did, I couldn't get her to let go of what appeared to be my groin. I didn't want to hit her so I tried to wrestle her off, but it wasn't happening. Before I knew it we had managed to make our way to the medium strip in the middle of the road, my mothers car was still at the red light with the door wide open, and during the tussle Tanja had ripped my sweatpants almost completely off (they were down to my ankles).

Someone driving by must have saw Tanja and I wrestling in the middle of the street with my pants down and called the police. When the police arrived, Tanja was still holding on to my pants. The police walked up and tried to break us apart. Finally Tanja let go. When she did, the police attempted to arrest me. "Someone called and said there's a guy out here trying to rape a girl!" the police said as he was putting my hands behind my back. Some dudes in another car pulled up and said "Let him go! We saw the whole thing! He didn't do anything to her. She was attacking him the entire time!"

The police officers looked at both Tanja and I and figured out that the guys were telling the truth. Right before letting us both go, the police asked for our IDs to check for warrants. I came back clean and was allowed to leave but Tanja did not. She had a warrant for a failure to appear in court and was arrested.

As I drove off, I called Chante to tell her what happened. I told her about the incident but did not tell her that I was still talking to Tanja. I used this incident to make Tanja look crazy in order to discredit anything she may have told Chante or would tell her in the future. Instead of going to Chante's that night, I hid my mother's car on another block and went to my mothers. Tanja was in an out-of-control rage, and I didn't know what she could do so I decided to stay low and out of sight just in case she tried to have one of her girlfriends track me.

The next day Tanja called me from jail asking me to help bail her out. I didn't have any money, so Tanja told me to go to her job (she had only been working there for two weeks and quit- daycare center) and pick up her paycheck. I did just that and bailed Tanja out with her own money. When she walked out of Central Bookings, I was outside waiting to take her home. When we arrived at Tanja's place we sat down and had a long talk. That's when she told me about the Bags incident, the text message she sent (that Chante deleted) as well as what happened when she ran out of the club. She also told me something that John (Sisqo's studio engineer and one of the beginning partners of Holla Back Ent) told her that stuck with me for a very long time.

John sometimes worked in construction as well so when Tanja was on the job painting for Bags, John was there also. The two of them began to talk one day and Tanja told him that we were no longer seeing each other. John then said to Tanja "You know, Cooli is no different than Kidd! They both are the same except Cooli moves in a more settle way!"

I was so pissed to hear that John said this. I looked at Kidd as being a manipulator that would purposely hold back someone else for his own advancement and I was nothing like that (Or was I?).

Sidenote: Years later after reflecting, I realized what John was saying. I must admit, I was a manipulator, but I never held anyone back or hated on another person's movement. I manipulated for the greater cause and that cause was to advance my music career which in return help everyone that I had to manipulate to get there. I'll explain more later.

Later that day, I called Butch and told him what Tanja said about Bags making advances on her. Butch admitted that he knew about it and told Bags he was wrong. That night when we all met up at the studio, Bags pulled me to the side so we could talk. Butch must have told him that I knew and wasn't happy. Bags explained to me that he thought we were not dealing with each other anymore, which was true and that I had went completely back to Chante. "Yo being as though Smirl (the nickname we all called Tanja) was the chick on the side, I didn't look at it as disrespect. I would have never tried that with Chante! I apologize my nigga!" Bags said. We both shook hands and went back into the studio.

After speaking with Bags, I decided to do one more new freestyle for Elliott's Ways. The mixtape was done but I wanted to add one more track to put the icing on the cake. I didn't have a song with Sisqo on it so I decided this would be the one. I chose one of Tupac's tracks "Until the End of Time" and basically spilled my guts about everything that had been recently going on in my life. I addressed everything from not being signed yet, to Big Flood and Sisqo's chain, to losing Chante, to Bags making advances at Tanja. I left no stone unturned.

Since it was always like pulling teeth to get Sisqo to get on a song, I decided to write the chorus tailored to him. Sisqo would always say to me, quoting a line from the movie Gladiator "Win the people and you'll win your freedom!" I put that quote in the chorus to increase the chance that he would like it and sing the hook. My plan worked successfully. I sung the hook for Sisqo and he liked it and agreed to sing. Sisqo was just getting over a cold so he brought some tea down to the studio and sipped on it as he sung the chorus.

The next day after listening to what he recorded, Sisqo told me that he didn't like how he sounded and wanted me to erase it. "Yo my voice wasn't right. I sound congested. Delete it and I will sing it again." Sisqo said. I agreed but said to myself "I'm not deleting it UNTIL he sings it over!" If I would have deleted and he never came back downstairs to re-sing it, I would have been stuck without a hook. Sisqo never came back to re-sing the hook so I kept the vocals that I had. I also got Chinky to sing backgrounds and I used a clip from one of my mothers favorite gospel groups, The Mighty Clouds of Joy as an interlude to the song. I named the song "Faith."

Once "Faith" was completed, I sat down with Teddy (a studio engineer- RIP Teddy) and strategically pieced together the entire mixtape. The skits, accapella freestyles, Big Flood's hosting and talking parts were scattered all over the place on different tracks. I told Big Flood as well as others to just go in the booth and say whatever was on their mind. So I had numerous tracks of everyone saying all types of things on several tracks. I grabbed what I thought highlighted the moment and placed their vocals throughout the mixtape to bring my vision to light. I placed Big Flood voice before and after songs to make it all make sense and showcased his vivid personality. I took Shawn's accapella freestyle and spread it over the duration of the mixtape to show him stumbling on his verse and finally getting it right at the end (actually that was one track that I chopped up). Once I completed the layout, Teddy mixed and mastered it and Elliott's Ways was complete!

Once Elliott's Ways was completed it was then time to press up copies and get them out into the street. To do so, money and resources were needed. My plan was to press up two thousand copies and start from there. I didn't personally have all the money to make this happen, so I went to everyone that was involved in the project and took up a collection. Everyone contributed but the main contributors were Ole Man Joe, Donny, Barrs and of course me.

After the CD's were pressed up, I gave everyone (Crown Vic Click) whatever amount of CD's they felt comfortable with and told them to sell. Then I hit the streets myself and sold hand to hand to as many as I could. I hit every barbershop, car wash and local clothing line store in town.

As time went on, the mixtape began to pick up steam and the streets were loving it however there were a few members within my team that wasn't feeling it. I was told that some didn't like all of the skits and plug ins between the songs and that the CD was too long. I respected their opinion, but it wasn't going to change what I had envisioned.

I remembered a while ago, not to long after Holla Back Entertainment dissembled, I had a listened party at Sisqo's house. The house was packed with all the fliest diva's in town as well as the creditable guys. As I played my songs, the crowd was initially into them but maybe after the 5th or 6th song, they began to disconnect and small conversations began to brew as my songs played and as an artist, that's the worst thing someone can do (talk while your song is playing). Before I knew it, the entire room was talking and conversating and I had lost the room musically. I was devastated. Once everyone left, Sisqo pulled me to the side and said "Yo don't sweat what just happened. I told you before, you make the kind of records that require a machine (record label) to push the narrative. You also make the kind of songs that live forever! You're before your time! They might not get it now, but one day they will!"

Like a lot of my music, Elliott's Ways had a deeper hidden meaning. It was a way to keep my grandfather's name alive and it was a way to show the world how my family and I were raised, what inspired us and how we lived. For those that didn't initially get it, I understood but I knew that this mixtape would stand the test of time and still be relevant many years after its release, especially to the members of the Jones family.

Sidenote: I took an old picture of my grandfather from my mother's photo album and used it to create the CD cover. I accidentally tore the picture when removing it from the book so that's why it's a white discoloring on the CD cover. I also put his date of birth and expiration date on the cover and got Tanja's aunt to recite his obituary in the background on the introduction skit.

*Elliott's Ways is available for streaming on Sound Cloud!

While in the mix of pushing Elliott's Ways all over the city, I was still dealing with the drama torn between Chante and Tanja. I was technically back with Chante but occasionally still seeing Tanja; similar to before the big incident but the difference was Chante now knew about Tanja and the two of them were talking and comparing notes.

As all of this was going on, my mother was observing from a distance and didn't like it at all. One day, Tanja being fed up with all of the back and forth asked me if I could meet her on a shopping center parking lot so I could return some of her things and I agreed. What I didn't know was Tanja and Chante arranged this meeting and had planned on jumping me or something because they both planned to meet me on this parking lot.

Since a young child my mother always told me that she would sometimes have visions. She used to tell my father things when they were together (about him) that would scare him. He used to joke with my mother and tell her that she should charge people money and reveal things about them for a living.

When I was leaving out the house to meet Tanja, my mother said to me, "Don't go to that parking lot. They are trying to set you up!" How she knew, I'll never know. Despite my mothers warning, I went to the parking lot anyway, but all my antennas were up (meaning I was watching my surroundings).

When I arrived, Tanja was already there. She got out of her car and walked over to my driver's side door. She then handed me her phone which had Chante on the other end. I believe she was trying to prove to Chante that I was recently at her house because I agreed to meet her to return something that I must have gotten while I was there. When Tanja gave me her phone and I heard Chante's voice on the other end and spooked from what my mother told me, I hit the gas and took off. Tanja attempted to grab her phone back as she ran beside the car as long as she could. Then she jumped in her car and followed me in a high-speed chase.

As I sped off with Tanja in hot pursuit on my trail, I was on Tanja's phone trying to explain why I was there meeting to return items that I should have never had. Chante screamed in my ear as I drove recklessly though Baltimore City, trying to shake Tanja. I even went down a one-way street dodging oncoming traffic (like a scene in a movie) and when I looked in my rear view, Tanja was right on my heels! After Chante finally hung up on me, I decided that the safest place to go was to a police station. I led Tanja to the Southwestern Baltimore Police Station, parked and walked into the station. Tanja and one of her girlfriends parked across the street and waited for me to return to my car. I went in and told the police officer at the desk what was going on. The policeman went outside to confront Tanja. Tanja told the officer that she wasn't breaking any laws by sitting in her car and that he couldn't make her leave. After a long lengthy conversation, Tanja agreed to leave but only after I returned her phone. The policeman gave Tanja her phone and she left.

About a week or so later, Tanja and I were back to ourselves again. One night after leaving the studio, I stopped at Tanja's house for a visit. Normally I would park blocks away or on the other side of some close by apartments but this night I was being lazy and decided to shake the dice. I parked on some grass directly across from where Tanja lived but hidden behind a large tree hoping this wouldn't be a night when Chante decided to drive by.

I was at Tanja's for maybe about 20 minutes or so before we began to get intimate when suddenly we heard a soft knock on the door. Immediately from the sound of the knock, I knew it was Chante. When I went to the door and opened it, no one was there. I went outside and saw Chante sitting in her car. She looked at me and shook her head in disgust. Then she began to call Tanja all kinds of names attacking her character as a woman. I believe Chante felt betrayed by Tanja because she believed that Tanja played her by pretending to be against me but at the same time still sleeping with me but in Tanja's defense, she didn't owe Chante anything. They didn't know each other and were not friends. After Chante called Tanja every name under the sun in a calm hurtful way, she drove off. Tanja surprisingly didn't say a word. I jumped in my car (well my mother's car) and followed Chante home.

The next day Chante came to me with a very calm demeanor and asked me what I wanted. I knew this was it. I had to make a final decision and stop playing with the both of them. I was completely torn down the middle. Chante was the perfect girl for Dwayne, yet Tanja was perfect for Cooli Hi. The question was, who was I? Was I Cooli Hi or Dwayne? If I was Dwayne, was I ready to bury Cooli Hi and vice versa?

The year was still 2005 and Cooli Hi was in full control of my physical being. Nothing or no one (with the exception of my kids, Peanut and Darrian) could trump my musical journey. I was determined and border lined obsessed with making my musical dream come true. I was like this even before I met Sisqo and once I got a taste of the music life (a real taste) there was almost nothing I wouldn't do, no one I wouldn't cross nor no battle I wouldn't fight to get it back. I had seen and experienced too much and came too close to let it slip out of my fingers.

Despite all of my reservations about Tanja, her three kids, sleeping with Kidd and Baldy prior to me, and her reckless personal affairs, I told Chante that I didn't think it was going to work between us and moved forward with Tanja. If someone was building a perfect woman for a man, Chante would have been the example, checking all of the boxes but unfortunately the perfect woman for the average man wasn't what was needed. Dwayne was and afterthought. Cooli Hi was the priority. I believed that if Cooli Hi didn't work, Dwayne could never exist. Dwayne could never bring in the income that Cooli Hi could. Cooli Hi took me places that Dwayne could only imagine. Dwayne needed Chante but Cooli Hi needed Tanja. Unfortunately for Chante, Cooli Hi was running the show so the final choice was Tanja.

Sidenote: I once read or heard somewhere that when a man is in pursuit of a dream or goal, he's no good to any woman because she will always come second to that pursuit. Prime example.

Chapter 41 - Local Moves

It was official. Tanja and I were together as a couple. Chante and I were now co-parenting, the same as me and Anna. Ironically Chante and Anna began hanging out with each other and became close friends. Meanwhile I was back on my grind trying to get Elliott's Ways in every hand as possible.

After selling as many Elliott's Ways as I possibly could, I started giving them away to flood the streets with my music. Then I thought to myself, if I'm going to give my music out for free, I should be giving it out in a market where it could possibly fall in someone's hand that could help me so I decided to take a trip to New York.

Donny, Ole Man Joe and I drove to New York with a box full of Elliott's Ways and walked the streets of Manhattan giving away CD's. While passing out CD's in Manhattan, some New Yorkers suggested that we went to Harlem for better results so we walked to Harlem and passed out CD's there as well. I remember being in an area where a lot of stores were when we bumped into Pete

Rock (from Pete Rock & CL Smooth) and gave him a CD. I was determined not to leave until every CD was gone. I figured the chances of my music falling into the right hands were 10 times higher than handing out CD's in Baltimore. As we continued to walk through Harlem we approached some projects and started giving out CD's there as well. A group of guys saw us giving out the CD and yelled out a challenge from across the street. "Yo, do you want to battle my man for some cash" one of the guys asked. Me being from where I was from knew that that wasn't a good idea. Win or lose, that appeared to be a set up for a robbery! I could have been wrong, but I knew how my neighborhood back in Baltimore would treat someone walking around from out of town, so I figured they would do the same to us. "Naw, I'm good" I responded. We finished handing out as many CD's as we could and then we returned to Baltimore.

The next day, instead of going to the studio, I stayed home and thought about how things were moving musically. Since the breakup of Holla Back, I had been sending off packages which included my CD, a one sheet and or bio and business card/ contact info (back then I had to send my music/ CD's through Fed X. Email and social media wasn't an option) three to four times a week to every executive I knew. I practically lived at Fed X and the post office because I was always there sending off music. I had been recording nonstop as well as putting out visual content also and now I'm sitting at my mothers kitchen table, tired from walking New York streets the day before.

Then it hit me, talent and good music can only take you so far. It has a ceiling and I reached it a long time ago. I needed someone with a music business mind and connections that could take my career to where it needed to go. It was also at that moment when I realized what Kidd brought to the table when we were working together. Granted, he couldnt do what I did as far as making and performing songs but now I realized that I couldn't do what he did and what he did was way more important than what I did. Talented artist come a dime a dozen, but the executive music mind is rare and hard to come by. I knew at that moment that I needed to connect with another "Kidd" if I wanted to bypass this ceiling I was hitting.

I was already casually working with Cliff Jones but Cliff had a lot of artist and the majority of them were major signed artist so of course the majority of his attention was going to them because they were bringing in the checks (or the bag as Cliff would say). I needed someone that had the time and energy to focus on me. I also wanted to deal with someone that was hands on and accessible not like Demetrius Spencer, Kenneth Crear and Huggy Carter that all lived in California and had bigger acts they were focusing on (Nothing against those guys. They all helped me as much as they could). I needed someone local but not local. Someone I could work with face to face. After brainstorming my options I decided to reach out to a local guy, an DJ icon in Baltimore that turned exec, named Shawn Ceasar.

Shawn Ceasar was a former DJ that now managed almost every DJ in Baltimore city under his record label and management team called Unruly Records. I met Shawn Ceasar (Ceez) back in the mid 90's when I was a part of Shock Trauma performing in his talent shows. Ceez was also known for throwing "record pools" where all the DJ's and artist in the DMV area would meet once a month to showcase new music and network. When Kidd and I started Holla Back, Ceez's record pool was our first showcase as a new record label and Ceez also distributed my Crown Victoria album's through DTLR (Downtown Locker room).

I reached out to Ceez and as always, he was open to take a meeting with me. When we met at his office, I told him that I was looking for management and thought he would be the perfect guy. At the time Ceez didn't manage any artist at all. He only managed DJ's. After I pitched my proposal, Ceez told me that he would get back to me after talking to his partners (one of which was Scottie B- another iconic DJ in Baltimore city). Ceez wanted to make sure that if he took on the task of being my manager, he and his Unruly team could deliver, and I respected that. A few days later Ceez called me and said yes. He and his Unruly team were willing and able to manage me moving forward.

Sidenote: I already knew that Ceez didn't manage any artist before I even reached out to him. That was one of the main reasons I did. I wanted to be top priority; The other reason was

Ceez managed all of the DJ's from Quick Silver to K Swift (a female DJ and radio personality- RIP) to Jay Claxton (just to name a few) so I figured if I was the only artist on a team full of DJ's, how could I lose. My records would be played non-stop!

Now that I had Shawn Ceasar and Unruly as my management, my decisions were very strategic as to what new music I recorded. You see, I had lots of songs that I had recorded over the years that had never been released so content was never a problem. My strategy now was to record with a purpose! Instead of just going to the studio every night making new songs, I now only wanted to record if the song was a potential single or with a producer that had a buzz or a certified club banger! For years I had been recording song after song, filling up my hard drive with records that didn't have any legs. Now I only wanted to record songs that had a goal or purpose, with all the musical political boxes checked before I even arrived at the studio. Ceez and I were on the same page. Ceez wanted me to work with some of K Swifts producers (one in particular- a producer named Black Starr) to get the ball rolling.

While waiting to meet up with K Swift and her production team to get new tracks, I slowed down a bit in regard to going to Sisqo's house every night. Instead I stayed home and thought of ways to get my business side to match my talent side of my musical body. It had been 5 years since the release of Unleash the Dragon and Sisqo's light was beginning to fade within the music industry. Things were scarce and although Return of

Dragon went platinum, only true Sisqo and Dru Hill fans ever knew the album existed so my day in the light from Can I Live was practically null and void.

One day while sitting on my mothers porch with Ole Man Joe, Mouse and a few others, I saw a car creeping down the block at a slow speed. Then the car stopped directly in front of my mother's porch. We all stopped talking as we stared at the car trying to figure out who it was. Then the drivers side door opened and the driver got out of the car. I couldn't believe my eyes! It was none other than Marlon (Slice) hopping out of the car with a smile.

I hadn't seen Marlon in about 6 or 7 years. The last time I saw him was when he, Mouse and I stole the tire and got arrested. Marlon went back into the Army before we went to court, skipping town which caused a bench warrant for his arrest. He spent a lot of time in Germany and Colorado in which he was stationed at the time. I hadn't spoken to him in years.

When Marlon got out of the car, we greeted each other with the biggest pound and hug you could imagine. Mouse and Ole Man Joe followed up with the same. After the greetings, I noticed that Marlon was smiling but something was wrong. I asked him, "Slice what are you doing here!?" That's when I found out why his smile looked tainted. "Man, I got some bad news. My Mom passed away" Marlon said. It felt like I swallowed a brick when I heard Marlon say that.

You see, this entire time while Marlon was away in the Army, his Mom (Ms. Brenda) who I also called Mom only lived 10 minutes away from my house (well my mothers house). In the past 6 or 7 years since Marlon was gone, I hadn't visited her one single time. It wasn't because of any other reason but my tunnel vision for music and my quest to be a rap star. So to hear that she had passed away knowing that I never took the time to check on her or visit broke my heart.

For the next couple of days while Marlon was in town I did absolutely nothing relating to music. I was with my brother all day everyday in his time of need. We hung out everyday, just talking and running errands leading up to the day of the funeral.

One day Marlon and I went to his mothers bank to close her account. Ms. Brenda was always known for saving lots of money so Marlon wanted to close her bank account because he believed that some of his family members might try to withdraw money from his Moms account. Since Marlon wasn't listed on the account, the bank wouldn't give him any information, nor would they give him access to the account. Marlon became so upset that I actually thought he was going to hit the bank rep. Instead, after being irate, Marlon gathered himself and explained to the guy that he did not want whatever was in the account. He just didn't want anyone taking advantage of his deceased mother. Once the bank rep realized that Marlon wasn't trying to withdraw money, he agreed to close the account. He then went on to tell Marlon the steps to take to retrieve what was in the account. "Sir whatever's in there, I don't want it. I don't need it. My mother is gone. Yall can keep it! I just don't want anyone taking advantage of my mother" Marlon said. Then we both walked out.

That was typical Marlon. He never cared about money. On several occasions Marlon and I had been in stores and Marlon would randomly pay for the person's things before or after us. One time he did this in a grocery store when a young lady's card kept being declined. Marlon paid for all her groceries and asked for nothing in return. He was selfless like that. But the initial frustration from the bank rep led him to want a drink so we stopped at a liquor store to get his favorite- Absolute.

The liquor store we stopped at was in a treacherous neighborhood in East Baltimore and had a gang of guys hanging out in front of the store. Marlon double parked in front of the store, hopped out and walked through the guys slightly bumping into the ones that didn't want to move out of the way. I followed behind him just in case something popped off. When we got back into the car, I said to Marlon "Boy you crazy for walking through them guys like that!" Marlon then said to me "Man if you saw the things that I've seen fighting in the war, nothing would phase you. These situations can't compare to the battles I've been in overseas." Then Marlon went on to tell me about the amount of people he had to kill while in the war and his mind set while doing so. He told me stories of how small children would have bombs strapped to their bodies and he and his squad had to "take care of it" before the bomb detonated. The he said something that I will never forget. "Yo every night after we've been in the field fighting, the next morning when it was time for roll call, we all would look from left to right to see if someone's bunk was empty. It was always very sad to see an empty bunk because we knew what that meant. I always got choked up when the horn soldier came out and started playing that sad theme song they play when soldiers die (then Marlon began to hum the theme). I was good until I heard that damn horn! It broke me every time."

Later that day, after the drinks kicked in, Marlon and I began to talk about my music career. Marlon told me how proud he was when he heard me rapping on Can I Live and saw me on the BET Award Show. He bragged to his platoon about being my brother and said some of them didn't believe him. To prove he wasn't lying, Marlon had to pull out some old pictures of us.

He then went on to say "Man when you dropped your solo album, I had it shipped to me and as I listened to the songs, I was reading your shoutouts and thankyous in the CD booklet. I was all excited reading the shoutouts waiting to read my name and before I knew it, I was done reading and wasn't mentioned at all! I was hurt. How could you forget about me!?" I was speechless. I didn't forget my brother. This was a classic example of out of sight, out of mind. I hadn't seen Marlon in years and at that time in my life, I lived and breathed with musical blinders on. Marlon saw the uncomfortable look on my face so he lightened up the mood by cracking a joke but I could tell that being left out of the thankyous bothered him a little.

A few days had passed of Marlon and I kicking it the same as back in our high school days and finally the day of the funeral had arrived. I was very worried about how Marlon would react when seeing his mom in the casket. Marlon and Ms. Brenda were extremely close. Before the funeral started, Marlon had been drinking heavily.

When it was time to approach for the last time before closing the casket, I walked up with Marlon to say our final goodbye's. As Marlon looked down at his mom, one of his twin daughters on the front row began to cry. Marlon looked back at his daughter and gave her a very hard stare suggesting that she stopped crying immediately. Marlon's daughter immediately stopped crying. Marlon never sheded one tear the entire service.

Sidenote: Marlon had three kids. Jennifer (named after his baby sister that passed away) Jessica and Dominic. When kids, Marlon and I made a pack, similar to the one the two brothers made in the Five Heartbeat's Movie. We said the first one to have a boy child would name the child after the other. Marlon had his son first and at the time he was stationed in Colorado or Germany. When Marlon told me his son's name was Dominic, I figured that he may have forgotten about our childish promise and it wasn't a big deal. Years later I learned that Dominic's middle name was Dwayne!

The next day Marlon and some of his family members cleared out the remaining things in his moms apartment (the things Marlon and I previously didn't move). Once that was completed Marlon, along with his wife and kids returned to Florida but before doing so, we promised each other that we would do a better job at keeping in touch no matter what!

After Marlon left, I immediately went back into Cooli Hi mode. I was in desperate need of a new single but not just any single, the right single that had all the political boxes checked-meaning the right producer that's linked to the right people connected to the right machine. I met with my now manager Shawn Ceasar and he connected me with K Swift which whom he managed also. K Swift had several Baltimore Club Music producers signed to her, so she gave me a CD with several tracks on it to choose from. Shawn Ceasar and K Swift- my political boxes were officially checked.

After listening to the tracks, I chose a Baltimore Club track produced by K Swifts' producer named Black Star. I wrote the chorus along with my verses but to add a little spice I needed a female rapper so I reached out to my homegirl Ms. Kitty to deliver the final blow (I also got Big Flood to speak on the record also to piggyback off the Elliott's Ways movement). The record turned out to be exactly what I was trying to accomplish. I needed a party/ club track that made people want to dance and this record did just that. The name of the song was "Beat It Up."

After the song was mixed, mastered and ready to be released, I went to Ceez to find out the next move. I thought that since Ceez managed all the DJ's, that all was needed was for him to give them the record and the DJ's would begin to play it (since we were all on the same team). Unfortunately for me, it didn't go that way at all.

After I turned the song in to Ceez, he gave it to all of his DJ's including a full DJ blast to all he had connections with but days had passed and I didn't hear my song played anywhere. When I asked Ceez what was going on, it seemed like he wanted to tell me something but didn't know how to say it. After reading his vibe, I knew what was needed to make things move. I vaguely suggested to Ceez that if I needed to grease a palm or two to make things happen, I was willing to do so. After I spoke on the unspoken, the conversation opened up and I was told what was needed to get my record played.

After I was given a number, I then went to my team to discuss the matter with them. I didn't go to everyone; I only went to the ones that I could depend on for large amounts of cash. At this time, I had no legal form of income. I was selling marijuana to make ends meet. There were two opinions that I valued the most and that was the opinion of Pig and Ole Man Joe's. Payola wasn't something that we subscribed to but we all agreed that at this point of my career it was worth the possible reward.

After putting up as much as we had collectively, we still didn't reach the number that was given so I called the only person I knew that could help. I called Kenneth Crear. Ken was still doing big things in the music industry managing the likes of 112, Cierra and Janet Jackson just to name a few. I called Ken and explained to him that I had a single and needed money to get it moving. Ken asked me how much I needed. I gave Ken a number. Ken agreed to give me half of the number I gave him.

Sidenote: Knowing Ken and how he operated, I knew he wouldn't give me the amount I asked for so the number I gave him was actually double of what I needed so when he agreed to give me half, he actually agreed to give me exactly what I needed. Chess never checkers.

When I received the money from Ken, I placed the cash in the appropriate person's hands and the very next day, "Beat It Up" was approved and being played on 92Q in the mix shows. I was told that every Tuesday at the radio station, all the DJ's along with the program director sat in a meeting, listened to new music and voted on what songs would be added to the mix show. The vote had to be unanimous for the record to be approved. With the help of Ken, when Beat It Up was played, everyone voted yes. I was also told that the DJ's really liked my record but business was business. Some would only give the yes vote if they were being compensated, no matter how much they liked the record.

It was July 2005 and finally I was back on the radio. I hadn't heard my voice on the radio since my Holla Back days back in 2003 and finally, I was back but only on the mix shows. Being played on the mix shows was always the first step but the ultimate goal was to get into rotation. For several weeks "Beat It Up" was being played in the mix shows every night and the record received a great response. The only problem was I didn't have the revenue to push and break the record. I needed the record to be played in the clubs simultaneously while being played on the radio, along with street promotion to even have a chance of breaking it but instead all I had was the mix show and even that had an expiration time that was approaching quickly.

Before I knew it, the money I paid had ran its toll and it was either time to make another payment or move on to another record. I met up with Ceez (something we did one a week) and we mapped out my next move. "Beat It Up was a club record that was perfect for the mix shows but we need a real hip hop record to follow up with" Ceez said, and I agreed.

Sidenote: The CD that K Swift gave me that had a lot of tracks for me to chose from, had a track on it that I chose before choosing the "Beat It Up" track but K Swift told me that someone had just purchased it a few days before I chose it. The record turned out to be a huge hit in Baltimore entitled "Jiggle It" by an artist named Young Leek.

Hearing Ceez say that he wanted a real hip hop record was like heaven to my ears. I liked "Beat It Up" but to me the record was political. The sound, who produced it, and who he was connected to were all the right moves. I remembered in the past when I would take songs to the radio I would always get rejected because the records weren't attached to the "right" people. "Beat It Up" checked all of the boxes but I would have never recorded it, if I had things my way. Now that I had a little buzz going and the green light from Ceez to get back to Hip Hop and could now do a record of my liking.

While meeting with several producers trying to get the right track for the moment, I was still performing everywhere I could to keep my name relevant. One night I had a big show, opening for Juvenile at a night club. As always, I took my entire crew with me to perform but I left Tanja home. Normally she would be the only girl with us, right by my side but for some reason I decided not to bring her.

Everyone on my team had on all black Cooli Hi T-shirts and it was anywhere between 10 – 15 of us. While back stage waiting to go on, I bumped into someone from Young Leeks team (maybe his father or uncle) and we began to talk. He told me that he admired my style and music. He also told me that he advised Young Leek to study how I made my songs and that I was the example of what a true hip hop artist should be. It felt good to hear that coming from someone outside of my circle especially because at the time Young Leek was the hottest thing smoking and had just signed a deal with Def Jam Recordings.

Moments later I took the stage along with Lil Flood (as my hype man) and we blazed the show. Afterwards we hung out for a few and decided to leave. As we were leaving, I saw a guy that I had saw prior to performing standing in the middle of the dance floor trying to pick fights with everyone. Earlier when I saw him, he was doing the same thing; trying to antagonize people. Me and my crew walked right by him and didn't pay him any mind.

When we got outside to the parking lot, we all began to (dap each other up) shake hands and head to our individual cars that were parked away from each other causing our tight crew to split up. In addition to my immediate crew (Crown Vic Click- with the exception of Bags) I had my friend Black with me also.

Sidenote: I was reacquainted with Black through his cousin KP and KP was a guy I met through Ole Man Joe. KP was an inspiring manager that I occasionally worked with that booked gigs for me from time to time. Black had been in jail for 13 years and had recently been released. Ironically, Black and I grew up in the same neighborhood, but I was a lot younger than him. When he was released from prison, KP told him that we were working together and played my music for him. One of the songs KP played was a song I wrote dedicated to my hood called "Brighton and Rosedale" from the Elliott's Ways CD. In the beginning of the song, I shouted out some notorious gangsters from my neighborhood and when Black heard the names being shouted out, he knew that we were connected. When we met up, we instantly connected and have been friends ever since.

Black was a notorious gangster known all over Baltimore City as someone you didn't want to play with. As we all went our separate ways, Black walked with me to my car as a precaution because he knew I didn't have anything on me, but he did. Once I got to my car, we shook hands and then he went to his car and we both left. Little did I know, Big Flood, Lil Flood and Tim Brown were still on the parking lot, in their cars attempting to leave.

While inching through traffic, preparing to pull out of the parking lot, the same guy I saw in the club was walking through the parking lot slapping people's side view mirrors as he passed their cars. As he walked past my cousin's car, he slapped their mirror also which caused them to jump out and confront him.

As always, once my cousins were face to face with the guy, talking was very limited and Tim Brown immediately punched the guy the face. Lil Flood followed up and hit the guys partner in the face also. As the fight continued, the guy that started the altercation pulled out a gun. He pointed it at Big Flood initially and then pointed it at Tim Brown and then he squeezed the trigger. Miraculously nothing happened. When Tim Brown saw that he wasn't shot, he hit the guy again and when he hit him the guy dropped the gun, and it went off! Everyone then ran for cover, jumped in their cars and sped off.

The next day when my cousins told me the story, we all counted our blessings. This could have turned out bad in so many ways. For one, it was nothing short of a miracle that the gun did not go off when the guy pointed and squeezed at Tim Brown and two if Black hadn't pulled off when he did it would have definitely been a disaster on that parking lot.

Another fact that stood out was, I didn't know then but the entire night, the guy that was antagonizing everyone kept going up to people in my crew asking which one of us was Cooli Hi. Everyone responded like we always responded, "We're all Cooli Hi. Why what's up!?" Now that this guy has been beaten up by my team, I now had to burden the load because like always, all that guy knew was he was beefing with "them Cooli Hi dudes." So now when I'm out and about with my kids, Tanja or my family and I just so happen to be wearing my Cooli Hi paraphernalia, I had to be careful because "Cooli Hi" was on so many revenge lists. My team beat up a lot of people at clubs, in addition to Bags and his antics and all the victims knew one thing, and one name- Cooli Hi.

About a week later, I was at Sisqo's in the studio working on some stuff with Murda and his new crew "The Greedy Boys" when Barrs came through and introduced me to one of his friends. The guy's name was Kevin Kid. Kevin Kid was a manager of producers that owned a studio in Odenton, MD. Kevin came through to play some tracks for us to see if we could collaborate and do business. After listening to his producers tracks, I was very impressed, so we exchanged information and not long afterwards I was going to his studio and working with his producers.

Kevin's studio was about 30 – 45 minutes away from Sisqo's and resided on top of a pizza shop. No matter how high he had the air conditioning on, in the summer we would burn up because of the pizza being made down below. Ironically, the name of his establishment was Heat Studios.

Kevin's producers were just what I needed at the time. I was running out of valuable track options to choose from. My name and my affiliation with Sisqo were all I had to work with because I didn't have a budget for purchasing tracks. My motto was the same as it was when I was with Holla Back; everyone will get paid on the back end- there's no upfront money. Kevin understood that and was willing to work with me because he believed in me.

Kevin Kid and his production company (Double Up Entertainment) had an abundance of hot tracks, all at my disposal. One day while at his studio listening to tracks, I heard a particular one and fell in love with it. "This is the one I've been looking for! This will be my next Hip-Hop single" I said to myself.

In order to make it work I had to take the track to my home studio, which was at Sisqo's, so I could have the right vibe when recording. I wrote the song based off a feeling I had one day when Tanja and I were at a Comedy Show.

One day Tanja came across some free tickets to an amateur comedy show. The show was at a high school close to my old neighborhood- Walbrook High. I didn't want to go to the show because I never heard of any of the comedians, or the promoter and I thought it would be packed with hood locals and I didn't want to be in there alone with just me and Tanja. Tanja was beautiful and drew a lot of attention and that didn't mix well with us sitting in the pit of this hood show. I knew the vultures would be out and I would have to deal with all of the stares and maybe a slick word or two coming from the mouth of an asshole. But what was weighing more than anything on my brain was I had just re- up'd (received a new package of weed) and I wanted to go back to Tanja's apartment and bag up my marijuana. Pig, Donny, Murda and I had put our money together and just bought a large amount of weed from our New York connect (who was affiliated with Mr. Cheeks and The Lost Boys). Tanja was so stuck on going to this show that I gave in and went. The entire time while there, I couldn't hear any of the jokes being told because all I could think about was bagging up my weed and selling it. Tanja saw the look on my face while there and decided we should leave. She was so pissed at me but I didn't care. When we got back to her apartment, she laid across the bed and gave me the silent treatment while I sat on the floor and bagged up my weed.

I used this experience and wrote a song called "Get Money". It was originally called "I'm a Hussler" but I changed the name because Cassidy had a song with the same title. I recorded it at Sisqo's and to pay homage, I got Tanja to do the intro to the song. Once the song was done, I gave it to Ceez and he loved it! Now it was time to get my money up for round two of the radio shenanigans.

Being as though I exhausted all my monetary options on my first song with Ceez, Beat It Up, I didn't know where to turn to get more cash for my latest single "Get Money." After brainstorming for a day or two it finally hit me. I decided to ask Marlon for the money. I called Marlon and asked him for the money I needed to get my song on the radio. Without hesitation Marlon wired me the money the next day. Once I received the money, I placed it in the appropriate hands once again and the next day "Get Money" was on the radio in the mix shows.

Every night like clockwork "Get Money" was being played in the 9 o'clock mix and the city, especially the hood, was really feeling the record. I really needed this song to graduate from the mix shows and make its way into rotation fast because I was all out of options for more money for payola. In order to get closer to my goal of rotation, I needed "Get Money" to be played on the 5 o'clock mix show as well. Of all the DJ's that were included in my first transaction, there was only one DJ that didn't take part in it nor would he play any of my two records. That DJ was Jay Claxton.

Jay Claxton was a popular DJ in Baltimore and was managed by Ceez also. I asked Ceez why Jay wouldn't play my records and I was told that Jay moved to the beat of his own drum, meaning if I wanted him to play my records, I had to come to him separately, outside of what I had going on with K Swift. Jay and I met up shortly afterwards, came to an "agreement" and the following day "Get Money was being played on the 5 o'clock mix show as well.

Everything was now in place. I asked everyone I knew to call the radio station continuously and request my song. Of all the family and friends I had, I believe that no one did this. People will say that they will but after a call or two, that was it. The only person I knew of that did this on a consistent basis was Tanja and that was one of the many reasons why I loved her so much. One night while I was live on a radio show called "Rap Attack" Tanja called the radio station (continuously until she got through) and debated with the host of the show, Pork Chop on how she believed I was better than any of the national artist the station was currently playing, live on air!

With my song in both mix shows and only Tanja burning up the phone waves, I knew something had to break quickly before my time ran out (especially because one of my political boxes weren't checked- the producer of "Get Money" was one of Kevin Kidds people and not one of K-Swifts). In an attempt to keep my flame lit after a few weeks of being played on both mix shows, Ceez arranged for me to perform on a local 92Q promoted inner city tour called "The Baltimore Believe" Tour. This tour helped revived my song when it was fading away because the radio station had to play it in order to promote the tour. The only problem was the tour was not catered to my audience.

The shows were outside at parks and school yards, opened to the public. The radio station would build a stage in the middle of an open field and have vendors set up stations. It was a very family and kid orientated event so the radio station as well as the city's representatives advocated no cursing.

At the very first show, I invited Ms Kittie to join me and perform "Beat It Up" but when I saw what Ms Kittie was wearing right before we hit the stage, I knew it was a mistake. Ms. Kittie wore a very provocative outfit and when she performed, she performed for an adult audience. I watched the parents faces while Ms. Kittie performed as well as the kids in the audience and I knew at that moment I wouldn't perform "Beat It Up" again on this tour. Several shows later I still was trying to find my nitch but I just couldn't. My latest two single were not for kids and the majority of my songs were not for kids also. I eventually got kicked off the tour for slipping up and cursing a few times as well as having too many guys on the stage. Soon afterwards, the payola ran out and "Get Money" was no longer being played on the radio. I tried to go for a 3rd single and linked up with Black Star again and recorded a song called "Take Down" featuring Black Star but I never released the record. I just didn't have enough money to continue to play the radio games. Shawn Ceasar and I remained friends, but the business relationship came to an end.

Chapter 42 - Falling Apart

It was the fall of 2005 and I had no clear direction of where to go. I had come to the realization that it didn't matter how hot of a song I made, if I didn't have the money to break the record, it wouldn't go anywhere. It would just be another song blasted in the studio after being made and then on repeat in the car. To add insult to injury, Kidd had resurfaced and got behind another local artist named Boss Man and had his song blasting all over the Baltimore airwaves called "Land of the O." I didn't feel bad or good about the success Kidd was having with his new artist. I actually didn't feel anything at all. I was so focused on trying to achieve my goals that the success of Kidd's new movement didn't matter.

Feeling defeated and somewhat in a slight depression, I decided to push myself even harder. One thing I knew and always knew from the beginning was I had the talent but just needed the other parts to make things come together. Whenever I felt depressed like I was falling into some sort of slump and had thoughts of throwing myself a pity party, I always thought it was the devil trying to kill my drive so as soon as I recognized what was going on with me, I would immediately push myself even harder because I always believed that I had to be close to accomplishing my goals. In my mind, that was the reason why the devil was attacking me. I decided that I needed to push even harder to get my music in every important hand that I could.

Around this time a lot of the local rappers in Baltimore were showing up on the HBO hit show "The Wire" being casted in small roles. Shanna was the first to tell me about this as she played the role of a girl at a house party that overdosed on Season One. Instead of trying to get an acting role on the show, one day I decided to go where they were shooting and just mingle and see if I could meet someone who was someone.

While in between shooting scenes, I saw one of the stars of the show leaning against a wall watching all that was going on. I went over to him with the intentions of sparking up a conversation. When he saw me walking over to him, he extended his hand and said "What's up." I shook his hand and spoke as well and then I asked him if he wanted to buy one of my CD's. I gave him one of my Crown Victoria CD's and he looked at the front and began to read the credits on the back. "Aye man, I don't have any money on me right now because we are filming but if you come back tomorrow, I promise I will support you and buy one." the star said. "Sure, no problem" I replied.

The next day I returned to the set but for some reason, I didn't have any CD's with me. The day before, I felt out of place walking around with a bunch of CD's in my hand. It made me look desperate and I didn't like that so this time I came without any. I also didn't believe that the star would stick to what he said. I looked at it as Hollywood/ industry talk. People say things they don't mean all the time in this business. As I stood to the side watching a scene being filmed, out of nowhere I heard someone say "Yo" and then I felt a tap on my shoulder. It was the star! The star then reached in his pocket and pulled out some money. "Alright, I'm ready to grab that CD from you. How much do I owe you?" he said. "I don't even have any on me today" I replied. "Ah man, I told you I was going to get one from you. Its all-good bro. Maybe next time!" the star said. We both smiled and shook hands and went our separate ways. The star was none other than Idris Elba!

Sidenote: While working on the set of the wire, Idris Elba would DJ at night clubs here in Baltimore and he was also managed by Shawn Ceasar as well.

After showing up on the set of the wire a few times, I decided to move on by selling my CD's. I had no legal form of income. I was getting by from selling weed, in addition to money my Dad would give me for taking him on his monthly errands and I also was receiving help from Evette. This was a very dark time for me financially. To make money, I would go almost anywhere to sell my CD's.

I would go from barbershop to barbershop, beauty salon's anywhere where there was a crowd selling CD's. I would even walk through the malls pushing my CD's until the Security Guards put us out. Though the entire process, Ole Man Joe was always right there with me along with a few others. After getting put out of so many malls and almost arrested a few times, I started renting space at the Patapsco Flee Market every week and sold my CD's there as well.

The money I was making selling my CD's hand to hand was okay but not nearly enough to make a difference business or personally. Since there was no outline on how to make things happen, I would always refer to other success stories I would hear or read about. One common denominator in a lot of success stories was the artist music somehow fell into the "right" hands. It was obvious that the hands I was selling my CD to were not the hands that could help me pass the $10 purchase so I decided to target a white audience. I began to brainstorm and think of where I could find a large amount of white people collectively in Baltimore City and then it hit me- The Baltimore Preakness!

Ole Man Joe, Mouse and I went to the Baltimore Preakness where 100K people came out to watch and bet on horse races and the majority of them were white. We stood in the center of the crowd approaching everyone that made eye contact soliciting my CD. The goal was to of couse sell the CD but hopefully the CD would possibly fall into the "right" hands.

Not only were we selling CD's, we also were selling cold waters and Mouse was renting out his mother's backyard as a parking space. The sales were going good and everything seemed to be going according to plan until one person I attempted to sell a CD to made a comment that I will never forget. I approached a random guy and gave him my pitch to sell. The guy asked to see my CD. He read the song list on the back and saw all of the features. Then he asked the million dollar question. "If you have all of these celebrities on your CD, why are you here selling CD's at the Preakness?" I was stuck. I had no answer. The guy saw Sisqo and Dru Hill's name and thought like any other person would think. When I didn't give an answer, the guy gave me back my CD and walked away.

After the Preakness, not knowing what else to do, I decided to release all the songs I did that I thought needed to be heard as an album. I entitled the album, "Crown Victoria- The Sequel". I didn't have the money to professionally press up the album so I hired a graphic designer to create a basic CD cover and I pressed up the minimum order 500 CD's. Crown Victoria- The Sequel never made it to the stores. It was only distributed hand to hand in the streets. Many of my fans never knew the album ever existed.

Sidenote: Crown Victoria- The Sequel is now available on all digital platforms.

Musically, things were beginning to look grimmer and grimmer as each day passed. Sisqo's light was continuing to dim which made the little "Can I Live" light I had fade even more. The house, (Sisqo's house) was beginning to go downhill in morale as well as appearance. The once prestigious studio and basement was beginning to fall apart. Speakers weren't working, the computer kept crashing, and the tidiness was null and void. Often there were Hennessy and Corona bottles filled with cigarette and blunt ashes everywhere. Sisqo, being a neat freak, the same as I, hated this. He almost never came downstairs during our sessions but the next morning, after everyone had left, he would come downstairs to a disastrous mess! Then we would have to hear about it that night when we returned. Often, he would threaten to shut down the studio and sometimes he did but just like a parent with their children, a few days later he would give in and we all would be right back. I believe although Sisqo hardly ever joined us in the basement, he enjoyed having us there. True musicians love music so I believe he enjoyed hearing what we created downstairs blasting through his vents and like always if he heard something that really got his attention, he would come running.

I wasn't coming to the studio as much as before (when I was pushing singles and out selling CD's) so the control of the house/ studio was shifting over to Murda. Murda lived with Sisqo so he was there all the time. Now that I had released Crown Victoria- The Sequel, I needed to reload my catalog with new material to have current records. Now when I went to the studio, sometimes I would have to wait because Murda and his crew "The Greedy Boys" might be recording. Pig didn't like this at all and started pushing the narrative that it was time for us "Crown Vic" to get our own studio.

As this was going on, I began to analyze my entire crew to find out what needed to change. I had Ole Man Joe, who was a true friend, gave money whenever asked and was always there every step of the way but didn't contribute anything on the musical nor business side. I had my cousins, the reasoning for the Crown Vic Click, that didn't contribute anything musically nor business wise, but they were my inspirations when creating songs. Whenever I wrote a song or even a feature verse, I always had their opinion in mind. I always asked myself, would they like this and I often wrote and said things to ensure they would. I didn't care about anything or anyone one else. If they approved it, I was good. Then I had Butch and Hot (also Big Status at a distance) who were good friends but only brought lyrical content when needed. Nothing on the business side. Murda, Barrs and Holla were once affiliated with us but had now branched off as the "Greedy Boys." Then I had Donny, my childhood friend that would contribute financially from time to time and Pig who did a little bit of everything from contributing revenue, to finding me tracks to write to, helped come up with logo's and always had a good word of advice musically for the most part. All of these people were important in my movement but none of them had what was needed to take my movement to the next level and I knew that. I needed someone that had what Kidd had (without the Blade issues). Kidd had the gift of power and finance mixed with influence and that was hard to come by. He made people feel like they needed to be attached to what he was doing or else they would lose out. The only one on my immediate team that was remotely close to what Kidd had was Jamal but he moved to New York to work for HBO. The final piece to the Crown Vic puzzle was Bags who brought "Bags type of things" to the table that had nothing to do with music.

I had love for all of these guys, but I knew I couldn't go far with this team. In addition to their short comings as it relates to the music business, some of them didn't like each other. Bags didn't like Hot nor Murda at (times) and Ole Man Joe didn't like Murda, just to name a few. On several occasions Bags plotted on fighting Hot and Murda individually but somehow, I would always catch wind of the plot and defuse it before it happened.

One night before a big show I had at a club called Club One, I had been drinking and as we were preparing to leave Sisqo's and head out, I told everyone that we weren't giving out any passes that night. If anyone remotely came close to violating, we were going to tear the club apart. Everyone loved the energy I gave especially Bags. They were so used to me telling everyone to chill (because I didn't want to get banned out of clubs for meaningless fights) and finally they could get busy if needed. This was back when I just released "Out of Control" featuring Dru Hill on vinyl records. I remember after saying that Tanja pulling me to the side asking "Why would you say that!? They're going to go down there (the club) and act a pure fool!"

Needless to say, this energy sparked something in the crew and now everyone was on edge. What I didn't know was Bags had plans on picking a fight with Hot and my energy sparked it. Bags, using what I had just said, decided to act like he was so pumped up, that he started open hand smacking Hot across the chest. Hot didn't initially respond thinking Bags was just in the moment but after the second smack hot got upset and punch Bags twice in the chest. Afterwards he immediately walked out of the room in anger. Bags looked like he was ready for the fight but me along with others jumped in and defused the situation. It was so many incidents where me and the crew would be out, and I wouldn't know if we would get into a fight with another crew or fight each other and Bags was always at the center of it all. It had come to a point where I thought I could read Bags actions a little better because I was around him so much until one night, I received an alarming call from Butch as I was on my way to Sisqo's.

On this night, Pig and I were driving to Sisqo's when suddenly my phone rang. When I answered it was Butch on the other end. Butch immediately asked where I was. "Me and Pig are on our way out to the house" I said to Butch. "Butch then said "Yo you're not going to believe whats happening right now as we speak. Bags and Tony are at Blondie's (Sisqo) house right now robbing him!" As Butch was telling me this, I was literally pulling up in Sisqo's driveway. "Alright cool" I said to Butch and then we hung up. I didn't tell Pig what Butch had just told me because I didn't want to scare him, nor did I want him to walk in the house with a shook look on his face. Bags would have immediately noticed that and knew that we knew what was going on.

When we walked in, I didn't know what to expect. I knew Bags and Tony had guns and weren't afraid to use them. I wasn't sure if Bags had everyone tied up, shot, or dead but everything appeared to be normal as I headed for the kitchen. When I walked in the kitchen, Bags was standing by the refrigerator while Sisqo was sitting on the couch playing video games. Tony was upstairs pretending to fix some doorknobs on one of Sisqo's bedroom doors. "Cooli motherfucking Hi" Bags said as I walked in. I walked over to him and we shook hands. Butch told me that Bags and Tony were pretending to fix some doors upstairs in Sisqo's house but actually they were planning to rob him. They had already had all of his jewelry by the time I had arrived. Bags didn't know that I knew what was going on. "Yo Cool, let me holla at you outside" Bags said to me. I agreed. Bag and I walked outside and then he said "Yo lets go over here and talk real quick." The area Bags was leading me to was in a very dark portion of Sisqo's driveway that no one could see. Me knowing what kind of dude Bags was, plus knowing what Butch had just told me, in addition to all of the jealousy and envy he had towards me, practically infatuated with my girl Tanja and knowing he had his gun, all added up to me being killed if I followed him into this blind spot of the driveway yet still I went.

Once we both were in the darkest spot of the area, Bags began to talk about whatever was on his mind. I didn't hear one-word Bags said. I was so focused on his body movement that everything he said to me was muffled. I stood extremely close to him as he talked because I didn't want to give him any room to reach for his gun. As soon as he made a sudden move, I would have moved too and we would have fought for that gun. The entire time he talked, I stood in his face and looked him dead in the eye and watched his body language. After a few minutes or so, Bags was done talking so we both returned to the house. I stayed for another 30 minutes or so and then Pig and I left. Pig had no idea of what was going on.

The next day, Butch told me that Bags changed his mind about robbing Sisqo and put all of his jewelry back. Sisqo never knew what was actually happening that night. Bags also told Butch that he had a newfound respect for me after the scene in the driveway. "Yo I had Cool in a very compromising situation where almost any nigga would have been shook but Cool was solid. He didn't flinch." Bags told Butch. Little did Bags know but I was scared out of my mind! I just knew that Bags was going to attempt to kill me that night. I say attempt because as I said before, I was anticipating for him to reach for his gun and was prepared to go all out to get to it before he did. I guess

664 | Dwayne Jones - Almost Famous

my poker face held up because Bags had no idea that I feared for my life but was also willing to fight for it.

I've been a lot of places and met a lot of people but I can honestly say that I had never came across anyone like Bags before. I honestly believe that nothing was off limits when it came down to what he would do. I was once told by a very reliable source that Bags and his girlfriend actually had a threesome with his girlfriends under age daughter!

There was one point and time when Butch and Tony was looking for Bags for days and couldn't find him. The three of them did home improvement work together and one day Bags just went missing. After a few days or so Bags finally resurfaced and it later came out that Bags was in a crack house on a smoke binge. When I heard this I immediately thought back to when we all were at JI 900's studio and the guy thought Bags was a junky and offered him crack. The guy was right. He saw the "look" in Bags eyes and Bags was exposed and got offended. With crack mixed in with the mental disorders Bags was probably dealing with explained why he was so unpredictable.

Not long after the crack house incident Bags moved to a part of Baltimore called Brooklyn and started selling drugs in the neighborhood. He didn't know anyone in the area at the time. Somehow he must have met someone and decided to trust that person by giving them his drugs to sell for him. Of course the person ran off with the drugs and didn't give him any of the money made. For days Bags searched all over for the guy but couldn't find him. Finally somehow Bags found out where the guy lived and kicked in his door looking for him. Once Bags was inside he shot the guy and two of his pitbull dogs and ran out.

After the incident, Bags called and told us what had just happened. He was officially on the run again. Later that same night Bags left town. A few days later Bags was caught somewhere in Texas. He was with a white girl and was asleep in the backseat while she was driving. She must have been speeding and once they were pulled over it was a wrap. They flew Bags back to Maryland to face his charges and ironically Sisqo and Murda saw bags at the airport shackled from head to toe as they were returning from one of Sisqo's shows.

We didn't have money to bail Bags out (actually I'm not sure if he even had a bail) so he had to sit and wait for his trial date. Everyday Bags would call my mothers house and speak with either her or myself. My mother actually liked Bags. Well, she like the version he presented to her. She had no idea of what he was actually in to.

A month had passed and one day I was returning from the barbershop when all of a sudden my phone rang. When I answered, it was my mother. "Dwayne you wouldn't believe who's sitting here with me" my Mom said. "Who" I asked. My mother replied "Bags!" and then she passed him the phone. When I heard his voice my heart dropped from my chest to the floor of the car. All kinds of thoughts were racing through my mind. How did he get out? Why was he at my mothers house? Was he planning on hurting her? Did this guy escape? He didn't get bailed out! He had an attempted murder charge and killed two dogs!?

I almost turned my mother's car over in an attempt to get back to her house. When I arrived Butch was pulling up as well. We all walked down the block to talk so my mother could hear what was going on. Bags said somehow the people at the jail made a mistake and let him go. Made a mistake? Are you serious? Butch and I asked. Bags assured us that he was telling the truth. I believed him because he didn't know anyone in Baltimore except for us so he couldn't have snitched on someone and even if he did snitch he still wouldn't have been released so soon. The jail system actually made a mistake and released a natural born killer!

Bags didn't waste any time getting out of town. He said he just wanted to stop at my mothers house to say goodbye to everyone before he left. A few hours later bags left town headed to Florida. That was the last time I saw Bags.

Sidenote: A few years later Bags was found dead on his couch from an overdose. The girl that he was living with at the time called and told Butch but by the time she told him, the state had already had his body for quite some time. We collectively didn't have the money to ship him back to Baltimore or New York (where he was originally from) so the state of Florida cremated him. RIP Bags.

As I continued to record new songs as well as freestyles to keep my skills sharp and to add to my catalog my primary goal was to join forces with someone that could take me to the next level. Another Kidd. I began working closely with Kevin Kidd and his Double Up Production team and before I knew it a great situation surfaced. Kevin Kidd had somehow connected with Lavar Arrington, a star NFL football player for the Washington Redskins. Lavar must have been looking to start a record label or wanted to get into the music business, like a lot of athletes and was looking for talent. Kevin Kidd played my music for Lavar Arrington and he loved it. Like many people he especially loved my song called "Always" often referenced as "the song about your son."

When Kevin brought this to my attention, I was very excited. Lavar had millions of dollars and was a NFL superstar at the time so with his power and influence and my artistry together was a perfect match for success. There was only one problem. Kevin kept a wall up between Lavar and me to ensure he didn't get cut out of the deal.

Whenever I asked Kevin about meeting Lavar, it was always some sort of an excuse why it couldn't happen. The situation reminded me of Mouse and Sisqo back in the day. Everything that was told to me from Lavar came from Kevin and vice versa. Kevin was determined to negotiate the deal. One day Kevin called me with Lavar on the phone also (on a three-way call) and we all talked. Lavar sounded very excited about working with me and I was pleased to hear that. He went on and on about how much he loved my song "Always" and about how he saw the music video being played out in his head. Lavar saw the video I had but he had plans of doing another video on a much larger scale. Before that call, all of Lavar's words came from Kevin's mouth so it was refreshing to hear it straight from Lavar. Before the call ended Lavar invited us to have lunch with him so we could finally meet in person.

On the day of the lunch, I along with Kevin Kidd of course, drove to Washington DC and met Lavar at a fancy restaurant along with many others and we all had lunch. It was anywhere between 12 – 15 people there so I really didn't get a chance to have a one-on-one conversation with him. When the lunch was over Lavar and I shook hands and said that we would talk more in detail on our next meeting. That meeting never came. That was the last time I heard from or saw Lavar Arrington. Rumor has it says that Kevin Kidd was asking Lavar for big upfront money (six figures), speaking on my behalf, and the number scared Lavar off.

The same thing happened with another investor that Kevin Kidd was affiliated with by the name of Terry. Terry was heavy into real estate, was very well off and wanted to get into the music industry. As always whenever Kevin Kidd ran into situations like this, he always pitched my project because I was the most polished artist that he had access to and because of my credentials. Having learned from the Lavar Arrington situation I didn't allow Kevin Kidd to keep his wall up between us so the first chance I got we exchanged numbers and I dealt with him personally along with Kevin Kidd. Nothing came out of this situation, but Terry did tell me that Kevin Kidd asked him for a check for 50K to push my project.

Both situations taught me very valuable lessons. For one, people that have money but are not grounded in music usually look at it as a hobby, just something to do and although they may talk a good game, they hardly ever cut the check because in the music business, especially when trying to break an artist, there are no guarantees. You must really have a passion for this and be willing to take a loss but for most athletes, investors etc. taking a loss is not an option. Also, the middleman can make or break any business situation so it's best not to have a middleman at all. Avoid them at all costs if possible.

There were other managers that came and went during that time such as Tony- Ray Lewis from the Baltimore Ravens head of security and G Money- Doug E Fresh personal assistant but nothing ever flourished. Finding that missing piece was beginning to feel like it was damn near impossible.

Meanwhile on a personal note, my life was a beautiful mess. The holidays were approaching (Christmas 2005) and I had no money to buy gifts for my children. The stress of my musical career was beginning to take a toll on my physical health causing the skin on my hands to peel. My weed sales were beginning to dry up because a lot of my regular customers were beginning to buy ounces at a time which hurt my sales because I was selling them dimes and $20 bags. The smaller the bags I sold, the more money I made off an once as well as the money kept coming. By my customers buying ounces at a time, I hardly saw any money and didn't hear from them for days afterwards.

Tanja and I were still madly in love with one another, but the dynamics of our relationship had changed. Since we were official, the excitement of us messing around when we weren't supposed to be was gone. Instead of sneaking off having spontaneous and passionate sex, we were now home in her apartment making love in a bedroom like normal couples do. Once every so often we would go to DC to a sex club, have sex in the car and come back home to Baltimore just to keep things a little spicy. That year 2005 on my birthday, Tanja got my name tattooed on her butt "Cooli Hi" that almost covered her entire left cheek. So now Tanja had my initials on her wrist and my name on her butt. In my mind, it was pretty safe to say that she wasn't going anywhere.

Chante had moved on and was now seeing and older guy almost twice her age. The guy seemed to be well off financially and Chante and my son Darrian had moved in with him. Although I was in a relationship with Tanja, I hated the fact that Chante and Darrian lived with another man. I felt like I gave away my perfect family. I subconsciously resented Tanja for this because I felt like she forced me to make a choice and although I made the choice that I made, I knew I could never be completely happy with Tanja.

Before, Tanja and I were in a relationship, it was just us having fun and enjoying each other's company but now that we were officially together, I was now a part of her everyday life which meant I was around her children even more. I never wanted to be the guy that was seeing someone else's children more than I was seeing my own so sometimes I would stay away from Tanja till it was close to her kids bedtime and then I would come over. I was so conflicted. I really loved Tanja but I felt like I sacrificed Darrian for my relationship with her and that bothered me constantly. Nothing changed with Anna and I so my relationship with Peanut wasn't affected but my time with Darrian drastically changed. I also felt guilty about how I hurt Chante and to see her with this older guy made my skin crawl. I knew that he wasn't good for her and that he was manipulating her, but I had no one to blame but myself. I always looked at Chante's situation as a line that Jay Z said in a song called "Song Cry" that goes, "Once a good girls gone bad, she's gone forever. I'll mourn forever. I gotta live with the fact that I did you wrong forever!"

Christmas was right around the corner, and I still wasn't in position to get my boys anything. Tanja had just recently moved into her apartment and had a good paying job in DC. One day she asked me to go with her to the toy store so she could Christmas shop for her kids. When we got to the store, she grabbed a cart. When I went to follow behind her, she told me to grab a cart too. "You know I'm not going to allow you to not get your kids anything for Christmas, right?" Tanja said. Christmas 2005 was a Christmas that I will never forget because Tanja bought my boys every toy that I gave them that year. Tanja had 3 kids of her own and received no help from her ex-husband. The toys she bought my kids could have gone to her kids but she was selfless enough to help me at my time of need. I'm forever grateful to Tanja for this and I will never forget.

Chapter 43 - Gut Blow

The year 2006 started off promising but ended up being the worst year of my life. Sisqo had just hired a new manager by the name of Keith who was determined to change how things were being ran at the house. Keith came in with a "lets clean some thing up" approach which ruffled a lot of feathers within the Dragon Family. Since I was still looked upon as the top hip hop artist in the family, my access wasn't affected as much but to others the studio wasn't as available as it once was before. No one liked it but had no choice but to accept it.

Soon after Keith's arrival on the scene there were talks of Sisqo releasing a new single brought to the table by of course Keith entitled "Who's Your Daddy." The song was on fire and everyone was excited about Sisqo releasing new music once again. "Who's Your Daddy" had a breakdown on the record that required a rap verse and I along with Barrs got the call. "Finally, another chance to jump back on the scene" I thought to myself. "This time I'll be sure to say my name in the verse just in case I'm not mentioned as a feature like on Can I Live" I also thought.

When I wrote my verse to "Who's Your Daddy" as always I used a familiar situation. I decided to write the verse about Tanja. Every single line was specifically about her except for the line about 3 kids with 3 different fathers. I did this to show my appreciation and love for her for holding me down all this time. I thought this song as well as myself was about to blow but I was sadly mistaken.

After the song was completed and it was time to do the paperwork, Keith came to me with a proposal that almost made me want to punch him in the face. Keith proposal for my contribution to the song was a $100 work for hire!

Sidenote: Work for hire in the music business means you receive one payment (in this case $100) and that's it. You don't receive any publishing and you sign away any rights that you might have to the song.

When Keith told me what he proposed, I looked at him like he was crazy. I explained to him that on Can I Live, I received 15K along with my percentage of the publishing and that was with the iconic Teddy Riley! If Teddy Riley was willing to give me my publishing, why wouldn't the producers of this song (which were not known producers) give me my publishing? Also what the hell is $100?? I felt so insulted. I told Keith $100 is gas money. I would rather for him to say there is no upfront money rather than to offer $100! Keith's explanation was that the writer and producer didn't feel the song needed a rap verse therefore they didn't want to share any of the publishing. Having a rapper on the song was Sisqo's call. I got up from the table and walked away.

Keith must have told Sisqo his version of how our conversation went and a few days later Sisqo and I had a one on one. I told Sisqo that I could never charge him for anything. He had helped and did so much for me, how could I even think of charging him? However, the $100 offer felt like a slap in the face from Keith, not Sisqo. Who offers someone $100? That's unheard of. I just wanted the publishing because I knew how important it was. Sisqo and I talked and everything ended on a good note but when the song was finally released neither me or Barrs was on it. They decided to go without the rap verse in order to keep all of the publishing.

After being removed from the "Who's Your Daddy" record, I began to start taking more frequent trips to New York to meet with anyone that I could. I would call a guy named Jaha Johnson, a former Def Jam executive that was now at the time working with Arista (I believe) and set up meetings with him. So many times I would catch a train or bus to New York to meet with Jaha and when I got there he would tell me "Yo Cooli I have another meeting I have to attend. Come back tomorrow and we can talk!" Feeling deflated I would leave his office and then call everyone I knew in New York attempting to get a same day meeting just to make the best out of the trip. But sometimes it didn't work out and before I knew it, I was back on the bus headed back to Baltimore, only being in New York for 20 minutes.

After several weeks of this madness, one day Jamal (childhood friend and Holla Back & Crown Vic affiliate) called me and said that he wanted me to meet a friend of his that worked at BMI by the name of Wardell Malloy. Jamal wanted us to meet so that Wardell could hear my records and possibly help me with a ghost writing type of situation for other rap artist. I wasn't a fan of ghosting writing for people but at this point I was willing to try almost anything to get my foot back in the door.

A few days later, I was back in New York at BMI in Wardell's office. I played all my best records for him and as I played each record, I watched Wardell's demeanor and noticed that his attention rose when I had singers singing my choruses. After I played about 6 or 7 records, Wardell stopped me and asked "Who wrote the singing choruses on these records?" "I did" I responded. Then Wardell asked a question that would change the direction of my musical career forever. Wardell asked, "Have you ever considered writing an entire R&B song?" "No I haven't but I'm willing to give it a try." I responded. Wardell burned me a CD of tracks and gave it to me. "See if you can come up with something to one of these tracks!" he said. I took the CD and returned to Baltimore.

The very next day, I listened to the CD all day trying to see if something came to mind. As I listened, I began to brainstorm and think of who I could get to sing whatever I came up with. I looked at this situation as a unique challenge. You see even before I wrote my very first rap back when I was 10 years old, I always wrote R&B songs (using my words with other popular songs melodies) and even during the current times when I wrote my choruses, I always enjoyed writing the singing parts. But I knew that no matter what I wrote, the success of the record all depended on who sung it.

Although I told Wardell that I never wrote and entire R&B song, actually I did. I just wasn't too proud of it. Back in the DeMartim Record days I wrote a few songs for Lia. One of the songs I wrote for her that I actually liked was a song called "Welcome Home." The song was about a female celebrating her man being released from jail. Later, not too long after the release of my Crown Victoria album, I wrote a song to one of Murda's tracks (the interlude on my album) entitled "Crazy About You." I also wrote a verse or two on a few records that Kidd and Butta worked on back in the day but nothing that I can remember. One thing I learned when writing these songs and even when I wrote choruses for my hip hop songs was the singer will make or break what was written.

Sidenote: Often I was asked the question "Since I needed singers, why didn't I reach out to my immediate musical family which was Dru Hill/ Sisqo or Lovher/ Chinky. Here's why I didn't. Although Dru Hill and Lovher were my family, sometimes you must step outside of your own circle in order to get what you want accomplished. You see Dru Hill, Sisqo and Chinky respected me as a rapper but not as an R&B songwriter. They were very high on the R&B food chain so if I wanted them to respect me as a songwriter, I had to earn their respect and the best way to do that was to get things done on my own and bring back a polished successful project and that was my intention.

One of the first songs I wrote from the CD that Wardell gave me was a song entitled "I Wanna Go Back." The song was for a female, and it talked about wanting to take a relationship back to when the two of them didn't have anything but each other. I always had to give my songs some sort of underlying subject matter. Subjects and specific topics were always my thing.

To sing what I wrote, I reached out to a singer named Tamika, the girl who sung the chorus on my song "My Life" from my Crown Victoria album. Tamika sung the song and did well but it just didn't sound like I heard it sounding in my head when I was writing it so I never played it for anyone. I tried to have another singer by the name of Nena take a shot at it and still it wasn't coming across as I expected.

One day I went to Kevin Kidds studio to work on some new hip hop material, and I ran into a guy I knew named Steve. Steve was a part of our street team at Holla Back Entertainment. Even back during the Holla Back days Steve had an entrepreneur's spirit and I always knew that it was just a matter of time before that kid took off. Steve and I talked and caught up for a few and then I asked what he was doing there at Kevin's studio. "I'm here with one of my artists that I manage" Steve replied. "His name is J Rome. He's in the booth recording now!"

I went into the main room with Steve, sat on the couch and began to listen to Steve's artist sing. The voice I heard coming from the monitors was like no other voice that I had ever heard before! "Yo Steve, what's your artist's name again" I asked. "His name is J Rome and he's from PG (Prince Georges County). He's dope, isn't he?" Dope was an understatement. J Rome's voice was absolutely amazing! Since he was in the middle of recording a song, I didn't get a chance to hear the finished product, but I had heard enough to know that I wanted to work with him in some capacity. I continued to listen to J Rome sing for a few and then I left.

The next day while in the shower, I began listening to another track that was on Wardell's CD that also caught my attention. I had this track playing on repeat and before I knew it the melody of the chorus was playing in my head. As I began to hum the melody out loud while still in the shower the words began to come to me. By the time I was out of the shower I had the entire chorus, lyrics and melody written in my head.

After I got dressed, I called Steve and told him I wanted to work with his artist. Steve was very excited due to my status and of course my affiliation with Sisqo so he told J Rome and we scheduled a date and time for a studio session.

A few days later we were at Sisqo's house recording the song I wrote while in the shower. The name of the song was "Sunday Morning". When recording the record, the first thing we did was record the chorus. J Rome laid down his unison parts first. As soon as he sung the first harmony note on the chorus, I knew I had something special. By the time all the harmony notes were recorded, I was completely blown away! I must have listened to the chorus accapella at least 50 times before we laid down the verses. Once the record was done, I knew I had to get it mixed and sent to Wardell immediately. In my mind, this song was going to change my life!

That night after the studio session, I went to Tanja's and played the record for her. As Tanja listened to the song her eyes opened very wide when the chorus came in. "This song is fucking incredible!" Tanja said. Tanja's comment confirmed what I felt in my soul; that I had something special.

Once the song was mixed, I immediately sent it to Jamal and Wardell for their opinion. They both absolutely loved it!! Wardell began to brainstorm and tried to find a good match for the song to be placed on someone's album. The track for "Sunday Morning" was produced by Shea Taylor a known producer who worked with the likes of Neo and many others.

Sidenote: The track was produced by Shea Taylor but the actual record was produced by me. For a long time I didn't even know that I was producing my own records, both hip hop and R&B because I thought producing was creating the track/ music but its not. Producing a record means putting everything in place on a song to bring it to life and completion which meant I produced 95% of all my songs because I hardly ever had the person who made my tracks there with me at the studio. Shea Taylor made the track but Sunday Morning was produced by myself and arranged by me, J Rome and a friend of J Rome's by the name of Vernell.

Sunday Morning had my name ringing in the BMI Publishing office and soon after I was being invited to BMI showcases where all the producers and writers met up to network. The host of the showcase would introduce a song as well as the songwriter and producer and then play about 60 seconds of the record for the entire room to hear. I remember the first showcase I attended, Old Man Joe and I were there. When Sunday Morning came on, it paralyzed the entire room! Afterwards, I was bombarded with producers asking for my contact information so we could collaborate and I could write to their music. Even some songwriters approached me for co-writing purposes. Wardell had placed "Sunday Morning" on a BMI sampler CD so everyone in the room had access to what I had to offer. I felt so honored to be on that sampler because not everyone made it. Of maybe 100 entries, only 12 were selected and I was one of the 12.

After the internal BMI success of Sunday Morning, I continued to push. The next song I wrote was to another track on the CD Wardell gave me that I named "I'm In Love" and of course J Rome was the singer. "I'm In Love" was the song that taught me about harmonies, notes and vocal arrangements, all things that I never had to deal with when creating Hip Hop records and a lot of this was taught to me by J Rome's friend Vernell. I watched and observed as he would give J Rome notes when adding harmonies to the chorus or whatever part that could use a harmony. That's also when I learned that there was so much more to writing R&B than just the lyrics. The vocal arrangement was just as important as what was actually being said!

After "I'm In Love" the next song I wrote was a record I called "Know Your Name". Sunday Morning and I'm In Love were love songs/ ballads but Know Your Name was the first up-tempo/ pop record that I wrote. The track was produced by an old school rapper by the name of Kwame' (known for his hit singles "The Rhythm" and "Only You"). "Know Your Name" was my Dad's favorite record of mine. So now I had 3 records swimming through the pools of BMI and I was just patiently waiting for one of them to land on someone's upcoming album.

Sidenote: When the hype of Sunday Morning didn't land an immediate placement, I started to worry about a theory Kidd shared with me a while ago when he was trying to get songs placed and had Butta singing the reference tracks. Kidd told me that sometimes it hurts the songwriter/ producer to have an amazing singer reference the song because the actual artist, the one who would be professionally releasing the song, may feel intimidated by the reference track. The artist might love the song but if they feel like they can't sing it as good as the person who referenced it, they wont touch it. I started thinking maybe that was the hold up with my records. If an artist heard what J Rome did on the record, they might not want to touch it because they might think they can't do better than the reference but that was the chance I was willing to take because there was no way I was not going to use J Rome.

Meanwhile on the home front, between running back and forth to New York for the BMI Songwriters showcases my personal life was falling apart and I didn't even know it. Chante's new boyfriend had convinced her that since I wasn't consistently giving her money for our son, that she should take me downtown and put me on child support. In addition to filing a claim for child support, she stopped allowing me to see Darrian after we got into a physical altercation at my mother's house.

One day I was at my mothers talking to my friend Black on the phone. Chante came over to pick Darrian up after a few hours of him being there with my mom and I. At this time Chante was financially on top of the world because her new boyfriend was financially well off. Almost every time Chante would come over with Darrian, she would be driving a different car. My money on the other hand didn't exist and Chante began to look down on me because of my financial status. Cheap shots were thrown around a lot but I chose to ignore them. Out of spite, (I believe) Chante would suggest that we put Darrian in some overpriced expensive day care or educational program because she knew I couldn't afford it and it would hurt my pride.

On this particular day, Chante came through the door on her high horse per usual. When I came downstairs still talking to my friend Black on the phone, she told me "Get off the phone now and get Darrian's things. I have to go!" Me being fed up, I snapped and told her not to talk to me like that in an aggressive way. Chante jumped in my face and before I knew it we were tussling in my mother's living room (all while I was still on the phone with Black). I could hear my friend Black yelling "Yo Cool, chill!" while I had one hand on the phone and the other hand on Chantes shoulder. No punches were thrown but it was an ugly pushing match all in front of our son Darrian. My mother intervened and we both let go. After that, Chante wouldn't allow me to see Darrian.

Since I knew where Darrian's daycare was I went there one time to pick him up because I hadn't seen him in a few weeks. Chante had removed my name from the list. The next day Tanja had just so happened to be driving past Darrian's day care and saw Chante leaving out with Darrian and had her boyfriend with her almost like a bodyguard. Seeing this really made Tanja angry passed the point of return.

Tanja now wanted desperately to fight Chante but I didn't allow it to happen. Often Tanja would get upset with me because she felt like I was protecting Chante. "All the shit this girl is doing to you and you're still looking out for her!" Tanja would say. Tanja knew how important it was for me to see and be involved in my kid's life and for someone to take that away from me made Tanja furious. Also, Tanja was still pissed about when Chante called her every name under sun (when she caught me at Tanja's house) and couldn't let it go although she and I were together.

One day Chante was going over to visit Anna (ironically these two became good friends) and was getting out of her car headed to Anna's porch. Tanja was driving by because my son Peanut and Tanja's kids attended the same school. When Tanja saw Chante getting out of the car, she called me and said "I'm about to fight your baby mother and there's nothing you can do or say to stop it!" It took everything in me to talk Tanja into not getting out of her car to fight Chante but eventually I did. Chante never saw or knew Tanja was there.

Tanja was right. I was protecting Chante. It didn't matter what Chante did or said to me. I felt guilty for how I left her, and our son and that guilt made me vulnerable to her. Chante was a sweet innocent girl and now because of me she's dating a guy that was old enough to be her father and riding around with a red cup drinking all the time.

As for my relationship with Tanja, it was slowing diminishing right before my eyes. You see being as though I had guilt from the way I did Chante, I was never able to love Tanja like she deserved, or anyone deserved and in addition to the guilt, I was selfish. I was in a relationship with Tanja, but still occasionally sleeping with Shanna, Evette and once in a blue moon even Anna. Chinky and I flirted at times, and I also slept with another member of Lovher but it wasn't one of my best moments. It happened at Sisqo's house, and I was so nervous thinking Tanja was going to walk through the door any minute while it was happening that I wasn't myself.

At times Tanja would pour her heart out to me via text, email and verbally pleading for us to discuss and work out our issues but I ignored all of her actions. I was cocky and arrogant, and it had nothing to do with music. I was cocky as a person when it came to Tanja. In my mind I thought, she had my name tattooed on her wrist and all over her ass. Where was she going to go especially with three small kids? Also the arrogance in me made me believe that I was the only one that could completely please her sexually because of the intimate bond that we had. We lived, breathed, and slept each other. Both of our worlds revolved around each other. Where would she go to find better than what we had? So I took her for granted thinking that although she was gorgeous, no one would be able to connect with her like I did.

Whenever we got into the slightest argument, I would always suggest that we should take a break and she hated it. I used the fear of losing me as a way to control her and for a while it worked until suddenly things dramatically changed.

I remember one day Tanja and I were together at Walmart. We went in to get a few things and when we returned to the car, the tire was flat. Neither Tanja nor I had our own car at the time. We were in one of her father's cars. Tanja's father had a Lincoln Towncar and the wheel/ rim had a lock on it that required a special key. As Tanja and I both stood there looking clueless in regard to what to do, finally Tanja called her father for help. When Tanja's dad arrived and saw me standing there, he looked at me with so much disgust as if to say, "What good are you to my daughter if you cant figure out how to change a tire?" Now granted, I knew how to change flat tires, but I just didn't know how to unlock the rim on the Lincoln Towncars.

Sidenote: Looking back, I should have figured it out or got help on MY end. A tow truck, roadside assistance or something. Calling her father should have never happened or even been an option.

Tanja Dad fixed the tire and afterwards he left. He never looked at me the entire time while changing the tire. He treated me like I wasn't even there but the sad part about it was afterwards, I jumped in the passenger's seat with Tanja and rode off not feeling any way about it at all but I'm sure Tanja was embarrassed to say that I was her "man" to her dad after that incident.

This is just one of so many examples of me not knowing how to be a man to a woman. I would drive her car and be late bringing it back at times when she needed it, get money from her with no intentions of giving it back, eat and drink at her apartment, spending almost every night there and never gave her anything towards her bills and brought the weed that I bagged up and sold to her house and stashed it in her closet. And my justification for this behavior was that I was great in bed and our bond, connection and friendship could never be topped or duplicated.

It was Memorial Day 2006 and Tanja had plans to attend a cookout at her cousins house in Prince Georges County, MD. Tanja mentioned the cookout to me previously but never actually invited so me being cocky, invited myself. Tanja had planned to head out to the cookout around 2pm but I had a haircut appointment for the same time, so I took Tanja's car and went to the barbershop. I joked with my friend Dave (back from DeMartim Records and was now my barber) about how pissed Tanja was going to be because I was late bringing her car back. I got my haircut and arrived at Tanja's around 3pm. Tanja was so disgusted that she didn't say anything when I arrived. She just got in the car and we both headed to her cousin's house.

When we arrived, Tanja spoke to everyone but did not introduce me to her family members that I didn't know. I spoke to the ones I did know, and Tanja's sister introduced me to the one that I didn't know. After a few moments of socializing, I pulled Tanja to the side and asked her to take a walk with me. Tanja agreed by saying "Yes. Let's take a walk because we need to talk." As always whenever Tanja was upset with me, I was planning to use the "maybe we should take a break card" to scare her into acting "right" again but little did I know the roles were reversed.

Tanja's cousin lived closed to a lake and as we walked around the lake and talked, I could tell that something was different. I couldn't see "us" in Tanja's eyes anymore. She looked like she had completely disconnected from me. Me not knowing what I was seeing in her eyes decided to throw my "break" card out there anyway and Tanja replied, "Yes I agree because this isn't working at all."

When Tanja said those words, I immediately got angry. "Damn, thanks for wasting my time!" I replied. I walked away from Tanja thinking to myself "This is why I should have stayed with Chante. Now I have lost out on both ends of the spectrum!" We both returned to the cookout for about 10 minutes and then we left. We drove back to Baltimore in complete silence.

When we arrived at Tanja's apartment, she asked me to return her keys. That when it really started to hit me. Tanja was serious and had had enough. As I placed my keys in her hand I began to plead with her about working things out but Tanja wasn't trying to hear it. The part that bothered me the most was she wasn't mad. She was very calm; never raised her voice. I was the one getting emotional trying to stir her up but there was nothing to stir. Tanja had completely checked out.

As I looked in Tanja eyes and saw nothing there I tried to make myself cry in order to get her to show some form of emotions but the more I tried eventually I really started to cry, not a noisy cry but tears began to run down my face. Tanja hugged me as I cried but it was a feelingless hug. Then she gently let me go and started hanging up some clothes in her closet. Totally unbothered. Once I saw that my tears had no effect, I walked out the door and started heading home. I had no idea how I was going to get home. My plan was to catch the subway and then transfer to a bus because I had no other way. As I walked towards the subway, I heard Tanja voice say "Dwayne, wait. I'll take you home."

Hearing Tanja call me "Dwayne" almost made my heart stop. Honestly up until then I had never heard her call me Dwayne before. Before we were dealing with each other, she called me "Cool" and the moment we became intimate she had been calling me "Babe" ever since so to hear her say "Dwayne" was a death blow. Tanja drove me home, dropped me off and then pulled off. I went into my mothers house broken and devastated not knowing what next to do.

For the next couple of days, I was in total shock. Being connected to Tanja was a huge part of my daily life and now it was gone. Everyday day I would attend to my boys Peanut and Darrian durning the afternoon hours, get my mothers car in the evening after she had made her daily runs, go to the studio either Sisqo's house or Kevin Kidds place, go to Tanja's afterwards and spend the night and return my mothers car back to her the next morning. Now that Tanja had broken up with me, I had no where to sleep at night. My mother did foster care and had children in my old room so at night, I had no where to sleep besides on my mothers couch. In addition to not having a bed to sleep in, I didn't have a place to grieve. My heart was broken because I had lost my best friend, lover and soul mate and I was in my mothers house with my mom and her foster kids which meant I had no privacy at all. I didn't have a secluded place to think, mourn or even cry if I had to because people were always around so I had to lock myself in the bathroom for a moment of privacy.

One day, I was feeling very low about losing Tanja so I went into the bathroom to get away from everyone. I sat on the edge of the bathtub for a while but after an hour or so I began to get uncomfortable so I laid on the bathroom floor. My mom noticed that I had been in the bathroom for quite sometime and began to bang on the door. Still being in a state of depression, I ignored my mothers knocks and just laid there. My mother then went to the kitchen and retrieved a butter knife and forced her way through the locked door. When she saw me lying on the bathroom floor she asked me what was wrong. I told her that I was okay, got up and walked out of the bathroom. Like always when my mother sensed that I was going through something, she called my father and my dad asked me to come see him.

As I drove to my dads house, I began to play everything back in my head of the last time I was with Tanja on Memorial Day. "How could she just turn off all of the feelings we had for each other all of a sudden?" I asked myself and then it finally hit me. It wasn't "all of a sudden". Tanja had been pleading, suggesting, and sometimes even begging for a better relationship but I was so into myself I couldn't see it. I ignored all her cries until she finally reached a breaking point. So in actuality, it wasn't all of a sudden for Tanja, it was only all of a sudden to me!

I went to my dad's and sat on his couch, and we talked as usual and like always my dad made me feel 1000 times better. The only thing was, how long would this good feeling last. By the time I left my dad's and was halfway back to my mother's house, I was back in the depressive state that I was before. There was absolutely no way to shake what I was feeling.

Losing Tanja was by far the toughest thing that I ever had to emotionally deal with in my entire life. I couldn't eat or sleep and all I did was think of ways to get her back. I called, texted and emailed Tanja everyday so much that she started ignoring the calls and had long delays with replying to my messages. I began to pray to God to bring her back to me and I leaned on faith believing that one day soon she would return.

Sidenote: This process taught me that it doesn't matter how much you believe and pray, if what you're asking God for doesn't align with HIS will, it won't happen. Sometimes we as humans can pray and ask God for the wrong things or things that are not meant for us so it's not that God is ignoring us, its that HE who is GOD knows best!

All I could think about now was everything that I did wrong. Before I couldn't see it but now after losing Tanja, all of my flaws were crystal clear. "How could I be so careless with something that was so precious to me?" I kept asking myself. I mean I didn't even have to cheat when having a girlfriend like Tanja. On the same birthday when she got my name tattooed on her butt, Tanja rented us a hotel room and hired a personal misuse to give me a massage with an ending of oral sex from the misuse (while Tanja watched).

One day maybe a month before our breakup, I received an email from a random girl stating that she was a fan and loved my music. As the girl and I went back and forth with emails, suddenly she started flirting and asking to hook up. I asked the girl to send me a picture and she did. The girl was cute, not overly attractive but attractive enough for engagement.

For a second, I thought about taking the girls offer but then I thought to myself "I have the kind of girlfriend that I can bring this to and we both can decide on how to move forward."

I told Tanja about the girl and showed her the picture as well. Come to find out, it was Tanja the whole time testing me to see if I would have taken the bait! The average guy would have failed this test miserably but I passed because I didn't have a reason to cheat. Tanja was down for whatever as long as it made since. All the things I was doing on the side were just acts of greed.

Sidenote: Thinking back on it, this was probably Tanja trying to have a reason to break up with me other than "this isn't working anymore" because of the timing.

Time kept passing and I had prayed till I couldn't say a different prayer anymore (the words were exactly the same) so then I decided to do what I always did. I decided to use my pain to create songs. I began to write song after song all pulling from what I was going through with Tanja and had J Rome sing what I had written. The studio sessions were like therapy and little did J Rome know but he was singing more than just lyrics and melodies. He was singing what weighed heavily on my heart and his voice was practically saving my life.

Normally when writing a song inspired by someone or something, the writer hardly ever gives word for word about the inspiration. Its sometimes generalized but in some of my songs I wrote every word about Tanja. One particular song comes to mind that I wrote was called "Another Woman" where I asked "Where would I find another woman" like Tanja. My breakup with Tanja inspired some of the greatest songs that I had ever written.

About a few weeks had passed and I was still down in the dumps about losing Tanja. One day I had my son Peanut with me at my mothers and I was waiting for Anna to pick him up after she got off from work. When Anna arrived she could see the pain in my eyes. She asked me what was going on and for some reason, the ask broke me. I couldn't hold it anymore. Not only was I dealing with the loss of Tanja I was also not happy about how my life and music career was going. I was tired, broken and I felt like I had no where else to go. I sat on my mothers couch and began to cry. Anna told our son peanut to wait outside on the porch (so he wouldn't see me crying) and then she came and embraced me. As Anna embraced me, she rubbed my back and whispered in my ear "Dwayne you're going to be okay. You just lost your faith. Once you get it back, you're going to be fine!"

That night after my emotional breakdown with Anna brings us to how this novel started...

Chapter 44 - Rock Bottom

T he living room is completely dark with the exception of the streetlights shining through the windows, bouncing against the flawless white paint on my mother's ceilings and walls. Ironically the shadows from the trees are starting to look like dragons as they dance from wall to wall when the wind blows. My legs are hanging over one end of the couch as I'm constantly adjusting a couch pillow (that my mother would kill me if she knew I was laying on) against the arm rest on the other end. As I'm gazing at my prom pictures on my mother's mantel piece, I vaguely hear my mentally challenged neighbor outside on his porch talking to himself along with trains and passing cars. I can't sleep. My mind is going a hundred miles and running, and I want it to stop. I look over towards the hallway leading to the kitchen and notice a beige trench coat hanging from a coat hanger on the wall. I grab the coat, ball up on the couch and toss the coat over my head searching for complete darkness and silence. I close my eyes for a few and adjust the coat over my head enough so I can breathe. Every time I open my eyes, I find myself looking at my mother's mantel piece with all of the pictures. I start to wonder, what's Tracy and Teresa up to these days (my junior and senior prom dates)? I hear my mother upstairs telling one of her foster kids to turn their TV off... The tree shadow- dragon moves faster each time I take notice. I shut my eyes tighter trying to avoid my thoughts when suddenly I hear a thump coming from next door. When my eyes open this time, still in the direction of the mantel piece, instead of focusing on the prom pictures I noticed Sisqo's- Return of Dragon CD cover (that my mother framed). My eyes start to water and I think to myself, how did I get here...

It was July 2006 and I was at the lowest point of my life. Quoting a line from a song I wrote entitled Nobody But You, "I didn't want to live but I didn't want to die!" I was suffering from a severe case of depression and didn't even know it. I felt so alone because I didn't have anyone I could talk to about what I was going through. Although everyone around me knew that Tanja and I had broken up, I was so embarrassed that I couldn't fully open up to anyone because I feared being made fun of. I couldn't trust anyone, so I had to deal with everything I was going through internally and that was very mentally dangerous. I only felt comfortable sharing with people that I knew experienced what I was going through and it wasn't many. Sometimes I would talk to Mouse (because he was going through or had been through something similar with his wife at the time) and my barber Tyon Horne (now Pastor Ty). Ty had gone through the exact same thing that I was going through, but he eventually got back with his girl and now wife for over

20 years. Ty's testimony was my hope. I figured if God could do it for Ty, he could do it for me also. In regard to my career, I figured if I could just weather this storm and get back into grind mode, eventually things would improve, and I would be back on my feet again. Mouse and I had this saying, when dealing with this kind of pain; instead of taking it one day at a time, we said lets take it one HOUR at a time. Days were entirely too long when holding up a heavy heart.

At night, in order to fall asleep, I would ball up on my mother's couch and envision myself lying on a floor at Jesus's feet. In my subconscious, the room was all white and I was curled up in a ball at HIS feet as HE sat at HIS thrown watching over me. Till this day that vision still comforts me.

As I continued to attempt to show Tanja that I now was willing to be the man she was asking me to be, I still was writing songs trying to land a placement but more importantly using the songs as therapy to make it through the heartache I was experiencing. Around this time I was spending a lot of time at Kevin Kidd's studio recording with J Rome. Sisqo's house was still an option however Murda did a lot of producing and recording there and sometimes there was a conflict in scheduling. I pushed my way forward for several months in a deep state of depression wondering when or if it would ever end.

At times when I needed to talk to someone to prevent me from losing my mind, I would call Marlon. He would always talk me off the cliff and ensure me that I would get through this. I would feel better after talking to him but after an hour or so I would be back in my funk. With no one else to turn to I was forced to pray to God and weather the storm by myself.

At this time I had no source of income at all. I didn't even have any weed to sell. Right before Tanja and I had broken up, one night I had just re-up (purchased a large amount of weed) and was on my way to Tanja's house. As usual, Pig, Donny and I had put together to make a large purchase from our New York connect. We were all at Sisqo's house when we got our package so the task was to get it in the city without any interruptions. Sisqo lived in Randallstown, MD and back then Liberty Rd. (the main road that went from Randallstown to Baltimore City) was always infested with cops. The cops pulled us over all the time for the dumbest reasons on Liberty Road. So now we have all this weed, it around 2am in the morning and we have to get it in the city. I was riding with Donny (my childhood friend) on this particular night. To avoid being stopped by the police Donny and I decided to take the back roads to the city because we didn't want to risk going down liberty road with a trunk full of weed. As we were traveling down the back roads, we approached a stop sign. The street was quiet and it was pitch dark outside. Donny slowed down but didn't come to a complete stop before moving pass the intersection. Out of nowhere a cop pulled behind us and all I saw were blue flashing lights.

This was it I thought to myself. We are going to jail tonight. The smell of the weed in the trunk was so strong that we could smell it while we were driving. "When Donny passes that cop his driver's license he going to smell it and off to jail we go!" I thought to myself but that didn't happen. Donny gave the cop his license and registration, and he took it back to his patrol car. Two other cops pulled up as well so that really had me nervous because usually that definitely means someone is going to jail. While the one cop was running Donny's info, a second cop came to me and asked for my identification. When both of our ID's came back clean, they let us go. When I got to Tanja's house that night, I looked at that incident as a warning and vowed to never sell drugs again but only after I sold what I had. When I was done with that package, I never re'd up again but I always kept an ounce or two on me just to sell a few dime bags to keep a little money in my pocket. Now that Tanja and I were done, I didn't even have that anymore because I couldn't bring the weed in my mother's house because of the smell so I was officially broke.

Thing were looking pretty grim when suddenly I caught somewhat of a break. Donny had come into a lot of money stemming from a settlement and decided that he wanted to partner up with me and invest. Me knowing how inconsistent the actual sales of music and Cd's were, I didn't think it would be smart to spend a one-time lump sum on marketing or pushing a record. I wanted to be more strategic and put the money into something more tangible, something that had more of a guarantee to generate revenue so we decided to open our very own recording studio.

Donny and I went to the state office, formed an LLC and named the studio Brickhouse Studio's. We found a nice two room office place in Pikesville, MD, bought office furniture and recording equipment and even had a sound proof recording booth built from scratch. Our spot was official. We were fully up and running in less than 3 weeks.

Now instead of going to Sisqo's or Kevin Kid's place we had our very own. We owned everything. Our only expenses were the rent, the electric and the phone and internet. Donny and I owned the studio (Donny's money and my expertise) but Pig ran the daily operations. As always Ole Man Joe was there as well. Butch and Hot were beginning to drift away from music around this time and my cousins, the original Crown Vic Click were still around but at a distance because of a situation that occurred at Anna's house.

A few months prior, Big Flood told me that he was looking for a new place to live and asked if I had any suggestions or connections. At the time Anna was renting a house that had a vacant apartment style basement with no one in it. I asked Anna if she could talk to her land lord and ask him if he would rent the basement portion of the house to Big Flood. The land lord agreed.

Before I told Big Flood about the land lords decision, I told him that I would help him under one condition. Being as though my son Peanut and his mom was directly upstairs, please don't have all kinds of traffic running in and out of the house and I specifically told him not to have Shaggy there because I knew the two of them were still friends. Big Flood agreed to my terms and shortly afterwards, moved into Anna's basement apartment.

One day while I was at Anna's house after bringing Peanut home from school, I heard Big Flood in the basement through the vents talking and laughing with a few guys. As I continued to talk with Anna I couldn't help but to notice a very distinct laugh that belonged to one person that I knew. "That sounds like Shaggy's laugh" I thought to myself. "Naw, Big Flood wouldn't have him over here after I told him not to" I also said to myself.

About ten minutes later, Anna asked me to go down the basement and bring up a basket of clothes from the washing machine. As I walked down the basement steps, I heard the distinct laugh again and when I got to the bottom of the steps, there Shaggy stood. This was the first time we saw each other since the night he stole Sisqo's chain.

We stared at each other with the stone face until I finally said "What the fuck you looking at?" Shaggy replied by saying "What's up" in an aggressive way. Anna had a house rule that whenever someone came in her house, they had to remove their shoes in order to keep her carpet clean so I didn't have any shoes on. I went back up the steps, grabbed my shoes and began to put them on with the intentions of going back down the basement to fight Shaggy. Anna saw and heard what was going on and tried to prevent me from returning to the basement. Through all of the commotion of me trying to get back down the basement without physically hurting Anna to get there, somehow Anna had locked the basement door and removed the key. I then went outside and walked to the back of the house to see if Shaggy was out back in the alley. No one was there. Not knowing what to expect, I called my homie Black and told him what was going on. Within 10 minutes Black was at Anna house along with two of his homeboys and all of them were "ready" and down for whatever.

This situation was uncomfortable and embarrassing at the same time. Black couldn't believe that my blood cousins would have someone that I was beefing with in the same house as my young son and baby mother; not to mention still friends with the dude after all of what happened with Sisqo's chain. It made us look weak and divided. Big Flood and my cousins still being cool and hanging out with Shaggy never set well with me. I always thought "How can you still be cool with someone that that crossed your family!" I always knew that they secretly still hung out with Shaggy but to see him in Anna's house was heartbreaking. I felt like I couldn't fully trust Big Flood or any of my cousins anymore, so I dealt with them from a distance.

So, once we were in our new studio, my team was cut down to just me, Ole Man Joe, Pig and Donny. We passed out flyers everywhere we went to generate business and soon afterwards a few local rappers booked a few sessions which helped us make some money. When we didn't have clients booking studio time, I was recording new material of my own, hip-hop records, while still writing songs for J Rome to sing.

One day, just before I was about to leave my Mom's house and head to our studio, I received a phone call from someone I hadn't spoken to in years. The person on the other end of the phone was Kidd. We talked for a few and our conversation was just the same as it was years ago. No animosity, no grudges, just a lot of catching up. Right before the call ended Kidd told me that he was outside of my house and to come outside. When I came outside, Kidd was sitting in the driver's seat of a brand new 600 Benz. I got in the car and we began to talk some more. He told me that he had drove to Baltimore all the way from California and the trip had taken him 6 days to get here. We laughed and joked about old times for a few and then I played a few records for him. I maybe played one or two hip hop records but most of the songs I played for him were the songs I wrote with J Rome singing. Kidd was blown away by the J Rome's records and I could tell that I had his full attention. I also told him that I had my own studio now and invited him to come check it out. Kidd said he couldn't make it but would come out the next day.

The next day as promised, Kidd came out to our studio and immediately fell in love with the place. We were far away from the city in a secluded, clean location and that was ideal for Kidd. The location as well as the vibe was peaceful, and Kidd loved not having to watch his back from someone trying to rob him.

I played more records that I wrote for J Rome and then Kidd and I started devising a plan to get J Rome a record deal instead of trying to place songs on someone else's album. The next day and almost everyday afterwards, Kidd was at our studio overseeing the now new J Rome project. Kidd gave me new tracks from his connections and producers from LA to write to. Still depressed and grieving from the breakup with Tanja, I wrote more love songs inspired by the pain. Once we had a solid project completed, Kidd took J Rome to New York to a couple of meeting to see if he could land a deal. The A&R's Kidd met with liked the records but for some reason they passed on signing J Rome.

Sidenote: Kidd was the second strongest connect I had used to attempt to get J Rome a record deal. My strongest connect that I had previously used before Kidd came back around was Kenneth Crear. I sent Ken Sunday Morning and a few other songs and Ken absolutely loved the records but decided not to move forward with an offer.

When we couldn't land a deal for J Rome, our focus shifted back to Hip Hop. With the track record Kidd had for being successful with making things happen, every rapper in Baltimore City wanted to work with him. Kidd asked me how I felt about doing a project with two other male rappers as well as a female artist that we both knew by the name of April Love. I was down for trying anything at that time, so we all began to work on the project. We decided to call the 3 male 1 female group the Alliance.

After maybe 3 or 4 records the project came to an end simply because we all were solo artist on different pages. I could tell that Kidd wasn't into the project also. It was just something he was doing just to hang out at the studio and pass time.

One night after a studio session Kidd drove me home and while driving, he opened up to me about his current situation. Kidd told me that he was dating Raven Samone (which I had already knew) and the 600 Benz was a gift from her that she was trying to take back. Often while we were together in the studio or riding somewhere in his car, Raven Samone would call him, and they would begin to argue. It was very clear that she wanted him to return that car. A few weeks later Kidd was on his way back to California.

After Kidd returned to California, I went back into my usual grind. Some nights I would stay at the studio over night and sleep on the futon to avoid going to my mothers sleeping on the couch. A few times I invited Tanja to the studio to show her I had something promising going on. Sometimes she would come, and I would play the songs that I wrote inspired by what we were going through. She never said it, but I could tell that she liked being the center piece of the art I was creating but didn't like the fact that I was in a depression because of our breakup. When I spent the night at the studio, a few times she stayed with me.

As days and weeks were steadily moving on we began to find ourselves falling into a financial hole. Our bills were piling up and we didn't have any clients booking studio time therefore we didn't have any income coming in. Out of frustration from things not moving, I called Pig and told him that I wanted to do one last mixtape and put it all on the line. I decided to call this mixtape "Now or Never."

I took an insert from the movie "8 Mile" when Eminem said "If somethings going to happen with this shit, it needs to happen now!" and used it as the theme of the mixtape and instead of using Murda or Big Flood as the host, I decided to get one of the most popular DJ's in Baltimore City, 92Q's own DJ Squirrel Wyde. Pig was very influential in the making of this mixtape, the same as Elliott's Ways by supplying me with instrumentals and suggestions on what tracks to rap to but of course ultimately I made all of the final decisions.

Per usual, I aired out a lot of my dirty laundry making this mixtape but only one of the confession songs made the CD. The name of the song was "I Need Love" (also called "If I Died Tonight). The other songs didn't make the mixtape because they weren't mixed correctly and the hard drive that they were recorded on crashed so all I had was the rough versions of the songs. "I Need Love" almost didn't make it also because the instrumental had a glitch it in causing the track to skip as it played. The glitch was very annoying to hear as I wrote my lyrics to it but I figured maybe Teddy (my engineer) could fix the track before I recorded it. When Teddy told me he couldn't fix it, I loved what I wrote so much, I decided to record and use it anyway. Pig and Black advised me not to because of the glitch but my soul needed to release what I had written so I ignored their advice as well as the glitch and released the song. I even had J Rome come through and sing on it also.

"I Need Love" was written to LL Cool Jay's I Need Love instrumental and it described everything that I was feeling at the time from going through the financial struggles with both of my kid's mothers to losing Tanja. The bases of the song was if I died tonight, please know that I did my best at what I did best and all I ever asked for was love because I needed it to continue this lop sided fight with the music industry.

There were many other songs on Now or Never that I confessed and shared some personal thought but none like "I Need Love". On a lighter note, there's a freestyle on Now or Never called "Money In The Bank" where I played a real voicemail that Chante's boyfriend left me after we had our altercation in my mother's living room. What he considered a threat, I considered a joke and used his words as an opening skit to show there were no worries on my end at all.

While in the process of completing Now or Never I was still suffering from severe depression but kept it to myself. I also still was in hot pursuit to win back Tanja and soon my persistence started to pay off. Tanja began to be open to talking to me more and soon our talks turned into visits and the visits turned into us being intimate again. Almost every night when I left our studio, I would go to Tanja's father's house (that's where she was living at the time) and practically spend the night with her, leaving around 4 or 5am before her dad woke up and left for work.

A few consistent weeks of this had me thinking that I had won my girlfriend back and I was on top of the world. I was trying to do everything perfect to make sure I didn't fumble the ball again. When my mother noticed that I wasn't coming home at night and saw and heard me talking to Tanja again, she said to me "She's going to hurt you again!" I got so upset with my mother when she said that, that I abruptly cut her off and walked out of the house. That was the last thing that I wanted to hear, especially knowing that my mother was always right about these kinds of things.

When I didn't have money to take Tanja on dates, my OG Black would always help me out. Black hung out at a local bar not too far from my old neighborhood and I would go there to meet with him, and he would shake my hand and when I pulled away from the shake, a $100 bill was always in my hand.

Sidenote: Black would also arrange for me to get paid whenever I linked him with someone to purchase weight from him. He always came back and gave me some sort of compensation although I never asked for it. He bailed me out of a lot of financial holes as well as had my back when or if things took a turn for street shit and unlike Bags, Black was always the same. Never switched up plus he was smart.

One night after leaving the studio, I called Tanja to let her know that I was on my way to her house. Tanja told me not to come because she was going out to a party in DC. "A party in DC? Since when did you start partying in DC" I said to her. Tanja and I went back and forth for a moment and then Tanja hit me with a death blow by saying, "Kool, we're not together any more so you cant tell me what to do!" Then she followed up and said "You see, I knew I shouldn't have started this again. I think I may have been leading you to think that we are something that we're not! I'm about to go. I will talk to you another time!" When Tanja hung up the phone I felt like my entire world had come to an end. Again for the second time! My pain instantly returned to my heart and soul and I was now back to square one, where I initially started from on Memorial

Day and all I could hear was my mom saying "She's going to hurt you again!"

The next day I called Tanja over and over again and didn't get an answer. I got her voicemail so much that I decided to attempt to break the code. After several unsuccessful tries, I decide to call Nextel and try to manipulate a customer service rep to reset her voicemail password. My plan worked. I made up a story and told the customer service rep that Tanja was stranded somewhere out of town and needed her password reset. You see, I knew the rep wouldn't give me the password but I also knew that when the password was reset, it defaulted to the last four of the users social security number and I knew Tanja's. When the rep reset the password, hung up and used Tanja's last four of her social security number and I was in her voicemails.

As I checked her voicemails, my heart pounded so hard it felt like it was going to jump out of my chest. I didn't hear anything except messages from her sister and cousins until I got to the very last message. The last message was from some guy saying how much he enjoyed their time together and he was looking forward to seeing her again. Hearing that message almost made me throw up.

Later that day Tanja called upset about me changing her passcode and listening to her voicemails. We went back and forth arguing about me resetting her passcode and the guy

I heard on her voicemail. Once we both calmed down a little Tanja told me that she went on a date with a guy that she met on her new job in DC. She claimed it was nothing serious just a date. As much as I hated the fact of her being in another guy's presence in a romantic way, I didn't want to push too hard because I didn't want her to disappear and stop taking my calls again. I needed her to at least be open to speaking with me because that was the only chance I had of winning her all the way back.

A little over a week had passed and I hadn't heard from Tanja at all. Then out of nowhere I received a call from her.

Sidenote: Seeing her name flashing on my phone as an incoming call was like air to me after going days without breathing. Usually, it was me calling her but when I received a call, it gave me life.

Tanja called and said she needed a big favor. Her kids were at the sitter's house and needed to be picked up by a certain time. Tanja said that she and her co workers were going out for drinks and she needed to be there for networking purposes. Tanja asked me if I could pick up her kids and watch them while she hung out and "networked" with her coworkers.

Immediately I thought about the guy I heard on the voicemail. "Will I be watching her kids while she went out on a date with that guy?" I thought to myself. Nevertheless, I agreed and picked up her kids.

I didn't have anywhere to take them after I picked them up, so I took them to the park and let them run around and play until Tanja returned. The next day and the day afterwards Tanja asked me to do the same and I did, trying to land browning points and to show Tanja that I had changed because there was no way in the world that the old me would have thought twice about doing something like that. After the third or fourth time I decided enough was enough. It wasn't that much networking in the world.

Finally, after pushing through depression and heartache, Now or Never was complete. I pressed up a couple of thousand professional copies and was ready to hit the streets. Being as though in my mind this was my last swing of the bat, I wanted to make sure I took the best swing possible of hitting a home run with this mixtape. I needed this project to reach the right persons hands and I knew those hands were not in Baltimore. Kidd was out in California, and I had plans to eventually get there but the next best place that was feasible to me was Atlanta.

I spoke with Pig and Ole Man Joe and told them about the idea. Both agreed that that was the best move. Not only did they agree, but they also said that they were willing to go with me. My uncle Curley lived in Atlanta so I called him and asked if me Old Man Joe and Pig could stay with him until we got things going in Atlanta. With open arms, my uncle said yes. It was now official. I was moving to Atlanta to take one last swing at bat.

A few days before we were scheduled to leave for Atlanta, I told Tanja about my plans. Tanja wrote me a long email saying how she wished me the best and how she thought it was a good move for my mental state as well as my career. She also told me that she loved me (something I hadn't heard from her in a long time) but it came off in a friendly way. Part of me wanted Tanja to ask me to stay but by her pushing me off into the sunset solidified my move even more. My children Peanut and Darrian meant the world to me but at that point in my life, I could offer them anything. My spirit was broken as well as my pockets. Drastic times called for drastic measures so off to Atlanta we went.

Sidenote: The bad part about this move was I was still in partnership with Donny and the studio. We were behind in all of the bills and were on the brink of being evicted. I didn't even tell Donny that I was leaving. None of us did. We just packed up our bags and the CD's and left Donny with all of the responsibility. In my head, I figured that I would make things right with Donny after my career jumped off by moving to Atlanta. That was my thought process with EVERYONE and EVERYTHING! I'll make up for all of my short comings when I blow! When Donny realized that we were gone, he sold all of our studio equipment to recoup some of his money back and shut down the studio. This is one of my many regrets. I should have at least sat down and told Donny what I had planned. Instead, I ran off like a coward and left him hanging. Till this day, I still owe him an apology.

Chapter 45 - Welcome to Altanta

It was the Fall of 2006 and Ole Man Joe, Pig and I were officially living in Atlanta. My uncle Curley had a spare room and all three of us shared that one room. He lived in College Park. I didn't want us to be a burden to my uncle, so I tried to stay out of his house as much as possible. Our goal was to only sleep there. The rest of the time we had plans to be out in the streets of Atlanta trying to meet the right people that could help catapult my career.

As soon as we touched down in Atlanta, we asked my uncle where all the hot spots were so we could hit the streets. The first place my uncle suggested was Old National Highway. Ole man Joe, Pig and I went to Old national Highway and posted up at a gas station directly across the street from a big motorcycle club. Our goal was to sell my Now or Never CD to any and everyone willing to buy it. This was going to be our way to financially survive while being in Atlanta. If we didn't sell any CD's we couldn't eat or have gas to get from one place to another. We drove Pig's car there and that was our form of transportation.

Our selling price for each CD was only $5 but if we came across a celebrity or someone musically important, we would give it to them for free. We all stood outside of the minimart at the gas station and pitched our saying to everyone we came across by saying "Would you like to help support a local artist?" A potential buyer would then ask, "How much?" and we would always reply by saying "the cost is $5.00 but we will take whatever you think is fair." Sometimes people would give us 2 or 3 dollars but most of the time, they would give 5 or even more. We had some people give us as much as $20 just to show support. I learned very quickly that people in the south were much more friendly and were willing to support others more than the folks back home up north. I also learned that you shouldn't always give things out for free. People don't put any value on things that are free but if they buy it, even for the smallest amount, they now look at it differently.

We posted up at that gas station every day until the owners made us leave. When we were forced to leave, we would just drive around and find another gas station and do the exact same thing there. As time went on, we were beginning to meet people and they would tell us about more hotspots to sell and place my music in the right hands. Before we knew it, we were going everywhere from the Underground to Lennox Mall and everywhere in between.

As stated before, we only slept at my uncle's house. We would wake up every morning, hit all our normal spots where we knew we could sell some CD's and then return to my uncles at night. We ate McDonalds every sing day, ordering off the dollar menu but occasionally if we had a good day selling, we would treat ourselves to a bucket of chicken.

One day while following leads going from one place to another, somehow, we ended up on the campus of Georgia University. As usual we were in grind mode trying to sell CDs to everyone we came across before some form of security made us leave. As I stood on the corner soliciting my CD, this guy came up and asked where I was from. I told him that I was from Baltimore. Ironically, he was from Baltimore too. We shook hands and I told him my name. The guy replied and said his name was Mike Lowery. As we continued to talk, he told me that he worked for a marketing company, and we should link up and discuss doing business. He also bought a CD. Mike and I exchanged information, he left, and I continued to sell CD's until a security guard made us leave and we were off to the next spot.

For the next couple of days Mike called everyday just to check on us and see if we were making any progress. I wasn't used to anyone involved in the music business being generous so I immediately pegged Mike as someone trying to get us to lower our guards so he could sell us some kind of service his marketing team offered so at times I wouldn't take his call.

One day it was raining when me and the guys woke up, so we decided not to go out in the streets. As we all sat around feeling like a fish out of water (because we never just sat around in my uncle's house) suddenly my phone rung. It was Mike and he asked what we were getting into that day. I told Mike that we didn't have plans to go out because of the rain. Mike then replied "Yo are you actually telling me that you're letting rain stop you from getting on your grind today. You guys drove all the way here from Baltimore and are sitting in the house because of rain with all of these opportunities out here at your fingertips?" Mike's comment immediately sparked a fire in me, so I told Ole Man Joe and Pig to get dressed; we're hitting the streets.

Mike was on the panel of some music convention that day that costed $250 per person for entry. Of course, we had nothing close to that, so we decided to go there just to hang out and possibly meet people coming in and out of the building but somehow Ole Man Joe tricked someone at the door to let us in for free. Once inside, I was able to network and meet several big producers one of which was Brian Michael Cox. I only brought anywhere between 50 – 100 R&B CD's (the songs I wrote sung by J Rome) to Atlanta, so my primary push was me as a hip-hop artist, but I always kept a few R&B CDs on me. Mike knew about my days with Sisqo and was familiar with my rap CD's but had no idea that I wrote R&B songs. I gave Mike as well as every major producer I came across an R&B CD hoping to land a writing spot on someone's team.

The next day after listening to the R&B CD, Mike called me completely blown away. He absolutely loved every song on the CD! "Yo your hip-hop albums and mixtapes are good, but this R&B CD is incredible!" he said. Mike and I continued to talk about the R&B CD, and I told him how it all came about as well as who's voice was singing the songs. "You and J Rome are a musical match made in heaven bro! Trust me when I say this. I'm going to do everything in my power to make sure your music is heard!"

Days continued to go by and me, Old Man Joe and Pig were still hitting the Atlanta streets every single day. At night when we were not out, we would hang out with my uncle at his house. I reached out to every single contact I knew that had relocated to atlanta, from Huggy Carter (formally Sisqo's road manager and currently Mary J. Blige's road manager) to Tera (Sisqo's ex-girlfriend).

One day I was talking to my cousin Reese back home in Baltimore and she told me that our cousin from Florida named "X" was now in Atlanta and I should reach out to him. My cousin "X" was one of those cousins that I barely knew. He grew up in Florida so I hardly ever saw him growing up. The last time I saw him was when he was in Baltimore doing security for Ghost Face Killa. I met up with him at Shawn Ceasars office where GhostFace was doing drops for radio stations (drops are when you here an artist on the radio say something like "Yo this is Ghost Face Killa and you're now listening to X105.7!"

before a song plays). Cousin "X" introduced me to Ghost Face and even got Ghost Face to do a drop for my Purple Haze II Mixtape.

Cousin "X" was known throughout the family to be affiliated with a lot of big time celebrities usually doing security for them. He was 6'4" and weighted at least 250 pounds, darked skinned with a bald head which was very intimidating to the average person. I called cousin "X" and told him that I was in Atlanta and he immediately came to my uncles house to pick us up.

Ole Man Joe, Pig and I jumped in my cousins truck and he took us to the strip club call Onyx. I remember when we got in his truck heading for Onyx, he was driving so fast, I thought we were going to flip over every time we entered a curve. Cousin "X" Florida accent was so strong that I could hardly understand was he was saying. I told him what I was in town for and he said that he could introduce me to a lot of people that could help me. From that night moving forward, I would sell CD's during the day and hang out with cousin "X" at night.

Every night while hanging out with my cousin I began to notice more and more of the impact my cousin had in Atlanta. For starters he always had his gun on him and he never hid the fact that he had it. Me coming from Baltimore, Maryland, I looked at him like he was insane, not knowing that Georgia may have had different carrying laws there. Sometimes I would get in my cousins car and he would have an AK 47 in the back seat. He had guns everywhere.

I also noticed how everywhere we went, people knew him and he had the red carpet laid out for him. There were clubs that required shoes and slacks for entry and he and I would walk straight to the front of the long line, jumping in front of everyone with jeans and timberlands on and walk straight in the club. The owners practically kissed his feet when we walked in and that happened at every single club we went to. After a few nights of partying, my cousin pulled me to the side and said that moving forward he only wanted me to roll with him. He didn't have anything against Ole Man Joe and Pig but he just didn't know them and didn't want them around anymore. This actually worked out fine because Ole Man Joe and Pig were beginning to feel uncomfortable moving around with my cousin because of the guns and how wild his lifestyle was. It kind of reminded me of being back home hanging out with Black. Some of the guys didn't feel comfortable being around Black also because they were afraid that some sort of retaliation could happen at any time. Me on the other hand, had no worries in both situations.

Once my cousin and I started hanging just the two of us, he began to reveal how he was able to do the things that he did. My cousin showed me a tattoo he had covered up that said "BMF" under the covering. At the time, I had no idea what BMF was. Cousin "X" didn't go into details, but he just said he was a part of a family that did but didn't exist anymore.

Later that night we linked up with some guys that were in his "family". I knew this because whenever we ran into someone and he introduced us, sometimes he would introduce the person as his homeboy but when it was a "family member" he would introduce them as his "brother". Me, my cousin and about 50 of his family members all met up at a strip club called Magic City. Once inside my cousins family took over the entire club. There were so many celebrities there that night I couldn't begin to name them all but my cousin and his family stood high above them all. Of the 50 of my cousins family members, one of them was a famous football player by the name of Adam "PacMan" Jones. I'm not sure if he was a part of my cousins "family" but he was there with us partying the entire night.

After balling out of control (dollar bills flying everywhere, so much that you could barely see what was in front of you) in Magic City, we all went to the next club and then the next. We must have ran through about 4 to 5 different clubs and all of them treated us the same way. Like royalty. I never seen anything like this in my entire life; even when I was rolling with Sisqo. Sisqo had power when going places but nothing compared to 50 goons walking straight up to every club door, walking in without paying or getting patted down, totally violating dress codes at times, popping bottles and throwing money EVERYWHERE!

After we hit the last club, my cousin's "family" decided they wanted to go and get something to eat. This was when I really knew these guys were different. We all pulled up to a closed restaurant around 4am. "This spot is closed" I thought to myself. "Maybe they're just waiting to meet some other people here on this parking lot and then head out to eat at some waffle house" I also said to myself. Suddenly, everyone started getting out of their cars and heading for the restaurant doors. "Come on Cuz" my cousin said to me.

When we got to the front door, the owner came out of nowhere and let us all in. The owner had some waitresses with him along with a few cooks. He pulled the shades down so no one could see inside and the owner and his staff served us at 4am in the morning as if it was 6pm! They took our orders and provided stellar service through the entire night (or morning I should say). I couldn't believe what I was seeing. These guys had the influence of opening a closed restaurant and getting served like it was regular business hours. While eating and socializing I met another celebrity in the mist of the family, that had been with us all night, a rapper name Maino.

The following night, (like every night) my cousin came and picked me up and we went to his condo. This was the first time he brought me to his place. When we got there, he took me into one of his walk in closets where he had sneakers as far as the eye could see. "What size shoe do you wear Cuz" he asked. I told him I wore a size 13. "Go in there a grab anything that you want" he then said. I went in the closet and picked out about two or three pair of sneakers. "What are you doing Cuz" he asked in a laughing tone. My cousin grabbed a huge trash bag and began to throw sneakers in the bag up until it could barely close. He stuffed at least 10 pair of brand-new sneakers in that bag.

When we left his condo headed out for the streets, I noticed my cousins phone kept ringing, but he was ignoring the call. After about 4 or 5 back to back calls finally he said to me "Cuz look at this shit. The basketball dude Amari Stoudemire is blowing up my phone because he wants to hit the clubs up tonight." I thought to myself "Why would Amari Stoudemire blow up my cousins phone just to go out clubbing?" Then it hit me. He was doing this because he didn't want to go out in these Atlanta streets by himself so he needed my cousin and some of his "family members" to go with him for protection.

My cousin and I met up with Amari Stoudemire along with a few others and we went into a very high scaled club where the crowd was very diverse as well as the music and even at a club like this my cousin got the same respect and treatment. After partying for a few with Amari Stoudemire, we then ventured off to the next spot where we ran into Ray J. From the vibe of their conversation, I could tell that my cousin and Ray J knew each other very well. My cousin introduced me to Ray J and I started to pitch my spill of being a songwriter to him but I decided not to. Simply because of the setting. Ray J was in party mode and from the glassy look in his eyes I could tell he had a few drinks. On top of that it was extremely loud in the club and that wasn't a good time to pitch. I figured from the conversation I saw my cousin have with Ray J, access to him was just a phone call away.

Later at that same club we bumped into Brandon, one of the twins in the R&B group Jagged Edge. My cousin grabbed Brandon and told him "Yo my cousin writes R&B music. He used to work with Dru Hill. Give him you number!" Without hesitation Brandon came to me and gave me his number.

Sidenote: I called Brandon a few times after that night meeting him, but he never answered. I believe he gave me his number that night out of fear for my cousin.

My cousin was trying to link me with everyone he came across. He had plans on taking me to TI's house to meet and politic with him, but TI was in California at the time filming American Gangster with Denzel Washington. The next day my cousin told me that he had to take care of some business in Florida and that he would be back in a few weeks. My cousin jumped on a plane headed for Florida and I went back into full grind mode with Ole Man Joe and Pig with the selling of the CD's.

As time continued to go by, our money was beginning to run low. Pig had suggested that we get part time jobs in order to keep afloat. I didn't want to get a job because I knew if I took a job in Atlanta, I was definitely there to stay. You see the entire time while in Atlanta, I had Chante and Anna thinking that it was just a music trip and I would be back soon but as more time went by they began to question if I had actually moved to Atlanta and abandoned my boys. Peanut and Darrian meant the world to me and I couldn't function without them. I would call them every night and talk to them before they went to bed. Conversation with my children gave me the fuel I needed to keeping pushing hard so I could make the right connection and get back to my boys.

One night after being in the Atlanta streets networking and selling CD's I called both Anna and Chante to speak to my kids and got no answer. The next morning I called the both of them again and still no answer. Finally after several calls with no answer, I received a text message from Anna saying that I couldn't speak to Peanut anymore because she heard that I had moved to Atlanta. Chante was doing the same as well. The two of them decided to cut my ties with my children because they felt like I was abandoning them for Atlanta. In addition to that alarming news, when I went into my uncle's kitchen to get a glass of water, I saw that he purposely left his home phone bill on the kitchen table, implying that it was time for us to start paying a bill.

Sidenote: I learned a long time ago that when you're an aspiring artist with no money, you're always working with a limited amount of time when dealing with "normal" people. Mother, father, sister, brother, significant other, family members, friends, it doesn't matter. It's like a hourglass when the sand slowly makes its way to the bottom. People will believe in you, love you to the moon and back as well as support you but eventually all of that runs dry if the goal isn't accomplished in a certain amount of time. A man without income can't survive anywhere and no matter how good of a person he is, he's looked at as less of a man if his finances aren't in order. So we as artist usually ride situations until the wheels fall off and then move on to the next one. Its not that we use people or take advantage, it's just that we are cut from a different cloth and on a mission. Your time is not our time.

The time had come for me to make a big decision. We were at a crossroad. It was simple. Either get a job and stay in Atlanta or return to Baltimore. There was only one thing that came before my career and music and that one thing was my kids. I knew that if I stayed in Atlanta, Chante and Anna would cut me out of my boy's life so it was a no brainer. I decided that we would pack our bags and move back to Baltimore. We were in Atlanta for about 5 or 6 months.

While driving back to Baltimore, I had a long talk with Ole Man Joe and Pig. I had told them both before but I just felt the need to reiterate the subject again. I told them both that they should look into doing something solid and had value in the music business. Just being my friend wouldn't be enough.

When or if someone did decide to work with me and if asked what do Ole Man Joe and Pig do, I wouldn't have an answer except for they're my friends which holds no value. Like my cousin did, people will see no purpose of having them around.

From the looks on Old Man Joe and Pig's face, I could tell what I was saying was hitting home. When I was pushing my R&B CD with Mike at that music conference, I could tell that Pig wasn't too fond of it because when I did R&B, Ole Man Joe and Pig didn't fit in. Hip- hop and Cooli Hi was a collective movement but me as a songwriter was only a "me" movement. Ole Man Joe on the other hand didn't care how the door was opened. He just wanted to see me win. Almost to a fault, he didn't even look out for himself. He just wanted me to win and just look out for him when I made it big. Pig showed interest in being an A&R but Ole Man Joe showed no interest in doing anything musically at all. He was just a loyal friend that was there for the ride no matter where the ride took us. Years later Ole Man Joe finally took an interest in songwriting.

While still in route heading to Baltimore, we stopped at a gas station in North Carolina. Pig was driving at the time and he felt a little tire so he asked Ole Man Joe to drive. Ole Man Joe told Pig that he wasn't driving and out of nowhere he started yelling out insults to Pig trying to provoke him to fight. I had to get in between the two of them and to defuse the situation, I decided to drive.

Pig had no idea why Ole Man Joe was so upset about him asking him to drive but I knew exactly where that energy was coming from. A few weeks prior to us leaving Atlanta, one day we were out selling CD's as usual. Around this time Pig was pressing hard about coming up with ways to get more money. Pig was always known for hussling (since the first day I met him) and he was thinking about trying to make moves in Atlanta but Old Man Joe and I shut that down quickly.

Pig had a little hidden compartment in his car that he normally would use to stash things in and on this day, something told Old Man Joe to look in the compartment. When Ole Man Joe went into the compartment, he found lots of one and five dollar bills loosely balled up, just thrown into the compartment. Ole Man Joe immediately came to me and told me what he saw. "Yo Pig is skimming off the CD sales!" Pig was in a store while this was happening so I went back to the car and saw exactly what Old Man Joe had described. It appeared to me that Pig was keeping some of the CD sales for himself. We all were always together so it looked like he would just throw the money in that compartment whenever he could.

Ole Man Joe and I immediately confronted Pig about the money we found in the compartment. Pig claimed that it was his personal money and it had no connection with the CD sales but us seeing the money scattered all over the compartment made it look like he was stashing money. Ole Man Joe couldn't get over it but I decided to over look it.

Dealing with folks in the music industry taught me that when people get desperate, they'll almost do anything to keep from sinking. This was nothing new to me. I now knew what I was dealing with. It didn't make him a bad person. The lack of money and the fear of not surviving will bring out the worst in almost anyone and I was glad that I was able to see this on a smaller scale instead of a much larger one. We all jumped back into Pigs car, with me now driving and before you knew it, we were back home in Baltimore.

Chapter 46 - Fix the Broken Pieces

Now that I was back home, I decided it was time for me to fix my life. My credit score was in the dumpster, I owed thousands of dollars in parking tickets, had several car insurance violations, broken leases from apartments and child support all waiting for me to resurface back into "regular" life. The year was 2007 and I hadn't had a 9 to 5 job in 7 years. I remember a conversation that I had with Shanna one time when I said to her that I would never work another 9 to 5 ever again in life. This was right after Holla Back Entertainment fell apart. Well a lot had changed since then (in regards to the way I thought) and I decided that it was now time for me to get a job.

Before I went on my job hunt, I first went looking for a new car. I knew in order to get a job with decent pay, I had to have transportation. I received a lawsuit settlement from a car accident that I was involved in and went to the car auction with my cousin Tavon and bought a green Dodge Caravan. I had to put my van in my mother's name because I owed so much in insurance violations and parking tickets.

Once I had transportation, it was now time to search for employment. I applied for a job as a customer service rep for a financial institution called HSBC and after a few excruciating interviews, I got the job. The job was in White Marsh, MD so I decided that I needed to live as close to the job as possible, just in case this van I just bought from the auction breaks down; I would be close to the money. I searched around in the area of my new job and found a one-bedroom apartment in a very nice complex. I moved in the same week I started the job which was the first week of April 2007.

When I moved in my apartment, I had nothing but my clothes. When I earned my first paycheck, I fully decorated my bathroom (because that was the easiest room to complete). Following the advice of my oldest aunt, Aunt Gertie, I didn't settle or compromise on any of my purchases. I bought exactly what I wanted no matter how much it costed. Aunt Gertie always said, "When furnishing your house, get what you want! The cost is going hurt anyways so you might as well love what you paid for!" I had the flyest bathroom ever but every other room in the apartment was bare. I later bought a TV and a DVD player from Walmart and one DVD and that was "Get Rich or Die Trying". I couldn't afford cable at the time so whenever I wanted to watch TV, I would watch "Get Rich or Die Trying" over and over again.

One day I was at my mother's house and decided to walk up the street to the neighborhood basketball court. While there I saw a girl with her young son, and I began to talk to her. As me and the girl were talking, my phone rang. It was my mother. She asked me to come home right away and the tone of her voice sounded upset.

When I walked in the house, my mother was standing there in the living room with a very disturbed look on her face. By her facial expression, I thought my mother found some old marijuana that I was selling and had misplaced but when she said what she said it explained exactly why that look was on her face. My mother told me that my best friend, my brother Marlon was killed in Iraq. As she told me this she burst out crying and ran into the kitchen. I sat in the living room in total shock. I couldn't believe what my mother had just told me. After sitting there alone listening to my mother cry in the kitchen, I went upstairs to the bathroom, closed the door, and began to cry.

Initially we were told that Marlon was hit with a grenade and the only way he was identified was through his tattoo's, but we later found out that that wasn't the case. Marlon was shot in the chest and died almost instantly. I had just spoken with him maybe a month or so prior. We laughed and talked for a long time on the phone, and he told me how on the last day when he was scheduled to go home from Iraq, they extended him for another tour. Marlon said he and his platoon were so upset about the extension, the next day they went out wrecking shop, shooting everything in sight. He told me that he had a lot of souvenirs that he wanted to bring back home with him, but he knew they wouldn't allow him. We laughed and joked all through the conversation and then we ended by saying that we loved each other, and we would link up when he returned to the states. Marlon was in his 3rd tour when he was killed.

The next few days were very tough for me. I was still in my probationary stage at my new job so I couldn't take off. The local new stations wanted to interview me regarding Marlon, but I declined. They called my mother on several occasions looking for me, but I never returned the call. At night, I couldn't sleep. I couldn't believe that my best friend and brother was gone. Since high school Marlon and I had this ongoing joke that suggested that we had something that it was rumored that twins have, when one person experiences something and the other feels whatever the first person is experiencing. We joked so much about it, we started to believe it so when I learned of Marlon's death I asked myself, "Why didn't I feel something when he was shot?"

Marlon's wife Stacy decided to have his funeral here in Baltimore but afterwards she was taking him to Florida (where they resided) to be buried. On the day of the funeral, I left work early and picked up my mother from her house and then we went to the funeral home. I bought a pint of Absolute Vodka, Marlon's favorite before I picked up my mother and was drinking it straight from the bottle up until my mom got in the car.

When we arrived at the funeral home, I told my mother to go in and that I would be coming in shortly. I sat in the car alone and finished off the bottle of vodka. Even after drinking, still couldn't get out of the car. I just didn't want to see my brother laying in a casket. After some time, finally I got the nerve to get out of the car.

When I walked in the funeral and began to walk down the middle isle, I could feel everyone looking at me. Marlon's family and everyone there knew that I was going to take this very hard. When I approached the casket, I looked over at Marlon's wife Stacy and we both burst out crying. I looked at Marlon's face for a second and then my head almost went down into his chest as I continued to cry. My mother came up beside me, rubbed my back and said some encouraging words in my ear. I heard my mother but didn't hear her because I was so upset. With the help of my mother, I was able to walk to a seat. I sat in one spot with my head in my lap for the entire service. I never looked up.

Being as though I drank a whole bottle of vodka before the funeral a lot of details were fussy afterwards, but I do remember Anna calling me while the service was going on. When I answered, I told her where I was and she could hear the pain in my voice. Before I knew it, as I continued to hold my head in my hands on my lap, someone was holding me from behind consoling me as I cried. It was Anna. She left wherever she was when she called me and came to the funeral home to support me. Anna never said a word. She just held me from behind as I cried.

At the end of the service, the military trumpet guy started to play that infamous sad tune when soldiers die and all I could think about was when Marlon said how he cried when he heard the trumpet playing for someone he knew. Now the trumpet was playing for him.

When the service was over, I stayed around for a few to socialize with Marlon's family. My mother had left along with Anna. I didn't have an appetite, so I just sat at the table while everyone else ate. I knew I wouldn't see any of them again because Ms. Brenda was gone, Stacy and the kids were going back to Florida and now Marlon was gone. I didn't want to feel any additional pain by saying goodbye to everyone, so I snuck out without saying a word. My dad had come also but I had just missed him.

A few weeks later, still grieving Marlon's death, I decided to pour all my energy into songwriting and sat hip hop completely to the side. By doing this, I eliminated the musical need of others like Ole Man Joe and Pig. As a songwriter, I only needed my pen. I reunited with Cliff Jones once again and played the songs I wrote for J Rome. Cliff loved what me and J Rome had done and wanted to sign him to his production company and then shop him to a major record label. Every day when I got off from work, I would drive to Prince Georges County and pick up J Rome and then we would drive to DC to Cliff Jones's studio. Cliff loved the records that we did but you know how the game goes. Cliff had nothing to do with the tracks J Rome and I recorded prior, so it was imperative that we recorded new songs to tracks Cliff Jones was affiliated with. I got tracks from Cliff's producer Davey Boy and wrote some of my best songs ever.

One record that stood out from them all was a song I wrote called "I've Changed". No one in particular inspired the writing of the song. I actually pulled from within myself. The way I viewed relationships was changing so I decided to write about it. I remember when recording the song, normally I would always have to push J Rome to get him to sing with the emotion needed to sell a song but, on this record, I didn't have to. At the end of the song when J Rome was singing his leads over the last chorus, J Rome broke down and began to cry as he was singing, and his tears were felt vocally on the song.

Sidenote: Till this day "I've Changed" is one of my favorites but J Rome told me later that he either sung the record in the wrong key or it was mixed in the wrong key. I couldn't and still can't hear what singers hear. All I knew and know was how the record made me FEEL and that's all that mattered to me.

After recording about 5 to 6 new records produced by Cliff's producer Davey Boy, Cliff shopped J Rome around to several major labels but no one offered a deal. Eventually over time, J

Rome decided to move on but I continued to work with Cliff. I decided to join Cliff's team and began to write songs for anyone that needed a record, teaming up with Cliff's producer Davey Boy. Cliff would bring the clients through the door, Dave would create the track and I would write the song. I was the only one from Baltimore on Cliff's Soul World Entertainment team. Cliff and I were close before, but this process made us even closer. Cliff trusted me so much that he gave me my own set of keys to his office/ studio.

Now when I got off from work, instead of picking J Rome up in PG County, I drove straight to DC to Cliffs studio. The drive one way was about a 90-minute drive. I would work on whatever song that needed to be worked on till the wee hours of the morning and then take the 90-minute drive home. So many times, I fell asleep at the wheel and was awoken by the sound of my tires rolling over the grooves beyond the painted lanes where cars are not supposed to be. It was only the grace of God that got me home safely on several nights returning from DC. I would sleep for a few hours and then I was back up headed to work to repeat the same process all over again.

Sidenote: This was why I never wanted to work another 9 to 5 job ever again. The 9 to 5 jobs are like shackles to an artist. The job will either drain your body or your mind (sometimes both) and after you got off from work, you had no energy to be creative. Also, when in the music business timing is everything. Things happen on the drop of a dime, and you must be able to move without hesitation. A job kills your freedom to move when needed to and it drains you mentally. That why working a job and being an artist, in my opinion is damn near impossible.

As time continued to go by, the late-night drives began to take their toll on me as well as my used caravan. At times when driving to and from DC, I thought my van was going to break down because it started hesitating as if the transmission was dying but somehow, I made it through. When it got to the point when I knew for sure I couldn't make it to and from DC, I stopped working with Cliff and Dave.

Sidenote: I was able to make some good upfront money working with Cliff. Through several small projects I was able to make enough money to purchase a new dining room set for my apartment. I previously received a check from my publishing on "Can I Live" and bought a King size bed, some matching nightstands, and lamps so all my apartment was now missing was a living room set.

Around this time, I was dating a married woman that I met that was from Chicago. Her husband treated her very badly by constantly cheating on her and leaving her home alone. She and her husband relocated to Baltimore because of his job. She didn't know anyone in Baltimore besides me and the people she worked with.

"Chi Town" (I called her) played a very influential part in my musical pursuit as well as personal life at that time. Her husband was financially well off, so she didn't have to work. The only reason she worked a job was because she was bored a needed something to do. Chi Town didn't have any kids. Whenever I needed to be in New York for a songwriters showcase or a meeting, Chi Town would take me because of course my Caravan wasn't good enough to withstand the trip. On several occasions when my van broke down and I was stranded on the beltway, Chi Town would come pick me up. Not only did she pick me up, often she would pay for my car repairs to get me back on the road.

When child support got wind that I was working and had an income, they came and demolished my paychecks causing my tight budget to be even tighter. When I moved in my apartment, I planned my finances without including the garnishment of child support so when that happened my whole world changed. One bad financial decision and I was going to be out on the streets. Living paycheck to paycheck was an understatement. Chi Town was my financial savior whenever I fell short. When my cell phone got turned off, she would pay the bill and get it turned back on. When I didn't have food, she would get us takeout. Again, being as though she was married, we never went out on dates. She would always come to my apartment when she got off from work. She couldn't spend the night but would leave around 12am on the weekdays and maybe 1 or 2am on weekends.

Chi Town did these things for me and in return, I was her escape from an unhappy home. At times when my van was in the car repair shop for weeks at a time, Chi Town was my only means of transportation. A few times when we went to New York for whatever reason, Ole Man Joe went with us. She was very cool and supportive but just married. Chi Town knew that there was a limit to how far we could go so she would always tell me "Dwayne, I understand that you're a single guy and by me being married, I can't give you all that you need. My only ask from you is when the time comes and you feel like you're ready to move on, just be honest and let me know. You don't ever have to lie to me!"

During this time, I was still trying to get over Tanja. I wasn't as bad off as I was initially, but I definitely wasn't over her yet. One day Tanja and I were talking on the phone, and she was explaining to me about how she was having a hard time getting settled into her new place. While I was in Atlanta, Tanja's fathers house (where she lived at the time) burned down in a fire causing her to lose everything that she owned. She was bouncing around from house to house till finally her brother-in-law allowed her to live in one of his houses that he wasn't occupying. The only thing was the house needed work before she could move in, and the home improvement guys were moving at a slow pace.

I told Tanja that she and her kids could come and stay with me whenever she wanted to. Tanja had done so much for me over the years that offering her a place to stay wasn't even a second thought. Besides, I wanted to show Tanja that all the things she was asking of me when we were together, I was finally getting a grasp of. I wanted her to see what I was capable of in just a short amount of time.

After a little convincing Tanja agreed to not live but occasionally stay with me when needed. The first night she came to my apartment, when she walked in, I could tell that she was impressed. Im a neat freak, been that way since a child so my apartment was spotless and smelled like heaven. I told Tanja that she and her kids could have my bed and I would sleep on the floor. Not exactly sure what was going on with her that night, but she and her 3 kids arrived at my place very late (after 1am) so we didn't talk much. She and her kids were tired, and I had to work the next morning so we all went to sleep.

That morning before I left for work, I gave Tanja a key to my apartment and told her to lock the door when or if she left. I was hoping that she stayed. My goal was to show Tanja that I finally understood and was becoming the man that she always wanted me to be. I couldn't see it when I had her but losing her opened my eyes clearly. Tanja was very thankful not to mention impressed but when I came home from work that evening, Tanja and her kids were gone. She called me later that night and we talked. I told her to keep the key so that whenever she ran into a jam and didn't have a place to stay, she could always come to my place.

After giving Tanja a key to my apartment, I reached out to Chi Town and told her the situation. Chi Town of course didn't like it, but she appreciated the fact that I was honest with her and stepped away without any drama.

A few days went by, and I didn't hear from nor saw Tanja then one night around 12:30am I heard my doors being unlocked. Tanja walked in, came into my bedroom, and whispered "Surprise!" We both burst out in laughter and then began to talk. The first night Tanja came she brought her kids but this time she came alone. Tanja and I sat on my living room floor and talked all night long. We talked about everything from the beginning of our relationship till the hurtful end. Tanja expressed how worried she was about me when we first broke up because I had lost so much weight.

Sidenote: Throughout the entire time after Tanja and I broke up, every so often we would hook up and have these talks and sometimes (not often because she was trying to break it completely off) we would sleep together. One day as she was on her way to my mother's house to visit, she told me that she had her tattoo with my name covered up. I was floored when she told me that because to me, that meant that she had found someone else, and they were being intimate. Then I began to think about it. "She has my initials on her wrist and my full name (Cooli Hi) tattooed on her ass!" I just prayed that the wrist tattoo was the one she covered because if she covered the one on her ass that definitely meant she was planning on or already sleeping with someone else. When Tanja arrived at my mothers, I looked at her wrist and my initials were still there. I felt like I wanted to die. We slept together that day and when I looked at her ass, my name was blended away in a cover up.

Tanja and I talked about all of this and by now she had the wrist tattoo filled in as well (but if you look closely, you could still see my initials clear as day- DJ). Tanja asked if I was seeing anyone and I told her about Chi Town. I wanted to see how she would respond but Tanja's poker face is like none other so I couldn't read if me seeing someone else affected her or not. We talked and reminisced about everything except her current situation regarding who she was seeing. I didn't want to know. We didn't go to bed till the sun was coming up.

The next day, being tired from being up talking all night, I called out from work. When we finally woke up that afternoon, Tanja and I slept together but this time it was different. As I said before, after our breakup, we had slept together plenty of times and although we were going through, our connection was still the same but this time something was off. Tanja took a shower afterwards, got dressed and left. That was the last time Tanja, and I was intimate.

Being fluttered with all kinds of thoughts swimming around in my head, I decided to pour it all out in songs but this time I didn't want to write any love songs. I wanted to spit bars! I wanted to rip a track to shreds!

I called Pig and told him that I was putting the R&B to the side and jumping back into the hip hop seat. Pig was happy to hear this because although he liked the R&B, he absolutely loved me as an artist and as I stated before, whenever I did hip hop, others could be involved.

Pig began to find me all kinds of instrumentals and being as though he was around so much, he knew my style and what kind of tracks I would like. We decided that we would take it back to where we started and began going to Sisqo's studio again. I reunited with Chi Town after the Tanja episode so whenever my van wasn't running, Chi Town was my transportation to and from Sisqo's.

Being as though I was now working a 9 to 5 job, I didn't have time to write lyrics. I would get off from work and head straight to Sisqo's house and Pig would meet me there. I had Peanut and Darrian on the weekends, worked during the week so there was no time for writing. Often while picking up my boys driving from one place to another, I would have instrumentals beats playing, trying to come up with concepts while driving. My boys hardly ever listened to the actual radio while with me. It was always instrumentals.

Since I didn't have time to write, I had to freestyle every song that I did during that time. Pig would be at the board playing the track, ready to record me and I would think of and record each bar, line by line. Pig and I recorded and entire mix CD using that format. I never wrote a single word on that project.

Sidenote: This project was a release for me. I had a lot of anger and frustration built up and needed to let it go. I spoke on several songs about Marlon here and there within my lyrics but I never did a full song about him. I had plans to but the emotions were too overbearing. That's why I always mentioned him in a bar or two but then I would move on.

After I recorded about 13 or 14 freestyles using the non-writing format, the project abruptly came to a halt. I realized as I was approaching the end of the project that I didn't have the means to financially complete the project. The "Crown Vic Click" had dwindled down to just two people, me, and Pig. Ole Man Joe had moved back to Atlanta with a girl that he met while we were out selling CD's. I didn't have any financial wiggle room due to child support coming out of my checks and Pig was struggling as well. Combined, we couldn't even afford to get the project mixed down, not to mention designing a CD cover and getting them pressed up. I came to the conclusion that I couldn't afford to do hip hop any more. My hip hop projects required money and a team of people to push the project and I didn't have either of the two. Based on my financial situation, it was best for me to go back to songwriting where the overhead hardly existed.

I began working with every producer in the Baltimore area that I knew and wrote songs to their tracks. From Jarod "King Beatz" Barnes to Kevin "KP" Prigden, I went from one studio session to another, writing songs with the goal of landing a placement. I also continued to work with Kevin Kidd and his producers as well as One Up Entertainment, Rich and Loren. Whenever I got tracks from Wardell Malloy or someone I met at the writer's showcases in New York, I would go to the third member of One Up Entertainment, Kevin's house/ studio and record there also.

My primary focus at this time was to land a placement on an established artist. While in New York, I met several people that I made a point to stay in contact with like, Dolly Turner, LaRonda Sutton and Tony Perez just to name a few. At one point Tony Perez was considering signing me as a writer. One day after a writer's showcase, I hung out with him, and his crew and he introduced me to a team of producers called the Basic Apes. At the time the Basic Apes were Solange's band and they were touring with her. We went to Solange's rehearsal and after it was over, I was introduced to them. The Basic Apes lived in LA and invited me to come out and work with them as soon as Solange's tour was over. I gladly accepted the offer.

It was now March of 2008, and I was still working my customer service job at HSBC, living in my one-bedroom apartment, spending my weekends with Peanut and Darrian, still dating Chi Town, and writing songs trying to land a placement. One day while at work, I was in the breakroom when suddenly one of my co workers walked in. My co workers name was Cheryl. Cheryl and I had worked together back in 1999 at a company called Credit Trust and now nine years later back working together again. After we spoke, Cheryl told me that someone in the section where her desk was wanted to say hi to me. I asked Cheryl who was it, but she just smiled and walked away. When I came out of the break room, I looked at the area where Cheryl sat and saw a bunch of elderly woman. As I continued to scan the area I saw one younger girl, maybe mid or late 20's sitting at her desk. "She's got to be the one Cheryl was talking about" I said to myself.

The girl I assumed Cheryl was talking about was a girl that I would see from time to time and had interest in. The only problem was we worked different shifts so I didn't see her as often as I would have liked but when I did see her, it was always sporadic, and I was never able to approach her without making a scene because she was either walking fast trying to get to her desk or with a group of people.

"If she's the girl that Cheryl's speaking of, I need to know today!" I said to myself. The music business had my approach to everything intensified. In my eyes, there literally was no such thing as tomorrow! Aggressive was my middle and last name so there was no time for procrastinating. Everything was now and today but also like the music business, every move was calculated!

My plan was to wait until the girl went into the breakroom and then I would make my approach but as time continued to pass, she never came. Before I knew it, it was lunch time. Being on a tight budget, I didn't buy lunch. Instead, since I only lived 10 minutes away from my job, I would go home, eat lunch and then return back to work. When I returned to work from lunch, as I searched for a parking spot, I saw the girl getting something out of her trunk on the parking lot as well. We were the only two there. "Jackpot" I thought to myself. My timing couldn't be more perfect. I parked in the first spot that I saw available and attempted to approach the girl while she was still at her car but by the time I got out of my car, she had rushed back in the building. "Damn, I missed a perfect opportunity" I said to myself but I wasn't done yet.

I went in the building, sat at my desk and like before, waited for her to make her way to the breakroom. Time continued to pass and still no signs of her coming to the breakroom. The day was winding down and soon our shift was about to be over. It was a Friday and I knew if I didn't make a move, I would have to wait until Monday to see her again.

Around 4pm I decided that she wasn't coming into the breakroom therefore I had to make a power move. When working at a call center, everyone was always in each other's business, so people tried to keep their dealings with others very low key. I knew this as well as all of the other unsaid call center rules, yet still I decided that I was going into the lion's den by walking up to her desk to talk to her before her shift ended.

As I walked down the aisle headed towards her desk, I looked, and her desk was empty. I knew she hadn't left for the day because her purse was still there. I continued to walk down the aisle headed towards another breakroom in the building and out of nowhere she came out and we almost ran into each other. "How are you" I said to her. She answered, "I'm fine" and then walked back into the breakroom. I went into the bathroom just so she didn't think I was following her, waited for a few and then went into the breakroom as well. She was at a phone booth talking on the phone. Me being in attack mode, I walked up to her and began to talk, totaling disregarding the fact that she was on the phone. She put her finger up as if to say, "Give me a second." I waited for a few for her to finish her call but when it appeared that she was going to be a while, I left and went back to my desk. About 10 minutes later Cheryl came over to my desk, slipped me a piece of paper and said "Shhhhh!" When I unfolded the piece of paper, it had her name and number on it. The girl's name was Erica.

I never considered myself as a guy that had a "type" but if I had to describe my "type" or preference, Erica was it. She was a beautiful brown skinned petite young woman with beautiful long hair. On our first phone conversation she blew me away with her outgoing personality, joking about how I approached her at the phone booth. "Why did you walk up on me like that! Boy you scared me" Erica joking said literally 10 seconds into our first conversation. Erica also admitted to purposely running into the building when we were outside on the jobs parking lot as well as pretending to be on the phone at the phone both. She said no one was on the other end of the phone. "Boy you were in hot pursuit! You made me nervous!" she jokingly said. Ninety percent of Erica's conversation went that way. She said the wildest, most craziest things; things that almost always caught you off guard. Erica's style of conversation made it challenging for me to be flirtatious with her because she would always deflect and make a light joke but me being who I was continued to press and go after her.

After conversating on the phone for a few days, one night I invited Erica over to my apartment and she agreed to come. She was in the middle of doing her hair that night so when she came over her hair was blown out. Erica came in with her lively energy and we sat in my bedroom and talked. I showed her a photo album that I had when I began to tell her about my music journey. As Erica looked through my photo's suddenly she stopped on a page with a surprised look on her face. I immediately thought she saw something relating to my music accomplishments that wild her but that wasn't the case. "That's Chante!" Erica said. "Wow, I haven't seen her in years!" I was completely shocked because Chante didn't deal with a lot of people therefore no one I ever came across knew her and now the girl that I'm pursuing knows her. Erica went on to explain that Chante and one of her childhood friends grew up as step siblings because Chante's Dad and the girlfriend's mom dated for a while. They all were small children at the time, but Erica recognized Chante as an adult.

Erica and I continued to talk about everything under the sun from both of our past relationships to what was going on currently in our lives. Erica told me that she wasn't seeing anyone and at that time Chi Town was still around, but our dealings were very light. Chi Town had just quit her job and was planning to move back to Chicago.

After talking for a few hours, instead of returning home, Erica spent the night with me. From that night moving forward, we were inseparable. Day after day night after night, we were always together. At times while we were at work, we would take paid time off, just to go back to my apartment and make love. The more time we spent together, the stronger our feelings began to grow for one another.

Soon we introduced each other to our kids, I met her daughter Akiya and I introduced her to Peanut and Darrian as well as we met each other's mothers. Erica's mothers name was Carmalita and from the first time meeting her I could see where Erica got her colorful personality from. Ms. Carmalita was a very friendly, outspoken woman with a big heart. I loved to hear her talk because her voice texture reminded me of Edith Bunker voice from an old TV Sitcom called All In The Family.

Everything was going well with Erica and I but I wasn't sure if I wanted to commit into a relationship with her until I took her to my mothers church. The first time I took Erica to church almost immediately she stood up and was very interactive in the service, clapping her hands, singing songs and praising God. When I saw this, it was right then that I knew I found someone special.

Afterwards whenever we were in an intimate moment, I would always whisper in Erica's ear "You know where this is going right?" and she would whisper back "Yes". It wasn't much longer that both Erica and I agreed to a committed relationship.

Now that Erica and I were in a committed relationship, I thought it was important for her to know who I was entirely. You see Erica knew Dwayne from HSBC and although I played songs for her and showed her music videos and pictures, she didn't really know who Cooli Hi was and it was imperative that she did. So, I decided to take her to Sisqo's house one night so she could see me in my element. Nothing major happened that night. Just a normal recording session but I just wanted to give her a taste of who I really was. Dwayne at HSBC was plan B but Cooli Hi and music was and always would be top priority in regard to my career and who I was. My thought process was no job or 9 to 5 would ever come before my purpose in life (whatever that entailed).

Erica and I officially became a couple in March 2008 and everything was going well. A few months had passed and one day (June 2008) while at work, everyone was told to stop what they were doing, and the entire call center gathered in a huddle for a major announcement. Due to the Great Recession/Financial Crisis of 2008, our job HSBC was shutting down and relocating to Delaware. We were offered a severance package or a job in Delaware. As expected, my co-workers were devastated by this news. Some even broke down and started crying but I couldn't have been happier. This was an opportunity for me to take one last full swing at my music career. I figured if I took the severance package and received unemployment, I could continue to stay at my apartment but at the same time be free and accessible to travel and be wherever I needed to be to advance my musical career.

Shortly after the announcement, HSBC had closed its doors and Erica and I had received our severance packages and were now unemployed receiving unemployment. My severance package wasn't as large as Erica's because she had been with the company for 10 years compared to my 1 year. At HSBC I was a customer service rep that relied on selling identity theft protection to break even after paying my bills which meant, if I didn't sell, I would be out on the streets. Again, this was because child support was garnishing my paychecks. The bonuses I received from sales, balanced out my finances.

One month, not too long before the closing of the business announcement, I came short of my sales goal causing me to miss my bonus payout for that month. When that happened, I wasn't able to pay my rent causing me to fall behind and as we all know, once you fall behind and are living paycheck to paycheck, its almost impossible to catch back up. Now that I was getting unemployment, I knew my time was limited so I had to make something happen fast before the unemployment ran out and I had to go back to work.

Being committed to a job, put shackles on my music movement but now I was officially free! The first move I made was reaching out to the Basic Apes (Solange's band). The tour was over and they were now back home in LA. I reached out to Mike (one of the members of the Basic Apes) and told him that I would be in LA soon and we should link up and work on some records. Mike gladly agreed.

Sidenote: This was how I approached everything when it came to meeting with people in the music industry. When speaking with executives or producers, it was all about positioning. I never asked anyone for anything or permission to do something. I simply said it and encouraged them to co sign my decision. I wasn't going to "just so happen to be in LA", but

I made it seem that way to the Basic Apes. That's how I landed a lot of meetings. I made it seem like I had several things going on and meeting with them was just one of the things but 99% of the time, it was the only thing.

Once I got the green light from the Basic Apes, I called Mike Lowery from Atlanta to see if he could hook me up with a round trip buddy pass flight from Baltimore to LA. Mike Lowery agreed and got me the tickets.

Sidenote: Ever since Pig, Ole Man Joe and I returned from Atlanta, Mike had been reaching out and keeping in contact with me. Initially I would ignore his calls because I thought he was out for something (like almost everyone is in this music business) but when I started taking his calls, I discovered his motives were genuine and we became good friends.

Mike booked me the tickets for a few weeks in advance and while I awaited my LA trip, Erica and I learned that she was pregnant. She and her daughter Akiya were pretty much staying with me at my apartment, spending time with Peanut, Darrian, and I ever since we were laid off from HSBC and during this time our child was conceived.

I reached out to Kidd and told him I was heading to LA and needed a place to stay, and he agreed. Kidd was working at My Space Records as a VP/ A&R Rep and was doing very well for himself. I flew out to LA and when I got off the plane and went to retrieve my one suitcase, I noticed that it wasn't at baggage claim. I searched everywhere but couldn't find my suitcase. I went to the office to report my suitcase missing when suddenly I saw a suitcase taped up with Southwestern Tape all over the bag. As I looked closer, I noticed it was my suitcase. Apparently, my cheap suitcase must have busted when the flight team was throwing my bag on or off the airplane so now I'm walking through LAX with a suitcase draped in Southwestern tape (very embarrassing).

Kidd was still at his office when I arrived in LA. He told me he couldn't pick me up from the airport, so I had to catch a cab to his office. When I arrived at his office, I was embarrassed all over again because I had to walk in with my suitcase practically falling apart. When Kidd saw me, all he could do was laugh.

We left Kidd's office and headed to his condo so I could drop off my bag and he could change his clothes. Kidd had plans of going out that night and of course I was going with him. When we arrived at his house, I was completely blown away. Kidd had a two car garage, 3 bedroom condo that was laid out with the finest of everything. His spot looked like something you would see in a magazine. His next door neighbor was Eva (the winner of America's Next Top Model & now Radio Host on the Rickey Smiley Morning Show).

When Kidd told me about the plans for going out, I decided to change my clothes as well. When I came downstairs dressed and ready to go, Kidd looked at me and then went into his closet. He then came back with some Gucci shoes and said, "Yo put these on." I changed into the Gucci shoes Kidd gave me and we headed out. Kidd probably figured, if I was going to roll with him, I had to look a certain way and what I initially had on wasn't up to par, especially in LA.

Speeding down the LA highway in his brand new 745 BMW, Kidd told me how he got the job at My Space records. He explained to me how he kept in contact with someone that was around back in when we were recording Sisqo's 2nd album "Return of Dragon" but no one paid too much attention to because he probably was an intern. Kidd and the guy remained friends and as time went on, that intern climbed up the ladder and was now a heavyweight in the music business. That intern was Shawn "Tubby" Holiday. Tubby gave Kidd the position at My Space Records and basically gave him the blueprint for success as an executive.

Kidd and I conversated the entire drive until finally we arrived at some fancy restaurant. When we walked in, I could tell it was a very high scaled restaurant because there were movie stars everywhere. As we approached our table, there were a few people already there, one of which was a familiar face, Demetrius Spencer (our almost former manager when we were the Associates). Demetrius and I greeted each other with pleasantries and then Demetrius introduced me to the two others that were sitting at the table as well. The two people he introduced me to were Cedric the Entertainer and Melissa Ford. The five of us eat dinner, had drinks, and laughed and talked the entire night.

The next day, when Kidd went to his office, I stayed at his house and began to plan my time in LA. The main purpose of the trip was to connect with the Basic Apes. I called Mike from the Basic Apes and told him I was in town and ready to work. Mike invited me to their home where they recorded all their music. When we told each other where we were, Mike told me that I was an hour and a half away from where he lived. He asked if I had a car and I told him no, but I would find a way to get to his house.

When Kidd came home that evening, I told him about my situation with the Basic Apes. Kidd heard me but I could tell by his demeanor, he had no intentions of helping me. All Kidd wanted to do was party. That night as well as the few nights to follow, all we did when he came home from the office was party.

After 5 straight nights of partying, I told Mike about my dilemma and reluctantly he decided to drive to Kidds house to pick me up. Once we arrived at the Basic Apes house (3-hour ride for Mike) we immediately began to work. Mike gave me some tracks to vibe to and I went in one of the writing/bedrooms and began to write. While vibing to one of their tracks trying to come up with a concept suddenly I heard a knock on the bedroom door. When I opened it, it was the famous actor,

Malik Yoba. Malik Yoba was there working downstairs with the Basic Apes on a solo project. Up until then I had no idea that he could sing. Malik and I talked for a few and then he went back downstairs to continue to work on his song.

Once I finished writing the song I was working on, Mike decided to drive me back to Kidd's house because we didn't have a female singer available to demo the song. Mike had scheduled for one of Solange's backup singers, a girl named Jade, to come by and demo the song a few days later. When I arrived back at Kidd's house, he and his girlfriend was there. I cant remember her name but what I do remember was she looked semi Latino and had a beautiful smile. She prepared dinner for us that night and afterwards we all just chilled out at the house and didn't go out.

A few days passed and me and Kidd's girlfriend grew fond of each other in a plutonic way. We laughed and talked about everything. One day we were having a conversation and she asked me what made me come out to LA. I told her I was a songwriter, and I was there to work with some producers called the Basic Apes. Kidd's girlfriend then replied, "Wow, how ironic! I work for a publishing company!" She then went on continuing to speak but honestly, I didn't hear a word she said after publishing company. I thought to myself, "Kidd knows why I'm out here in LA and to know that his girlfriend is or knows who the connection is to catapult me to the next level, but he didn't mention a word. The whole time I'm here in LA looking for the connect and she's right here at my fingertips under the same roof!

Later that night after she left, I asked Kidd why he didn't tell me that his girlfriend worked for a publishing company? Kidd gave me a bull crap explanation saying that she only worked with established writers with lots of placements and since I didn't have any placements as a songwriter, it didn't make since to mention it. I thought his explanation was bull crap. Even if what he said was true, about working with established writers, she could have at least help me link up with other up and coming writers and producers that could have led to something in the near future. I believe Kidd didn't connect us two because he didn't want to musically help me. As before he was cool with me just being his homeboy that would always need him. Instead of putting people in position to catch their own fish, Kidd would rather spoon feed the fish to his peers accordingly. That way he controls when or if everyone ate.

Sidenote: I often would suggest to Kidd that he started his own production team and signed people like myself and other writers and producers. That way he could still have the control that he desperately needed but at the same time everyone ate but he never acted on it. Again, Kidd just wanted to have it all and have everyone else around him, needing him.

After about a week, the Basic Apes called and told me the singer was ready to record our song and asked if I could find a way back to their house. Mike said that he couldn't come and get me this time. That's when I realized that having a car in LA was a necessity. I asked Kidd if he would take me to the session and he refused saying it was too far. Not knowing what to do, I started brainstorming thinking of everyone I knew that lived in LA. Then it hit me. I decided to call an old friend Corey Grant, the director of my first two music video's Always and Off the Chain. I called Corey, explained to him my situations and without hesitation Corey came and picked me up from Kidds house and drove me to the session at the Basic Ape's. I recorded a pop record called "Unhappy" with Solanges back up singer Jade that night and after the session a caught a cab to the airport to return to Baltimore.

When I arrived at the airport, it was late and only one flight was leaving headed to Baltimore. I had a buddy pass ticket so in order for me to catch that flight an empty seat had to be available. Unfortunately, there wasn't an empty seat and the next flight to Baltimore wasn't until the next morning. I could have called Kidd and asked him to come pick me up from the airport but instead I decided to spend the night at the airport. I was just tired of depending on people to take me here, drop me off there, put in a good word for me and so on, that the processed had drained me. I was able to record a hot record with the Basic Ape's as well as got some tracks from them to bring back to Baltimore, so I felt like I accomplished what I came to do. I slept on the airport benches the entire night and the next morning returned to Baltimore.

A few weeks later I was talking on the phone with Kidd and he suggested that I should come back to LA because he had a lot going on that I could benefit from. Without hesitation, I booked another flight and flew back to LA almost immediately. When I arrived, I caught a cab to Kidd's house knocked on his door but no one answered. I then called his phone, and he didn't pick up. I sat outside of his door for a few and then I started calling his phone back to back, nonstop. Finally Kidd answered. "Yo where you at! Im at your front door!" I said. "Get the fuck outta here." Kidd replied. Kidd couldn't believe that I sporadically jumped on a plane and came back to LA. "Yo I'm dead ass serious. I'm at your front door. Where are you?" Kidd replied "Alright cool. I'm on my way" About 2 hours later Kidd showed up and laughingly said "Yo I was damn near in Vegas! I can't believe you just came out here winging it!" I then replied, "You said there was some opportunities out here and I came to see what was up!" We both laughed and walked into his house.

I asked Kidd about his girlfriend and the publishing situation, and he told me the two of them had broken up.

Sidenote: When I first found out that Kidd's girlfriend worked for a publishing company, I often thought about pitching my music directly to her going around Kidd but I didn't because to me it was a bad idea. You see the move had to come from Kidd because if it didn't, it wouldn't hold any value. Meaning, if I would have gone directly at her, she would have immediately thought "If this is Kidds friend from his hometown, why wouldn't he mention that he was a songwriter to me and he knows I'm in the business of signing songwriters? Something must not be right with him because if it was, Kidd would have brought him to me!" Knowing this is why I never went directly at her. I knew that I needed to be recommended by Kidd or it would have made me look flawed.

After I put my bags in the house, Kidd and I hit the LA streets per usual but this time instead of going to party or to get something to eat, we went to a casino. When we walked inside, I noticed that almost all of the dealers at the casino knew who Kidd was. That alarmingly told me that Kidd frequent this place a lot which could mean he had a gambling problem.

Kidd placed huge bets which meant he won big and lost big that night. Not sure if he came out on top or not. I couldn't afford to lose anything I had so I just stood on the sidelines and watched. After about an hour or so we left.

As we drove to our next destination, Kidd explained to me how he would flip income at the casino. He told me that whenever he received a large amount of money from a project he worked on, he would go to the casino and try to flip it. If he won, he would go to the clubs and ball out with the earnings but if he lost, he would just go home. Since we were on our way to the club, that told me he must have won that night.

While in route to the club, Kidd drove recklessly through the LA streets almost as if he was drunk. Not sure why he felt the need to drive that way but I never said a word. He swerved around every car he approached sometimes even going head on into on coming traffic just for the rush. Finally we arrived at the club where Tubby and a few others were there waiting on us.

We partied that night and had a good time but the night ended on a bad note when Kidd and R&B singer Tank got into an altercation and had to be separated. Initially I thought the two of them were just talking but then their body language shifted and it was clear the conversation took a turn for bad. When the night was over and we were headed to the next spot, Kidd told me the beef had something to do with his ex-girlfriend.

Before we headed home, Kidd called up a few girls that he saw at the club and asked them if they wanted to get something to eat. The girls met us at an all night diner. It was roughly around 3am. While ordering our food, Kidd and I noticed that NBA basketball player Lamar Odom was sitting at the bar eating breakfast alone. Kidd looked at me and said "Yo, I'm about to go see if I can get Lamar Odom to invest in a few projects I'm working on." I replied by saying "Huh, Yo you're straight with My Space. Why would you need Lamar Odom?" Kidd then said "You can never get too comfortable in the business. You always got to be looking for the next move in order to stay ahead." Kid went over to Lamar, sat beside him and the two of them talked for hours. The girls and I finished our food and then they went home leaving me at the table alone waiting for Kidd. Finally after about two hours or so, Kidd returned to our table and we left.

The next couple of days in LA with Kidd were starting to look like the same as before. Kidd would wake up in the morning, go to the office and then return wanting me to run the streets with him. I kept telling Kidd that I didn't come to LA to party. I needed to make the best of my time before my unemployment ran out and my musical run was over but Kid wasn't trying to hear it. To pour salt over the wound, Kidd would go meet with important people and purposely leave me at the house (so I wouldn't meet or have access to them) and then return to pick me up to go party.

To show off, Kidd would show me text messages from him and big celebrities such as Ric Ross, Brandi and Cierra just to name a few. When we went out at night, we would always link up with his friend Cudda (a big wheel in the music industry at the time who had serious ties with Mase). Cudda managed Tierra Marie and Pleasure P from the R&B group "Pretty Ricky" so they were with us every night also. So like clockwork when Kidd came home from the office, he would pick me up, head to the casino and afterwards Kidd, myself, Cudda, Tierra Marie and Pleasure P (along with a few others) would club hop every single night.

One day while Kidd was at the office, I became fed up with all of the partying and hanging out so I decided to take matters into my own hands. I called up a friend I knew, Makeba Riddick-Woods and told her what was going on and how I didn't come all the way to LA for this.

Makeba was a big songwriter from Baltimore as well. Her brother (Kevin) and I were homies (I mentioned the two of them earlier when I said Kevin had a sister that worked with Diddy at Bad Boy Records but at the time, I didn't believe him). Makeba knew Kidd as well and the two of them had a very rocky past therefore she wasn't so fond of him anymore. When I told her what was going on Makeba came and picked me up from Kidds house and instead of taking me to parties and restaurants, Makeba took me to the studio's where she frequented the most.

Every studio she took me to, she introduced me to everyone there and told them that I was a songwriter unlike Kidd. Whenever I went somewhere with Kidd, he never introduced me to anyone. It was always an awkward silence when we initially came together and eventually, I introduced myself to whomever we were around. Makeba on the other hand did the total opposite. Not only did she introduce me and told people I was a songwriter, but she also suggested that they should work with me. I met and exchanged contact information with more people in the few hours I hung out with Makeba than the entire two LA trips combined hanging out with Kidd. Later that night Makeba took me back to Kidd's house but then we all met back up later that night at some club again and partied in a section with Paris Hilton.

Up until the day I hung out with Makeba I thought this LA trip was a bust, but once I connected with the producers Makeba introduced me to, it made the trip worth being there. A few days later I returned to Baltimore.

Once I returned to Baltimore, I began writing and recording songs to the tracks I received from Makeba's connects. One of the producers she linked me with was a producer name Infamous (who was known for producing tracks for Lil Wayne and many others). I hooked up with J Rome and recorded one of my favorite up-tempo R&B songs that I'd ever written, a song called "I Gotta Hate Her".

In addition to writing songs to the tracks Infamous gave me, I also wrote to a few tracks Makeba sent me as well. Once I completed a record, I would immediately send it back to the producer or whoever gave me the track to show them that I worked fast and didn't sit on their tracks. Then I would leave it up to them to place the record because they all had 10 times more connections than I had.

Around this time J Rome began to travel a lot trying to enhance his career so I then had to find other male singers to demo my records. I started to use Scola from Dru Hill when J Rome wasn't available and when Scola was out of town, I would use a singer/ producer that I met through Kevin Peck (Dru Hill's manager) named Dudley.

Time was steady passing by and I didn't land a placement yet. I had a black and white composition notebook and I wrote down every single name of anyone of value that I ever met. I tracked how many times I called them as well as met with them face to face. I did this because I wanted to make sure I explored every option that was available to me. Keeping a log ensured that no contact would slip through the cracks.

One day after making my routine calls, I got in touch with my former A&R rep at RCA named Darrale Jones. Per usual I told Darrale that I would be in New York and asked if it was cool to stop by and played some records for him. Darrale agreed. I also called everyone else I knew in New York attempting to set up as many meetings as I could while I was there. Lots of people told me yes but when I arrived in New York and called them I didn't get an answer. Things like this happen in the music business all of the time. People will agree to have lunch with you that morning and by lunch time your calls are going straight to voicemail. Then when you finally get them on the phone that evening, they pretend the lunch episode never happened. You had to have very tough skin to deal with this kind of behavior, especially when you're riding 4 hours on the bus or train coming from out of town.

On this trip to New York, all of my meetings canceled on me except for Darrale. When I arrived at his office, we reminisced for a few and talked about the Sisqo days and then I started playing my records for him. From his facial expression, Darrale was feeling my writings but I could tell he wasn't all the way sold. After the 4th or 5th record, darrale stopped me and said "Yo all your songs are about love and breakup's. That's cool but people don't want to hear that anymore. People want to hear songs that make them want to fuck! Bring me some records that make people want to fuck."

When I returned to Baltimore, I took Darrale's advice and began to write very sexual songs as well as songs suggesting that the two involved keep their feeling to themselves. I wasn't a big fan of these types of records, but my time was running out. Unemployment wasn't going to last forever, and I needed to land a placement fast.

Not long after returning from New York and writing a new style of music, I received an unexpectant call from Darrale Jones. Darrale called and said he had an opportunity for me. He had a track that he was working on for his artist Lupe Fiasco that needed a hot chorus. Ironically, the producer that made the track was a guy that I met in Atlanta and was already working with by the name of Myke Snoody. Darrale sent me the track and I immediately started working on it. Within 30 minutes I had the hook done. All I needed to do now was record it.

I booked a session at KP's (Kevin Prigden) studio and Scola came through and sung what I had written. The chorus came out amazing! Everyone that was there in the studio that night assured me that I had a certified hit on my hands. In my mind, this was the one! The next day I sent the record to Darrale and Myke Snoody. Myke called me and said he liked the chorus, but he wasn't as excited as I would have liked for him to be. I never heard anything from Darrale. A few weeks later while driving to my mom's house, I was listening to the radio and all of a sudden, I heard the track playing but it didn't have my chorus on it. Once again, I was devastated and heartbroken. Darrale decided to use another chorus. The name of the song was "Out of My Head" Lupe fiasco featuring Trey Songz.

More time passed and it was now the fall of 2008. I was still writing songs to every track that came my way trying to land a placement before my unemployment ran out and I had to return to work. Around this time I was 2 months behind on my rent and there was no way I could make two payments at once to catch up. When it was time to renew my lease, the apartment complex that I was renting from decided not to offer me another year on my lease. They informed me due to all the late payments, I had to vacate my apartment at the end of the lease.

I had maybe about a month or two before I had to be out of my apartment. Since I was already struggling trying to pay the rent with my unemployment checks, I figured why wait.

Why give these people my last dollar, knowing I must leave in 60 days? I might as well take my rent money and buy a plane ticket to somewhere I need to be. That's when I made the decision to pack up my things and leave.

Leaving my one-bedroom apartment was one of the hardest things I ever had to do. I loved that place but more importantly, I loved what I had accomplished there. That was the first place that I had all to myself, and that I got and took care of all on my own. I had other apartments before but it was always shared with a girlfriend or a roommate, but this was all mine and I was very proud of it. Nevertheless, I packed up all my belongings, put them in storage and moved back in with my mother. As I was moving out of my apartment, Erica was moving into her own apartment, but I decided not to move in with her initially. Erica was my girlfriend and pregnant with my child but I didn't want to commit to anything financially after just getting out of my financial ties with my apartment. If I did, I might as well have stayed in my own apartment. I needed to be financially free, just for a moment because I knew my time was expiring and I had to make the best out of the little time that I had.

Sidenote: Around this time Chante and I were on good terms. Before my job closed its doors, whenever Chante thought I was in a financial bind, she would actually give me back the child support that came out of my check. Child support hadn't caught up with my unemployment yet, but I was expecting it to happen any day now and when that happened my financial freedom would be over. Years later, Chante decided to remove me from Child Support after I almost was arrested for driving on a suspended license.

One day while going through my important contacts, making my routine calls, I spoke to a guy named Courtney that I met in New York at one of the BMI writing showcases. While conversating, Courtney said "Yo Cooli, you live in Maryland, right? I know a producer that lives in Frederick, Maryland and he's looking for a good writer. You two should link up!" Of course I was willing to do so. Courtney gave me the producers number. I called the producer and we set up a date and time for me to come to his house and get to work. The producer's name was Shawn Campbell.

A few days later, I drove to Shawn's house out in Frederick MD about 2 hours away from where I lived. When I arrived Shawn was there, with his wife and I believe he had a very young son. Shawn took me to his studio but before he played any tracks for me, we just talked. I told him about my background, how I worked with Sisqo and he told me about how he got started producing.

Shawn said a lot but one testimony he shared stuck with me even till this day. Shawn told me a few years prior he was doing very bad financially. Bills pilled to the sky and he had no income due to his dedication and pursuit of reaching his musical goals. Shawn said he was so pressed for money at the time that he began "hacking" around Baltimore City.

Sidenote: Hacking in Baltimore simply means being an illegal cab driver. Before Uber and Lyft, we (Baltimore natives) would catch "hacks". Hacks were people in regular cars that drove around the city looking for people that may need a ride. If you were outside walking down the street, all you had to do was throw your hand in the air as you walked and eventually someone would pull over and ask you if you needed a "hack". Very dangerous but that's what we did (and some of us still do).

Before things got so bad for Shawn he submitted a CD full of tracks to an A&R at a record label trying to land a placement. One day while out hacking (In a snowstorm) Shawn said he had just picked up someone off the street and as he drove off he vaguely heard what sounded like one of his tracks on the radio. When he turned up the volume, he noticed it was his track and it was being used by Missy Elliott. The name of the record was "She's A Bitch". Shawn's life changed forever after that moment and needless to say, he didn't have to ever "hack" again.

This story inspired and reminded me to never give up. Just as you think there's no hope, a seed that you'd planted some time ago could out of no where blossom and change your life forever. That's why till this day, I always put content out in the atmosphere because you just never know what it could lead to.

After Shawn and I talked for a while, he then told me what he was currently working on. He said he had a young kid from Australia that he was working with that could possibly be the next Justin Bieber. The kid and his father had just arrived in town and was scheduled to be there the next day to record some records. Without hesitation I immediately began to work on some songs for him.

The next day I when I arrived at Shawn's house, the kid and his father were already there. Shawn introduced me to them both and then the kid and I began to record what I had written for him the night before. The young kid had a very nice voice. He was kind of quite and shy but I could tell that the young girls would love him because of how he looked as well as his Australian accent. He also played the guitar.

Every night for about a week or so, I would drive out to Shawns house and record with the kid. Afterwards, Shawn's wife would cook dinner for everyone and Shawn, his wife, the kid, his father and I would sit down and eat. I recorded maybe about 5 or 6 records with the kid. The last night that I was with them, Shawn told me that he was taking the kid to LA, the next morning, with hopes of getting him signed to a major record company. That night when I drove home, I remember thinking I wasn't going to make it home because it had began to snow and the tires on my van were extremely bald. The highway (Route 70) was extremely dark with deer's running frantically across the roads and I just knew I was going to wind up in a ditch somewhere. It took me forever but with God's grace I made it home.

Sidenote: Years later, I'm sitting on my couch watching TV and I see a white young male singer with fans going crazy over him. I didn't pay too much attention to him at first. I thought he was just another heart throb pop singer that all the kids loved but when he spoke, he got my attention. I recognized his Australian accent. As I looked closer at the TV, I realized it was the kid at Shawn's house that I was working with. I asked my kids what his name was and if he was from Australia. My kids told me his name and said yes. I couldn't believe my eyes. I told my kids that I worked with him when he was younger, and they were completely blown away from excitement. The kid was none other than pop star Cody Simpson. As my kids went crazy from hearing that I worked with or "knew" Cody Simpson, I got up off my couch, went upstairs to my bedroom and laid down in silence. I felt like I dropped the ball and missed a golden opportunity once again.

It was now the winter of 2008 heading into 2009 and the pressure was on. Erica and I were expecting a baby boy and decided to name him Donovan (suggested by my cousin Keacha). On top of that, Erica knew Dwayne from HSBC and still wasn't too familiar with Cooli Hi and his sometimes-irrational decisions. Although I had grown tremendously from the person I used to be, I still had a drive in me that would never go away.

One day I sat Erica down and attempted to give her some insight on how I would be perceived. I said to her, "Listen. A lot of your family and friends will not understand what I am doing. They're going to question why I'm not working or looking for a job. They're not going to understand why I'm spending so much time out of town. Its not going to make sense to them but I want to make sure it makes sense to you. This is who I am. I'm an artist with dreams and the key to my dreams, unfortunately are not here in Baltimore. I will never abandon you but please know, to accomplish what I'm trying to do, requires me to move this way." Erica's response told me that she didn't quite understand where I was coming from so that enhanced the pressure even more.

In March 2009 Erica gave birth to my 3rd son Donovan so I now have 3 kids with 3 different women. I was still receiving unemployment due to President Obama extending the time periods, but I could feel my run coming to an end. Around mid-May 2009, I decided to go back to Atlanta to focus only on songwriting as opposed to hip hop and songwriting. At this point, my Crown Vic Click didn't and hadn't existed for quite some time now, including Pig and Ole Man Joe. I was all alone. I didn't have the money for a plane ticket so I had to catch the bus which was very uncomfortable. I'm 6'4" so I didn't have any leg room at all on the 14 hours hot, smelly bus ride.

When I arrived, Mike Lowery was there to pick me up. Mike had started his own car service business and was now chauffeuring celebrities while they were in town (Atlanta). Often while driving, Mike would play my R&B CD as he and whatever artist or executive he chauffeured, rode around town. When my music played, often, he would be asked the question, "Who is this?" and that's when Mike would mention my name.

Now that I was back in Atlanta, I rode around with Mike as he chauffeured his celebrity clients but only the one's Mike had personal relationships with because some people weren't cool with their driver bringing along someone with him. I would also from time to time hang out with my cousin (Cousin X) but the more I did that, the more I realized that hanging out with him was similar to what I was doing in California with Kidd. We just partied and had a good time. The only difference was my cousin genuinely tried to help me but the people he linked me with were so intimidated by him that they wouldn't respond to me after the initial meeting. Kidd on the other hand never had intentions on helping me at all.

Rolling around Atlanta with Mike, I met some amazing people. One of which was an up-and-coming music executive by the name of Sickamore. Mike, Sickamore and I would ride around Atlanta, taking Sickamore to wherever he needed to be, talking about everything, and listening to music. Of course, Mike would play my music and Sickamore loved it. He would always say, "You're a dope writer Cooli. One day soon, we will work together." From my observation, it appeared that Sickamore executive career was in the making, so I figured once he got to where he was trying to go, hopefully he would reach back out and give me an opportunity.

Another person I met while riding with Mike was rapper Lil Scrappy. Lil Scrappy was very cool and down to earth. We all rode around Atlanta so much, it didn't feel like Mike was his driver. It was almost like were all were just hanging out. Lil Scrappy always had one of his friends, cousins or even sometimes his girlfriend (which was a female rapper named Diamond at the time) with him. He had just signed with Ludacris label DTP so a few times we even went to the studio with him. While at the studio, I never mentioned to Scrappy that I rapped. I just sat back and observed the scene and tried to figure out who were the top dogs so I could focus on them instead. I learned a long time ago that the person that can make the power moves is rarely the artist. The artist is mainly focusing on themselves and seldom has any business sense at all. It's usually some low-key person with a phone in their hand typing or up to their ear making everything you see happen.

Sidenote: One day Mike and I were picking Lil Scrappy up from a Disturbing the Peace (Ludacris record label) photo shoot and Scrappy and his mom were outside waiting. When we got out of the car Scrappy introduced me to his mom and almost immediately, I could see the showmanship in her personality. Scrappy's mom and Mike began to talk, and her slick mouth had everyone laughing as she said the wildest and craziest things. I said to myself "That lady is a natural star!"

Year's later Lil Scrappy landed a job on VH1's Love & Hip Hop- Atlanta (Reality Show) and brought his mom with him who we all know now as Momma Dee! I can confirm that what you see on the show is not an act! From what I saw outside at that photoshoot, that's really her personality.

One day after riding around town all day with Scrappy, the night was coming to an end, and we were taking Scrappy home. After Mike and I dropped Scrappy off at his house, we were now headed to take Scrappy's cousin home who was sitting in the back of Mike's Escalade Cadillac truck. For some reason, when we left Scrappy's house, Mike began to drive uncharacteristically reckless and fast. As soon as we got on a major street out of no where we saw police lights. Mike pulled over and we all waited for the police to approach the truck. Scrappy and his cousin were smoking weed before Scrappy was dropped off, so the car smelled like weed and Scrappy's cousin had weed on him.

When the officer came to the car, he smelled the weed and said "I know yall were smoking but is there any more weed in this truck that I should know about?" Me, Mike and Scrappy's cousin replied "No" "Are you sure?" the officer asked. We all doubled down and said no. The officer then asked us all to step out of the truck as two other patrol cars pulled up.

We all sat on the curb and watched as the police officers searched Mike's truck from top to bottom. As they were searching, I asked Scrappy's cousin "Where did you put it?" Scrappy's cousin replied, "I tucked it deep into the crease of the backseat." Right then I knew it was just a matter of time before they found it.

After 15 minutes of searching, the officer came over to us with his findings. "I asked yall several times was there any more weed in this truck and yall said no!" the officer said as he held about an ounce of weed in his hand. He then asked us "Who's weed is this?" None of us replied. "Now yall don't have anything to say huh. I'll tell you what. I'm going to walk over here and talk to my partners. When I come back, whoever this belongs to is going to tell me and that person is going to jail tonight. If none of you say anything, all of you are going to jail!" the officer said.

When the officer walked away, Scrappy's cousin said to me and Mike "I'm on probation. I can't take that charge!" Mike then said "Its your weed! If you don't say anything, they are going to arrest all of us and you're still going to violate your probation!" Mike and Scrappy's cousin went back and forth till finally the officer came back over to us. "So, what's the verdict?" the officer asked. Again no one said anything. When the officer realized that we weren't going to talk, he told us to get up and he and his partners began to place hand cuffs on us. It was about 3am and all I could think about was I didn't know anyone in Atlanta phone number from memory so I wouldn't be able to call for help after I was arrested. One of my worst fears was being arrested in a different state and it appeared that it was about to happen. Then after the officers huddled up one last time, they decided to only arrest the owner of the vehicle and driver (since no one would say anything) which was Mike. The cops arrested Mike and let me and Scrappys cousin go free. Me driving Scrappy's cousin home was a very awkward car ride. He kept trying to explain to me why he couldn't take his charge, but I wasn't trying to hear it. Mike was on his way to jail because of him. I dropped him off and then went to my uncle's house. The next day Mike was released from jail and the charges were later dropped.

Outside of riding around Atlanta with Mike, I also would go to the BMI office in Atlanta to record new songs. I didn't have a studio to use while in Atlanta so I would use a room in the BMI office to record songs. I would go to Craigs List to find singers and pay them to record the songs I wrote. One song that stands out that I recorded in the BMI office was a song called "Paralyze the Room" This song stands out because after I recorded it, I didn't like the way the female singer sung the record, so I sent it to Chinky to re-do it. At the time, Chinky was living in California. Chinky re-did my record and gave it the soul I was initially looking for. Chinky sung choruses and ad libs on many of my hip hop songs but that was the first time she sung one of my R&B records and although we had relations in the past and were still close friends, I admired her as an artist and was honored to have her singing one of my records.

I also told all of my New York connects that I had moved to Atlanta so that when they were thinking of linking a producer with a songwriter in Atlanta, my name would at least be an option. I didn't move there but it was important for them to think I did because it enhanced my opportunities. For several weeks I went back and forth from Baltimore to Atlanta until finally I couldn't afford to do so anymore.

My money was starting to run low and my final weeks of unemployment were dwindling down. While in Baltimore, I pretended to still be in Atlanta whenever I spoke to someone of importance on the phone. My plan was if someone wanted to meet up, I would simply say that I was booked for that day but could link up with them the next day. If they agreed, I would jump on the bus and return to Atlanta.

One day while in Baltimore, Mike called me and said that Sickamore was in Atlanta and wanted to meet with me. Instead of getting a bus ticket, I decided to rent a car and drive to Atlanta so I would get there in a better time. I didn't want to take the 12 hour drive alone so I called around asking people if they would ride with me. No one was willing to take the ride, not even Pig and Ole Man Joe (who had just moved back to Baltimore). It was at that very moment that I realized that I was really all by myself when it came to my musical journey. Afraid that I would fall asleep on the long drive, I took my little cousin Deontay (Keacha's oldest son) along for the ride to keep my company. He wasn't old enough to drive so he couldn't help in that department, but he was someone to talk to and that's all I needed so I wouldn't fall asleep at the wheel.

We made it to Atlanta safely that night and the next day, I met with Sickamore. The meeting went well. I played some new records for him that he hadn't heard because he was fond of my previous songs because Mike constantly played them for him. Sickamore liked the new as well as the old records but nothing ever came out of the meeting. The very next day, I drove back to Baltimore alone. My little cousin stayed in Atlanta with his mom.

Once back in Baltimore, I had about four weeks remaining of unemployment benefits and afterwards I had to go back into the work field. Per usual, I called all of my contacts in my notebook that were in New York and began going there once and sometimes twice a week. I would set up meetings with A&R's and executives only to get all the way to New York, call them and get their voicemail.

One time while in New York, going from building to building, I ran into a woman I met at a BMI songwriters showcase named

LaRonda Sutton. At the time LaRonda worked closely with Jamie Foxx. As I was entering the doors of a building LaRonda and a few of her collegues, one of which was Jamie Foxx was coming out.

LaRonda and I greeted and spoke to each other and then I continued to go in the building as she and her entourage headed for their car. When I realized that Jamie Foxx was with her, I turned around and tried to catch up with them before they pulled off. I wanted to give Jamie Foxx one of my many press kits I had with me. As I ran, trying to catch up with them, I arrived at their car door just as Jamie Foxx sat in the car. I reached out my hand with my press kit attempting to hand it to Laronda and Jamie when suddenly I tripped over the curb and fell in the car, directly on Jamie Foxx's lap. Although embarrassed from the fall, I still managed to hand them the press kit.

Days later I continued to travel back and forth to New York. I found out about a bus called the Mega Bus where you could book a one-way ticket to New York for one dollar! I began booking as many bus trips as I could. Lots of times I would go to New York with my bookbag filled with press kits and CD's with absolutely no where to go. I would sit outside of the Def Jam Records office and just watch and wait to see if anyone I recognized came out or in the building. When I saw someone, I knew I would approach them and attempt to give them my press kit or CD. I once saw Jay Z and attempted to give him a CD but he told me he couldn't take it and to give it to the receptionist/ security person at the front desk.

I remember one time I looked up Puff Daddy's (Diddy) studio address and walked there from Manhattan (well where I thought the studio was located). When I arrived at the location, it didn't look like a studio at all, but I still stood there waiting for someone, anyone to walk in or out that looked like Hip Hop. Gold chains, sweatsuits, New York Yankee hats, anyone who looked like someone in the music industry was getting approached but unfortunately after hours of standing outside alone, no one was spotted. Till this day, I'm not even sure if I was at the right place.

Chapter 47- Gracefully Bowing Out

inally, after all of the New York trips, placing my music in every hand possible, my unemployment benefits had run out and it was time for me to get a job. I went to a temporary agency, and they found me an assignment working in a small call center as a financial aid counselor. Right before I took the job, one day as I was pulling up to Erica's mothers house for a visit, my phone rang. To my surprise it was Tanja.

Tanja didn't want anything specific. We hadn't talked in quite sometime and she was just calling to see how things were going. I told Tanja about Erica, our new baby and how things were going with me, and she told me about her new guy and updated me on how her kids were doing. After conversating for a few, it appeared that whatever transformation I made during the time Tanja and I were together up until that point, Tanja could sense it. I told her that it took our breakup for me to finally realize what she was asking of me all along. Tanja agreed and then joked about how our breakup made me a better man for someone else. "If only you could have gotten it a little sooner, who knows where we would be" she said. We both laughed but I could tell it was some truth in that joke.

Tanja was right. Our breakup combined with where I was in my music career literally almost killed me. But it also made me better and stronger. Before that time, I couldn't see who I truly was. I feel like God had to strip me down from everything I knew to be right, take it all away and rebuild me piece by piece. Not only did I hit rock bottom, I had to stay there for a long time, years, so that when I made my way to the top, I would remember the lessons learned.

I started the temporary job which led to me being hired permanently after a few months. Shortly after that I applied and got a job at another company where I'm currently employed today.

As for everyone else Butch gave up music, got married and is now a Jehovah Witness. He also has his own construction company. Hot gave up music as well and currently works as a Long Shoreman. Kidd is currently serving time in Federal prison for drug charges and recently was indicted on a murder charge in Texas.

My cousins Big Flood, Lil Flood (Shawn), Tim Brown, Chop and Kebo are still around. That will never change. My relationship with Big Flood took a while to repair though. For years, I would never go to his house because there's no telling who would be there. In order to avoid an uncomfortable situation, I decided to stay away. Till this day, whenever Kebo gets drunk (which is quite often) he will bring up the chain incident and then all of us will talk and argue about what happened all over again. Each time I found out more information than I already knew. Just recently after all these years, Big Flood finally "got it" and apologized for how he conducted himself during the "Sisqo's Chain" incident with Shaggy. Also, Shaggy was just recently shot and is currently fighting for his life.

Ole Man Joe is still around as my brother/ friend, but Pig has moved on. After I went back to work, Pig and I worked on a few hip-hop projects together at his apartment/ studio and shot a few videos as well. Shortly afterwards, Pig moved out of town. We don't speak often but when we do, we laugh and talk as if no time gap has passed.

The girls Lovher, have all gone their separate ways. Chinky now goes by the name of Shire' and currently lives in California. Murda had a health scare which led him to working out and now is a personal trainer as well as a barber. From time to time he still goes out on the road with Sisqo.

Sisqo is still touring as a solo artist as well as with Dru Hill. He doesn't live in Baltimore anymore so the only times I get to see him is when he has a show in the area. On holidays and birthdays, we text each other and occasionally talk on social media. Although things didn't work out as planned, I could never thank Sisqo enough for all that he's done for me and my career. I've learned so much from him that I can't even begin to list. He was the vessel that God placed in my life that changed my life forever and for that, I'm totally grateful. Till this day, whenever I do anything musically, he's the first person I send it to. Out of respect, it's a must for me that he hears or see's it first.

Shanna sadly passed away in 2010 from cancer. I remember one of the last conversations she and I had when she told me that she didn't fear death. Her energy was very bright and full of spunk. After beating cancer, the first time, Butch and I wrote and dedicated a song to her celebrating her victory over cancer. Not long afterwards cancer came back a second time which caused her demise. Hopefully through memories, songs, and video's her legacy will live on forever.

Tanja married the guy she met in DC at her job but is now divorced. I hardly ever see or talk to her anymore except for comments under pictures on social media. Although the most painful, I'm very thankful for the experience I had with Tanja. If it wasn't for what I went through with her, I would have never seen who I was back then therefore I still would be the same person. I had to be broken in order to be fixed. This experience also taught me that people can change because I changed. They just don't change on their own. Something must force the change or ignite it.

Anna and Chante are both married and we're all on good terms. For years I felt so guilty for what happened with Chante and me. I felt like I threw her to the wolves, and I couldn't forgive myself no matter how hard I tried. From an outside eye, it may have appeared that I was a push over for her and that I jumped at her every begging call, but it was all because of the guilt I felt so subconsciously I always gave her a pass. I've now learned how to forgive myself, so the guilt doesn't bother me anymore. As for Anna, we hardly ever had any drama after we broke up back in the late 90's. Co-parenting with her wasn't difficult at all.

I didn't mention these two as much as I planned but my mother and father were the invisible backbone to my entire life. My mother never said the words "I love you" but her actions told me every single day. I know for a fact that her going to God in prayer on my behalf saved my life plenty of times and kept me out of unfortunate situations. Although she seldomly did it, her prophecies were never wrong, and they gave me the heads up in a lot of situations.

My Dad was my hero. I never met a man as wise as my dad. No matter what I was going through, he always knew exactly what to say and gave me sound advice on a consistent basis. I was never Cooli Hi around my dad. I was always Dwayne no matter how much popularity I had or didn't have. He always kept me grounded. Unfortunately, my dad passed away in 2011 from cancer but before he died, he instilled in me everything I needed to survive. Job well done Dad.

As for me, Erica and I made it official and got married in 2012. Combined we have a blended family that consist of 4 children, Peanut, Akiya, Darrian and Donovan. My wife and I are homeowners with jobs, cars and living a middleclass life and although things may seem like everything is in place, at times I feel the void.

You see, during my music run, I distance myself from almost all my childhood, high school and college friends. It wasn't on purpose, but I was so focused on my dreams that if you weren't attached to it in some way, there was no need to be around you. Dwayne is a chill, reserved kind of guy but Cooli Hi is a selfish monster (when he needs to be) but the two balance each other out. Now all I have is music associates and they're only relevant when I'm doing something relating to music which isn't often so a lot of times, I'm alone with my memories and my thoughts but I'm okay with that. When I'm in social gatherings, depending on the topic of discussion, I get bored very easily and shut down. People often think that I'm quite or shy but that's not the case at all. Sometimes when a person has seen and done so much its hard to get excited about average things. You don't want to come off as if you're better than anyone, but your stimulation bar has been set so high because of the lifestyle you've witness and lived and there's no turning back from that so a lot of times you just sit there, surrounded by many but actually alone in your bubble.

Often, I feel like I'm an alien or weird because I'm wired different than the average person. I've been blessed with the gift and curse of artistry. When most people listen to music, they hear the beat and the voice of the singer or rapper but when I listen to music, I hear EVERYTHING! I hear every instrument playing in the background, I hear harmonies, the ad libs and notes, I hear when rappers overlap their bars and use another track to get punched in, I hear their stacks on the last word of their bars, I hear reverb and auto tune on voices, I hear everything!

When I watch movies, I watch through the director's eyes, not what I actually see on the movie or TV screen. I study the angles and ask my self "What made the director shoot from this angle?" I also watch the mouths of the actors when the edits bounce back and forth from frame to frame, to see if the mouth of the actor the scene is not focusing on, is matching up with what I am hearing.

When dealing with new people I'm usually quite because I'm studying the person. In the music business, the quicker you figure someone out, the quicker you can manipulate them! I learned a long time ago that if you let a person talk, they will tell you everything you need to know and not even know it! I've subconsciously manipulated so many in my past, not for malicious purposes but only to achieve my ultimate goal. I know that I have a date with karma for my past actions, so I have no choice but to welcome her with open arms.

The insane drive that I had still burns in me but instead of aiming it at music, I channel it into other areas. None of my kids got bit by the musical bug (which I thank God for) but my two youngest son's Darrian and Donovan took a liking to basketball. So now my insane drive is focused on pushing them to pursue their hoop dreams. I'm always in the gym with them, coaching them from the sidelines and putting them in positions to be successful. I always tell them "I know firsthand what it takes to get something one out of a million people get because I did it without a road map!" I always compared my drive to a fire hydrant shooting water out in the hood. The pressure of the water is my drive. It never stops. It only shifts directions when someone shifts the water to whatever they're aiming for. But the pressured water continues to go hard at whatever it aimed for.

Occasionally I release new music and shoot videos from time to time. The goal isn't to make money but to stamp my presence in history. I do this because I want my name and music to live forever. I also do it because I cannot stop, even if I wanted to. As long as I am physically and mentally able, I will always release some type of artistry into the universe but as of now my main focus is my family and helping my kids accomplish whatever goals they're after. Peanut and Akiya aren't into sports, but I support them and their goals just the same.

When thinking back on it all, I honestly don't have any regrets. I believe I did everything that I could have possibly done (expect turning my back on my children) to accomplish my goal. It just didn't happen (yet) and I'm cool with that. If I had to call out a reason, I would probably say it was because I never had the right team behind me. I remember when I would see local rappers in the clubs and they always were backed by some dude with lots of cash, usually drug money so the only thing the artist had to focus on was being the artist. I never had this luxury. The closest thing I had to this was the Holla Back situation with Kidd, but I had to fight him off weekly from wanting to be the artist himself! Sometimes I even think that the deal we had with RCA was all about putting some quick money in Kidd's pocket because I don't think they were ever going to release an album on us, 9/11 or not. I was just trying to get all I could out of every situation I was involved in.

The people around me were only focused on themselves and not winning as a team. Talent can only take you so far. It has a ceiling, and a business team takes you the rest of the way. Unfortunately for me, I never had that business team. I came very close on numerous occasions, was around a lot of the "right people" but for some reason, things didn't turn out as I would have liked. Just a lot of cameras, bright lights and action. But I must admit, it was one hell of a ride!

About the Author

Dwayne "Cooli Hi" Jones originally started his musical career as a hip hop recording artist. What distinguished this Baltimore native from other artists in that genre is the compelling subject matter, smooth delivery, and unique lyrical content. With his baritone laden rhymes, he gives his fans an incredible visual experience as he narrates stories of common urban tales and life experiences. Overall, it's his dynamic ability to add a touch of pure human emotions that turns even the toughest hip hop skeptic into a fan. So it's no surprise that songwriting was this talented artist's next exploration.

In 2001 Cooli Hi was featured on Sisqo's Hit Single "Can I Live" Produced by Teddy Riley. Since his debut on the single from the multi-platinum album, Return of the Dragon, Cooli Hi has performed with such notable groups as Dru Hill and The Backstreet Boys. This experience gave him the opportunity to perform on MTV's Total Request Live (TRL), CBS This Morning and the historic 1st Annual BET Music Awards. In addition to countless performances in the United States, Cooli Hi has entertained audiences all over the world; from

Africa to Scotland to London - including a performance on Top Of The Pops, a syndicated show in London that features the biggest acts in Hip Hop, Rock and Pop music.

In 2006 a childhood friend introduced him to a BMI executive with the intentions of showcasing his hip hop writing talents. As the BMI executive listened, he periodically stopped the music, curious to find out who wrote the chorus's on the tracks. When he discovered that Cooli Hi wrote and arranged all of the choruses, he asked a question that unleashed one of Cooli's many hidden talents. "Have you ever considered writing an entire R&B song?" That simple inquiry undoubtedly unlocked the initiative for this exceptional musician to transition from writing hooks, to writing breathtaking songs that cover an array of music genres. As with hip hop, his lyrics still target the pulse of everyday life and the foundation for every song starts with the consciousness and passion of pure human sentiment. As you listen to songs written by Cooli Hi, your emotions will connect as the phrases turn, and the melodies soar! That is his formula for timeless music!

Realizing his strengths in Songwriting, and combining that with a style influenced by great artists of the past Dwayne "Cooli Hi" Jones continues to touch the hearts and souls of many with his gift and never follows a trend. His past experiences have molded an artist who realizes that music is not an avenue to wealth, but an outlet of expression that holds the power to touch lives and lift spirits. More importantly, for him, music is a way of life!

www.ingramcontent.com/pod-product-compliance
Lightning Source LLC
Chambersburg PA
CBHW070854120626
46546CB00001B/3